Coastal
California

Sara Benson

Alison Bing, Andy Bender, Nate Cavalieri, John A Vlahides

REDWOOD NATIONAL & STATE PARKS (p145)
Disappear into Tall Trees Grove, hike through Fern Canyon and watch Roosevelt elk rut

LOST COAST (p127)
Ditch civilization and obey the tides along a wild shoreline that time truly has forgotten

AVENUE OF THE GIANTS (p129)
Wend your way beneath the world's tallest trees as they glisten with sunrise dew

POINT ARENA (p111)
Spot the San Andreas Fault atop an early-20th-century lighthouse

POINT REYES NATIONAL SEASHORE (p98)
Commune with nature in near-perfect solitude, spotting migratory whales off the peninsula's soulful, wind-battered beaches

SAN FRANCISCO (p51)
Eat your way through the Ferry Building Marketplace and ascend dizzying hills on iconic cable cars

LEGEND

Tollway
Freeway
Primary Road
Secondary Road
Tertiary Road
Unsealed Road

0   60 miles
0   100 km

ELEVATION

13,000ft
11,000ft
9,000ft
7,000ft
5,000ft
3,000ft
1,000ft
0

Idaho

Utah
Mountain Time Zone
Pacific Time Zone

Nevada

Oregon

Mountain Time Zone
Pacific Time Zone

Cascade Range

Sierra Nevada

Sacramento Valley

Coast Range

Sacramento River

San Joaquin

Eel River

Klamath River

Feather River

Lake Tahoe

Pyramid Lake

Goose Lake

Clear Lake

Shasta Lake

Carson Sink

Mono Lake

Lassen Volcanic National Park

Lava Beds National Monument

Mt Shasta 14,179ft

Yosemite National Park

Redwood National Park

Twin Falls
Burns Junction
Lakeview
Grants Pass
Medford
Klamath Falls
Crescent City
Klamath
Trinidad
Arcata
Eureka
Scotia
Ferndale
Redway
Garberville
Leggett
Redding
Red Bluff
Westport
Fort Bragg
Caspar
Mendocino
Elk
Manchester
Point Arena
Anchor Bay
Sea Ranch
Gualala
Guerneville
Bodega Bay
Inverness
Point Reyes
Bolinas
Olema
Santa Rosa
Napa
Vallejo
Sausalito
San Francisco
Pacifica
Half Moon Bay
Farallon Islands
Davis
SACRAMENTO
Stockton
Modesto
Oakland
Palo Alto
San Jose
Rafael
Wells
Elko
Eureka
Austin
Battle Mountain
Winnemucca
Fallon
CARSON CITY
Reno
Hawthorne
Tonopah
Ely
Bishop

Mountain Time Zone
Pacific Time Zone

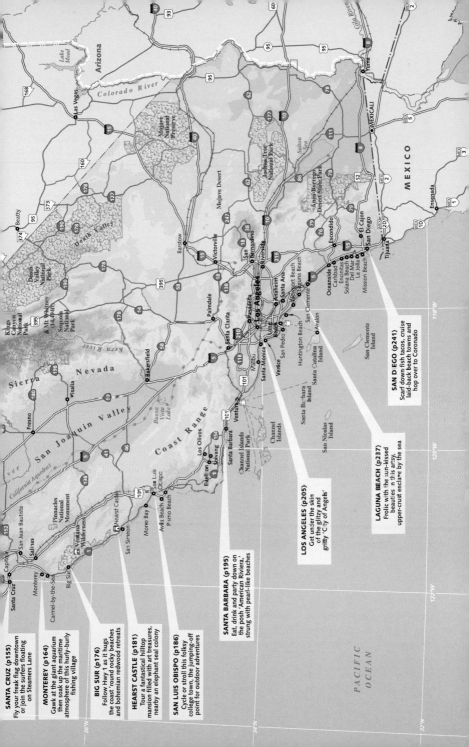

SANTA CRUZ (p155)
Fly your freak flag downtown or join the surfers floating on Steamers Lane

MONTEREY (p164)
Gawk at the giant aquarium then soak up the maritime atmosphere of this hurly-burly fishing village

BIG SUR (p176)
Follow Hwy 1 as it hugs the coast 'round rocky beaches and bohemian redwood retreats

HEARST CASTLE (p181)
Tour a fantastical hilltop mansion filled with art treasures, nearby an elephant seal colony

SAN LUIS OBISPO (p186)
Cycle or stroll this folksy college town, the jumping-off point for outdoor adventures

SANTA BARBARA (p195)
Eat, drink and party down on the posh 'American Riviera,' strung with pearl-like beaches

LOS ANGELES (p205)
Get under the skin of the glitzy and gritty 'City of Angels'

LAGUNA BEACH (p237)
Frolic with the sun-kissed beauties in this artsy, upper-crust enclave by the sea

SAN DIEGO (p241)
Scarf down fish tacos, cruise laid-back beach towns and hop over to Coronado

On the Road

SARA BENSON Coordinating Author
That's me, taking a break from researching this guide at the 52nd Monterey Jazz Festival (p169). It's just one of dozens of unique events and hidden places on the Central Coast that make me thankful to live and work here, in the often forgotten 'flyover' country between San Francisco and LA.

ANDY BENDER Yes, LA is a big city, with big city stresses. But it's hard to imagine another city where it's so easy to find a way to release that stress, whether it's partying like a grownup on the Sunset Strip (p221) or partying like an eight-year-old on Santa Monica Pier (p214).

ALISON BING I'm proudly supporting the historic Castro Theatre (p73), to which I walked an entire three blocks from home to research. Fifteen years of living here, and I still well up hearing the Castro's Wurlitzer play 'San Francisco, Open Your Golden Gates'…

NATE CAVALIERI After spending an afternoon wilting in the merciless sun of Hwy 101 on a bicycle, I took a plunge into a Smith River (p153) swimming hole. That look of terror is not staged; even at the peak of the summer, the icy water seems to stop your heart for a second.

JOHN A VLAHIDES Hiking the coastal bluffs around the Golden Gate (p55) means uncertain weather. One minute it's foggy and cold, the next minute it's sunny and hot – which is why I always carry a backpack full of layers when trekking the coast.

For full author biographies see p293.

Coastal California Highlights

From towering coast redwoods in foggy Northern California to the perfectly sun-kissed surf beaches of Southern California, the scenery that unfurls along coastal California's highways is always a knockout. And so are the people. They're no less astoundingly diverse than the landscape, as you'll soon find out. Hang with radical tree-sitting lefties in the Humboldt Nation, hipster bohemians in San Francisco's kaleidoscopic neighborhoods or glam TV and silver-screen celebrities with their entourages in Los Angeles. When the San Andreas Fault shakes, rattles and rolls, think of it as just a small reminder of how wild every moment of being here is. Make sure you take advantage of it all, starting with some of our fave spots.

MICHAEL AW

1 BIG SUR

Here's exhilarating proof that California actually is falling off the edge of the continent. In Big Sur (p176), craggy cliffs tilt helter-skelter down to the Pacific, where growling white-capped waves splash against fallen rocks and waterfalls. Meanwhile, California condors fly overhead and redwood trees make their stand against the ravages of time at the mossy borderline of true wilderness.

Sara Benson, Lonely Planet Author

CHRISTINA LEASE

CAMPING IN THE REDWOODS

Climbing out of the tent and into the ethereal fog of the Redwood National Park (p145) is an awe-inspiring (and downright creepy) way to start the day in one of California's most spectacular natural areas. Without cellphone reception or another person in sight, this is my favorite place to get lost.

Nate Cavalieri, Lonely Planet Author

2

HOLLYWOOD BOULEVARD, LOS ANGELES

I've taken hundreds of visitors to Grauman's Chinese Theatre (p219) over the years, and even the most jaded comes away impressed. How could you not, literally standing in the footsteps of screen legends from Judy Garland to Daniel Radcliffe? Then we follow the Hollywood Walk of Fame to the long colonnade of the Kodak Theatre, home of the Academy Awards. On its columns are inscribed the titles of Oscar-winning movies, perhaps providing inspiration for the legends of tomorrow.

Andy Bender, Lonely Planet Author

3

NICHOLAS PAV

PAUL KEN

4

ORANGE COUNTY BEACHES

Northern California beaches are all about crashing waves, tidepools, rock collecting and (oftentimes) solitary strolls along the water's edge, but for the full-on Baywatch experience you need to head south. Bust out the bikini once you hit Santa Barbara. I especially love the warm water, soft sand and palm trees at Orange County beaches like Laguna Beach (p237).

Suki Gear, Lonely Planet Staff

NORTH BEACH, SAN FRANCISCO

Get under the skin of San Francisco's cafe culture along Columbus Ave in North Beach (p73).

John A Vlahides, Lonely Planet Author

5

6

MONTEREY

You know those sun-soaked Hollywood images of California beach life you've been hypnotized by? Forget all about 'em in this hurly-burly, working-class fishing village (p164). Hop aboard a whale-watching bay cruise, visit the renowned aquarium and the West Coast's oldest operating lighthouse, and amble the cobblestone streets evocatively captured by 20th-century novelist John Steinbeck.

Sara Benson, Lonely Planet Author

HEARST CASTLE

When I visit Hearst Castle (p181), I picture myself as Marion Davies – attending an exclusive week-long party, sipping champagne by the gilded pool, wearing gowns Hearst has had sent over from France. Charlie Chaplin is playing cards with Greta Garbo, Buster Keaton is dancing with Jean Harlow, Errol Flynn is drinking with Joan Crawford in the wine cellar. Hearst may have banned sex and scandal from his movies, but there was plenty to be had at his house.

Jennye Garibaldi, Lonely Planet Staff

7

CHILDREN'S POOL, LA JOLLA

By just doing what seals do, this colony illustrates the eternal tug-of-war between nature and human-kind on the California coast. The pool (p256) was designated a park for the kids of La Jolla, but the seals thought differently and made it their own; animal-rights groups petitioned to let the seals stay but courts said they could not. Problem is, nobody knows the best way to keep them away...

Andy Bender, Lonely Planet Author

8

SANTA BARBARA

Never mind those highly charged partisan debates that locals have about whether it's better to live in Northern California (NorCal) or Southern California (SoCal). That question becomes irrelevant in the lotus land of the Central Coast. Perhaps no other place claims the best of both worlds as well as Santa Barbara (p195), with its cultured charms, chic restaurants and shopping, and balmy beaches fringed by palm trees.

Sara Benson, Lonely Planet Author

10

9 **POINT REYES NATIONAL SEASHORE**

Step across the San Andreas Fault at Point Reyes (p98), where you can hike among herds of tule elk and explore windswept beaches.

John A Vlahides, Lonely Planet Author

Contents

Regional Map Contents

North Coast (p100)

San Francisco & the Bay Area (p50)

Central Coast (p154)

Los Angeles & Orange County (p204)

San Diego Area (p240)

Destination Coastal California

Welcome to the way-out western edge of Western civilization. Coastal California has a way of capturing the imagination unlike any other place in America, thanks partly to the often fantastical, sometimes laughable, comic-book proportions of the culture. In what other state can an action-movie star and bodybuilder get himself elected to the governor's office – and then surprisingly get re-elected? It boggles the mind.

Go-go Los Angeles really is just like in the movies, with palm-tree-lined boulevards, Mercedes-Benz convertibles and Botoxed blondes awaiting their big breaks. Check out SoCal's parade of hotties on Orange County's sandy beaches, where way-cool dudes and bikinied babes strut and preen as if auditioning for spots on Baywatch. If you prefer goofy grins to chiseled chests, head to Northern California, land of free love and go-it-alone politics. Frolic au naturel in the crashing surf of a nude beach. Scream your face off aboard a rickety, wooden roller coaster on the boardwalk in Santa Cruz. Get lost in the redwood forests of Big Sur, a haven for artists, poets and modern-day beatniks. Or hang out with all the hipsters and tech-savvy digerati in San Francisco, and eat like a prince on a pauper's budget.

The biggest wow in Coastal California firmly remains its spectacular scenery – here, thousand-foot cliffs plunge into the sea, the world's tallest trees cling precipitously to near-vertical hillsides and lonely lighthouses stand sentinel while giant gray whales breach offshore. This is where America ends and the vast blue Pacific begins. There's something magical about being on the shore of the largest body of water on Earth, hypnotized by the play of color and light, your view restricted only by the curvature of the planet. And that's the one thing that Californians agree on: all stand in awe of the coast's limitlessness and seductive mystery. You will, too.

Recently the Golden State has been sinking under a massive budget crisis, exacerbated by the USA's economic downturn following the collapse of the subprime mortgage-lending market, which sent seismic shocks through the world's economy. Governor Arnold Schwarzenegger (aka 'The Governator'), once hailed as a centrist Republican who understood many Californians' desire to lead the nation in environmental policy and progressive social politics, has made some staggering compromises. In 2009, Schwarzenegger slashed the state's annual operating budget by $489 million, unilaterally taking away funding from education, medical and social services, and California State Parks. Over one-third of the entire state-parks system was threatened with closure – including over 100 public beaches, redwood forest preserves, historic sites and more. To the chagrin of local residents who vigorously protested the closures, several state parks have started closing their gates on weekdays and reducing their opening hours until the economy recovers or the next gubernatorial election in 2010.

In other environmental news, California has a lot at stake in the unfolding global-warming crisis. Its water comes from snowfall in the Sierra Nevada Mountains. If global warming continues unchecked, precipitation will fall there as rain instead of snow, undermining the state's natural water-storage system. Of course, nothing has shaped California like its ongoing water wars (as witnessed by private investigator Jake Gittes in the 1974 neo-noir and all too true-to-life film *Chinatown*, set in Los Angeles). In general, coastal Southern California has money and political power, while inland Northern California has (or in some cases, had) water. For years, SoCal's insatiable thirst has emptied ancient lakes and diverted major waterways as far north as the Oregon border, but Northern Californians are fed up. There's even talk of decommissioning dams on the Klamath River, the state's second-largest river. Although this wouldn't directly affect SoCal, it doesn't bode well for the region's growth: if there's no water, you can't build new houses. Southern California has never subscribed to a slow-growth political ideology, but soon it may have to. Or at least it will have to give up green lawns and golf courses, which would go a long way toward reducing water consumption. Agriculture remains California's largest industry, and as the popular political slogan says, 'Food grows where water flows.' Nobody can eat golf balls, you know.

Meanwhile, gasoline prices are on everyone's mind, as news articles and bloggers declare 'Pain at the Pump.' The website for CBS 2 in Los Angeles has a dedicated front-page module for gas prices, listing the latest news on the subject as well as the 20 cheapest places to find gasoline. But prices in big cities like LA aren't nearly as painful as in less urban areas of the Central and North Coast, which are usually at the top of the list for the most expensive gasoline sold in America. More and more Californians are trading in their SUVs for fuel-efficient hybrid vehicles. (One quarter of all hybrids in the US are driven in California.) In 2006, Governor Schwarzenegger signed into law legislation capping greenhouse gas emissions, the first law of its kind in the US; the goal is to reduce such emissions by 25% before the year 2020.

When it comes to social issues, nothing is more hotly debated than gay marriage. San Francisco Mayor Gavin Newsom started the uproar in 2004 by officiating at California's first same-sex marriages. In 2008, the California Supreme Court struck down pre-existing statutes that limited marriage to couples of opposite genders. Proposition 8, which proposed a state constitutional ban on same-sex marriage, was narrowly approved by voters later that same year. Civil-rights activists have since taken the fight to overturn Prop 8 to court. Although recent polls show that a small majority of Californians support same-sex marriage, it's likely to be an uphill battle to legally guarantee the civil rights of every Californian to marry, regardless of sexual orientation.

Getting Started

Ready and rarin' to go for an epic trip? Just remember that California is huge, and it takes time to get around. It's easy to get overambitious, blow your budget and spend more time getting to sights than actually seeing them. You can take the train or buses between coastal cities and some towns, but you'll need a car to reach many gorgeously remote areas. Outside of metropolitan areas it's easy to navigate, and your biggest problem will be keeping your eyes focused on the road and not on the beautiful scenery. If you've got kids with you, fret not: there's plenty for them to do. And despite the glut of high-cost lodgings along the coast, budget travelers can sniff out deals along the way. Although they are helpful during the peak summer travel season, don't let a lack of reservations stop you from hitting the road whenever you like. Spontaneity and a hang-loose attitude are what visiting coastal California is all about.

WHEN TO GO

See Climate Charts (p275) for more information.

Just about any month is a good time to be traveling somewhere in coastal California. Visitors and locals alike throng the coast in summer, from June through August, crowding tourist attractions and causing room rates to spike, even at motels. If you come in summer, try to travel midweek, when crowds are thinner and rates cheaper. Traveling the weekend before or after major holidays (eg Memorial Day, 4th of July, Labor Day) can also help salvage your vacation budget – and your sanity. For year-round festivals and special events, see p277; for holidays, see p279.

Expect summertime fog anywhere north of Santa Barbara, nicknamed 'May gray' and 'June gloom,' though it may last into July or August. It gets chilly, but never cold. (If you crave summer heat, head south of Santa Barbara to escape the fog.) During spring and fall, this coastal fog clears, providing the best opportunity to capture famous ocean vistas on film. Balmy 'Indian summer' stretches through September and October. Swimming is only comfortable at the height of summer in Northern California and from May to October in Southern California (SoCal), though surfers and divers hit the waters year-round in wet suits. You can canoe, kayak and do most other outdoor activities from spring through fall. Summer is pretty darn hot for hiking or cycling in SoCal.

DON'T LEAVE HOME WITHOUT...

- A sweater in summer, a raincoat in winter and sunscreen year-round
- Hotel (p274), hostel (p273) or camping (p273) reservations for the places where you really want to stay, especially in peak summer season
- A good playlist for your iPod and games for long car rides, especially with kids (p274)
- A leash and portable water bowl for your faithful, four-legged travel companion (p282)
- A handful of credit cards – they're often easier and safer than cash, and are sometimes necessary (eg for hotel reservations, car rentals)
- Your driver's license and an automobile association membership card (p289)
- Sufficient travel, medical and car insurance (p279)
- If necessary, a passport and US visa (p280)

Visiting in winter (November to February) is iffy, since storms may ruin the views, but you can score great rates on lodgings. Just remember that winter can be pretty chilly, especially north of San Francisco, and it definitely isn't the time for a beach vacation, even in SoCal. Though it rains frequently in winter, the coast never freezes, and the hills turn emerald green; from March through May, they're dotted with spring wildflowers before summertime drought turns them golden-brown again. Winter is the prime whale-watching season, when gray whales migrate down the coast from Alaska (see p43).

COSTS & MONEY

Coastal California is undoubtedly pricey. Your biggest travel costs will likely be accommodations and transportation, followed by food and drink and then sightseeing. If you're a student or senior, traveling with children or just wanting to keep your costs down, always ask about discounts (p277).

The easiest way to tour California is by car, although many cities and towns from San Francisco south to San Diego are also accessible by Amtrak train (p287) or Greyhound bus (p287). Car rentals cost at least $200 week, plus insurance costs of $15 to $30 per day, depending on the coverage selected. Gasoline averages over $3 per gallon in summer, and is more expensive in remote areas like Big Sur – as much as a dollar per gallon extra compared with metropolitan areas. For more tips for traveling the coast by car and motorcycle, see p287.

Lodging costs peak between Memorial Day (late May) and Labor Day (early September). Basic motels (p274) start at around $75 a night, but top out over $250 for ocean-view rooms and suites. Hotels cost $100 to $200, or over $500 for luxurious top-end resorts. To save cash, head inland and choose motels near freeways for savings of up to 50%. Hostels (p273) are few and far between, charging between $25 and $30 per night for a dorm bed. Coastal camping (p273) is plentiful, with sites costing $10 to $65 per night, but occasionally they're free. B&Bs (p273) range from $100 to $300 per couple. Note that only peak-season lodging rates are given in this guide during the off-season (ie winter), ask about discounts.

If you don't insist on sit-down meals, you won't spend much money on food. Eat at simple, hole-in-the-wall restaurants, seafood shacks or taquerias (taco shops) and you'll pay $10 or less. For more substantial meals, lunch is cheaper than dinner. A two-course dinner with one drink at a midrange restaurant costs $20 to $30 per person. Remember to add taxes and a 15% to 20% tip (see p280). Families can ask about cheaper children's menus. Seniors sometimes get smaller discounts of 10% to 15%.

Many museums have an admission-free period once a month. Parking at state parks and beaches costs $4 to $15 per vehicle, usually valid for one day; pedestrians and cyclists are often admitted free or for a nominal fee.

TRAVELING RESPONSIBLY

You can reduce your carbon footprint while you travel and help fight California's air pollution problems by using public transportation to get around, rather than flying or driving. Amtrak's *Coast Starlight* and *Pacific Surfliner* routes (p287) reward carbon-conscious travelers with epic scenery. Although riding Greyhound buses (p287) lacks the romance of the rails, you'll definitely meet a diverse cross-section of Californians to give you insight into the real 'state of the state,' something drivers cocooned inside their cars won't get. Some cities offer car-free tourism discount incentives, like in Santa Barbara (see p195), to encourage bus-hopping or rail-riding weekenders and ambitious long-distance cyclists (p288) alike.

HOW MUCH?

Motel room by the beach $100-250+

Theme park day pass $30-69

Movie ticket $10

Local phone call 35-50¢

Small iced latte with soy milk $3.50

For more everyday prices, see the Lonely Planet Index inside the front cover.

TOP 10

San Francisco
COASTAL CALIFORNIA
Los Angeles
San Diego

PARTIES & PARADES

Californians love a good party. Here are our top picks for the most unusual, oddball and unique celebrations. See p277 for more ideas.

1 Bay to Breakers (San Francisco; p74)

2 Kinetic Grand Championship (Arcata–Ferndale; p132)

3 San Francisco Pride (p74)

4 Summer Solstice Celebration (Santa Barbara; p199)

5 Comic-con International (San Diego; p259)

6 Sunset Junction Street Fair (Los Angeles; p223)

7 Reggae on the River (Garberville; p126)

8 Woodies on the Wharf (Santa Cruz; p160)

9 Pageant of the Masters (Laguna Beach; p237)

10 Rose Parade (Pasadena; p222)

BEAUTIFUL HIDDEN BEACHES

Coastal California has over 1100 miles of coastline and hundreds of beaches. Many are unbelievably crowded, but here are some gorgeous patches of sand where you can still find room to breathe:

1 Manchester State Park (p112)

2 Gold Bluffs Beach (p147)

3 San Mateo Coast Beaches (p85)

4 Pfeiffer Beach (p178)

5 Lands End (p64)

6 Black Sands Beach (p127)

7 McClures Beach (p99)

8 Jalama Beach County Park (p194)

9 Silver Strand (p253)

10 Black's Beach (p257)

OUTDOOR ADVENTURES

Dude, there's so much more than surfing waiting for you here in coastal California. Just you wait and see! For the complete lowdown on getting outdoors, see p39.

1 Canoeing up the Big River outside Mendocino (p115)

2 Navigating the tide charts to trek the dramatic Lost Coast (p127)

3 Learning to surf perfect waves off Huntington Beach (p234)

4 Diving in the crystal waters embracing Santa Catalina Island (p216)

5 Hiking amid the tallest trees on earth at Redwood National & State Parks (p145)

6 Kayaking among sea otters and seabirds at Elkhorn Slough (p164)

7 Spotting northern elephant seals at Point Piedras Blancas (p182)

8 Snorkeling the rich kelp beds of Channel Islands National Park (p202)

9 Hang gliding or paragliding off Torrey Pines in La Jolla (p259)

10 Mountain biking with eye-popping Pacific views in the Marin Headlands (p87)

Water is at the heart of many conflicts between agricultural, urban and environmental interests in California, which is no stranger to drought. Tourism development contributes to perennial water shortages, but some hotels have taken steps to reduce water waste (eg installing low-flush toilets). For our picks for sustainable travel options, including ecofriendly lodging, see our 'GreenDex' (p302), which lists environmentally, socially and culturally responsible businesses, services and nonprofit organizations that travelers can support. Our GreenDex list includes restaurants that serve seasonal, organic produce and/or are committed to sourcing food from local vendors. If you're cooking for yourself, you'll find vibrant farmers markets in many coastal cities and towns, including San Luis Obispo (p188).

For 'green' hybrid rental cars and car-sharing services, see p290. While hitchhiking is always risky and we do *not* recommend it, ride-sharing using online bulletin boards such as **Craigslist** (www.craigslist.org) is not uncommon. Craigslist also has listings for vacation rentals and housing sublets, short-term jobs, community activities and free classified ads for anything you might want to buy, sell or barter during your trip, whether a surfboard or a bicycle. For volunteering opportunities, see p284.

TRAVEL LITERATURE

The lively anthology *My California: Journeys by Great Writers*, edited by Donna Wares and Mark Arax, takes you surfing, roller skating and cruising across the Golden State as interpreted by Pico Iyer, Michael Chabon and others.

In *Where I Was From*, Joan Didion piercingly dissects the mythology of life in California, from the early pioneers (of whom she is a descendant) to the state's newest arrivals and their shared shut-the-door-behind-me mentality.

Pulitzer Prize-winning author Marc Reisner's *A Dangerous Place: California's Unsettling Fate* is part scientific investigation, part fictionalized vision about what living through coastal California's impending 'big one' (earthquake) might be like.

Bill Barich's *Big Dreams: Into the Heart of California* amusingly narrates an ultimately heart-breaking trip from the Oregon border down Mexico way, searching for the elusive American Dream so many California immigrants fail to find.

Writing Los Angeles, edited by David Ulin, is an ambitious collection of fiction and nonfiction excerpts by great writers about the glitz of the City of Angels and its perhaps even more seductive noir side.

By a former *Los Angeles Times* reporter, Mark Arax' collection of essays, *West of the West: Dreamers, Believers, Builders, and Killers in the Golden State*, is an intimate look at idiosyncratic characters living in modern California today.

In Jack Kerouac's semi-autobiographical book, *Big Sur*, he boomerangs back and forth between bohemian San Francisco and the peaceful beauty of the remote, rugged Big Sur coast, where he befriends a Buddhist poet.

John Steinbeck's *Cannery Row* is a true-to-life novel set in Monterey when California's first capital was populated by adventurers and hooligans, heroes and whores. Some of the places described are still recognizable today.

INTERNET RESOURCES

California Travel & Tourism Commission (www.visitcalifornia.com) Hundreds of trip-planning ideas, travel tools and free e-guides in nine languages.

California State Parks (www.parks.ca.gov) Indispensable site for information about outdoor activities and camping in all state parks.

Caltrans (www.dot.ca.gov) For driving in California, including route planning, maps and current highway and weather conditions.

Lonely Planet (www.lonelyplanet.com) Offers travel news and summaries, the Thorn Tree travel forum and links to other Web resources.

Los Angeles Times (http://travel.latimes.com) Newspaper travel site is 'taking Southern California on vacation' along with the rest of the state, too.

Theme Park Insider (www.themeparkinsider.com) Breaking news and reviews of rides and attractions at California's major theme parks.

Itineraries
CLASSIC ROUTES

A TALE OF TWO STATES
Two Weeks/San Francisco to San Diego

Northern and Southern California couldn't be more different. Observe the cultural divide as you cruise south. Get a primer on the left-leaning NorCal scene in **San Francisco** (p51) before driving down Hwy 1 along the edge of the continent. Consider the merits of socialism on the beach in surf-savvy **Santa Cruz** (p155) before donning hiking boots and going off the grid in **Big Sur** (p176). Once you've dropped your jaw at **Hearst Castle** (p181) and let it all hang out in collegiate **San Luis Obispo** (p186), pull yourself together in oh-so-civilized **Santa Barbara** (p195) with its *Sideways* wine country revolving around **Los Olivos** (p193). Shop for strappy sandals and trip on the star-maker machinery in **Los Angeles** (p205), then question the nature of happiness at the 'happiest place on Earth,' **Disneyland** (p231). Bronze your bod on golden sands and ride the waves off Orange County's **Huntington Beach** (p234), then dig the arts in picture-perfect **Laguna Beach** (p237). It's almost always 68°F (20°C) and sunny in **San Diego** (p240), America's best-looking city where nothing much ever happens.

It's not just the land that changes as you cruise 600 miles down the coast from NorCal to SoCal. Two weeks is enough to get a sense of place but, if you want to take sides in the culture wars, you'll need more time.

NORTH INTO THE REDWOOD EMPIRE

10 Days/
San Francisco to Crescent City

To discover what makes Northern California tick, just over a week is barely enough time, but it'll do. Once you're out of the big City by the Bay, just trade your Italian-leather jacket for a sporty fleece pullover, and then don't worry, you'll blend right in.

Delve into the tapestry of neighborhoods in **San Francisco** (p51). Heading north, snap killer pictures of the **Golden Gate Bridge** (p55) from the **Marin Headlands** (p87). At windy **Point Reyes National Seashore** (p98), watch herds of elk meander and whales breach offshore, then greet the harbor seals of riverside **Jenner** (p105). Set up housekeeping in a seaside cottage at **Anchor Bay** (p110) and climb **Point Arena Lighthouse** (p111) to scout out hikes on the coastal bluffs. Take your inner artist on a retreat in boho-chic **Mendocino** (p113) and learn to see beauty in the fog.

Next say hello to redwood country. You may feel dwarfed on the Avenue of the Giants, as if you're driving along in a Matchbox car, or when you wander among the cathedral of trees inside **Humboldt Redwoods State Park** (p129). Ditch civilization on the **Lost Coast** (p127), then reemerge into a time warp in Victorian **Ferndale** (p131). After a few nights in the woods, you may appreciate a hot clawfoot-tub bath in one of the town's incredibly quaint B&Bs.

Knock back microbrews as you inhale the salty maritime air of **Eureka** (p134). Ogle critter-packed tide pools at **Trinidad** (p142) and **Patrick's Point State Park** (p145) before disappearing beneath the canopy of tall trees of **Redwood National Park** (p145), **Prairie Creek Redwood State Park** (p146) or **Del Norte Coast Redwood State Park** (p149). Spot eagle and osprey vying for river salmon at **Klamath** (p147) before exploring the wild canyons of **Smith River National Recreation Area** (see boxed text, p153).

The moody, fog-shrouded North Coast extends northward from San Francisco in a patchwork of misty coves, giant redwood forests and tiny coastal towns straight out of a Hitchcock movie. This almost-mystical 400-mile route lets you in on all the secrets of NorCal boho life.

CENTRAL COAST SEASIDE JAUNTS   One Week/San Luis Obispo to Malibu

If you like a bodacious mix of outdoor activities and in-town culture, you'll find primo spots and myriad ways to indulge your passions here, from farm-fresh gourmet fare and organic, biodynamic wines to surfing, sea kayaking and rugged coastal hikes.

Start your week in **San Luis Obispo** (p186), at its most rambunctious during its Thursday-night farmers market. Pull on your hiking boots to summit **Bishop's Peak** (p188) then go mountain biking and peak bagging in **Montaña de Oro State Park** (p186), with its spectacular ocean vistas, or paddle around that big ol' rock in **Morro Bay** (p185). Soak your tired muscles in the hot springs of **Avila Beach** (p190) then catch a soulful sunset at **Pismo Beach** (p192), where you can dig into buckets of fresh seafood and sourdough-bread bowls filled with clam chowder.

Heading south on a little-traveled stretch of Hwy 1, gaze awestruck at the massive shifting sands of the **Guadalupe Dunes** (p194) and find out where Cecil B DeMille buried his enormous *Ten Commandments* movie set. In bucolic **Santa Barbara wine country** (p193), get lost on winding back roads among seemingly endless vineyards. Strut down State St in **Santa Barbara** (p195) and climb to the top of the courthouse for bird's-eye views. Down at Stearns Wharf, meet local hotties in a pickup game of volleyball on **East Beach** (p198), or take your sweetheart to prettily romantic **Butterfly Beach** (p198).

If you crave solitude and wilderness, hop on a boat to **Channel Islands National Park** (p202) and devote days to exploring 'California's Galapagos.' Back on dry land, cruise south to starstruck **Malibu** (p214) for paparazzi-worthy celeb spotting, world-famous surf spots and the amazing antiquities of the hilltop **Getty Villa** (p215), cradled by flowering bowers.

Don't just speed on by: the idyllic Central Coast perfectly blends outdoor sports and more sybaritic pleasures. If you long to spend your days kayaking and hiking, but never want to be too far from a good bottle of Pinot Noir, take this 175-mile jaunt.

GOLDEN SOCAL SANDS   One Week/Santa Monica To San Diego

So, you've got a problem. You just can't stop dreaming about lying on movie-perfect beaches under a seductive sun, while sublimely toned surfer girls and boys launch into the Pacific's frothy azure waters? Well, Southern California (SoCal) is definitely the place you're thinking of.

Give yourself a couple of days to get acquainted with California's largest city, **Los Angeles** (p205). Pay your respects to newly glam-again **Hollywood** (p219), then soak up the arts and culture of **Downtown** (p219) and museum-packed **Mid-City** (p221). Cruise the coast, from the hilltop **Getty Center** (p215), past **Santa Monica Pier** (p214) and crazy-as-all-get-out **Venice** (p215), the TV-worthy beaches of the **South Bay** (p217) and more down-to-earth **Long Beach** (p216) with its family-friendly attractions. It's just a quick drive inland to **Disneyland** (p231), a kiddie theme-park paradise.

Keep hugging the coast as it snakes southbound through Orange County (aka 'the OC'), the star of countless TV shows and movies. **Huntington Beach** (p234) claims the title of 'Surf City USA,' while wealthy **Newport Beach** (p235) has soap opera–worthy environs, and artsy **Laguna Beach** (p237) couldn't be more picturesque. Take time to tour **Mission San Juan Capistrano** (p239), a beautifully restored Spanish colonial mission.

Keep rolling south into San Diego County, where pearl-like beaches stretch from the **North County Coast** (p267) down to the Mexico border. Get new-agey in **Encinitas** (p269), bet on horse races in **Del Mar** (p268), dive or snorkel in **La Jolla** (p258), ride the Giant Dipper roller coaster in **Mission Beach** (p255) and make it funky in **Pacific Beach** (p255). Climb the **Old Point Loma Lighthouse** (p253) for sweeping views, or just drive over the bridge to **Coronado** (p252). Head inland to San Diego's museum-loaded **Balboa Park** (p249), hipsterville **Hillcrest** (p252), the after-dark **Gaslamp Quarter** (p248) and atmospheric Spanish-Mexican **Old Town** (p251).

Life is good down in sunkissed SoCal, where the Pacific Coast Hwy is bookended by two exhilarating cities: Los Angeles, a jigsaw puzzle of independent neighborhoods, and San Diego, California's lotusland. You could drive the 175 miles in a day, but why rush? Take a week.

TAILORED TRIPS

FREAKS & WEIRDOS UNITE!

This *is* California after all; if you can't be odd here, where can you be?

Around **Santa Cruz** (p155) bumper stickers read, 'Keep Santa Cruz Weird.' Indeed. Meet like-minded freaks on the town's **beach boardwalk** (p155) and eavesdrop on conspiracy theorists at **Cafe Pergolesi** (p161). Nearby, bohemian **Big Sur** (p176) has been an alt-cultural haven ever since the Beat generation. Tap into the bohemian scene at the **Henry Miller Library** (p178).

In **San Francisco** (p51), visit the **Haight** (see boxed text, p73) to see who's still

pining for 1967's 'Summer of Love,' then join a drumming circle in **Golden Gate Park** (p56). Meet the gay community in the **Castro** (see boxed text, p80). Meanwhile, the **Mission** (see boxed text, p73) district is San Francisco's most bubbling melting pot, especially for artists and literati.

On the North Coast, **Garberville** (p125) is pot-growing country – 'nuff said. But no place embraces freaks like **Arcata** (p138) – wander around downtown's plaza or head to **Humboldt State University** (p138) to find your own lost tribe.

Down in SoCal, there's no shortage of weirdos in LA's arty **Venice** (p215), especially along the surreal **boardwalk** (p215). **Ocean Beach** (p253) is an island of tattoo parlors, vintage shops and alt-minded coffeehouses in conservative San Diego.

KITSCHY CALIFORNIANA

Before Disney corporatized the theme park, quirky roadside attractions were everywhere in California. Many have long since disappeared, but you'd be surprised how many wacky spots remain. Where else can you drive through a carved-out redwood tree or stroll through an ersatz Danish village, complete with faux windmills?

On the North Coast, squeeze your Subaru through Leggett's **Chandelier Drive-Thru Tree Park** (p124), then play tricks on gravity at **Confusion Hill** (p124) and at Klamath's **Trees of Mystery** (p148), where you can ride a gondola through the redwood canopy. Look for chainsaw carvers along Hwy 101, too.

In San Francisco, shove quarters into the opium den at the **Musée Méca-**

nique (p63) and be wowed by the cliffside **Camera Obscura** (p64). Heading south, spin a compass in Santa Cruz at the **Mystery Spot** (p157), check out the bizarre waterfall in the men's room of the **Madonna Inn** (p188) in San Luis Obispo, discover the 'Lost City of DeMille' at **Guadalupe Dunes** (p194) and chase windmills in compulsively cute, Dane-esque **Solvang** (p193).

In LA, blur the edges of reality at the Museum of Jurassic Technology or have a cocktail and catch an outdoor movie at a celebrity cemetery, Hollywood Forever. Finally, what could be kitschier than America's first theme park? Head to quaint **Knott's Berry Farm** (see boxed text, p234) and fatten up on good ol' fried chicken.

FOR TREE HUGGERS & NATURE LOVERS

California's national parklands (see p37) richly abound along the coast. In the north, crane your neck up at the world's tallest trees in **Redwood National Park** (p145). Tip: get the lock combination to the gate to **Tall Trees Grove** (p146). Wintertime whale-watching is fantastic at **Point Reyes National Seashore** (p98) and down south at **Cabrillo National Monument** (p253) in San Diego. Take a boat to reach untamed **Channel Islands National Park** (p202), off the Ventura County coast near Santa Barbara.

State parks and beaches also bless the coast, even amid SoCal's sprawl – witness San Diego's **La Jolla Cove** (p257), which beckons to snorkelers and scuba divers. Some coastal state parks have awesome hiking and mountain-biking trails. Around San Luis Obispo, you can summit peaks and ride atop ocean bluffs at **Montaña de Oro State Park** (p184). Further north, the redwood-forested state parks of **Big Sur** (p176) hide lacy waterfalls and wild, remote beaches for frolicking.

The picture-postcard views of the craggy North Coast are awesome at **Sonoma Coast State Beach** (p105), **Salt Point State Park** (p109) and the rocky **Mendocino Headlands** (p114). Further north, canoe up the tidal estuary of **Big River** (p115) or kayak the calm waters of **Humboldt Lagoons State Park** (p145). Finally, disappear from civilization along the **Lost Coast** (p127).

COASTIN' WITH KIDS

Coastal California is chockablock with old-fashioned boardwalks, futuristic theme parks, eco-educational zoos and aquariums, and tons of other family-friendly attractions to keep little ones entertained for days.

In SoCal, you gotta see **Disneyland** (p231), but **Knott's Berry Farm** (see boxed text, p234) also merits a visit for its thrill rides. If you have preteens, make a beeline for **Legoland** (p270) in Carlsbad, then detour to the **San Diego Wild Animal Park** (see boxed text, p270), where giraffes and zebras roam free. In the heart of San Diego, check out puppet shows and the model-train museum at **Balboa Park** (p249), home to the **San Diego Zoo** (p251). In LA, take a spin on the solar-powered Ferris wheel at **Santa Monica Pier** (p214).

On the Central Coast, watch otters and penguins cavort at the **Monterey Bay Aquarium** (p166) and touch tidepool critters at Santa Cruz's **Seymour Marine Discovery Center** (see boxed text, p159). Ride the vintage wooden roller coaster at the **Santa Cruz Beach Boardwalk** (p155) and jump on the **Roaring Camp Railroad** (see boxed text, p159) for a ride up into the redwoods. In San Francisco, experience a tropical rainforest dome at Golden Gate Park's **California Academy of Sciences** (p56) then push buttons at the **Exploratorium** (p64), another interactive science museum – reserve tickets for its way-cool Tactile Dome.

On the North Coast, kiddie fun is mostly DIY: ascend the **Point Arena Lighthouse** (p111) or play make-believe in the prehistoric-looking world of **Fern Canyon** (p147).

24

History

THE FIRST PEOPLES

If you don't fancy tackling Kevin Starr's epic seven-volume series, pick up the professor's compact *California: a History*, an insightful tour de force that narrates the state's story from indigenous tribes to the 'Governator.'

Immigration is hardly a new phenomenon here, since people have been migrating to California for millennia. Archaeological sites indicate this geographical region was first inhabited soon after people migrated across the long-gone land bridge from Asia during an ice age at least 20,000 years ago. Many archaeological sites have yielded evidence, from large middens of seashells along the beaches to campfire sites on the Channel Islands, that people have been living along this coast for around 8000 years.

Archaeological evidence paints a clear picture of the diversity of indigenous peoples living here at the time of first European contact. Native peoples spoke over 60 different languages and numbered as many as 300,000. They mostly lived in small groups, often migrating with the seasons from the coast up into the mountains. Acorn meal was their dietary staple, supplemented by small wild game and seafood.

Traditionally, indigenous peoples made and used earthenware pots, fish nets, bows, and arrows and spears with chipped-stone points. Animal skins and plant fibers were used for clothing. The most developed native craft was weaving baskets decorated with intricate geometric designs. Some baskets were so tightly woven they could hold water. You can view some of the native plants used in basket weaving at Sumêg, a reproduction of a Yurok village in Patrick's Point State Park (p145) on the North Coast.

A NEW WORLD FOR EUROPEANS

DID YOU KNOW?

Traces of a sophisticated Native American culture can be seen in the rock art and writing inside Chumash Painted Cave State Historic Park, near Santa Barbara.

Following the conquest of Mexico in the early 16th century, the Spanish turned their attention toward exploring the edges of their new empire. In 1542 the Spanish crown engaged Juan Rodríguez Cabrillo, a Portuguese explorer and retired conquistador, to lead an expedition up the West Coast to find the fabled golden land beyond Mexico's west coast. He was also charged with finding the equally mythical Strait of Anian, an imagined sea route between the Pacific and the Atlantic.

When Cabrillo sailed into San Diego Bay in 1542, he and his crew became the first Europeans to see mainland California. Staring back at them from shore were the Kumeyaay – to learn more about this coastal tribe, visit San Diego's Museum of Man (p250). Cabrillo's ships sat out a storm in the harbor, then sailed northward. They made a stop at the Channel Islands where, in 1543, Cabrillo fell ill, died and was buried. The expedition continued as far as Oregon, but returned with no evidence of a sea route to the Atlantic, a city of gold or islands of spice. The unimpressed Spanish authorities forgot about California for the next 50 years.

TIMELINE

20,000 BC	AD 1542	1769
The continent's early inhabitants arrive from Asia, likely after having migrated over a land bridge across the Bering Strait; nomadic groups eventually settle in California.	Portuguese navigator Juan Rodríguez Cabrillo and his Spanish crew become the first Europeans to sight the mainland of New Spain's west coast, allegedly named California after a mythical paradise.	Spain attempts to colonize California when Father Junípero Serra and Captain Gaspar de Portolá lead an expedition to establish the first Catholic missions, starting with Mission San Diego de Alcalá.

The English privateer Sir Francis Drake sailed up the California coast in 1579. He missed the entrance to San Francisco Bay, but pulled in near what is now called Point Reyes (p97) to repair his ship, which was bursting with the weight of plundered Spanish silver. He claimed the land for Queen Elizabeth, named it Nova Albion (New England) and left for other adventures, starting with journeying north up the Pacific Coast to Alaska.

THE MISSION PERIOD

Around the 1760s, as Russian ships came to California's coast in search of sea-otter pelts, and British trappers and explorers spread throughout the West, King Carlos III of Spain grew worried that these other newcomers might pose a threat to Spain's claim. Conveniently for the king, the Catholic Church was anxious to start missionary work among the indigenous peoples, so church and state combined forces to found missions inside presidios (military forts).

Ostensibly, the presidios' purpose was to protect the missions and deter foreign intruders. The idea was to have Native American converts live inside the missions, learn trade and agricultural skills, and ultimately establish pueblos (small towns). But these garrisons created more threats than they deterred, as the soldiers aroused local hostility by raiding Native American camps to sexually assault and kidnap women. Not only were the presidios militarily weak, but their weaknesses were well known to Russia and Britain, and didn't strengthen Spain's claims to California.

Ultimately, the mission period was pretty much a failure. The Spanish population remained small; the missions achieved little more than mere survival; foreign intruders were not greatly deterred; and more Native Americans died than were converted. Most of California's missions are still standing today, though a few are in ruins. Beautifully restored Mission San Juan Capistrano (p239) is among California's original chain of 21 missions, the earliest of which were founded by peripatetic Franciscan priest Junípero Serra.

FROM MEXICO TO MANIFEST DESTINY

When Mexico gained independence from Spain in 1821, many of the new nation's people looked to California to satisfy their thirst for private land. By the mid-1830s the Spanish missions had been secularized, with a series of Mexican governors doling out hundreds of free land grants, or ranchos, that were largely given over to livestock to supply a profitable trade in hide and tallow. The new landowners, called rancheros or Californios, quickly prospered and became the social, cultural and political heavyweights of Alta (Upper) California.

American explorers, trappers, traders, whalers, settlers and opportunists showed increasing interest in California, seizing on prospects that

DID YOU KNOW?

The precise etymology of 'California' has never been convincingly established, though many think it derives from a Spanish novel about a gold-rich island paradise ruled by Queen Califia.

To learn more about the cultural influence and historical significance of Spanish colonial missions built in California between 1769 and 1823, visit www .californiamissions.com.

1821	1848	1850
Mexico gains independence from Spain, and California falls under Mexican rule. Alta (Upper) California is reorganized into *ranchos* (land grants) and Spanish Catholic missions are forcibly secularized, except for Mission Santa Barbara.	After winning the Mexican-American War, the US takes control of Alta California, just as gold is discovered in the Sierra Nevada foothills. The population jumps from under 15,000 to more than 90,000 in two years.	After a protracted debate about whether it would be a slaveholding or free state (Congress decides on the latter), California finally becomes the 31st US state on September 9, 1850.

BEAR FLAG REPUBLIC

When the US annexed Texas in 1845, Mexico broke off diplomatic relations and ordered all foreigners without proper papers to be deported from California. Outraged Northern California settlers revolted, captured the nearest Mexican official and, supported by a company of US soldiers led by Captain John C Frémont, declared California's independence from Mexico in June 1846 by raising their 'Bear Flag' over the town of Sonoma. The Bear Flag Republic existed for less than one month. The banner lives on, however, in the California state flag.

---

the rancheros ignored. Some of the Americans who started businesses converted to Catholicism, married locals and assimilated into Californio society. Impressed by California's potential wealth and hoping to fulfill the promise of Manifest Destiny (the USA's imperialist doctrine to extend its borders from coast to coast), US President Andrew Jackson sent an emissary to offer the financially strapped Mexican government $500,000 for California in 1835. Though American settlers were by then showing up by the hundreds, especially in Northern California, Jackson's emissary was tersely rejected.

In 1836 Texas had seceded from Mexico and declared itself an independent republic. On May 11, 1846, the US declared war on Mexico following disputes over the former's annexation of Texas. By July, US naval units occupied every port on the California coast, including Monterey, the capital of Alta California. When US troops captured Mexico City in September 1847, ending the war, the Mexican government had little choice but to cede much of its northern territory to the US. The Treaty of Guadalupe Hidalgo, signed on February 2, 1848, turned over what is now California, Nevada, Utah and parts of Arizona, New Mexico, Colorado and Wyoming to the US. Two years later, California was admitted as the 31st state of the United States.

The website www.ca.gov /about/history.html has extensive links for history buffs, from maps of California missions and photos of the 1906 earthquake to audio clips of 20th-century folk music.

THERE'S GOLD IN THEM THAR HILLS

By remarkable coincidence, gold was discovered at Sutter's Creek, about 120 miles northeast of San Francisco, little more than a week before the signing of the Treaty of Guadalupe Hidalgo that ended the Mexican-American War. By 1849, surging rivers of wagon trains were creaking into California filled with miners, pioneers, savvy entrepreneurs, outlaws and prostitutes, all seeking their fortunes.

Population growth and overnight wealth stimulated every aspect of California life, from agriculture and banking to construction and journalism. But mining damaged the land: hills were stripped bare, erosion wiped out vegetation, streams silted up and mercury washed down rivers into San Francisco Bay. San Francisco became a hotbed of gambling, prostitution, drink and chicanery, giving rise to its moniker 'the Barbary

1869	**1906**	**1927**
A golden spike is nailed in Utah, completing the first transcontinental railroad linking California and the East Coast. The event is reported using a new invention, the telegraph, in the world's first real-time communication.	A massive earthquake levels entire blocks of San Francisco in less than a minute, setting off fires that rage for three days without adequate water supply or fire breaks. Survivors start rebuilding immediately.	*The Jazz Singer* premieres in Los Angeles as the world's first 'talkie' movie, signaling the decline of the silent-film era. Hollywood, already the epicenter of the US motion-picture industry, booms.

Coast,' whose last vestiges live on today in the strip joints in SF's North Beach neighborhood (p73).

In 1860, California vicariously experienced a second boom after the discovery of the Comstock silver lode, though that lode was located east of the Sierra Nevada range in what would soon become the state of Nevada. Exploiting the lode required deep-mining techniques, which necessitated companies, stocks, trading and speculation. San Francisco made more money speculating on silver than Nevada did mining it: huge mansions sprouted on the city's Nob Hill, and California business tycoons became renowned for their unscrupulous audacity.

DID YOU KNOW?

In 1873, Levi Strauss received a patent for his hard-wearing, riveted denim pants, originally designed for gold prospectors – and, voilà! – American blue jeans were born.

RICHES FROM RAILROADS, FARMS & OIL FIELDS

Opening the floodgates to massive migration into the West, the transcontinental railroad drastically shortened the trip from New York to San Francisco from two months to five days, profitably linking markets on both coasts. Tracks were laid simultaneously from east and west, dramatically converging with the driving of a golden spike at Promontory Point in Utah in 1869. Los Angeles was not connected to the transcontinental railroad until 1876, when Southern Pacific Railroad laid tracks from San Francisco south to the fledgling city.

By this time, rampant speculation had raised land prices in California to levels no farmer or immigrant could afford; the railroad brought in products that undersold goods made in California; and some 15,000 Chinese laborers – no longer needed for railroad construction – flooded the labor market. A period of unrest ensued, which culminated in anti-Chinese discrimination and the federal 1882 Chinese Exclusion Act banning Chinese immigration. The act was not repealed until 1943.

Much of the land granted to the railroads was sold in big lots to speculators who also acquired, with the help of corrupt politicians and administrators, a lot of the farmland intended for new settlers. A major share of the state's agricultural land thus became consolidated as large holdings in the hands of a few city-based landlords, establishing the pattern (which continues to this day) of industrial-scale 'agribusiness' rather than small family farms. These big businesses were well placed to provide the substantial investment and the political connections required to bring irrigation water to the farmland. They also solidified an ongoing need for cheap farm labor.

In the absence of coal, iron ore or abundant water, heavy industry developed slowly in California, though the 1892 discovery of oil in central Los Angeles by Edward Doheny stimulated the development of petroleum processing and chemical industries. By the year 1900, California was producing 4 million barrels of oil per year and the population of LA had doubled to over 100,000 people.

The Oscar-winning 2007 film *There Will Be Blood* is adapted from Upton Sinclair's book *Oil!*, about fictional California oil magnate Daniel Plainview, whose story is based on real-life SoCal tycoon Edward Doheny.

1941	1967	1976
Following a surprise attack by Japanese forces on Pearl Harbor on December 7, the US enters WWII. In February 1942, US Executive Order 9066 banishes 120,000 Japanese Americans to inland internment camps, including in California.	San Francisco's 'Summer of Love' kicks off with the 'Human Be-In' in Golden Gate Park, witnessing the blowing of conch shells and minds and the lighting of draft cards used as rolling papers for weed.	The first personal computer, the Apple I, is designed and hand-built in Silicon Valley. It sells for $666.66. Apple's first iPod won't appear on the market until 25 years later.

GROWING INTO THE 20TH CENTURY

John Steinbeck's Pulitzer prize–winning novel *The Grapes of Wrath* (1939) narrates the epic journey of the Joad family as they struggle to escape the Dust Bowl and reach California by motoring along Route 66.

The population, wealth and importance of California increased dramatically throughout the 20th century. The great San Francisco earthquake and fire of 1906 decimated the city, but it was barely a hiccup in the state's development. The revolutionary years in Mexico, from 1910 to 1921, caused a huge influx of immigrants from south of the border, reestablishing Latino communities that had been smothered by Anglo dominance. The Panama Canal, completed in 1914, made shipping more feasible between the East Coast and West Coast, opening up new markets for California's farms. Meanwhile, SoCal's oil industry boomed in the 1920s and Hollywood entered its so-called 'Golden Age,' which lasted through the 1950s.

The Great Depression saw another wave of immigrants, this time from the impoverished Great Plains states of the Dust Bowl. Outbreaks of social and labor unrest led to rapid growth of the Democratic Party in California, as well as trade unions for blue-collar workers. Many of the Depression-era public works projects sponsored by the federal government had lasting benefits, from San Francisco's Bay Bridge to the restoration of historic missions statewide, notably Mission La Purísima Concepción (p194) near Santa Barbara.

A noir film masterpiece, *Chinatown* (1974) is the fictionalized yet surprisingly realistic account of the brutal early-20th-century water wars that were waged to build LA and San Francisco.

WWII had a major impact on California. Women were co-opted into wartime factory work and proved themselves in a range of traditionally male jobs. Anti-Asian sentiments resurfaced, many Japanese Americans were interned, and more Mexicans crossed the border to fill labor shortages. Some military servicepeople who passed through California liked the place so much that they returned to settle after the war. In the postwar decade, the state's population jumped by 40%, reaching 13 million by 1955.

RADICALS, TREND-SETTERS & TECHNOLOGY

Unconstrained by tradition, California has long been a leader in new attitudes and social movements. During the affluent postwar years of the 1950s, the Beat movement in San Francisco's North Beach railed against the banality and conformity of suburban life, instead choosing bohemian coffeehouses for jazz, poetry and pot.

When the postwar baby boomers came of age, many took up where the Beat generation left off, heeding 1960s countercultural icon Timothy Leary's counsel to 'turn on, tune in, and drop out.' Their revolt climaxed in San Francisco's Haight district (p73) during the 1967 'Summer of Love.' Sex, drugs and rock-and-roll ruled the day. With the foundation for social revolution already laid, gay liberation exploded in San Francisco in the '70s. Today San Francisco remains one of the world's most exuberantly gay cities – just take a stroll through the Castro district (p80).

1989	1992	2000
The 6.9-magnitude Loma Prieta Earthquake hits near Santa Cruz and collapses a San Francisco freeway and a Bay Bridge section, killing 42. The Bay Bridge seismic retrofit is expected to be completed by 2013.	After the videotaped 1991 beating of African American motorist Rodney King by white police officers, three of four officers involved are acquitted by a predominantly white jury. LA endures six days of riots.	On March 10 the Nasdaq crashes, dramatically ending the dot-com boom. Traditional industry wonks gloat over the burst bubble, until knock-on effects lead to a devalued dollar and a later NYSE slide.

In the 1980s and '90s, California catapulted to the forefront of the healthy lifestyle, with more aerobics classes and self-actualization workshops than you could shake a shaman's stick at. In-line skating, snowboarding and mountain biking rose to fame here first. Be careful what you laugh at, though: from pet rocks to soy burgers, California's flavor of the month will probably be next year's fad sweeping the nation.

As digital technology continually reinvents our world view, California has also led the world in developing computer technology. In the 1950s, Stanford University needed to raise money to finance postwar growth, so it built an industrial park and leased space to high-tech companies like Hewlett-Packard, which formed the nucleus of Northern California's Silicon Valley. In 1971 Intel invented the microchip, and in 1976 Apple invented the first personal computer. In the fat years of the late 1990s, companies nationwide jumped on the dot-com bandwagon following the exponential growth of the web. Many reaped huge overnight profits, fueled by misplaced optimism, only to crash with equal velocity at the turn of the millennium.

> The Oscar-winning film *Milk* (2008) tells the story of San Francisco's first openly gay city supervisor who, on a dark day in 1978, was murdered by political opponent Dan White.

OUTLOOK FOR THE 21ST CENTURY

No place in America was more affected by the demise of the dot-coms in 2000 than California. That same year also brought widespread power shortages and rolling blackouts to California, which were caused by Enron's illegal manipulation of markets. But before the truth came out, Republican malcontents fingered then-Governor Gray Davis and called for a special recall election that ousted him.

Enter Arnold Schwarzenegger – Californians will always forgive a movie star more easily than a politician. Although a Republican, Schwarzenegger's actions during his first term suggested that he intended to govern from California's political center, notably when it came to environmental issues. He fought to pass legislation that helped California lead the nation in cutting greenhouse emissions, even as US President and fellow Republican George W Bush rejected the Kyoto Protocol.

In 2006, Schwarzenegger won another gubernatorial term, and San Francisco congresswoman Nancy Pelosi became the Speaker of the House in Washington DC. But the next year saw the start of the unraveling subprime mortgage-lending crisis, which triggered the US stock market crash of 2008 and caused the entire nation to sink into a recession. Massive unemployment devastated California, once the world's sixth-largest economy. By 2009 the state was so broke that it issued IOU slips to creditors. The 'Governator' played hardball during the budget crisis, making massive cuts to social services, education and state parks funding.

> **DID YOU KNOW?**
>
> The very first item sold on eBay, the online auction site invented in San Jose, California, in 1995, was a *broken* laser pointer. The winning bid? $14.83.

> LA once had a wonderfully efficient system of streetcars, until General Motors allegedly conspired to destroy it: search Google for 'General Motors streetcar conspiracy' and make up your own mind.

2003	2007	2009
Body builder, movie star and Republican, Arnold Schwarzenegger, becomes Governor of California; his wife Maria Shriver is an influential Kennedy clan member.	With winds gusting up to 85mph, wildfires sweep across drought-stricken Southern California. One million people evacuate homes from Santa Barbara to San Diego as military personnel, state prisoners and Tijuana firefighters curb the blazes.	Five years after San Francisco Mayor Gavin Newsom first officiates same-sex marriages, California's Supreme Court upholds a constitutional ban on same-sex marriages that voters narrowly passed in 2008. Legal challenges are pending.

The Culture

If you happen to overhear some California slang you're totally confused by, log onto www .urbandictionary.com for all the uncensored, street-worthy definitions. Word out.

The rest of America shakes its head in wonder at California, never quite sure how to categorize it. It's best not to try, since the Golden State is forever reinventing itself. Remember, this is the place that gave the world both hippies *and* Ronald Reagan.

REGIONAL IDENTITY

It's best to think of California as two states: Southern California (SoCal) and Northern California (NorCal, *not* NoCal). Although nobody can agree on exactly where to draw the line between the two, it falls somewhere between San Francisco, with its liberal-minded hipsters, and Los Angeles, the glitzy but tarnished 'City of Angels.'

In any case, believe everything you've ever heard about Californians, so long as you realize the stereotypes are always exaggerated. Sure, tweens snap chewing gum in the shopping malls of the San Fernando Valley north of LA, blond surfers shout 'Dude!' across San Diego beaches, hippies and Rastafarians gather for drum circles in San Francisco's Golden Gate Park, and tree huggers toke on joints in the North Coast woods but, all in all, it's hard to peg the population. Bear in mind that the following explorations of identity merely address trends, not hard-and-fast rules.

Woodsy types live in the north. Think buffalo-plaid flannel. There aren't a lot of people way up there – and there's not a lot of money floating around either. Conservative radio stations shout on several strong frequencies. At the other end of the spectrum, you'll also find some of the state's most progressive liberals and borderline fanatics up north. If you spot a beat-up old diesel Mercedes-Benz chugging along the highway, chances are it's running on biodiesel, possibly recycled French-fry grease from fast-food restaurants. There's a lot of ingenuity 'round here.

In the Bay Area, the politics are liberal and the people open-minded, with a strong live-and-let-live ethic and an often passionate devotion to the outdoors. In overwhelmingly wealthy and white Marin County, there's a tremendous sense of civic pride that sometimes borders on narcissism. San Francisco is more of a melting pot, but there aren't a lot of lower-income citizens since rents are so high. The East Bay, Alameda County, which covers Oakland and Berkeley, has more ethnic diversity.

In We Tell Ourselves Stories in Order to Live (2006), Joan Didion's essays capture the essence of California's history and contemporary culture, from early women pioneers to the psychology of driving LA freeways.

The hard-to-classify Central Coast, with its smaller pockets of population, starts near wacky, left-of-center Santa Cruz and stretches all the way south to surreally beautiful, sexily posh Santa Barbara. Along the way, Hwy 1 winds past working-class Monterey, made famous in John Steinbeck's novels; the bohemian Big Sur coast; the conservative upper-crust villages of Carmel-by-the-Sea and Cambria, where the 'newly wed and nearly dead' have multimillion-dollar homes; and the laidback, liberal college town of San Luis Obispo, midway between SF and LA.

LA has a reputation for racial tension, possibly because it's so much more diverse. Yet the unease also likely reflects the disparity between haves and have-nots, for example, from Beverly Hills and South Central. Composed of dozens of independent cities, it's impossible to generalize about LA, but one thing is for sure: almost everybody drives. You're nothing – and sometimes nowhere – without a car.

Between LA and San Diego lies Orange County, aka 'the OC,' where beautifully bronzed, buff bodies soak up rays on the sands. But make no mistake about it: it's no beach bums' paradise. The politics 'behind the Orange Curtain' are notably conservative. Here Republicans are welcomed with open arms at $2000-a-plate fundraising dinners. Many people live in gated communities and have limited tolerance for (or exposure to) outsiders. The conservative politics extend south to San Diego, partly due to its sizeable military population.

LIFESTYLE & POPULATION

So, what about that sun-kissed beach lifestyle you've been dreaming about? Most coastal Californians wouldn't recognize that life as their own. In major cities, more residents rent than own, although that balance has lately been shifting following the bursting of the housing-market bubble. As the economic recession continues, home prices continue to fall, making housing more affordable for the middle-class, despite the fact that California's median home price of $246,000 is still almost 50% more than the US average. In addition, California's median household income is only $60,000, less than 20% above the national average, which makes their sky-high mortgage payments even more difficult to pay.

Political correctness thrives along the coast. In fact, most everyone is so determined to get along that it can be hard to find out what somebody really thinks. This increases the further south you go. Sometimes it's annoying. If you stick around one of the larger metropolitan areas for a while, you'll inevitably exchange telephone numbers with a person who expresses interest in seeing you again. In most parts of the world that means, 'Call me.' Not in California. It may be just a nicety. Often the other person never calls and, if you make an attempt, you may never hear back.

Some might say that you're 'codependent' for having expectations of your new friend. Self-help jargon has thoroughly infiltrated the daily language of coastal Californians. For example, the word 'issue' is constantly bandied about. Generally this is a way to refer to someone else's problems without implying that the person has…well, problems. The mantra seems to be: 'can't we all just get along, man?'

Of course, this all flies out the window with an extended middle finger on busy freeways. Road rage has become a serious hazard. If you plan to do any driving, take a deep breath before you put the key in the ignition, and meditate on remaining calm. Expect to encounter irrational and unpredictable drivers who won't hesitate to cut you off, then flip you the 'bird,' especially in major metropolitan areas.

California ranks as the most populous state in the US, with over 36 million residents. The state has more than double the US average population density, with 217 people per square mile. In fact, 25% of California residents live in LA County alone. California is one of the fastest-growing states, with three million new residents just since 2000. Its racial makeup continues to shift: Hispanic, Latino and Asian populations steadily increase, while Caucasians (non-Hispanic) decline. At least one in four California residents is foreign-born (including Governor Schwarzenegger) and 40% speak a language other than English at home, primarily Spanish.

If you visit a coastal city, you're sure to encounter homeless people, sometimes begging on the streets, beaches and at well-trafficked intersections. Many suffer from medical or psychiatric problems, or the effects of alcohol and drug abuse; some are scammers. Most are harmless, although verbally harassing passersby, especially women, is common. It's an individual judgment call whether to give them money – you might just offer food if you have it. If you want to contribute toward a long-term solution, consider donating to a reputable charity that cares for the homeless.

Can San Diego's outwardly carefree appearance belie a seamy noir underbelly? Get the dirt in *Under the Perfect Sun: The San Diego Tourists Never See* (2003), by Mike Davis, Kelly Mayhew and Jim Miller.

Eight of the 10 most-expensive US housing markets are found in California. La Jolla, a beachfront community in northern San Diego County, tops the list.

The NorCal coast has scores of nude beaches (apparently, people aren't so willing to get nekkid outside in SoCal). To find out where you can frolic au naturel, browse www.sfbg.com/nudebeaches.

ARTS

Thanks to the movie industry, perhaps no other city can claim the pop-cultural influence that LA exerts worldwide. Meanwhile, writers and musicians have been seeking inspiration in gritty LA and bohemian San Francisco for decades. Southern California in particular has proved to be fertile ground for new architectural styles.

Literature

The Beat generation of writers fired up San Francisco's North Beach literary scene during the 1950s, including with Allen Ginsberg's epic poem *Howl* (1956) and Jack Kerouac's iconic novel *On the Road* (1957).

The West Coast has long drawn artists and writers, and today California's resident literary community is as strong as ever with such talent as: Alice Walker, Pulitzer prize-winning author of *The Color Purple* (1982); progressive feminist poet Adrienne Rich; Chilean-American novelist Isabel Allende; Amy Tan, author of such popular fiction as *The Joy Luck Club* (1989); Maxine Hong Kingston, coeditor of the landmark anthology *The Literature of California* (2000); Dave Eggers, the hipster behind *McSweeney's* quarterly literary journal; and Michael Chabon, author of the Pulitzer prize-winning *The Amazing Adventures of Kavalier and Clay* (2000).

Few writers nail California culture as well as Joan Didion. She's best known for her collection of essays, *Slouching Towards Bethlehem* (1968), which takes a caustic look at 1960s flower power and Haight-Ashbury. Tom Wolfe also put '60s San Francisco in perspective with *The Electric Kool-Aid Acid Test* (1968), which follows Ken Kesey's band of Merry Pranksters, who began their acid-laced 'magic bus' journey near Santa Cruz. Charles Bukowski's semiautobiographical novel *Post Office* (1971) captures down-and-out Downtown LA. Richard Vasquez' *Chicano* (1971) takes a dramatic look at LA's Latino barrio.

For a frothy taste of 1970s San Francisco, the serial-style *Tales of the City*, by Armistead Maupin, collars the reader as the author follows the lives of several colorful, fictional characters, gay and straight.

Back in the 1930s, San Francisco and LA became the capitals of the pulp detective novel, often made into classic noir films. Dashiell Hammett (*The Maltese Falcon*, 1930) made San Francisco's fog a sinister character. The king of hard-boiled crime writers was Raymond Chandler (*The Big Sleep*, 1939), who thinly disguised Santa Monica as shadowy Bay City. A renaissance of noir crime fiction has been masterminded by James Ellroy (*LA Confidential*, 1990) and Walter Mosley (*Devil in a Blue Dress*, 1990), whose Easy Rawlins detective novels are set in LA's South Central 'hood.

Cinema & Television

California's major export – film – is a powerful presence in the lives of not only Americans but people around the world. Images of California are distributed far beyond its borders, ultimately reflecting back upon the state itself. Few tourists arrive without some cinematic reference to the place – nearly every street corner has been or perhaps will be a movie set. With increasing regularity, Hollywood films feature California as both a setting and a topic and, in some cases, almost as a character. LA especially loves to turn the camera on itself, often with a film-noir angle. California is also a versatile backdrop for edgy cable TV dramas, from Showtime's *Weeds*, about a pot-growing SoCal widow, to cop show *The Closer*, and also reality shows including MTV's *The Hills*, about rich, gorgeous 20-somethings in LA.

California Babylon: A Guide to Sites of Scandal, Mayhem and Celluloid in the Golden State (2000) by Kristan Lawson and Anneli Rufus is a bizarre guide to infamous locations throughout the state. It's a guilty pleasure.

The Industry, as it's called, grew out of the humble orchards of Hollywoodland (the original name for Hollywood's residential area). The silent-movie era gave way to 'talkies' after 1927's *The Jazz Singer* premiered in Downtown LA, ushering in Hollywood's glamorous Golden Age. Today Hollywood is no longer the focus. The high cost of filming in LA has sent location scouts beyond the San Fernando Valley (where most movie and TV studios are found) and north of the border to Canada, where they're welcomed with open arms in 'Hollywood North.' A few production companies are still based in San Francisco, including Francis Ford Coppola's American Zoetrope and George Lucas' Industrial Light & Magic, made up of high-tech gurus who produce computer-generated special effects for Hollywood blockbusters. Pixar Animation Studios, makers of *Toy Story* and *Wall•E*, are just across the Bay in Emeryville.

Music

From smoky jazz clubs that once filled San Francisco's North Beach to hard-edged West Coast rap and hip hop born in South Central LA, California has rocked the world.

In the 1930s and '40s, swingin' big bands toured LA. After WWII, the bebop of Charlie Parker and Charlie Mingus made LA swoon, while the West Coast blues sound developed up north in Oakland. In the '50s, the cool West Coast jazz of Chet Baker and Dave Brubeck evolved in San Francisco's North Beach, where Beat poets echoed improvisational riffs.

The first homegrown rock-and-roll talent to make it big in the '50s was Richie Valens, whose 'La Bamba' was a rockified version of a Mexican folk song. In the '60s, Sam Cooke's record label attracted soul and R&B talent to LA, where Jim Morrison and The Doors busted onto the Sunset Strip. Meanwhile, San Francisco launched the psychedelic-rock revolution with big-name acts such as the Grateful Dead and Janis Joplin.

The late '70s and early '80s birthed California's own brand of punk. In LA, the rockabilly-edged band X stood out, while Black Flag led the hard-core way with singer Henry Rollins. San Francisco produced the Dead Kennedys and the Avengers. The Red Hot Chili Peppers exploded out of LA in the late '80s with a highly charged, funk-punk sound, while the early '90s generated pop punksters blink-182 in San Diego and Green Day in the Bay Area.

LA today is the hotbed for West Coast rap and hip hop. Eazy E, Ice Cube and Dr Dre released the seminal NWA (Niggaz With Attitude) album, *Straight Outta Compton*, in 1988. Death Row Records, cofounded by Dr Dre, has since launched such artists as Long Beach bad-boy Snoop Dogg and the late Tupac Shakur, who launched his rap career in Marin County, of all places. At the turn of the 21st century, the Bay Area was producing underground artists such as E-40 and birthed the 'hyphy movement,' a reaction against the increasing commercialization of hip hop.

Architecture

California's architecture, a fruitful jumble of styles, is as diverse as the state's population.

In the late 18th and early 19th centuries, Spanish colonial missions were built around courtyards with materials that were on hand: adobe, limestone and grass. Southern California's Mission San Juan Capistrano (p239) and Mission La Purísima Concepción (p194) are among the best-restored examples. Later settlers adapted mission architecture to create the rancho adobe style, as seen at El Pueblo de Los Angeles (p219) and in San Diego's Old Town (p251).

During the mid-19th-century Gold Rush, California's nouveau riche started constructing grand mansions. Victorian architecture, especially the showy Queen Anne style, is most prevalent in NorCal cities such as San Francisco (p74), Ferndale (p131) and Eureka (p134), yet one of the finest examples of Victorian whimsy is San Diego's Hotel del Coronado (p252).

With its simpler, classical lines, Spanish colonial revival style – also called mission revival style – was an early-20th-century rejection of frilly Victorian

Director Alfred Hitchcock set some of his best thrillers in San Francisco, including *Vertigo* (1958), with unforgettable shots of the Golden Gate Bridge and Muir Woods, and *The Birds* (1963), mostly filmed in Bodega Bay.

Listen online to KCRW (www.kcrw.com/music), Santa Monica's National Public Radio (NPR) affiliate, or download podcasts of its award-winning music shows for a slice of the California soundscape.

California Crazy and Beyond: Roadside Vernacular Architecture (2001) by Jim Heimann is for anyone enamored of hot dog–shaped fast-food stands, windmill-shaped bakeries and other kitschy architectural treasures that reach their zenith in SoCal.

design. Union Station train depots in LA and San Diego showcase this style, as do many buildings in downtown Santa Barbara (p195) and San Diego's Balboa Park (p249), a legacy of the 1915 Panama-California Exposition.

Simplicity was also the hallmark of the arts-and-crafts style, a reaction against the mass production of the Industrial Revolution. Arts-and-crafts bungalows emphasized handcrafted details and erased definitive lines between indoor and outdoor spaces. They were especially popular in Southern California, and in Oakland and Berkeley. Julia Morgan, California's first licensed female architect, worked with the arts-and-crafts style in the Bay Area and on the Monterey Peninsula at Asilomar (p173).

Art deco took off during the 1920s and '30s, with vertical lines and symmetry creating a soaring effect. Heavy ornamentation featured floral motifs, sunbursts, zigzags and other embellishments inspired by Ancient Egypt, Greece and Rome, as well as African, Indian and Mesoamerican designs. Downtown Oakland (p62) has a wealth of art-deco buildings. Around the same time period, Julia Morgan was starting work on over-the-top Hearst Castle (p181), a quirky mix of Moorish, Spanish and Mediterranean revival styles.

Modernism, also called the International Style, was initiated in Europe by Bauhaus architects Walter Gropius, Ludwig Mies van der Rohe and Le Corbusier. Its characteristics include boxlike building shapes, open floor plans, plain facades and abundant glass. After moving to LA, Austrian-born Richard Schindler and Richard Neutra adapted this minimalist style to residential houses that reflected SoCal's see-and-be-seen culture.

Postmodernism was partly a response to the starkness of the International Style, and sought to reemphasize the structural form of the building and the space around it. Richard Meier transcended postmodernist vision with LA's Getty Center (p215). Canadian-born Frank Gehry is known for his deconstructivist buildings with almost sculptural forms and distinctive facade materials, as seen in the high-profile Walt Disney Concert Hall (p219) in Downtown LA.

SPORTS

California boasts more professional sports teams than any other state. If you're in LA, San Francisco, Oakland or San Diego, depending on the season you'll have your pick of NFL football, NBA basketball or MLB baseball action. Pro games can sell out – especially San Francisco 49ers, Oakland Raiders and San Diego Chargers football, LA Lakers basketball and LA Kings hockey matches – so buy tickets early. You probably won't have to sell your firstborn child to score a ticket to pro hockey in Anaheim, pro soccer in LA, or pro baseball action in any coastal city, however.

Pro beach volleyball tournaments take place every summer at Hermosa and Manhattan Beaches in LA and Huntington Beach in the OC. Check www.avp.com for schedules.

Intercity and intracity rivalries can be intense, so when football's San Francisco 49ers play the Oakland Raiders, basketball's LA Lakers play the LA Clippers, or baseball's San Francisco Giants play the LA Dodgers, or when the Oakland A's take on Anaheim's Angels, you best just stand back. Patrons of college-sports rivalries, such as UC Berkeley's Cal Bears versus the Stanford Cardinals, or the USC Trojans against the UCLA Bruins, are even more insane. In 2005, there was SoCal outrage over the Anaheim Angels renaming themselves the LA Angels of Anaheim, which is stretching the point geographically. Anaheim's civic leaders, who had custom-built the Angels' stadium in the 1960s, sued the team but lost.

Excepting championship play-offs, the regular season for major-league soccer runs from March to October, major-league baseball April to September, NFL football September to January, NHL ice hockey October to March and NBA basketball November to April.

Environment

Much of coastal California has a Mediterranean climate, with warm, dry summers and mild, wet winters. That makes it a haven for diverse plants and animals. In fact, 30% of all plant and reptile species and almost half of all of the bird and mammal species that inhabit the USA can be found right here in the Golden State. At the same time, California is the most-populous US state (with over 70% of its residents living in coastal counties) and it has the highest projected growth rate in the nation, all of which puts a tremendous strain on its natural resources. So, is it paradise found or lost? The answer is undeniably complex.

The California state flower is the orange-yellow California poppy, and it's illegal to pick them. Besides, they wilt almost instantly when plucked from the ground.

THE LAND

The third-largest state after Alaska and Texas, California covers nearly 156,000 sq miles, making it larger than Germany or the UK. The state's northern edge lies at about the same latitude as Cape Cod, Massachusetts, and Rome, Italy, while its southern edge lies at the same latitude as Savannah, Georgia, and Tel Aviv, Israel.

California sits on one of the world's major earthquake fault zones, on the dramatic edge of two moving plates: the Pacific Plate, consisting of the Pacific Ocean floor and much of California's coastline, and the continental North American Plate. The primary boundary between the two is the infamous San Andreas Fault, which runs for over 650 miles and has spawned numerous smaller faults that extend their fingers toward the shoreline. Walk the Earthquake Trail at Point Reyes National Seashore (p98) for an up-close lesson in plate tectonics. Earthquakes are common, although most are too small or too remote to be detected without sensors. For safety advice, see p276.

California claims both the highest point in the contiguous US (Mt Whitney summit, 14,505ft) and the lowest elevation in North America (Badwater, 282ft below sea level, in Death Valley).

Capturing winter storms and summertime fog, the north–south Coast Ranges run along most of California's coastline, plunging into the Pacific to the west and rolling gently toward the sea-level Central Valley to the east. San Francisco Bay divides these ranges roughly in half, with towering redwoods thriving from the Oregon border all the way south to Big Sur on the Central Coast. Three-quarters of the way down the state, the Coast Ranges are joined to the Sierra Nevada by a series of east–west mountains called the Transverse Ranges. These mountains, which extend toward the coast as far north as Santa Barbara, officially divide the state into Southern and Northern California. Further south, the desert-like Los Angeles Basin fronts the ocean while being surrounded by mountains on three sides. San Diego, on the edge of this plateau about 120 miles south of Los Angeles, borders Tijuana, Mexico.

WILDLIFE
Animals

Spend even one day along the coast and you're likely to spot some sort of amusingly lively sea otter or pinniped, likely a harbor seal or California sea lion. See them all frolic along the Central Coast at Point Lobos State Reserve (p174) near Carmel or on the Channel Islands (p202) offshore from Ventura County. In San Francisco, you can see sea lions up close at Pier 39 (p63). Between December and April, everyone wants to watch gray whales breach offshore during their annual migration between Alaska and Mexico's Baja California. For whale-watching tips and viewpoints, see p43.

According to the US Geological Survey, the odds of a magnitude 6.7 or greater earthquake hitting California in the next 30 years is over 99%.

Over 350 bird species migrate through California along the Pacific Flyway, one of North America's principal migration routes, so there's a changing roster of birds overhead from fall through spring. Birders can bust out binoculars almost anywhere along the coast, but birding hot spots include Lake Earl (p152), Humboldt Bay National Wildlife Refuge (p134), Arcata Marsh (p139), Point Reyes National Seashore (p98), Audubon Canyon Ranch (p96), Morro Bay (p185), Andrée Clark Bird Refuge in Santa Barbara (p195) and the Channel Islands (p202). Year-round avian residents include gulls, grebes, terns, cormorants, sandpipers and little sanderlings that chase receding waves along the shore, looking for critters in the freshly turned sand.

Monarch butterflies are gorgeous orange creatures that follow amazing long-distance migration patterns in search of milkweed, their only source of food. They spend winter in California by the tens of thousands, mostly on the Central Coast, famously at Pismo Beach (p192), Pacific Grove (p171) and Santa Cruz (p155).

Plants

Coastal ecosystems range from drenched to parched. Northern Coast Ranges support stands of coast redwoods, the world's tallest trees (see p143). These towering giants with spongy red bark, flat needles and olive-size cones rely on fog as their primary water source. On the lush forest floor beneath them, look for sword ferns, redwood sorrel and deep green mosses.

Along the Central Coast, the Monterey cypress and Monterey pine have thick, rough, grayish bark; long, reaching branches growing in clusters from the top of the trunk; and long needles. Depending where they stand, they're sometimes contorted by the coast's frequent and powerful wind. They too derive much of their water from the billowing coastal fog.

Southern California, by comparison, is much more arid. Look for live oak, with holly-like evergreen leaves and sweet acorns; aromatic California bay laurel, with long slender leaves that turn purple; and manzanita, tree-like shrubs with burgundy bark and small berries. The Torrey pine, a species adapted to sparse rainfall and sandy, stony soils, is extremely rare. Look for it north of San Diego (p257) and on Santa Rosa Island in the Channel Islands National Park (p202).

Throughout California, both along the coast and inland, the hills turn green in winter, not summer. Because it almost never freezes, the dried-out brown grasses spring to life with new growth as soon as the late autumn or early winter rains arrive. Wildflowers pop up as early as February, and March is nicknamed the 'emerald month.' All along the coast, look for California poppies, which bloom until May.

Threatened & Endangered Species

The coastline of California – indeed, much of the state – has been drastically altered by development. Imagine almost all of the coast from the Oregon border to Santa Cruz covered with stands of giant redwoods. Today only about 4% remain, yet they provide an important habitat: in recent years scientists have discovered that the complexity of these old-growth forests matches that of the tropical rainforests.

Along the North Coast, the most famous casualty of logging in recent years is the northern spotted owl. A threatened species, these owls are protected inside **Headwaters Forest Reserve** (☎ 707-825-2300 for reservations) outside Eureka. It's open to the public for guided hikes from mid-May through mid-November.

CALIFORNIA'S COMEBACK CONDORS

When it comes to endangered species, one of the state's biggest success stories is the California condor. These gigantic, prehistoric birds weigh over 20lb with a wingspan of up to 10ft, enabling them to fly great distances in search of carrion. They're easily recognizable by their naked pink heads and large white patches on the black undersides of each wing.

So rare did this big bird become, mostly due to poisoning by the insecticide DDT from industrial waste runoff, that in 1987 there were only 27 left in the world, and all were removed from the wild to special captive-breeding facilities. There are now 356 California condors alive and thriving, with increasing numbers of captive birds being released back into the wild, where it is hoped that they will begin breeding naturally.

The entire Big Sur coast offers excellent opportunities for observing this majestic bird in flight. Stop by the Big Sur Discovery Center (p178) at Andrew Molera State Park for an up-close look at condor ecology, species-recovery plans and bird-banding and monitoring efforts.

All along the coast, you'll hear about threatened western snowy plovers, tiny birds that nest in the sand and scare easily. When approached by hikers or dune buggies, they take off, leaving their eggs, which burn in the sun. Some state beaches partially close during the plovers' nesting season from March through September. The Monterey Bay Aquarium (p166) is working to restore their habitat by rescuing abandoned eggs and pairing the chicks with adult males, who raise the young.

Hunted to the edge of extinction in the 19th century for their oil-rich blubber, threatened northern elephant seals began reappearing on California beaches in the 1950s. North of Santa Cruz, Año Nuevo State Reserve (p86), and Point Piedras Blancas (p182), just north of Hearst Castle, are now home to the world's largest colonies of northern elephant seals, which also breed along the Point Reyes National Seashore.

> The peak mating season for northern elephant seals along the Pacific coast just happens to coincide with Valentine's Day (February 14).

Introduced & Invasive Species

Once a biodiverse 'island' protected by the ocean and the Sierra Nevada Mountains, California has been overrun by introduced species. Ice plant, the ropy green groundcover plant with purple-and-white flowers that creeps over beach dunes, originally came from South Africa. During construction of 19th-century railways, fast-growing eucalyptus trees were imported from Australia to make railroad ties, but the wood proved poor and split when driven through with a stake. The trees now grow like weeds, fueling summertime wildfires with their flammable, explosive seed capsules. Even snails come from far away, brought here in the 1850s from France to produce escargot. Now they're everywhere, along with Atlantic crabs, which also destroy native oyster beds.

> The Sierra Club (www.sierraclub.org/ca) was the USA's first conservation group and it remains the nation's most active, offering educational programs, organized trips and volunteer vacations.

NATIONAL & STATE PARKS

The **National Park Service** (NPS; www.nps.gov/state/CA) protects spectacular stretches of coastline in California, including Redwood National Park (p145) on the North Coast. In the San Francisco Bay Area, the Golden Gate National Recreation Area protects Alcatraz Island (p55), Ocean Beach (p64), the Marin Headlands (p87), Muir Woods National Monument (p95) and Stinson Beach (p96), among other sites. Further north, the Point Reyes National Seashore (p98) is another haven for wildlife. Offshore from Ventura in Southern California, the Channel Islands National Park (p202) is remote and largely undeveloped. The islands, nicknamed 'California's Galapagos,' are prized for their rich marine life and unique ecology. Further south in San Diego, the Cabrillo National

> The California State Parks website (www.parks.ca.gov) is a one-stop trip-planning tool, featuring themed itineraries and downloadable maps, brochures and trail guides.

Monument (p253), where European explorers first landed on the West Coast, is a spectacular vista point.

California State Parks (☎ 916-653-6995, 800-777-0369; www.parks.ca.gov) protects nearly a third of the coastline, along with 3000 miles of hiking, biking and equestrian trails. Although recent budget cutbacks by the state government and Governor Arnold Schwarzenegger had forced widespread closures (hopefully, temporarily) throughout the entire state park system at press time, California's nature preserves and historical sites are still a diverse bunch, including underwater marine reserves, coastal dunes, lagoons, lighthouses and seemingly endless beaches. Redwood National Park together with Prairie Creek Redwoods State Park (p146), Del Norte Coast Redwoods State Park (p149) and Jedediah Smith Redwoods State Park (p152) is California's only Unesco World Heritage site.

> California sports 40 National Wildlife Refuges (NWRs), with over a dozen near the coast – for descriptions, check the US Fish & Wildlife Service website (www .fws.gov/refuges).

In coastal California, the entrance fee for national parks varies from free to up to $5 per person or vehicle and may be good for unlimited entries over seven consecutive days. At most state parks, there's a day-use parking fee of $4 to $15 per vehicle, but often no charge or a minimal entry fee if you arrive on foot or bicycle. At both state and national parks, organized tours and transportation operated by private concessionaires normally cost extra.

ENVIRONMENTAL ISSUES

California's development has often come at the expense of the environment. Pollution from mining washes into waterways that find their way to the ocean, polluting wetlands along the Pacific Flyway. Tons of particulate matter spews into the air from automobile and diesel emissions, reducing air quality and hiding the sun in urban areas, especially around LA. The ocean is overfished, land is disappearing beneath asphalt and landfills, and tankers occasionally leak oil into the sea.

> Southern California would not exist as it does today without water. Marc Reisner's must-read *Cadillac Desert: The American West and Its Disappearing Water* examines the contentious, sometimes violent, water wars that gave rise to modern California.

But the news isn't all bad. Californians maintain a high awareness of environmental matters and often vote for preservation. Take San Francisco for example. The city plans to recycle *all* of its trash by the year 2020 and has already instituted citywide composting of perishable organic matter; it also recently installed carbon-offset vending-machine kiosks at San Francisco International Airport. Meanwhile, Californians have voted to fund construction of solar power plants that currently produce 500 megawatts of electricity statewide. There's even talk of harnessing the tremendous tidal flows of the Pacific Ocean to generate more 'clean' energy. In late 2009, Governor Schwarzenegger signed an executive order mandating that California get 33% of its energy from renewable resources by 2020, so far the most ambitious target of any state.

Along the coast air pollution isn't too bad, due mainly to the prevailing westerly winds that blow in clean air off the ocean. But travel inland, especially across the LA Basin, and the air takes on a thick haze, obscuring vistas and creating health hazards. Fortunately California leads the nation in both automobile emissions control and ownership of hybrid and alternative-fuel vehicles. That said, given their love affair (some say obsession) with cars, Californians aren't likely to give up driving en masse anytime soon.

> The nonprofit organization Coastwalk (www.coastwalk.org) is dedicated to finishing the 1200-mile California Coastal Trail; check the website for guided hikes and volunteer beach clean-up days.

Of equal concern is water. There never seems to be enough to satisfy demand by coastal cities and inland farms. Most of it comes from the Sierra Nevada Mountains, in the eastern part of the state, but global warming and droughts both affect winter snowpack. If it doesn't snow in the Sierra – or if it only rains – there's nothing left in spring to melt into the reservoirs that supply inland farms and coastal cities. Out of necessity, Californians are slowly learning how to conserve. And you will too: look for low-flow showerheads and low-flush toilets in hotel rooms.

Coastal California Outdoors

Though you'll feel plenty of wind through your hair and sun on your face while cruising Hwy 1, you'll need to get those muscles moving and adrenaline pumping to fully grasp the coast's spectacular riches. Californians know they're spoiled silly, so they express their gratitude by taking every chance to hit the trails, hop into the saddle or grab a paddle. Now it's your turn: go kayaking under sea arches and along rocky coastlines, launch your paraglider off a cliff and float over the glistening ocean, spot a whale breaching off the bow of your boat or make your California dreamin' come true with a surfing lesson. This state may be where car and mall culture gained a foothold, but the wise among us know that in reality, it's all about the great outdoors.

With a database that's searchable by destination or activity, www.away .com has ideas for scores of active adventures in coastal California, featuring content from *Outside* magazine.

SWIMMING

If lazing on the beach and taking quick dips in the Pacific is what you've got in mind, look to Southern California (SoCal). Northern California waters are unbearably cold year-round, with a dangerously high swell in places and rocky beaches that make swimming uninviting. Once you get far enough south, let's say Santa Barbara, the beaches become golden and sandy, and the weather and the waters turn balmy. By the time you hit Los Angeles, Orange County (aka 'the OC') and San Diego, you'll find SoCal beach culture in full swing – at least during summer, that is. Even SoCal beaches can be chilly and too stormy for swimming in winter.

The biggest hazards along the coast are riptides and dangerous ocean currents. Obey all posted signs on beaches. If you get caught in a riptide, which pulls you away from shore, don't fight it or you'll get exhausted and drown. Instead, swim parallel to the shoreline and, once the current stops pulling you out, swim back to shore.

The illustrated *California Coastal Access Guide* (University of California Press, 2003) gives comprehensive driving directions and maps to every public beach, reef, harbor, overlook and coastal campground in the state.

SURFING

Surf's up! Are you down? Even if you never set foot on a board – and we like, totally recommend that you do, dude – there's no denying the influence of surfing on every aspect of California beach life. Invented by Pacific Islanders, surfing first washed ashore in 1907, when business tycoon Henry Huntington invited Irish Hawaiian surfer George Freeth to LA to help promote real-estate developments – California has never been the same since.

The state has plenty of easily accessible world-class surf spots, with the lion's share in SoCal. You won't find many killer spots north of the San Francisco Bay Area, but if your travels take you up there, check out www.northerncaliforniasurfing.com. Famous surf spots southbound include Mavericks (p84), past Half Moon Bay; Steamers Lane (p157) in Santa Cruz; Rincon Point (p199), outside Santa Barbara; Surfrider (p214) in Malibu; and Trestles, south of San Clemente in the OC. All are point breaks, known for their consistently clean, glassy, big waves.

Generally speaking, the most powerful swells arrive in winter (especially at Mavericks, world-famous for its big-wave surfing competition), while early summer sees the flattest conditions (except at Trestles, which still goes off then) but also warmer waters. Speaking of which, don't be

COASTAL CALIFORNIA OUTDOORS

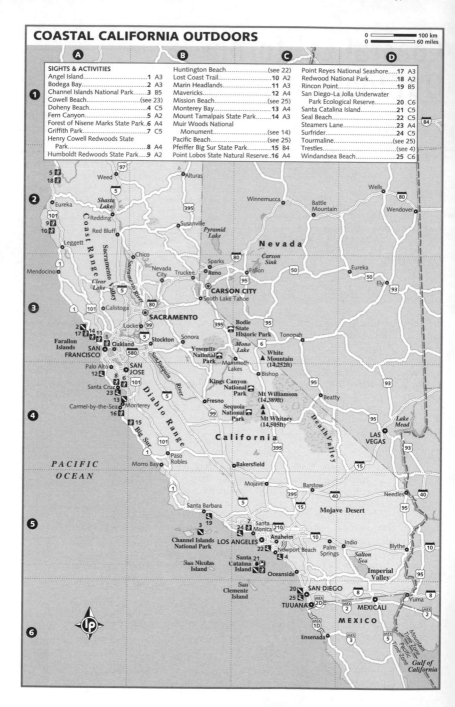

TWO GIRLS FOR EVERY BOY

Learning to surf can be intimidating, but don't let those hot-shot boys keep you off the waves. Surf outfitters that specialize in women-only lessons taught by female instructors include:

- **Aloha Surfer Girls** (☎ 858-427-0644; www.alohasurfergirls.com; 735 Santa Clara Pl, San Diego) In San Diego, LA and Santa Barbara.
- **Paradise Surf Shop** (☎ 831-462-3880; www.paradisesurf.com; 3961 Portola Dr) In Santa Cruz (p157).
- **Surf Diva** (☎ 858-454-8273; www.surfdiva.com; 2160 Avenida de la Playa) In La Jolla, San Diego (p258).

---

fooled by all those images you've seen of hot blonds surfing in just a bathing suit. You'll likely freeze your ass off in the water anywhere but SoCal in summer. Bring or rent a wet suit.

Crowds can be a problem in many places, as can overly territorial (even violent) surfers, notably at Malibu, San Diego's Windansea Beach (p257) near La Jolla and the OC's Huntington Beach (p234). Befriend a local surfer for an introduction – and protection – before catching any waves.

If you're a beginner, the best places to learn surfing are at beach breaks or long, shallow bays where waves are small and rolling. Mission Beach, Pacific Beach and Tourmaline, all in San Diego (p258), are good beginner spots, as are Seal Beach and Doheny Beach, both in the OC, as well as Santa Barbara (p199), Cayucos (p184) and Santa Cruz' Cowell Beach (p157), all on the Central Coast.

You'll find surfboard rental stands on just about every patch of sand where surfing is possible. Expect to pay about $20 per day for a board, with wet suit rental another $10. Two-hour group lessons for beginners start at $75 per person, more for private instruction. If you're ready to jump in at the deep end, many surf schools offer weekend clinics (from $150) and week-long 'surfari' camps (from $350).

Safety issues to watch out for include riptides, which are powerful currents of water that pull you away from the shore (see p39). Sharks do inhabit California waters but attacks are extremely rare. Most take place in the so-called Red Triangle, or Shark Belt, between Monterey on the Central Coast, Tomales Bay north of San Francisco and the offshore Farallon Islands.

Like cyclists, surfers can benefit from good maps to plan a coastal surfing adventure. **Surf Report** (www.surfmaps.net) maps, which detail surf breaks and provide information on seasonal weather and water temperatures, are sold by county ($8) or in a Southern California set ($40). Water quality varies from beach to beach and day to day; for current conditions check the statewide 'Beach Report Card' at www.healthebay.org. Enlightened surfers may also want to check out **Surfrider** (www.surfrider.org), a grassroots nonprofit organization working to protect the coastal environment.

WINDSURFING & KITESURFING

Experienced windsurfers tear up the waves up and down the coast, while newbies (or those who want a mellower ride) skim along calm bays and protected beaches. There's almost always a breeze – with the best winds from April through October – but the water is cold year-round and, unless you're a polar bear, a wet suit is a necessity. Any place that has good windsurfing has good kiteboarding. Look for surfers doing aerial acrobatics while parachute-like kites propel them over the waves.

In San Diego, beginners should check out Mission Bay (p253) near Santa Clara Point. The winds are steady and most of the time they blow

Surfline (www.surfline.com) has an atlas of California surf spots with detailed descriptions, weather reports and live surf cams, plus surfing news, tips and women-only features.

For the lowdown on surfing, pick up *Surfer Magazine*'s guides to Southern, Central and Northern California surf spots, featuring water-resistant covers and published by Chronicle Books.

The first person to ever surf Mavericks in 1975, Jeff Clark also co-founded Mavericks' famous annual big-wave surfing contest (www.mavericksurf.com). Check out the awesome competition footage archived online.

For wind reports, 'windcams' and video feeds, weather forecasts, classified ads and discussion forums, windsurfers can click to www.iwindsurf.com, while kitesurfers browse www.ikitesurf.com.

toward the shore – perfect if you're a first-timer. Santa Barbara's Leadbetter Beach (p199) is another good spot for beginners, as is Belmont Shores, near Long Beach (p216) in LA. The Bay Area has some of the most spectacular windsurfing backdrops in all of California, but winds can be fierce and the water much colder. San Francisco's Crissy Field (p64) is a favorite spot for experienced boarders, where the wind literally howls as it squeezes into the bay. Further north, Bodega Bay (p103) is another place to learn how to skim or to perfect your skills; sites vary from 'mild to wild,' as one local outfitter put it.

The learning curve in windsurfing is steeper than other board sports – imagine balancing on a fast-moving plank through choppy waters while trying to read the wind and angle the sail just so. Lessons are available in most of the windsurfing hot spots, especially along the coast between LA and San Diego, costing from $110 for a half-day beginner's lesson. Windsurfing rentals start around $20 per hour for a beginner's board, plus $15 to $25 for a wet suit and harness for the day.

Some windsurfing businesses at least dabble in kiteboarding and many offer training for a full course (usually two or three lessons, $300 to $450 including equipment hire). The first day is usually spent learning kite control on the beach and the second day gets you into the water. Shops typically won't rent kiteboarding gear to people who aren't taking lessons.

SCUBA DIVING & SNORKELING

All along the coast, rocky reefs, shipwrecks and kelp forests teem with sea creatures ready for their close-up. In the warmer waters of SoCal, the fantastic San Diego-La Jolla Underwater Park Ecological Reserve (p258), Santa Catalina Island (p216) and Channel Islands National Park (p202) are hot spots for diving and snorkeling. Thanks to the Monterey Bay National Marine Sanctuary, Monterey Bay (p169) offers year-round, world-renowned diving and snorkeling, though you'll need to don a wet suit. Nearby Point Lobos State Reserve (p174) is another diving gem. North of San Francisco, dive boats depart from windy Bodega Bay (p103).

If you've got the time and the money to get your PADI certification, basic open-water classes cost from $350 and are often held over two successive weekends. If you're already certified, you can rent one-tank dive outfits for $55 to $80; two-tank half-day boat dives cost from $100. It's wise to reserve at least a day in advance.

The website http:// ladiver.com lists dive sites, rental shops, instructors and weather conditions for the LA area, with links for every other coastal California county, too.

Snorkeling kits can be rented from most dive shops for $15 to $40 a day, but if you're going to be taking the plunge more than twice, it's worth buying your own snorkel and set of fins. When you head out snorkeling, don't go alone, don't touch anything and don't forget to put sun block on your back (or toss on a T-shirt)!

KAYAKING

Few watersports are as accessible and or as much fun for the whole family as kayaking. Prior experience is rarely necessary. Lots of rental outfitters can be found along the Central Coast, for example in Morro Bay (p185), whose waters are protected by a gorgeous 4-mile sand spit, and from Monterey (p169) north to Santa Cruz (p159), especially around Elkhorn Slough (p164). Sausalito (p90) in Marin County is a mere paddle's-length away from San Francisco's skyline, while sheltered Tomales Bay at Point Reyes National Seashore (p99) and Bodega Bay (p103) are also popular spots. As you head farther up the chilly North Coast, various small towns offer challenging put-in points for experienced sea kayakers. On the Redwood Coast, you can take a scenic spin around Humboldt Bay, Trinidad

Cove or Humboldt Lagoons State Park, with outfitters in Eureka (p134) and Arcata (p138). Meanwhile, SoCal's warmer waters beckon sea kayakers to Santa Catalina Island (p216) and Channel Islands National Park (p202) offshore, and San Diego's Mission Bay and La Jolla (p259).

Most outfitters offer a choice between sit-upon (open) kayaks and sit-in (closed-hull) ones, the latter usually requiring some training before you head out. Kayak rentals average $30 to $45 per day. A reputable outfitter will make sure you're aware of the tide schedule and wind conditions on your proposed route. Most kayaking outfitters offer introductory group lessons (from $50) and a variety of half-day ($25 to $75) or day-long (from around $100) excursions, many with a theme like full-moon paddling or a kayak-and-hike combo. The best tours take small groups and have guides with a background in natural history or marine biology.

Kayak Online (http:// kayakonline.com /california.html) has links to kayaking outfitters, schools and organizations, and helpful resources for beginner and expert paddlers alike.

WHALE-WATCHING

During summer, majestic gray whales feed in the Arctic waters between Alaska and Siberia, and every October they start moving south down the Pacific coast to the sheltered lagoons of the Gulf of California in Mexico's Baja California. While there, pregnant whales give birth to calves weighing up to 1500lb (who go on to live up to 60 years, grow to 50ft in length and weigh up to 40 tons). Around mid-March, these whales turn around and head back to the Arctic. Luckily for us, during their 12,000-mile round-trip, these whales pass just off the California coast.

Mothers tend to keep newborn calves closer to shore for safety, so your best chances of catching a glimpse may be during the whales' northbound migration. You can try your luck from shore (free, but you're less likely to see anything and are more removed from the action) or by taking a boat cruise. A few of the best dockside spots from which to point your binoculars include Point Reyes Lighthouse (p98), Point Pinos Lighthouse (p173) on the Monterey Peninsula, and Cabrillo National Monument (p259) at San Diego's Point Loma.

Just about every coastal California port town worth its salt offers whale-watching boat cruises. Half-day excursions (from $30 to $45 per adult, $20 to $35 per child) last from 2½ to five hours. Look for a tour that limits the number of people and has a trained naturalist or marine biologist on board. Many companies will let you go again for free if there are no sightings during your trip, and some have minimum age requirements, so check on this before the tears start. Binoculars are a must.

A whale's age can be determined by counting the layers of wax in its ears, similar to counting the rings of a tree.

Spotting whales is a simple combination of patience and timing. Spouting, the exhalation of moist warm air, is usually the first sign that a whale is about. A series of spouts may be followed by a sight of the creature's tail as the whale dives. If you're lucky, you may see whales spyhopping (sticking their heads out of the water to look around) or even breaching (leaping clear out of the water).

And it's not only gray whales that make appearances along the coast. Blue, humpback and sperm whales (not to mention schools of dolphins) pass by in summer and fall, but these sightings tend not to be as predictable.

CYCLING & MOUNTAIN BIKING

Top up those tires and strap on that helmet! California is outstanding cycling territory, whether you're off for a leisurely spin by the beach, an adrenaline-fueled mountain ride or a multiday cycling tour along the Pacific Coast Highway (p65).

Just across the Golden Gate Bridge from San Francisco, the Marin Headlands (p87) offer a bonanza of trails for fat-tire fans. Other classic,

For a helpful guide for bicycle touring in California with links to free downloadable maps, visit the California Association of Bicycling Organizations' website (www.cabobike.org).

If you're serious about long-distance cycling in coastal California, consider purchasing the detailed full-color maps with elevation profiles published by the Adventure Cycling Association (www.adventurecycling.org).

top-rated single-track rides include Prairie Creek Redwoods State Park (p146) on the North Coast and Montaña de Oro State Park (p186) near San Luis Obispo.

California's cities are not terribly cycle-friendly, although there are exceptions, notably San Francisco (p51), Arcata (p138), Santa Cruz (p155), San Luis Obispo (p186) and Santa Barbara (p195). Even LA has some good cycling turf in the Santa Monica Mountains and along the beachy South Bay Trail (p222). On the Central Coast, the Monterey Peninsula Recreation Trail (p168) travels along the waterfront, while road-cycling enthusiasts tackle the famously scenic 17-Mile Drive (p175). But nothing surpasses coastal Hwy 1, stretching from the Redwood Coast all the way down to the OC – the dizzying stretch through Big Sur (p176) alone is epic.

With few exceptions, mountain biking is not allowed in wilderness areas or on trails in national or state parks, but you may usually cycle on paved or dirt roads that are open to cars. Redwood National Park (p145) and Humboldt Redwoods State Park (p129) are a couple of bike-friendly parks where you'll be two-wheeling among giant trees. More state parks for recreational cyclists and mountain bikers include Crystal Cove State Park (p236) in Orange County, El Capitán and Refugio State Beaches (p198) near Santa Barbara, Montaña de Oro State Park (p186) near San Luis Obispo, and Wilder Ranch (p159) outside Santa Cruz. Mountain bikers are allowed on single-track trails in national forests and Bureau of Land Management (BLM) land, but must yield to hikers and stock animals.

All coastal cities and some towns have at least one bike-rental outfitter. Prices range from $8 to $10 per hour or $20 to $30 per day (more for high-tech mountain bikes), depending on the type of bike and the rental location. Before heading out, be sure to check tire inflation and ask about hiring a lock and helmet. To get the inside scoop on local cycling routes, ask the knowledgeable staff at specialist cycle shops.

California's Coastal Parks (John McKinney, 2005) is a resource for independently discovering coastal hikes both short and long, famous and hidden, and also gives natural and cultural history contexts for exploring land and sea.

For road rules, safety tips and information about buying and selling bikes and taking them on public transportation, see p288. The **Adventure Cycling Association** (☎ 406-721-1776, 800-775-2453; www.adventurecycling.org) is an excellent resource for bike routes, information and gadgets, and also maintains a cyclists' yellow-pages directory online.

HIKING

With its unparalleled scenery, coastal California is perfect for exploring on foot. This is true whether you've got your heart set on climbing sand dunes, rambling among the world's tallest trees or beachcombing accompanied by booming surf. Wherever you go, expect encounters with an entire cast of furry, feathered and flippered friends (see p35).

Near San Francisco, the Marin Headlands (p87), Mt Tamalpais (p94), magical Muir Woods National Monument (p95), Point Reyes National Seashore (p98) and Henry Cowell Redwoods and Forest of Nisene Marks State Parks (p159) are all crisscrossed by dozens of superb trails. In LA, you can ditch the car in Griffith Park (p220) and on Santa Catalina Island (p216).

The website www.trails.com has downloadable topographic maps, guidebook excerpts and user reviews for hundreds of trails in coastal California, designed for nearly 20 different sports.

On the Central Coast, there's excellent hiking in Big Sur, most popularly in redwood-studded Pfeiffer Big Sur State Park (p178). On the North Coast, stroll through impossibly lush Fern Canyon (p147), which made its cinematic debut in *The Lost World: Jurassic Park*. Redwood National Park (p145) offers misty walks through groves of old-growth redwoods, as do several nearby state parks. Dozens of trails beckon off the aptly

---

GIMME MORE, MORE, MORE

Almost no matter what your adrenaline fix, you'll find it in coastal California, either on land or at sea. If you've got energy to burn after trying everything else in this chapter, maybe it's time for:

- **Ballooning** Almost anywhere you'll find vineyards in California, there are hot-air balloon flights taking off in the pre-dawn light. Ocean-view flights are a trademark of Del Mar (p268), north of San Diego.

- **Birding** Ideally positioned along the Pacific Flyway (see p36), coastal California offers an incredible diversity of habitats for birders to work on their life lists. For birding checklists, maps and links to organizations and festivals statewide, check www.birding.com or the **Audubon California** (http://ca.audubon.org) website.

- **Fishing** You'll find folks casting a line off just about every pier and booking sportfishing charter boats all along the coast, from San Diego north to Crescent City. For fishing regulations and the required licenses (available for purchase online), contact the **California Department of Fish & Game** (☎ 916-445-0411; www.dfg.ca.gov).

- **Golfing** Tee off at dozens of windy, water hazard–filled courses along the coast. You can walk in the pros' footsteps at Pebble Beach (p175) on the Monterey Peninsula or Torrey Pines (p255) in La Jolla, north of San Diego.

- **Horse Riding** California's Wild West days may be long gone but there are still plenty of places along the coast where you can saddle up for a romantic ride on the sand, including in Big Sur (p178).

Check out the website www.caoutdoors.com for even more outdoor adventures, from bungee jumping and sky diving to beach volleyball.

---

named Avenue of the Giants winding through Humboldt Redwoods State Park (p129). Up for more of a challenge? Tackle the truly wild beaches of the multiday Lost Coast Trail (p129).

National and state parks and national forests almost always have a visitors center or ranger station with clued-in staff ready with route suggestions and trail-specific tips. They also stock trail maps, which may be necessary depending on the length and difficulty of your hike. Always ask about the local weather forecast and current wildfire conditions before heading out.

> Hikers can break out in a rash after being exposed to the urushiol oil in poison oak, even when the plant's distinctive tripartite leaves are missing.

HANG GLIDING & PARAGLIDING

For a memorable, fly-like-a-bird experience – and perhaps the most expensive 20 minutes of your life so far – you can't beat gliding. Very roughly speaking, paragliding is to hang gliding as a plane is to a hot air balloon.

Some of the most unbelievable vistas and best gliding schools are found on the California coast. A tandem flight (the only kind you can do as a first-timer) either paragliding or hang gliding costs $150 to $200 a pop, with the former on the cheaper side of the spectrum. Most companies won't allow kids under 12 to take the leap.

Popular gliding spots include Torrey Pines Gliderport (p259) in La Jolla, north of San Diego, and Santa Barbara (p198). Even if you have no intention of going up yourself, you can swing by and watch the fun. For more gliding locations up and down the California coast, check www.caoutdoors.com for listings.

> At the website www .californiacoastline.org, you can browse nearly 30,000 aerial photographs of the California coast, attempting to capture every mile of shoreline from Oregon to Mexico.

Food & Drink

California produces nearly all the nation's grapes and almonds, 75% of its strawberries and half its tomatoes. Dairy products are the real cash cow, bringing in $6 billion annually.

Many of the nation's great foodie trends began in the kitchens of coastal California. San Francisco and Los Angeles constantly play off each other, ever expanding the genre of California cuisine. The organic, Slow Food and locavarian movements are all booming along the coast, with season-regional cooking also growing in popularity. North America's only indigenous beer-brewing style originated in California, while grapes are grown from Santa Barbara all the way north to San Francisco and beyond. Fresh-caught seafood, farmers markets' fruits and vegetables, and ethnic delicacies from around the globe are just some of the delights you'll find to bite into here.

STAPLES & SPECIALTIES

You name it, California grows it. The Golden State provides almost all of the USA's tomatoes and artichokes, most of its lettuces and cabbages, and a lot more besides. The most common way to eat vegetables is in salad – served with a crusty loaf of freshly baked sourdough bread, it's a classic meal. Though salad was once thought of as 'rabbit food' by much of the rest of the nation, mainstream America has now followed suit – if only with iceberg lettuce (also grown here). In California, where ripe avocados, fresh fruits and crunchy nuts originate, there's always something unusual thrown into the salad bowl, too.

Founded by influential Bay Area chef Alice Waters, the restaurant Chez Panisse (p62) in Berkeley is considered the birthplace of California cuisine.

With California's 1100 miles of Pacific coastline and innumerable rivers and streams, it's no wonder Californians love seafood. Fishing is not only a huge industry, but a recreational sport. As you travel along the coast from spring through fall, you'll see salmon on every restaurant menu, much of it locally caught. (Try it cooked in the traditional Pacific Northwest style, on a cedar plank – so juicy.) On the far North Coast, pick up salmon jerky to nibble on in the car. Oysters, too, are very popular, although most indigenous species have been decimated or have vanished altogether. Look for oyster farms, such as at Drakes Bay (p98) near Point Reyes. On the Central Coast around Cayucos (p184), farm-raised red abalone is a delicacy.

Although California is often associated with vegetarianism (see p48), many locals ardently love meat. For decades the paradigm for beef was corn-fed cattle from the Midwest. In California, however, prime restaurants now serve grass-fed beef from local free-range cattle raised without dietary or hormonal supplements. Not only does this improve the meat's texture and flavor, but it's more environmentally friendly, since cattle aren't forced to consume a crop that requires vast amounts of water, fuel and electricity to grow and process into feed.

Monterey Bay Aquarium (www.monterey bayaquarium.org) publishes a 'Seafood Watch: West Coast' downloadable pocket guide that lists good picks – ie sustainably harvested seafood – and stuff to avoid on restaurant menus.

'Organic' meats and produce have taken off in California among savvy food lovers and environmentalists alike. It's kind of ironic, since California's giant agribusiness companies produce huge amounts of genetically modified foods in the Central Valley. But the cognoscenti won't buy it. Top chefs now insist on organics, claiming that they're not only environmentally safer, but taste better and can be more nutritious. That's what pioneering 'locavarian' chef Alice Waters, a champion of fresh, locally grown and organic ingredients, has been saying since the early 1970s.

As you drive through California's coastal agricultural regions, especially in Marin and Monterey Counties, stop at little farm stands and buy whatever is in season – see if you can't taste the organic difference, too. Farmers markets with organic and artisan food vendors are immensely popular in many coastal cities and towns, especially at San Francisco's Ferry Building (p54), in pastoral San Luis Obispo (p188) and seaside Santa Monica (p214).

Californians adore culinary trends. Some crazes are silly and doomed to failure (eg chocolate pasta), others are good but overused (eg foams), while still others get integrated from foreign countries, skyrocket in popularity and become a part of the California repertoire (eg seafood paella, Chinese dim sum). Perhaps no one has done as much to popularize California's healthy-minded, fusion-style cuisine nationwide as peripatetic Austrian-born chef Wolfgang Puck, who began his career as a celebrity restaurateur in LA.

DRINKS

Californians love wine. Ever since Stag's Leap Cabernet Sauvignon and Chateau Montelena Chardonnay, both hailing from the Napa Valley, beat French rivals at the 1976 Judgment of Paris, California vintages have merited international attention. From Mendocino south to Santa Barbara, you'll only need to detour a short distance inland to discover some of the world's greatest wine-growing regions (see the boxed text, p48).

Unlike in France, locally made wine can be expensive – and some prefer to drink beer. During the 19th-century Gold Rush, men wanted lager but couldn't brew it without refrigeration. Instead they devised a way to brew lager as one would brew ale, at higher temperatures. The result: steam beer, which has characteristics of both stout and lager. Although beer is no longer made this way in California, the coast overflows with equally innovative modern-day craft brewers, from San Diego north to Oregon. Some of the most famous labels are found in Northern California, including San Francisco's Anchor Brewing, the Anderson Valley Brewing Company (p116), Fort Bragg's North Coast Brewing Co (p121), organic-certified Eel River Brewing (p131) in Fortuna, and Eureka's Lost Coast Brewery (p137).

On the nonalcoholic front, many vintners have started bottling their unfermented wine as grape juice. Look for it on restaurant menus and at grocery and liquor stores. At coffeehouses and cafés – which are everywhere in coastal California – don't be ashamed to wrinkle your nose at weak, stale brews, like those served in roadside diners. Most baristas respect those who like their java potent.

WHERE TO EAT & DRINK

Whenever possible pick a restaurant where the chef is also the owner. It often makes all the difference in consistency and quality. These days, there really is no such thing as a typical 'California cuisine' restaurant. Many chefs draw influences from Europe, Asia or both. There are no rules, except that the food is extremely fresh, minimally processed and perfectly prepared. The point? To let the ingredients' natural flavors sing. Many restaurants now proudly advertise the names of their local, often organic-certified suppliers on the menu.

At all restaurants in California, smoking is illegal indoors, though lighting up at sidewalk or patio tables may be tolerated. Cell (mobile) phones are a big annoyance in restaurants, so excuse yourself and step outside to make or take a call. For typical restaurant opening hours, see p274; for average meal costs, p278; and for tipping, p280.

An exposé of corporate-driven food-production methods in the USA today, the hard-hitting documentary *Food, Inc.* (2008) investigates the side effects of big agribusiness on everyday Americans' diets.

Bottle Shock (2008) is a nostalgic romp through the early days of winemaking in California's Sonoma and Napa Valleys, ending with California wines beating the French at the 1976 Judgment of Paris.

The outlandish film *Sideways* (2004) captures the folly and passion of California's wine-snob scene. Pinot Noir, a highly sensitive grape, becomes a metaphor for the beleaguered, middle-aged main character, Miles, brilliantly played by Paul Giamatti.

VEGETARIANS & VEGANS

Chowhound (www
.chowhound.com) is
'for those who live to
eat.' Come here to ask
locals about hot foodie
issues, like finding the
tastiest taco trucks in San
Francisco.

California may have more vegetarians and vegans per capita than any other state, but outside the Bay Area and greater LA, strictly vegetarian restaurants are few and far between. Take heart: vegetarians may go to virtually any proper sit-down restaurant in California and order a satisfying meal from the regular menu. Most restaurants have obligatory vegetable pasta dishes, salads, portobello-mushroom burgers, baked squash and eggplant, pilafs and rice bowls. Dishes of steamed, mixed vegetables dressed with olive oil or an emulsion sauce are popular, and cooks do astonishing things with tofu. Many Chinese and Mexican restaurants offer vegetarian dishes – just ask to make sure lard isn't used. For top-notch vegetarian cuisine, legendary Greens (p77) in San Francisco and Ravens (p118) in Mendocino are stand-out choices.

EATING WITH KIDS

HappyCow (www
.happycow.net) is a
free online directory of
vegetarian, vegan and
veg-friendly restaurants
and health-food stores,
with countless listings in
coastal California.

If you're traveling with kids, most restaurants will be happy to see you and provide high chairs and booster seats. Ask about a discounted children's menu; which is sometimes printed on a take-home placemat for kids to color. In some casual, family-style restaurants, children under a certain age occasionally eat free.

High-end restaurants are not often child-friendly, however. Meals in such places last two hours or more – too long to expect little ones to sit without squirming or screaming. At fine restaurants, always call ahead to ask if it's appropriate to bring children.

For more family travel tips, see p274.

HABITS & CUSTOMS

In California, the main meal of the day is dinner. Breakfasts are traditionally hearty, though busy lifestyles have cut into the eggs-and-bacon tradition; these days, it might just be a latte and a pastry. Lunch tends to be light – typically a sandwich, perhaps soup and salad. Californians are still big snackers. If you're looking for huge, American-style meals, high-end restaurants – where the idea is to savor, not gorge – may disappoint, but diners and coffee shops usually won't. At most

---

GRAPE ESCAPES FROM THE COAST

Weary of the pretentious Napa Valley? Us too. If you'd rather visit more down-to-earth and off-the-beaten-path wineries, detour inland to:

- **Sonoma County** (p106) – lazy Russian River days with bottles of Pinot Noir, plus Syrah and Zinfandel in the Dry Creek and Alexander Valleys
- **Mendocino County** (www.truemendocinowine.com) – not far from Napa and Sonoma, follow back roads through the Anderson Valley (p116) for stellar Syrah and Riesling
- **Santa Cruz Mountains** (www.scmwa.com) – some of California's oldest, most revered winemakers hide among the redwoods, a mecca for Pinot Noir
- **Paso Robles** (www.pasowine.com) – California's fastest-growing wine region crafts superb Zinfandel and Cabernet Sauvignon (see p184)
- **Edna Valley** (www.slowine.com) – crisp Chardonnay and smoky Syrah vintages, just south of San Luis Obispo
- **Santa Ynez & Santa Maria Valleys** (www.sbcountywines.com) – starting from Los Olivos (p193) north of Santa Barbara, wander along the Foxen Canyon Wine Trail (p193)

TOP PICKS: COASTAL CALIFORNIA'S FOOD & WINE FESTIVALS

Of course, almost every wine country, county fair and farm town has its own festival or food competition, too. For more epicurean celebrations, see the destination chapters. Here are just a few of our faves:

- **San Francisco Chronicle Wine Competition** (☎ 415-391-2000; www.winejudging.com) The world's stiffest competition of American wines, with gourmet food and drink vendors galore. Held in February.
- **Rhône Rangers Grand Wine Tasting** (☎ 800-467-0163; www.rhonerangers.org) Scores of American Rhône-style wine producers, with Bay Area artisanal food producers. Held in San Francisco in March.
- **California Strawberry Festival** (☎ 888-288-9242; www.strawberry-fest.org) Family-fun festival with recipe cook-offs and star chefs' demos. Held near Ventura in May.
- **Castroville Artichoke Festival** (☎ 831-633-2465; www.artichoke-festival.org) Classic car show, 3D 'agro-art' sculptures and a wine expo. Held near Monterey in May.
- **Cooking for Solutions** (☎ 866-963-9645; www.montereybayaquarium.org) Celeb chefs show how to cook using sustainably farmed ingredients. Held in Monterey in May.
- **California Festival of Beers** (☎ 805-544-2266; www.hospiceslo.org/beerfest) All profits go to charity at this brewmeisters' summit. Held near San Luis Obispo in May.
- **Organic Planet Festival** (☎ 707-445-5100; www.organicplanetfestival.com) Live entertainment, all-natural food vendors and the world's largest organic salad. Held in Eureka in August.
- **California Avocado Festival** (☎ 805-684-0038; www.avofest.com) The world's largest vat of guacamole – 'nuff said. Held near Santa Barbara in October.
- **Pismo Beach Clam Festival** (☎ 805-773-4382; www.pismochamber.com) Chowder cook-offs, a kids' clam dig and plenty of fried mollusks. Held near San Luis Obispo in October.
- **San Diego Bay Wine & Food Festival** (☎ 877-808-9463; www.worldofwineevents.com) Tastings, wine-maker dinners, classes and demos. Held at various locations in November.

---

popular restaurants, the peak dining hour is 7pm to 8pm; always make reservations, even on weekdays.

COOKING COURSES

Some high-end cookware shops like **Williams-Sonoma** (www.williams-sonoma.com) and **Sur la Table** (www.surlatable.com) offer introductory cooking classes.

Balboa Park Food & Wine School (☎ 619-557-9441; www.balboawinefood.com; 1549 El Prado, San Diego; from $35) Quickie demonstrations, hands-on classes and wine tastings with local chefs.

California Sushi Academy (☎ 310-231-4499; www.sushi-academy.com; 1131 Nebraska Ave, LA; from $80) Apprentice in the art of finessing raw fish, Japanese macrobiotic cooking and sake tasting.

Cavallo Point Cooking School (☎ 888-651-2003; www.cavallopoint.com; 601 Murray Circle, Fort Baker, Sausalito; from $85) Seasonal, sustainable-themed cooking classes featuring farmers-market fare and local chefs.

Laguna Culinary Arts (☎ 949-494-0745; www.lagunaculinaryarts.com; 845 Laguna Canyon Rd, Laguna Beach; from $85) Home-chef classes occasionally indulge in wine pairings.

New School of Cooking (☎ 310-842-9702; www.newschoolofcooking.com; 8690 Washington Blvd, Culver City; from $50) Learn ethnic cooking from around the world in LA.

Relish Culinary Adventures (☎ 707-431-9999, 877-759-1004; www.relishculinary.com; 14 Matheson St, Healdsburg; from $39) Demonstration and hands-on classes, including at farms and vineyards, in NorCal's Wine Country.

It's fast and easy to make dining reservations for free online at www .opentable.com, serving hundreds of restaurants in coastal California, including metro areas.

Starring Meryl Streep, the delicious drama *Julie & Julia* (2009) is based on the real-life adventures of TV chef and French cookbook author extraordinaire Julia Child, who was born in Pasadena, an LA suburb.

San Francisco & the Bay Area

If you've ever wondered where the envelope goes when it's pushed, here's your answer. Natural beauty and license to be outlandish continues to draw free-thinkers and wild parrots into the San Francisco Bay Area, today America's fifth-largest metropolitan region. Psychedelic drugs, newfangled technology, gay liberation, green ventures, free speech and culinary experimentation all became mainstream long ago in the Bay Area.

Never afraid to go for broke, the region has lost fortunes but never its spirit in Gold Rush panics, dot-com crashes and earthquakes. Losing your shirt has become a favorite local pastime, with surfers stripping down right in Santa Cruz parking lots, marchers at San Francisco's Pride Parade and pretty much anyone on hot weekends in clothing-optional Berkeley. This is no place to be shy: out here among eccentrics of every stripe, no one's going to notice a few tan lines.

With its fault lines and free thinkers, the Bay Area keeps only a tentative hold on the planet, not to mention the continental US. Stick around and you'll catch the continental drift, with breezes laced with Pacific salt, perpetually blooming flowers and a tantalizing whiff of unlimited possibility. Breathe in, and brace yourself: other places in California may surprise you, but only in the San Francisco Bay Area will you surprise yourself.

HIGHLIGHTS

- Tasting Northern California's seasonal bounty at the **Ferry Building Marketplace** (p54)

- Conquering SF's hills for top-of-the-world views – or taking the **cable car** (p84)

- Butterflies alighting on your shoulders in the Rainforest Dome at the **California Academy of Sciences** (p56)

- Watching fog drift over the Golden Gate Bridge from the **Marin Headlands** (p87)

- Hiking beneath the world's tallest trees at **Muir Woods National Monument** (p95)

- Exploring the wind-swept peninsula of **Point Reyes National Seashore** (p98)

- Biting into fresh-picked organic strawberries at **Swanton Berry Farm** (p86)

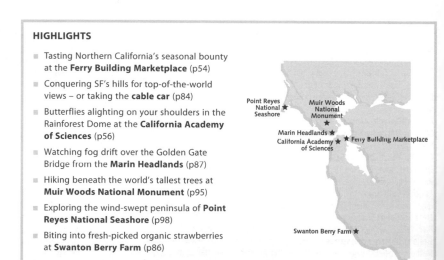

Point Reyes National Seashore ★
Muir Woods National Monument ★
Marin Headlands ★
California Academy of Sciences ★
★ Ferry Building Marketplace
Swanton Berry Farm ★

SAN FRANCISCO

pop 744,041

Welcome to the bubble, America's most liberal city, where you can say what you like and act like a freak without anyone noticing. 'Eclectic' doesn't begin to describe a town where you can begin your day with a leisurely breakfast of *huevos rancheros* in the Mission sun, picnic on Italian *panini* among parrots and poets on North Beach stairway gardens, get goose bumps watching the fog billow over the Golden Gate Bridge from a nude beach, dine Downtown on cutting-edge cuisine inspired by California's cornucopia of produce, and end up still partying at 5am with South of Market (SoMa) clubsters in a universal groove. So long, inhibitions; hello San Francisco.

Once you've ogled Victorians, ridden the cable cars and sailed to Alcatraz, explore the off-the-beaten-path neighborhoods to get a true sense of place. Don't underestimate poet George Sterling's 'cool, gray city of love': a couple of weeks here and you may start shopping for apartments – or at least a pair of chaps.

ORIENTATION

Compact San Francisco sits at the tip of a 30-mile-long peninsula and measures 7 miles by 7 miles. To the west lies the Pacific, to the east San Francisco Bay.

The city can be divided into three sections. Downtown resembles a generous slice of pie, its edges delimited by Van Ness Ave and Market St, with the rounded edge being the waterfront. Major downtown neighborhoods include the Financial District (FiDi), North Beach, Chinatown, Union Square, Nob Hill, Russian Hill and Fisherman's Wharf. To find numbered piers, note that even-numbered piers extend southward of the Ferry Building, and odd-numbered piers northward.

The area south of Market St is aptly called South of Market (SoMa). South of SoMa past Division is the hip, gritty Mission district.

West of Van Ness Ave to the Pacific are historic neighborhoods, including posh Pacific Heights and the Marina, Japantown, the Castro (the city's gay center) and the Haight district (of 1960s fame). Also here are the city's best parks – the Presidio, Lincoln Park and Golden Gate Park.

FAST FACTS

- **Average temperature low/high in San Francisco** January 46/58°F, September 56/71°F

- **San Francisco to Los Angeles** 382 miles, six to eight hours

- **San Francisco International Airport to downtown San Francisco** 14 miles, 20 to 45 minutes

- **Downtown San Francisco to downtown Napa** 48 miles, 60 to 90 minutes

- **Golden Gate Bridge to Muir Woods** 11 miles, 20 to 40 minutes

---

INFORMATION
Bookstores

A Different Light Bookstore (Map p61; ☎ 415-431-0891; www.adlbooks.com; 489 Castro St; 10am-11pm) Gay-specific titles.

Adobe Books (Map p61; ☎ 415-864-3936; http://adobebooksbackroomgallery.blogspot.com; 3166 16th St; 11am-midnight) Glorious chaos of used books complete with cat, sofas and back-room art gallery.

Books Inc (Map p61; ☎ 415-864-6777; www.booksinc.net; 2275 Market St; 10am-10pm) General interest with several branches in SF; check out the local bestsellers section.

Bound Together Anarchist Book Collective (Map p63; ☎ 415-431-8355; www.boundtogetherbooks.com; 1369 Haight St; 11:30am-7:30pm) All-volunteer nonprofit bookstore stocked with anti-superhero comics, organic farming manuals and other radical notions.

ourpick City Lights (Map pp58-9; ☎ 415-362-8193; www.citylights.com; 261 Columbus Ave; 10am-midnight) A free-speech landmark, bookseller and publisher; literature main floor, nonfiction cellar, legendary Beat poetry loft.

Fog City News (Map pp58-9; ☎ 415-543-7400; www.fogcitynews.com; 455 Market St) Stellar selection of magazines, international periodicals and gourmet chocolate.

Get Lost (Map pp58-9; ☎ 415-437-0529; 1825 Market St) Tops for travel books and maps.

Modern Times (Map p61; ☎ 415-282-9246; www.mtbs.com; 888 Valencia St; 10am-9pm Mon-Sat, 11am-6pm Sun) Good in-store events; great for politicos.

Omnivore (Map p61; ☎ 415-282-4712; www.omnivorebooks.com; 3885a Caesar Chavez St; 11am-6pm Mon-Sat, noon-5pm Sun) Signed cookbooks by SF's top chefs, vintage recipe books and standing-room-only foodie events.

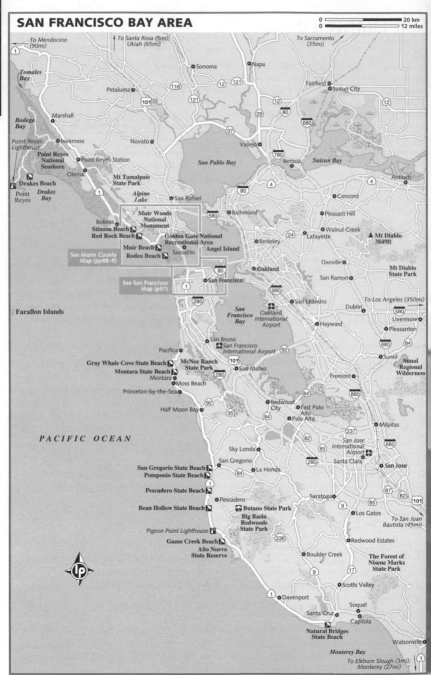

SAN FRANCISCO BAY AREA

| 0 | 20 km |
| 0 | 12 miles |

To Mendocino (90mi)

To Santa Rosa (5mi); Ukiah (65mi)

To Sacramento (35mi)

Tomales Bay

Sonoma

Napa

Fairfield

Suisun City

Petaluma

Marshall

Bodega Bay

Point Reyes Lighthouse

Inverness

Novato

Vallejo

Point Reyes National Seashore

Point Reyes Station

Olema

San Pablo Bay

Benicia

Suisun Bay

Drakes Beach

Point Reyes

Drakes Bay

Mt Tamalpais State Park

Alpine Lake

San Rafael

Antioch

Concord

Muir Woods National Monument

Bolinas

Stinson Beach

Red Rock Beach

Golden Gate National Recreational Area

Richmond

Pleasant Hill

Walnut Creek

Mt Diablo 3849ft

Muir Beach

Rodeo Beach

Sausalito

Angel Island

Berkeley

Lafayette

See Marin County Map (pp88–9)

Oakland

Danville

San Ramon

Mt Diablo State Park

See San Francisco Map (p57)

San Francisco

San Leandro

To Los Angeles (350mi)

Dublin

Livermore

Farallon Islands

San Francisco Bay

Oakland International Airport

Pleasanton

Hayward

Sunol

San Bruno

San Francisco International Airport

Fremont

Sunol Regional Wilderness

Pacifica

Gray Whale Cove State Beach

McNee Ranch State Park

Montara State Beach

Montara

San Mateo

Moss Beach

Princeton-by-the-Sea

Half Moon Bay

PACIFIC OCEAN

Redwood City

East Palo Alto

Palo Alto

Milpitas

San Jose International Airport

Santa Clara

Sky Londa

San Gregorio

San Gregorio State Beach

Pomponio State Beach

La Honda

San Jose

Pescadero State Beach

Saratoga

Los Gatos

Bean Hollow State Beach

Pescadero

Butano State Park

Big Basin Redwoods State Park

To San Juan Bautista (45mi)

Pigeon Point Lighthouse

Gazos Creek Beach

Año Nuevo State Reserve

Redwood Estates

The Forest of Nisene Marks State Park

Boulder Creek

Scotts Valley

Davenport

Soquel

Santa Cruz

Capitola

Natural Bridges State Beach

Watsonville

Monterey Bay

To Elkhorn Slough (3mi); Monterey (27mi)

Internet Access

Wi-fi finds you in SF, with 370 free hot spots citywide – connect for free in Union Sq, most cafes and hotel lobbies. Check the phone book for nearby **FedEx Office** (☎ 800-463-3339; www.fedex.com) branches.

Apple Store (Map pp58-9; ☎ 415-392-0202; www .apple.com/retail/sanfrancisco; 1 Stockton St; ☯ 10am-9pm Mon-Sat, 11am-7pm Sun; 💻 📶) Free wi-fi access and internet terminal usage.

Brain Wash (Map pp58-9; ☎ 415-255-4866; www.brain wash.com; 1122 Folsom St; ☯ 7am-10pm Mon-Thu, 7am-11pm Fri & Sat, 8am-10pm Sun; 💻 📶) Multitaskers rejoice: do laundry, drink beer, watch live music or update Facebook (per 20 minutes $3, free wi-fi).

Café Flore (Map p61; ☎ 415-621-8579; http://cafe flore.com; 2298 Market St; ☯ 7am-2am; 📶) Free wi-fi and eye candy in the Castro's sunny all-glass corner venue (see also p79).

Cole Valley Café (Map p63; ☎ 415-668-5282; www .colevalleycafe.com; 701 Cole St; ☯ 7am-8pm; 📶 🔌) Powerful coffee, free wi-fi and gourmet sandwiches in the Haight.

Main Library (Map pp8-9; ☎ 415-557-4400; cnr Larkin & Grove Sts; 💻 📶 🔌) Six first-come, first-served terminals on the 1st floor, for 15-minute free sessions.

Internet Resources

Bay Guardian (www.sfbg.com) Features primers on politics and local events.

Craig's List (www.craigslist.org) SF's definitive community bulletin board.

National Weather Service (www.wrh.noaa.gov/mtr)

SF Gate (www.sfgate.com) Online edition of the *San Francisco Chronicle*.

SF Weekly (www.sfweekly.com) Covers 400 things to do today in SF.

SAN FRANCISCO IN...

Stretch your dollars and ditch the car: bus fare and calf muscles let you see SF at its best.

One Day

Cruise to Alcatraz early in the day, so you can make your getaway in time for lunch at the chef's table at **Boulette's Larder** (p77). Witness the next breakthroughs in photography and new media art at **SFMOMA** (p55), then head over to the **Asian Art Museum** (p56), where art transports you across centuries and oceans within an hour. Spirits are lifted by Michael Tilson Thomas conducting Beethoven down the block at **Davies Symphony Hall** (p82), and by cocktails around the corner at **Jardinière** (p78). End the night singing along to classic musicals at the **Castro Theatre** (p73) or being showered with glam-rock glitter at the converted speakeasy of **Café du Nord** (p81).

Two Days

Take an eye-opening walking tour of Mission murals with **Precita Eyes** (p74), and fuel up like a local at **La Taqueria** (p76). Load up on pirate supplies and tall tales at **826 Valencia** (p82) on your way to the Haight for flashbacks at vintage clothing boutiques. From here, follow starry-eyed hippies to the Summer of Love site: **Golden Gate Park** (p56). Go global with arts and crafts from around the planet at **MH de Young Museum** (p56), then take a walk on the wild side in the rainforest dome of the **California Academy of Sciences** (p56). End your all-natural, cross-cultural San Francisco adventure with a fitting feast: Korean-inspired organic small plates at **Namu** (p77).

Three Days

Leave San Francisco on a high note: climb stairway walks lined with cottage gardens and trees filled with wild parrots to Coit Tower, then follow your rumbling stomach downhill to the Italian deli sandwiches at **BaoNecci** (p76). For more stunning views, hike uphill to Diego Rivera murals and take in sweeping vistas of the Golden Gate Bridge at George Sterling Park, then recharge with tea and scones downhill at **Crown and Crumpet** (p77). Along the wharf, you can valiantly fight off Space Invaders at the **Musée Mecanique** (p63), experience underwater stealth mode aboard the **USS Pampanito** (p63) or sunbathe with sea lions along **Pier 39** (p63). Follow the waterfront west for more natural highs: kite-flying in **Crissy Field** (p64), scientific discoveries at the **Exploratorium** (p64) and sensational vegetarian chili at **Greens** (p77).

Urban Daddy (www.urbandaddy.com/home/sfo) Blogging the new and now in SF.

Media

Northern California's largest daily, the *San Francisco Chronicle* is ailing, but still the best source for general news; check the Sunday edition's 'Datebook' for entertainment resources.

SF has two intelligent free weeklies, the *San Francisco Bay Guardian* and *SF Weekly*, both published Wednesdays with excellent events listings and in-depth articles.

The *Bay Area Reporter* (*BAR*) and the *Bay Times* are free GLBT community papers distributed in the Castro and surrounding neighborhoods.

Medical Services

California Pacific Medical Center (Map p57; ☎ 415-600-3333; www.cpmc.org; 2333 Buchanan St) The city's calmest ER; short waits but high fees without insurance.

City Clinic (Map pp58-9; ☎ 415-487-5500; www.sfcityclinic.org; 356 7th St; ☯ 8am-4pm Mon, Wed & Fri, 1-6pm Tue, 1-4pm Thu) For treatment of sexually transmitted diseases.

Haight Ashbury Free Clinic (Map p63; ☎ 415-746-1967; www.hafci.org; 558 Clayton St; ☯ 1-9pm Mon, 9am-9pm Tue-Thu, 1-5pm Fri) For nonemergencies, payable on a sliding scale. Appointments required, except at drop-ins (4:45pm Monday and Tuesday, 8:45am Tuesday and Wednesday); arrive at least 30 minutes early.

Pharmaca (Map p63; ☎ 415-661-1216; www.pharmaca .com; 925 Cole St; ☯ 8am-8pm Mon-Fri, 9am-8pm Sat & Sun) Pharmacy plus naturopathic remedies and weekend chair massage.

San Francisco General Hospital (Map p57; ☎ 415-206-8000; www.sfghf.net; 1001 Potrero Ave) For severe trauma, go directly to one of the country's best trauma units; but it's often full and you might wait hours. Enter the ER from 23rd St.

Walgreens The Castro (Map p61; ☎ 415-861-6276; 498 Castro St); The Marina (Map p60; ☎ 415-931-6417; 3201 Divisadero St) A 24-hour pharmacy.

Money

Banks and ATMs are ubiquitous.

Travelex (Map pp58-9; ☎ 415-362-3453; 75 Geary St, Union Sq; ☯ 9am-5pm Mon-Fri, 10am-6pm Sat, 10am-5pm Sun) Currency exchange; there's another branch at SFO's International Terminal.

Post

Civic Center Post Office (Map pp58-9; ☎ 415-563-7284, 800-725-2161; 101 Hyde St; ☯ 9am-5pm Mon-Fri)

To receive poste restante mail, address it with: your name, c/o General Delivery, Civic Center Post Office, 101 Hyde St, San Francisco, CA 94142 USA.

Union Square Post Office (Map pp58-9; downstairs, Macy's department store, 170 O'Farrell St, Union Sq; ☯ 10am-5:30pm Mon-Sat, 11am-5pm Sun)

Tourist Information

California Welcome Center (Map p60; ☎ 415-981-1280; www.visitcwc.com; 2 Pier 39; ☯ 10am-5pm) Statewide information, brochures, maps and help with accommodations bookings (fees cost up to $5).

San Francisco Visitors Information Center (Map pp58-9; ☎ 415-391-2000; www.onlyinsanfrancisco. com; lower level, Hallidie Plaza, cnr Market & Powell Sts; ☯ 8:30am-5pm Mon-Fri, 9am-3pm Sat & Sun) Carries maps, guidebooks, brochures and accommodations information. Operates a 24-hour automated phone line with recorded information (☎ 415-391-2001).

DANGERS & ANNOYANCES

Keep your city smarts and wits about you, especially at night in SoMa, the Mission, Haight and all parks. Unless you know where you're going, avoid the Tenderloin, bordered by Polk St (west), Powell St (east), Market St (south) and O'Farrell St (north). To cut through the Tenderloin, take Geary or Market Sts – still seedy, but tolerable. Avoid 6th St (aka Skid Row) between Market and Folsom Sts.

Expect to be asked for spare change often, but don't feel obliged – to address the causes of homelessness instead of the symptoms, consider a donation to a nonprofit organization such as the **Haight Ashbury Food Program** (Map p63; ☎ 415-566-0366; www.thefood program.org; 1525 Waller St).

SIGHTS & ACTIVITIES

If you're here awhile, get Lonely Planet's *San Francisco* or *San Francisco Encounter* for comprehensive coverage.

The Embarcadero & Ferry Building

Stroll or bike the eastern waterfront from SoMa to Fisherman's Wharf along wide-open sidewalks and take in picture-perfect views of Treasure Island and the Bay Bridge. At the foot of Market St, SF's historic 1898 transport hub now houses San Francisco's monument to slow food: the **Ferry Building Marketplace** (Map pp58-9; ☎ 415-983-8000; www.ferry buildingmarketplace.com; ☯ most shops 10am-6pm), which showcases gorgeous local, sustainable and regional foods by such culinary celebs as Cowgirl Creamery, Hog Island Oyster Co and Acme Bread, and farmers whose names you'll recognize on locavore restaurant menus. But the breakout star is the **farmers market** (see boxed text, p76), which wraps around the building. Sample the goods then stop for lunch at one of several acclaimed on-site restaurants. Ferries to Sausalito with the **Golden Gate Ferry** (☎ 415-455-2000; www.goldengate.org) and to Tiburon with the **Blue & Gold Fleet** (☎ 415-705-8200; www.blueandgoldfleet.com) dock out the back.

For drop-dead vistas, take your goodies south to **Pier 14** (Map pp58–9), a narrow pedestrian pier extending 600ft into the bay. Vintage streetcars run along the Embarcadero from Fisherman's Wharf to the Ferry Building, then up Market St to the Castro district.

Golden Gate Bridge

Soaring symbol of the city and the Golden Gate National Recreation Area (GGNRA), the 1937 **Golden Gate Bridge** (Map p57; ☎ 415-921-5858; www.goldengatebridge.org; ⏱ pedestrian walkway 5am-9pm early Mar-Oct, to 6pm Nov-early Mar, bicycles 24hr; ♿) is a marvel of 20th-century engineering and a beauty besides. Those stunning looks take work: at nearly 2 miles long and with a main span of 4200ft, the bridge gets touched up with about 10,000 gallons of 'international orange' paint annually.

Start your tour from the parking lot at the bridge's southern end (via Lincoln Blvd through the Presidio; or via Hwy 101 northbound to the 10mph hairpin exit marked 'Last SF Exit,' just before the toll plaza). There's a lookout here, along with a gift shop and a must-see cutaway of the 3ft-thick suspension cable. Follow the path to the bridge sidewalk. (If you're on a bicycle, follow signs to the appropriate westbound sidewalk.) Bring a jacket, even if it's sunny inland. MUNI buses 28 (from Golden Gate Park) and 29 (from the Marina) run to the toll plaza.

If you drive across, stop at the first exit north of the bridge marked **Vista Point** for superb views of the city. Cars pay a $6 toll to return, except if you're carpooling with three or more people during weekday rush hours of 5am to 9am and 4pm to 6pm (there's no outbound toll).

Alcatraz Island

America's most notorious prison from 1933 to 1963, 12-acre Alcatraz Island sits isolated by chilly waters and strong currents. Tour 'The Rock' by booking a ferry and tour through **Alcatraz Cruises** (Map p60; ☎ 415-981-7625; www.alcatrazcruises.com; ferry & audio tour adult/child 5-11/family $26/16/79; ♿). On the self-guided audio tour of the cellblock, former guards and prisoners recall attempted prison breaks, visiting days and the library (no books with cursing, kissing or violence allowed). Native American leaders took over the island from 1969 to 1971 to protest US occupation of Native lands, and their standoff with the FBI is preserved in 'This Is Indian Land' water tower graffiti and an oral history centre. Reservations are essential, especially for popular night tours (adult/child five to 11 $33/19.50): at peak summer periods, the parks service turns away 2000 people a day.

Downtown, South of Market & Civic Center

The commercial heart of Downtown SF, **Union Sq** (Map pp58–9), is ringed with hotels, department stores, designer boutiques and theaters.

SF's cultural cutting edge is South of Market (SoMa) in the Yerba Buena Arts District, anchored by **San Francisco Museum of Modern Art** (SFMOMA; Map pp58-9; ☎ 415-357-4000; www.sfmoma.org; 151 3rd St; adult/child under 12/student $15/free/$9; ⏱ 10am-5:45pm Fri-Tue, 10am-8:45pm Thu; ♿), designed by Mario Botta. Around a central lightwell are massive mural installations, an outstanding photography collection, a new rooftop sculpture garden and breakthrough shows by new media mavericks such as Matthew Barney, who debuted his Vaseline-smeared videos here. Thursday

---

SF'S COOLEST EPHEMERAL SIGHT

Golden Gate Bridge isn't the only local landmark – though the other one tends to hide. As summertime afternoon fog blows in, look westward to Sutro Tower, the double-spiked radio tower atop Twin Peaks. When the rolling clouds reach its midsection, the tower magically transforms into a two-masted schooner sailing across a sea of fog. Fabulous.

evenings are half-price; the first Tuesday of the month is free.

Within a block are three other contemporary museums. The **Cartoon Art Museum** (Map pp58-9; ☎ 415-227-8666; www.cartoonart.org; 655 Mission St; adult/child 6-12 $6/2; ⊙ 11am-5pm Tue-Sun; ♿) caters to fanboys and comix-chicas of all ages with original *Watchmen* covers, too-hot-to-print political cartoons and events with Oscar-winning, Oakland-based Pixar animators. On this same block is the always-moving **Museum of the African Diaspora** (Map pp58-9; ☎ 415-358-7200; www.moadsf.org; 685 Mission St; ⊙ 11am-6pm Wed-Sat; ♿), tracing connections among African communities through art, storytelling and technology. Architect Daniel Liebskind reshaped San Francisco's 1881 brick power plant with a blue steel extension into the Hebrew word *l'chaim* (to life) – a fitting home for the vibrant **Contemporary Jewish Museum** (Map pp58-9; ☎ 415-655-7800; www.jmsf.org; 736 Mission St at 3rd; adult/senior & student/child under 18 $10/free/8; ⊙ 11am-5:30pm Fri-Tue, 1-8:30pm Thu; ♿), where standout shows have included Chagall's theater backdrops and soundscapes based on the Hebrew alphabet by Lou Reed and Laurie Anderson.

Rest those weary museum legs by the Martin Luther King waterfall fountain in **Yerba Buena Gardens** (Map pp58-9; ☎ 415-820-3550; www.yerbabuenagardens.com; ⊙ 6am-10pm), or take the kids indoors for ice-skating, a bowling alley, and the handcarved 1906 **Looff carousel** (Map pp58-9; cnr 4th & Howard Sts; tickets $2; ⊙ 10am-6pm; ♿). Child prodigies prefer **Zeum Art & Technology Center** (Map pp58-9; ☎ 415-822-3320; www.zeum.org; 221 4th St; adult/child 4-18 $7/5; ⊙ 11am-5pm Tue-Sun Jun-Aug, 1-5pm Wed-Fri & 11am-5pm Sat & Sun Sep-May; ♿) where they can play live-action video games, make claymation music videos and take CGI workshops with Silicon Valley innovators.

Up Market St in a perpetually 'transitional' (read sketchy) neighborhood, Civic Center is graced by the gilded Beaux-Arts **City Hall** (Map pp58-9; ☎ 415-554-6139; cnr Van Ness Ave & Grove St; ⊙ 8am-8pm Mon-Fri), modeled after St Peter's Basilica in Vatican City. Wander in and see the grand rotunda, where anti-McCarthy protesters were hosed off the stairs in the first sit-in of the '60s and same-sex weddings were celebrated in 2004. Opposite City Hall, the **Asian Art Museum** (Map pp58-9; ☎ 415-581-3500; www.asianart.org; cnr Larkin & McAllister Sts; adult/child/youth 13-17/student $12/free/7/8; ⊙ 10am-5pm Tue-Wed & Fri-Sun, 10am-9pm Thu)

transports you across Asia via an escalator in the Gae Aulenti-converted library, with exhibits ranging from ancient Persian miniatures to contemporary Chinese landscapes made entirely from toy dinosaurs. First Thursdays from 5pm to 9pm, the hipsters are in charge at Matcha events featuring Korean hip hop and Japanese swordplay demos.

Golden Gate Park

A mile-wide, 48-block stretch of the imagination, Golden Gate Park reaches nearly halfway across the peninsula. Pick up information on park features at **McLaren Lodge** (Map p63; ☎ 415-831-2700; www.parks.sfgov.org; park's eastern entrance, cnr Fell & Stanyan Sts; ⊙ 8am-5pm Mon-Fri).

Architect Renzo Piano's 2008 landmark LEED-certified **California Academy of Sciences** (Map p57; ☎ 415-379-8000; www.calacademy.org; 55 Concourse Dr; weekday adult/child 7-11/youth 12-17 $24.95/14.95/19.95, 3rd Wed of the month free, 6-10pm Thu over 21 only $12; ⊙ 9:30am-5pm Mon-Sat, 11am-5pm Sun; ♿) houses 38,000 weird, wonderful animals under a 'living roof' of California wildflowers. Kids squeal in the Eel Forest and butterfly-filled Rainforest Dome, but adults love NightLife, the Thursday-night open house with DJs, cocktails and penguins dozing off to a faux sunset. Across the music concourse is another showstopper: Herzog & de Meuron's sleek, copper-clad **MH de Young Fine Arts Museum** (Map p57; ☎ 415-750-3600; www.famsf.org/deyoung; adult/child over 13/senior $10/6/7, $2 discount with Muni ticket, 1st Tue of the month free; ⊙ 9:30am-5:15pm Tue-Sun, to 8:45pm Fri Jan-Nov) is oxidizing green to blend into the park. Inside are standout shows that celebrate inspired handiwork, from Andy Warhol's silkscreened pop-star portraits to Oceanic ceremonial masks.

The **Japanese Tea Garden** (Map p57; ☎ 415-752-1171; Hagiwara Tea Garden Dr; adult/child under 12 $5/2; ⊙ 9am-6pm Mar-Oct, 8:30am-5pm Nov-Feb) is stunning in spring when cherry trees and wisteria bloom, but its stone-studded Zen Garden, vintage footbridges and bonsai grove make it picturesque year-round. For $4, revive with *genmaicha* (green tea with roasted brown rice) and fortune cookies – invented in SF a century ago for the inauguration of this tea garden.

(continued on page 62)

SAN FRANCISCO

INFORMATION	
California Pacific Medical Center	1 C2
San Francisco General Hospital	2 D4
SIGHTS & ACTIVITIES	
Alamo Sq Park	3 C3
California Academy of Sciences	4 B3
California Palace of the Legion of Honor	5 A3
Camera Obscura	(see 6)
Cliff House	6 A3
Fort Point National Historic Site	7 B1
Golden Gate Bridge	8 B1
Golden Gate Park Bike & Skate	9 B3
Japanese Tea Garden	10 B3
MH de Young Fine Arts Museum	11 B3
Stow Lake Boathouse	12 B3
Strybing Arboretum & Botanical Gardens	13 B3
Sutro Baths	14 A3
Tank Hill	15 C4

EATING	
Humphry Slocombe	16 D4
Louis'	17 A3
Namu	18 C2
Tataki	19 C2
Warming Hut	20 B2

ENTERTAINMENT	
Boom Boom Room	21 C3
Bottom of the Hill	22 D3
Cafe Cocomo	23 E4
Fillmore	24 C3
Yoshi's	25 C3

SHOPPING	
Crossroads	26 C2

SAN FRANCISCO & THE BAY AREA

DOWNTOWN SAN FRANCISCO

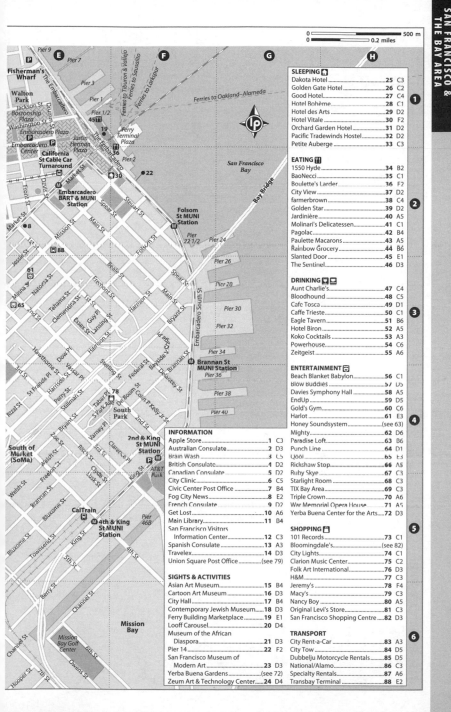

0 ————————— 500 m
0 ————————— 0.2 miles

SLEEPING 🛏
Dakota Hotel	**25**	C3
Golden Gate Hotel	**26**	C2
Good Hotel	**27**	C4
Hotel Bohème	**28**	C1
Hotel des Arts	**29**	D2
Hotel Vitale	**30**	F2
Orchard Garden Hotel	**31**	D2
Pacific Tradewinds Hostel	**32**	D2
Petite Auberge	**33**	C3

EATING 🍴
1550 Hyde	**34**	B2
BaoNecci	**35**	C1
Boulette's Larder	**36**	F2
City View	**37**	D2
farmerbrown	**38**	C4
Golden Star	**39**	D2
Jardinière	**40**	A5
Molinari's Delicatessen	**41**	C1
Pagolac	**42**	B4
Paulette Macarons	**43**	A5
Rainbow Grocery	**44**	B6
Slanted Door	**45**	E1
The Sentinel	**46**	D3

DRINKING 🍷🍺
Aunt Charlie's	**47**	C4
Bloodhound	**48**	C5
Cafe Tosca	**49**	D1
Caffe Trieste	**50**	C1
Eagle Tavern	**51**	B6
Hotel Biron	**52**	A5
Koko Cocktails	**53**	A3
Powerhouse	**54**	C6
Zeitgeist	**55**	A6

ENTERTAINMENT 🎭
Beach Blanket Babylon	**56**	C1
Blow Buddies	**57**	D5
Davies Symphony Hall	**58**	A5
EndUp	**59**	D5
Gold's Gym	**60**	C6
Harlot	**61**	E3
Honey Soundsystem	(see 63)	
Mighty	**62**	D6
Paradise Loft	**63**	B6
Punch Line	**64**	D1
Qõõl	**65**	E3
Rickshaw Stop	**66**	A5
Ruby Skye	**67**	C3
Starlight Room	**68**	C3
TIX Bay Area	**69**	C3
Triple Crown	**70**	A6
War Memorial Opera House	**71**	A5
Yerba Buena Center for the Arts	**72**	D3

SHOPPING 🛍
101 Records	**73**	C3
Bloomingdale's	(see 82)	
City Lights	**74**	C1
Clarion Music Center	**75**	C2
Folk Art International	**76**	D3
H&M	**77**	C3
Jeremy's	**78**	F4
Macy's	**79**	C3
Nancy Boy	**80**	A5
Original Levi's Store	**81**	C3
San Francisco Shopping Centre	**82**	D3

TRANSPORT
City Rent-a-Car	**83**	A3
City Tow	**84**	D5
Dubbelju Motorcycle Rentals	**85**	D3
National/Alamo	**86**	C3
Specialty Rentals	**87**	A6
Transbay Terminal	**88**	E2

INFORMATION
Apple Store	**1**	C3
Australian Consulate	**2**	D3
Brain Wash	**3**	C5
British Consulate	**4**	D2
Canadian Consulate	**5**	D2
City Clinic	**6**	C5
Civic Center Post Office	**7**	B4
Fog City News	**8**	E2
French Consulate	**9**	D2
Get Lost	**10**	A6
Main Library	**11**	B4
San Francisco Visitors Information Center	**12**	C3
Spanish Consulate	**13**	A3
Travelex	**14**	D3
Union Square Post Office	(see 79)	

SIGHTS & ACTIVITIES
Asian Art Museum	**15**	B4
Cartoon Art Museum	**16**	D3
City Hall	**17**	B4
Contemporary Jewish Museum	**18**	D3
Ferry Building Marketplace	**19**	E1
Looff Carousel	**20**	D4
Museum of the African Diaspora	**21**	D3
Pier 14	**22**	F2
San Francisco Museum of Modern Art	**23**	D3
Yerba Buena Gardens	(see 72)	
Zeum Art & Technology Center	**24**	D4

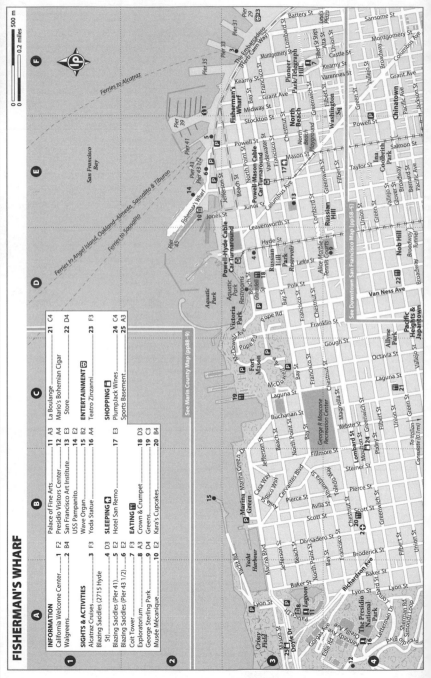

THE CASTRO & THE MISSION

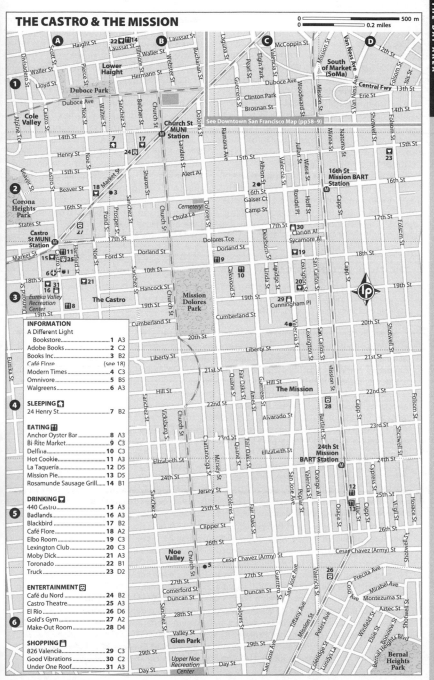

SAN FRANCISCO &
THE BAY AREA

(continued from page 56)

Plants thrive within the park's mild microclimates, and the 70-acre **Strybing Arboretum & Botanical Gardens** (Map p57; ☎ 415-661-1316; www.sfbotanicalgarden.org; Martin Luther King Dr; admission free; ☯ 8am-4:30pm Mon-Fri, 10am-5pm Sat & Sun) includes species from around the world in its Garden of Fragrance, the California Collection of Native Plants and the Japanese Moon-Viewing Garden. Stop by the botany bookstore – a must for gardeners and naturalists – at the entrance for details on daily tours.

Carnivorous plants and outer-space orchids reveal a wild side to the upright 1879 Victorian **Conservatory of Flowers** (Map p63; ☎ 415-666-7001; www.conservatoryofflowers.org; adult/child 5-11/senior & youth 12-17 $7/2/5; ☯ 9am-5pm Tue-Sun), flanked on the east side by the **Dahlia Garden**, where spiky hybrids contributed by SF's avid amateur horticulturalists are at their bodacious best in August. The 1960s beat goes on thanks to the drum circle at **Hippie Hill**, while strollers find a moment's peace in the contemplative valley of the **AIDS Memorial Grove**.

The park is packed with sporting facilities, including 7.5 miles of bicycle trails, countless miles of jogging trails, 12 miles of equestrian trails, an archery range, fly-casting pools, a nine-hole golf course, lawn-bowling greens, four soccer fields, 21 tennis courts, and baseball and softball diamonds (conveniently backed by pagan altars, for prayers between innings). Rent rowboats and pedal boats from the **Stow Lake boathouse** (Map p57; ☎ 415-752-0347; per hr $13-17; ☯ 10am-4pm; ♿).

THE OTHER SIDE OF THE BAY

San Franciscans rarely cross the water, but there are damn cool spots in the East Bay. In **Oakland**, start in the Rockridge neighborhood, on the skirts of the East Bay hills; park your car and wander College and Piedmont Aves for indie shops, fun bars and bustling restaurants. Or take BART to Rockridge station.

Smack in the middle of downtown Oakland, **Lake Merritt** is ideal for an urban jog or nature walk. You'll spot hundreds of Canada geese (and their droppings) along a 3.5-mile perimeter path. Rent a boat and float beside Oakland's revitalized downtown. Kids love cute-as-a-button **Children's Fairyland** (☎ 510-452-2259; www.fairyland.org; 699 Bellevue Ave; admission $7; ♿), which apparently inspired Walt Disney to create Disneyland.

Also near the Lake Merritt BART station, the **Oakland Museum of California** (☎ 510-238-2200; www.museumca.org; adult/child/senior & student $8/free/5; ☯ 10am-5pm Wed-Sat, noon-5pm Sun; ♿) has fantastic exhibits on California history, science and art.

It's a short walk to the bayside **Jack London Square** (☎ 510-645-9292; www.jacklondonsquare.com), at the foot of Broadway, along the city's revitalized waterfront. (From I-880, exit at Broadway/Alameda; or take the ferry from SF.) Though it feels like an outdoor mall, there's good waterside strolling. The Bay Area's premier jazz venue is **Yoshi's** (☎ 510-238-9200; www.yoshis.com; 510 Embarcadero West; ☯ shows nightly), which doubles as a Japanese restaurant. For rock, hit **Uptown** (☎ 510-451-8100; www.uptownnightclub.com; 1928 Telegraph Ave). Or take in a show – maybe Pink Floyd or the Oakland Symphony – at the gorgeous art deco **Paramount Theatre** (☎ 510-465-6400; www.paramounttheatre.com; 2025 Broadway).

Berkeley (aka Berserkeley) was ground zero for 1960s radicalism and remains a bastion of liberalism – though it's no longer legal to walk around nude. (Take BART to Downtown Berkeley, or I-80 to University Ave.) Wander the wooded 178-acre **UC Berkeley Campus** (☎ 510-642-5215; www.berkeley.edu) and tour historic buildings and museums. Extending southward from UC, grungy **Telegraph Ave** is chockablock with shops, with great bargains on books and music. The clean-hands crowd prefers the northern stretch of Telegraph, aka the Gourmet Ghetto. The star attraction and birthplace of California cuisine is Alice Water's **Chez Panisse** (☎ 510-548-5525; www.chezpanisse.com; 1517 Shattuck Ave; prix fixe menu $65-95; ☯ Mon-Sat), which wows diners with seasonal, ingredients-driven cooking, available in prix fixe dinners in the dining room (reservations essential) or at the more casual upstairs **Café at Chez Panisse** (☎ 510-548-5049; mains $18-26; ☯ lunch & dinner Mon-Sat). For classic Indian, venture down University Ave to **Vik's Chaat Corner** (☎ 510-644-4432; 2390 4th St; meals under $8; ☯ 11am-6pm Tue-Fri, 11am-8pm Sat & Sun), our cheap-eats favorite.

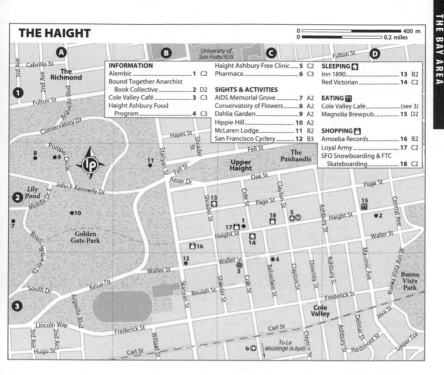

THE HAIGHT

0 _____ 400 m
0 _____ 0.2 miles

INFORMATION
Alembic..**1** C2
Bound Together Anarchist
   Book Collective.......................**2** D2
Cole Valley Café.........................**3** C3
Haight Ashbury Food
   Program..................................**4** C3

Haight Ashbury Free Clinic......**5** C2
Pharmaca......................................**6** C3

SIGHTS & ACTIVITIES
AIDS Memorial Grove................**7** A2
Conservatory of Flowers..........**8** A2
Dahlia Garden.............................**9** A2
Hippie Hill..................................**10** A2
McLaren Lodge...........................**11** B2
San Francisco Cyclery..............**12** B3

SLEEPING
Inn 1890.....................................**13** B2
Red Victorian.............................**14** C2

EATING
Cole Valley Café.....................(see 3)
Magnolia Brewpub...................**15** D2

SHOPPING
Amoeba Records.......................**16** B2
Loyal Army................................**17** C2
SFO Snowboarding & FTC
   Skateboarding.......................**18** C2

On Sunday, John F Kennedy Dr closes to traffic and hordes of in-line skaters, cyclists and street-hockey players fill the roadway. Lindyhoppers flip in the band shell on the Music Concourse, and old-school skaters bust synchronized moves at 6th Ave and Kennedy Dr.

Rent skates from **Golden Gate Park Bike & Skate** (Map p57; ☎ 415-668-1117; www.goldengate parkbikeandskate.com; 3038 Fulton St, cnr 6th Ave; skates per hr/day $5/20, in-line skates $6/24; ☼ daily, weather permitting); rent bikes from **San Francisco Cyclery** (Map p63; ☎ 415-379-3870; 672 Stanyan St; per 2/8hrs $15/30; ☼ 10am-6pm Wed-Mon).

Fisherman's Wharf

North of the Embarcadero, **Pier 39** marks the beginning of **Fisherman's Wharf** (Map p60), the epicenter of (bland) tourism and home of the city's fishing fleet. Not much of a working wharf any more, it better resembles a waterfront shopping mall. Locals are baffled that tourists are drawn here. But two cable-car lines end here, there are attractions for kids, and you can get fresh Dungeness crab from fish stands. Hamming it up off Pier 39's western end, a **sea-lion colony** barks, belly-flops and sets the SF standard for beach bumming.

Over six tours of duty, the WWII submarine **USS Pampanito** (Map p60; ☎ 415-775-1943; www.maritime.org/pamphome.htm; Pier 45; adult/child 6 12/senior/family $9/4/5/20; ☼ 9am-6pm Sun-Thu, 9am-8pm Fri & Sat mid-Oct–May, 9am-8pm Thu-Tue, 9am-6pm Wed Jun–mid-Oct) sunk six Japanese ships (including two carrying British and Australian POWs), battled three others, and survived to tell the tale. Take a self-guided tour of the beautifully restored, extra-tight quarters, booth-sized bathroom and ship-shape kitchen; pay $2 extra for the audio tour, with *Pampanito* servicemen describing tense days in underwater stealth mode.

On the docks you can guillotine a man for a quarter at the **Musée Mécanique** (Map p60; ☎ 415-346-2000; www.museemecaniquesf.com; Pier 45; admission free; ☼ 10am-7pm Mon-Fri, 10am-8pm Sat & Sun), where 19th-century arcade games like the macabre French Execution compete for your spare change with Ms Pac-Man.

On fog-free days, rent a bicycle from **Blazing Saddles** (Map p60; ☎ 415-202-8888;

www.blazingsaddles.com; from per hr/day $7/28; ☺ from 8am), ride over the Golden Gate Bridge and return via ferry from Sausalito. There are branches at Pier 41, Pier 43 1/2 and 2715 Hyde St.

On the Wharf's western end, **Aquatic Park** has rest rooms and a sandy beach where only die-hard and Neoprene-clad swimmers brave the Bay's icy waters.

The Marina

West of Aquatic Park, a footpath traverses a wooded hill toward the Marina, a neighborhood of multimillion-dollar homes on seismically unstable ground. Stroll past the yacht harbor onto **Marina Green**, a six-block-long esplanade great for kite-flying, picnicking, skating and watching windsurfers and kiteboarders (who look like giant mosquitoes zipping up and down).

Bordering the Presidio, Bernard Maybeck's artificial Roman ruin of the **Palace of Fine Arts** (Baker St at Bay St) was built for the 1915 Panama-Pacific Exposition, but has a timeless romantic look and a rotunda frieze with a recurring SF theme: 'Art Under Attack by Materialists, with Idealists Leaping to Her Rescue.' Test the physics of skateboarding, learn the science of cuteness, and grope your way through the Tactile Dome to enlightenment at the **Exploratorium** (Map p60; ☎ 415-561-0360; www.exploratorium.edu; 3601 Lyon St; adult/child 4-12/student $14/9/11, Tactile Dome $17; ☺ 10am-5pm Tue-Sun; ♿), SF's hands-on discovery museum. Reservations (☎ 415-561-0362) are strongly recommended for the Dome and you must be at least seven years old.

The Presidio & Fort Point

Army sergeants would surely be scandalized by the frolicking in former army bases in the Presidio, founded in 1776 by Spanish explorers and now a 1480-acre National Parks Services (NPS) and GGNRA playground for rare shorebirds, kite-flyers and nudist lollygaggers. The generals might approve of one tenant however: George Lucas of *Star Wars* fame has his digital studio headquarters here; look for the **Yoda statue** (Map p60; 1 Letterman Dr). Get your bearings at the **Presidio Visitors Center** (Map p60; ☎ 415-561-4323; www.nps.gov/prsf; Officers' Club Bldg 50, Moraga Ave; ☺ 9am-5pm).

Along the bay, former military airstrip **Crissy Field** (Map p60; ☺ sunrise-sunset; ♿) has been restored to a tidal marsh, with hiking and biking trails, picnic areas with BBQs and a grassy former airstrip for pooches and kite-flying. When the fog rolls in, the **Warming Hut** (Map p57; ☺ 9am-5pm) serves fair trade coffee and organic pastries within walls insulated with old denim. Get knock-your-socks-off bridge views on the fishing pier opposite the Warming Hut – especially at night.

Directly under the southern span of the Golden Gate Bridge, the **Fort Point National Historic Site** (Map p57; ☎ 415-556-1693; www.nps.gov/fopo; ☺ 10am-5pm Fri-Sun) never actually used those guns in the 1861–65 Civil War, but made a killer backdrop for Alfred Hitchcock's *Vertigo*.

Along the ocean side of the peninsula, **Baker Beach** (Map p57; ☺ sunrise-sunset) features wind-sculpted pines, breathtaking bridge views, a dangerous undertow and a lot of skin – the northern end is clothing-optional.

Lincoln Park, Point Lobos, Ocean Beach & Fort Funston

Golden Gate Park ends in blustery **Ocean Beach** (Map p57; ☺ sunrise-sunset; ♿), too chilly for bikinis but ideal for beachcombing or watching pro surfers brave rip tides (casual swimmers beware). Bonfires are allowed in designated pits, but consult regulations first (online at www.parksconservancy.org) or call **park police** (☎ 415-561-5505).

At **Point Lobos**, the city's westernmost tip, the latest incarnation of the **Cliff House** (Map p57; ☎ 415-386-3330; www.cliffhouse.com) restaurant looks like a mausoleum. But along the cliff's edge is the mesmerizing 1946 **Camera Obscura** (Map p57; ☎ 415-750-0415; admission $2; ☺ 11am-sunset; ♿), Leonardo da Vinci's invention that projects the view from outside the building onto a giant parabolic screen inside.

Follow the trail above the splendid ruin of the 1896 **Sutro Baths** (Map p57), where Victorian dandies once converged for bracing baths and workouts, and visit **Lands End** (Map p57; ☺ sunrise-sunset; ♿) for postcard-worthy views of Marin Headlands and the Golden Gate Bridge. The trail leads to the **California Palace of the Legion of Honor** (Map p57; ☎ 415-750-3600; www.thinker.org; 34th Ave at Clement St adult/senior/youth 13-17 $10/6/7, $2 discount with MUNI ticket, 1st Tue of the month free; ☺ 9:30am-5.15pm Tue-Sun; ♿), which mixes blockbuster exhibits of Fabergé eggs with shows of Max

(continued on page 73)

Pacific Coast Highway

Coastal poppies along PCH in Los Padres National Forest (p177)

JAN STROMME

Fill up the gas tank and buckle up: it's time to hit the road. Everyone knows the Pacific Coast Highway (aka 'PCH') is the West Coast's ultimate road trip. Snaking for over 1000 miles along dizzying sea cliffs, past redwood forests and old-fashioned beach towns, PCH connects the dots between coastal California's big three cities: offbeat San Francisco, glam Los Angeles and surfin' San Diego. When pounding the pavement starts to feel claustrophobic, it's super easy to jump back onto PCH and cruise the coast highway north or south, wherever your wanderlust leads.

During summer (June through August), vacationing crowds descend on PCH. Beaches are at their warmest and most beckoning then, but everywhere along the coast north of San Luis Obispo may be socked in by fog (nicknamed 'June gloom,' though it can last into July or August). September and October usually see clearer skies and more sunshine in Northern California (NorCal), while Southern California (SoCal) beaches are less jam-packed. Or you can take a trip in early spring after the winter rains end, when wildflowers bloom, usually in April. For more advice on when to go, see p14.

For more coastal California road-tripping ideas, turn to p18. For travel books to toss in your beach bag, see p17.

top five

INLAND DETOURS OFF PCH

Golden Gate Bridge (p55) at sunset   NICHOLAS PAVLOFF

SAN FRANCISCO TO THE OREGON BORDER

Once you've had enough of coffeehouses and big-city culture, plot your escape from San Francisco over the soaring Golden Gate Bridge (p55). Ditch the car to walk across the bay's art-deco landmark, braving blustery winds for the sake of killer vacation snapshots.

North of the bridge lies Marin County (p87), just about the densest collection of gorgeous beaches, grassy headlands and thick forests anywhere in California. This is where Hwy 1 starts to get squirrelly, as it twists along the coast, flung west of Hwy 101. Go hiking at Point Reyes, devour some fresh oysters or make a quick detour inland to Sonoma's Wine Country (p106).

Made famous by Hitchcock's thriller *The Birds*, Bodega Bay (p103) is where things really start to get wild. Not just a watersports mecca, it's also the gateway to more windswept beaches strung along the Sonoma Coast (p105), an ecological haven. Keep going north past Sea Ranch resort, Point Arena Lighthouse and the blink-and-you-miss-it town of Elk, with its singular sea stacks.

Just when you think Hwy 1 couldn't get any more remote, the quaint 19th-century New England–style village of Mendocino (p113) pops up like a welcoming beacon. Soak up the arty atmosphere, go kayaking on the Big River, and sleep cozily inside a Victorian B&B. Scout for sea-polished souvenirs at Glass Beach in maritime Fort Bragg, then zip north up the last lonely stretch of Hwy 1 beyond sleepy Westport.

At Leggett (p124), Hwy 1 rejoins Hwy 101 and the redwood empire begins. Bordered by old lumber towns and latter-day hippie hamlets, Hwy 101 journeys north to the Oregon border and beyond. En route you'll pass bewitching parklands where you can get lost among coast redwoods, the tallest trees

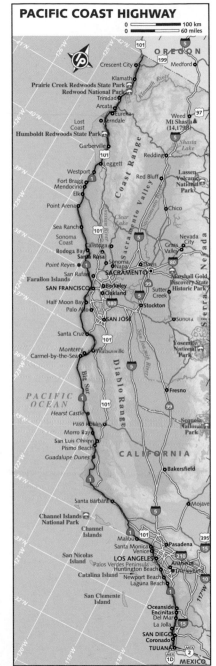

PACIFIC COAST HIGHWAY

Carson Mansion (p135), Eureka

JOHN ELK III

on earth. North of Garberville, the 32-mile Avenue of the Giants (p129) is like a mini road trip itself, diving into a forested fairyland where sunlight splashes against morning mist and verdant ferns.

To truly get off the beaten path, detour along the nearly roadless Lost Coast (p127). When you crave civilization again, visit Victorian-era Ferndale, with its quaint B&Bs; the salty sea-dogs' lair of Eureka; the trippy, hippie-dippy university town of Arcata; or postcard-perfect Trinidad (p142), nestled among retro 20th-century vacation cottages.

Then it's onward into the redwoods. Make time for Redwood National Park's Tall Trees Grove and the Newton B Drury Scenic Parkway in Prairie Creek Redwoods State Park, which hides blustery Gold Bluffs Beach. Klamath (p147), a rustic riverside outdoor-adventure base camp, and Crescent City are places to stock up on supplies before exploring Northern California's farthest reaches, where more redwood groves and wild and scenic rivers await.

SAN FRANCISCO TO LOS ANGELES

Wrongly considered 'flyover' country by urbanites shuttling between San Francisco and LA, the Central Coast unlocks hidden natural delights: redwood forests, lacy waterfalls, hot springs and laid-back surf haunts. Of course, there's superb wildlife watching, too – from

KEEPING THE LIGHTS ON

All along the California coast, you'll stumble across enchanting historical lighthouses, over a dozen of which are still open to the public. Most date from the mid-19th century, after the shipping boom of the Gold Rush era, built to warn mariners of the dangers of rocks. Among coastal California lighthouses still standing, only the North Coast's Point Arena (p111) lets you climb to the tippy-top. You can stay overnight in the former lightkeepers' quarters there or at Point Cabrillo (p114) near Mendocino. Traveling on a budget? In the San Francisco Bay Area, the Point Montara (p84) and Pigeon Point (p86) lighthouses luckily have been converted into spic-and-span youth hostels. On the Central Coast, Point Sur Lightstation (p177) offers moonlight tours from spring through fall, while tour guides at Point Piedras Blancas Lightstation (p181) occasionally don historical costumes. San Diego's Point Loma (p253) and Marin County's Point Bonita (p90) and Point Reyes (p98) lighthouses boast some of the most sweeping sea views anywhere in California. On the Monterey peninsula, Point Pinos (p173) is the West Coast's oldest continuously operating lighthouse, though the lighthouse on San Francisco's infamous Alcatraz Island (p55) was built first. San Pedro's Point Fermin Lighthouse (p216) in LA was, unusually, built out of California redwoods. Near the Oregon border, island-bound Battery Point Lighthouse (p150) is reputedly haunted by ghosts, despite still having a live-in lighthouse keeper.

endangered California condors and the coast's largest colony of northern elephant seals to kaleidoscopic tide-pool communities and underwater canyons rich in sea life.

Life moves more slowly here, so savor the drive – much as you would a knockout vintage from the Santa Cruz Mountains, Paso Robles, San Luis Obispo or Santa Barbara Wine Countries you'll pass along the way. Take your time following Hwy 1 along the coast, far from speedier inland Hwy 101. Just driving from San Francisco to Santa Cruz via Half Moon Bay (p84) often feels like you're dangling off the edge of the world.

If you thought San Francisco was bohemian, you haven't seen anything yet, not until you've spent an afternoon in wacky Santa Cruz (p155). No-nonsense Monterey has the rough-and-ready seafaring atmosphere of a John Steinbeck novel, with the peaceful charms of Pacific Grove and posh Carmel nearby. South of Point Lobos, Hwy 1 plunges into Big Sur (p176), where modern-day beatniks and alternative thinkers homestead.

Emerging from redwood forests, Hwy 1 passes by Hearst Castle (p181), a monumental mansion perched high above the sea. 'SLO' down for San Luis Obispo (p186), an energetic university town that abounds with outdoor pursuits, from hiking volcanic peaks to sea kayaking and whale-watching nearby.

top five

SECRET SEA VIEWS OFF PCH

Jalama Beach County Park (p194)

Tomales Point (p99)

Moonstone Beach, Trinidad (p142)

Jade Cove (p179)

Carbon Beach, Malibu (p214)

Elephant seal at Piedras Blancas (p182)

DOUGLAS STEAKLEY

The beach at Santa Cruz (p155) JOHN ELK III

Street art in San Luis Obispo (p186) JUDY BELLAH

From Pismo Beach, Hwy 101 speeds south to Santa Barbara, passing the Santa Maria and Santa Ynez Valley Wine Countries, while Hwy 1 detours out to the monumental sand dunes of Guadalupe and magically isolated beaches.

Whichever way you approach Santa Barbara (p195), you'll fall under the spell of its sunny Mediterranean climate, picturesque red-tiled roofs and golden beaches. You'll suddenly realize that you've already crossed over the invisible dividing line between NorCal and SoCal. Sail out to Channel Islands National Park to really get away from it all. Or keep cruising south over the Ventura County line right into star-studded Malibu (p214), where celebrity sightings are as predictable as the tides. Then, you'll be truly ready for LA.

PLAYLIST: CALIFORNIA THROUGH THE DECADES

Get in the groove for your coastal road trip with the classic California sounds of:

- 'Surfer Girl' by the Beach Boys (1963)
- 'California Dreamin'' by the Mamas and the Papas (1965)
- '(Sittin' on) The Dock of the Bay' by Otis Redding (1968)
- 'Going to California' by Led Zeppelin (1971)
- 'Low Rider' by War (1975)
- 'Hotel California' by the Eagles (1977)
- 'California Sun' by Dick Dale (1994)
- 'California Love' by 2Pac (1995)
- 'Santa Monica' by Everclear (1995)
- 'Dani California' by the Red Hot Chili Peppers (2006)

LOS ANGELES TO THE MEXICO BORDER

This lazy, sun-lovin' stretch of coastal highway from LA to San Diego through Orange County may be the shortest leg of your trip, but it has something found nowhere else: the official Pacific Coast Highway, legally speaking. Over time PCH has come to popularly refer to California's entire coastal highway, and even Hwy 101 reaching into Oregon and Washington. Yet, this slice of Hwy 1 through SoCal is technically where it's at. Here you can dive headfirst into a dreamscape of bodacious beaches, paradisiacal surf waves and glam ocean-view enclaves where Hollywood-inspired dreams really do come true.

On weekends, the irresistible attraction of posh Santa Monica (p214) makes it seem as if every Angeleno is at this very same beach. Take a spin on the solar-powered Ferris wheel at Santa Monica Pier, incidentally the endpoint of Route 66 (but that's a road trip for another book). Neighboring Venice is as far-out, wacky and weird as anywhere in California – just take a stroll along the boardwalk, a nonstop freak show (and we say that with love). Fashionistas, surfers and beach-volleyball stars head to LA's trio of South Bay beaches – svelte Manhattan Beach, funky Hermosa Beach and touristy Redondo Beach. Follow Hwy 1 as it snakes around the privileged Palos Verdes Peninsula (p217), with its epic sea views, to workaday Long Beach, famous for its aquarium and HMS *Queen Mary*.

Don your strappy sandals and Gucci sunglasses as you cruise into Orange County (p230), aka 'the OC,' which looks exactly like it does on TV and the silver screen. Although Santa Cruz might beg to differ, Huntington Beach claims the title of 'Surf City USA.'

top five

SEAFOOD SHACKS ALONG PCH

Reel Inn (p225)

Spud Point Crab Company (p104)

Splash Cafe (p193)

Drakes Bay Oyster Farm (p98)

Ruddell's Smokehouse (p185)

A classic car in Huntington Beach (p234)   CHRISTINA LEASE

Newport Beach is filled with yachties and public white-sand beaches open to anyone who cares to dally. A former artists' colony, ritzy Laguna Beach is so movie-star beautiful – not just its ocean views, but also its youthful denizens – that you may never want to leave.

Easy does it as you slide into San Diego County. On the North County Coast (p267) play with giant blocks at Legoland, get in touch with your spiritual side in Encinitas and bet on a horse race in Del Mar. Be rejuvenated by La Jolla, with its nature reserves and oh-so-classy downtown scene. Or join everyday people at funky Pacific Beach, ride the roller coaster at Mission Beach and take a pier walk in bohemian Ocean Beach.

Don't miss seeing Point Loma, with its hilltop lighthouse panoramas, before heading inland to explore San Diego (p241). Wander historic Old Town, Balboa Park and the Gaslamp Quarter. Then fly high across the bridge to Coronado and grab a swanky sunset cocktail at the celebrated Hotel Del. After an epic road trip like this, you've definitely earned it.

Highway 1, Big Sur (p176)

EDDIE BRADY

A DEVIL OF A ROAD

The Pacific Coast Hwy is infamous for its hairpin turns, steep cliffside drop-offs and rocky and muddy landslides, especially when winter storms drench the hillsides or when late summer wildfires wreak havoc. Some of the riskiest sections of PCH (thrilling!) are from Jenner north to Mendocino, farther north around Redway, the Devil's Slide in Pacifica and everywhere in Big Sur, where the Bixby Bridge didn't safely connect the bohemian retreat to the rest of California until 1935.

Here are a few pieces of advice, to make sure your road trip is happy-go-lucky:

- Check road conditions before heading out with CalTrans (☎ 800-427-7623; www.dot.ca.gov).
- Fill up the tank whenever possible, as gas stations can be few and far between – not to mention shockingly high-priced!
- Check the spare tire, tool kit (eg jack, jumper cables, ice scraper, tire-pressure gauge) and emergency equipment (eg reflective light signals) in your car.
- Join an automobile association (p289) for 24-hour roadside assistance, free driving maps (hey, you can't always rely on that GPS unit...) and valuable travel discounts at motels etc.
- For more advice about dealing with foggy weather, rockfalls, wildlife and never-ending road construction, see p291.

(continued from page 64)

Klinger's obscure, macabre 19th-century *Waking Dream* etchings. Check out works on paper from post-impressionists through to pop at the Achenbach Foundation for Graphic Arts, and the Rodin-rich sculpture garden donated by the Legion's benefactor, 'Big Alma' Spreckels, whose socialite career started as a nude sculptor's model. The museum is surrounded by an 18-hole **golf course** (☎ 415-750-4653, 415-221-9911).

One and a half miles south of Ocean Beach, watch hang gliders float above **Fort Funston** (Map p57; ☽ sunrise-sunset; 🅰) and hike along windswept cliffs to the beach below.

THE NEIGHBORHOOD CRAWL

Like San Franciscans themselves, this city's neighborhoods do not adhere to obvious boundaries. But as in medieval Italy, you might be able to tell where you are based on some combination of what's on the menu, what people are drinking, where they're headed and what they're wearing. Here's what you'll probably spot where in San Francisco:

North Beach

- Drink of choice: cappuccino at **Caffe Trieste** (p79)
- Style signature: guitar from **101 Records** (p82)
- Local eats: sandwich with housemade salami from **Molinari's Delicatessen** (p79)
- Headed to: poetry reading at **City Lights** (p51)

Chinatown

- Drink of choice: tea with breakfast, lunch and dinner – and maybe Irish coffee afterwards at **Cafe Tosca** (p79)
- Style signature: *erhu* (Chinese violin) from **Clarion Music Center** (p82)
- Local eats: dim sum from **City View** (p77)
- Headed to: jam session at a culture center in historic **Spofford Alley** (see p74)

The Castro

- Drink of choice: happy hour specials at **Café Flore** (p79)
- Style signature: $200 jeans for $70 from **Jeremy's** (p82)
- Local eats: Dungeness crab cakes at **Anchor Oyster Bar** (p77)
- Headed to: 1930s film retrospective at the **Castro Theatre** (Map p61; ☎ 415-621-6120; 429 Castro St)

The Mission

- Drink of choice: Anchor Steam beer on tap at **Zeitgeist** (p79)
- Style signature: pirate's patch from **826 Valencia** (p82)
- Local eats: burrito from **La Taquería** (p76)
- Headed to: the wee hours at the **Endup** (p81)

The Haight

- Drink of choice: house microbrews at **Magnolia Brewpub** (p77)
- Style signature: skateboard from **FTC Skateboarding** (p83)
- Local eats: smoked duck sausage with mango chutney from **Rosamunde Sausage Grill** (p76)
- Headed to: the Hippie Hill drum circle in **Golden Gate Park** (p56)

DRIVING TOUR: 49-MILE SCENIC DRIVE

What to See

San Francisco covers 49 square miles – and the 49-mile Drive provides a smart overview of the city's best sights, from historic Victorians to windswept beaches. In a few hours you'll cover **Civic Center** and **Downtown**, the northern waterfront and the **Golden Gate Bridge**, as well as various local neighborhoods including the **Mission** and **Castro**. Leave time to linger in **Golden Gate Park** and plan to snap pix at **Twin Peaks** – assuming it's not sopped in with fog.

The Route

Street signs (with seagulls on them) indicate the route, but it's tricky to find without the 49-mile Drive map; get one at the **San Francisco Visitors Information Center** (p54) or download a copy at their website (www.onlyinsanfrancisco.com/maps/49miledrive.asp). Specific sights are bulleted on the map, along with commentary. Do not attempt the drive during rush hour. Some stops are silly – like the airport – so plan to stray and make your own discoveries.

Time & Mileage

The route is 49 miles; plan on three to four hours. Add time for lunch and stops along the way. To avoid traffic, set out at 9am or 10am.

TOURS

The visitors information center (Map pp58–9) has a complete list of tour operators.

Chinatown Alleyway Tours (☎ 415-984-1478; www.chinatownalleywaytours.org; adult/child 6-9/student 10-17 $18/5/12; ☺ 11am-1pm Mon-Sat by appointment; ♿) Teens who grew up in the neighborhood lead two-hour tours through Chinatown's historic backstreets.

City Guides (☎ 415-557-4266; www.sfcityguides.org; ♿) Sponsored by the San Francisco Public Library, City Guides offers free walking tours led by savvy local historians: Art Deco Marina, Gold Rush Downtown, Pacific Heights' Mansions and more. See the website for meeting times and locations.

Oceanic Society (☎ 415-474-3385; www.oceanic-society.org; per person $48-120; ♿) Whale-watching trips from San Francisco, Bodega Bay and Half Moon Bay (December to May), plus trips to the Farallon Islands (May to November).

Precita Eyes Mission Mural Tours (☎ 415-285-2287; www.precitaeyes.org; public tour adult/student/child under 12 $10-12/2/5; ♿) Local artists lead two-hour tours on foot or bike, covering 60 to 70 murals within a six- to 10-block radius of mural-bedecked Balmy Alley. Tours depart 11am weekdays and 1:30pm weekends.

Victorian Home Walk (☎ 415-252-9485; www.victorianwalk.com; per person $25; ☺ 11am; ♿) Two-and-a-half-hour architectural walking tours ranging from Edwardian cottages to Queen Anne mansions, plus 'Painted Lady' Victorians with TV credits. Cash only.

FESTIVALS & EVENTS

Chinese New Year Parade (☎ 415-986-1370; www.chineseparade.com) Chase the 200ft dragon with toddler martial artists and frozen-smile runners-up for the Miss Chinatown title through town in late January/early February.

SF International Film Festival (☎ 415-561-5000; www.sffs.org) Popcorn and paparazzi kick off the nation's oldest film festival for two weeks in late April.

Bay to Breakers (☎ 415-359-2800; www.baytobreakers.com) Thousands run costumed, naked and/or clutching beer from Embarcadero to Ocean Beach on the third Sunday in May.

Carnaval (☎ 415-826-1401; www.carnavalsf.com) Brazilian, or just faking it with a wax and a tan? Shake your tail feathers in the Mission the last weekend of May.

SF Gay Pride Month (☎ 415-864-0831; www.sfpride.org) A day isn't enough to do SF proud: June begins with the Gay & Lesbian Film Festival, and goes out in style the last weekend with Pink Saturday and the half-million-strong Pride parade, trailing boas and bridal veils by the mile.

Folsom Street Fair (☎ 415-777-3247; www.folsomstreetfair.com) Wear your heart on your sleeve but not much else, and enjoy public spankings for local charities the last weekend of July.

LitQuake (☎ 415-750-1497; www.litquake.org) Authors spill true stories and trade secrets over drinks at the legendary Lit Crawl, held the second weekend in October.

SF Jazz Festival (☎ 415-398-5655; www.sfjazz.org)

Old-school greats and breakthrough talents blow horns and minds in late October.

Diá de los Muertos (☎ 415-821-1155; www.dayofthe deadsf.org) Party to wake the dead with costume parades, sugar skulls and fabulous altars in the Mission on November 2.

SLEEPING

Staying Downtown, by Union Sq, puts you near all public transportation. It's a neighborhood of high-rises, not Victorians. Watch your back in the Tenderloin (see p54). North Beach is exciting, but street parking is impossible – use hotel garages.

Rates in this section are published high-season prices; you can often do better. The San Francisco Visitors Information Center (p54) runs a **reservation line** (☎ 888-782-9673; www.onlyinsanfrancisco.com).

Budget

Hostelling International (HI; www.sfhostels.com) has three locations in SF. Lombard St, in the Fisherman's Wharf area west of Van Ness Ave, is motel row – good when you show up without reservations.

Pacific Tradewinds Hostel (Map pp58-9; ☎ 415-433-7970, 888-734-6783; www.sanfranciscohostel.org; 680 Sacramento St; dm $24-26; ✪ reception 8am-11:30pm; 🖳 🛜) The city's spiffiest all-dorm hostel sports a nautical theme, with ultraclean shared bathrooms, spotless showers and full kitchen. Great service, but no elevator and three flights of stairs.

Hotel San Remo (Map p60; ☎ 415-776-8688, 800-352-7366; www.sanremohotel.com; 2237 Mason St; r $75-99; 🖳 🛜) Long on Old West charm, the vintage 1906 San Remo has simple rooms with shared bathrooms. Cheapest rooms face the hallway; for air and light request one with a window.

24 Henry Street (Map p61; ☎ 415-864-5686, 800-900-5686; www.24henry.com; 24 Henry St; r incl continental breakfast with/without bathroom from $85/129; 🛜) A modest 19th-century house on a quiet, tree-lined lane, 24 Henry's rooms are simply decorated with cast-off antiques and utilitarian furniture. Ideal for unfussy, gay travelers.

Dakota Hotel (Map pp58-9; ☎ 415-931-7475; 606 Post St at Taylor St; r $98-110; 🖳 🛜) Upgrade from hostel to hotel at this vintage 1920s downtowner with clean, basic rooms with microwave, fridge and clawfoot bathtubs. Temperamental elevator.

Midrange

Good Hotel (Map pp58-9; ☎ 415-621-7001, 800-738-7477; www.jdvhotels.com; 112 7th St; r $109-169; 🔀 🛜 ☺) With a focus on green practices, Good Hotel is decorated with reclaimed and recycled fixtures. The candy-color paint jobs and low-slung platform beds make rooms look like the dorm you wish you'd had in college.Rooms on Mission St are loud; book in back. Some air-conditioned rooms are available. Parking is free for hybrid vehicles (all others $20).

Inn 1890 (Map p63; ☎ 415-386-0486, 888-466-1890; www.inn1890.com; 1890 Page St; r incl breakfast with/without bath from $129/99, ste $169-189; 🖳 🛜) A stately 16-bedroom Victorian mansion with little ornamentation, Inn 1890 sits on a quiet residential street in the Upper Haight. Book a fireplace room for romance. There's also a big communal kitchen, so you can save money by eating in.

Hotel des Arts (Map pp58-9; ☎ 415-956-3232, 800-956-4322; www.sfhoteldesarts.com; 447 Bush St; r with/without bathroom from $139/89; 🛜) Art freaks take note: every wall in specialty rooms at Hotel des Arts has been painted with jaw-dropping murals by up-and-coming underground street artists – it's like sleeping inside a painting. Standard rooms are less exciting, but clean and good value.

Red Victorian (Map p63; ☎ 415-864-1978; www.redvic.net; 1665 Haight St; r incl breakfast with/without bath from $149/89; 🛜) The '60s live on at the tripped-out Red Vic. Individually decorated rooms pay tribute to peace, ecology and friendship. Only four have baths; breakfast is in the organic cafe. Wi-fi in lobby.

Golden Gate Hotel (Map pp58-9; ☎ 415-392-3702, 800-835-1118; www.goldengatehotel.com; 775 Bush St; r with/without bathroom $165/105; 🖳 🛜) Like an old-fashioned *pensione*, the Golden Gate has kindly owners and simple rooms with mismatched furniture inside a 1913 Edwardian, safely up the hill from the Tenderloin. Great homemade cookies.

Petite Auberge (Map pp58-9; ☎ 415-928-6000, 800-365-3004; www.jdvhospitality.com; 863 Bush St; r incl breakfast $169-219; 🛜) Like a country inn, this French-provincial charmer has cheerful rooms (some come with gas fireplaces) that include breakfast and a nightly wine-and-cheese hour, served fireside in the cozy salon.

ourpick Hotel Bohème (Map pp58-9; ☎ 415-433-9111; www.hotelboheme.com; 444 Columbus Ave; r $174-194; ☎) Like a love letter to the jazz era, the Bohème is decorated in moody color schemes – orange, black and sage-green – nodding to the late 1950s. Inverted Chinese umbrellas hang from the ceiling, and Beat-era photos decorate the walls. Rooms are smallish, and some front on noisy Columbus Ave, but the hotel sits smack in the middle of North Beach's vibrant street scene. For quiet, book rooms in back.

Top End

Orchard Garden Hotel (Map pp58-9; ☎ 415-399-9807, 888-717-2881; www.theorchardgardenhotel.com; 466 Bush St; r $179-249; ☒ ☐ ☎) San Francisco's first all-green-practices hotel, opened in 2006, uses sustainably grown wood, recycled hypoallergenic fabrics and chemical-free cleaning products. The look is soothingly swank, with muted colors and deluxe touches like fancy bedding and flat-screen TVs. Great location.

Hotel Vitale (Map pp58-9; ☎ 415-278-3700, 888-890-8688; www.hotelvitale.com; 8 Mission St; r $239-339; ☒ ☐ ☎ ☻) Mid-century modern meets contemporary chic at the coolly minimalist Vitale, Downtown's sexiest hotel. Rooms

are done in a soothing spa theme, and beds have silky-soft 450-thread-count sheets. Splurge on a bay-view room.

EATING
Budget

La Taquería (Map p61; ☎ 415-285-7117; 2889 Mission St at 25th; burritos $5-6.50; ☻ 11am-9pm Mon-Sat, 11am-8pm Sun; ☻) No debatable tofu, saffron rice, spinach tortilla or mango salsa in these burritos and tacos: just classic tomatillo or mesquite salsa, marinated, grilled meats and flavorful beans inside a flour tortilla.

Rosamunde Sausage Grill (Map p61; ☎ 415-437-6851; 545 Haight St; sausages $5.50-6.50; ☻ 11:30am-10pm; ☻) Impress a dinner date with $10: load up classic Brats or duck-fig links with complimentary roasted peppers, grilled onions, whole-grain mustard and mango chutney, then enjoy with your choice of 100 beers at Toronado next door.

BaoNecci (Map pp58-9; ☎ 415-989-1806; www.caffe baonecci.com; 516 Green St; sandwiches $6.50-8; ☻ 9am-5pm Tue-Sun; ☻) Pull up a sidewalk chair in sunny North Beach for bold Southern Italian *panini* on house-baked ciabatta or focaccia. Taste buds sit up and pay attention to the Studente, a ham-and-cheese sandwich slathered with hot

---

DIY DINNERS: SF FARMERS' MARKETS

Year-round

Ferry Building (Map pp58-9; www.cuesa.org; ☻ 10am-2pm Tue & Thu, 8am-2pm Sat; ☻) California-grown produce, meat, seafood and eggs, plus local artisan cheeses, chocolates, olive oils and other gourmet prepared foods; excellent range of organics and sustainably harvested foods; moderate to premium prices.

Alemany (www.sfgov.org/site/alemany; 100 Alemany Blvd; ☻ 6am-4pm Sat; ☻) Since 1945, the city-run market for local produce, with flowers, fish, eggs and food stalls for ready-to-eat foods; bargain prices and a good range of organics and sustainably harvested foods.

Heart of the City (Map pp58-9; UN Plaza; ☻ 7am-4pm Wed, to 5pm Sun; ☻) Local produce, including excellent selection of lesser-known varietals, plus prepared food stalls; bargain prices, some organics.

Crocker Galleria (Map pp58-9; 50 Post St; ☻ 11am-3pm Thu) Local fruit and vegetables, and some organics, at premium prices.

Island Earth (Map pp58-9; www.islandearthfarmersmarket.org; Yerba Buena Gardens entrance, lower level, Metreon; ☻ 10am-7pm or 8pm) Local produce, food artisans and wine tasting; indoors, occasionally with live DJ; some organics, moderate prices.

Seasonal (usually May–November)

Inner Sunset (Map p57; parking lot btwn 8th & 9th Ave, off Irving; ☻ 9am-1pm Sun; ☻ ☻) Local produce and artisan foods, live music, some organics and bargain to moderate prices.

Castro (Map p61; Market at Noe; ☻ 4-8pm Wed; ☻ ☻) Local produce and artisan foods, some organics, moderate prices.

Calabrese red-pepper paste and green-olive spread.

Golden Star (Map pp58-9; ☎ 415-398-1215; 11 Walter Lum Pl; meals $7-9; ⏰ 10am-9pm; ♿) Elementary school cafeterias could outclass this Chinatown standby for atmosphere – but they get gold stars for *pho* (Vietnamese rice noodle soup). Five-spice chicken *pho* is rivaled only by *bun* (rice vermicelli) topped with thinly sliced grilled beef, imperial rolls, mint and ground peanuts.

Louis' (Map p57; ☎ 415-387-6330; 902 Pt Lobos Ave; dishes $7-10; ⏰ 6:30am-4:30pm Mon-Fri, to 6pm Sat & Sun; ♿) Try Louis' for decent burgers and Point Lobos views at half the price of nearby Cliff House. Hold out for a booth overlooking the splendid ruin of the Sutro Baths.

Pagolac (Map pp58-9; ☎ 415-776-3234; 655 Larkin St; dishes $7-10; ⏰ 10am-10pm Mon-Sat) The sweet spot of 'Little Saigon' along gritty Larkin St, Pagolac has the richest *pho* and great char-grilled meats, with candlelit niches and smiles all around.

Sentinel (Map pp58-9; ☎ 415-284-9960; www.the sentinelsf.com; 37 New Montgomery St; sandwiches $8-9; ⏰ 7:30am-2:30pm Mon-Fri) Acclaimed chef Dennis Leary is revolutionizing Downtown lunchtime takeout: tuna salad gets radical with chipotle mayo and crisp fennel, and roast beef does an about-face with horseradish cream cheese. Menus change daily; expect 10-minute waits.

La Boulange (Map p60; ☎ 415-440-4450; www .baybread.com; 1909 Union St; lunch under $10; ⏰ 7am-6pm; ♿) Splurge at Union St boutiques and save on lunch: half a *tartine* (open-faced sandwich) with soup or salad and a fresh-baked macaroon for $10, plus Nutella and cornichons gratis at the condiment bar. Other locations: Hayes Valley (500 Hayes St at Octavia St) and Haight (1000 Cole St at Parnassus).

Midrange

City View (Map pp58-9; ☎ 415-398-2838; 662 Commercial St; small plates $3-5; ⏰ 11am-2:30pm Mon-Fri, 10am-2:30pm Sat & Sun; ♿) Hail carts piled to teetering with impeccable shrimp-and-leek dumplings and crisp Peking duck for decadent dim sum lunches at this sunny Chinatown restaurant. Three to four plates usually make a good meal.

Crown & Crumpet (Map p60; ☎ 415-771-4252; www .crownandcrumpet.com; 207 Ghirardelli Sq; tea & cake $8-12, 5-course tea service $32; ⏰ 10am-6pm Mon-Thu, 9am-10pm Fri, 9am-9pm Sat, 9am-6pm Sun; ♿) Girlfriends rehash hot dates over scones with strawberries and champagne, and dads and daughters clink teacups with crooked pinkies and finger sandwiches. Reservations recommended; large parties, request the corner table with Golden Gate Bridge views.

Greens (Map p60; ☎ 415-771-6222; www.greens restaurant.com; Bldg A, Fort Mason; lunch $8-16, dinner $16-25; ⏰ 8am-8pm Mon-Thu, 8am-5pm Fri & Sat, 9am-4pm Sun; Ⓥ) Inventive cooking so savory, even hard-core meat eaters leave sated and dazzled by Golden Gate Bridge views. On weekends, enjoy takeout black-bean chili with *crème fraîche* and pickled jalapeños at redwood-stump cafe tables or on sunny docks.

Magnolia Brewpub (Map p63; ☎ 415-864-7468; www.magnoliapub.com; 1398 Haight St; mains $8-19; ⏰ noon-midnight Mon-Thu, noon-1am Fri, 10am-1am Sat, 10am-midnight Sun) A Haight staple named after a Grateful Dead song, serving organic salads, homebrew samplers and grass-fed Prather Ranch burgers big enough for stoner appetites at chatty communal tables and shy-hippie booths.

our pick **Namu** (Map p57; ☎ 415-386-8332; www .namusf.com; 439 Balboa St; small plates $9-15; ⏰ 5-10:30pm Mon-Fri, 10am-3pm & 5:30-10:30pm Sat & Sun) SF's unfair culinary advantages are showcased in organic, Korean-inspired small plates of buttery *kampachi* with chili oil and *fleur de sel*, meltaway spare ribs, and Niman Ranch Kobe beef with organic vegetables in a sizzling stone pot.

Anchor Oyster Bar (Map p61; ☎ 415-431-3990; www.anchoroysterbar.com; 579 Castro St; mains $14-25; ⏰ 11:30am-10pm Mon-Fri, noon-10pm Sat, 4-9:30pm Sun) Well hello, sailor: since 1977, Anchor has been the port of call for post-workout Castro boys craving local oysters, crab cakes, Boston clam chowder and Bloody Marys.

farmerbrown (Map pp58-9; ☎ 415-409-3276; www .farmerbrownsf.com; 25 Mason St; mains $15-24; ⏰ 5-11pm Sun-Thu, 5pm-midnight Fri & Sat, bar open to 2am) Putting soul back into soul food with ribs that stick to yours, Tilamook cheddar grits, and coleslaw with a kick – all with ingredients sourced from local, organic and African American farmers. Downsides are harried service and a location on the wrong side of the block; upsides are shotgun-shack decor and $15 all-you-can-eat brunches with live music.

Boulette's Larder (Map pp58-9; ☎ 415-399-1155; www.bouletteslarder.com; 1 Ferry Bldg; mains $15-28;

9am-3pm Mon-Fri, noon-3pm Sat, 11am-3pm Sun) Dinner theater doesn't get better than Boulette's lunchtime communal table, strategically placed inside a working kitchen. Inspired by their truffled eggs and chili-dusted watermelon salads? Get spices and mixes to go at the pantry counter.

1550 Hyde (Map pp58-9; ☎ 415-775-1550; www .1550hyde.com; 1550 Hyde St; dishes $16-19; dinner Tue-Sun) Watch cable cars clang past as you savor Cal-Mediterranean slow food with local, sustainable ingredients with *Wine Spectator*–acclaimed selections under $40. Go Sunday to Thursday for the $29.95 three-course dinner and $15 wine flights, and be seduced.

Delfina (Map p61; ☎ 415-552-4055; www.delfina sf.com; 3621 18th St; mains $18-26; 5:30-10pm Mon-Thu, 5:30-11pm Fri & Sat, 5-10pm Sun) Simple, sensational, seasonal California fare: Sonoma duck with Barolo-roasted cherries, wild-nettle tagliatelle pasta, profiteroles with coffee gelato and candied almonds. Reserve ahead, or settle for Delfina Pizza next door.

Top End

Reserve well ahead for all restaurants in this section.

ourpick Tataki (Map p57; ☎ 415-931-1182; www .tatakisushibar.com; 2815 California St; small plates $4-13; lunch & dinner Mon-Fri, 5-11:30pm Sat, 5-9:30pm Sun) Pioneering sustainable sushi chefs Kin Lui and Raymond Ho rescue dinner and the oceans with sustainable delicacies: silky arctic char drizzled with *yuzu* (Japanese citrus) and capers happily replaces at-risk wild salmon, and the Golden State Roll is a local hero, featuring spicy line-caught scallops, Pacific tuna, organic apple slivers and edible gold leaf.

Slanted Door (Map pp58-9; ☎ 415-861-8032; www .slanteddoor.com; Ferry Bldg; lunch $9-18, dinner $15-28; lunch 11am-2:30pm Mon-Sat, 11:30am-3pm Sun, dinner 5:30-10pm) James Beard Award–winning chef Charles Phan's Cal-Vietnamese landmark has looks and smarts, too: corner windows overlooking the bay and a menu blending Saigon street eats with NorCal ingredients, sourced locally and sustainably. Lunches are ideal for a leisurely pace, lower prices, and mesmerizing bridge-view vistas. When the place is booked, get Dungeness crab noodles from the Out the Door window, and enjoy Bayside.

Jardinière (Map pp58-9; ☎ 415-861-5555; www .jardiniere.com; 300 Grove St; mains $22-35; 5-10:30pm Tue-Sat, 5-10pm Sun & Mon) Iron Chef champ Traci Des Jardins has a way with organic vegetables, free-range meats and sustainable seafood, topping succulent octopus with crispy pork belly, and drizzling Sonoma lavender

---

JUST DESSERTS

■ **Humphrey Slocombe** (Map p57; ☎ 415-550-6971; www.humphryslocombe.com; 2790 Harrison St; noon-9pm Tue-Sun;) The Mission's indie-rock ice cream may permanently spoil you for Top 40 flavors: once balsamic vinegar caramel and olive oil have rocked your taste buds, cookie dough seems so obvious.

■ **Kara's Cupcakes** (Map p60; ☎ 415-563-2253; www.karascupcakes.com; 3249 Scott St; 10am-8pm Mon-Sat, 10am-6pm Sun;) Watch Proustian nostalgia wash over fully grown adults as they bite into retro-1970s carrot cake with cream-cheese frosting, or recall magician birthday parties over chocolate-marshmallow cupcakes.

■ **Mission Pie** (Map p61; ☎ 415-282-1500; www.missionpie.com; 2901 Mission St; 7am-9pm Mon-Thu, 7am-10pm Fri, 8am-10pm Sat, 9am-9pm Sun;) Like mom used to make, only better: from savory quiche to all-American apple, all pie purchases support a nonprofit sustainable farm where city kids learn about nutrition and cooking.

■ **Paulette Macarons** (Map pp58-9; ☎ 415-864-2400; www.paulettemacarons.com; 437 Hayes St; 11am-7pm Tue-Sat, noon-6pm Sun & Mon;) Sorry, Oreo: the competition for the ultimate sandwich cookie is down to Paulette's Sicilian pistachio and passion fruit French macaroons.

■ **Hot Cookie** (Map p61; ☎ 415-621-2350; 407 Castro St; 11am-11pm Mon-Thu, 11am-1am Fri & Sat, 11am-11:30pm Sun) If this place seems familiar, that says something about your taste in cookies or entertainment. After adult film scenes were shot here, Hot Cookie became the place to be photographed for porn stars – hence the signed Hot Cookie underwear, and customers eating chocolate chip cookies with a certain gusto.

honey over squash blossoms bursting with molten sheep's cheese. Go Mondays, when $4 scores three courses with wine pairings, or hit the mood-lit lounge for an affordable bar menu with seasonal cocktails.

Groceries & Quick Eats

Bi-Rite Market (Map p61; ☎ 415-241-9760; 3639 18th St) A showcase for local farmers, vintners, chocolatiers and cheese-makers. Take sandwiches to Dolores Park up the street, with organic ice cream across the street at Bi-Rite Creamery – trust us on the salted caramel.

Rainbow Grocery (Map pp58-9; ☎ 415-863-0620; 1745 Folsom St; Ⓥ) A worker-owned cooperative, Rainbow offers no meat but a huge selection of natural foods, local organic veggies, Sonoma cheeses, breads, wines and organic skincare; this is the best spot to buy vitamins and supplements.

Molinari's Delicatessen (Map pp58-9; ☎ 415-421-2337; 373 Columbus Ave) Plan a gourmet Italian picnic with salami, olives, bread and buffalo mozzarella at this famous delicatessen, and head to Washington Sq Park.

DRINKING
Cafes

Caffe Trieste (Map p60; ☎ 415-392-6739; 601 Vallejo St; 🛜) The West Coast's first espresso bar and former Beat hangout still has poetry graffiti in the bathroom. This is North Beach at its best, with Sinatra on the jukebox and monthly Saturday accordion shows.

Café Flore (Map p61; ☎ 415-621-8579; 2298 Market St; 🛜) Nicknamed the 'floor show' for its gorgeous parade of regulars, the Flore's outdoor patio is a cool scene on a sunny day. At night it's a mellow spot quiet enough for conversation. Good food too. Wi-fi Monday to Friday.

Bars

For pub crawls, hit the Mission (around 16th and Valencia Sts), North Beach, the Haight, and Polk St (north of Geary St).

Bloodhound (Map pp58-9; ☎ 415-863-2840; 1145 Folsom St) Bloodhound feels vaguely Nordic, with white wood, antler chandeliers and fantastic art. Top-shelf ingredients. Killer jukebox. Best weeknights or before midnight on weekends.

Zeitgeist (Map pp58-9; ☎ 415-255-7505; 199 Valencia St) *The* hangout for urban bikers – pedal-and motor-powered – has an enormous

back patio with pot smoke lingering in the air. Heavy pours and good beers.

Hotel Biron (Map pp58-9; ☎ 415-703-0403; 45 Rose St) Our favorite wine bar for an intimate tête-à-tête has a French-underground vibe and great cheese plates; it gets impossibly crowded on weekends.

Koko Cocktails (Map p57; ☎ 415-885-4788; 1060 Geary St) This retro-cool cocktail lounge makes a snappy start to a pub crawl, and spins reggae, soul and sometimes hip hop.

Cafe Tosca (Map pp58-9; ☎ 415-986-9651; 242 Columbus Ave) A classic 1919 bar with old-world character, Tosca has a great jukebox with Rat Pack and Tin Pan Alley-American songbook classics. If you're stalking Sean Penn, start here.

Alembic (Map p57; ☎ 415-666-0822; 1725 Haight St) Haight St's spiffiest bar has an impressive array of whiskeys and mixology drinks, appealing to bon-vivant 30-somethings who jam the tiny space nightly.

Elbo Room (Map p61; ☎ 415-552-7788; 647 Valencia St) Shoot pool downstairs with Mission-district scenesters or hear DJs and live bands upstairs. Dig the photo booth.

Toronado (Map pp58-9; ☎ 415-863-2276; 547 Haight St) Beer mavens dig the 50-plus microbrews, with hundreds more in bottles. Stumble next door to Rosamunde (p76) for sausages.

ENTERTAINMENT

Pick up *SF Weekly* for listings; look online at **Nitevibe** (www.nitevibe.com), **SF Station** (www.sfstation.com) and **SF Gate** (www.sfgate.com); and strike up conversations with locals to gather tips.

Clubs & Live Music

Qoöl (Map pp58-9; ☎ 415-974-1719; www.qoolsf.com; 111 Minna St; ⊙ 5-10pm Wed) SF's coolest weekly dance party is a Wednesday-evening techno happy hour in an art gallery. Afterward, follow the crowd to Satellite, at Anu (43 6th St), for techno-dance till 2am.

Ruby Skye (Map pp58-9; ☎ 415-693-0777; www.rubyskye.com; 420 Mason St; admission $10-25; ⊙ 9pm-late Fri & Sat, sometimes Thu & Sun) The city's premier-name nightclub hosts the who's who of the world's DJs on a state-of-the-art Funktion-One sound system. The very-mainstream crowd sometimes gets messy.

Mighty (Map pp58-9; ☎ 415-626-7001; www.mighty119.com; 119 Utah St; admission $10-20; ⊙ 10pm-4am Fri, Sat & occasional weeknights) Mighty packs a

GAY & LESBIAN SAN FRANCISCO

The mothership of gay culture, San Francisco is America's pinkest city, the easiest place in the US to be gay and where 'mos are accepted as part of mainstream society. (Remember, this is where gay marriage first became reality in the US.) New York Marys may label SF the retirement home of the young – indeed, the sidewalks roll up early – but when it comes to sexual outlaws and underground weirdness, SF kicks New York's ass.

The intersection of 18th and Castro Sts is the heart of the gay scene, and there are bars a go-go, but most are predictably middlebrow. Dancing queens and slutty boys head South of Market (SoMa), the location of most thump-thump clubs and sex venues. Cruise Castro by day, SoMa by night. On sunny days, Speedo-clad gay boys colonize the grassy hill at 20th and Church Sts, overlooking downtown. Be prepared for pot smoke: SF is stoner central. Sexy ladies connect on Valencia St, south of 16th St, in happening cafes, thrift stores and bookshops. Check Get Your Girl On (http://gogetyourgirlon.com) for concerts and parties; or plug into the A-gay scene on Betty's List (www.bettyslist.com). The *San Francisco Bay Times* (www.sfbaytimes.com) has good resources for transsexuals; the *Bay Area Reporter* (aka BAR; www.ebar.com) has gay news and listings.

Bars

The place on Sunday afternoons, the **Eagle Tavern** (Map pp58-9; ☎ 415-626-0880; www.sfeagle.com; 398 12th St) serves all-you-can-drink beer ($10) from 3pm to 6pm. Wear leather and blend right in. Thursday through Sunday are best at **Powerhouse** (Map pp58-9; ☎ 415-552-8689; www.powerhouse-sf. com; 1347 Folsom St), an almost-rough-trade SoMa bar; patrons smoke out and get cozy on the back deck. **Truck** (Map pp58-9; ☎ 415-252-0306; www.trucksf.com; 1900 Folsom St) draws a happening crowd of local gay-boy scenesters, especially Sunday evenings; get the password for Tuesday night's speak-easy (no girls). The hands-down best drag show happens at 10pm Friday and Saturday nights at **Aunt Charlie's** (Map pp58-9; ☎ 415-441-2922; www.auntcharlieslounge.com; 133 Turk St), the classic urban-grit dive bar.

In the Castro, cologne-wearing 20-somethings (and gay-boy-loving straight girls) queue up nightly to dance in the light of flickering videos at **Badlands** (Map p61; ☎ 415-626-9320; 4121 18th St) – if you're over 30, you'll feel old. A better bet for cocktails is see-and-be-seen **Blackbird** (Map p61; ☎ 415-503-0630; 2124 Market St); wear a tight T-shirt. Shy types and A&F boys shoot pool in the glow of the fish tanks at neighborhood-esque **Moby Dick** (Map p61; ☎ 415-861-1191;

no-bullshit wallop with its awesome sound system, underground dance beats, urban vibe and cool local crowd that doesn't fuss about dress codes.

Harlot (Map pp58-9; ☎ 415-777-1077; www.harlotsf .com; 46 Minna St; admission $10-20, 5-9pm Wed-Fri free; ⚑ 5pm-2am Wed-Fri, 9pm-2am Sat) Velvet curtains and intense red lighting lend a Goth-erotic-chic look – think vampire's den. Before 9pm it's a lounge, after 9pm a club. Wednesdays and Thursdays are best; weekends get suburban. Dress smart or don't get in.

Triple Crown (Map pp58-9; ☎ 415-863-3516; www .triplecrownsf.com; 1760 Market St) A storefront bar with adjoining black-box rooms, Triple Crown hosts DJs spinning everything from '60s soul and '80s pop to down-tempo funk and hip hop. Upbeat, cool local crowd. Tuesdays: gay.

Fillmore (Map p57; ☎ 415-346-6000; www.the fillmore.com; 1805 Geary Blvd) Hendrix, Zeppelin,

the Who – they all played the Fillmore. Its 1250 capacity means you're close to the stage. Dig the priceless collection in the upstairs poster-art gallery.

Yoshi's (Map p57; ☎ 415-655-5600; www.yoshis .com; 1300 Fillmore St) San Francisco's definitive jazz club draws the world's top talent and occasionally hosts rare appearances; advance bookings recommended.

Bottom of the Hill (Map p57; ☎ 415-621-4455; www.bottomofthehill.com; 1233 17th St; ⚑ shows after 8:30pm Tue-Sat) On lower Potrero Hill, this indie-rock institution showcases happening local acts. Shoot pool in back and smoke on the outdoor patio.

Boom Boom Room (Map p57; ☎ 415-673-8000; www.boomboomblues.com; 1601 Fillmore St; ⚑ Tue-Sun) John Lee Hooker owns this vintage '30s blues and jazz club, which hops six nights a week. Advance tickets are necessary for major acts.

4049 18th St); extroverts and gym queens prefer **440 Castro** (Map p61; ☎ 415-621-8732; 440 Castro St).

For *grlz*, the Mission-hipster spot is down-and-dirty **Lexington Club** (Map p61; ☎ 415-863-2052; www .lexingtonclub.com; 3464 19th St), which has SF's best bathroom graffiti. Expect catfights. Softball dykes go to off-the-beaten-path **Wild Side West** (off Map p57; ☎ 415-647-3099; 424 Cortland St), but boys come to gab in the lush garden. Start the night at **Café Flore** (p79), a cool gay coffeehouse and bar.

Clubs

Juanita More (www.juanitamore.com) throws fierce parties attended by sexy boys (especially on Pride). **Cockblock** (www.cockblocksf.com), at the **Rickshaw Stop** (Map pp58-9; ☎ 415-861-2011; www .rickshawstop.com; 155 Fell St), draws a happening gay-boy-and-girl crowd the second Saturday of the month. **Fresh** (http://freshsf.com), at Ruby Skye (p79), is the monthly circuit party. For gay salsa try Cafe Cocomo (below) on the third Friday of the month.

Ladies: log on to **Craigslist** (www.craigslist.org) and click on women-seeking-women to search for monthly parties or post a query. Mango, from 3pm to 9pm the fourth Saturday of the month at **El Rio** (Map p61; ☎ 415-282-3325; www.elriosf.com; 3158 Mission St), is blazing hot. Hit the Lexington Club (above) to inquire about roving-party Flourish – when dykes actually dress up. Hipster gals pack Stay Gold the last Wednesday of the month at the **Make-Out Room** (Map p61; ☎ 415-647-2888; www.makeoutroom.com; 3225 22nd St).

Every Thursday the art-school-boy crowd crams divey-chic Aunt Charlie's (opposite) for Tubesteak Connection to cruise and grind to vintage bathhouse disco; Tuesday they're at Chilidog Disco at Triple Crown (opposite). Sunday nights, groove to obscure disco and German techno at **Honey Soundsystem** (Map pp58-9; ☎ 415-252-5018; www.honeysoundsystem.com; Paradise Loft, 1501 Folsom St). When it's time to get laid, head to the Disneyland of cock, **Blow Buddies** (Map pp58-9; ☎ 415-777-HEAD; www .blowbuddies.com; 933 Harrison St; admission $12, plus $8 membership fee; ☽ Thu-Sun nights, call for details). No cologne: sweat is the preferred scent.

Gyms

To get your workout on, head to **Gold's Gym** (www.goldsgym.com; admission $15; Market St Map p61; ☎ 415-626-4488; 2301 Market St; Brannan Map pp58-9; ☎ 415-552-4653; 1001 Brannan St). Pretty boys go to Market St; testosterone-y daddies go to Brannan.

Café du Nord (Map p57; ☎ 415-861-5016; www .cafedunord.com; 2170 Market St) The former speakeasy in the basement of the Swedish-American Hall rocks revelers with a cool changing lineup; check its calendar.

Starlight Room (Map pp58-9; ☎ 415-395-8595; www .harrydenton.com; 450 Powell St; ☽ 8:30pm-2am Tue-Sat, 11am-4pm Sun) The 21st-floor views are mesmerizing at the Sir Francis Drake hotel, where khaki-clad tourists dance to live music. Safe space for tipsy dorks and conservative parents. Sunday's drag-show brunch is kooky.

Cafe Cocomo (Map p61; ☎ 415-824-6910; www .cafecocomo.com; 650 Indiana St; ☽ 7pm-midnight Mon, 6pm-midnight Thu, 6pm-2am Sat) Kick-ass salsa bands play Thursday and Saturdays, and hundreds pack the dance floor. Mondays there's no band, but those who come dance hard. Lessons precede parties.

Endup (Map pp58-9; ☎ 415-646-0999; www.theendup .com; 401 6th St; ☽ 10pm-4am Mon-Thu, 11pm-11am Sat, 10pm Sat-10pm Sun) When you're grinding your teeth, desperate for a place to dance till noon on Saturday or Sunday, you've one choice. The crowd is tweaky, but the place an institution.

Theater

TIX Bay Area (Map pp58-9; ☎ 415-433-7827; www.tixbay area.org; Union Sq; ☽ Tue-Sun) This free-standing kiosk on Powell St at Geary St sells half-price, day-of-performance tickets and full-price advance tickets. Cash only for same-day seats.

Beach Blanket Babylon (Map p60; ☎ 415-421-4222; www.beachblanketbabylon.com; 678 Green St; tickets $25-80) If you see only one show, make it hilarious Beach Blanket, where larger-than-life performers brilliantly spoof contemporary culture. And those hats! – legendary.

Teatro Zinzanni (Map p57; ☎ 415-438-2668; http:// zinzanni.org; Pier 29; tickets $145-195) A rotating cast of celebs star in Zinzanni's 19th-century, European-style circus – a sort of comedic Cirque du Soleil – with a surprisingly good five-course meal.

The world-renowned San Francisco Symphony performs in **Davies Symphony Hall** (Map pp58-9; ☎ 415-864-6000; www.sfsymphony .org; cnr Grove St & Van Ness Ave). The beautiful **War Memorial Opera House** (Map pp58-9; ☎ 415-864-3330; 301 Van Ness Ave) hosts the San Francisco Opera and the **San Francisco Ballet** (☎ 415-865-2000; www.sfballet.org). **Yerba Buena Center for the Arts** (Map pp58-9; ☎ 415-978-2787; www.ybca.org; cnr Howard & 3rd Sts) hosts excellent contemporary performing arts.

For comedy, head to the **Punch Line** (Map pp58-9; ☎ 415-397-4337; www.punchlinecomedyclub. com; 444 Battery St; tickets $12-23 plus 2 drink minimum).

Sports

San Francisco 49ers (☎ 415-656-4900; www.sf49ers .com; admission $25-100) The 49ers play NFL football at Candlestick Park, south of the city, but will likely move to Santa Clara in 2014.

San Francisco Giants (☎ 415-972-2000; www.sf giants.com; admission $5-135; ♿) The Giants play Major League Baseball at AT&T Park.

SHOPPING

If you've forgotten underwear or a sweater, head to Union Sq, anchored by good-for-basics **Macy's** (Map pp58-9; ☎ 415-397-3333; 170 O'Farrell St; ♿) and **Original Levi's Store** (Map pp58-9; ☎ 415-501-0100; www.us.levi.com; 300 Post St), the flagship of SF's historic denim inventor. Off the square is a Frank Lloyd Wright–designed building that looks like a mini-Guggenheim inside and, since 1979, has housed **Folk Art International** (Map pp58-9; ☎ 415-392-9999; www.folkartintl.com; 140 Maiden Lane; ♾ 10am-6pm Tue-Sat).

Bloomingdale's (Map pp58-9; ☎ 415-856-5300; 845 Market St) is the main attraction in the **San Francisco Shopping Centre** (Map pp58-9; cnr Market & 5th Sts; ♿), but for cheap and chic it's hard to beat **H&M** (Map pp58-9; ☎ 415-986-4215; 150 Powell St). Designers unload sample and runway-worn fashion at **Jeremy's** (Map pp58-9; ☎ 415-882-4929; www.jeremys.com; 2 South Park Ave) – for as much as 90% off.

For original fashion statements, get hip to Hayes St between Franklin and Laguna Sts in Hayes Valley (Map pp58–9). Acquire that fogged-in SF glow with organic skincare 'tested on boyfriends, never animals'

TOP FIVE SF SOUVENIR UPGRADES

Sure, you could settle for San Francisco snow globes from souvenir shops along Chinatown's Grant St – but neighborhood stores supply only-in-SF finds like these:

■ **Castro:** Martini glasses etched with the SF skyline from Under One Roof (opposite)

■ **Haight:** T-shirt of a grumpy thundercloud in a happy San Francisco fogbank from Loyal Army (below)

■ **Hayes Valley:** Travel-sized Butch & Fem scents from Nancy Boy (below)

■ **Noe Valley:** Signed Alice Waters cookbook at Omnivore (p51)

■ **Pacific Heights:** Psychedelic shirt actually worn during the Summer of Love from Crossroads (below)

---

from local maker **Nancy Boy** (Map pp58-9; ☎ 415-552-3802; www.nancyboy.com; 347 Hayes St). Chic boutiques and gift shops also line Union St, between Franklin and Fillmore Sts (Map p57).

Fashionistas shop the Pacific Heights boutiques along Fillmore St (Map p57) between Bush and Sacramento Sts and sell never-worn designer clothes and mint vintage at **Crossroads** (Map p57; ☎ 415-775-8885; www.crossroadstrading.com; 1901 Fillmore St; ♾ 11am-7pm Mon-Thu, 11am-8pm Fri & Sat, noon-7pm Sun). For vintage finery and T-shirts with cartoon California rolls bragging 'That's how we roll!' from **Loyal Army** (Map p63; ☎ 415-221-6200; www.loyalarmy.com; 1728 Haight St; ♾ 10am-8pm Mon-Sat, 11am-7pm Sun), hit Haight St.

Groove to your own beat at **Amoeba Records** (Map p63; ☎ 415-831-1200; 1855 Haight St; ♾ 10:30am-10pm Mon-Sat, 11am-9pm Sun), with SF's best selection of new and used CDs, or load up on vintage vinyl and guitars at **101 Records** (Map pp58-9; ☎ 415-392-6369; 1414 Grant Ave; ♾ 10am-8pm Tue-Sat, noon-8pm Sun), the secret stash of Tom Waits, Carlos Santana and local DJs. For a real musical challenge, try the *erhu* (Chinese violin) at **Clarion Music Center** (Map pp58-9; ☎ 415-391-1317; www.clarionmusic.com; 816 Sacramento St; ♾ 11am-6pm Mon-Fri, 9am-5pm Sat).

In the Mission, Valencia St between 16th and 24th Sts features locally designed clothing, Mexican folk art and pirate supplies at **826 Valencia** (Map p61; ☎ 415-642-5905; www

.826valencia.org; 826 Valencia; ⏰ noon-6pm), where sales of eye patches, anti-scurvy lemondrops and McSweeney's publications fund youth writing workshops. For more feel-good shopping, Castro's volunteer-run **Under One Roof** (Map p61; ☎ 415-503-2300; www.underoneroof .org; 518a Castro St; ⏰ 10am-9pm) sells gifts donated by local businesses, with 100% of proceeds donated to AIDS service organizations ($11 million to date!). But to feel *really* good about your purchase, try **Good Vibrations** (Map p61; ☎ 415-522-5460; 603 Valencia St) for sex-positive adult toys – Margaret Cho's on the board, so you know they're not shy.

Sporty types can gear up before they split town near Golden Gate Bridge at **Sports Basement** (Map p60; ☎ 415-437-0100; www .sportsbasement.com; 610 Mason St; ⏰ 9am-9pm Mon-Fri, 8am-8pm Sat & Sun), which sells every conceivable shoe and rents ski gear. Go for big air and big style from local maker **SFO Snowboarding & FTC Skateboarding** (Map p63; ☎ 415-626-1141; www.sfosnow.com; 1630 Haight St; ⏰ 11am-7pm).

GETTING THERE & AROUND
Air
The Bay Area has three airports: **San Francisco International Airport** (SFO; ☎ 650-821-8211, 800-435-9736; www.flysfo.com), 15 miles south of the city via Hwy 101 or I-280; **Oakland International Airport** (OAK; ☎ 510-563-3300; www.fly oakland.com), 12 miles southeast, via the Bay Bridge and I-880; and **San Jose International Airport** (SJC; ☎ 408-277-4759; www.sjc.org), 45 miles south. Most international flights arrive at SFO.

To/From the Airports
Take **Bay Area Rapid Transit** (BART; ☎ 415-989-2278; www.bart.gov) directly from SFO or OAK into Downtown San Francisco ($8.10, 30 minutes).

Taxis charge about $40 to $45 for a trip into the city, plus 15% gratuity.

Door-to-door shuttle vans leave the departures level outside terminals. Try **Lorrie's** (☎ 415-334-9000; www.gosfovan.com) and **Super Shuttle** (☎ 415-558-8500; www.supershuttle.com). Fares are about $15. Call ahead for city pick-ups.

Buses are cheapest. From SFO, take **SamTrans** (☎ 800-660-4287; www.samtrans.org) express-bus KX (adult $4.50, 30 minutes) or bus 292 ($1.75, 60 minutes); buses depart from the lower level.

For services from OAK, reserve 48 hours ahead with **Bayporter Express** (☎ 415-467-1800; www.bayporter.com; 1st passenger $32, each additional passenger $15).

To get from SJC to San Francisco, take the **Valley Transit Authority** (VTA; ☎ 408-321-2300; www.vta.org) bus 10, the Airport Flyer ($1.75), to the Santa Clara Caltrain Station and ride the train to San Francisco ($7.75).

Bus
Intercity buses operate from the **Transbay Terminal** (Map pp58-9; 425 Mission St at 1st St). Take **AC Transit** (☎ 510-891-4700; www.actransit.org) to the East Bay, **Golden Gate Transit** (☎ 415-455-2000; www.goldengate.org) to Marin and Sonoma counties, and **SamTrans** (☎ 800-660-4287; www .samtrans.org) buses to points south.

Greyhound (☎ 415-495-1575, 800-231-2222; www .greyhound.com) operates nationwide buses; see p289 for more details about intra-California routes. Some typical one-way fares are: San Francisco to LA $39 to $50; SF to Santa Cruz $12 to $18; and SF to Arcata $42 to $56.

Train
CalTrain (☎ 800-660-4287; www.caltrain.com; cnr 4th & Townsend Sts) operates commuter lines down the peninsula. MUNI's N-Judah streetcar line serves the station.

Amtrak (☎ 800-872-7245; www.amtrak.com) stops in Emeryville and Oakland, with connecting bus services to San Francisco's Ferry Building. Trains depart for Sacramento, Los Angeles and the east. For details about intra-California routes and fares, see p292.

Car & Motorcycle
Avoid driving; parking in SF is trying. When parallel parking on hills, back your wheels against the curb or face fines.

Parking restrictions are strictly enforced, so read the signs. For towed vehicles, call **City Tow** (Map pp58-9; ☎ 415-621-8605; Room 145, 850 Bryant St).

Rent a car for excursions out of town. For good service, go to **National/Alamo** (Map pp58-9; ☎ 415-292-5300; www.nationalcar.com, www .alamo.com; 320 O'Farrell St) or **City Rent-a-Car** (Map pp58-9; ☎ 415-359-1331; www.cityrentacar.com; 1433 Bush St). Alternatively, try Zipcar (p290). For 4WDs and convertibles, try **Specialty Rentals** (Map pp58-9; ☎ 800-400-8412; www.specialtyrentals .com; 150 Valencia St).

To rent a motorcycle, contact **Dubbelju Motorcycle Rentals** (Map pp58-9; ☎ 415-495-2774; www.dubbelju.com; 689a Bryant St).

Public Transportation

MUNI (☎ 415-673-6864; www.sfmuni.com) runs buses, streetcars and cable cars. Get the *Street & Transit Map* ($2.50) at newsstands around Union Sq. Buses cost $2, cable cars $5 (or $10 all day). Transfers are valid for three trips within 90 minutes, except on cable cars. Buy multiday passes at the Visitors Information Center or Union Sq TIX kiosk (p81). Children under four travel free; there's a discount for youths aged five to 17.

BART (☎ 415-989-2278; www.bart.gov) runs trains beneath Market and Mission Sts, linking San Francisco and the East Bay. One-way fares start at $1.75 (children under four are free).

Taxi

Taxi fares start at $3.10 for the first fifth of a mile and cost 45¢ per fifth of a mile thereafter. Be warned: taxis are almost impossible to find during the Friday-evening rush. Call **Luxor Cab** (☎ 415-282-4141), **Arrow Cab** (☎ 415-648-3181) or **Green Cab** (☎ 415-626-4733), a worker-owned collective with fuel-efficient hybrids. You can hail taxis on the street, or your hotel doorman will call one for you for a tip.

SOUTH OF THE BAY

Considering that the Bay Area is America's fifth-largest metropolitan area, it's amazing how much of the land along the Pacific side of the peninsula is undeveloped. The peninsula's eastern side is a tangle of suburbs, bisected by Hwy 101, but on the pastoral western side, along Hwy 1, all is quiet but for the roaring sea and whooshing wind. Leave time to explore hidden beaches and small towns, and stop at farm stands in between. The 68-mile drive from SF to Santa Cruz takes roughly 90 minutes.

PACIFICA TO HALF MOON BAY

Fifteen miles from Downtown San Francisco, Pacifica marks the end of coastside suburbs. It's a nothing-special town but has two sandy beaches: **Rockaway Beach** to the north, popular for fishing, and **Pacifica State Beach**, big with surfers (beware riptides). The latter has outdoor showers and restrooms.

Just south of town, Hwy 1 emerges from eucalyptus forests onto an unstable cliff called Devil's Slide. The road often washes out during winter rains but, wow, it's breathtaking.

A half-mile south of Devil's Slide is **Gray Whale Cove State Beach**, a sandy crescent and one of the coast's most popular clothing-optional beaches. Park on the inland side of Hwy 1; take care crossing the road.

Montara State Beach (the locals' favorite) lies a mile south and has pristine sand and good whale-watching November to May. Adjacent is **McNee Ranch State Park**, a northern section of the Santa Cruz Mountains, with stellar wildflowers in spring. To ascend the hills, hike the trails leading from the Martini Creek parking lot on the inland side of Hwy 1.

Point Montara Lighthouse HI Hostel (☎ 650-728-7177; www.norcalhostels.org; cnr Hwy 1 & 16th St; dm $23-25, r $63-105; ☑ reception 7:30am-10:30pm; ☐ ☎) stands next to a lighthouse built in 1900; make reservations.

our pick **Fitzgerald Marine Reserve** (☎ 650-728-3584; www.fitzgeraldreserve.org; ☑), at Moss Beach, protects exquisite tidepools packed with colorful marine life, from anemones to star fish. Check the website for current tide tables. Observe posted regulations; some of the critters will perish if mishandled. From Hwy 1 in Moss Beach, turn west onto California Ave.

Just to the south, Princeton-by-the-Sea stretches around Pillar Point Harbor. Eat fried fish and coleslaw at **Barbara's Fishtrap** (☎ 650-728-7049; 281 Capistrano Rd; dishes $8-28). At the west end of Pillar Point, **Mavericks** (www.maverickssurf.com) attracts the world's top surfers to its huge, steep and incredibly dangerous waves. The annual Quiksilver/ Mavericks surf contest happens sometime between December and March, depending on conditions.

HALF MOON BAY

pop 12,430

Farms unfurl around Half Moon Bay, which feels worlds away from San Francisco, even though it's only 45 minutes south. Wander Main St and poke your head into home-furnishings and country-crafts shops – all rather vanilla, but quaint nonetheless. Agriculture is the major industry, and pumpkins dot the landscape orange in autumn, when otherwise-quiet farms transform into roadside attractions with corn mazes and jack-o-lanterns. Santa Cruz is 40 miles south.

Orientation & Information

Hwy 92 connects Half Moon Bay to inland freeways; avoid Hwy 92 during commute hours though, unless you are traveling against the traffic. Locally, Hwy 1 is called Cabrillo Hwy.

Shops, cafes and restaurants line five-block-long Main St, just east of Hwy 1. The **Half Moon Bay Coastside Chamber of Commerce** (☎ 650-726-8380; www.halfmoonbaychamber.org; 235 Main St; ❂ 9am-4pm Mon-Fri) provides visitor information and details on its website about ecofriendly businesses.

Sights & Activities

Half Moon Bay State Beach (☎ 650-726-8819; per car $10; ☖) gets crowded but it has bathrooms – ideal for kids who constantly have to pee; access via Kelly Ave or further north at Venice Blvd. We recommend heading further south.

To hit the water, contact **Half Moon Bay Kayaking** (☎ 650-773-6101; www.hmbkayak.com; Pillar Point Harbor; rentals s/d per hr $20/40, guided trips $65-150), which rents kayaks and leads stellar guided wildlife and sunset paddles.

Celebrate harvest at the October **Art & Pumpkin Festival** (☎ 650-726-9652), which kicks off with the World Championship Pumpkin Weigh-Off; the winning pumpkins exceed 1500 lb. (Yes, you read that right.)

Sleeping & Eating

San Benito House (☎ 650-726-3425; www.sanbenito house.com; 356 Main St; r from $70; ☜) Rent folksy, modest, Americana-style rooms above an old-fashioned bar and steakhouse. Downstairs is a deli (10am to 5pm) with sandwiches on good bread (lunch under $10).

Old Thyme Inn (☎ 650-726-1616, 800-720-4277; www.oldthymeinn.com; 779 Main St; r incl breakfast $155-325; ☜) This 1898 inn has cheerful B&B rooms, some with Jacuzzis and fireplaces.

Mill Rose Inn (☎ 650-726-8750, 800-900-7673; www.millroseinn.com; 615 Mill St; r incl breakfast $175-360; ☜) The Mill Rose B&B is over-decorated

but provides cushy touches and the town's most eye-popping gardens.

Flying Fish Grill (☎ 650-712-1125; cnr Hwy 92 & Main St; dishes $4-10; ❂ 11am-8pm; ☖) This tiny fish shack makes delicious, inexpensive fish tacos and seafood plates to eat in or to go.

Cameron's Restaurant & Inn (☎ 650-726-5705; www.cameronsinn.com; 1410 S Cabrillo Hwy; dishes from $9; ☖) Eat pub grub, swill beer and shoot darts at Cameron's, a century-old, atmospheric English-style pub. If you don't mind bar noise, rent a room upstairs (from $99).

Sam's Chowder House (☎ 650-712-0245; www.samschowderhouse.com; 4210 N Cabrillo Hwy; dishes $12-32; ❂ 11:30am-9pm) In the tradition of big Cape Cod waterside fish houses, Sam's makes a mean bowl of chowder, whole steamed crab (in season), traditional lobster-clambake with all the fixin's, steaks and a knockout lobster roll – to find better, fly to Maine. Full bar. Great ocean views.

Getting There & Away

SamTrans (☎ 800-660-4287; www.samtrans.com) bus 294 operates from the Hillsdale CalTrain station to Half Moon Bay, and up the coast to Moss Beach and Pacifica, daily until about 6pm ($1.75, 30 minutes).

HALF MOON BAY TO SANTA CRUZ

Santa Cruz is covered in the Central Coast chapter, starting on p154.

State beaches and parks run the length of the coast between Half Moon Bay and Santa Cruz; all charge $10 per car. The following are in north to south order. **San Gregorio**, 10 miles south of Half Moon Bay, is a driftwood-strewn beauty with a long, sandy strand. Families stick to the main beach, where kids can build forts from branches washed down the little stream that meets the sand. Note: the northern end is private, charges a fee, and is gay and nude.

For a flashback to the Old West, turn inland on Route 84 from San Gregorio beach and go 1 mile to the **San Gregorio General Store** (☎ 650-726-0565; www.sangregoriostore.com; Stage Rd; ❂ 9am-6pm). It's the classic cowboy emporium, catering to local farmers and ranchers who drink booze at the counter. Endure their cold stares to browse Western hats, flannel shirts, crockery and woodstoves. We most love coming on Saturdays and Sundays when bluegrass and folk musicians jam; call ahead for schedules.

Pomponio and Pescadero State Beaches are small enough that you can keep an eye on kids; both have barbecue grills. An old farming village, **Pescadero** (www.pescaderovillage .com) lies 3 miles east of Hwy 1 (via Pescadero Creek Rd), between mountainous parks and forest preserves. It's a good spot to browse antiques and curio stores, but the best reason to come is to eat (see below).

Butano State Park, about 5 miles southeast of Pescadero Beach, is good for day hikes among redwoods; ascend to the top for ocean views. **Bean Hollow** is rocky and crescent-shaped – more like New England than California. Seals swim close to shore, and critter-packed tidepools emerge at low tide. This is the only dog-friendly beach in the county (leashes under 6ft long mandatory).

Five miles south of Pescadero, the stately **Pigeon Point Lighthouse** rises 115ft – the tallest lighthouse on the Pacific Coast. The tower is indefinitely closed because of damage sustained during a major storm in 2001, but you can wander the base and sit on the picket-fence-lined viewing deck to whale-watch, March to May. Down below there's a small beach with little tidepools; in springtime gorgeous wildflowers bloom. The former lightkeeper's quarters are a popular hostel (see below).

Gorgeous **Gazos Creek** beach, at the northern end of Año Nuevo State Reserve, has long rolling waves, wind-protected sand, views of Pigeon Point Lighthouse and wheelchair access. For a complete rundown of these beaches, check out the San Mateo Coast pages of this author's website: www.71miles.com.

our pick **Año Nuevo State Reserve** (☎ 650-879-0227; www.parks.ca.gov; per car $10), 10 miles south of Pigeon Point, is the breeding ground of hundreds of elephant seals that took over abandoned Año Neuvo Island. You can view them as they fight for dominance and submission, December to March, during which time reservations are essential for the 2½-hour, 3-mile guided walking tour ($7). The walk across the vast plateau passes through gorgeous grasslands with peerless views and zero highway noise. From April through November, you can take a self-guided walk; at trail's end, you emerge at a little beach within spitting distance of belly-to-belly seals molting (shedding skin and hair) on the sand. (Keep your distance.) Crowds come in winter, but we love it here in June and July when the trail is lined with ollalieberries (similar to blackberries) and you can gorge yourself till your tongue turns purple. Arrive by 3pm to gather the mandatory free trail permit. The opening hours change with the breeding season, so check the website before visiting.

South of Año Nuevo on the inland side, look for **Swanton Berry Farm** (☎ 831-469-8804; www.swantonberryfarm.com; Hwy 1, 2mi north of Davenport; ☺ self-pick 8am-6pm), where in spring and summer you can pick the Bay Area's best organic strawberries or pop into an old-fashioned, un-manned **farmstand** (☺ 8am-6pm spring, 8am-8pm summer) for flats of berries, berry pie, strawberry lemonade and hot chocolate – leave your money in the little box. Families gather at the picnic tables on the grassy lawns. This is old-school Northern California at its very best.

Sleeping & Eating

Pigeon Point Lighthouse (☎ 650-879-0633; www .norcalhostels.org/pigeon; 210 Pigeon Point Rd, Pescadero dm $23-25, s/d/tr from $53/61/84; ☺ reception 7:30am-

---

DETOUR: BIG BASIN REDWOODS STATE PARK

Big Basin (☎ 831-338-8860; www.bigbasin.org; 21600 Big Basin Way, Boulder Creek; day-use fee per car $10) became California's first state park in 1902, following heated battles between conservationists and loggers. Many old-growth redwoods in this 25-sq-mile park in the Santa Cruz Mountains have stood more than 1500 years. The hiking is exceptional – primordial forests fragrant with fir, cedar and bay; fern-lined waterfalls and high-mountain overlooks.

You can access the park from Hwy 1 at Waddell Creek Beach, but it's a 13-mile-long, steep climb (1000ft elevation gain) via the Skyline-to-the-Sea Trail. The main entrance is off Hwy 236, which connects with Hwy 9 about 15 miles north of Santa Cruz. The park has 146 family **campsites** (☎ 800-444-7275; www.reserveamerica.com; campsites $35) and 36 **tent cabins** (☎ 800-874-8368; www .bigbasintentcabins.com; cabins $65) with two double-bed platforms and wood-burning stoves.

For more redwood state parks closer to Santa Cruz, see p159.

10:30pm; 🖥 📶) The sound of the ocean lulls you to sleep at this former lightkeeper's house. There's also a blufftop oceanview hot tub. Bicyclists never turned away.

Costanoa (☎ 650-879-1100, 877-262-7848; www .costanoa.com; 2001 Rossi Rd; tent cabin without bath $115-175, cabin without bath $185-195, lodge r with bath $210-270, tents & RVs $40-65; 📶 🐾) Four miles south of Pigeon Point, Costanoa is part ecolodge, part campground, tucked between three state parks. Great for outdoor enthusiasts, it feels like summer camp for former hippies turned moms and dads, with hiking on gorgeous, wide-open hillsides and weekend activities like yoga and horse-riding. Accommodations range from comfy lodge rooms (with bath) to our favorite retreat-like modern duplex cabins (without bath), to tiny tent cabins with heated mattresses. Every room comes with extras like robes and aromatherapy soap; shared bath-houses also have saunas. On-site restaurant. No TVs.

Taqueria y Mercado de Amigos (☎ 650-879-0232; 1999 Pescadero Creek Rd; snacks $2-9; 🕑 lunch & dinner) Inside an orange-painted gas station, Mexican farmworkers and their families line up for the fish tacos, *carnitas* (braised or roasted pork) and *al pastor* (a Mexican meat dish similar to a kebab) amid the mini-mart's bags of tamale flour and gigantic cans of hominy.

Duarte's Tavern (☎ 650-879-0464; www.duartes tavern.com; 202 Stage Rd, Pescadero; dishes $16-23; 🕑 7am-9pm) A homey, country-pine-paneled roadhouse, which the James Beard Foundation named an 'American Classic,' Duarte's Tavern serves chops, steaks, deep-fried seafood, good sandwiches and the usual burgers, but it's the artichoke soup, fresh-fish dishes (such as sand dabs and cioppino), rich meaty pan gravies, and homemade flaky-crusted berry pies and sourdough bread that win our vote. There's a friendly lunch counter if you want to chat up locals. Make reservations on weekends.

MARIN COUNTY

Majestic redwoods cling to coastal hillsides, while the thundering surf carves new shapes into the cliffs. Miles of verdant trails crisscross the Point Reyes National Seashore, Muir Woods and Mt Tamalpais National Park. Marinites get outdoors every chance they get. But if there's one thing other than their intense love of the outdoors that binds the residents of Marin County, it's their equally passionate appreciation of the good life. And they can afford it. Marin is the 11th-wealthiest county in America, and locals pride themselves on their laid-back lifestyle. Towns may look like idyllic rural hamlets, but shops cater to cosmopolitan tastes – pity the naive restaurateur who tries to make a go of it using nonorganic ingredients.

Orientation

Hwy 101 heads north from the Golden Gate Bridge ($6 toll for southbound traffic), bisecting Marin's middle; bucolic, winding Hwy 1 winds along the coast. From San Rafael, Sir Francis Drake Blvd cuts west across Marin from Hwy 101 to the ocean. Tank up before heading toward the coast – from Mill Valley, the next gas is in Stinson Beach and Point Reyes Station.

Hwy 580 comes in from the East Bay over the Richmond–San Rafael bridge ($4 toll for westbound traffic) to meet Hwy 101 at Larkspur.

Information

Marin County Convention & Visitors Bureau (☎ 866-925-2060, 415-925-2060; www.visitmarin.org; 1 Mitchell Blvd, Suite B, San Rafael; 🕑 9am-5pm Mon-Fri) handles tourist information for the entire county. The Sausalito Visitors Center (p91) has local information and great historical exhibits. The **West Marin Chamber of Commerce** (☎ 415-663-9232; www.pointreyes.org) provides specifics on the Point Reyes region.

MARIN HEADLANDS

Immediately northwest of the Golden Gate Bridge, the rugged natural beauty of the Marin Headlands stand in stark contrast to Downtown San Francisco's towers, visible across the bay. Once you're hiking atop the rolling hills, beyond earshot of cars, you'll hear only cawing birds, crashing surf and wind whooshing through tall grass. With winter's rains the hills turn vibrant green; in summer they dry up and turn golden brown. Plan to hike, picnic, walk or mountain bike; there's also limited camping.

MARIN COUNTY

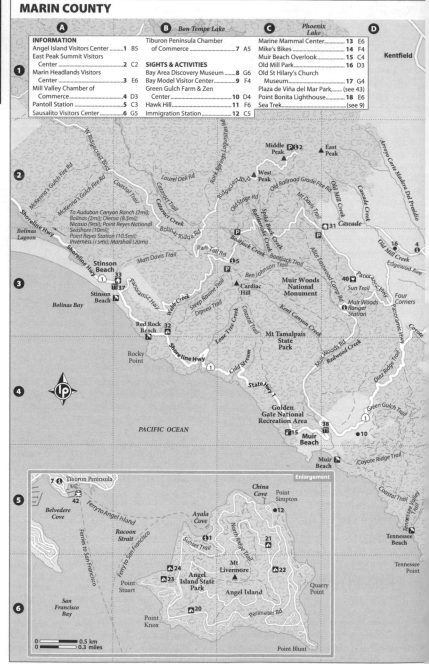

INFORMATION
Angel Island Visitors Center 1 B5
East Peak Summit Visitors
   Center 2 C2
Marin Headlands Visitors
   Center 3 E6
Mill Valley Chamber of
   Commerce 4 D3
Pantoll Station 5 C3
Sausalito Visitors Center 6 G5

Tiburon Peninsula Chamber
   of Commerce 7 A5

SIGHTS & ACTIVITIES
Bay Area Discovery Museum 8 G6
Bay Model Visitor Center 9 F4
Green Gulch Farm & Zen
   Center 10 D4
Hawk Hill 11 F6
Immigration Station 12 C5

Marine Mammal Center...............13 E6
Mike's Bikes 14 F4
Muir Beach Overlook 15 C4
Old Mill Park 16 D3
Old St Hilary's Church
   Museum 17 G4
Plaza de Viña del Mar Park.......(see 43)
Point Bonita Lighthouse 18 E6
Sea Trek ....(see 9)

Kentfield

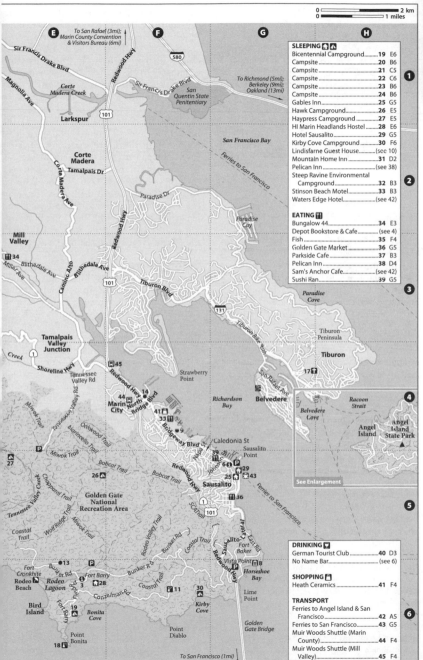

SLEEPING
Bicentennial Campground	**19**	E6
Campsite	**20**	B6
Campsite	**21**	C5
Campsite	**22**	C6
Campsite	**23**	B6
Campsite	**24**	B6
Gables Inn	**25**	G5
Hawk Campground	**26**	E5
Haypress Campground	**27**	E5
HI Marin Headlands Hostel	**28**	E6
Hotel Sausalito	**29**	G5
Kirby Cove Campground	**30**	F6
Lindisfarne Guest House	(see 10)	
Mountain Home Inn	**31**	D2
Pelican Inn	(see 38)	
Steep Ravine Environmental Campground	**32**	B3
Stinson Beach Motel	**33**	B3
Waters Edge Hotel	(see 42)	

EATING
Bungalow 44	**34**	E3
Depot Bookstore & Cafe	(see 4)	
Fish	**35**	F4
Golden Gate Market	**36**	G5
Parkside Cafe	**37**	B3
Pelican Inn	**38**	D4
Sam's Anchor Cafe	(see 42)	
Sushi Ran	**39**	G5

DRINKING
German Tourist Club	**40**	D3
No Name Bar	(see 6)	

SHOPPING
Heath Ceramics	**41**	F4

TRANSPORT
Ferries to Angel Island & San Francisco	**42**	A5
Ferries to San Francisco	**43**	G5
Muir Woods Shuttle (Marin County)	**44**	F4
Muir Woods Shuttle (Mill Valley)	**45**	F4

Orientation & Information

Conzelman Rd snakes into the hills, where it eventually forks with McCullough Rd. Conzelman Rd continues west, becoming a steep, one-lane road as it descends to Point Bonita. From there it continues to Rodeo Beach and Fort Barry. McCullough Rd heads inland, joining Bunker Rd, which goes west toward Rodeo Beach and east through a tunnel back toward the freeway.

Information is available from the **Marin Headlands Visitors Center** (☎ 415-331-1540; www.nps .gov/goga/marin-headlands; Bldg 948, Fort Barry; ☽ 9:30am-4:30pm) in an old church off Bunker Rd.

Sights & Activities

Every fall, migratory birds and raptors – including hawks, falcons and eagles – congregate at **Hawk Hill**. Because open water doesn't support the thermals that the birds need to stay aloft, they use the headlands to gain altitude for the 2 mile crossing of the Golden Gate. Bring binoculars. Go 1.8 miles up Conzelman Rd, park along the road and walk up the west side of the hill. For maps and details on which birds are there now, see www.ggro.org.

Near the end of Conzelman Rd is the still-operating **Point Bonita Lighthouse** (free tours at 12:30pm; ☽ 12:30-3:30pm Sat-Mon), a breathtaking half-mile walk from the parking area, ending at a suspension footbridge over the roiling surf (acrophobes beware). Looking west, the distant city skyline looks out of place.

The **Marine Mammal Center** (☎ 415-289-7325; www.tmmc.org; 4 Bunker Rd, admission free; ☽ 10am-4pm; ♿), on the hill above Rodeo Lagoon, is the largest marine-mammal hospital in the world. In 2009 the center opened its all-green solar-powered hospital, with observation decks for visitors to get close to the recovering patients (mostly seals and sea lions) before they're released back into the wild. Spring brings oh-so-cute new pups – and the most visitors. Kids love the hands-on exhibits and see-through glass walls to the science labs and animal rooms.

At the end of Bunker Rd sits black-sand **Rodeo Beach** (ro-*day*-oh), protected from wind by cliffs.

Sleeping

HI Marin Headlands Hostel (☎ 415-331-2777; www .norcalhostels.org/marin; Bldg 941, Fort Barry; dm/r $24/66; ☽ check-in 7:30am-11:30pm; ☐) Set amid towering eucalyptus trees, this friendly, eco-sensitive hostel has two parts: the main building (formerly a military infirmary), location of 76 dorm beds; and the cozier annex (formerly officers' housing), location of most private rooms. Picture windows overlook the lush landscape. It has a good game room and offers easy access to hiking.

There are four small campsites in the headlands, and all involve hiking at least 1 mile from the nearest parking lot. **Kirby Cove Campground** (☎ 800-365-2267; tent sites $25; ☽ Apr-Oct) is in a spectacular shady nook near the entry to the bay. There's a small beach with the Golden Gate Bridge arching over the rocks nearby. Hawk, Bicentennial and Haypress campgrounds are inland; camping is free but must be reserved through the Marin Headlands Visitors Center.

Getting There & Away

By car from San Francisco, take the Alexander Ave exit just after the Golden Gate Bridge, dip left under the freeway, and immediately before the bridge's southbound on-ramp turn right to ascend Conzelman Rd. Bicycles take roughly the same route. Alternatively, take Bunker Rd: from the Alexander Ave off-ramp, continue 1000ft to the left turn for Bunker Rd and go through the tunnel. Arriving from southbound Hwy 101, take the *second* Sausalito exit, and bear right onto Conzelman Rd.

Golden Gate Transit (☎ 415-923-2000; www.golden gatetransit.org) bus 10 runs from Mission St, the corner of 7th and Market Sts, or Van Ness Ave in Downtown San Francisco (one-way adult/child 6-18 $3.95/1.95, exact change required; dollar bills accepted); ask the driver for the first-possible stop after the bridge (it's just past the Alexander Ave off-ramp). Walk back under the freeway to Conzelman Rd (see driving directions, above). On Sundays and holidays **MUNI** (☎ 415-673-6864; www.sfmuni.com; one-way ticket $2) bus 76 runs from the CalTrain depot in SF to Fort Barry and Rodeo Beach.

SAUSALITO
pop 7330

Sausalito is the first town you hit after crossing the Golden Gate. Perched above Richardson Bay, it's known for galleries, window-shopping and picture-postcard vistas of SF and Angel Island. And it's often sunny: the Headlands block the fog most days. However cute, Sausalito becomes a victim of its charm and beauty on summer weekends, when day-trippers jam the sidewalks, pricey shops and restaurants, and locals get stuck in heavy traffic.

When it became the terminus of the train line down the Pacific coast, Sausalito was transformed into a busy lumber port. After the war a new bohemian period began, with a resident artists' colony living in 'arks' (houseboats moored along the bay). The town is still renowned for its houseboat community, one of the world's largest and most diverse, ranging from mansions to hippie hovels.

Orientation & Information

Sausalito's commercial district is essentially one street, Bridgeway Blvd, on the waterfront. For the locals' scene, wander up Caledonia St. The town is on Richardson Bay, a smaller bay within San Francisco Bay. The ferry terminal marks the town center. Housed in the old Ice House, the **Sausalito Visitors Center** (☎ 415-332-0505; www.sausalito.org; 780 Bridgeway Blvd; ☯ 11:30am-4pm Tue-Sun) has local information and exhibits.

Sights

Plaza de Viña Del Mar Park, near the ferry terminal, has a fountain flanked by 14ft-tall elephant statues from the 1915 Panama-Pacific Exposition in San Francisco.

Until computers rendered obsolete the system at the **Bay Model Visitor Center** (☎ 415-332-3871; 2100 Bridgeway Blvd; suggested donation $3; ☯ 9am-4pm Tue-Fri, 10am-5pm Sat & Sun; ☝), this enormous indoor 1.5-acre hydraulic model of the San Francisco Bay and delta helped scientists understand the effects of tides and currents on the land. A 24-hour period is represented in just 15 minutes. Look in the deepest water – under the Golden Gate Bridge – to grasp the force of tidal movement. This is a must-visit for geography buffs.

Famous **Heath Ceramics** (☎ 415-332-3732; www.heathceramics.com; 400 Gate Five Rd; ☯ 10am-5pm Sun-Wed, to 6pm Thu-Sat), founded by Edith Heath in the 1940s, crafts earthy tableware – and here it costs 30% off retail; free factory tours are offered weekends at 11am, Fridays at 12:30pm. Reservations requested.

Spread across half a dozen former bunkers just under the Golden Gate Bridge, the **Bay**

Area Discovery Museum (☎ 415-339-3900; www.baykidsmuseum.org; 557 McReynolds Rd; adult/child 1-17 $8.50/7.50; ☯ 9am-4pm Tue-Fri, 10am-5pm Sat & Sun; ☝) caters to the curious kindergarten set with hands-on science exhibits, musical instruments, festivals and camps.

Activities

To get out on the bay, rent kayaks from **Sea Trek** (☎ 415-332-8494 weekdays, 415-332-4465 weekends; www.seatrekkayak.com; 85 Liberty Ship Way, Sausalito; s/d per hr $20/35; ☯ 9am-5pm), which also guides monthly summertime trips to Angel Island ($85).

Sausalito is also perfect for **cycling**. If you venture across the Golden Gate Bridge, note that cyclists generally use the western side, except on weekdays between 5am and 3:30pm when they must share the eastern side with pedestrians (who have the right of way). After 9pm, cyclists can still cross the bridge on the eastern side through a security gate. For more information on biking the Bay Area, contact the **San Francisco Bicycle Coalition** (☎ 415-431-2453; www.sfbike.org).

Mike's Bikes (☎ 415-332-3200; www.mikesbikes.com; 1 Gate Six Rd; 1/24hr $10/40), at the northern end of Bridgeway Blvd near Hwy 101, rents road and mountain bikes. No reservations.

Sleeping & Eating

Hotel Sausalito (☎ 415-332-4155; www.hotelsausalito.com; 16 Fl Portal; r $155-195, ste $265-285; ☒ ☎) The guestrooms at this grand 1915 hotel are on the small side, but are decorated in soft golden and green hues, some with lovely stained-glass windows. Vouchers are provided for continental breakfast at the restaurant next door. Parking costs $12.

Gables Inn (☎ 415-289-1100, 800-966-1554; www.gablesinnsausalito.com; 62 Princess St; r incl breakfast $155-495; ☎) All nine rooms in this historic home have massive baths but the more expensive, upstairs rooms have Jacuzzi, fireplaces and balconies with spectacular views. Evening wine is also included. For families, several rooms have sleeper sofas, and there's a video library.

Golden Gate Market (☎ 415-332-3040; 221 2nd St; sandwiches around $6; ☯ 8am-9pm Mon-Sat, 9am-7pm Sun) Grab deli sandwiches, cheese and wine for picnics at this grocery/deli/liquor store on the town's southern side.

Sushi Ran (☎ 415-332-3620; www.sushiran.com; 107 Caledonia St; dishes $5-17; ☯ lunch Mon-Fri, dinner daily) One of the Bay Area's top sushi spots. A wine and sake bar ease the pain of long waits – and perhaps the bill.

Fish (☎ 415-331-3474; 350 Harbor Dr; mains $12-30; ☷ 11:30am-8:30pm; ☝) This kid-friendly dockside joint at the end of Harbor Rd hooks locals with sustainable, line-caught fish – some from their own boats – and down-home details like picnic-table seating and Mason-jar glasses. Sustainability has its price: the Saigon salmon sandwich will set you back $22 – but it's worth it. No credit cards.

Drinking

No Name Bar (☎ 415-332-1392; 757 Bridgeway Blvd) Live bands play most nights at this old-school boho dive. During the daytime, feed the jukebox and kick back with a game of Pictionary. Cash only.

Getting There & Away

We recommend taking a bike on the ferry from San Francisco to avoid awful weekend traffic. Driving to Sausalito from San Francisco, take the Alexander Ave exit (the first exit after the Golden Gate Bridge) and follow signs into Sausalito. There are five municipal parking lots in town – worth using as street-parking restrictions are strictly enforced.

Golden Gate Transit (☎ 415-923-2000; www.golden gatetransit.org) bus 10 runs daily to Sausalito from San Francisco (one-way adult/child 6-18 & senior $3.95/1.95). In San Francisco, you can catch this bus along Mission St, at the corner of 7th and Market Sts, or as it continues up along Van Ness Ave.

Ferry is the ideal way to reach Sausalito. **Golden Gate Ferries** (☎ 415-923-2000; http://golden gateferry.org; one-way adult/child 6-18 & senior $7.85/3.90) operate to and from the San Francisco Ferry Building nine times daily. **Blue & Gold Fleet** (☎ 415-773-1188; www.blueandgoldfleet.com; one-way adult/child 5-11 $9.50/5.20) sails daily from San Francisco's Pier 41. Both take 30 minutes; bicycles are welcome on both services.

TIBURON

pop 8671

With a Lilliputian-sized Main St lined with clapboard buildings, Tiburon has retained more of the original wharf-rat vibe than its upper-crust neighbor to the west. Its name comes from the Spanish Punta

de Tiburon (Shark Point). Take the ferry from San Francisco, browse the shops on Main St, grab a bite, and you've done Tiburon. The town is also the jumping-off point for nearby Angel Island.

Orientation & Information

The central part of town is comprised of Tiburon Blvd, with Juanita Ln and Main St arcing off. Along Main St, Ark Row is where old houseboats have been transformed into shops and boutiques.

The **Tiburon Peninsula Chamber of Commerce** (☎ 415-435-5633; www.tiburonchamber.org; 96b Main St; ☷ 8am-4pm Mon-Fri), on the lower level of Ark Row shops, provides information. Its hours can be spotty: if it's closed you can usually pick up a historic-walking-tour guide at Windsor Vineyards' tasting room (72 Main St).

Sights & Activities

Commanding splendid views from its perch, **Old St Hilary's Church Museum** (☎ 415-435-1853; 201 Esperanza St; admission free; ☷ 1-4pm Wed & Sun Apr-Oct) is one of the country's last examples of Carpenter Gothic architecture still in its original setting. The hillsides around the deconsecrated Catholic church comprise **St Hilary's Preserve**, which nurtures a treasure trove of rare wildflowers, including the black jewel flower and Marin dwarf flax. Best in spring.

The Angel Island-Tiburon Ferry offers **sunset cruises** (☎ 415-435-2131; www.angelislandferry .com; adult/child $20/10; ☷ Fri & Sat May-Oct). Pack a picnic dinner to enjoy on board. Reservations recommended.

Friday nights, May through October, Tiburon throws its Main St **block party**, kicking off at 6pm.

Sleeping & Eating

Waters Edge Hotel (☎ 415-789-5999; www.marin hotels.com/waters.html; 25 Main St; r $159-499; ☒ ☎) This smart 23-unit hotel extends over the bay, with a variety of room types and amenities. All have crisp white bedspreads and balconies (limited views, except in suites); some have fireplaces. Those with wood ceilings are most atmospheric. Complimentary in-room breakfast and evening wine and cheese.

Sam's Anchor Cafe (☎ 415-435-4527; 27 Main St; dishes $10-25; ☝) Everyone wants an outdoor

---

DETOUR: ANGEL ISLAND

Rising from the middle of the bay, **Angel Island State Park** (☎ 415-435-5390; www.angelisland. org) has served as a military base, immigration station, WWII Japanese internment camp and Nike missile site. In 2008, the island was devastated by a fire that burned 300 of the park's 740 acres. As you explore this domed beauty, all around you'll spot signs of the land repairing itself, especially in springtime when wildflowers carpet the hillsides.

Families tend to congregate at Ayala Cove, where you can picnic at the water's edge. But because the ferry schedule limits day-trippers' time on the island, we recommend exploring immediately on arrival. There are 13 miles of hiking trails and 8 miles of bike paths around the island, including a hike to the summit of 781ft Mt Livermore (no bikes) and a 5-mile perimeter trail. Wednesday to Sunday, the Immigration Station and its detention barracks, which operated 1910 to 1940, are open for **tours** (adult/child $7/5) but you must buy tickets in advance or on arrival, near the ferry dock at the Cove Cafe in Ayala Cove. The cafe also rents bikes (per hr/day $10/35, cash only).

For an overnight adventure, book campsites through the Angel Island website or through **Reserve America** (☎ 800-444-7275; www.reserveamerica.com; tent sites $30). All sites are walk-in; plan to lug your stuff a mile from the ferry.

To get to Angel Island from San Francisco, take **Blue & Gold Fleet** (☎ 415-773-1188; www .blueandgoldfleet.com; one-way adult/child 5-11 $7.50/4.25), which sails daily from Pier 41. From Tiburon, take the **Angel Island-Tiburon Ferry** (☎ 415-435-2131; 21 Main St, Tiburon; www.angelislandferry.com; round trip adult/child/bike $13.50/11.50/1).

---

table but you can't reserve the bay-front patio at this way-popular seafood and burger shack – the town's oldest restaurant (look for the trapdoor that was used to spirit booze straight from ship to saloon). Good cioppino. Expect seagulls to alight tableside.

Getting There & Away

Golden Gate Transit (☎ 415-923-2000; www.golden gatetransit.org) bus 10 travels daily from San Francisco (one-way adult/child 6-18 & senior $3.95/1.95) and Sausalito (one-way $2/1) to Tiburon, via Mill Valley.

By car, on Hwy 101, look for the off-ramp for Tiburon Blvd, E Blithedale Ave and Hwy 131; driving east, it leads into town and intersects with Juanita Lane and Main St.

Blue & Gold Fleet (☎ 415-773-1188; www.blue andgoldfleet.com; one-way adult/child 5-11 $9.50/5.25, bicycles free) sails daily from San Francisco's Pier 41 to Tiburon; ferries dock in front of Guaymas restaurant (5 Main St). From Tiburon, ferries connect to nearby Angel Island (see boxed text above).

MILL VALLEY

pop 13,286

Tucked beneath towering redwoods at the base of Mt Tam, the picturesque town of Mill Valley is a good stopover on a jaunt through Marin. Though the 1892 Mill Valley Lumber Company still greets motorists on Miller Ave, the former logging town has long since become a bedroom community of expensive homes and fancy boutiques. Its 1960s-era bohemian sensibility lingers though: in the central plaza, mothers breastfeed, goth kids sulk, alfresco painters dab, hippies hacky-sack and beret-wearing middle-aged men play backgammon. But the real draw is the network of trails ascending Mt Tam.

Gather information from the **Mill Valley Chamber of Commerce** (☎ 415-388-9700; www.mill valley.org; 85 Throckmorton Ave; ☻ 9am-noon Tue-Fri, or by appt).

Sights & Activities

Several blocks west of Downtown along Throckmorton Ave is forested **Old Mill Park**, ideal for a picnic.

our pick **Tennessee Valley Trail**, in the Marin Headlands (p87), is one of Marin's most popular hikes (expect crowds on weekends), providing spectacular views of the coastal prairie and sea, with wildflower displays in spring. The easy, level trail (1.7 miles one way) ends at an often-windy black-sand beach. Scamper up the adjacent Coastal Trail for hilltop vistas of the Pacific. From Hwy 101, take the Mill Valley-Stinson Beach Hwy 1 exit, and turn left onto Tennessee Valley Rd from the Shoreline Hwy; follow it 1.8 miles to the trailhead. Dogs aren't allowed on the main trail, but on-leash dogs are permitted on the Miwok Trail, which runs north 1.1 miles through the hills from the Tennessee Valley parking area. You can also take Fido on the Coastal Trail, from the parking area at Muir Beach (opposite).

Sleeping & Eating

Mountain Home Inn (☎ 415-381-9000; www.mtn homeinn.com; 810 Panoramic Hwy; r incl breakfast $195-345; 🤶) Set atop a ridgeline amid redwood, spruce and pines, Mountain Home is perfect for a romantic, woodsy retreat. All 10 rooms face east for brilliant sunrises; most have balconies and fireplaces. Some are tiny but cozy nonetheless. No TVs. Its **restaurant** (brunch $10-20, dinner $38; 🕙 Wed-Sun) serves dinner prix fixe.

Depot Bookstore & Cafe (☎ 415-383-2665; 87 Throckmorton Ave; meals under $10; 🕙 7am-7pm; 🤶) Adjoining the central plaza, the Depot occupies the former rail station and is the community's de facto gathering place. It serves coffee, drinks and light meals. The bookstore carries local trail guides.

Bungalow 44 (☎ 415-381-2500; 44 E Blithedale Ave; dishes $15-25; 🕙 dinner) Portions are huge and the heritage American at this intimate local bistro. We most like the appetizers – order a handful to share and call it a meal; the steak tartare is a perennial favorite. The front room gets loud; we prefer the relaxing enclosed fireside patio. Full bar.

Getting There & Away

From San Francisco or Sausalito, take Hwy 101 north to the Mill Valley-Stinson Beach Hwy 1 exit. Follow Hwy 1 (also called Shoreline Hwy) to Almonte Blvd (which becomes Miller Ave), then follow Miller Ave into Downtown. From the north, take the E Blithedale Ave exit from Hwy 101, then head west into Downtown Mill Valley.

Golden Gate Transit (☎ 415-923-2000; www .goldengatetransit.org; one way adult/child 6-18 & senior $3.95/1.95) bus 4 runs between San Francisco and Mill Valley, weekday commute hours; on weekends take bus 10, and transfer in Marin City to bus 17. The **West Marin Stagecoach** (☎ 415-526-3239; www.marintransit.org; adult/child 6-18 & senior $2/1) bus 61 connects Mill Valley with Marin City, Stinson Beach and Bolinas.

MT TAMALPAIS STATE PARK

Visible from almost everywhere in Marin, 2571ft Mt Tamalpais (*ta-mul-pie-us*) has panoramic views of ocean, bay and hills rolling into the distance. The coastal Miwok people, to whom Mt Tam was sacred, saw a figure of a sleeping maiden in its silhouette and, with enough squinting, you may too.

Mt Tamalpais State Park was formed in 1928 and its 6300 acres are home to deer, foxes, bobcats and 50 miles of trails. In 1896 the 'world's crookedest railroad' was completed from Mill Valley to the summit; today the Old Railroad Grade Fire Road is one of Mt Tam's most popular hiking and biking trails.

Pantoll Station (☎ 415-388-2070; 801 Panoramic Hwy) is the state park's headquarters, where you can get information and maps, but watch carefully or you'll miss the turn-off, just past Mountain Home Inn and Bootjack Creek on Panoramic Hwy. Overnight parking is available. You can dayhike from here – it's a beautiful 8.5-mile climb to

---

IS IT BEER O'CLOCK YET?

Those wholesome weekend-morning hikes in the mountains are enough to make you feel downright Teutonic. Which is why, when your calves are aching, you should hop-step it to the **German Tourist Club** (☎ 415-388-9987; www.touristclubsf.org; 30 Ridge Ave, Mill Valley; 🕙 1-5pm Sat & Sun, closed 2nd weekend of the month), aka Die Naturfreunde. It's technically a private club that shuns overexposure, but the kind folks there realize their beer patio – overlooking Muir Woods and Mt Tam – is too good to keep to themselves. A stein of German draft will set you back around $7. If you're here at the right time, traditional alpine festivals are held in May, July and September on the third Sunday of the month (admission around $6).

If you're car-bound, turn onto Ridge Ave from Panoramic Hwy, park in the gravel driveway at the end of the road, and start the 0.3-mile walk down the switchback driveway. Look to the right and you'll see the lodge through the trees. If you're hiking, the club is 1 mile into the Sun Trail from the Dipsea Trail.

East Peak Summit and back – or drive 4.2 miles along Ridgecrest Blvd to the **East Peak Summit Visitors Center** (parking $8), then climb the remaining quarter-mile to the summit.

From Pantoll Station, **Steep Ravine Trail** follows a wooded creek down to the coast (about 2.1 miles each way). For a longer hike, veer right (northwest) after 1.5 miles onto the **Dipsea Trail**, which meanders through woods for about a mile before ending at Stinson Beach.

One of the Bay Area's premier campgrounds lies about 1 mile south of Stinson Beach. **Steep Ravine Environmental Campground** (☎ reservations 800-444-7275; info 415-388-2070; 801 Panoramic Hwy, Mill Valley; tent sites/cabins $25/100) has drop-dead ocean views from a high promontory. Book rustic five-person cabins seven months ahead; campsites are easier to snag, but coveted nonetheless.

Public transportation (weekends only) goes only to the Mountain Home Inn; the rest you'll have to walk. From Marin City, Mill Valley, Bolinas and Stinson Beach, take the **West Marin Stagecoach** (☎ 415-526-3239; www.marintransit.org; adult/child 6-18 & senior $2/1).

MUIR WOODS NATIONAL MONUMENT

Coastal redwoods are the Earth's tallest living things, and exist only on the California coast, from Santa Cruz to just over the Oregon border. Only 4% of the original forest remains, but you can explore a glorious old-growth stand at **Muir Woods National Monument** (☎ 415-388-2595; www.nps.gov/muwo; adult/child under 16 $5/free; ☼ 8am-sunset, call ahead), 12 miles north of the Golden Gate Bridge. It gets crowded on weekends – come midweek if you can. Otherwise arrive in early morning or late afternoon, when tour buses leave. Even at busy times, a short hike gets you beyond the densest crowds, onto trails with mammoth trees and stunning vistas.

Hiking

The brochure you receive on arrival shows the basic loops. For more substantial hikes buy the comprehensive park map ($2) at the visitors center.

The 1-mile **Main Trail Loop** is easy, leading alongside Redwood Creek to 1000-year-old trees at **Cathedral Grove**; it returns via **Bohemian Grove**, where the park's tallest tree stands 254ft. The **Dipsea Trail** is a strenuous 2-mile hike to the top of aptly named **Cardiac Hill**, but

it's possibly the most beautiful hike for views – a half-mile steep grade through lush, fern-fringed forest leads from the canyon to an exposed ridge, from which you can see Mt Tamalpais, the Pacific and San Francisco. Gorgeous. You can also trek to Stinson Beach if you're up for a longer stint.

Getting There & Away

The least stressful option – on you and the environment – is the **Muir Woods Shuttle** (☎ 415-923-2000; www.goldengatetransit.org; adult/child 6-18 & senior $3/1) bus 66, which operates weekends and holidays, May to September, and runs about every 30 minutes from Marin City and Mill Valley, with limited service to the Sausalito ferry terminal. From Mill Valley, get the bus at Pohono St and Hwy 1; return trips from the woods drop passengers across the street at the Manzanita Park & Ride. Parking is free for shuttle users. From Marin City, pickup and dropoff is at Donahue St and Terners Dr, at the Gateway shopping center.

If you must drive, Muir Woods is 12 miles north of the Golden Gate. Exit the freeway at Hwy 1 and continue north along Hwy 1/Shoreline Hwy to the Panoramic Hwy (a right-hand fork). Follow that for about 1 mile to Four Corners, where you turn left onto Muir Woods Rd.

THE COAST

Unlike Marin's eastern side, the coast remains largely undeveloped. Craggy coves, rolling hills and sandy beaches extend northward from the Golden Gate, and the city feels a world away. A car gives you the most flexibility, but it's possible to take the bus to most of the destinations listed below (except Muir Beach). The **West Marin Stagecoach** (☎ 415-526-3239; www.marintransit.org; adult/child 6-18 & senior $2/1) operates bus 61 daily from Marin City to Stinson Beach and Bolinas, via Panoramic Hwy and Mt Tam. Bus 68 operates daily from San Rafael to Point Reyes Station, via Sir Francis Drake Blvd. On Tuesday, Thursday and Saturday, bus 62 runs up the coast, from Stinson Beach to Point Reyes Station.

Muir Beach

The North Coast's longest row of mailboxes marks the turn-off to Muir Beach from Hwy 1 (Mile 5.7). There's not much here, but the crescent-shaped beach is usually uncrowded. The Coastal Trail runs along the bluffs southeast toward Tennessee Valley (p93); leashed dogs are allowed.

Take in jaw-dropping views from the **Muir Beach Overlook**, 2 miles north of Muir Beach. During WWII, scouts kept watch from the surrounding concrete lookouts for invading Japanese ships. Amble to the end of the overlook and you may spot birds of prey; on a fog-free day, scan the horizon for the Farallon Islands, looming offshore.

The oh-so-English Tudor-style **Pelican Inn** (☎ 415-383-6000; www.pelicaninn.com; 10 Pacific Way; lunch $10-17, dinner $15-29, r from $190) is Muir Beach's only commercial establishment. Its timbered restaurant and cozy pub are perfect for a pint and to warm up fireside on foggy days. The British fare is respectable, but nothing mind-blowing – it's the setting that's magical. Upstairs are seven luxe rooms, each individually decorated in Tudor style with cushy half-canopy beds.

About 2 miles north of the Hwy 1/Muir Woods Rd intersection, **Green Gulch Farm & Zen Center** (☎ 415-383-3134; www.sfzc.org/ggf; 1601 Shoreline Hwy) is a secluded Buddhist retreat above Muir Beach, with magnificent redwoods standing sentinel. Its Japanese-style **Lindisfarne Guest House** (r with shared bath $90-180) has 12 simple rooms surrounding a 30ft-tall atrium. Rates include buffet-style vegetarian meals.

Stinson Beach

The premier beach along the Marin Coast draws big crowds on sunny weekends, when traffic through town grinds to a halt. The little bohemian village lacks sidewalks and locals amble around, often barefoot, without paying much mind to cars. Restaurants, inns, shops and bookstores line a short stretch of Hwy 1, but to bite into the local culture, drop by local cafes, where you may hear jazz or spoken-word, sometimes simultaneously. Compared with other coastal towns, Stinson feels downright cosmopolitan – until the sun sets, that is.

Stinson's 3-mile strand has decent surfing, though frequent fog reminds you that you're not in Southern California. Call ☎ 415-868-1922 for weather and surf conditions. When the sun does appear, escape the crowds by heading to the northern end, where a lovely slender sand spit looks out over Bolinas. Swimming is only safe from May to mid-September.

Around 1 mile south of Stinson Beach is **Red Rock Beach**, a clothing-optional beach that attracts smaller crowds, probably because you have to scamper down a steep trail from Hwy 1 to reach it.

About 3½ miles north of town on Hwy 1, climb the trails at **Audubon Canyon Ranch** (☎ 415-868-9244; www.egret.org; donations welcome; ⏰ 10am-4pm Sat, Sun & holidays mid-Mar–mid-Jul; ♿) to view great blue herons and snowy egrets feeding their newborn chicks in the treetops. The ranch supplies binoculars; from the hills you can watch these magnificent birds feed at low tide in the mudflats of **Bolinas Lagoon**.

The **Stinson Beach Motel** (☎ 415-868-1712; www.stinsonbeachmotel.com; 3416 Hwy 1; r $125-200) has eight tidy beach cottages and pretty gardens outside.

The **Parkside Cafe** (☎ 415-868-1272; 43 Arenal Ave; breakfast & lunch $7-12, dinner $19-24; ⏰ 7:30am-9pm Mon-Fri, 8am-9pm Sat & Sun) has both a snack bar and sit-down restaurant, with greasy-delicious burgers and shakes, and respectable steaks and seafood. We especially love the breakfasts.

Bolinas
pop 1246

Most known for its anti-tourism citizenry, who kept removing the directional road signs until the highway department finally gave up posting them, Bolinas is a community in a bubble. It supports a disproportionately large number of writers, artists and activists, a fact borne out all over town – the Lady of Bolinas Shrine on Wharf St, the fragments of art and poetry on the ramp down to the beach, and at least one barn sporting a giant peace sign. This homegrown NorCal authenticity makes Bolinas a great stopover for travelers on a coastal jaunt. To make nice with locals, hide your guidebook and don't speed as you drive into town.

Plan to stroll the small Downtown and poke into shops and galleries. From town you can walk to dog-friendly **Bolinas Beach**, but at high tide you'll be hard-pressed to find much sand. Further west are tidepools along 2 miles of coastline at **Agate Beach** around the end of Duxbury Point.

The **Point Reyes Bird Observatory** (☎ 415-868-1221; www.prbo.org; ⏰ 9am-5pm Mon-Fri), off

Mesa Rd west of town, has bird-banding and netting demonstrations, guided walks, a visitors center and a nature trail; call for activity schedules and dates.

A crusty old place dating to 1851, **Smiley's Schooner Saloon & Hotel** (☎ 415-868-1311; www .coastalpost.com/smileys; 41 Wharf Rd; r $79-89; ⊚) has six simple but decent rooms (no phone or TV). The bar is popular with grizzled Deadheads and salty dogs; live bands play on weekends.

On a sunny day, locals crowd the patio at **Coast Cafe** (☎ 415-868-2298; 48 Wharf Rd; mains $9-27; ⊕ Tue-Sun; Ⓥ ♿), whose long menu lists everything from big organic salads to grilled steaks, with plenty for vegetarians. Kids get their own menu.

Point Reyes Station

An Old West patina clings to West Marin's small-town hub. Dominated by dairies and ranches, the region was invaded in the '60s by artists, whose legacy remains in tie-dye shops and (ho-hum) galleries lining Main St. Plan to fuel up on gasoline and supplies.

A locavarian's delight, **Osteria Stellina** (☎ 415-663-9988; 11285 Hwy 1; mains $13-20; ⊕ 11:30am-2:30pm & 5-9pm Wed-Mon) is a cozy, heart-warming Downtown bistro. Everything on the forward-thinking California menu is fresh, seasonal and often organic,

from handmade *strozzapreti* (choke the priest) pasta to braised goat shoulder with herbed polenta. Don't skip the pastry chef's creamy and berrylicious desserts.

At **Cafe Reyes** (☎ 415-663-9493; 11101 Hwy 1; dishes $6-14; ⊕ noon-9pm; Ⓥ ♿) the Latin-Asian wraps, stir-fries, sandwiches and salads are solidly good, but the best thing is the view from the big outdoor deck.

Tomales Bay Foods & Cowgirl Creamery (☎ 415-663-9335; 80 4th St; ⊕ 10am-6pm Wed-Sun) stocks stellar picnic items. Cowgirl Creamery's famous organic, artisanal cheeses are made on the premises and run to about $20 a pound – splurge on the Mt Tam triple-cream. Factory tours ($5, reservations recommended) are held at 11:30am on Friday. The attached Cowgirl Cantina serves a daily-changing menu of gourmet soups, sandwiches and salads.

The **Point Reyes Lodging Association** (☎ 800-539-1872, 415-663-1872; www.ptreyes.com) has a good list of the region's many small inns and B&Bs. The only budget accommodations choice is the Point Reyes Hostel at nearby Point Reyes National Seashore (see p98).

Two miles south of Point Reyes Station in Olema, the **Bear Valley Inn** (☎ 415-663-1777; www.bearvinn.com; Sir Francis Drake Blvd & Bear Valley Rd; r $120-180, cottage $160-250; ⊚) has three snug B&B rooms inside a 1910 house, and a cottage that sleeps six. Breakfasts are organic and there's limitless nature at your doorstep. The owners knock off 15% if you cycle here – call for details on the 20-mile ride from the Larkspur ferry.

Twenty miles north of Point Reyes Station in tiny Marshall, **Nick's Cove & Cottages** (☎ 415-663-1033; http://nickscove.com; 23240 Hwy 1, Marshall; mains $14-30; ⊕ 8am-9pm) is the area's only destination restaurant. Celeb chef Mark Franz runs the kitchen at this vintage 1930s roadhouse perched over Tomales Bay, with trophy heads mounted on knotty-pine walls and a roaring fireplace. Book a window table to bird-watch while you sup on impeccable seafood, grilled meats and local oysters – all sustainably farmed. Reservations essential. The adjoining cottages are expensive ($355 to $700), but oh-so romantic.

Inverness
pop 995

The last outpost of civilization before Point Reyes National Seashore sits on the west shore of Tomales Bay and has some good

---

WHY IS IT SO FOGGY?

When the summer sun's rays warm the air over the chilly Pacific, fog forms and hovers offshore; to grasp how it moves inland requires an understanding of geography. Think of California as a giant bathtub, ringed by mountains that surround the vast Central Valley. As the inland valley heats up and the warm air rises, it creates a deficit of air at surface level, generating wind that gets sucked through the only sea-level break in the Coastal Range: the Golden Gate. But hills can block the fog's passage, especially at times of high atmospheric pressure. Because of this, weather forecasters speak of the Bay Area's 'microclimates.' In July it's not uncommon for inland areas to reach 100°F, while at the coast temps barely reach 70°F. But, as the locals say, if you don't like the weather, just wait a minute.

lodging-and-dining choices. Inverness Park is the tiny hamlet 3.5 miles south of Inverness.

Six miles west of town, stop for a picnic of oysters at **Drakes Bay Oyster Farm** (☎ 415-669-1149; www.drakesbayoyster.com; 17171 Sir Francis Drake Blvd; ☿ 8:30am-4:30pm); call ahead to make sure they're not sold out.

The great vegetarian sandwiches at **Perry's Delicatessen** (☎ 415-663-1491; 2301 Sir Francis Drake Blvd, Inverness Park; sandwiches $6-8; ☿ 6:30am-8pm) are made greater with the addition of bacon. Pop one in your backpack and enjoy it mid-hike from a high promontory.

There's good pizza (some with soy cheese) at **Priscilla's Pizza** (☎ 415-669-1244; 12781 Sir Francis Drake Blvd, Inverness; pizzas around $10; ☿ 11am-8pm Wed-Mon; 🅥 ♿); other dishes are so-so. In the morning there's coffee and pastries.

Upmarket **Motel Inverness** (☎ 866-453-3839, 415-236-1967; www.motelinverness.com; 12718 Sir Francis Drake Blvd; r $100-150; 🛜) has wonderful service and spiffy rooms with good beds. Alas, it was built backwards: rooms face the parking lot, but behind there are gorgeous wetlands. No matter – enjoy the view from the lovely great room, with its roaring fire and board games.

Brimming with architectural curiosities, **Blackthorne Inn** (☎ 415-663-8621; www.blackthorne inn.com; 266 Vallejo Ave, Inverness Park; r $225-325) is a treehouse-reminiscent, adults-only inn built around a four-story wooden spiral staircase. The inn's three rooms are lovely, but a stay in the octagonal Eagles' Nest is honeymoon-worthy, with private hot tub and a walkway connecting the Nest to the deck.

Stay in a fully equipped house at **Rosemary Cottages** (☎ 415-663-9338; www.rosemarybb.com), whose two cottages are designed in harmony with nature and come equipped with wood stoves and vintage appliances. Fir Tree (from $295) is a two-bedroom house; Rosemary Cottage (from $255) sleeps four in two cozy rooms. Guests share a secluded hot tub.

Point Reyes National Seashore

On an entirely different tectonic plate from the mainland, the windswept peninsula of Point Reyes juts 10 miles out to sea and lures marine mammals, migratory birds and whale-watching tourists. In 1579 Sir Francis Drake landed here to repair his ship, the *Golden Hind*. In 1595 the *San Augustine*

went down offshore, the first of scores of ships lost here; she was laden with luxury goods, including porcelain, and to this day bits of her cargo wash up on shore. Even now, despite GPS systems, the dangerous waters and treacherous rocks still claim the occasional vessel, adding to the peninsula's mystique.

Point Reyes National Seashore, established by President Kennedy in 1963, includes 110 sq miles of pristine ocean beaches, wind-tousled ridgetops and diverse wildlife. With excellent hiking and camping, Point Reyes is one of the Bay Area's top day-trip excursions, and its surrounding villages make a romantic spot for a quick overnight stay. Bring warm clothing: even the sunniest days can quickly turn cold and foggy.

INFORMATION

The park headquarters, **Bear Valley Visitor Center** (☎ 415-464-5100; www.nps.gov/pore; Bear Valley Rd, Olema; ☿ 9am-5pm Mon-Fri, 8am-5pm Sat & Sun) provides hiking maps, information and worthwhile exhibits. You can also get information at the Point Reyes Lighthouse and the **Ken Patrick Center** (☎ 415-669-1250; ☿ 10am-5pm Sat, Sun & holidays) at Drakes Beach.

SIGHTS & ACTIVITIES

our pick **Point Reyes Lighthouse** (☎ 415-669-1534; ☿ 10am-4:30pm Thu-Mon) sits at the end of Sir Francis Drake Blvd atop a rocky promontory that gets buffeted by ferocious winds. It's one of the best spots for **whale-watching** along the coast (peak season happens January and March, with calving late April into May). The lighthouse sits 600ft below the headlands, down 308 steps, so that its light can shine below the fog that usually blankets the point. Be prepared for a steep downhill walk. The lens room and clockworks are open as conditions permit.

Nearby **Chimney Rock** makes a lovely short hike, especially in spring when wildflowers are blossoming. A viewing area lets you spy on the park's braying elephant-seal colony.

On weekends during good weather, late December through mid-April, the road to Chimney Rock and the lighthouse is closed to private vehicles. Instead you must take a **shuttle** (☎ 415-464-5100 ext 2 then press 1; adult/child under 16 $5/free) from Drakes Beach. Buy tickets at the Ken Patrick Center.

At the park's northern tip, **McClures Beach** is a gem of a beach, with white sand, forceful surf and excellent tidepools at low tide. Start the steep half-mile trail down to the beach at the end of Pierce Point Rd, where you can also access the stunning 3-mile blufftop walk to **Tomales Point** – our favorite Point Reyes hike – which passes through herds of Tule elk (keep your distance).

Within easy walking distance of the Bear Valley Visitor Center, you'll find **Kule Loklo**, a replica of a Miwok village. Nearby is one of the park's coolest interpretive walks, the **Earthquake Walk**, smack dab on the San Andreas Fault. Point Reyes sits on the Pacific tectonic plate, the mainland on the North American plate, and the two grind against each other and occasionally trigger earthquakes. Along the Earthquake Walk, look for the fence that split and shifted a stunning 18ft during the 1906 earthquake. Amazing.

The Bear Valley Visitor Center is also the main trailhead for the park – at 11.5 miles the longest is the **Palomarin Trail**, which terminates in the park's southern reaches, near Bolinas. Other worthwhile hikes include **Arch Rock** (4.1 miles one way), **Sky Camp** (2.7 miles one way), **Wildcat Camp** (6.3 miles one way) and **Coast Camp** (8.9 miles one way).

Limantour Rd, off Bear Valley Rd about 1 mile north of Bear Valley Visitors Center, leads to the Point Reyes Hostel and to **Limantour Beach**. The **Inverness Ridge Trail** heads from Limantour Rd up to 1282ft Mt Vision.

You can also explore on horseback with **Five Brooks Stable** (☎ 415-663-1570; www.fivebrooks .com; 8001 Hwy 1, Olema; 1/2/3/6-hr rides $40/60/80/160; 9am-5pm), which also offers kids' pony rides ($15). To explore the peninsula from the water contact **Point Reyes Outdoors** (☎ 415-663-8192; www.pointreyesoutdoors.com; 11401 Hwy 1, Point Reyes Station; guided trips $85-110) or **Blue Waters Kayaking** (☎ 415-669-2600; www.bwkayak

.com; guided trips $68-98, rentals $40-120), which has two locations, one in Inverness, the other in Marshall. The bird-watching at Tomales Bay is superb mid-winter.

SLEEPING

Just off Limantour Rd, the rustic **Point Reyes Hostel** (☎ 415-663-8811; www.norcalhostels.org/reyes; off Limantour Rd; dm from $22; reception 7:30-10am & 4:30-9:30pm) lies in a secluded valley 2 miles from the ocean, and is surrounded by hiking trails. The one private room (from $64) is reserved for families traveling with a child under the age of six.

Point Reyes has four **campsites** (☎ 415-663-8054; tent sites $15) with pit toilets, untreated water and picnic tables (no fires). Permits required; reserve at Bear Valley Visitor Center or by telephone three months ahead. Reaching the campgrounds requires a 2- to 6-mile hike. One word: wildcat.

GETTING THERE & AWAY

The slowest and curviest way to Point Reyes is along Hwy 1, through Stinson Beach. From SF, it's more direct to take Hwy 101 to the San Anselmo exit and follow Sir Francis Drake Blvd to Point Reyes. If you're coming from the north on Hwy 101, take the Central San Rafael exit and go west on 4th St, which turns into Sir Francis Drake Blvd. By either route, it's about 75 minutes to Point Reyes Station from San Francisco.

Just north of the intersection of Hwy 1 and Sir Francis Drake Blvd, Bear Valley Rd runs west to the Bear Valley Visitor Center. To reach the peninsula itself, follow Sir Francis Drake Blvd through Point Reyes Station; it takes 45 minutes to reach the lighthouse from town.

West Marin Stagecoach (☎ 415-526-3239; www .marintransit.org) bus 68 will drop you at the Bear Valley Visitor Center.

North Coast

Forget the sun-drenched vision of the Beach Boys' California – in lieu of bikinis and bright, sunny skies the North Coast has banks of spectral fog, towering redwoods and cliffs that drop into a menacing roar of surf. Forget the jammed freeways of Southern California; the northern stretch of the coast is traveled mostly on winding two-lane blacktop, where the biggest traffic problem is encountered behind a dawdling Winnebago. The further north you travel, the more dominant the landscape becomes; interrupted only by two-stoplight towns that are departure points for the wilds surrounding you.

Here, you don't have to go too far off-track to feel like you're in an overgrown set of *Land Of The Lost*. Sun dapples the forest floor beneath towering redwoods, lighting up bristly ferns and shaggy beds of moss. Sea lions and elephant seals laze upon crags jutting out of the Pacific, barking and braying; beneath them sea cucumbers, starfish and anemones cling to the rocks, despite the relentless surf. In winter, migrating whales breach offshore while eagles, falcons and vultures arc overhead.

Best of all, you're likely to have the place mostly to yourself. There's a libertarian spirit on the North Coast that only begrudgingly accepts interlopers, with weed farmers and hippies staking out territory next to logging companies, and though they don't get along, they cut each other a wide swath. Mostly though, this is a place to get lost, and in doing so, find the majesty of California's untamed coast.

HIGHLIGHTS

- Standing in the shadow of trees over 40 stories high at **Redwood National Park** (p145)

- Watching the parade of tree-huggers, lumberjacks and college students around the **Arcata** (p138) town square

- Rolling the Chevy through the belly of a redwood at the **Chandelier Drive-Thru Tree** (p124)

- Navigating the tide charts to hike the black sands and ghostly beauty of the **Lost Coast** (p127)

- Renting a bicycle and pedaling the North Coast's best ride along the **Avenue of the Giants** (p129)

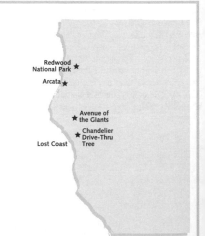

NORTH COAST

FAST FACTS

- **Temperature range at Redwood National Park** 40°–60°F, year-round

- **San Francisco to Mendocino via Hwy 1** 170 miles, four hours

- **San Francisco to Crescent City via Hwy 101** 355 miles, six hours

- **Bodega Bay to Leggett via Hwy 1** 151 miles, four hours

- **Ukiah to Crescent City via Hwy 101** 241 miles, 4½ hours

Getting There & Away

To make your way north fast, take Hwy 101, the inland route; Hwy 1 meanders along the coast then cuts inland and ends at Leggett, where it joins Hwy 101.

If you aren't traveling by car, Amtrak (p292) operates the *Coast Starlight* between Los Angeles and Seattle, with connecting bus services to several North Coast towns including Leggett, Arcata and Garberville. Note that the train runs inland, not along the coast. Alternatively, Greyhound (p289) operates a cheaper bus service up Hwy 101 from San Francisco to Santa Rosa. This trip takes about two hours and costs $19, stopping in several towns all the way up the coast.

In Santa Rosa, the regional transit hub for bus services, **Golden Gate Transit** (☎ 707-541-2000, 415-923-2000; www.goldengate.org) is the way to get up the coast on public transportation – which isn't speedy, but possible. Bus 80 goes to and from San Francisco's Transbay terminal for $9.25 one way, and the trip takes about 3½ hours. Bicycles are allowed. **Sonoma County Transit** (☎ 707-576-7433, 800-345-7433; www.sctransit.com) serves Sonoma County. **Sonoma County Airport Express** (☎ 707-837-8700, 800-327-2024; www.airportexpressinc.com) operates buses to the Bay Area's SFO and OAK airports.

The **Mendocino Transit Authority** (MTA; ☎ 707-462-1422, 800-696-4682; www.4mta.org) operates key long routes along the coast and to cities along Hwy 101 with reliable service and friendly drivers. It's possible, though hardly convenient, to use the MTA to travel all the way between Santa Rosa and Fort Bragg (3¼ hours) and many points between. The key long routes (once daily each way)

are the 65 (between Fort Bragg and Santa Rosa) and the 95 (connecting Point Arena and Santa Rosa, about one hour). If you're visiting Mendocino, the county's main attraction, you can use the MTA to visit Fort Bragg multiple times a day. All buses have racks for bicycles. No municipal transportation continues north from Fort Bragg.

North of Mendocino County, the **Redwood Transit System** (☎ 707-443-0826; www.hta.org) operates buses Monday through Saturday between Scotia and Trinidad (about two hours), stopping en route at Eureka and Arcata. **Redwood Coast Transit** (☎ 707-464-9314; www.redwoodcoasttransit.org) runs two buses a day, Monday to Saturday, between Crescent City, Klamath and Redwood National Park, with numerous stops along the way. The best deal going is the 'Redwood Rider' pass, which offers unlimited rides for five days between Eureka and points north for $35.

For those stout-hearted souls considering a visit via bicycle, the region is especially inviting, with a plethora of state camping facilities and drivers who are accustomed to cyclists. For detailed information about routes, visit the Caltrans website (www.dot.ca.gov) and search 'bicycle tourism,' which leads to printable PDFs of elevation and detailed maps.

COASTAL HIGHWAY 1

The coast between Bodega Bay and Fort Bragg is on the gorgeous, jagged edge of the continent, where cows graze on cliffs above the frothing, frigid roar of the Pacific. The metropolitan charms of San Francisco, only a few hours south, feel eons away. The snaking route that Hwy 1 takes along the North Coast is challengingly remote and real: white-knuckled drivers pass farms, fishing towns and hidden beaches, pausing on roadside pullouts where gusty cliffs overlook migrating whales. The drive takes four hours of daylight driving without stops. At night, and in the fog, it takes steely nerves and much longer.

In the 1960s, there were plans to turn the winding road into a four-lane freeway and subdivide the surrounding land into 2-acre parcels. Can you imagine? It would have become another Southern California–

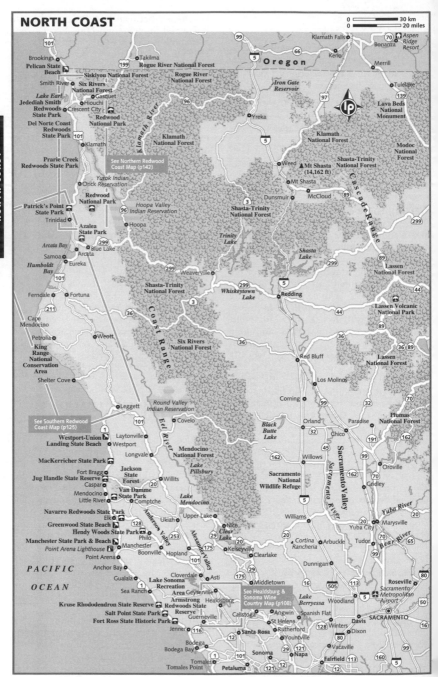

style ecological nightmare. Instead the land looks as it always has, with fog-shrouded coves, rolling hills and dense forests. North of Jenner, grassy table bluffs yield to sheer cliffs as the road climbs hundreds of feet in twisty turns: this is one of the premier coastal California drives (eat a fistful of crystallized ginger if you get car sick). The top destination is Mendocino (p113), but for every mile past Mendocino you venture, the Bay Area weekenders peel off exponentially, until you reach the remote, rugged Lost Coast (p127).

BODEGA BAY
pop 1423

Bodega Bay is the first pearl in a string of sleepy fishing towns and the setting of Alfred Hitchcock's terrifying 1963 avian horror flick, *The Birds*. The skies are free from bloodthirsty gulls today, though you'd best keep an eye on the picnic. It's Bay Area weekenders who descend en masse on the bed and breakfasts and extraordinary state beaches between here and Jenner, 10 miles further north.

Nowadays it looks more like an East Coast seaside tourist town, with kite shops, stands selling salt water taffy, and tour bus crowds who feast on local Dungeness crab. The gateway to the Sonoma Coast, Bodega Bay is somewhat center-less, making wandering around by foot a challenge, but it's a good base for exploring nearby beaches and dramatic coastal bluffs. If you have more than one night, there are prettier places to sleep further north, like Anchor Bay and Mendocino.

The town was saved from a terrible fate in 1962, when Pacific Gas & Electric (PG&E) attempted to build the world's largest nuclear power plant in the Bodega Bay Headlands – smack dab on the San Andreas Fault (oops!) – without permits from the Atomic Energy Commission (AEC). AEC halted the project, but you can still see the enormous hole PG&E dug in the headlands.

Orientation & Information

Hwy 1 runs along the east side of Bodega Harbor. On the west side, a peninsula resembling a crooked finger juts out to sea, forming the entrance to the harbor. The **Sonoma Coast Visitors Center** (☎ 707-875-3866; www.bodegabay.com; 850 Hwy 1; ☻ 9am-5pm Mon-Thu

& Sat, to 6pm Fri, 10am-5pm Sun) is opposite the Tides Wharf complex and provides information on the area north to Sea Ranch.

Sights & Activities

Most views from the mainland are of the harbor, but the view of the ocean opens up at **Bodega Head**, 265ft above sea level, where windswept grassy hills drop into the churning surf. Among several easy hikes the **Bodega Head trail** around the point is the most rewarding. Look southward to spot Tomales Point, the northern tip of Point Reyes – which is geologically related to Bodega Head – and east across the harbor. On a clear day, the views are superb and it's an excellent place to scan the water for whales (seasonal). The wind promises to be fierce, so bring a kite from one of the shops lining Hwy 1. To reach Bodega Head, go west from Hwy 1 onto Eastshore Rd, then turn right at the stop sign onto Bay Flat Rd.

For an easy 8-mile ride to the headlands, get some wheels at **Bodega Bay Cycles** (☎ 707-875-2255; www.bodegabaycycles.com; 1580 Eastshore Rd; ☻ 10am-6pm Mon & Wed-Sat, to 4pm Sun), a new bike shop that rents both adult and kids' bikes. As an example, cruisers cost $9 per hour, $25 for a half-day. They also employ a full-time mechanic. Serious cyclists should inquire about exceptional rides in the area.

For high romance, arrange a horseback ride on the beach with **Chanslor Riding Stables** (☎ 707-875-3333; www.chanslor.com; 2660 Hwy 1; ☻ 9am-5pm). Scenic group rides range from $30 to $70, though private tours can be arranged for a higher fee.

There's good seasonal surfing around Bodega Bay, depending on your level of expertise. **Bodega Bay Surf Shack** (☎ 707-875-3944; www.bodegabaysurf.com; 1400 Hwy 1; ☻ 10am-6pm Mon-Fri, 9am-7pm Sat & Sun) is the place to get information on conditions, rent boards and wet suits (both $13 per day) and get lessons ($85 for three hours). They also rent kayaks starting at $45 for four hours.

Bodega Bay Pro Dive (☎ 707-875-3054; www.bb prodive.com; 1275 Hwy 1) rents full gear for scuba diving ($70), but provides no instruction.

Make reservations for sport-fishing charters and, from December to April, popular whale-watching cruises. **Bodega Bay Sportfishing Center** (☎ 707-875-3344; www.bodega baysportfishing.com; 1410b Bodega Bay Flat Rd), beside the Sandpiper Café, organizes full-day fishing trips ($75) and whale-watching excursions (adult/child $30/25). It also sells bait, tackle and fishing licenses, and can arrange harbor cruises. Outdoor activities are the major draw, but the renowned collection of modern Japanese prints and California works at the **Ren Brown Collection Gallery** (☎ 707-875-2922; www.renbrown.com; 1781 Hwy 1; ☽ 10am-5pm Wed-Sun) is a tranquil escape from the elements.

Festivals & Events

The **Bodega Bay Fishermen's Festival and Blessing of the Fleet** (www.bbfishfest.com) in early to mid-April is the big annual event and includes a flamboyant parade of vessels, an arts-and-crafts fair, kite-flying and feasting. **Bodega Seafood, Art & Wine Festival** (www.winecountry festivals.com) is an outdoor festival in late August with local art vendors, beer and killer BBQ crab. The great **crab feed** takes place in February or March.

Sleeping

Though prices are targeting weekenders on a splurge from the Bay Area, Bodega Bay has no shortage of rooms if you plan ahead. For a complete list of lodgings and rentals, contact the visitors center. Campgrounds in Bodega Bay fill up early on weekends, so advance reservations are recommended.

Sonoma County Regional Parks (☎ 707-565-2267; www.sonoma-county.org/parks; campsites $22) operates Doran Regional Park (201 Doran Beach Rd), which has a few walk-in sites at the quiet Miwok Tent Campground, and Westside Regional Park (2400 Westshore Rd), which is best for RVs. It caters primarily to boaters and has windy exposures, beaches, hot showers, fishing and boat ramps. Excellent camping is also available at the Sonoma Coast State Beach (opposite).

Bodega Harbor Inn (☎ 707-875-3594; www .bodegaharborinn.com; 1345 Bodega Ave; r $80-155, cottages from $135; ☙) Half a block inland from Hwy 1, surrounded by grassy lawns and furnished with both real and faux antiques, this modest blue-and-white shingled motel is the town's most economical option. Pets are allowed in some rooms for a fee of $15 plus security deposit of $50. Freestanding cottages have BBQs.

Chanslor Guest Ranch (☎ 707-875-2721; www .chanslorranch.com; 2660 Hwy 1; furnished tents & eco-cabins $100-175, r $265-340) A mile north of town, this working horse ranch has three rooms and options for upscale camping. Wildlife programs and guided horse tours make this one sweet place, with sweeping vistas across open grasslands to the sea.

Bodega Bay Lodge & Spa (☎ 707-875-3525, 800-875-2250; www.bodegabaylodge.com; 103 Hwy 1; r $190, ste $430; ☎ ☙) As you come into town from the south, you'll pass this lodge overlooking marshlands and the sea. The more expensive rooms have more commanding views, but all have balconies, high-thread-count sheets, feather pillows and the usual amenities of a full-service hotel. The other pluses on-site include a golf course, Bodega Bay's best spa and a fine-dining restaurant, the Duck Club.

Eating & Drinking

Spud Point Crab Company (☎ 707-875-9472; 1860 Bay Flat Rd; dishes $4-10; ☽ 9am-5pm Thu-Tue; ☙) In the classic tradition of dockside crab shacks, Spud Point makes sandwiches and salty-sweet crab cocktails served at picnic tables overlooking the marina. Take Bay Flat Rd to get here.

Gourmet Au Bay (☎ 707-875-9875; 913 Hwy 1; ☽ 11am-7pm Sun-Thu, to 8pm Fri & Sat) Sit on the back deck of this wine bar with a glass of Zinfandel and enjoy the brackish air. During the high season, there's live jazz.

Sandpiper Dockside Café & Restaurant (☎ 707-875-2278; 1410 Bay Flat Rd; breakfast $7-14, mains $14-25; ☽ 8am-8pm Sun-Thu, to 8:30pm Fri & Sat; ☙) The classic tartar sauce and fried-fish joint, Sandpiper overlooks the bay and serves straightforward, middle-of-the-road seafood with no surprises. There's breakfast too. Turn seaward from Hwy 1 onto Eastshore Rd and then go straight at the stop sign to the marina.

Terrapin Creek Café & Restaurant (☎ 707-875-2700; www.terrapincreekcafe.com; 1580 Eastshore Dr; mains $18-30; ☽ lunch Thu-Sun, dinner 4:30-9pm Thu-Sun) Occupying the site of the much-beloved (now-defunct) Seaweed Café, this has quickly emerged as Bodega Bay's most exciting restaurant. Run by a husband-wife team, the elegant little cafe espouses the Slow Food movement and serves local dishes sourced from the surrounding area. Even modest comfort-food offerings like the pulled pork sandwich are artfully executed, though the Dungeness crab salad is fresh, briny and perfect. Jazz and warm light complete the atmosphere.

For the old-fashioned thrill of seafood by the docks there are two options: **Tides Wharf & Restaurant** (☎ 707-875-3652; 835 Hwy 1; breakfast $6-12, lunch $12-22, dinner $15-25; ☷ 7:30am-9:30pm Mon-Thu, 7:30am-10pm Fri, 7am-10pm Sat, 7am-9:30pm Sun; ☷) and **Lucas Wharf Restaurant & Bar** (☎ 707-875-3522; 595 Hwy 1; dishes $14-25; ☷ 11:30am-9pm Mon-Fri, 11am-10pm Sat; ☷). Both have views and similar menus of clam chowder, fried fish and coleslaw and markets for picnic supplies. Tides boasts a great fish market, though Lucas Wharf feels less like a factory. Don't be surprised if a bus pulls up outside either of them.

SONOMA COAST STATE BEACH

Stretching for 19 miles from Bodega Head to north of Jenner, the **Sonoma Coast State Beach** (☎ 707-875-3483) is actually a series of excellent beaches, a place to explore foggy coves, take in crumbling, rocky headlands, and picnic. However inviting the water seems, these are *not* swimming beaches. The surf is treacherous, with rip currents and unpredictable sneaker waves and it's often unsafe to wade. Never turn your back on the ocean, stay above the high-tide line and keep an eye on kids.

Heading north along the coast, notable beaches include **Miwok Beach**; 2-mile-long **Salmon Creek Beach**; sandy **Portuguese** and **Schoolhouse Beaches**; **Shell Beach** for tide-pooling and beachcombing; and, our favorite, the scenic **Goat Rock** (Mile 19.15) with its yawning colony of harbor-seals who lounge at the mouth of the Russian River. Volunteers protect the seals and educate tourists during pupping season, between March and August. To stretch the legs a bit, take the **Kortum Trail**, a well-marked 5-mile trip that's stunning.

The Sonoma Coast State Beach includes a plethora of options for camping. Best is **Bodega Dunes Campground** (☎ 800-444-7275; www.reserveamerica.com; campsites $35) right at the edge of the town of Bodega Bay. It has high sand dunes and hot showers near a long, sandy beach – but a foghorn sounds all night, so bring earplugs. Another 5 miles further north, year-round **Wright's Beach Campground** (☎ 800-444-7275; www.reserveamerica.com; campsites $35-45) doesn't offer much by way of privacy, but, situated between the cliffs

and pounding surf, it's a perfect launch pad for experienced sea kayakers. Others, be warned: the surf is *treacherous*. People drown here: stay out of the water!

On Willow Creek Rd, inland from Hwy 1 on the southern side of the Russian River Bridge, are two first-come, first-served **environmental campgrounds** (campsites $25): Willow Creek and Pomo Canyon. Willow Creek has no water; Pomo Canyon has cold-water faucets. Both are usually open April to November.

JENNER
pop 257

There's not much here, just a cluster of shops and restaurants dotting the hills where the Russian River meets the Pacific. Fifteen minutes north of Bodega Bay and a moment north of Goat Rock State Beach, tiny Jenner is more of a crossroads than a town, where Hwy 116 (aka River Rd) cuts inland along the Russian River to western Sonoma County's wine-growing regions (p106).

North of here, the wide terraces of southern Sonoma yield to the rugged cliffs of the North Coast. Highway 1 climbs and twists, with drop-dead vistas out to sea. Stay focused and use turnouts to allow locals to pass.

Sleeping & Eating

Jenner Inn & Cottages (☎ 707-865-2377, 800-732-2377; www.jennerinn.com; 10400 Hwy 1; creekside r $118-178, ocean view r $188-298, cottages $178-398; ☷ ☷) It seems like half the town belongs to this business, which offers everything from vacation houses and salt-weathered seaside cottages to river-view guest rooms. Rates include breakfast and afternoon tea. Most rooms have a balcony but no TV. The best of these have access to small hot tubs and saunas.

River's End (☎ 707-865-2484; www.ilovesunsets.com; 11048 Hwy 1; r & cabins $150-220, lunch $14-26, dinner $20-34) Here, there are simple ocean-view cottages and comfortable knotty pine-paneled rooms, with no TVs or phones: a good spot for an overnight hideaway. It has a good, but pricey, restaurant (with full bar) that serves ambitious local game and California coastal dishes.

Café Aquatica (☎ 707-865-2251; 11048 Hwy 1) This is the kind of North Coast coffee shop

NORTH COAST

DETOUR: HEALDSBURG & SONOMA WINE COUNTRY   *John Vlahides and Alison Bing*

Mention Wine Country and everyone thinks Napa, but you needn't fight inland traffic to sample some damn good California wines. Unless you're a Cabernet Sauvignon fetishist, stick to Sonoma County (Map p108), which is far less fussy and closer to the coast – and, unlike in fancy-pants Napa, nobody in Sonoma will care if you have a bad hair day.

From Jenner, head inland via Hwy 116, along the banks of the Russian River, 13 miles to Guerneville, where Main St turns into River Rd. Stop in Monte Rio at **Sophie's Cellars** (☎ 707-865-1122; www.sophiescellars.com; 20293 Hwy 116; ⏰ 11am-7pm Thu-Mon) for Sonoma cheeses, cult wines you won't find elsewhere and owner/connoisseur John Haggard's tasting itinerary suggestions – maybe even free tasting passes.

Continue eastward on River Rd for 5 miles, turn left onto Westside Rd and wind your way 13 miles to Healdsburg, with free tastings at two key Russian River Pinot pit stops: organic, solar-powered **Moshin** (☎ 707-433-5499; www.moshinvineyards.com; 10295 Westside Rd; ⏰ 11am-4:30pm) and the reclaimed bowling-alley-lane bar at Demeter-certified biodynamic **Porter Creek** (☎ 707-433-6321; www.portercreekvineyards.com; 8735 Westside Rd; ⏰ 10:30am-4:30pm; 🐾).

Along bucolic Westside Rd, you can picnic near the Japanese bonsai garden at **Arista** (☎ 707-473-0606; www.aristawinery.com; 7015 Westside Rd; tastings $5; ⏰ 11am-5pm) with a bottle of their crisp, lychee-tinged dry Gewurztraminer. Across the street, you can't miss the stone triple chimneys of century-old **Hop Kiln** (☎ 707-433-6491; www.hopkilnwinery.com; 6050 Westside Rd; tastings $5-7; ⏰ 10am-5pm), a national historic landmark built by 25 Italian masons. Step into the redwood-beamed tasting room to try signature red blends, but also lip-smacking artisan vinegars.

North of Healdsburg, Dry Creek Valley is a Wine Country dreamscape, with blossoming ground cover, grazing sheep and a sparkling stream amid the vines. For a spectacular country drive, take the meandering, tree-lined West Dry Creek Rd, especially if you're on a bicycle. At the valley's north end, spelunk as you taste velvety small-production Syrahs at **Bella** (☎ 707-473-9171, 866-572-3552; www.bellawinery.com; 9711 W Dry Creek Rd; tastings $5; ⏰ 11am-4pm), where the tasting bar is in caves burrowed right into Lilly Hill.

Across the road, **Preston Vineyards** (☎ 707-433-3327; www.prestonvineyards.com; 9282 W Dry Creek Rd; tastings $5, applicable to purchase; ⏰ 11am-4:30pm) is a picture-perfect 19th-century farm handcrafting food-complementary wines from certified organic estate grapes. Preston plants artichokes and radishes for pest control, so there's fresh produce to enjoy with Preston's own olive oil, fresh-baked bread and local cheeses.

With a tasting room in a windowless California garage, Demeter-certified biodynamic **Unti** (☎ 707-433-5590; www.untivineyards.com; 4202 Dry Creek Rd; ⏰ by appointment) offers a California-casual taste of Italy – its elegant Sangiovese smacks of bodacious Brunello, at a fraction of the cost. Unti's dedication to artisanal methods verges on obsession: a recent reserve Syrah was actually stomped twice underfoot, yielding only five barrels.

North of Healdsburg, head east off Hwy 101 into Alexander Valley, the last valley inland before Napa. Take in the scenery from the modern Frank Lloyd Wright–inspired tasting room at **Stryker Sonoma** (☎ 800-433-1944; www.strykersonoma.com; 5110 Hwy 128, Geyserville; tastings $5-10; ⏰ 10:30am-

---

you've been dreaming of: fresh pastries, fog-lifting coffee and chatty locals. The expansive view of the Russian River from the patio and strangely appropriate new age tunes are bonuses.

Cape Fear Café (☎ 707-865-9246; 10439 Hwy 1; breakfast & lunch $8-14, dinner $16-24; 🐾) If you feel the need for more substantive home-style cookin', head 10 minutes inland on Hwy 116 (River Rd) to Duncan's Mills and order a breakfast anchored by creamy grits or a thick burger.

FORT ROSS STATE HISTORIC PARK

Fort Ross State Historic Park offers a glimpse into the pre-American Wild West. Founded in March 1812 by a group of 25 Russians and 80 Alaskans (including members of the Kodiak and Aleutian tribes), it was the southernmost outpost of the 19th-century Russian fur trade on America's Pacific coast. The wooden fort they built near a Kashaya Pomo village was established as a base for sea-otter hunting operations and trade with Alta California

5pm), where 14 distinct Zins and 13 Cabs reveal the underlying traits of vineyards: sunny intensity from the valley floor and cascading flavors from volcanic Mount St. Helena.

Gourmet sandwiches, bottled strawberry crush and antique toys are draws at Anderson Valley's quaint, 1895 **Jimtown Store** (☎ 707-433-1212; www.jimtown.com; 6706 Hwy 128, Jimtown). But for wood-fired pizza worth the drive from SF or LA, big-boned Alexander Valley house red by the jug and stellar housemade Italian charcuterie, head directly to **Diavola** (☎ 707-814-0111; www .diavolapizzeria.com; 21021 Geyserville Ave; ◷ 11:30am-9pm).

With gracious Victorians gathered around a leafy central square called the Plaza, swanky little Healdsburg showcases its good taste in local produce and artisan cheeses at the twice-weekly summer–fall **farmers market** (☎ 707-431-1956; www.healdsburgfarmersmarket.org; ◷ 9am-noon Sat May-Nov, 4-6:30pm Tue Jun-Oct) held at North and Vine Sts on Saturday and at Healdsburg Plaza on Tuesday. Many people don't come to Sonoma for the wines, but for the cheese – and you can find out why at the **Cheese Shop** (☎ 707-433-4998; www.doraliceimports.com; 423 Center St; ◷ 10am-6pm Mon-Sat), from the crowd-pleasing mild Point Reyes Blue to the adventurously stinky aged-goat Capricious.

Only in Healdsburg would you find Slow Food at a bookstore cafe. **Bovolo** (☎ 707-431-2962; www.bovolorestaurant.com; 106 Matheson St; dishes $7-16; ◷ 9am-6pm Thu-Tue, 9am-9pm Sat & Sun, shorter winter hrs) uses farm-fresh produce and cures its own meats for tasty, seasonal antipasti, pizza and breakfast sandwiches. Pick up gooey sticky buns from **Downtown Bakery** (☎ 707-431-2719; www.downtownbakery.net; 308a Center St; ◷ 7am-5:30pm), followed by a cappuccino with a fern drawn in properly stiff foam at **Flying Goat Coffee** (☎ 707-433-9081; www.flyinggoatcoffee.com; 324 Center St; ◷ 7am-6pm). **Cyrus** (☎ 707-433-3311; www.cyrusrestaurant.com; 29 North St; fixed-price menu $102-132; ◷ dinner Wed-Mon) wins raves for Euro-Cal prix fixes in the dining room, but also à la carte dishes with seasonal cocktails at the bar.

If you decide to spend the night, the best motel in Healdsburg is the **Best Western Dry Creek Inn** (☎ 707-433-0300, 800-222-5784; www.drycreekinn.com; 198 Dry Creek Rd; r $115-139; ⊠ ⛾ ♿). Better yet, Victorian **Healdsburg Inn on the Plaza** (☎ 707-433-6991, 800-234-1425; www.healdsburginn.com; 110 Matheson St; r Mon-Fri $200-250, Sat & Sun $220-275; ⊠) has airy, high-ceilinged rooms with fine linens, gas fireplaces and some Jacuzzi tubs. Back in Guerneville, you'll find sweet deals: vintage cabins with woodstoves among the redwoods at **Dawn Ranch** (☎ 707-869-0656; www.dawnranch.com; 16467 River Rd; d incl breakfast $99-120; ⊠ ⛾ ♿) and **Boon Hotel & Spa** (☎ 707-869-2721; www.boonhotels .com; 14711 Armstrong Woods Rd; d $185-205, tr $225-250; ⊠ ⛾), a chic eco-retreat, with solar-heated cabanas alongside the chlorine-free pool and hot-stone massages.

For more Sonoma splendor, take Hwy 12 east of Santa Rosa into the heart of Sonoma Valley to Glen Ellen, and obey the call of the wild at **Jack London Historic State Park** (☎ 707-938-5216; www.jacklondonpark.com; 2400 London Ranch Rd; ◷ 10am-5pm Oct-Apr, 9:30am-7pm May-Sep), where you can explore the California novelist's estate on horseback. Take a shortcut to Napa: follow Trinity Rd from Glen Ellen to Oakville Grade, which ends in Oakville at the center of Napa Valley. Drive up the valley on slow-moving Hwy 29, then back down parallel Silverado Trail; you'll spot about 100 wineries along the way, many of them architecturally stunning.

and for supplying crops to Russian settlements in Alaska. While the Russians occupied it, it was the center of manufacturing in California. The fort was abandoned in 1842 because the sea-otter population had been decimated, agricultural production had never taken off and it was drowning in red ink.

Eleven miles north of Jenner, **Fort Ross State Historic Park** (☎ 707-847-3286; 19005 Hwy 1; per car $8; ◷ 10am-4:30pm) is a lovely reconstruction of the fort, situated around a grassy bailey. Though the original buildings were sold, dismantled and carried off to Sutter's Fort in Sacramento during the Gold Rush, the rebuilt chapel remains and is a National Historic Landmark. The **visitors center** (☎ 707-847-3437; ◷ 10am-4:30pm) has historical displays and an excellent bookstore on Californian and Russian history and nature. Ask about hikes to the Russian cemetery.

On **Fort Ross Heritage Day**, the last Saturday in July, costumed volunteers bring the fort's

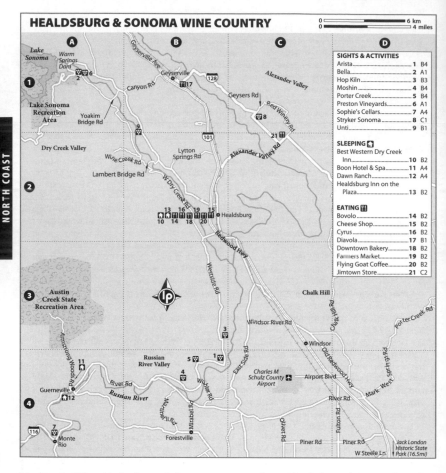

HEALDSBURG & SONOMA WINE COUNTRY

SIGHTS & ACTIVITIES		
Arista	1	B4
Bella	2	A1
Hop Kiln	3	B3
Moshin	4	B4
Porter Creek	5	B4
Preston Vineyards	6	A1
Sophie's Cellars	7	A4
Stryker Sonoma	8	C1
Unti	9	B1

SLEEPING		
Best Western Dry Creek Inn	10	B2
Boon Hotel & Spa	11	A4
Dawn Ranch	12	A4
Healdsburg Inn on the Plaza	13	B2

EATING		
Bovolo	14	B2
Cheese Shop	15	B2
Cyrus	16	B2
Diavola	17	B1
Downtown Bakery	18	B2
Farmers Market	19	B2
Flying Goat Coffee	20	B2
Jimtown Store	21	C2

history to life; check the website www
.parks.ca.gov or call the visitors center for
other special events.

Sleeping & Eating

Stillwater Cove Regional Park (☎ information
707-847-3245, reservations 707-565-2267; www.sonoma
-county.org/parks; 22455 N Hwy 1; campsites $22) Two
miles north of Timber Cove, the campsites
here (17 with reservations, three first-come,
first-served) have hot coin-operated showers
and there is hiking under Monterey pines. If
Reef is full, you can usually get a site here.

Reef Campground (☎ 707-847-3286; campsites
$25; ☺ Apr-Oct) Two miles south of the park,
this has first-come, first-served campsites
(no showers) in a sheltered seaside gully,

popular with abalone divers and surfers.
The hike up to Fort Ross from here passes
the old Russian cemetery.

Timber Cove Inn (☎ 707-847-3231, 800-987-8319;
www.timbercoveinn.com; 21780 N Hwy 1; r Sat & Sun
$219, ocean view from $270) This dramatic and
quirky '60s-modern seaside inn was once a
top-of-the-line luxury lodge and, though
the price remains high, it has slipped a bit.
The rustic architectural shell is still stunning, though, and a duet of tinkling piano
and crackling fire fills the lobby. The cozy,
quirky rooms facing the ocean feel a bit like
a tree house, with rustic redwood details,
balconies, fireplaces and lofted beds. Even
those who don't bunk here should wander
agape in the shadow of Benny Bufano's

93ft peace statue, a spectacular totem on the edge of the sea. The ambitious, expensive restaurant on-site is nothing to write home about.

SALT POINT STATE PARK

If you stop at only one park along the Sonoma Coast, make it 6000-acre **Salt Point State Park** (☎ 707-847-3221; per car $8), where sandstone cliffs drop dramatically into the kelp-strewn sea and hiking trails crisscross windswept prairies and wooded hills, connecting pygmy forests and coastal coves rich with tidepools. The 6-mile-wide park is bisected by the San Andreas Fault – the rock on the east side is vastly different from that on the west. Check out the eerily beautiful *tafonis*, honeycombed sandstone formations, near Gerstle Cove. For a good roadside photo op, there's a pullout at mile-marker 45, with views of decaying redwood shacks, grazing goats and headlands jutting out to the sea.

For views of the pristine coastline, walk to the platform overlooking **Sentinel Rock**; it's just a short stroll from the Fisk Mill Cove parking lot at the park's north end. Just south, **Stump Beach** has picnic areas with firepits and beach access. Further south, seals laze at **Gerstle Cove Marine Reserve**, one of California's first underwater parks. Tread lightly around tidepools and don't lift the rocks: even a glimpse of sunlight can kill some critters. Kids can check out an 'Adventure Pack' from the Gerstle Cove entrance station or the tiny **visitors center** (☺ weekend afternoons, when volunteer staff is available) and use it to ID animals and plants in tidepools.

If it's springtime, you *must* see **Kruse Rhododendron State Reserve**. Growing abundantly in the forest's filtered light, magnificent, pink rhododendrons reach heights of over 30ft, making them the tallest species in the world; turn east from Hwy 1 onto Kruse Ranch Rd and follow the signs.

Two campgrounds, **Woodside** and **Gerstle Cove** (☎ 800-444-7275; www.reserveamerica.com; campsites $35), both signposted off Hwy 1, have campsites with cold water. Inland Woodside is well protected by Monterey pines. Gerstle Cove's trees burned over a decade ago and have only grown halfway back, giving the gnarled, blackened trunks a ghostly look when the fog twirls between the branches. Walk-in **environmental campsites** (campsites $25) are half a mile from the parking area, on Woodside campground's east side.

SEA RANCH

pop 1200

Though not without its fans, the exclusive community of Sea Ranch might well be termed Stepford-by-the-Sea. The ritzy subdivision that sprawls 10 miles along the coast is connected with a well-watched network of private roads. Approved for construction prior to the existence of the watchdog Coastal Commission, the community was a precursor to the concept of 'slow growth,' with strict zoning laws requiring that houses be constructed of weathered wood only. According to *The Sea Ranch Design Manual*: 'This is not a place for the grand architectural statement; it's a place to explore the subtle nuances of fitting in…' Indeed. Though there are some lovely and recommended short-term rentals here, don't break any community rules – like throwing wild parties – or security will come knockin'. For supplies and gasoline, go to Gualala.

After years of litigation, public throughways onto private beaches have been legally mandated. Hiking trails lead from roadside parking lots to the sea and along the bluffs, but don't dare trespass on adjacent lands. **Stengel Beach** (Hwy 1 Mile 53.96) has a beach-access staircase, **Walk-On Beach** (Mile 56.53) provides wheelchair access and **Shell Beach** (Mile 55.24) also has beach-access stairs; parking costs $4. For hiking details, including maps, contact the **Sea Ranch Association** (☎ 707-785-2444; www.tsra.org).

Sea Ranch Lodge (☎ 707-785-2371, 800-732-7262; www.searanchlodge.com; 60 Sea Walk Dr), was a marvel of stark, '60s-modern California architecture, with elegant rooms and dramatic views. At press time the owners had just won zoning permission to knock the whole thing down and rebuild. The $50-million upgrade will promise sustainable building methods and sky-high rates. North of the lodge, stop for a meditation at Sea Ranch's iconic nondenominational **chapel** (Hwy 1 Mile 55.66), shaped like a wizard's hat. It's on the inland side of the highway.

Depending on the season, it can be surprisingly affordable to rent a house here; three good options are **Rams Head Realty**

NORTH COAST

(☎ 707-785-2427, 800-785-3455; www.ramshead-realty .com), **Sea Ranch Rentals** (☎ 707-884-4235; www .searanchrentals.com) and **Sea Ranch Vacation Rentals** (☎ 800-643-8899; www.searanchgetaway.com).

For crusty artisan breads and delicious seasonal pastries, venture east up the steep hill and follow the signs to **Two Fish Baking Co** (☎ 707-785-2443; www.twofishbakery.com; 355090 Verdant View Dr, off Annapolis Rd; ☺ 7am-3pm Wed-Sun). The sandwiches are worth the detour.

GUALALA
pop 1912

Most locals pronounce it 'Wah-*la*-la.' At just 2½ hours north of San Francisco, this little town is northern Sonoma coast's hub for a weekend getaway. Founded as a lumber town in the 1860s, the downtown stretches along Hwy 1 with a bustling commercial district that has a great grocery store and some cute, slightly upscale shops.

Redwood Coast Chamber of Commerce (☎ 707-884-1080, 800-778-5252; www.redwoodcoastchamber.com; 39150 Hwy 1; ☺ 11am-5pm Thu-Sat, 11am-2pm Sun) has local business information. In a clearing of redwoods stands the area's cultural hub, **Gualala Arts Center** (☎ 707-884-1138; www.gualala arts.org; 46501 Gualala Rd), with changing exhibitions, classes and musical performances. It organizes the lovely **Art in the Redwoods Festival** in mid-August. Head inland along Old State Rd, at the south end of town.

Sleeping & Eating

Ocean-view motels line the main drag and an abundance of nearby vacation rentals are available at the Redwood Coast Chamber of Commerce.

Gualala Point Regional Park (☎ 707-785-2377, reservations 707-565-2267; www.sonoma-county.org /parks; 42401 Hwy 1; per car $6, campsites $22) South of downtown, this 195-acre park has good camping and wooded hiking trails up the Gualala River.

Gualala River Redwood Park (☎ 707-884-3533; www.gualalapark.com; per car $5, campsites $33-40; ☺ Memorial Day-Labor Day) This is the more remote of the two camping options, along Old State Rd where you camp (and hike) among redwoods.

St Orres Inn (☎ 707-884-3303, dining room 707-884-3335; www.saintorres.com; 36601 Hwy 1; B&B $90-130, cottages $120-350, mains $40) Famous for its trippy, redwood, Russian-inspired architecture, there's no place quite like this hotel,

an eye-popping structure with dramatic rough-hewn timbers and copper domes. On the property's 90 acres, hand-built cottages range from rustic to luxurious. If you can swing it, eat at the inn's dining room, open for dinner only, which serves California cuisine in one of the coast's most romantic rooms. The nightly specials are exhaustive and delicious.

Trinks (☎ 707-884-1713; www.trinkscafe.com; 39410 S Hwy 1; mains $7-10; ☺ 7am-5pm Mon-Sat, 8am-4pm Sun; ☺) A solid bet for breakfast or lunch, Trinks uses fresh ingredients in its sandwiches (try the 'Paris,' stacked with ham, brie and homemade jam), baked goods and locally roasted coffee.

Bones Roadhouse (☎ 707-884-1188; 39350 S Hwy 1; mains $10-20; ☺ 11:30am-9pm Sun-Thu, to 10pm Fri & Sat) With bawdy bric-a-brac on the wall, savory smoked meats and a pulled pork sandwich designed for the Harley drivers, this is Gualala's best lunch. On weekends, they may even have a codgerly blues outfit growling out 'Mustang Sally.'

Surf Supermarket (☎ 707-884-4184; 39250 S Hwy 1) Of the two groceries, this is best, with choice wines, a friendly meat counter and a fresh salad bar. If you're barbecuing or self-catering, stock up here.

ANCHOR BAY
pop 176

Anchor Bay is little more than a wide spot in the road 3 miles from Gualala, and the perfect place to disappear. There's not much other than two exceptional inns, a grocery and, heading north, a string of secluded, hidden-away beaches. At night, you'll fall asleep to braying sea lions and the shush of the sea.

It'd be a crime to visit without a bit of beachcombing. Seven miles north of town, pull off at Mile 11.41 for **Schooner Gulch State Beach** (☎ 707-937-5804), where a trail leads down cliffs to a sandy beach with tidepools. Bear right at the fork in the trail to reach **Bowling Ball Beach**, the next beach north where (only at low tide) rows of big, round rocks resemble bowling balls. Consult tide tables for Arena Cove. The forecast low tide must be lower than +1.5ft on the tide chart; otherwise the rocks remain covered with water.

ourpick Mar Vista Cottages (☎ 707-884-3522, 877-855-3522; www.marvistamendocino.com; 35101 S Hwy

1; 1-bedroom cottages $140-205, 2-bedroom cottages $200-230; ⏏ 🚭 😸) This is our favorite escape on the entire California coast. All 12 brightly painted, 1930s fishing cottages were retrofitted with elegant simplicity: beds with feather-light duvets, polished hardwood floors, comfy reading chairs, wood-burning stoves and full kitchens. Chickens peck around the 9-acre grounds laying fresh eggs for breakfast. Guests may indulge in seasonal herbs and veggies from the open garden. Across the road there's a hidden beach. If you're looking for a retro-cozy hideaway cottage, look no further.

North Coast Country Inn (☎ 707-884-4537, 800-959-4537; www.northcoastcountryinn.com; 34591 S Hwy 1; r incl breakfast $189-225; 😸) Perched on a hillside beneath towering trees and lovely gardens, this lovely inn has six large, cozy rooms with open-beam ceilings, fluffy down duvets, fireplaces and private entrances. Some have kitchenettes. A hillside hot tub sweetens the deal.

POINT ARENA
pop 460

Thirty minutes north of Gualala, tiny downtown Point Arena looks like Main Street USA, but the centerpiece of the former fishing village is a windswept point crowned by the 1908 **Point Arena Lighthouse** (☎ 707-882-2777; www.pointarenalighthouse.com; ⏱ 10am-3:30pm; 🚭). Just 2 miles north of town, it's the only lighthouse in California you can ascend. Check in at the museum, then climb the 145 steps to the top and see the Fresnel lens and the jaw-dropping view which includes a bird's-eye glimpse of the San Andreas Fault (adult/child $7.50/1). You can also rent one of the former **Coast Guard homes** (☎ 877-725-4448; homes $125 225) next to the lighthouse. They look like tract houses and are simply furnished, but offer unreal views.

One mile down Lighthouse Rd from Hwy 1, look for the Bureau of Land Management (BLM) signs on the left indicating the 1132-acre **Stornetta Public Lands** (☎ 707-468-4000; www .blm.gov), which has fabulous bird-watching, hiking on terraced rock past sea caves and access to hidden coves. Scope your hike from atop the lighthouse.

The **Arena Cinema** (☎ 707-882-3456; 214 Main St) shows mainstream and art films in a beautifully restored movie house. Sue, the ticket seller, has been in that booth for 40 years. Got a question about Point Arena? Ask Sue.

Sleeping & Eating

Sea Shell Inn (☎ 707-882-2000; 135 Main St; r $55-70, tr $90; 🖳) Near downtown, this is the cheapest motel within 100 miles, though the rooms suffer from fairly dank shag carpet.

Wharf Master's Inn (☎ 707-882-3171; www.wharf masters.com; 785 Iversen Ave; s $105, d $135-195, ste $255, house $550) This stands on a cliff overlooking fish boats and a stilting pier. The rooms in this large, modern inn all have balconies and fireplaces.

Coast Guard House Historic Inn (☎ 707-882-2442; www.coastguardhouse.com; 695 Arena Cove; r $155-225) This 1901 Cape Cod–style house and cottage is a mile west of town at Arena Cove and has views of the water.

Franny's Cup & Saucer (☎ 707-882-2500; www .frannyscupandsaucer.com; 213 Main St; ⏱ 8am-4pm Wed-Sat) The cutest patisserie on this stretch of coast is run by Franny and her mother, Barbara (a veteran of Chez Panisse). The fresh berry tarts and rich chocolaty desserts seem too beautiful to eat, until you take the first bite and immediately order another. Between April and June, try to reserve ahead for their Sunday garden brunch (seatings at 10am and 1:30pm, $25).

For such a tiny population, Point Arena is ga-ga for quality organic groceries. There are two on the main drag: the newly opened

---

TOP FIVE COZY & CREATIVE EATS ON THE NORTH COAST

- **Terrapin Creek Café & Restaurant** Inventive California cuisine that explodes with freshness (p104)

- **Franny's Cup & Saucer** Baked goods to die for and elegant summer brunches (above)

- **Café Beaujolais** Mendocino's top dining room serves a local, organic and sustainable menu (p118)

- **La Petite Rive** Tiny and intimate, this is the North Coast's most romantic dining experience (p112)

- **3 Foods Cafe** A menu executed with enough waggish character to suit perfectly an eclectic college crowd (p141)

NORTH COAST

Arena Market & Café (☎ 707-882-3663; 183 Main St; ⏰ 7:30am-7pm Mon-Sat, 8:30am-6pm Sun) and **The Record** (☎ 707-882-3663; 265 Main St; ⏰ 7am-8pm Mon-Sat, 8am-6pm Sun; 🖥), which has a better deli and internet access.

MANCHESTER STATE PARK & BEACH

The surf positively roars at this 5-mile-long, windswept **state beach** (☎ 707-882-2463), where long, rolling breakers pound the driftwood-littered coastline, smack dab on the San Andreas Fault. If you're looking to spend the day at a beach, this one's tremendous. Take the turn-off 9 miles north of Point Arena.

Ross Ranch (☎ 707-877-1834; www.rossranch.biz) at Irish Beach, 5 miles north of the park, arranges two-hour horseback beach ($60) and mountain ($50) rides; be sure to make reservations.

Just before Manchester Beach, an excellent **campground** (campsites $25) has grassy sites with water. Ten unreservable **environmental campsites** (campsites $25) are hidden in the dunes and are a 1.5-mile walk from the parking area; these have untreated creek water.

If your idea of camping includes an espresso bar and a chlorinated hot tub, make for **Mendocino Coast KOA** (☎ 707-882-2375, 800-562-4188; www.manchesterbeachkoa.com; tent/RV sites from $33/43, cabins $61-77; 🖳). This magnet for RVs is hardly roughing it, but the cabins are tidy, the sites are nice enough and it's a good backup if it's getting dark.

ELK

pop 208

Thirty minutes north of Point Arena, itty-bitty Elk is famous for its stunning cliff-top views of 'sea stacks,' towering rock formations jutting out of the water. There is *nothing* to do after dinner, so bring a book – and sleeping pills if you're a night owl. And you can forget about the cell phone, too; reception here is nonexistent.

Orientation & Information

Elk's **visitors center** (5980 Hwy 1; ⏰ 11am-1pm Sat & Sun mid-Mar–Oct) has exhibits on the town's logging past. At the southern end of town, **Greenwood State Beach** (☎ 707-877-3458) has a path to the beach where Greenwood Creek meets the sea – an excellent launching point for kayaking. **Force 10** (☎ 707-877-3505; www.force10tours.com) guides worthwhile ocean-kayaking tours ($115) and can also arrange for longer outings.

Sleeping & Eating

Elk's inns have mesmerizing views; just try not to look at your credit card statement when you get home.

Griffin House (☎ 707-877-3422; www.griffinn.com; 5910 S Hwy 1; cottages $130-160, with ocean view $145-267; 🖳) Griffin House doesn't pretend to be more than it is – an unpretentious cluster of simple beachside cottages with low-pile carpeting, stunning views and wood-burning stoves. The little touches – complimentary wine, board games and an on-site pub – make this a favorite for couples on a getaway.

Harbor House Inn (☎ 707-877-3203, 800-720-7474; www.theharborhouseinn.com; 5600 S Hwy 1; r & cottages incl breakfast & dinner $316-490) Elk's finest inn is ideal for honeymooners. The 1915 Craftsman-style mansion has polished redwood interiors and stunning cliff-top gardens.

Queenie's Roadhouse Café (☎ 707-877-3285; 6061 S Hwy 1; dishes $6-10; ⏰ 8am-3pm Thu-Mon) Queenie's is the top choice for breakfast or lunch, with killer twists on standards like herbed biscuits under the eggs Benedict and wild rice waffles. Too bad it's closed for dinner.

Bridget Dolan's (☎ 707-877-1820; 5910 S Hwy 1; dishes $10-20; ⏰ dinner Fri-Tue) This dressed-down pub adjoining the Griffin House serves straightforward cookin', like pot pies and bangers and mash.

ourpick La Petite Rive (☎ 707-937-4945; www .lapetiterive.com; 7750 Hwy 1; 5-course prix fixe $24-35; ⏰ dinner Wed-Sun) Misty ocean views are only part of the reason this warmly romantic, French dining room in Little River (15 miles north of Elk) has become the talk of the North Coast. From the first exhilarating moment of the *amuse bouche*, through the following four courses of elegant, seasonal fare, it's the best food on the coast, north of San Francisco. It's also *tiny*. There are seven tables and two seatings – at 5:30pm and 8pm only – so reservations are crucial. Robert Redford drove over two hours for the tomato soup, waited in the parking lot and was turned away. Seriously.

VAN DAMME STATE PARK

Five minutes south of Mendocino, this gorgeous 1831-acre **state park** (☎ 707-937-5804, 707-937-5397; www.parks.ca.gov; per car $8; 🖥) draws divers, beachcombers and kayakers to its easy-access beach. It's also known for a **pygmy forest**, where the acidic soil and an impenetrable layer of hardpan just below the surface create a bonsai forest with decades-old trees half a foot high. There's a wheelchair-accessible boardwalk that provides access to the pine-scented forest; turn east off Hwy 1 onto Little River Airport Rd, a half-mile south of Van Damme State Park, and drive 3 miles. Alternatively, hike or bike up inland from the campground on the park's premiere trail, the lush 3.5-mile **Fern Canyon Scenic Trail**, which crosses back and forth over Little River beneath second-growth redwoods.

The **visitors center** (☎ 707-937-4016; 10am-4pm daily summer, Sat & Sun fall-spring) has a diorama of the park's marine conservation area and videos and interpretive programs; a half-hour marsh loop trail starts nearby. For sea-cave kayaking tours ($50), contact **Lost Coast Kayaking** (☎ 707-937-2434; www.lostcoast kayaking.com).

Ten **environmental campsites** (campsites $25) lie just under a 2-mile hike up Fern Canyon and they only have untreated creek water. However, there are two gorgeous **campgrounds** (☎ 800-444-7275; www.reserveamerica.com; campsites $35) with hot showers, one off Hwy 1, the other in a highland meadow. *Make reservations!*

MENDOCINO
pop 822

Mendocino is the North Coast's salt-washed gem, with B&Bs surrounded by rose gardens, white picket fences and New England-style redwood water towers leading out to a gorgeous headland. Here, visitors walk along the headland among berry bramble and wildflowers, where cypress trees stand guard over dizzying cliffs. Nature's power is evident everywhere; from driftwood-littered fields and cave tunnels to the raging surf. The town itself is full of cute shops – no chains – and has earned the nickname 'Spendocino,' for its upscale goods. Quasi-bohemian bourgeoisie with fat wallets love wandering the streets; most are up from San Francisco for the weekend. In summer, fragrant bursts of lavender and jasmine permeate the foggy wind, tempered by salt air from the churning surf, which is never out of earshot.

Built by transplanted New Englanders in the 1850s, Mendocino thrived late into the 19th century, with ships transporting redwood timber to San Francisco. The mills fell silent in the 1930s and the town suffered until it was rediscovered in the 1950s by bohemians. The years since have made the town an exclusive getaway where prices can run sky-high, and while the culturally savvy, politically aware citizens welcome visitors, they vigorously defend their turf from the construction of cell-phone towers, straighter roads and corporate interlopers.

Alas, Mendocino has become a victim of its own charms and, at times, seems a parody of itself: it's a magnet for young honeymooners but prohibitively expensive for young families. It's a town that espouses green-and-local trends though without sufficient infrastructure development to support its dominating hospitality trade, so that much of the water in the high season has to be imported. Even so, there's no arguing the stunning beauty of the place. Ideally, come midweek or off-season, when the vibe is pure – and prices are reasonable.

Information
Ford House Visitors Center & Museum (☎ 707-937-5397; www.gomendo.com; 735 Main St; donation requested $2; 11am-4pm) Maps, books, information and exhibits including a scale model of 1890 Mendocino. There's also hot cider, picnic tables and restrooms.
Gallery Books (☎ 707-937-2665; 319 Kasten St) History, nature, travel and children's books.
Mendocino Coast Clinics (☎ 707-964-1251; www.mendocinocoastclinics.org; 205 South St; Fort Bragg; 9am-6pm Mon-Fri, 9am-1pm Sat) For nonemergencies.
Mendocino Coast District Hospital (☎ 707-961-1234; 700 River Dr, Fort Bragg) Has a 24-hr emergency room.
Moody's Coffee Bar (☎ 707-933-4843; www.moodys coffeebar.com; 10450 Lansing St; per min $0.10, 5.30am-9pm) Internet access, good coffee and the *New York Times*.
Post office (☎ 707-937-1650; 10500 Ford St)
Savings Bank of Mendocino County (☎ 707-937-0545; 10500 Lansing St) 24-hr ATM.

Sights
Mendocino Art Center (☎ 707-937-5818, 800-653-3328; www.mendocinoartcenter.org; 45200 Little Lake St; 10am-5pm Apr-Oct, to 4pm Tue-Sat Nov-Mar) Behind a yard of twisting iron sculpture, the city's art center takes up a whole tree-filled block, hosting exhibitions, the 81-seat Helen Schonei Theatre and nationally renowned art classes. This is also where to pick up the *Mendocino Arts Showcase* brochure, a quarterly publication listing all

MENDOCINO

PACIFIC OCEAN

Agate Beach

Mendocino Headlands State Park

Mendocino Headlands State Park

Presbyterian Church

Mendocino Bay

Big River

0 ————— 300 m
0 ————— 0.2 miles

INFORMATION
Ford House Visitors Center & Museum.............................1 C3
Gallery Books.............................2 B3
Moody's Coffee Bar.............(see 30)
Post Office.................................3 B3
Savings Bank of Mendocino County.................................4 C3

SIGHTS & ACTIVITIES
Big River State Beach.............5 D3
Catch a Canoe & Bicycles, Too!....................................6 D4
Kelley House Museum...........7 C3
Kwan Tai Temple.....................8 B3
Mendocino Art Center...........9 B3

SLEEPING
Blackberry Inn......................10 C1
Coast Getaways.....................11 C3
John Dougherty House..........12 B3
Joshua Grindle Inn................13 C2
Mendocino Campground......14 D4
Mendocino Coast Reservations........................15 C2
Mendocino Hotel....................16 B3
Packard House.......................17 B3
Quartet..................................18 B3
Sea Gull Inn...........................19 C3
Stanford Inn by the Sea........20 D4

To Russian Gulch State Park (2mi);
Lighthouse Inn at Point Cabrillo (3.3mi);
Point Cabrillo Lighthouse (3.3mi);
Caspar (4mi);
Jug Handle State Reserve (5mi);
Fort Bragg (10mi);
Mendocino Coast Clinics (10mi);
Mendocino Coast District Hospital (10mi)

To Old Mill Farm School of Country Living (10.6mi)

To Comptche (15mi);
Orr Hot Springs (53mi);
Hwy 101 (62mi);
Ukiah (62mi)

Comptche-Ukiah Rd

Mendocino Headlands State Park

To Brewery Gulch Inn (0.5mi);
Van Damme State Park (3mi);
Little River (3mi);
Little River Inn (3mi)

EATING
Café Beaujolais.....................21 C3
Corners of the Mouth.............22 C3
Garden Bakery.......................23 C3
Harvest Market at Mendosa's.24 C2
Lu's Kitchen......................(see 30)
MacCallum House Restaurant.25 C3
Mendo Burgers........................26 C3
Mendocino Café................(see 19)
Moosse Café..........................27 C3
Patterson's Pub.................(see 29)
Ravens..............................(see 20)

DRINKING
Dick's Place...........................28 B3
Patterson's Pub.....................29 C3

SHOPPING
Lark in the Morning................30 C3
Out of this World...................31 B3
Twist.....................................32 B3
Village Toy Store....................33 C3

---

the happenings and festivals in town. Art galleries around town hold events on the second Saturday of each month from 5pm to 8pm.

Kelley House Museum (☎ 707-937-5791; www .mendocinohistory.org; 45007 Albion St; admission $2; 11am-3pm Thu-Tue Jun-Sep, Fri-Mon Oct-May) With a research library and changing exhibits on early California and Mendocino, the 1861 museum hosts seasonal, two-hour walking tours for $10; call for times.

Point Cabrillo Lighthouse (☎ 707-937-0816; www.pointcabrillo.org; Point Cabrillo Dr; 11am-4pm Sat & Sun Jan & Feb, daily Mar-Oct, Fri-Mon Nov & Dec;) Restored in 1909, this lighthouse stands on a 300-acre wildlife preserve north of town, between Russian Gulch and Caspar

Beach. Admission is free. The head lighthouse keeper's home is now a B&B (p117). Guided walks of the preserve leave at 11am on Sundays from May to September.

Kwan Tai Temple (www.kwantaitemple.org; 45160 Albion St) Peering in the window of this 1852 temple reveals an old altar dedicated to the Chinese god of war. Tours are available by appointment.

Activities
Mendocino Headlands State Park (☎ 707-937-5804) This park surrounds the village, with trails crisscrossing bluffs and rocky coves. Ask at the Ford House visitors center on Main St about guided weekend walks, including spring wildflower walks and whale-watching

walks. There are no camping facilities in the park.

Catch a Canoe & Bicycles, Too! (☎ 707-937-0273, 800-331-8884; www.stanfordinn.com; cnr Comptche-Ukiah Rd & Hwy 1; ☺ 9am-5pm; ♿) Situated on the bank of the Big River, this friendly shop rents bikes, kayaks and special outrigger canoes ($28 for three hours) for self-guided trips up the 8-mile Big River tidal estuary, the longest undeveloped estuary in Northern California. Without highways or buildings, it's exceedingly peaceful to float or roll past forests, frolicking otters or historic logging structures.

Old Mill Farm School of Country Living (☎ 707-937-0244, 707-937-3047; www.oldmillfarm.org; cabins $95) Literally and philosophically distant from the frou-frou places in town, this working organic farm is powered by biodiesel and offers a chance to shear sheep or harvest grapes. The farm is about 30 minutes from Mendocino; take Little Lake Rd east out of town for 6 miles. After the pavement ends, the road forks. Bear left on Road 408 and continue for another 3 miles, looking for signs. Check the website for info on farm events and workshops.

Big River State Beach (☎ 707-937-5804) Park behind the Presbyterian church on Main St and take the stairs down to the beach, where you can build beach fires and make driftwood forts.

Little River Inn (☎ 707-937-5942, 888-466-5683; www.littleriverinn.com; Hwy 1, Little River) Three miles south of town, you can play a round of golf (greens fees $25 to $40) and take in stunning views at this nine-hole course. The golf-pro here, Shelly, is a sweetheart.

Festivals & Events

For a complete list of Mendocino's many festivals, check with the visitors center or www.gomendo.com.

Mendocino Whale Festival (www.mendowhale.com) Early March, with wine and chowder tastings, whale-watching and music.

Mendocino Music Festival (www.mendocinomusic .com) Mid-July, with orchestral and chamber music concerts on the headlands, children's matinees and open rehearsals.

Mendocino Wine & Mushroom Festival (www .mendocino.com) Early November, guided mushroom tours and symposia.

Mendocino Coast Candlelight Inn Tour (www .mendocinoinntour.com) Christmas-time inn tours and caroling.

Mendocino Crab & Wine Days Late December to early February, with wine tasting, cooking classes, whale-watching and crab cruises.

Sleeping

Mendocino is downright cluttered with B&Bs (many of which come cluttered with the cabbage-rose wallpaper, lace-curtain aesthetic). Rates plummet in winter. Fort Bragg (p120) is cheaper, if less charming.

Mendocino Coast Reservations (☎ 707-937-5033, 800-262-7801; www.mendocinovacations.com; 45084 Little Lake St; ☺ 9am-5pm) can book vacation homes and B&Bs. The reliable **Coast Getaways** (☎ 707-937-9200; www.coastgetaways.com; 45061 Little Lake St; ☺ 9am-5pm Mon-Fri, 10am-4pm Sat) also books homes in the area; the properties are perfect for families requiring a bit more space. Unlike the listings at Mendocino Coast Reservations, the prices listed on the Coast Getaways website are all-inclusive.

BUDGET

Though you'll pass a handful of private campgrounds in the area catering to RVs, the state facilities are generally of higher quality.

Mendocino Campground (☎ 707-937-3130; www .mendocino-campground.com; Comptche-Uklah Rd; campsites $25-35; ☺ Apr-Oct; ♿) High above Hwy 1, this woodsy option has 60 sites (some with views), hot showers and forested trails.

Russian Gulch State Park (☎ reservations 800-444-7275; www.reserveamerica.com; campsites $35) After Van Damme State Park (p112), make this your first choice. In a wooded canyon 2 miles north of town, Russian Gulch has secluded drive-in campsites and hot showers, a sandy beach, small waterfall and Devil's Punch Bowl – a collapsed sea arch.

Sea Gull Inn (☎ 707-937-5204, 888-937-5204; www .seagullbb.com; 44960 Albion St; r incl breakfast $75-165, cottage $185) With a lovely garden and morning delivery of the organic breakfast, this centrally located small inn is one of the best deals in town. The cottage has TV and a refrigerator.

Mendocino Hotel (☎ 707-937-0511, 800-548-0513; www.mendocinohotel.com; 45080 Main St; r $95-115, with bathroom $135-165, ste $225-395) Built in 1878 as the town's first hotel, many of the Victorian guestrooms share bathrooms. For thicker walls, book a modern garden suite. If you book Room one, it's the cheapest spot in town with an ocean view. Look for the

NORTH COAST

ghost. (Fear not: she's mellow and lingers in the dining room.)

MIDRANGE

All prices include breakfast; most don't have TVs. These are a few favorites:

Blackberry Inn (☎ 707-937-5281, 800-950-7806; www.mendocinomotel.com; 44951 Larkin Rd; r $145) On a hill above town, the Blackberry looks like a row of Old West storefronts. Inside, the Americana-style rooms are comfy and have distant ocean views and fireplaces. Rates are best online.

John Dougherty House (☎ 707-937-5266, 800-486-2104; www.jdhouse.com; 571 Ukiah St; r $150-275) Decked out in a spiffy-looking, blue-and-white nautical theme that would do any gay sailor boy proud, rooms at this elegant,

---

DETOUR: ANDERSON VALLEY & HWY 128

What to See

If you're in a hurry to get to San Francisco or weary of the coast's chilly weather, cut inland through the Anderson Valley via twisty Hwy 128, passing vineyards, apple orchards, pastureland and oak-dotted prairies. You'll also go through two of the valley's plucky little towns, **Boonville** and **Philo**, which may have a combined population of only 1000 residents, but boast their own slang-riddled dialect, called Boontling.

Turning off Hwy 1, you'll first pass **Navarro Redwoods State Park** (☎ 707-895-3141), which extends 11 miles under second-growth redwoods before emerging in the Anderson Valley. Don't tell locals you read this here, but you can swim in the warm-water Navarro River at a great beach near mile-marker 3.66 on Hwy 128; walk through the woods to the river's sandy shore.

After you dry off, warm up with some of the region's wine. The valley's cool nights yield high-acid, fruit-forward, food-friendly wines like Pinot Noir, Chardonnay and dry Gewürztraminer. Most **wineries** (www.avwines.com) offer free tastings and are located outside Philo. **Navarro** (☎ 707-895-3686; 5601 Hwy 128; ☒ 10am-6pm) is the best option, and picnicking is encouraged. Romantic, tiny **Lazy Creek** (☎ 707-895-3623; 4741 Hwy 128) is up a half-mile dirt road; it's open when the gate is (call ahead). **Husch** (☎ 800-554-8724; 4400 Hwy 128; ☒ 10am-5pm) serves tastings inside a rose-covered cottage.

For other bevvies, visit **Anderson Valley Brewing Co** (☎ 707-895-2337; www.avbc.com; 17700 Hwy 153; tours $5), east of Hwy 128. They serve award-winning beers in a Bavarian-style brewhouse and also have a disc golf course on hand. Opposite the Boonville Hotel, **Boonville General Store** (☎ 707-895-9477; 17810 Farrer Lane; dishes $5-8; ☒ 9am-3pm Thu-Mon) is perfect for lunch – sandwiches on homemade bread, thin-crust pizzas and organic cheeses. Locals pack **Lauren's** (☎ 707-895-3869; 14211 Hwy 128, Boonville; mains $9-14; ☒ 5-9pm Tue-Sat) for homemade Cal-American cookin'.

Accommodations fill on weekends. **Anderson Valley Inn** (☎ 707-895-3325; www.avinn.com; 8480 Hwy 128, Philo; r $75-100, with kitchen $130-160) has fresh-looking motel rooms. Decked out in a contemporary American-country style that would make Martha Stewart proud, rooms at the **Boonville Hotel** (707-895-2210; www.boonvillehotel.com; 14040 Hwy 128; r $125-225, ste $180-275; ☒) are safe for urbanites who refuse to abandon style just because they've gone to the country. **The Other Place** (☎ 707-895-3979; www.theotherplaceboonville.com; cottages $175-250; ☒) rents secluded, private hill-top cottages surrounded by 500 acres of ranch lands. **Hendy Woods State Park** (☎ 707-937-5804, reservations 800-444-7275; www.reserveamerica.com; campsites $35, cabins $50) has wooded campsites by the Navarro River – with hot showers.

The Route

Hwy 128 originates 10 miles south of Mendocino and continues east on a twisting path to Hwy 101.

Time & Mileage

Driving the length of Hwy 128 between the coast and Hwy 101 only covers 58 miles, though the curvy route takes about 90 minutes without stops. If you're stopping along the way to taste some wine and soak up the sights, allow four hours.

uncluttered B&B have more contemporary style than others in town. Some have fireplaces and ocean views. Top choice for gay travelers, but all welcome. Ask about the **Packard House** (☎ 707-937-2677; www.packardhouse .com; 45170 Little Lake St; r $190-250), by the same owners.

Alegria (☎ 707-937-5150, 800-780-7905; www .oceanfrontmagic.com; 44781 Main St; r $159-189, with ocean view $179-299) The perfect romantic hideaway, Alegria's rooms have ocean-view decks and wood-burning fireplaces; outside there's private beach access, a rarity in Mendo.

Lighthouse Inn at Point Cabrillo (☎ 707-937-6124, 866-937-6124; http://mendocinolighthouse.point cabrillo.org; Point Cabrillo Dr; r $177-272) On 300 acres, in the shadow of Point Cabrillo Lighthouse, the lighthouse keeper's house and several cottages have been turned into B&B rooms, with atmospheric details like redwood paneling. At night, the light from the brilliant Fresnel lens sweeps overhead, making it a fabulous spot for a nighttime stroll. Rates include a private night tour of the lighthouse and a five-course breakfast.

TOP END

Joshua Grindle Inn (☎ 707-937-4143, 800-474-6353; www.joshgrin.com; 44800 Little Lake Rd; d $189-279, ste $359) The ideal choice for aficionados of historic accommodations, it's also Mendo's first B&B, with bright, airy, simply furnished rooms in an 1869 house, a weathered saltbox cottage and water tower. There are afternoon goodies, warm hospitality and gorgeous gardens. Singles rates available; ask when booking.

Brewery Gulch Inn (☎ 800-331-4752; www.brewery gulchinn.com; 9401 N Hwy 1; r $210) Just south of town, on a hill overlooking the ocean, this newcomer wins with fireplace rooms, private decks and hosts who pour heavily at the complimentary wine hour. They also leave sweets out for midnight snacking. The historic structure has been sustainably remodeled, but the floors are a bit thin, so book a room upstairs.

Stanford Inn by the Sea (☎ 707-937-5615, 800-331-8884; www.stanfordinn.com; Comptche-Ukiah Rd; r $240-295; 🖳 🕿 🐾) There's not a stitch of Victoriana at Mendo's first-choice lodge, where every rough-hewn, pine-paneled room has a wood-burning fireplace, top-quality mattress with fine linens and extras like stereos and fine art. On the 10 rolling acres, gorgeous organic gardens, with the Pacific as a backdrop, provide produce for the dining room. The solarium-enclosed pool and hot tub are open 24 hours. On-site spa. Free bicycles.

Eating

If it's late and you find yourself without a reservation, you'll have far better luck driving a bit further north to Fort Bragg (p121).

BUDGET

Mendo Burgers (☎ 707-937-1111; 10483 Lansing St; meals $6-9; 🕑 11am-4:30pm Thu-Tue; 🚼) Behind Mendocino Bakery, this old-fashioned lunch counter makes great burgers and handcut fries; veggie burgers too.

Lu's Kitchen (☎ 707-937-4939; 45013 Ukiah St; dishes $7-10; 🕑 11:30am-5:30pm; 🚼) Lu serves fab organic-veggie burritos and colorful salads out of this tiny shack. On warm days, the picture is completed by the outdoor seating in the adjacent garden lot that buzzes with lazy bumblebees.

MIDRANGE

Mendocino Café (☎ 707-937-6141; www.mendocino cafe.com; 10451 Lansing St; lunch $9-14, dinner $11-20; 🚼) A good-value choice for a sit-down garden lunch or mid-priced dinner, Mendocino Café's diverse menu weaves together Mexican, Asian and American cooking, like fish tacos, Thai burritos, steaks, pasta and seafood.

Patterson's Pub (☎ 707-937-4782; www.pattersons pub.com; 10485 Lansing St; mains $10-15 🕑 lunch-11pm) Just about the only unreserved eating option in town, you can wash down quality pub grub with cold beer and chat up locals. The only spoiler to the traditional Irish pub ambience is the plethora of flat-screen TVs. They serve until 11pm Friday and Saturday, 10pm weeknights. Brunch is served on Saturday and Sunday between 10am and 2pm.

TOP END

Moosse Café (☎ 707-937-4323; www.theblueheron .com; 390 Kasten St; lunch $10-14, dinner $20-25; 🕑 noon-2:30pm, 5:30-8pm Thu-Mon) The ideal spot for a lingering lunch, bright and airy Moosse Café serves creamy, delicious mac-'n'-cheese, housemade paté and Niçoise salads. At dinner, roast chicken and *cioppino*

NORTH COAST

are the standouts. Save room for chocolate pudding. Monday nights, three-course dinners cost $20 and there's no corkage fee.

Ravens (☎ 707-937-5615; www.stanfordinn.com; Stanford Inn, Comptche-Ukiah Rd; breakfast $8-15, dishes $20-28; ☽ breakfast 8-10:30am Mon-Sat, to 12:15pm Sun, dinner 5:30-8pm; **V**) Who knew vegetarian food could be so good? Omnivores may forswear meat after dining here, where the haute-contemporary menu features everything from pizza to sea-palm strudel. Produce comes from the inn's own organic gardens, where you can stroll after dinner. The breakfasts are Mendocino's best, when you can look over rolling hills to the sea beyond.

MacCallum House Restaurant (☎ 707-937-0289; www.maccallumhouse.com; 45020 Albion St; cafe dishes $6-12, mains $21-32; ☽ dinner) Once upon a time, this restaurant and the attached B&B were the finest in Mendocino, and though the sure-handed Euro-Cal dishes are high quality, they've been dethroned by Beaujolais and La Petite Rive (p112). The otherwise romantic dining room suffers from too many tables, too close together. Sit on the veranda or request a table on the wall.

Café Beaujolais (☎ 707-937-5614; www.cafe beaujolais.com; 961 Ukiah St; lunches $9-16, mains $24-36; ☽ lunch Wed-Sun, dinner daily) Mendocino's iconic, beloved country-Cal-French restaurant occupies an 1896 house restyled into a monochromatic urban-chic dining room, perfect for holding hands by candlelight. The refined and inspired cooking draws diners from San Francisco, who make this the centerpiece of their trip. Bring your credit card; you'll need it.

SELF-CATERING

Mendocino's best grocery store, **Harvest Market at Mendosa's** (☎ 707-937-5879; 10501 Lansing St; ☽ 7:30am-10pm), has an excellent salad bar, picnic foods, good meats and produce. Also worth trying is **Corners of the Mouth** (☎ 707-937-5345; 45016 Ukiah St; ☽ 9am-7pm), a co-op that carries organic food and which is housed in an old church. For the best pastries and good bread, go to the **Garden Bakery** (☎ 707-937-3140; 10450 Lansing St; ☽ 8:30am-4pm Wed-Sat); the entrance is off Albion St.

Drinking

Dick's Place (☎ 707-937-5643; 45080 Main St) A bit out of place among the fancy-pants shops downtown, but an excellent spot to check out the *other* Mendocino and do shots with rowdy locals.

Patterson's Pub (☎ 707-937-4782; 10485 Lansing St) Mendocino's most happening night spot, with good pub grub and lots on tap.

Shopping

Mendocino is all about local art and the galleries around town can be surprisingly affordable sources of one-of-a-kind gifts.

Lark in the Morning (☎ 707-937-5275; 45011 Ukiah St) In addition to a stock of fine acoustic guitars and banjos, the walls of this fantastic shop are lined with handmade and rare instruments from around the world – everything from hammer dulcimers and Celtic harps to African marimbas.

Out of this World (☎ 707-937-3335; 451000 Main St) Bird-watchers, astronomy buffs and science geeks: head directly to this telescope, binocular and science-toy shop.

Twist (☎ 707-937-1717; 45140 Main St) Twist stocks ecofriendly, natural-fiber clothing and trippy hand-blown 'tobacco-smoking accessories' (dude: that means bongs).

Village Toy Store (☎ 707-937-4633; 10450 Lansing St) Get a kite to fly on Bodega head or browse the old-world selection of wooden toys and games that you won't find in the chains – and hardly anything requires batteries!

Getting There & Away

See the Fort Bragg section (p122) for details on regional buses.

JUG HANDLE STATE RESERVE

Even if you're not a rock hound, Handle's **ecological staircase** is a fascinating place. Five wave-cut terraces ascend in steps from the seashore, each 100ft and 100,000 years removed from the previous, and each with its own distinct geology and vegetation. See it on a 5-mile (round-trip) self-guided nature trail. One of the terraces has a pygmy forest, similar to the popular one at Van Damme State Park (p112). Pick up a printed guide from the parking lot. If you're not that geologically curious, head directly for the headlands and whale-watch or lounge on the beach. The turn-off is just north of Caspar, halfway between Fort Bragg and Mendocino.

Should you yearn to get back to the land, **Jug Handle Creek Farm & Nature Center**

(☎ 707-964-4630; www.jughandlecreekfarm.org; camp-sites $12, r & cabins adult $35-40, child $13, student $23-30) is a nonprofit, 39-acre farm that has rustic cabins, and hostel rooms in a 19th-century farmhouse. Call ahead about work-stay discounts and environmental-education opportunities. Reservations recommended. Alternatively, **Annie's Jughandle Beach B&B** (☎ 707-964-1415, 800-964-9957; www.inntravels.com /usa/ca/anniesjughandle.html; Hwy 1, Mile 55; r incl break-fast $120-220), opposite the state reserve, is an 1880s farmhouse with cheery rooms, some with Jacuzzis and gas fireplaces.

FORT BRAGG
pop 7025

In the past, Fort Bragg was always Mendocino's ugly stepsister, home to a lumber mill, a scrappy downtown and blue-collar locals who gave a cold welcome to outsiders. Since the mill closure in 2002, the town has started to reinvent itself, slowly warming to a tourism-based economy. What to do with the seaside mill site is the talk of the town, running the gamut from progressive ideas like a marine research center or university to disastrous ones like a condo development, a world-class golf course or (gasp!) another mill. Regardless of what happens, the effect on Fort Bragg is likely to be profound. Follow the progress at www.fortbraggmillsite.com.

In the meantime Fort Bragg's downtown continues to develop as an unpretentious alternative to Mendocino, even if the southern end of town is hideous: unlike the *entire* franchise-free 180-mile stretch of Coastal Hwy 1 between here and the Golden Gate, southern Fort Bragg sprawls, with McDonald's and Starbucks polluting the coastal aesthetic. Put on blinders and don't stop till you're downtown, where you'll find way better hamburgers, locally roasted coffee, old-school architecture and residents who are eager to show off their cute little town.

Orientation & Information

Twisting, nausea-inducing Hwy 20 connects with Hwy 101. Most facilities are near Main St, a 2-mile stretch of Hwy 1. Shops, a movie theater and the post office are along Franklin St, which runs parallel, one block east. Fort Bragg's wharf, with its fishing-boat docks and seafood restaurants, lies

at Noyo Harbor – the mouth of the Noyo River – south of downtown.

Fort Bragg–Mendocino Coast Chamber of Commerce (☎ 707-961-6300, 800-726-2780; www.fort bragg.com, www.mendocinocoast.com; 332 N Main St; ☺ 9am-5pm Mon-Fri, to 3pm Sat) provides information about Fort Bragg, Mendocino and surrounding areas.

For nonemergency medical treatment, go to **Mendocino Coast Clinics** (☎ 707-964-1251; www.mendocinocoastclinics.org; 205 South St; Fort Bragg; ☺ 9am-6pm Mon-Fri, 9am-1pm Sat).

Mendocino Coast District Hospital (☎ 707-961-1234; 700 River Dr, Fort Bragg) has a 24-hour emergency room.

Sights & Activities

Skunk Train (☎ 707-964 6371, 866-457-5865; www .skunktrain.com; Laurel St; ♿) is a popular historic logging train that chugs between Fort Bragg (departs 10am daily) and Willits (p124), passing stunning redwood mountains, rivers and through deep mountain tunnels en route to Northspur, the midway point, where it turns around – a plenty-long 3½-hour trip. Price per adult $39 to 47, child three to 11 $22. There's also a 90-minute jaunt if you're tight on time. The depot is downtown at Laurel St, west of Main St.

The stunning displays of native flora at **Mendocino Coast Botanical Gardens** (☎ 707-964-4352; www.gardenbythesea.org; 18220 N Hwy 1; ☺ 9am-5pm Mar-Oct, to 4pm Nov-Feb) impress all year round, as visitors follow serpentine paths on 47 seafront acres south of town (admission prices adult/child/teen/senior $10/ 2/4/7.50). Primary trails are wheelchair-accessible.

Glass Beach is named for (what's left of) the sea-polished glass in the sand – once a city dump, now part of MacKerricher State Park (p122). Take the headlands trail from Elm St, off Main St, but leave the glass; as a part of the park system, visitors are not supposed to pocket souvenirs.

The **Larry Spring School Of Common Sense Physics** (☎ 707-964-2116; www.larryspring.com; 225 Redwood Ave) opens for classes by appointment under the codgerly tutelage of 94-year-old Larry Spring, a retired TV repairman who has been working to disprove the hooey of Einstein's relativity theory for the majority of his life. The hours are erratic, but the window display looks like the *Jetsons* prop shop, with an assortment of solar-powered doohickeys and nostalgic old machines.

Fort Bragg is the unlikely home to the world's leading organic, raw, vegan culinary training center, the **Living Light Culinary Arts Institute** (☎ 707-964-2420; www.rawfoodchef.com; 301b N Main St) under the direction of raw food pioneer Cherie Soria. Day-long knife skills classes are the most affordable at $145, but the intensive two-day fundamental course in raw food ($475) is a popular introduction for all experience levels. Call for details about their inn and internship possibilities. They also operate an excellent vegan cafe (opposite).

Even if you don't have plans to get inked at the renowned **Triangle Tattoo & Museum** (☎ 707-964-8814; www.triangletattoo.com; 356b N Main St; ☽ noon-7pm), the passionate scholarship and catholic approach to the art might make you think twice.

Literally and figuratively on the other side of the street from Triangle Tattoo is the **Guest House Museum** (☎ 707-964-4251; 343 N Main St; admission $2; ☽ 11am-2pm & 1-4pm Sat & Sun Jun-Oct, 11am-2pm Thu-Sun Nov-May), a majestic 1892 Victorian house displaying relics of Fort Bragg's history.

Small boats at Noyo Harbor offer coastal and whale-watching cruises and deep-sea fishing and crabbing trips. Prices per person from around $65 for fishing trips, from $25 for two-hour cruises. Try **Noyo Fishing Center** (☎ 707-964-3000; www.fortbraggfishing.com; 32440 N Harbor Dr) or **All-Aboard Adventures** (☎ 707-964-1881; www.allaboardadventures.com; 32400 N Harbor Dr).

Festivals & Events

See www.fortbragg.com for details of the following and other festivals/events.
Fort Bragg Whale Festival Third weekend in March, with microbrew tastings, crafts fairs and whale-watching.
Rhododendron Show Late April or early May.
Paul Bunyan Days Celebrates California's logging history with a logging show, square dancing, parade and fair, Labor Day weekend.

Sleeping

Though still dominated by B&Bs, Fort Bragg has a much wider spectrum of lodging options than Mendocino, including large corporate chains and midcentury motels along noisy Hwy 1 at the south end of town. The following don't have noise problems. Summer weekends sell out, so book ahead.

BUDGET
California Department of Forestry (☎ 707-964-5674; www.fire.ca.gov/php/rsrc-mgt_jackson.php; 802 N Main St; ☽ Mon-Fri) Come here for maps, permits and camping information for the Jackson State Forest, east of Fort Bragg, where camping is free!

Colombi Motel (☎ 707-964-5773; www.colombi motel.com; 647 Oak St; 1- & 2-bedroom units $45-70) The Mendocino Coast's best bargain has sparkling-clean, two-room units with either a bedroom and kitchen or two bedrooms. Check in at the Market at Oak and Harold Sts. Launderette next door.

Anchor Lodge (☎ 707-964-4283; www.anchor-lodge .com; 32260 N Harbor Dr; r $65, with ocean view $100, with kitchen $135) Fishermen and salty dogs favor this motel under the Wharf Restaurant at Noyo Harbor. Some rooms have water views, some have kitchens.

Grey Whale Inn (☎ 707-964-0640, 800-942-5342; www.whalewatchinn.com; 615 N Main St; r incl breakfast $99-195) Situated in a historic building on the north side of town, this comfortable, family-run inn has simple, straightforward rooms that are great value – especially for families. The owner/operator, Mike, plucks herbs from the organic garden to punch up breakfast and provides excellent local information.

MIDRANGE
Beachcomber Motel (☎ 707-964-2402, 800-400-7873; www.thebeachcombermotel.com; 1111 N Main St; r $109-119, with ocean view $119-149, with kitchen $159) Fussier travelers who want an ocean-view motel with upgraded furniture should choose this. Book upstairs for maximum privacy.

Rendezvous Inn (☎ 707-964-8142, 800-491-8142; www.rendezvousinn.com; 647 N Main St; r incl breakfast $110, cottage $170) One of the North Coast's best chefs cooks your breakfast at this simple B&B; good for low-maintenance travelers. A cottage out back sleeps four.

Weller House Inn (☎ 707-964-4415, 877-893-5537; www.wellerhouse.com; 524 Stewart St; r incl breakfast $155-195) Fort Bragg's top-choice B&B is a beautifully restored 1886 Victorian with a fabulous redwood ballroom on the top floor, where guests take breakfast and play cards. Rooms have fluffy down comforters and period details. The water tower is the tallest structure in town – and has a hot tub inside!

Eating

Headlands Coffeehouse (☎ 707-964-1987; www
.headlandscoffeehouse.com; 120 E Laurel St; dishes $4-8;
☽ 7am-10pm) This happening cafe serves
Belgian waffles at breakfast and good, if
pricey, sandwiches. The atmosphere and
nightly music schedule is a godsend for idle
Fort Bragg teens.

Living Light Café (☎ 707-964-2420; 444 N Main St;
dishes $5-11; ☽ 8am-7pm Mon-Sat; **V**) Before you
junk the stove and sign up for classes at the
Living Light Culinary Institute (opposite),
try the excellent organic raw food at this
bright cafe. The tasty to-go menu is a sight
better than bland crudités, like the Sicilian-
style pizza on a spouted seed crust, raw
desserts and tangy cold soups.

Laurel Deli (☎ 707-964-7812; Depot Shopping
Center, 401 N Main St; mains $6-8; ☽ 7am-3pm; 🚹)
Locals pick the Laurel for cheap breakfasts
and sandwiches; kids *love* the giant, real
locomotive parked in the middle of the
cavernous room.

ourpick Piaci Pub & Pizzeria (☎ 707-961-1133;
120 W Redwood Ave; pizza $8-12; ☽ lunch Mon-Fri,
dinner 4-9pm Sun-Thu, to 10pm Fri & Sat) Fort Bragg's
must-visit pizzeria is the place to chat up
locals while enjoying regional wines and
microbrews and a menu of fantastic wood-
fired, brick-oven pizza. The 'Gustoso' – an
immaculate selection with Chevre, pesto
and seasonal pears – hints at the carefully
orchestrated thin-crust pies. The room is
tiny, loud and fun, but expect to wait at
peak times.

North Coast Brewing Co (☎ 707-964-3400; 444 N
Main St; mains $8-25; ☽ noon-9:30pm Sun-Thu, to 10pm
Fri & Sat) Though thick, rare slabs of steak
and a list of specials demonstrate that they
take the food as seriously as the bevvies,
it's burgers and garlic fries that soak up the
fantastic selection of handcrafted brews.

Mendo Bistro (☎ 707-964-4974; www.mendobistro
.com; 301 N Main St; dishes $14-22; ☽ dinner 5-9pm;
🚹) This dining option gets packed with
a young crowd on the weekend, offering a
choose-your-own-adventure menu, where
you select a meat, a preparation and an
accompanying sauce from a litany of
options. The loud, bustling 2nd-story room
is big enough for kids to run around and
nobody will notice.

Nit's (☎ 707-964-7187; 322 N Main St; lunch $8-13,
dinner $18-22; ☽ 5:30-9pm Wed-Sun) Mains are
pricey, but plates are huge, beautifully

presented and dynamically spiced at this tiny
French-Thai storefront cafe run by a Thai-
born chef-owner. After the Rendezvous
Inn (below), Nit's serves the town's best
lunch. Cash only.

Rendezvous Inn (☎ 707-964-8142; www.rendezvous
inn.com; 647 N Main St; mains $24-29; ☽ 5:30-8:30pm
Wed-Sun winter, to 9pm summer, closed Jan & Feb) The
North Coast's lauded dining room sits in a
converted redwood-paneled Craftsman-style
house, where chef-owner Kim Badenhop
(a protégé of Michelin-three-star-rated,
celebrity French chef Georges Blanc) showcases seasonal, regional ingredients like
lavender, wild boar, blackberries and venison
in his down-to-earth, French-provincial
menu. Make reservations and bring a
sweater: the old house gets drafty.

For unpretentious harbor grub, try **Heron's
by the Sea** (☎ 707-962-0680; 32096 N Harbor Dr;
lunch $6-17, dinner $11-24; ☽ breakfast 8-10am, lunch
11am-3pm, dinner 5-9pm), a pretty little dockside
fish grotto with picnic tables outside. For
fried fish, coleslaw and fries, skip the pricey
Wharf restaurant and head next door to
Cap'n Flint's (☎ 707-964-9447; 32250 N Harbor Dr;
☽ 11am-9pm; 🚹) and get (nearly) the same
food for half the price.

For self-caterers and those in search of
a quick meal, try **Harvest Market** (☎ 707-964-
7000; cnr Hwys 1 & 20; ☽ 5am 11pm), which has the
best groceries; or the once-a-week **Farmers
Market** (☎ 707-937-4330; cnr Laurel & Franklin Sts;
☽ 3:30-6pm Wed May-Oct) downtown.

Drinking & Entertainment

Headlands Coffeehouse (☎ 707-964-1987;
www.headlandscoffeehouse.com; 120 E Laurel St; 📶)
The town's informal cultural center features live music nightly – jazz, folk and
classical – and jazz jam sessions on Sunday
afternoons.

North Coast Brewing Company (☎ 707-964-
3400; 444 N Main St; 📶) Of all the many brew-
eries up the coast, this might be the most
serious, with an arsenal of handcrafted, bold
brews that include award-winning stouts
and ales. If you order the sampler, designate
a driver.

Caspar Inn (☎ 707-964-5565; www.casparinn.com;
14957 Caspar Rd) To bust out of the Scrabble
scene at your B&B, head south of Fort
Bragg, off Hwy 1, where the Caspar Inn
has live music every night but Monday.
The cover for the omnivorous schedule is

modest and big names occasionally show up unannounced. If you have too many, there's a basic inn upstairs.

Opera Fresca (☎ 707-937-3646, 888-826-7372; www.operafresca.com) This ambitious company performs fully staged operas year-round, and also hosts a Christmas sing-along *Messiah*.

Shopping

There's plenty of window-shopping in Fort Bragg's compact downtown, including a string of antique shops along Franklin St.

Outdoor Store (☎ 707-964-1407; www.mendooutdoors.com; 247 N Main St) If you're planning on camping on the coast or exploring the Lost Coast (p127), this is the best outfitter in the region, stocking detailed maps of the region's wilderness areas, fuel for stoves and high-quality gear.

Mendocino Vintage (☎ 707-964-5825; www.mendocinovintage.com; 344 N Franklin St) Of the antique shops on Franklin, this is the hippest by a long shot, with a case full of vintage estate jewelry, antique glassware and old local oddities.

Getting Around

Mendocino Transit Authority (MTA; ☎ 707-462-1422, 800-696-4682; www.4mta.org) operates Route 5, 'BraggAbout' buses, weekdays between Noyo Harbor and downtown. Bus 60 operates weekdays to Mendocino ($1, 30 minutes). Bus 65 operates daily to Willits ($3.25, one hour), then heads south along Hwy 101 via Ukiah to Santa Rosa ($20, three hours), where you can connect with Golden Gate Transit to San Francisco (see the San Francisco chapter, p83).

MACKERRICHER STATE PARK

Lose yourself in the roaring surf and wide-open sight lines of **MacKerricher State Park** (☎ 707-964-9112; www.parks.ca.gov; 🅿), 4 miles north of Fort Bragg, where rocky headlands, tidepools, sandy beaches and pristine dunes unfurl for nine gorgeous miles up the coast. The **visitors center** (🕑 10am-6pm Sat & Sun Jul-Sep, 11am-3pm Sat & Sun Oct-Jun) has information about the park's features, including coastal hikes and the easy boardwalk around **Lake Cleone**, a 30-acre freshwater lake stocked with trout. At nearby **Laguna Point** an interpretive boardwalk overlooks seals and, December to April, migrating whales. Or

you can ride bikes south along a dedicated **bicycle path** that includes passage over a train trestle leading to Fort Bragg. **Ricochet Ridge Ranch** (☎ 707-964-7669; www.horse-vacation.com; 24201 N Hwy 1) offers horseback-riding trips through redwoods or along the beach ($45, 90 minutes). Guides are terrific, the horses top quality.

Popular **campgrounds** (☎ 800-444-2725; www.reserveamerica.com; campsites $30), nestled in pine forest, have hot showers and water; the first-choice reservable campsites are numbers 21 to 59. Ten superb, secluded walk-in campsites (numbers 1–10; campsites $35) are first-come, first-served.

WESTPORT
pop 200

If sleepy Westport feels on the peaceful edge of nowhere, that's because it is. The last hamlet before the Lost Coast (p127), on a twisting 15-mile drive north of Fort Bragg, it is the last town before Hwy 1 veers inland on the 22-mile ascent to meet Hwy 101 in Leggett. (For details on accessing the Lost Coast's southernmost reaches from Westport, see entry on Usal Beach Campground, p128.)

Sleeping & Eating

Westport-Union Landing State Beach (☎ 707-937-5804; campsites $25) This beach extends along 3 miles of rugged coastline. It's mostly a primitive campground (with water), but a rough hiking trail passes by tidepools and streams, accessible at low tide.

Westport Inn & Deli (☎ 707-964-5135; 37040 N Hwy 1; r $60) For in-town accommodations, the recently remodeled inn has six simple rooms. This makes a good, uncomplicated staging area for the Lost Coast.

Howard Creek Ranch (☎ 707-964-6725; www.howardcreekranch.com; 40501 N Hwy 1; r $75-125, ste $155-185) This rugged B&B occupies 60 stunning acres of forest and farmland abutting the wilderness and is a genuinely isolated getaway. Guests stay in an 1880s farmhouse or carriage barn, all with detailed redwood rooms handcrafted by the owners. If you're in a hurry or expecting the frilly B&B thing, look elsewhere, as the proprietress, Sally, moves at her own pace. In the spring, there's usually a couple of heart-melting baby lambs in the barnyard. All room rates include breakfast.

INLAND HIGHWAY 101

To get into the most remote and wild parts of the North Coast on the quick, eschew winding Hwy 1 for inland Hwy 101, which runs north from San Francisco as a freeway, then as a two- or four-lane highway north of Sonoma County, occasionally pausing under the traffic lights of small towns. If you're on a budget, consider staying along 101 – but understand that you're trading atmosphere for price.

Know that escaping the Bay Area at rush hours (weekdays between 4pm and 7pm) ain't easy. You might sit bumper-to-bumper through Santa Rosa or Willits, where trucks bound for the coast turn onto Hwy 20.

HOPLAND
pop 2231

One hundred miles north of San Francisco, little Hopland is a quaint gateway to Mendocino County's Wine Country, with worthy tasting rooms. Spend an hour getting lost in (and eating your way through) the **Fetzer Vineyards Organic Gardens** (☎ 800-846-8637; www.fetzer.com; 13601 Eastside Rd; ☒ 9am-5pm), possibly the most gorgeous meandering gardens in Northern California, attached to a winery that sets a high standard for sustainable wine growing; from Hwy 101, turn east onto Hwy 175 and drive one mile. The progressive, futuristic 12-acre campus of **Real Goods Solar Living Center** (☎ 707-744-2100; www.solarliving.org; 13771 S Hwy 101; ☒ 10am-7pm; ♿) greets visitors at the south end of town. There's no charge but the suggested donation is $1 to $5.

If you're spending the night in town, your only choice is a good one: the 1890 **Hopland Inn** (☎ 707-744-1890, 800-266-1891; www.hoplandinn.com; 13401 S Hwy 101; r $110-140; ☒). Enjoy bevvies from the full bar downstairs in their cozy, wood-paneled library. For no-frills American fare in burly portions, hit the **Bluebird Café** (☎ 707-744-1633; 13340 S Hwy 101; breakfast & lunch $5-10, dinner $10-15; ☒ 7am-2pm Mon-Thu, 8am-8pm Fri-Sun; ♿).

UKIAH
pop 15,497

As the county seat and Mendocino's largest city, Ukiah is mostly a utilitarian stop for travelers to refuel the car and get a bite.

But, if you have to stop here for the night, you could do much worse; there are a plethora of cookie-cutter hotel chains, some cheaper midcentury motels and a handful of good dining options. The coolest attractions, a pair of thermal springs and a sprawling campus for Buddhist studies, lie outside the city limits.

Sights & Activities

The warm springs at the **Vichy Hot Springs Resort** (☎ 707-462-9515; www.vichysprings.com; 2605 Vichy Springs Rd; RV campsites $20, lodge s/d $135/195, creekside r $195/245, cottages from $280; ☒ ♿) are the only naturally carbonated mineral baths in North America; two-hour day-use costs $30, all day runs to $38. There's a communal kitchen. Unlike Orr, it also requires swimwear (you might be thankful).

If you can't imagine soaking with a suit on, **Orr Hot Springs** (☎ 707-462-6277; hotwater@pacific.net; campsites $45-50, dm $55-65, s $100-175, d $135-155, cottages $185-215; ☒ 10am-10pm), the crunchy cousin to Vichy, is *the* place for back-to-the-land hipsters and backpackers who like to get naked. Rates include access to the communal redwood hot tub, private porcelain tubs, outdoor tile-and-rock heated pools, sauna, spring-fed rock-bottom swimming pool, steam, massage and magical gardens. There's also a communal kitchen. Day use costs $25; reservations are required. From Hwy 101 in Ukiah, take N State St exit, go north a quarter of a mile to Orr Springs Rd, then 9 miles west. The steep, winding mountain road takes 30 minutes to drive. (Continue westward, via Comptche–Ukiah Rd and you'll wind up in Mendocino, p113.)

City of Ten Thousand Buddhas (☎ 707-462-0939; www.cttbusa.org; 2001 Talmage Rd; ☒ 8am-6pm) is a sprawling 488-acre Chinese-Buddhist community on the grounds of a former state mental hospital, three miles east of Ukiah, via Talmage Rd. Don't miss the temple hall (which really does have 10,000 Buddhas!) or lunch in the vegetarian **restaurant** (4951 Bodhi Way; dishes $6-9; ☒ 11am-3pm Mon, Wed & Thu, to 6pm Fri-Sun; Ⓥ).

Sleeping & Eating

Our favorite two places to stay in the area are Vichy Hot Springs Resort or Orr Hot Springs (above), but there are plenty of options for those just passing through. The bright lights of chains draw cars from the highway, but the best independent options are the budget-friendly **Sunrise Inn** (☎ 707-462-6601; www.sunriseinn.net; 650 S State St; r $48-68; 🐾) and **Discovery Inn Motel** (☎ 707-462-8873; www .5motels.com; 1340 N State St; r $85-90; 🐾 🖹) with a big pool and clean (if tired-looking) rooms.

For tasty dishes, and sandwiches on crusty bread, **Schat's Courthouse Bakery & Café** (☎ 707-462-1670; 113 W Perkins St; lunch $3-7, dinner $8-14; ☺ 6am-8:30pm Mon-Sat) is a good option, but for the most fun dining in town you can visit the **Ukiah Brewing Company** (☎ 707-468-5898; www.ukiahbrewingco.com; 102 S State St; dinner mains $15-25; ☺ 5:30-9pm Tue-Sat, 11:30am-2pm Thu&Fri; 🛜), where the brews are better than the food, but the dance floor rocks to live music on the weekend. Ukiah's upscale option, **Patrona** (☎ 707-462-9181; www.patronarestaurant.com; 130 W Standley St; dishes lunch $11-19, dinner $15-30; ☺ 11am-9pm Tue-Sat), serves organic, seasonal Euro-Cal cooking, but the service is a bit uneven.

WILLITS
pop 5073

Twenty miles north of Ukiah, Willits mixes tie-dyed NorCal bohos with loggers and ranchers (the high school has a bull-riding team). It's the last town before the best of the redwoods and the eastern terminus of the **Skunk Train** (☎ 707-459-5248, 866-457-5865; www .skunktrain.com), which runs between Willits and Fort Bragg (for details, see p119).

Willits is silly with motels, but choose carefully as some are downright dank. Cheaper options to consider include the way-dated but clean **Edgewood Motel** (☎ 707-459-5914; fax 707-459-4875; 1521 S Main St; r $50-60; 🐾); **Best Value Inn Holiday Lodge** (☎ 707-459-5361, 800-835-3972; www .bestvalueinn.com; 1540 S Main St; r $69-99; 🖵 🛜 🖹); or the Old West–themed **Old West Inn** (☎ 707-459-4201, 800-700-7659; fax 707-459-3009; 1221 S Main St; r $69-89; 🐾 🖹). The upmarket option, **Baechtel Creek Inn & Spa** (☎ 707-459-9063, 800-459-9911; www .baechtelcreekinn.com; 101 Gregory Lane; r $109-149; 🐾 🖵 🛜 🖹 🐾), is further off the highway (quieter) and has a surprisingly nice day spa.

Breakfast at **Ardella's Kitchen** (☎ 707-459-6577; 35 E Commercial St; meals $5-8; ☺ 6am-noon Tue-Sat) might be the best reason to spend the night in town. Try the smoked pork and eggs with homemade crispy tortilla strips or a triple smoked omelet with gouda, smoked chicken and bacon. It's all sided with crunchy toast and homemade seasonal jams.

SOUTHERN REDWOOD COAST

There's some real magic in the loamy soil and misty air 'beyond the redwood curtain'; it yields the tallest trees and most potent herb on the planet. North of Fort Bragg, Bay Area weekenders and antique-stuffed B&Bs give way to lumber wars, pot farmers and an army of carved bears. The 'growing' culture here is intense and the huge profit it brings to the region has evident cultural side effects – an omnipresent population of transients who work the harvests, a chilling respect for 'No Trespassing' signs and a political culture that is an uneasy balance between gun-toting libertarians, ultra-left progressives and typical college-town chaos. Nevertheless, the reason to visit is to soak in the magnificent landscape, which runs through a number of pristine, ancient redwood forests.

LEGGETT
pop 350

Hwy 1 ends and redwood country begins at Leggett, home to little more than an expensive gas station, a good pizza joint with beer, and two markets. The town center is just off Hwy 1, though if you don't need to gas up, keep moving.

The first (and best) of the drive-thru trees in the region, **Chandelier Drive-Thru Tree Park** (☎ 707-925-6363; Drive-Thru Tree Rd; per car $5; ☺ 8am-dusk; 🔥) boasts a 315ft-tall, 2000-year-old redwood with a square driveway carved out, large enough to accommodate a Chevy Suburban. It sits among 200 private acres of virgin redwoods with pretty picnicking and some domesticated geese.

The 1949 tourist trap of **Confusion Hill** (☎ 707-925-6456; www.confusionhill.com; 75001 N Hwy 101; adult/child gravity house $5/4, train rides $7/5; ☺ 9am-6pm summer, 10am-5pm winter; 🔥) is an enduring curiosity and the most elaborate of the old-fashioned stops that line the route north. The gravity house challenges queasy visitors to keep their balance while standing at a 40-degree angle (a rad photo op). Kids and fans of kitsch go nuts for the playhouse quality of the space and the narrow-gauge train rides are exciting for toddlers.

Peg House (☎ 707-925-6444; 69501 Hwy 101; ☺ 8am-9pm), just north of Leggett, is the best supplier of groceries, sandwiches and cookies. It also offers BBQ food in the garden most afternoons. For diner food and pizza, head to the center of town.

RICHARDSON GROVE STATE PARK

Fifteen miles north, **Richardson Grove** (☎ 707-247-3318; Hwy 101; per car $8; 🤝) occupies 1400 acres of virgin forest. Many trees are over 1000 years old and 300ft tall, including one of the 10 tallest trees in the world. The hiking trails are better further north, but plunging into Eel River's chilly South Fork is a thrilling way to beat the heat of the drive. The park is primarily a **campground** (☎ reservations 800-444-7275; www.reserveamerica.com; campsites $35-45) and has three separate areas with hot showers; some remain open year-round. Summer-only Oak Flat on the east side of the river is shady and has a sandy beach.

BENBOW LAKE

On the Eel River, 2 miles south of Garberville, the 1200-acre **Benbow Lake State Recreation Area** (☎ summer 707-923-3238, winter 707-923-3318; per car $8) exists when a seasonal dam forms the 26-acre Benbow Lake, mid-June to mid-September. In mid-August, avoid swimming in the lake or river until two weeks after the Reggae on the River festival (p126), when 25,000 people use the river as a bathtub. The water is cleanest in early summer. The year-round riverside **campground** (☎ reservations 800-444-7775; www.reserveamerica.com; campsites $35-45) is subject to wintertime bridge closures due to flooding.

A monument to 1920s rustic elegance, **Benbow Inn** (☎ 707-923-2124, 800-355-3301; www.benbowinn.com; 445 Lake Benbow Dr; r $135-489, cottages $395; 🟦 🟦) is a national historic landmark and the Redwood Empire's first luxury resort. Hollywood's elite once frolicked in the Tudor-style resort's lobby, where you can play chess by the crackling fire and enjoy complimentary afternoon tea and evening hors d'oeuvres. Rooms are appointed with antique furniture, a decanter of sherry and a basket of paperbacks. The window-lined dining room (breakfast and lunch $10 to $15, dinner mains $22 to $32) serves good Euro-Cal cuisine and Sunday brunch. There's an adjoining golf course and tidy RV park.

GARBERVILLE
pop 2403

The main supply center for southern Humboldt County is the primary jumping-off point for both the Lost Coast, to the west, and the Avenue of the Giants, to the north. There's an uneasy relationship between the old-guard loggers and the

TOP FIVE ROMANTIC HIDEAWAYS ON THE REDWOOD COAST

- **Tides Inn** (p128)
- **Historic Requa Inn** (p149)
- **Benbow Inn** (p125)
- **Carter House** (p136)
- **Casa Rubio** (p153)

---

hippies, many of whom came in the 1970s to grow sinsemilla (potent, seedless marijuana) after the feds chased them out of Santa Cruz. At last count, the hippies were winning the culture wars, but it rages on: a sign on the door of a local bar reads simply: 'Absolutely NO patchouli oil!!!' Two miles west, Garberville's ragtag sister, Redway, has fewer services, but a noteworthy restaurant. Garberville is about four hours north of San Francisco, one hour south of Eureka.

Information

Garberville-Redway Area Chamber of Commerce (☎ 707-923-2613, 800-923-2613; www.garberville.org; 784 Redwood Dr; ☼ 8am-4pm Mon-Fri, 10am-4pm Sat & Sun Jul-Sep) Inside the Redwood Drive Center; has tourist information.

KMUD FM91 Find out what's really happening by tuning in to community radio.

Friends of the Eel River Information Center & Gift Shop (☎ 707-923-2146, www.eelriver.org; 915 Redwood Dr, Ste E; ☼ 8am-4pm Mon-Fri, 10am-4pm Sat) An excellent resource on enjoying the river with sensitivity for the environment.

Sights & Activities

The area's sights and activities are in surrounding parks and on the Lost Coast (opposite). If you want to kayak down the Eel River, visit **Tsunami Surf & Sport** (☎ 707-923-1965; www.tsunamisurfandsport.com; 445 Conger; ☼ Mon-Sat).

Festivals & Events

Reggae on the River (☎ 707-923-4583; www.reggae ontheriver.com) in early August draws huge crowds of dreadlocked world music lovers who camp along and swim in the river. Three-day passes ($175) go on sale March 1 and sell out fast; no single tickets. This is by far the North Coast's biggest event.

Other annual events:

Avenue of the Giants Marathon (www.theave.org) Early May. One of the most scenic foot races in the world.

Summer Arts & Music Festival Early June event at Benbow Lake.

Harley-Davidson Redwood Run (www.redwoodrun .com) Held in mid-June.

Humboldt Hempfest Celebrate all things hemp in mid-November.

Sleeping

Prices drop significantly in winter. Though generic, the **Best Western Humboldt House Inn** (☎ 707-923-2771, 800-528-1234; 701 Redwood Dr; r $119-129; ☒ ☒) is by far the best place in town, with good beds, upgraded furnishings and refrigerators. Call ahead, as it fills nearly every night in summer. **Redwoods Getaway** (☎ 707-923-2061; www.redwoodsgetaway.com; Redway; house $200) is a three-bedroom house right on the Eel River; book in advance.

For cheaper lodging, there are two satisfactory motels. First try **Sherwood Forest** (☎ 707-923-2721; www.sherwoodforestmotel.com; 814 Redwood Dr; r $66-84; ☒ ☒), then **Humboldt Redwoods Inn** (☎ 707-923-2451; www.humboldt redwoodsinn.com; 987 Redwood Dr; r $59-95; ☒ ☒), but the desk clerks are hardly ever there, so call ahead.

Eating

Chautauqua Natural Foods (☎ 707-923-2452; 436 Church St; sandwiches & lunch plates $5-10; ☼ Mon-Sat) Sells natural groceries. It has a small dining area and a great bulletin board.

Nacho Mama (☎ 707-923-4060; 375 Sprowel Creek Rd; meals under $6; ☼ 11am-7pm Mon-Sat) This tiny shack on the corner of Redwood Dr has organic fast-food Mexican. Tops for budget eats.

Calico's Deli & Pasta (☎ 707-923-2253; 808 Redwood Dr; dishes $6-13; ☼ 11am-9pm; ☖) Calico's has house-made pasta and sandwiches, which is good if you're with kids or want a hot dinner for 10 bucks, but don't be surprised if there's water on the plate under your noodles.

Woodrose Café (☎ 707-923-3191; 911 Redwood Dr; meals $7-11; ☼ 7am-1pm; ☖) Garberville's beloved cafe serves organic omelettes, veggie scrambles and buckwheat pancakes with *real* maple syrup in a cozy room. Lunch brings crunchy salads, sandwiches with all-natural meats and good burritos. There's lots for vegetarians too. Too bad it's closed at dinner. No credit cards.

Mateel Café (☎ 707-923-2030; 3342-3344 Redwood Dr, Redway; lunch $8-12, dinner $20-26; ☺ 11:30am-9pm Mon-Sat) The big, diverse menu of this Redway joint includes a rack of lamb, stone-baked pizzas and terrific salads. There's pleasant patio seating out back.

Cecil's New Orleans Bistro (☎ 707-923-7007; 733 Redwood Dr; dinner $20-26; ☺ dinner Thu-Mon) After the Woodrose and the Mateel Café (in Redway), Garberville's best by a long shot is this 2nd story eatery that overlooks Main St and serves ambitious dishes that may have minted the California-Cajun style. The fried green tomatoes are a good place to start before launching into the smoked boar gumbo. The cocktail menu is also excellent and they frequently host live music.

LOST COAST

The North Coast's superlative backpacking destination is a rugged, mystifying stretch of coast where narrow dirt trails ascend rugged coastal peaks and volcanic beaches of black sand, ethereal mist hovers above the roaring surf and majestic Roosevelt Elk graze the forests. Here, the rugged King Range boldly rises 4000ft within 3 miles of the coast between where Hwy 1 cuts inland north of Westport to just south of Ferndale. The coast became 'lost' when the state's highway system deemed the region impassable in the early 20th century.

The best hiking and camping is within the King Range National Conservation Area and the Sinkyone Wilderness State Park, which make up the central and southern stretch of the region. The area north of the King Range is more accessible, if less dramatic.

In autumn, the weather is clear and cool. Wildflowers bloom from April through May and gray whales migrate from December through April. The warmest, driest months are June to August, but days are foggy. Note that the weather can quickly change.

Information

Aside from a few one-horse villages, Shelter Cove, the isolated unincorporated town 25 long miles west of Garberville, is the option for services. Get supplies in Garberville, Fort Bragg, Eureka or Arcata. The area is a patchwork of government-owned land and private property; visit the Bureau of Land Management office (p128) for information, permits and maps. There are few circuitous routes for hikers, and rangers can advise on reliable (if expensive) shuttle services in the area. A few words of caution: lots of weed is grown around here and it's wise to stay on trail to respect no trespassing signs, lest you find yourself at the business end of someone's right to bear arms. Also, pot farmers don't pose the only threat; you'll want to check for ticks (Lyme disease is common) and keep food in bear-proof containers, which are required for camping.

SHELTER COVE

pop 500

The only sizable community on the Lost Coast, Shelter Cove is surrounded by the King Range National Conservation Area and abuts a large south-facing cove. It's a tiny seaside subdivision with an airstrip in the middle – indeed, many visitors are private pilots. Fifty years ago, Southern California swindlers subdivided the land, built the airstrip and flew in potential investors, fast-talking them into buying seaside land for retirement. But they didn't tell buyers that a steep, winding, one-lane dirt road provided the *only* access and that the seaside plots were eroding into the sea.

Today, there's still only one route, but now it's paved. Cell phones don't work here: this is a good place to disappear. The town is a mild disappointment, with not much to do, but stunning **Black Sands Beach** stretches for miles northward.

Sleeping

Shelter Cove has some plain motels and decent inns, but camping is far and away the best way to spend the night here.

Shelter Cove RV Park, Campground & Deli (☎ 707-986-7474; 492 Machi Rd; tent/RV sites $25/35) The services may be basic, but the fresh gusts of ocean air can't be beat – the deli has good fish and chips.

Shelter Cove Beachcomber Inn (☎ 707-986-7551, 800-718-4789; www.sojourner2000.com; 412 Machi Rd; r $65-105) Slightly inland, the Beachcomber Inn has some rooms with kitchens and wood-burning stoves; all have BBQ and picnic tables. They could use upgrades, but they're a bargain.

Oceanfront Inn & Lighthouse (☎ 707-986-7002; www.sheltercoveoceanfrontinn.com; 10 Seal Court;

r $135-165, ste $195) The tidy, modern rooms here have microwaves, refrigerators and balconiesoverlooking the sea. The decor is spartan so as not to detract from the view. Splurge on a kitchen suite; the best is upstairs, with its peaked ceiling and giant windows.

our pick **The Tides Inn** (☎ 707-986-7900, 888-998-4377; www.sheltercovetidesinn.com; 59 Surf Point Rd; r $155-345; ☎ ⚕) Perched above tidepools teeming with starfish and sea urchins, this is the top-choice indoor sleeping in Shelter Cove. The squeaky clean rooms offer excellent views (go for the mini suites on the 3rd floor). The suite options are good for families, and kids are greeted warmly by the innkeeper with an activity kit.

Inn of the Lost Coast (☎ 707-986-7521, 888-570-9676; www.innofthelostcoast.com; 205 Wave Dr; r $160-250) This recently remodeled inn has breathtaking ocean views and clean rooms; downstairs there's a serviceable take-out pizza place.

Eating

Be warned: there isn't a single joint open for breakfast in Shelter Cove; self-catering is essential. The first-choice place to eat, **Cove Restaurant** (☎ 707-986-1197; 10 Seal Court; dishes $6-19; ☷ dinner Thu-Sun), has everything from veggie stir-fries to New York steaks. For those who are self-catering, **Shelter Cove General Store** (☎ 707-986-7733; 7272 Shelter Cove Rd) is 2 miles beyond town. Get groceries and gasoline here.

SINKYONE WILDERNESS STATE PARK

Named for the Sinkyone people who once lived here, this 7367-acre wilderness extends south of Shelter Cove along pristine coastline. The **Lost Coast Trail** continues here for another 22 miles, from Whale Gulch south to Usal Beach Campground, taking at least three days to walk as it meanders along high ridges, providing bird's-eye views down to deserted beaches and the crashing surf; side trails descend to water level. Near the park's northern end, the (haunted!) **Needle Rock Ranch** (☎ 707-986-7711; campsites $35) serves as a remote visitors center. Register here for the adjacent campsites ($25 to $35). This is the only source of potable water. For information when the ranch is closed (most of the time), call **Richardson Grove State Park** (☎ 707-247-3318).

To get to Sinkyone, drive west from Garberville and Redway on Briceland-Thorn

Rd, 21 miles through Whitethorn to Four Corners. Turn left (south) and continue for 3.5 miles down a very rugged road to the ranch house; it takes 1½ hours.

There's access to the **Usal Beach Campground** (campsites $25) at the south end of the park from Hwy 1 (you can't make reservations): north of Westport, unpaved County Rd 431 begins from Hwy 1's Mile 90.88 and travels 6 miles up the coast to the campground. The road is graded yearly in late spring and is passable in summer via two-wheel-drive vehicle. Most sites are past the message board by the beach. Use bear canisters or keep food in your trunk. Look for giant elk feeding on the tall grass – they live behind sites No 1 and 2 – and osprey by the creek's mouth.

North of the campground, Usal Rd (County Rd 431) is much rougher and recommended only if you have a high-clearance 4WD and a chainsaw. Seriously.

KING RANGE NATIONAL CONSERVATION AREA

Stretching over 35 miles of virgin coastline, with ridge after ridge of mountainous terrain plunging to the surf, the 60,000-acre area tops out at namesake King's Peak (4087ft). The wettest spot in California, the range receives over 120 inches – and as much as 240 inches – of annual rainfall, causing frequent landslides; in winter snow falls on the ridges. (By contrast, nearby sea-level Shelter Cove gets only 69 inches of rain and no snow.) Two-thirds of the area is awaiting wilderness designation.

Nine miles east of Shelter Cove, the **Bureau of Land Management** (BLM; ☎ 707-986-5400, 707-825-2300; 768 Shelter Cove Rd; ☷ 8am-4:30pm Mon-Sat Memorial Day-Labor Day, 8am-4:30pm Mon-Fri May-Sep) has maps and directions for trails and campsites; they're posted outside after hours. For overnight hikes, you'll need a backcountry-use permit. Don't turn left onto Briceland-Thorn Rd to try to find the 'town' of Whitethorn; it doesn't exist. Whitethorn is the BLM's name for the *general* area. To reach the BLM office from Garberville/Redway, follow signs to Shelter Cove; look for the roadside information panel, 0.25 miles past the post office. Information and permits are also available from the BLM in Arcata (p138).

Fire restrictions begin July 1 and last until the first soaking rain, usually in November.

During this time, there are no campfires allowed outside developed campgrounds.

Hiking
The best way to see the Lost Coast is to hike. Some of the best trails start from Mattole Campground, near Petrolia. It's at the ocean end of Lighthouse Rd, 4 miles from Mattole Rd (sometimes marked as Hwy 211), southeast of Petrolia.

The **Lost Coast Trail** follows 24.7 miles of coastline from Mattole Campground in the north to Black Sands Beach at Shelter Cove in the south. The prevailing northerly winds make it best to hike from north to south; plan for three or four days. In October and November, and April and May, the weather is iffy and winds can blow south to north, depending on whether there's a low-pressure system overhead. The best times to come are summer weekdays in early June, at the end of August, September and October. The trail will often have hikers; busiest times are Memorial Day, Labor Day and summer weekends. Only two shuttles have permits to transport backpackers through the area, **Lost Coast Trail Transport Services** (☎ 707-986-9909; www.lostcoast trail.com) or the more reliable **Lost Coast Shuttle** (☎ 707-223-1547; www.lostcoastshuttle.com). Neither is cheap; prices for the ride between Mattole and Black Sands Beach start at $100 per person with a two-person minimum.

Highlights include an abandoned lighthouse at Punta Gorda, remnants of early shipwrecks, tidepools and abundant wildlife including sea lions, seals and some 300 bird species. The trail is mostly level, passing beaches and crossing over rocky outcrops. Along the Lost Coast Trail, **Big Flat** is the most popular backcountry destination. Carry a tide table, lest you get trapped: from Buck Creek to Miller Creek, you can only hike during an outgoing tide.

A good **day hike** starts at the Mattole Campground trailhead and travels 3 miles south along the coast to the Punta Gorda lighthouse (return against the wind).

People have discovered the Lost Coast Trail. To ditch the crowds, take any of the (strenuous) upland trails off the beach toward the ridgeline. For a satisfying, hard 21-mile-long hike originating at the Lost Coast Trail, take Buck Creek Trail to King Crest Trail to Rattlesnake Ridge Trail.

The 360 degree views from **King Peak** are stupendous, particularly with a full moon or during a meteor shower. Note that if you hike up, it can be hellish hot on the ridges, though the coast remains cool and foggy; wear removable layers. Carry a topographical map and a compass: signage is limited.

Both Wailaki and Nadelos have developed **campgrounds** (campsites $8) with toilets and water. There are another four developed campgrounds around the range, with toilets but no water (except Honeydew, which has purifiable creek water). There are multiple primitive walk-in sites. You'll need a bear canister and backcountry permit, both available from BLM offices.

NORTH OF THE KING RANGE
Though it's less of an adventure, you can reach the Lost Coast's northern section year-round via paved, narrow Mattole Rd. Plan three hours to navigate the sinuous 68 miles from Ferndale in the north to the coast at Cape Mendocino, then inland to Humboldt Redwoods State Park and Hwy 101. Don't expect redwoods: the vegetation is grassland and pasture. It's beautiful in spots – lined sweeping vistas and wildflowers that are prettiest in spring.

You'll pass two tiny settlements, both 19th-century stage-coach stops. **Petrolia** has an all-in-one **store** (☎ 707-629-3455; ⊙ 9am-5pm) which rents bear canisters and sells supplies for the trail, good beer and gasoline. **Honeydew** also has a **general store** (☎ 707-629-3310; ⊙ 9am-5pm). The drive is enjoyable, but the Lost Coast's wild, spectacular scenery lies further south in the more remote regions.

There's creekside camping with flush toilets and cold showers at the developed **AW Way County Park** (☎ 707-445-7651; Mattole Rd; per vehicle $15), which is 6 miles southeast of Petrolia, on the road toward Honeydew.

HUMBOLDT REDWOODS STATE PARK & AVENUE OF THE GIANTS
Of all of California's redwood parks, **Humboldt Redwoods State Park** (☎ 707-946-2409) packs the biggest punch, if only because it's easily accessible by car. The park covers 53,000 acres – 17,000 of which are old-growth – and protects some of the world's most magnificent trees, including 74 of the 100 tallest.

If you're anywhere near the area, exit Hwy 101 at the **Avenue of the Giants** to travel through the park. The incredible 32 miles of two-lane blacktop is parallel to Hwy 101, under the canopy of the world's tallest trees. All perspective gets lost in the shadow of these stately trunks; suddenly the other cars on the road seem like toys. If you have the inclination, the route is perfect for cycling, with smooth pavement and moderate elevation changes. A string of small towns line the drive, with chances to get deli food, gas up and shop for redwood carved knick-knacks. Free guides are at roadside sign-boards at the Avenue's southern entrance, 6 miles north of Garberville (Hwy 101 Exit 645), and at the northern entrance, south of Scotia (Hwy 101 Exit 674); there are access points off Hwy 101. Driving the Avenue instead of Hwy 101 adds only 15 minutes to your northbound travel time.

South of Weott, a volunteer-staffed **visitors center** (☎ 707-946-2263; ◷ 9am-5pm summer, 10am-4pm winter; ♿) has picnic areas, a small **museum** littered with cool taxidermy, exhibits and seasonal kids' programs. The *pièce de résistance* is the historic 1917 'Travel Log,' a full-size RV made from the trunk of a carved-out redwood.

Primeval **Rockefeller Forest**, 4.5 miles west of the Avenue via Mattole Rd, appears as it did a century ago. It's the world's largest contiguous old-growth redwood forest and contains about 20% of all such remaining trees. In **Founders Grove**, north of the visitors center, the **Dyerville Giant** was knocked over in 1991 by another falling tree. A walk along its gargantuan 370ft length, with its humongous trunk towering above, helps you appreciate how huge these ancient trees are.

Walking Trails

The park has over 100 miles of trails for hiking, mountain biking and horseback riding. Trails are muddy and may be brush-covered until mid-June, when seasonal river bridges go up. Easy walks include short nature trails in Founders Grove and Rockefeller Forest and the **Drury-Chaney Loop Trail**. The **Bull Creek Flats Trail** is the only trail that loops through the heart of the contiguous old-growth forest – and it's moderately easy. Schedule half a day and plan to swim in the creek (summer only). The most challenging is the **Grasshopper Peak Trail**, south of the visitors center, which climbs to the 3379ft fire lookout.

Sleeping & Eating

Several towns along the avenue have simple motels – but choose wisely: some are a bit creepy and some are run by people not exactly tolerant of difference. Those with the right equipment may prefer to camp. If you're not traveling with gear, look into a rental at REI (www.rei.com; p274) or Northern Mountain Supply in Eureka (p135).

Campgrounds (☎ reservations 800-444-7275; www .reserveamerica.com; tent sites $5-20, campsites $35-55) The park runs three campgrounds with hot showers, two environmental camps, five trail camps, a hike-bike camp and an equestrian camp. One of the three, Burlington, is beside the visitors center and

---

CHOP IT, CARVE IT, DRIVE A CAR THROUGH IT: REDWOOD ODDITIES

Driving along the Redwood Coast is a bit like taking a time machine back to the days when the concept of conserving redwoods was as absurd as driving a car through one seems today. Aside from gaping at the region's majestic wood, here are some alternative ways to spend time in the redwoods, literally.

■ **Chandelier Drive-Thru Tree Park** (p124) Our favorite drive-through tree, one of three up the coast. If you miss it on the ride north, look for other redwoods to drive through in Meyer's Flat and Klamath.

■ **Confusion Hill** (p124) The giant bear totem that stands in front of this corny tourist trap is the largest freestanding redwood chainsaw carving in the world.

■ **Trees of Mystery** (p148) Is that Abe Lincoln with an axe? No! It's Paul Bunyan. Here, one of the world's largest trees was carved into the world's largest lumberjack.

■ **Curly Redwood Lodge** (p150) This entire motel was carved from a single redwood and has been restored in mid-century modern style.

is open year-round. It's near trailheads and the road, but it's in the redwoods and kids like it. The other two are open mid-May to early autumn. Hidden Springs, 5 miles south, is on oak mountainsides with sites surrounded by brush; it has more privacy and the best swimming. Albee Creek, on Mattole Rd past Rockefeller Forest, is the prettiest, with meadows and apple orchards where wildlife comes to feed; it's nearest the backcountry trailheads.

Riverwood Inn (☎ 707-943-3333; www.riverwood inn.info; 2828 Ave of the Giants, Phillipsville; r $78-95; ✷ 4:30-10pm Mon-Thu, 11am-10pm Fri-Sun). Harley riders love this raucous, haunted roadhouse near Garberville. The bar turns out potent drinks and Mexican food, which is good but probably not quite the advertised 'best in the world.' Rooms are clean enough but not recommended if a band is banging out blues downstairs.

Miranda Gardens Resort (☎ 707-943-3011; www .mirandagardens.com; 6766 Ave of the Giants, Miranda; cottages $105-185, with kitchen $165-265; ✷) One of the best resorts in the area and family friendly. The cozy, slightly rustic cottages have redwood paneling; some have fireplaces. They're a tad musty – as is everything under the redwoods – but the bathrooms are clean and there's a pool. Across the street there's a family restaurant.

our pick Vacation House in the Redwoods (☎ 707-722-4330; www.floodplainproduce.com; 31117 Ave of the Giants, Pepperwood; house $135) This is a lovely one-bedroom cottage surrounded by a sunny flower farm. It sleeps up to five. A hammock, deck and hot tub sweeten the deal.

Avenue Café (☎ 707-943-9945; 6743 Ave of the Giants, Miranda; ✷ 8am-9pm Mon-Sat, to 1pm Sun; ✷) With a straightforward menu and a cheery staff, they turn out good burgers and one helluva breakfast burrito ($7).

Eternal Treehouse Café (☎ 707-722-4247; 2650 Ave of the Giants, Redcrest; ✷ 8:30am-6:30pm; ✷) With stick-to-your-ribs biscuits and gravy, and dinner staples, this is an old-school stop along the Avenue that's good for families. The 'Hungry Logger' breakfast ($8) is not to be trifled with.

SCOTIA
pop 1117

For years, Scotia was California's last 'company town,' entirely owned and operated by the Pacific Lumber Company, which built cookie-cut houses and had an open contempt for long-haired outsiders who liked to get between their saws and the big trees. They recently went belly up, sold the mill to another redwood company and, though the town still has a creepy *Twilight Zone* vibe, you no longer have to operate by the company's posted 'Code of Conduct.' A history of the town awaits at the **Scotia Museum & Visitors Center** (☎ 707-764-2222; www .palco.com; cnr Main & Bridge Sts; ✷ 8am-4:30pm Mon-Fri summer), at the town's south end. The museum's **fisheries center** is remarkably informative – ironic, considering that logging destroys fish habitats – and houses the largest freshwater aquarium on the North Coast.

There are dingy motels and diners in **Rio Dell** (aka 'Real Dull'), across the river. Back in the day, this is where the debauchery happened: because it wasn't a company town, Rio Dell had bars and hookers. In 1969, the freeway bypassed the town and it withered.

As you drive along Hwy 101 and see what appears to be a never-ending redwood forest, understand that this 'forest' sometimes consists of trees only a few rows deep – called a 'beauty strip' – a carefully crafted illusion for tourists. Most old-growth trees have been cut. **Bay Area Coalition for Headwaters Forest** (www.headwaterspreserve.org) helped preserve over 7000 acres of land with public funds through provisions in a long negotiated agreement between the Pacific Lumber Company and state and federal agencies.

Up Hwy 101 there's a great pit stop at **Eel River Brewing** (☎ 707-725-2739; 1777 Alamar Way, Fortuna; ✷ 11am-midnight, to 11pm Sun), where a breezy beer garden and excellent burgers accompany all-organic brews.

FERNDALE
pop 1400

The North Coast's most charming town is stuffed with impeccable Victorians – known locally as 'butterfat mansions' because of the dairy wealth that built them. There are so many, in fact, that the entire place is a state and federal historical landmark. When Hollywood location scouts came to Ferndale, hoping to use the local fairgrounds to film *Seabiscuit,* locals balked at the idea of suspending the Humboldt County Fair, which has been held in the

NORTH COAST

same spot every year, rain or shine, since 1896. Dairy farmers built the town in the 19th century and it's still run by the 'milk mafia': you're not a local till you've lived here 40 years. A stroll down Main St offers galleries, old-world emporiums and soda fountains. Although Ferndale relies on tourism, it has avoided becoming a tourist trap – and has no chain stores. Though a lovely place to spend a summer night, it's dead as a doornail in winter.

Information

Look for free copies around town of the souvenir edition of the *Ferndale Enterprise* for walking and driving tours.

Ferndale Chamber of Commerce (☎ 707-786-4477; www.victorianferndale.com) The website has current information, or use the phone service.

Ferndale Library (☎ 707-786-9559; 807 Main St; noon-5pm & 7-9pm Tue-Thu, noon-4pm Fri, noon-5pm Sat) Free internet access, one-hour limit.

Sights & Activities

The 'butterfat' palaces that you'll want to check out should start with the **Gingerbread Mansion** (400 Berding St), an 1898 Queen Anne-Eastlake and the town's most photographed building. **Shaw House** (703 Main St) was the first permanent structure in town and houses the first post office. The 1866, 32-room **Fern Cottage** (☎ 707-786-4835; www.ferncottage.org; Centerville Rd; 10am-4pm Wed-Sun Jul-Sep), west of town, was originally a Carpenter Gothic that grew as the family did. Only one family ever lived here, so nothing got thrown away and it's all been preserved. Admission: adult/student/senior $5/2.50/4; child free. Call ahead for winter hours.

Ferndale has two museums that are very different in style. Though little ones might get a bit antsy from the pile of artifacts, slightly cheesy installations and working seismograph at the **Ferndale Museum** (☎ 707-786-4466; www.ferndale-museum.org; cnr Shaw & 3rd Sts; donation requested; 11am-4pm Wed-Sat, 1-4pm Sun), the museum's light-up diorama-style dollhouses spark the imagination. Quite a contrast is the **Kinetic Sculpture Museum** (www.kineticgrandchampionship.com; 580 Main St; 10am-5pm Mon-Sat, noon-4pm Sun;), housing fanciful, astounding kinetic sculptures used in the town's annual Kinetic Grand Championship (see the boxed text, below). This place is a real trip, and admission is free.

Half a mile from downtown via Bluff St, tramp through fields of wildflowers, along ponds, redwood and eucalyptus trees at 110-acre **Russ Park**. The **cemetery**, also on Bluff St, is worth exploring. Five miles down Centerville Rd, **Centerville Beach** is one of the few off-leash dog beaches in Humboldt County.

Festivals & Events

Contact the chamber of commerce for details of the town's festivals.

Kinetic Grand Championship (www.kineticgrandchampionship.com) The famous race is held during the Memorial Day weekend (see boxed text, below).

Humboldt County Fair (www.humboldtcountyfair.org) In mid-August; horse racing is the big event. This is an unexceptionally good county fair.

Sleeping
BUDGET
Though Ferndale's B&Bs can be heavy on the Victorian frill, it's not all old-world frou-frou.

CRAZY CONTRAPTIONS

The Kinetic Grand Championship (formerly the Kinetic Sculpture Race) was born in 1969 when Ferndale artist Hobart Brown decided to spruce up his son's tricycle to make it more interesting, creating a wobbly, five-wheeled red 'pentacycle.' Initially, five odd contraptions raced down Main St on Mother's Day, and a 10ft turtle sculpture won. The race was expanded in the early '70s and has now blossomed into a three-day, amphibious event with contraptions competing over 38 miles from Arcata to Ferndale. Held over Memorial Day weekend (late May), the race attracts thousands of spectators and usually at least a few dozen entrants (one year there were 99). Cities around the world have followed in Ferndale's footsteps, with far-flung places like Perth, Australia, now holding their own kinetic races.

A few of the race rules are as bizarre as the entrants, including 'It is legal to get assistance from the natural power of water, wind, sun, gravity and friendly extraterrestrials (if introduced to the judges prior to the race).'

Francis Creek Inn (☎ 707-786-9611; 577 Main St; r $73-83) This motel has four well-kept, pretty rooms, but shares a lot with a convenience store.

Hotel Ivanhoe (☎ 707-786-9000; www.ivanhoe -hotel.com; 315 Main St; r $95-145) Ferndale's oldest hostelry opened in 1875 and retains its Old West style for excellent value. The 2nd-floor porch overlooking downtown is perfect for morning coffee.

MIDRANGE

Collingwood Inn B&B (☎ 707-786-9219, 800-469- 1632; 831 Main St; r $110-215, cottage $300; 🛜 🐾) The cute-as-a-button 1885 Hart House has four rooms with extras like featherbeds, bathrobes, coffee delivered to your door and breakfast at your convenience. Gay friendly.

Shaw House (☎ 707-786-9958, 800-557-7429; www .shawhouse.com; 703 Main St; r $120-175, ste $200-260; 🛜 🐾) California's oldest B&B and Ferndale's first home, this storybook place is perched atop a grassy hill behind a white picket fence. The three parlors are lovely, as are the original details. Book a full breakfast or cheaper continental breakfast in advance. Pets allowed in some rooms, $35 per night.

Gingerbread Mansion Inn (☎ 707-786-4000, 800- 952-4136; www.gingerbread-mansion.com; 400 Berding St; r $160-400; 🛜) Ferndale's iconic B&B drips with gingerbread trim. The 11 exquisitely detailed rooms are decked out with high-end 1890s Victorian furnishings. Rates include high tea service, evening wine and a three-course breakfast. No kids under 12.

TOP END

Victorian Inn (☎ 707-786-4949, 888-589-1808; www .a-victorian-inn.com; 400 Ocean Ave; r $155-245, ste $245-295; 🛜) With 16ft ceilings and bright rooms, this large B&B sits in the middle of town like a big Victorian cake. Wine and cheese mingling, high-count threads and an excellent breakfast (included) make it Ferndale's most popular.

Eating

Main Street's bakeries, cafes and old-school lunch counters are a dream for families and a nightmare for those on a low-carb diet.

Ferndale Pizza Co (☎ 707-786-4345; 607 Main St; meal $5; 🕑 11am-9pm Tue-Sun; ♿) This little pizzeria turns out piping hot, crusty pies and pitchers of beer. The meatball pizza is a hedonistic highlight.

Poppa Joe's (☎ 707-786-4180; 409 Main St; dishes $5-7; 🕑 6am-2pm Mon-Fri, to noon Sat & Sun; ♿) At this wacky local mainstay, you'll go shoulder-to-shoulder with a cadre of waggish old farmers – just don't interrupt their dice game! Pancakes and breakfast burritos are excellent.

Curley's Grill (☎ 707-786-9696; 400 Ocean Ave; dishes $8-21; 🕑 11:30am-9pm Sun-Thu, to 10pm Fri & Sat) Spare yourself the trip to Eureka by ordering from a Cal-American/comfort food menu, served on bright Fiestaware and big oak tables. It can be a bit inconsistent, but when you hit it right, it's spot-on. The bar? Never misses.

Hotel Ivanhoe (☎ 707-786-9000; 315 Main St; mains $14-30; 🕑 dinner Wed-Sun) Chicken marsala is the specialty at this Victorian dinner-house and pub, but when it's available, lamb is the standout. There's prime rib on Friday and Saturday (and sometimes Sunday), and on Tuesday great beef stroganoff made with the weekend's leftover prime rib. There's a small-portions menu ($10 to $14), also available at the bar. Top choice for dinner.

Entertainment

Ferndale Repertory Theatre (☎ 707-786-5483; www.ferndale-rep.org; 447 Main St) This theater produces worthwhile shows and musicals year-round.

Shopping

Ferndale's main drag is great for window shopping and unique gifts.

Golden Gait Mercantile (☎ 707-786-4891; 421 Main St) The shelves of this old-fashioned store are filled with yesteryear's goods, as well as fun bric-a-brac and tasty jams.

Blacksmith Shop & Gallery (☎ 707-786-4216; www.ferndaleblacksmith.com; 455 & 491 Main St) From wrought-iron art to hand-forged furniture, this is the largest collection of contemporary blacksmithing in America. Of all Ferndale's shops, this one's not to be missed.

Gazebo (☎ 707-786-9853; 475 Main St) It's easy to get lost in the shelves of tasteful local crafts, mixed media art and gifts – our favorite on Ferndale's main drag.

Hobart Gallery (☎ 707-786-9259; 393 Main St) The steel, brass and copper works of the late Hobart Brown, father of kinetic racing, are stunning. It's a cozy space to shop or browse.

HUMBOLDT BAY NATIONAL WILDLIFE REFUGE

Even if you're not into bird-watching, this wildlife refuge (☎ 707-733-5406; ☼ sunrise-sunset) at the southern end of Humboldt Bay is impressive: more than 200 species of birds have habitats here, a key stop on the migratory route between North and South America. In one single day in 2004, there were a whopping 26,000 Aleutian cackling geese counted outside the visitors center!

Gulls, terns, cormorants, pelicans, egrets and herons come year-round. Peak season for waterbirds and raptors runs September to March, for black brant geese and migratory shorebirds mid-March to late April. Look for harbor seals offshore; bring binoculars.

Pick up a map from the **visitors center** (1020 Ranch Rd; ☼ 8am-5pm). It highlights two 30-minute interpretive walks. Exit Hwy 101 at Hookton Rd (Exit 696), 11 miles south of Eureka, and turn north along the frontage road on the freeway's west side. In April, look for the **Godwit Days festival** (www.godwitdays.com).

EUREKA

pop 26,097
One hour north of Garberville, on the edge of the giant Humboldt Bay, lies Eureka, the largest bay north of San Francisco. With strip-mall sprawl surrounding a lovely historic downtown, it wears its role as the county seat a bit clumsily. Despite a diverse and interesting community of artists, writers, pagans and other free-thinkers, Eureka's wild side slips out only occasionally; mostly, it goes to bed early. Make for Old Town, a small district with colorful Victorians, good shopping and a revitalized waterfront. For night life, head to Eureka's trippy sister up the road, Arcata.

Orientation & Information

Streets lie on a grid; numbered streets cross lettered streets. For the best window-shopping, head to 2nd St between D and G Sts. There's a California Welcome Center in Arcata (p138).

Eureka Chamber of Commerce (☎ 707-442-3738, 800-356-6381; www.eurekachamber.com; 2112 Broadway; ☼ Mon-Fri) This is the main visitors information center and is located on Hwy 101.

Eureka-Humboldt County Convention & Visitors Bureau (☎ 707-443-5097, 800-346-3482;

www.redwoods.info; 1034 2nd St; ☼ Mon-Fri) Has maps and brochures.

Going Places (☎ 707-443-4145; 328 2nd St) Travel-oriented bookstore. One of three excellent bookshops in Old Town.

Pride Enterprises Tours (☎ 707-445-2117, 800-400-1849) Local historian leads outstanding personalized tours. Licensed to guide in the national parks.

Six Rivers National Forest Headquarters (☎ 707-442-1721; 1330 Bayshore Way; ☼ Mon-Fri) Has maps and information.

Sights

The free *Eureka Visitors Map*, available at tourist offices, details architectural and historical walking tours and drives. Old Town, along 2nd and 3rd Sts, from C St to M St, was once Eureka's down-and-out area, but has been refurbished into an inviting pedestrian district of galleries, shops, cafes and restaurants. The F Street Plaza and Boardwalk run along the waterfront at the foot of F St.

The **Romano Gabriel Wooden Sculpture Garden** (315 2nd St) is the coolest thing to gawk at – a collection of whimsical outsider art that's enclosed by glass, between D and E Sts. For 30 years, wooden characters in Gabriel's front yard delighted locals. After he died in 1977, the city moved the collection here.

The hands-on **Discovery Museum** (☎ 707-443-9694; www.discovery-museum.org; 517 3rd St; admission $4; ☼ 10am-4pm Tue-Sat, noon-4pm Sun; ♿) is the best of its kind on the North Coast and ideal for little kids.

To get to the source of the area's Victorian charm, come to **Blue Ox Millworks & Historic Park** (☎ 707-444-3437, 800-248-4259; www.blueoxmill.com; 1 X St; adult/child $7.50/3.50; ☼ 9am-4pm Mon-Sat; ♿). This millworks is one of a small handful of such places in the United States that uses antique tools and mills to produce authentic gingerbread trim and decoration for Victorian buildings. One-hour self-guided tours take you through the mill and surrounding historical buildings, including a blacksmith shop and recreated 19th-century skid camp. Kids love the oxen. Master craftsman Eric Hollenbeck does everything by hand, manufactures his own stains and runs the show with a quick wit.

Clarke Historical Museum (☎ 707-443-1947; www.clarkemuseum.org; 240 E St; admission free; ☼ 11am-4pm Wed-Sat) is the best community historical museum on this stretch of the coast and it houses a set of typically musty relics – needlework hankies and paintings of the area's history-making notables (in this case Ulysses Grant, who was once dismissed from his post at Fort Humboldt for drunkenness) – but its best collection is that of intricately woven baskets from local native tribes. One look at the scenes of animals and warriors that unfold in the weave and you'll quickly understand the Pomo saying that 'every basket tells a story.'

The most famous of Eureka's Victorians is the **Carson Mansion** (134 M St), the ornate 1880s home of lumber baron William Carson, designed by Samuel and Joseph Newsom, notable 19th-century architects. It took 100 men a full year to build. Today, it's a private club. The pink house opposite, the **Wedding Mansion** (202 M St), is an 1884 Queen Anne Victorian by the same architects, built as a wedding gift for Carson's son.

Who says they don't build 'em like that anymore? **Carter House** (cnr 3rd & L Sts) was built in the 1980s by *bon vivant* Mark Carter, using 19th-century blueprints he'd found in an antique store. He's a local celeb; you can meet him at the Hotel Carter, across the street.

The **Morris Graves Museum of Art** (☎ 707-442-0278, events 707-442-9054; www.humboldtarts.org; 636 F St; donation requested; ☽ noon-5pm Wed-Sun), Eureka's cultural hub, has rotating exhibitions by California artists inside a 1904 Carnegie library, the state's first public library. It hosts weekend jazz, dance and spoken-word performances (September to May).

Sequoia Park (☎ 707-442-6552; 3414 W St; donation requested; ☽ 10am-7pm Tue-Sun May-Sep, to 5pm Oct-Apr; ✦) is a 77-acre old-growth redwood grove with biking and hiking trails, and playground and picnic areas. It also has a well-kept small zoo.

Activities

At **Hum-Boats Sail, Canoe & Kayak Center** (☎ 707-443-5157; www.humboats.com; Startare Dr; ✦) you can rent kayaks (half-day/full day $40/50) and sailboats and they also offer lessons and tours (including some ecotours).

The 1910 *Madaket* owned by **Harbor Cruise** (☎ 707-445-1910; www.humboldtbaymaritimemuseum .com; F St; ☽ May-Oct; ✦) originally ferried mill passengers until the Samoa Bridge was built in 1972, making it North America's oldest continuously operating passenger vessel. These days, the passengers are joyriders: the $10 sunset cocktail cruise serves from the smallest licensed bar in the state. Other cruises: adult/child five to 12/junior and senior $18/10/16.

The internet supplier **Northern Mountain Supply** (☎ 707-445-1711; www.northernmountain.com; 125 W 5th St) has *everything* you might need in the wilds and rents camping and backpacking gear (two-person tents from $35 for a two-day rental). It's an ideal supply point for those heading to the Lost Coast (p127).

Festivals & Events

Taking place on the first Saturday every month, 'Arts Alive!' is a progressive gallery tour. Summer concerts are held at the F

THE INDIAN ISLAND MASSACRE

In 1860, Eureka had been settled only 10 years. Like many frontier settlements, hostilities between the Native Americans and white settlers were common. On the night of February 25, 1860, the Wiyot tribe had just finished a celebration on Indian Island, across Humboldt Bay, and the tribal men set out on a hunting expedition, leaving the women and children alone. Under cover of night, a militia of settlers bearing hatchets stormed the island and viciously murdered 100 women, children and elders. The militia continued up the coast, and by the time the killing spree was over, the tribe had been decimated. The immediate outcry came not from the community, which did nothing, but from young journalist Bret Harte, who lived in Union (now Arcata). In a front-page editorial, he accused the settlers of 'barbarity' – and within two weeks he was run out of town.

It took Eureka more than 120 years to acknowledge the massacre, though some still deny it ever happened. The Wiyots – what's left of them – are now at Table Bluff, next to Humboldt Bay National Wildlife Refuge. You can see an abstract mural memorializing the event on the wall of the **Eureka Theater** (612 F St), next to the Morris Graves Museum, entitled *The Sun Set Twice on the People That Day*.

Street Pier. Contact the visitors bureau for details on festivals.

Redwood Coast Dixieland Jazz Festival (www .redwoodjazz.org) Late March-early April.

Rhododendron Festival Late-April flower festival.

Sleeping

Rates are high midsummer; you might find cheaper in Arcata.

BUDGET

There are a couple of private RV parks in the area, but superior camping is on Samoa Peninsula or on the nearby Lost Coast (p127). Motels line Hwy 101. Most cost $70 to $100 and rarely have air-conditioning: get back from the road for less noise. The cheapest are south of downtown on the suburban strip.

MIDRANGE

Bayview Motel (☎ 707-442-1673, 866-725-6813; www .bayviewmotel.com; 2844 Fairfield St; r $104, ste $170; 🐾) There's some noise from nearby Hwy 101, but the upscale Bayview has spotless rooms and patios overlooking Humboldt Bay. Jacuzzi suites have fireplaces.

Abigail's Elegant Victorian Mansion (☎ 707-444-3144; www.eureka-california.com; 1406 C St; r incl breakfast $125-190; 🛜) Outclassing the frilly faux Victorian fuss of most B&Bs, this National Historic Landmark is practically a Victorian museum, stuffed with carefully selected period pieces. The sugar sweet innkeepers dote on everyone, and offer a trip around town in a 1920s ride.

The Ship's Inn (☎ 707-444-3344; www.shipsinn.net; 821 D St; r incl breakfast $130-175; 💻 🛜 👌) In a quiet residential neighborhood, blocks from Old Town, this elegant little three-room inn is a favorite for its tasteful nautical decor and warmly hospitable host, Genie.

Cornelius Daly Inn (☎ 707-445-3638, 800-321-9656; www.dalyinn.com; 1125 H St; r $130, with bathroom $170-180; 🛜) This impeccably maintained 1905 Colonial Revival mansion has individually decorated rooms with turn-of-the-20th-century antiques.

Hotel Carter (☎ 877-443-7583; www.carter house.com; 301 L St; r $165-225, ste $275-350; 🛜 🐾) This standard-bearing luxury North Coast inn was recently constructed in period style – a Victorian lookalike without drafty windows. Stylish without being fussy, rooms have top-quality linens, unfinished pine

antiques and modern amenities; suites have in-room whirlpools and marble fireplaces. Rates include made-to-order breakfast, plus evening wine and hors d'oeuvres.

Upstairs at the Waterfront (☎ 707-444-1301, 888-817-5840; www.upstairsatthewaterfront.com; 102 F St; r $175, ste $225) A grand Victorian apartment above the cafe, this rental has superb details, and a fabulous shared kitchen divides the space into two. Pictures on the website don't do it justice. You can rent just a bedroom, but the suite's the thing, with a *huge* living room overlooking the harbor. If you're two couples, book the whole place.

TOP END

Carter House Inns (☎ 707-444-8062, 800-404-1390; www.carterhouse.com; r $100-285, ste $350-450, cottage $595) Stay in one of three sumptuously decorated houses: a single-level 1900 house, a honeymoon-hideaway cottage or a replica of an 1880s San Francisco mansion (p135). Unlike elsewhere, you won't see the innkeeper unless you want to. Guests can have an in-room breakfast or eat at the adjacent hotel's elegant restaurant.

Eating
BUDGET

Smug's Pizza (☎ 707-268-8082; 626 2nd St; dishes $6-14; 🕑 11am-late) Though this small local chain is unlikely to win your nomination of best slice ever, this place has a killer lunch special: a slice, soda and cookie for $3.75.

La Chapala (☎ 707-443-9514; 201 2nd St; dishes $6-14; 🕑 11am-9pm; 👌) For Mexican, family-owned La Chapala is consistently good and has dirt-cheap margaritas. Don't get so hammered you miss the homemade flan.

Hole In The Wall (☎ 707-443-5362; 1331 Broadway St; lunch $7-10; 🕑 11am-4pm) Tucked behind a Chinese restaurant, this bright little sandwich shop is the busiest take-out lunch in Humboldt for good reason: they stack corned beef and other fresh meats thick and dress them up with piles of crunchy veggies.

MIDRANGE

Waterfront Café Oyster Bar & Grill (☎ 707-443-9190; 102 F St; lunch $8-13, dinner $13-20; 🕑 9am-9pm) With a nice bay view and baskets of steamed clams, fish and chips, oysters and chowder, this is a solid bay-side lunch.

Top spot for Sunday brunch, with jazz and Ramos fizzes.

Roy's (☎ 707-442-4574; 218 D St; dishes $14-20; 🕙 dinner Tue-Sat; 🔆) If Eureka had a Mafia, they'd tie on their bibs at Roy's. The five-cheese ravioli and balsamic vinaigrette are delicious, but avoid complicated dishes.

Kyoto (☎ 707-443-7777; 320 F St; dishes $15-25; 🕙 dinner Wed-Sat) With new ownership, this once-top sushi spot has added lots of Americanized rolls, though it still offers the freshest fish around. Make reservations, as it's tiny.

Hurricane Kate's (☎ 707-444-1405; www.hurricane kates.com; 511 2nd St; mains lunch $9-14, dinner $16-26; 🕙 11:30am-2pm, 5-9pm Tue-Sat) The favorite spot of local *bon vivants*, Kate's open kitchen pumps out pretty good, eclectic, tapas-style dishes ($10 to $14) and roast meats, but the wood-fired pizzas are the standout option. Full bar.

TOP END

ourpick **Restaurant 301** (☎ 707-444-8062; www .carterhouse.com; 301 L St; breakfast $11, dinner $20-34, 4-course menu $45; 🕙 breakfast & dinner) Eureka's top table, romantic, sophisticated 301 serves a contemporary California menu, using produce from its organic gardens (tours available). Mains are pricey, but the four-course prix-fixe menu ($45) is a good deal.

SELF-CATERING

There's a **farmers market** (☎ 707-441-9999; Old Town Gazebo, cnr 2nd & F Sts; 🕙 10am-1pm Tue Jun-Oct), cafes and sandwich shops in Old Town, the best neighborhood for following your nose. Pick up groceries at **Eureka Natural Foods** (☎ 707-442-6325; 1626 Broadway; 🕙 7am-9pm Mon-Sat, 8am-8pm Sun) or **Eureka Co-op** (☎ 443-6027; cnr 4th & A Sts; 🕙 6am-9pm).

Drinking

The Shanty (☎ 707-444-2053; 213 2nd St; 🕙 noon-2am) Chill on the patio with hipsters at this cool dive, where you can play Donkey Kong, pool or Ping Pong and knock back $3 beers.

Lost Coast Brewery (☎ 707-445-4480; 617 4th St; 🕙 11am-midnight; 🛜) Another great North Coast brewery. The Downtown Brown and Great White are both delicious and there's pub grub – fries, wings and good burgers (mains $6 to $14) – all day.

Entertainment

The **Morris Graves Museum of Art** (☎ 707-442-0278, events 442-9054; www.humboldtarts.org; 636 F St) hosts performing-arts events, September to May, Saturday evenings and Sunday afternoons. Housing the Eureka Symphony, performing arts and second-tier crooners, the **Arkley Center** (☎ 707-442-1956; www.arkleycenter .com; 412 G St) is a newly restored theater with a schedule full of surprises. The **Broadway Cinema** (☎ 707-444-3456; Broadway) screens first-run movies and can be found near 14th St. For gay events, log onto **Queer Humboldt** (www.queerhumboldt.com).

Getting There & Around

Horizon Air (☎ 800-547-9308; horizonair.alaskaair.com) and **United Express** (☎ 800-241-6522; www.united .com) serve **Arcata/Eureka Airport** (ACV; ☎ 707-839-5401; http://co.humboldt.ca.us/aviation), 20 miles north. Horizon is a better option if you're flying from LA (3½ hours, flights every day except Thursday) and United is better from the Bay Area (two hours), though either is cheap; prices start at around $500 for the short flights. Buses between Trinidad, Arcata, Eureka, Fernbridge (near Ferndale) and Scotia are operated, Monday to Saturday, by **Redwood Transit Service** (☎ 707-443-0826; www.hta.org). The trip from Arcata to Fernbridge takes about 45 minutes. Buses to Arcata cost $2.50 and stop along 5th St at D, H, K, O and U Sts. The **Eureka Transit Service** (☎ 707-443-0826; www.hta.org/ets) operates local buses around town, Monday to Saturday.

SAMOA PENINSULA

Grassy dunes and windswept beaches extend along the half-mile-wide, 7-mile long Samoa Peninsula, Humboldt Bay's western boundary. Stretches of it are down-right spectacular, particularly the dunes, which are part of a 34-mile-long dune system – the largest in Northern California – and the wildlife viewing is excellent. The shoreline road (Hwy 255) is a backdoor route between Arcata and Eureka.

At the peninsula's south end, **Samoa Dunes Recreation Area** (☎ 707-825-2300; 🕙 sunrise-sunset) is good for picnicking and fishing. For wildlife, head to **Mad River Slough & Dunes**; from Arcata, take Samoa Blvd west for 3 miles, then turn right at Young St, the Manila turn-off. Park at the community center lot, from where a trail passes mudflats, salt marsh and tidal channels. There are over 200 species of birds: migrating waterfowl in spring and fall, songbirds in spring and summer, shorebirds in fall and winter, and waders year-round.

The 475-acre **Lanphere Dunes Preserve** at the peninsula's north end protects one of the finest examples of dune succession on the entire Pacific coast. These undisturbed dunes reach heights of over 80ft. Because of the environment's fragility, access is by guided tour only. **Friends of the Dunes** (☎ 707-444-1397; www.friendsofthedunes.org) leads 2½-hour rain-or-shine Saturday guided walks at 10am through Lanphere Dunes and Manila Dunes. Visit the website for departure locations and information. A couple of miles south from Lanphere Dunes, the 100-acre **Manila Dunes Recreation Area** (☎ 707-445-3309; 🐾) has trails through beach pines and allows dogs on-leash. The **Ma-Le'l Dunes** (☎ 707-825-2300; 🐾), immediately south of Lanphere Dunes, allow dogs to run free. Access is from Young Lane, at the northern end of the peninsula, off Hwy 255.

The lunch place on the peninsula is the **Samoa Cookhouse** (☎ 707-442-1659; www.humboldt dining.com/cookhouse; off Samoa Blvd; breakfast/lunch/dinner $9/10/14; 🍽), the last surviving lumber camp cookhouse in the West, where you can shovel down all-you-can-eat family meals at long red-checkered tables. Kids eat for half-price. The cookhouse is five minutes northwest of Eureka, across the Samoa Bridge; follow the signs. From Arcata, take Samoa Blvd (Hwy 255).

ARCATA

pop 16,500

There's no place in California quite like Arcata, the North Coast's most progressive town, set around a tidy central square that fills with an agreeable mix of college students, campers, the slightly disheveled and tourists. Sure, it occasionally reeks of patchouli and its politics may lean toward the far left (in April 2003, the City Council did not simply vote to condemn the USA Patriot Act, it outlawed voluntary compliance with it), but its earnest embrace of sustainability has long harbored some of the most progressive civic action in America. Here, garbage trucks run on biodiesel, recycling gets picked up by tandem bicycle, wastewater gets filtered clean in marshlands and almost every street has a bike lane.

Founded in 1850 as a base for lumber camps, Arcata is today defined by two major elements: its college and its marijuana. Humboldt State University (HSU), on the north part of town, ensures a fluctuating population of students. A 1996 state proposition that legalized marijuana for medical purposes has helped Arcata become what one *New Yorker* article recently referred to as the 'heartland of high grade marijuana,' a claim evident in the recent housing shortage that stems from indoor 'grow houses.' Regardless of their method, this is a place where scruffy 20-somethings come to expand their minds.

Orientation & Information

Streets run on a grid, with numbered streets traveling east to west and lettered streets north to south. G and H Sts run north and south (respectively) to HSU and Hwy 101. The plaza is bordered by G and H and 8th and 9th Sts. Eureka is 5 miles, or 10 minutes, south on Hwy 101. Or, take Samoa Blvd to Hwy 255 for a scenic route around Arcata Bay.

Arcata Eye (www.arcataeye.com) Free newspaper listing local events; the 'Police Log' column is hysterical.

Bureau of Land Management (BLM; ☎ 707-825-2300; 1695 Heindon Rd) Has information on the Lost Coast.

California Welcome Center (☎ 707-822-3619; www .arcatachamber.com; 1635 Heindon Rd; 🕙 9am-5pm) Two miles north of town, off Giuntoli Lane, Hwy 101's west side. Operated by the Arcata Chamber of Commerce. Provides local and statewide information. Get the free *Official Map Guide to Arcata*.

Northtown Books (☎ 707-822-2384; 957 H St) New books, periodicals, travel maps and guides.

Redwood Peace & Justice Center (☎ 707-826-2511; http://rpjc.net; 1040 H St) Ground zero for grassroots political actions and resources.

Tin Can Mailman (☎ 707-822-1307; 1000 H St) Used volumes on two floors; excellent for hard-to-find books.

Sights

Around **Arcata Plaza** are two National Historic Landmarks: the 1857 **Jacoby's Storehouse** (cnr H & 8th Sts) and the 1915 **Hotel Arcata** (cnr G & 9th Sts). Another great historic building is the 1914 **Minor Theatre** (1013 10th St), which some local historians claim as the oldest theater in the US built specifically for showing film.

Humboldt State University (HSU; ☎ 707-826-3011; www.humboldt.edu) is on the northeastern side of town. The Campus Center for

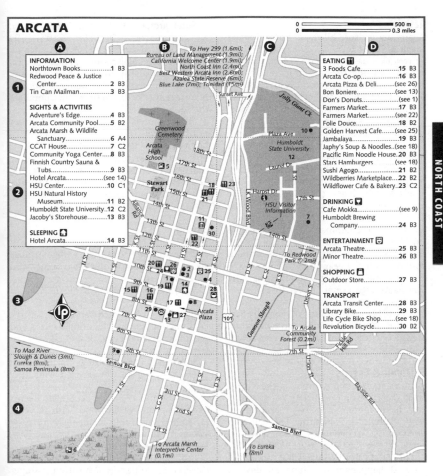

ARCATA

0		500 m
0		0.3 miles

INFORMATION
Northtown Books...............1 B3
Redwood Peace & Justice
  Center.........................2 B3
Tin Can Mailman..............3 B3

SIGHTS & ACTIVITIES
Adventure's Edge..............4 B3
Arcata Community Pool......5 B2
Arcata Marsh & Wildlife
  Sanctuary....................6 A4
CCAT House.....................7 C2
Community Yoga Center......8 B3
Finnish Country Sauna &
  Tubs...........................9 B3
Hotel Arcata..............(see 14)
HSU Center....................10 C1
HSU Natural History
  Museum......................11 B2
Humboldt State University.12 C2
Jacoby's Storehouse.........13 B3

SLEEPING
Hotel Arcata..................14 B3

EATING
3 Foods Cafe.................15 B3
Arcata Co-op.................16 B3
Arcata Pizza & Deli.......(see 26)
Bon Boniere...............(see 13)
Don's Donuts.............(see 1)
Farmers Market.............17 B3
Farmers Market...........(see 22)
Folie Douce.................18 B2
Golden Harvest Cafe.....(see 25)
Jambalaya...................19 B3
Japhy's Soup & Noodles..(see 18)
Pacific Rim Noodle House.20 B3
Stars Hamburgers........(see 18)
Sushi Agogo.................21 B2
Wildberries Marketplace...22 B2
Wildflower Cafe & Bakery.23 C2

DRINKING
Cafe Mokka.................(see 9)
Humboldt Brewing
  Company....................24 B3

ENTERTAINMENT
Arcata Theatre..............25 B3
Minor Theatre...............26 B3

SHOPPING
Outdoor Store...............27 B3

TRANSPORT
Arcata Transit Center.......28 B3
Library Bike..................29 B3
Life Cycle Bike Shop......(see 18)
Revolution Bicycle..........30 D2

To Mad River
Slough & Dunes (3mi);
Eureka (8mi);
Samoa Peninsula (8mi)

To Hwy 299 (1.6mi);
Bureau of Land Management (1.9mi);
California Welcome Center (1.9mi);
North Coast Inn (2.4mi);
Best Western Arcata Inn (2.6mi);
Azalea State Reserve (6mi);
Blue Lake (7mi); Trinidad (15mi)

To Redwood
Park (0.2mi)

To Arcata
Community
Forest (0.2mi)

To Eureka
(8mi)

To Arcata Marsh
Interpretive Center
(0.1mi)

NORTH COAST

Appropriate Technology (CCAT) is a world leader in sustainable technologies; on Fridays at 2pm you can take a self-guided tour of the **CCAT House** (☎ 707-826-3551; Buck House, HSU; ☼ 9am-5pm Mon-Fri; ♿), a converted residence that uses only 4% of the energy of a comparably sized dwelling. The **HSU Natural History Museum** (☎ 707-866-4479; www .humboldt.edu/~natmus; 1315 G St; adult/child $3/2; ☼ 10am-5pm Tue-Sat; ♿) has kid-friendly interactive exhibits of fossils, live animals, a beehive, tidepool tank and cool tsunami and seismic displays; .

Arcata Marsh & Wildlife Sanctuary, on the shores of Humboldt Bay, has 5 miles of walking trails and outstanding birding – and it doubles as the city's (nearly) odor-free

wastewater treatment facility. Friends of Arcata Marsh guide tours Saturdays at 2pm from the **Arcata Marsh Interpretive Center** (☎ 707-826-2359; www.arcatamarshfriends.org; 600 South G St; ☼ 9am-5pm Tue-Sun, 1-5pm Mon; ♿). The **Redwood Region Audubon Society** (☎ 707-826-7031; www.rras.org) offers guided walks of the marsh on Saturdays at 8:30am, rain or shine, from the parking lot at I St's south end. These are free, but donations are welcome.

At the east end of 11th and 14th Sts, **Redwood Park** has beautiful redwoods and picnic areas. Adjoining the park is the **Arcata Community Forest**, a 575-acre old-growth forest crisscrossed by 10 miles of trails, with dirt paths and paved roads good for hikers and mountain bikers.

NORTH COAST

Activities

A nirvana for sore hikers, at **Finnish Country Sauna & Tubs** (☎ 707-822-2228; cnr 5th & J Sts; ◷ noon-10pm Sun-Thu, to 12:30am Fri & Sat) you can sip chai by the fireside or in meditative gardens, and rent a private open-air redwood hot tub ($9 per half hour) or sweat in a sauna. Reserve ahead, especially on weekends.

HSU Center Activities (☎ 707-826-3357; www .humboldt.edu/~cntract) sponsors myriad activities, workshops, outings, sporting-gear rentals and consignment sales; nonstudents are welcome. It's in the University Center, beside the campus clock tower.

Adventure's Edge (☎ 707-822-4673; www .adventuresedge.com; 650 10th St; ◷ 9am-6pm Mon-Sat, 11am-5pm Sun) also rents, sells and services outdoor equipment. The **Outdoor Store** (☎ 707-822-0321; 876 G St; ◷ 10am-6pm Mon-Sat, noon-5pm Sun) is another great retail option, with high-quality gear.

For some locally based exercise, the **Community Yoga Center** (☎ 707-440-2111; www .innerfreedomyoga.com; 890 G St) offers drop-in classes ($12) and the **Arcata Community Pool** (☎ 707-822-6801; 1150 16th St) has lap swimming, a coed hot tub, sauna and exercise room. (Admission: adult/child/senior $6/5/4.)

Festivals & Events

Arcata's most famous event is the **Kinetic Grand Championship** (www.kineticgrandchampionship .com), held on Memorial Day weekend (late May). People on self-propelled contraptions travel the 38 miles from Arcata to Ferndale (see the boxed text, p132).

The **Arcata Bay Oyster Festival** (www.oyster festival.net) happens in mid-June. Sundays in August and September bring the **Summer Music & Art on the Plaza** (www.arcatamainstreet.com). **North Country Fair** is in late-September.

Sleeping

Arcata lodgings are limited, though it's a good base for exploring parks further north. There are a few private RV lots, but better camping facilities up the road in Trinidad (p142) and Patrick's Point State Park (p145). With **Arcata Stay** (☎ 707-822-0935, 877-822-0935; www.arcatastay.com; apt $165-175; 🛜) you can live like a local in a beautifully furnished apartment or cozy cottage; most apartments in this lodging network are within walking distance of the plaza and have kitchens, wi-fi and lots of privacy.

Hotel Arcata (☎ 707-826-0217, 800-344-1221; www.hotelarcata.com; 708 9th St; r $90-105, ste $111-156) The renovated 1915 Hotel Arcata anchors the plaza. The small rooms are nice enough, but the best reason to roost here is to spy on the hippies, nerds, skaters, stoners, hikers, rednecks and retirees that populate the square.

Other motels and chains are 2 miles north of Hwy 101's Giuntoli Lane exit.

North Coast Inn (☎ 707-822-4861, 800-406-0046; 4975 Valley West Blvd; r $80-85; 🐾 🖳 🕮) Satisfactory chain option, with on-site restaurant and airport transfers.

Best Western Arcata Inn (☎ 707-826-0313, 800-528-1234; www.bestwestern.com; 4827 Valley West Blvd; r $109; 🐾 🖳 🕮 🉑) First choice motel.

Eating

Being a left-leaning college town, cheap eats are everywhere. Browse with your nose along G St, north of the town center and around the square.

Japhy's Soup & Noodles (☎ 707-826-2594; 1563 G St; dishes $3-6; ◷ 11:30am-8pm Mon-Fri) The budgeteers first choice serves big salads, tasty coconut curry, cold noodle salads and great homemade soups. Best of all, you can fill up for about $6.

Sushi Agogo (☎ 707-601-1000; 15th & G Sts; rolls $3-10; ◷ 11:30am-9pm Mon-Sun; Ⓥ) This tiny little cart is just off the northwest corner of 15th St and G St and accurately deems itself the future of fast food, with all vegetarian and vegan rolls featuring homemade sauces, fresh veggies and nut butters. Best, the packaging is all ecofriendly.

Pacific Rim Noodle House (☎ 707-826-7604; 1021 I St; dishes $4-7; ◷ 11am-7pm Mon-Sat) Super-duper noodles, rice bowls, potstickers and sushi rolls are mainstays at this take-out favorite with outside tables.

Wildflower Cafe & Bakery (☎ 707-822-0360; 1604 G St; dishes $5-8; ◷ 8am-8pm Mon-Sat, 9am-1pm Sun; Ⓥ) *The* place for vegetarians, Wildflower serves fab frittatas, pancakes and big crunchy salads. At dinner there's mushroom stroganoff, veggie lasagna and other substantial dishes.

Golden Harvest Cafe (☎ 707-822-8962; 1062 G St; breakfast $4-8, lunch $5-12; ◷ 6:30am-3pm Mon-Fri, 7:30am-3pm Sat & Sun) Tops for breakfast with a hangover (it's windowless), Golden Harvest serves classic Benedicts, four-egg omelettes and pancakes with *real* maple syrup. Alas, the coffee sucks.

Jambalaya (☎ 707-822-4766; 915 H St; lunch $7-9, dinner $15-20; ☺ lunch Mon-Fri, dinner nightly) Probably the most vibrant dining option in town, Jambalaya serves a mishmash of Caribbean-influenced dishes – at lunch Cuban sandwiches, at dinner wild salmon and (of course) jambalaya. The menu also rules, with fresh fruit cocktails and a great beer selection. As if this wasn't fun enough, they also host Arcata's best live music scene.

3 Foods Cafe (☎ 707-822-9474; 835 J St; brunch $8-14, dinner $10-30; ☺ 5:30am-10pm Tue-Thu, to 11pm Fri & Sat, to 9pm Sun) This newcomer fits perfectly into the Arcata dining scene: whimsical, creative, worldly dishes (think Korean beef in a spicy chili sauce) at moderate prices (a prix fixe is sometimes available for $20 and the 'Times Are Tough Tuesday' menu features all-you-can-eat pasta for a measly $5). The lavender infused cocktails start things off on the right foot. For a $1 fee, you can get your attending wait staff to do a silly walk.

Folie Douce (☎ 707-822-1042; 1551 G St; dinner $23-32; ☺ 5:30-9pm Tue-Thu, to 10pm Fri & Sat) Folie Douce presents a short but inventive menu of seasonally inspired bistro cooking, from Asian to Mediterranean, with an emphasis on local organics. Wood-fired pizzas ($12 to $18) are a specialty. Reservations are essential.

Other good cheap eats where $7 or less brings a decent meal include the following: **Arcata Pizza & Deli** (☎ 707-822-4650; 1057 H St; ☺ 11am-1am Sun-Thu, to 3am Fri & Sat) Fill up after bar hopping.

Bon Boniere (☎ 707-822-6388; 791 8th St; ☺ 11am-10pm; ☺ ☺) Inside Jacoby's Storehouse; get ice-cream sundaes here.

Don's Donuts (☎ 707-822-6465; 933 H St; ☺ 24hr) Get a Southeast-Asian sandwich.

Stars Hamburgers (☎ 707-826-1379; 1535 G St; burgers $3-5; ☺ 11am-8pm Mon-Thu, to 9pm Fri, to 7pm Sat, noon-6pm Sun; ☺) Uses grass-fed beef to make fantastic burgers.

There are fantastic **farmers markets** (☎ 707-441-9999; Arcata Plaza ☺ 9am-2pm Sat Apr-Nov; outside Wildberries ☺ 3:30-6:30pm Tue Jun-Oct), and **Wildberries Marketplace** (☎ 707-822-0095; 747 13th St; ☺ 7am-11pm) is Arcata's best grocery, with natural foods, a good deli, bakery and juice bar. **Arcata Co-op** (☎ 707-822-5947; cnr 8th & I Sts; ☺ 6am-10pm) carries natural

foods and has a good butcher working grass-fed beef.

Drinking

Dive bars and cocktail lounges line the plaza's northern side. Arcata is awash in coffeehouses.

Humboldt Brewing Company (☎ 707-826-2739; 856 10th St; pub grub $5-10) This popular beer house has been elegantly remodeled and has a huge selection of carefully selected beer taps, fish tacos and buffalo wings. Live music nightly.

Cafe Mokka (☎ 707-822-2228; cnr 5th & J Sts; snacks $4) Bohos head to this cafe at Finnish Country Sauna & Tubs (opposite) for a mellow,old-world vibe, good coffee drinks and homemade cookies.

Entertainment

An exquisite remodeling has revived the **Arcata Theatre** (☎ 707-822-1220; www.arcatatheater .com; 1036 G St), a classic movie house, which shows art films, rock documentaries, silent films and more. Plus, they serve beer! **Center Arts** (☎ 707-826-4411, tickets 707 826 3928; www .humboldt.edu/~carts) hosts events on campus and you'd be amazed at who shows up: from Diana Krall and Dave Brubeck to Lou Reed and Ani Difranco. The place to buy tickets is at the University Ticket Office in the HSY Bookstore on the 3rd floor of the University Center. There's also the **Minor Theatre** (☎ 707-822-3456; 1013 H St), which screens first run and classic films.

Getting There & Around

Eureka is 10 minutes south. See p137 for airport information and details of the **Redwood Transit System** (☎ 707-443-0826; www .hta.org). Redwood, **Greyhound** (☎ 800-231-2222; www.greyhound.com) and **Arcata city buses** (☎ 707-822-3775; adult $1.40; ☺ frequently 7am-10pm when HSU is in session, to 6pm during breaks in the academic calendar) stop at the **Arcata Transit Center** (☎ 707-825-8934; 925 E St at 9th St). For shared rides, read the bulletin board at the Arcata Co-op (left).

Cyclists: Hwy 101 entering town from the north is scary because you have to cross the freeway on-ramps. Here's an alternate route: from McKinleyville in the north, take Murray Rd west from Hwy 101, to the Hammond Trail south (a dedicated bike route), to Mad River Rd south into Arcata.

Only in Arcata: borrow a bike from **Library Bike** (☎ 707-822-1122; www.arcata.com/green bikes; 865 8th St) for a $20 deposit, which gets refunded when you return the bike – up to six months later! They're beaters, but they ride. **Revolution Bicycle** (☎ 707-822-2562; 1360 G St) and **Life Cycle Bike Shop** (☎ 707-822-7755; 1593 G St; ❂ Mon-Sat) rent, service and sell bicycles.

NORTHERN REDWOOD COAST

Congratulations, traveler, you've reached the middle of nowhere, or at least the top of the middle of nowhere. Here, the trees are so large that the tiny towns along the road seem even smaller. The scenery is pure drama: cliffs and rocks, native lore, legendary salmon runs, mammoth trees, redneck towns and RVing retirees. It's certainly the *weirdest* part of the California Coast. Leave time to dawdle and bask in the haunting grandeur of it all and, even though there are scores of mid-century motels, you simply must make an effort to sleep outdoors if possible. Good rental options for tents are abundant in Eureka (p134) and Arcata (p138).

TRINIDAD

pop 310

Twenty-three miles north of Eureka, picture-perfect Trinidad sits on a bluff overlooking a glittering blue-water harbor, with gorgeous hiking and lovely sand beaches. Several water-view B&Bs make terrific romantic getaways. The town gained its name when Spanish sea captains arrived on Trinity Sunday in 1775 and named the area La Santísima Trinidad (The Holy Trinity). Trinidad didn't boom, though, until the 1850s, when it became an important port for miners. Schooners from San Francisco brought supplies for inland gold fields and carried back lumber from the North Coast. Today, tourism and fishing keep the economy going.

Orientation & Information

Trinidad is tiny. Approach via Hwy 101 (exit at Trinidad) or from the north via Patrick's Point Dr (which becomes Scenic Dr further south).

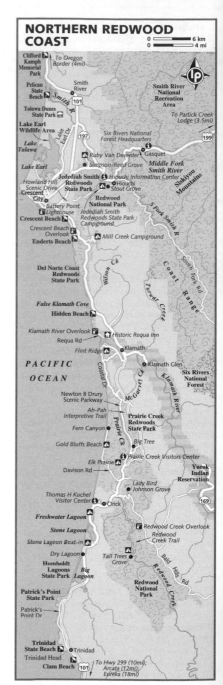

Beachcomber Café (☎ 707-677-0106; 363 Trinity St; per hr $5; ⏰ 7am-4pm Mon-Thu, to 9pm Fri, 9am-4pm Sat & Sun; 🛜) Internet access.

Information kiosk (cnr Patrick's Point Dr & Main St) Just west of the freeway, pick up the pamphlet *Discover Trinidad*, which has an excellent map.

Sights & Activities

Overlooking the bay on a bluff at the foot of Main St, **Trinidad Memorial Lighthouse** (cnr Trinity & Edwards Sts), is a replica of an 1871 structure. It opens rarely to visitors, except during the annual **Trinidad Fish Festival** in mid-June. For kids who love fish, the **HSU Telonicher Marine Laboratory** (☎ 707-826-3671; www.humboldt .edu/~marinelb; Ewing St; ⏰ 9am-4:30pm Mon-Fri, noon-4pm Sat & Sun Sep–mid-May; ♿) is an interesting place to spend an hour or two. There's a touch tank, several aquariums (look for the giant octopus), an enormous whale

jaw and a cool 3-D map of the ocean floor. Tours are by arrangement; admission $1 for self-guided tour.

The free map available from the information kiosk shows several good hiking trails, especially the definitive **Trinidad Head Trail**, which affords superb coastal views and great whale-watching opportunities (April to June and December to February). Stroll along an exceptionally beautiful cove at **Trinidad State Beach**; take Main St and bear right at Stagecoach, then take the second turn left (the first is a picnic area) into the small lot.

Eroding Scenic Dr twists south along coastal bluffs. About two miles south of town, **Baker Beach** is nude. Take the marked trail through the grass, opposite No 1237 Scenic Dr. A third of a mile past Baker, Scenic Dr leads to broad **Luffenholtz Beach**

COAST REDWOODS: THE TALLEST TREES ON EARTH

Though they covered much of the northern hemisphere millions of years ago, redwood trees now grow only in China, two areas of California and a small grove in Oregon. Coast redwoods (*Sequoia sempervirens*) are found in a narrow, 450-mile-long strip along California's Pacific coast between Big Sur and southern Oregon. They can live for 2200 years, grow to 370ft tall and achieve a diameter of 22ft at the base, with bark up to 12 inches thick.

In summer 2006, researchers found three new record-breaking trees in Redwood National Park. The tallest, Hyperion, measures a whopping 378ft – that's nearly 40 stories tall! Coming in a close second and third are Helios at 376ft and Icarus at 371ft. These trees displace the old record-holder, the 370ft-high Stratosphere Giant in Rockefeller Forest (p130). But the trees bear no signs, so you won't be able to find them – too many boot-clad visitors would compact the delicate root systems.

The tallest trees reach their maximum height between 300 and 700 years. Because they're narrow at their bases, they generally aren't the ones you notice as you walk through the forest. The dramatic, fat-trunked giants, which make such a visually stunning impact from the ground, are ancient, as much as 2000 years old. But they're not as tall as the younger ones because their tops have been blown off in intense storms that have occurred over the centuries.

The structure of coast redwoods has been compared to a nail standing on its head. Unlike most trees, coast redwoods have no deep taproot and their root system is shallow in relation to their height – only 10ft to 13ft deep and spreading out 60ft to 80ft around the tree. The trees sometimes fall due to wind, but they are very flexible and usually sway in the wind as if they're dancing.

What gives these majestic giants their namesake color? It's the redwoods' high tannin content. It also makes their wood and bark resistant to insects and disease. The thick, spongy bark has a high moisture content, too, enabling the ancient trees to survive many naturally occurring forest fires.

There's a whole ecosystem in the canopy of the trees. Critters and birds like the wandering salamander, marbled murrelet and the famous northern spotted owl spend their entire existence high above the forest floor, where they need not fight for food, nor get caught by predators.

Today, only 4% of the North Coast's original two million acres of ancient redwood forests remain standing. Almost half of these old-growth forests are protected in Redwood National and State Parks.

(accessible via the staircase), where the bathers wear suits.

Trinidad is famous for fishing. Arrange a trip through **Salty's Surf 'n' Tackle Tours** (☎ 707-677-0300; 332 Main St) or **Trinidad Bay Charters** (☎ 707-839-4743, 800-839-4744; www.trinidadbay charters.net). The harbor is at the bottom of Edwards St, at the foot of Trinidad Head. Five-hour trips cost $80. **North Coast Adventures** (☎ 707-677-3124; www.northcoastadventures.com) gives sea- and river-kayaking lessons ($50/90 per two hours/day) and guided ecotrips (including tidepool tours) around the North Coast.

Sleeping

Clam Beach (☎ 707-445-7491; campsites per vehicle $12) South of town off Hwy 101, Clam Beach has excellent beach camping. Pitch your tent in the dunes (look for natural windbreaks). Facilities include pit toilets, cold water, picnic tables and fire rings.

View Crest Lodge & Campground (☎ 707-677-3393; www.viewcrestlodge.com; 3415 Patrick's Point Dr; tent/RV sites $25/35, 1-bedroom cottages $115-165; ☎ ☒) On a hill above the ocean on the inland side, these modern, well-maintained cottages are a bargain. Some have views and Jacuzzis; most have kitchens. There's also a good campground.

Trinidad Inn (☎ 707-677-3349; www.trinidadinn .com; 1170 Patrick's Point Dr; r $75-110) The rooms are sparklingly clean and attractively decorated at this gray-shingled, single-story motel – Trinidad's best. Most rooms have kitchens.

Bishop Pine Lodge (☎ 707-677-3314; www.bishop pinelodge.com; 1481 Patrick's Point Dr; cottages $110-150, add $10 for kitchen use) It feels like summer camp at Bishop Pine, where you can rent freestanding redwood cottages in a grassy meadow on a sunny hillside. All but two have kitchens and woodsy, retro charm.

Trinidad Retreats (☎ 707-677-1606; www.trinidad retreats.com; per day from $150; ☒) Rents local houses, good for vacationing families.

Trinidad Bay B&B (☎ 707-677-0840; www.trinidad baybnb.com; 560 Edwards St; r $225-300; ☎) On bluffs overlooking the harbor and Trinidad Head, this cute little Cape Cod–style saltbox is the only lodging downtown, with four individually decorated rooms done in a cozy, inviting, beach-house style with classy white furniture (parents beware). One room has a kitchen; two others have fireplaces. There's homemade honey at breakfast.

Lost Whale Inn (☎ 707-677-3425; www.lostwhale inn.com; 3452 Patrick's Point Dr; r incl breakfast $225-250, ste $300; ☒) Fall asleep to the sound of braying sea lions at this spacious, modern cliff-top B&B surrounded by flowering gardens. The ocean views are mesmerizing and there's a 24-hour hot tub. Rooms have knotty-pine trimmings, redwood floors and homey touches like country quilts. Kids welcome.

Eating

Kahish's Catch Café (☎ 707-677-0390; 355 Main St; mains $6-9; ☒ 11am-7pm Tue-Sun; ☒) Across from the Chevron, this fun little hippie joint makes good food fast, using mostly organic ingredients – from pizzettas and 'grass-fed' burgers to brown rice and veggies. Order at the counter and then sit outside.

Seascape Restaurant (☎ 707-677-3762; Trinidad Harbor; breakfast & lunch $8-10, dinner $11-22; ☒ 7am-10pm; ☒) Vinyl booths overlook the harbor at this character-filled greasy spoon. The breakfasts are good and the seafood-based menu is best when everything is batter fried. It's open shorter hours in winter.

Trinidad Bay Eatery (☎ 707-677-3777; cnr Parker & Trinity Sts; breakfast & lunch $7-12, dinner $17-23; ☒ 7am-3pm Mon & Tue, to 8pm Wed-Sun; ☒) Chowder and blackberry cobbler are the standouts at this serviceable diner.

Larrupin Café (☎ 707-677-0230; 1658 Patrick's Point Dr; mains $20-30; ☒ dinner Thu-Tue) Most locals will point to the Larrupin for upscale eats. Warmed by Moroccan rugs and a cozy atmosphere of noodling lovers, the menu boasts consistently good mesquite-grilled seafood and meats. In the summer, book a table on the garden patio. Cash only.

At **Katy's Smokehouse & Fishmarket** (☎ 707-677-0151; www.katyssmokehouse.com; 740 Edwards St; ☒ 9am-6pm) they use line-caught seafood to make their own chemical-free smoked and canned fish, plus some vacuum-packed for convenient transportation.

Drinking

Beachcomber Café (☎ 707-677-0106; 363 Trinity St; ☎) If you really want to know what's happening in Trinidad, talk to Jackie and Melissa, the fun owners of this sweet little cafe that makes good organic coffee, sandwiches, bagels and homemade cookies.

Moonstone Grill (☎ 707-677-1616; Moonstone Beach; ☒ Wed-Sun) For drop-dead sunset views over a picture-perfect beach, have cocktails at fancy-pants Moonstone. Call for directions.

PATRICK'S POINT STATE PARK

Although it is only a single square mile, **Patrick's Point** (☎ 707-677-3570; 4150 Patrick's Point Dr; per car $8; 🚻) has a little of everything: dense hemlock forests open onto golden meadows, and sandy beaches abut dramatic headlands. Five miles north of Trinidad, it has easy access to dramatic coastal bluffs, making it a top choice for families. The set of scenic overlooks are stunning and you can climb giant rock formations to watch whales to a soundtrack of braying sea lions and squawking gulls.

An authentic reproduction of a Yurok village, **Sumêg**, has been created within the park, with hand-hewn redwood buildings where Native Americans gather for traditional ceremonies. (Local Native Americans built solid structures, instead of temporary ones, because the land here is so productive that tribes didn't need to migrate with the seasons.) In the native plant garden you'll find species for making traditional baskets and medicines.

On **Agate Beach** look for bits of jade and shiny sea-polished agate. Follow the signs to **tidepools**. Tread lightly and obey regulations. The 2-mile **Rim Trail**, a former Yurok trail around the bluffs, circles the point with access to huge rocky outcroppings. Don't miss **Wedding Rock**, one of the park's most romantic spots. Other trails lead around unusual formations like **Ceremonial Rock** and **Lookout Rock**.

The park's three well-tended drive-in **campgrounds** (☎ reservations 800-444-7275; www .reserveamerica.com; campsites $35-45) have coin-operated hot showers. Penn Creek and Abalone campgrounds are more sheltered than Agate Beach. There is also a site for hikers and bikers.

HUMBOLDT LAGOONS STATE PARK

Hwy 101 drops out of the forest at **Humboldt Lagoons** (☎ 707-488-2041), where long, sandy beaches stretch for miles. Two large coastal lagoons – **Big Lagoon** and **Stone Lagoon** – have stellar bird-watching and kayaking (rent boats in Arcata, p140). Of all the places to kayak on the Redwood Coast, this is a favorite. Sunsets are spectacular, with no manmade structures in sight.

About a mile north, **Freshwater Lagoon** is also great for bird-watching. Picnic at its north end near the Thomas H Kuchel Visitor Center of Redwood National Park (p146). South of Stone Lagoon, itty-bitty **Dry Lagoon** (actually a freshwater marsh) has a fantastic hike. Park at Dry Lagoon's picnic area and hike north on the unmarked trail to Stone Lagoon, which skirts the southwestern shore and ends up at the ocean, passing through woods and marshland rich with birds and wildlife. It's about 2.5 miles one way, mostly flat and nobody takes it because it's unmarked.

The state park runs two first-come, first-served **environmental campgrounds** (tent sites $20; 🕙 Apr-Oct); bring water. Stone Lagoon has six canoe-in environmental campsites; Dry Lagoon, off Hwy 101, has six walk-in campsites. Check in at Patrick's Point State Park (left), at least 30 minutes before sunset. **Humboldt County Parks** (☎ 707-445-7651; campsites $18) operates a lovely cypress-grove picnic area and campground beside Big Lagoon, a mile off Hwy 101, with flush toilets and water, but no showers.

Redwood Trails RV & Campground (☎ 707-488-2061; http://rv4fun.com/redwood.html; Hwy 101; tent/RV sites $15/26), opposite the turn-off to Dry Lagoon, has a general store, bakery, arcade, horseback rides and, if you're lucky, elk lazing in the meadow outside.

REDWOOD NATIONAL PARK

Sure, if you've explored southern areas of the California coast, you may *think* that you've experienced the majesty of the redwoods, but this is the big show: the world's tallest living trees will stagger the mind, predating the Roman Empire by over 500 years and standing as an imposing reminder of nature's pure grandeur. In the summer of 2006, researchers found a trio of trees here that were bigger than any they'd ever measured before; the biggest one, Hyperion, is nearly 40 stories tall.

Unlike California's other National Parks, it's difficult to know when exactly you're within the borders of the park, as it's jointly administered by the state and federal agencies. Redwood National and State Parks are actually a string of parks that were set aside by one agency or another and spared from the lumber wars. It starts in the north at Jedediah Smith Redwoods (p152) and continues south 70 miles to include Del Norte Coast Redwoods (p149), Prairie Creek Redwoods (below) and Redwood National Park. Together, these parks have been declared an International Biosphere Reserve and World Heritage Site.

You'll pass through teensy **Orick** (population 650) at the southern tip of the park. As the only settlement on the 40-mile stretch between Trinidad and Klamath it should be a bustling supply center, but has withered. Locals blame the park for their demise. A one-sided telling of the tale is spelled out in *Orick 911*, which you can rent free from the local video store.) If you need to gas up, stop here; otherwise, keep moving.

Orientation & Information

There are no fees and no entrance stations, so it's imperative to pick up the free official map either at the park headquarters (p150) in Crescent City or at the **Thomas H Kuchel Visitor Center** (Redwood Information Center; ☎ 707-465-7765; www.nps.gov/redw; Hwy 101; ⏰ 9am-6pm summer, 9am-4pm winter; 🏾) in Orick, where there's a 12-minute introductory video. Rangers issue permits here for Tall Trees Grove (below). For in-depth redwood ecology, buy the official parks handbook ($7.50). Outside are ocean-view picnic areas and boardwalks over the dunes – a great spot to let kids run.

Reserve campgrounds in advance, or run the risk of getting stuck in one of the unattractive RV parks nearby.

Sights & Activities

Just north of the visitors center, turn east onto Bald Hills Rd then it's 2 miles to **Lady Bird Johnson Grove**, one of the park's most beautiful groves, accessible via a gentle 1-mile loop trail. Follow signs. Continue another 5 miles up Bald Hills Rd to **Redwood Creek Overlook**. On the top of the ridgeline at 2100ft elevation, you'll see over the trees and the entire watershed – provided it's not foggy. Past the overlook lies the gated turn-off for **Tall Trees Grove**, the home to some of the world's tallest trees. Rangers issue only 50 vehicle permits per day, but they rarely run out. Pick one up, along with the gate-lock combination, from the Thomas H Kuchel Visitor Center (above) or park headquarters in Crescent City (p150). Allow four hours for the round-trip, which includes a 6-mile drive down a rough dirt

road (speed limit 15mph) and a steep 1.3-mile one-way hike, which descends 800ft to the grove.

The 4.5-mile **Dolason Prairie Trail** drops 2400ft in elevation, passing through various ecological zones, from open grasslands high above the trees into the lush forest below. The trailhead is 11 miles up Bald Hills Rd from Hwy 101; catch a shuttle car at Tall Trees Grove and spare yourself the uphill return.

The 2.7-mile **Emerald Ridge Trail** originates 600ft from the Tall Trees trailhead and drops to Redwood Creek, crisscrossing the stream and gravel bars (bring appropriate footwear and attempt this trail in summer only, when the water is low). Instead of following trail markers downstream, make an *upstream* detour for swimming holes, stunning scenery and total solitude.

There are several longer trails, including awe-inspiring **Redwood Creek Trail**, which also reaches Tall Trees Grove. You'll need a free backcountry permit to camp along the route, which is accessible only from Memorial Day to Labor Day, when footbridges are up. Otherwise, there's no way across the creek. (Note that there are more automobile break-ins at Redwood Creek trailhead than anywhere else in the park. Hide valuables.)

There's primitive camping in the park; inquire at visitors centers.

PRAIRIE CREEK REDWOODS STATE PARK

Famous for virgin redwood forests and unspoiled coastline, this 14,000-acre section of Redwood National and State Parks has 70 miles of hiking trails and spectacular scenic drives. Pick up information and sit by the fire at **Prairie Creek Visitors Center** (☎ 707-465-7354; per car $8; ⏰ 9am-5pm Mar-Oct, 10am-4pm Nov-Feb; 🏾), which has the best bookstore of all the redwood parks' visitor centers – including park headquarters. Kids love the taxidermy dioramas and their push-button, light-up displays. Outside, Roosevelt elk roam grassy flats.

Sights & Activities

Newton B Drury Scenic Parkway parallels Hwy 101 and is a worthy 8-mile detour through untouched ancient redwoods. Numerous trails branch off from roadside pullouts to allow visitors to wander agape under the canopies.

There are 28 mountain-biking and hiking trails through the park, from simple to strenuous. If you're tight on time or have mobility impairments, stop at **Big Tree**, an easy 100yd walk from the parking lot. Several other short nature trails start near the visitors center, including the Revelation Trail, Five-Minute Trail, Elk Prairie Trail and Nature Trail. If you only have a few hours, try the 3.5-mile **South Fork–Rhododendron–Brown Creek Loop**, particularly if it's spring when rhododendrons and wildflowers bloom. The best all-day option is the 11.5-mile **Coastal Trail**, though you'll want to approach from the Brown Creek to South Fork direction to spare a grueling incline. Another option for the conservation-minded wanderer is the **Ah-Pah Interpretive Trail** at the park's north end, where you can stroll a recently reforested logging road.

The **Coastal Drive** follows Davison Rd to access Gold Bluffs and Fern Canyon. Go west 3 miles north of Orick and doubleback north over corrugated gravel for 3.5 miles over the coastal hills, where you'll find the often-unmanned **fee station** (per vehicle $6). Up the coast is the lovely **Gold Bluffs Beach Campground**, where you can picnic or camp. One mile ahead, hike through **Fern Canyon**, where 60ft fern-covered sheer-rock walls can be seen from Steven Spielberg's *Jurassic Park 2: The Lost World*. This is one of the most photographed spots on the North Coast – damp and lush, all emerald green – and *totally* worth getting your toes wet to see.

Sleeping & Eating

Welcome to the great outdoors: without any motels or cabins, the choice sleeping here is to pitch a tent in the campgrounds at the southern end of the park. Look for rentals in nearby Eureka (p134).

Elk Prairie Campground (☎ reservations 800-444-7275; www.reserveamerica.com; campsites $35) Elk roam this popular campground, where you can sleep under redwoods or at the prairie's edge. The camp has hot showers and some hike-in sites. There's also a shallow creek to splash in. Sites 1 to 7 and 69 to 76 are on grassy prairies and get full sun; sites 8 to 68 are wooded. To camp in a mixed redwood forest, book sites 20 to 27.

Gold Bluffs Beach Campground (campsites $35) This campground sits between 100ft cliffs and wide-open ocean, but there are some windbreaks and solar-heated showers. Look for sites up the cliff under the trees. There are 29 first-come, first-served sites, with enough basic amenities to satisfy a family; you can't make reservations.

KLAMATH

pop 687

Giant metal-cast golden bears stand sentry at the bridge across the Klamath River announcing Klamath. Without them, you'd likely drive right by. With a gas station/market, a great diner and a casino, Klamath is basically a wide spot in the road. The Yurok Tribal Headquarters is here and the entire town and much of the surrounding area is the tribe's ancestral land. Klamath is roughly an hour north of Eureka.

August's **Salmon Festival** is the biggest event in town. Contact the **Klamath Chamber of Commerce** (☎ 800-200-2335; www.klamathcc.org). For hiking maps, stop by the Redwood National and State Parks Headquarters in Crescent City (p150) or the Thomas H Kuchel Visitor Center in Orick (opposite). **Blue Creek Guide Service** (☎ 707-482-0579, 707-951-1284; www.yurokfishingguides.com) is a Yurok-owner-operated company that leads excellent, custom-designed expeditions on the river.

Sights & Activities

The mouth of the **Klamath River** is dramatic. Marine, riparian, forest and meadow ecological zones all converge: the birding is exceptional! For the best views, head north of town to Requa Rd and the **Klamath River Overlook**, where you can picnic on high bluffs above driftwood-strewn beaches. On a clear day, this is one of the most spectacular viewpoints on the North Coast (no exaggeration) and one of the best whale-watching spots in California. For a good hike, head north along the Coastal Trail. You'll have the sand to yourself at **Hidden Beach**; access the trail at the northern end of **Motel Trees** (p149).

Just south of the river, on Hwy 101, follow signs for the scenic **Coastal Drive**, a narrow, winding country road (unsuitable for RVs and trailers) that skirts cliffs over the ocean. If it's foggy, forget it; you'll hardly see 20ft forward.

Paul Bunyan and his pal Babe the Blue Ox tower over the parking lot at Cheese of… er, **Trees of Mystery** (☎ 707-482-2251, 800-638-3389; www.treesofmystery.net; 15500 Hwy 101; ☑ 8am-7pm Jun-Aug, 9am-4pm Sep-May; ♿), a shameless, kitschy, mid-century tourist trap with a gondola running through the redwood canopy (adult/child/senior $13.50/6.50/10). The **End of the Trail Museum**, hidden behind the gift shop, has an amazing collection of Native American arts and artifacts – and it's *free*.

Sleeping & Eating

Woodsy Klamath is cheaper than nearby Crescent City, but there aren't as many places to eat or buy groceries and there's nothing to do at night but play cards.

Flint Ridge Campground (☎ 707-464-6101; campsites free) Four miles from the Klamath River Bridge via Coastal Drive, this tent-only, hike-in campground sits among a wild, overgrown meadow of ghostly, overgrown ferns and moss, a five-minute walk east, uphill from the dirt parking area. No water; pack out trash. And it's free!

Kamp Klamath (☎ 707-482-0227, 866-552-6284; www.kampklamath.com; tent/RV sites $20/30; ☐ ☎) If park campgrounds are full, pitch a tent on the river's south shore at this well-shaded RV park, with bicycle rentals and family-friendly events like all-you-can-eat Saturday BBQs and campfire songs. There's an on-site store with beer and camping equipment and a basic restaurant, the Big Foot Grill. RV sites have hookups.

Ravenwood Motel (☎ 707-482-5911, 866-520-9875; www.ravenwoodmotel.com; 131 Klamath Blvd; r/ste with kitchen $58/105; ☎) This is the best midrange motel within many, many miles, decorated

---

SALMON & THE DAMMED KLAMATH

Yurok elders will tell a story of the great salmon runs of their youth, when the spawning fish running the Klamath made the whole river appear to be silver and running away from the ocean. So how could it happen that the 2006 salmon-fishing season was almost canceled altogether, threatening the livelihood of the same tribes? There simply weren't enough fish. The problem lay not so much with overfishing – salmon fishing is heavily regulated – but habitat destruction by hydroelectric dams and logging.

The crisis began 100 years ago with major dam construction on the Klamath and large-scale logging. Dams blocked spawning adults and killed weak, immature fish in giant rotating hydroelectric turbines. They also caused diminished flows downriver, which caused water temperatures to rise, and sparked the growth of oxygen-depriving blue-green algae blooms, a persistent and serious problem to this day. Logging caused silt runoff from deforested hillsides, filling in the clear, cold-water pools and gravel beds that salmon require for spawning. By the 1970s there were five dams along the Klamath.

And while the tribes and fishermen on the coast saw the fish population deplete, it got worse in 2002 when the Bureau of Reclamation began to divert huge amounts of Klamath River water to inland farmers, some of whom grow crops in the desert. When the salmon returned to spawn that autumn, there wasn't enough water in the river, and that which did flow got so warm that it killed the fish. Over 30,000 spawning salmon died on the muddy banks. Because newborn fish don't spawn for approximately four years, the effects of the kill weren't fully felt until 2006. The local tribes, fishermen, sport anglers and tourism agencies still have not recovered.

The situation is not without hope, though. In March 2006, the US District Court in Oakland set caps on how much water could be diverted from the Klamath to farms, in order to protect migrating salmon. And the growing momentum to decommission some or all of the dams along the lower Klamath (a sentiment seen in the 'Undam the Klamath' bumper stickers) began to work: in 2007, the federal government required PacifiCorp, the dam owners, to install fish ladders at a cost of $300 million, and a year later the company signed a nonbinding agreement to decommission three dams by 2020. In 2009, PacifiCorp drafted a plan for the removal of four dams, a key breakthrough long sought after by environmental activists.

To learn the latest, search back issues online at the **Times-Standard** (www.times-standard.com) or ask a local member of the Yurok, Karuk or Klamath tribe, which has water rights to the lower Klamath.

with tasteful modern furnishings. The beds and bedding are high quality and they have BBQs. Call ahead, as it tends to fill.

Motel Trees (☎ 707-482-3152, 800-848-2982; www .treesofmystery.net; 15495 Hwy 101 S; d/q $60/103; ☎) Opposite Trees of Mystery, Motel Trees has standard-issue rooms and theme rooms. The restaurant (open 8am to 8pm in summer, closed Tuesday and Wednesday in winter) serves plain-old American cooking.

Steelhead Lodge (☎ 707-482-8145; Hwy 169; r $65, mains $16-25; ☯ dinner nightly summer, Fri-Sun Feb-Jun, closed Nov-Jan) Locals speak of the high-octane 'fishbowl' margaritas that come over the U-shaped redwood bar with a rueful reverence. This local joint 3 miles upriver in Klamath Glen has *a lot* of flavor, though less so in its meat and potatoes dinners. If you drown in the fishbowl, there are clean, basic motel rooms with kitchens..

ourpick Historic Requa Inn (☎ 707-482-1425, 866-800-8777; www.requainn.com; 451 Requa Rd; r $99-159 incl breakfast) A woodsy country lodge on bluffs overlooking the mouth of the Klamath, the 1914 Requa Inn is one of our North Coast favorites and – a cherry on top – it's a carbon neutral facility. Many of the charming country-style rooms have mesmerizing views over the misty river, as does the dining room, where guests have breakfast. After a day hiking, play Scrabble by the crackling fire in the common area and chat with other travelers.

Klamath River Cafe (☎ 707-482-1000; meals $8-12; ☯ breakfast & lunch) With excellent homemade baked goods, a daily pie special and excellent breakfast food, this shiny new place is the best diner food within miles. The breakfasts are killer. Seasonal hours vary, so call ahead. If you arrive around dinner time, cross your fingers – they're open sporadically for dinner.

DEL NORTE COAST REDWOODS STATE PARK

Marked by steep canyons and dense woods, 6200 acres of this **park** (per vehicle per day $8) are virgin redwood forest, crisscrossed by 15 miles of hiking trails. In December 2005, the park grew by 25,000 acres of logged-out land purchased from a lumber company. Now the entire ecologically important Redwood Creek watershed is fully protected – good news for salmon, since the watershed is one of the biggest spawning areas in all

of Northern California. Unfortunately, it's currently closed to the public.

Pick up maps and inquire about guided walks at the Redwood National and State Parks Headquarters in Crescent City (p150) or the Thomas H Kuchel Visitor Center in Orick (p146).

At the park's north end, watch the surf pound at **Crescent Beach**, just south of Crescent City via Enderts Beach Rd. Continue uphill to **Crescent Beach Overlook** for picnicking and wintertime whale-watching. Hike via the Crescent Beach Trail (or along the Coastal Trail from the south) to **Enderts Beach** for magnificent tidepools at low tide.

Tall trees cling precipitously to canyon walls that drop to the rocky, timber-strewn coastline. It's almost impossible to get to the water, except via the gorgeous but steep **Damnation Trail**. If you don't want to hike, head south to **False Klamath Cove**, where you can picnic and stretch your legs on the sand.

Mill Creek Campground (☎ 800-444-7275; www .reserveamerica.com; campsites $35) has 145 sites in a redwood grove, 2 miles east of Hwy 101, 7 miles south of Crescent City. It's quieter than Jedediah Smith Redwoods (p152), but it's in a second-growth, not old-growth forest. Sites 1 to 74 are woodsier; sites 75 to 145 sunnier. Hike-in sites are prettiest.

CRESCENT CITY
pop 7542

Though Crescent City was founded as a thriving 1853 seaport and supply center for inland gold mines, the history was quite literally washed away in 1964: half the town was swallowed by a tsunami. Somehow, this disaster has become a point of civic pride, evidenced by the tsunami-logo flags decorating downtown lampposts and historical placards (see boxed text, p151). Of course, they rebuilt (though mostly with the utilitarian ugliness of ticky-tacky buildings). Crescent City remains California's last big town north of Arcata, though the constant fog (and sounding fog horn) and damp, '60s sprawl makes it about as charming as a wet bag of dirty laundry. At least there's cell-phone reception. Considering the entire town is on the water, city planners blew it when it came to maximizing the views – except at Beachfront Park and along Pebble Beach Dr, the town's only pretty residential neighborhood. The economy depends heavily on shrimp and crab fishing, hotel tax and on Pelican Bay maximum-security prison, just north of town, which adds tension to the air and lots of cops on the streets.

Orientation & Information

Hwy 101 splits into two parallel one-way streets, with the southbound traffic on L St, northbound on M St. Front St runs west toward the lighthouse. The tiny downtown is centered along 3rd St.

Crescent City–Del Norte Chamber of Commerce (☎ 707-464-3174, 800-343-8300; www.delnorte.org; 1001 Front St; ☷ 9am-5pm daily Jul-Sep, Mon-Fri Oct-Jun) Pick up local information here.

Redwood National & State Parks Headquarters (☎ 707-465-7306; 1111 2nd St; ☷ 9am-5pm) On-staff rangers and information about all four parks under its jurisdiction. This place is key for all wilderness adventures in the area. On the corner of K St.

Sights & Activities

Battery Point Lighthouse (☎ 707-464-3089; www .delnortehistory.org/lighthouse) at the south end of A St is among the last-remaining light stations with a live-in lighthouse keeper. It sits on a tiny, rocky island that you can reach at low tide; though, even then, sneaker waves have soaked many. April to October, tour the **museum** (☷ 10am-4pm Wed-Sun May-Sep, Sat & Sun Dec-Feb); hours vary with tides and weather. Phone ahead, or check the bulletin board in the parking lot (adult/child $3/1). Six miles offshore, the **St George Reef Lighthouse** (☎ 707-464-8299; www.stgeorgereeflighthouse.us; ☷ Oct-May) is visible on clear days. The only way to visit is via helicopter ($195); you need to book ahead.

The **North Coast Marine Mammal Center** (☎ 707-464-6265; www.northcoastmmc.org; 424 Howe Dr; ☷ 10am-5pm; ☷) is the ecologically minded foil to Ocean World: the clinic treats injured seals, sea lions and dolphins and releases them back into the wild (donation requested). **Beachfront Park** (Howe Dr), between B & H Sts, has a great harborside beach for little ones (no waves), picnic tables and a bicycle trail. Further east on nearby J St, you'll come to **Kidtown** (Howe Dr), with slides and swings and a make-believe castle and a walk-thru tree. For a scenic drive, head north on Pebble Beach Dr, which ends at

Point St George, where you can stroll over grassy dunes.

Crescent City is a very mellow place to learn to surf. The best waves for beginners are on South Beach, where you can rent a board ($25 per day) and wet suit ($10) from the friendly and helpful folks at **South Beach Outfitters** (☎ 707-464-2963; www.southbeachoutfitters .net; 128 Anchor Way). On Friday between 10pm and midnight, patrons enjoy glow-in-the-dark Cosmic Bowling ($13 per person) at **Tsunami Lanes** (☎ 707-464-4323; www.tsunamilanes .com; 760 L St).

Festivals & Events

The best reason to visit may be the **Aleutian Goose Festival** (www.aleutiangoosefestival.org), at the end of March, to see the dawn sky fill with thousands of migrating geese. Less impressive, the **Del Norte County Fair** (http://dnfairgrounds .com) takes place in early August.

Sleeping

Since this is a popular stop between Portland and San Francisco, hotels are a sellers' market: a drab little motel can charge getaway prices. In winter, it's a different story entirely and prices hit rock bottom. If you stay for more than a day, investigate vacation rentals. For motels, ones on the south side of town are quietest. Also see Pelican State Beach (p153).

Campgrounds (☎ 707-464-7230; campsites $10) The county operates two campgrounds just outside town: Florence Keller Park (3400 Cunningham Ln) has 50 sites in a beautiful redwood grove (take Hwy 101 north to Elk Valley Cross Rd and follow the signs); Ruby Van Deventer Park (4705 N Bank Rd) has 18 sites along the Smith River, off Hwy 197.

Curly Redwood Lodge (☎ 707-464-2137; www .curlyredwoodlodge.com; 701 Hwy 101 S; r $65-70) The Redwood Lodge is a marvel; entirely built and paneled from a single curly redwood tree which measured over 18' thick in diameter. Progressively restored and polished into a gem of mod '50s kitsch, the inn is a delight for retro junkies. Rooms are clean, large and comfortable (request one away from the road). For truly modern accommodations look elsewhere.

Bayview Motel (☎ 707-465-2050, 800-446-0583; www.bayviewmotel.com; 310 Hwy 101 S; r $91-104, tr $130; ☷ ☷)This nondescript two-story motel has clean and standard modern facilities and is further from the road, providing maximum quiet. It accommodates small pets.

Crescent Beach Motel (☎ 707-464-5436; www .crescentbeachmotel.com; 1455 Hwy 101 S; no view r $70, ocean-view s/d $92/98; 🌐) Just south of town, this basic, old-fashioned motel is the only place in town to stay right on the beach, offering views that distract you from the somewhat plain indoor environs. Try here first, but skip rooms without a view.

Lighthouse Inn (☎ 707-464-3993, 877-464-3993; www.lighthouse101.com; 681 Hwy 101 S; s/d/tr $99/119/ 160; 🔲 💻 🌐) A good choice for families, the rooms are big and spotless at this three-story motel. The lobby has too many frilly details (think dollhouses), but rooms have refrigerators and microwaves.

Eating & Drinking

Restaurants close early, before 9pm. A trio of quality restaurants await travelers on the South Bay pier.

Beacon Burger (☎ 707-464-6565; 160 Anchor Way; dishes $6-10; 🕙 11:30am-8:30pm Mon-Sat) This scrappy little one-room burger joint has been here forever, square in the middle of a parking lot overlooking the South Bay. It looks like it might invite a health inspector's scorn, but you'll quickly forgive after ordering a burger – perfectly greasy and mysteriously wonderful. They come sided with potato gems and a menu of thick shakes.

Perlita's (☎ 707-465-6770; 297 Hwy 101 S; mains $5-12; 🕙 11:30am-8:30pm) The carnitas are savory and smoky and the Tex-Mex-style tamales are expertly made. With cheap taco specials and strong drinks, it's the favorite Mexican joint in town.

Good Harvest Café (☎ 707-465-6028; 575 Hwy 101 S; dishes $7-10; 🕙 7am-9pm Mon-Sat, from 8am Sun; 👶) This popular local cafe recently moved into a spacious new location across from the harbor. They also added a dinner menu on a par with the quality salads, smoothies and sandwiches that made them so popular in the first place. Good beers, a crackling fire and loads of vegetarian options make this the best dining spot in town.

The Chart Room (☎ 707-464-5993; 130 Anchor Way; dinner mains $9-23; 🕙 6:30am-7pm Sun-Thu, to 8pm Fri & Sat; 👶) At the tip of the South Harbor pier, this joint is renowned far and wide for its fish and chips: batter caked golden beauties which deliver on their reputation. It's often a hive of families, retirees, Harley riders and local businessmen, so grab a beer at the small bar and wait for a table.

Bistro Gardens (☎ 707-464-5627; 110 Anchor Way; lunch $8-11, dinner $17-27; 🕙 7am-8pm Mon-Tue to 4pm) This upscale option for Crescent City serves a fish-heavy menu, filet mignon and saucy continental fare. The ocean views are good, but the best option is to grab one of their pre-made picnic lunches (the five options include fancy cold salads, appetizers and deserts) and head to the beach.

Getting There & Around

United Express (☎ 800-241-6522; www.united.com) flies into tiny **Del Norte County Airport** (CEC; ☎ 707-464-7229), aka Jack McNamara Field, north of town. Rent a vehicle, by reservation only,

---

CRESCENT CITY'S GREAT TSUNAMI

On March 28, 1964, most of downtown Crescent City was destroyed by a tsunami. At 3:36am, a giant earthquake occurred on the north shore of Prince William Sound in Alaska. Measuring a whopping 9.2 on the Richter scale, the quake was the most severe ever recorded in North America. The first of the ensuing giant ocean swells reached Crescent City only a few hours later.

Officials warned the sheriff's office, and at 7:08am evacuation began. The waves arrived an hour later. The first two were small, only 13ft above the tide line, and many thought the worst had passed. Then the water receded until the bay was empty, leaving boats that had been anchored offshore in the mud. Frigid water surged in, rising all the way up to 5th St, knocking buildings off their foundations, carrying away everything in its path. By the time the fourth and final wave receded, 29 blocks of town were destroyed, 300 buildings were displaced, five gasoline storage tanks exploded and eleven people died, three of whom were never found.

Many old-timers are still remembered for heroic acts during the event, helping to save their neighbors and rebuild. Today, the modern little downtown shopping center that replaced many of the destroyed buildings bears an unusual but appropriate name – Tsunami Landing.

at **Hertz** (☎ 707-464-5750, 800-654-3131; www.hertz .com), or at the local **Two Guys Car Rental** (☎ 707-464-6818, 800-308-7813). **Redwood Coast Transit** (☎ 707-464-9314, 707-464-6400; www.redwoodcoast transit.org) operates two daily buses (except Sunday) between Crescent City and Arcata for $20 one way, or $30 for a five-day pass. It also serves Klamath and Smith River. Service between Klamath and Crescent City costs $1 and takes about 40 minutes. (The transit company's website is woefully inadequate; call for up-to-date information.)

TOLOWA DUNES STATE PARK & LAKE EARL WILDLIFE AREA

Some 10,000 acres of terrain of this naturalist's playground lie five minutes north of Crescent City via Northcrest Dr. The **park and wildlife area** (☎ 707-465-2145; ☘ sunrise-sunset) is a major stopping point along the Pacific flyway for Aleutian geese, encompassing wetlands, dunes, meadows, wooded hillsides and two connected (and misnamed) lagoons, **Lake Earl** and **Lake Tolowa**. They're the biggest coastal lagoons in California, attracting over 250 species of birds, including peregrine falcons. Out near the shore, you'll see harbor seals, sea lions and – if you're lucky – a whale.

The 20 miles of hiking and horseback trails are mostly level, but sandy. The best wetland trails lie in the northern portion of the park, where a number of endangered and threatened species populate freshwater and marine habitats. Pick up information from the Crescent City–Del Norte County Chamber of Commerce or the Redwood National and State Parks office in Crescent City (p150). Since the winter is marshy and wet, and the summer is bone dry, the best time to visit is spring and early summer, while everything is green and the wildflowers are lovely.

The park and wildlife area are split into a patchwork of lands administered by California State Parks and the Department of Fish & Game (DFG); it's hard to tell where one area begins and another ends. The DFG focuses on single-species management, hunting and fishing, while the State Parks focus on ecodiversity and recreation. Thus you might be hiking a vast expanse of gorgeous and pristine dunes, with peerless views of mountains and sea, when out of nowhere you'll hear a shotgun in the woods. Fear not: there are strict regulations limiting where and when you can hunt and such places are clearly marked.

There are two primitive **campgrounds** (campsites $10): a walk-in environmental campground (no water) and an equestrian campsite (non-potable well water). Both are first-come, first-served. Register at Jedediah Smith (below) or Del Norte Coast Redwoods State Park (p149) campgrounds. Bring firewood and be prepared for mosquitoes in late spring and early summer.

JEDEDIAH SMITH REDWOODS STATE PARK

Bald eagles fly lazy circles above the sparkling Smith River in the state's northernmost redwood park, **Jedediah Smith** (per day $8). Ten miles northeast of Crescent City (via Hwy 101 east to Hwy 197), it's home to California's only undammed major river. The **visitors center** (☎ 707-465-2144; ☘ 10am-4pm daily summer, Sat & Sun fall & spring) sells hiking maps and nature guides, but if you prefer to ride, try the outstanding 11-mile **Howland Hill Scenic Drive** which cuts through otherwise inaccessible areas (take Hwy 199 to South Fork Rd; turn right after crossing two bridges). It's a rough, unpaved road, impassable for RVs over 22ft and it gets graded only once every spring, but if you can't hike it's the best way to see the forest.

The **Simpson-Reed Grove** has a good interpretive trail, though there is more of a challenge in the longer **Mill Creek Trail**, off Howland Hill Scenic Dr, which passes through redwoods and along a creek before ending at the park's campground on the Smith River. **Boy Scout Tree Trail** leads through the lush woods to a 20ft waterfall (December to May), the only waterfall in any of the redwood parks. There's a terrific **river beach** and picnic area near the park entrance, off Hwy 199, 5 miles east of Hwy 101. An easy half-mile path, departing from the far side of the campground, crosses the Smith River via a summer-only footbridge, leading to **Stout Grove**, the park's most famous grove.

The popular **campground** (☎ reservations 800-444-7275; www.reserveamerica.com; tent sites $5 (walk-in), campsites $35) has hot showers and sits beneath giant redwoods beside the river. Fabulous. Make reservations.

Just east, the **Hiouchi Information Center** (☎ 707-464-6101, ext 5064; ☘ 9am-5pm mid-Jun–mid-Sep)

DETOUR: SMITH RIVER NATIONAL RECREATION AREA

West of Jedediah Smith Redwoods, the Smith River, the state's last remaining undammed waterway, runs right beside Hwy 199. Originating high in the Siskiyou Mountains, its serpentine course cuts through deep rock canyons beneath thick forests. Chinook salmon and steelhead trout annually migrate up its clear waters. Camp, hike, raft and kayak; check regulations if you want to fish. **Lunker Fish Trips** (☎ 707-458-4704, 800-248-4704; 2590 Hwy 199) leads excursions and rents inflatable kayaks. (Note that when it rains, the water rises fast because the riverbed is mostly rock; but it recedes fast too.) Stop by the **Six Rivers National Forest Headquarters** (☎ 707-457-3131; www.fs.fed.us/r5/sixrivers; 10600 Hwy 199, Gasquet; ⏲ 8am-4:30 daily summer, Mon-Fri fall-spring) to get your bearings; opening hours can vary. Pick up pamphlets for the **Darlingtonia Trail** and **Myrtle Creek Botanical Area**, both easy jaunts into the woods where you can see rare plants and learn about the area's geology. The **South Fork & Middle Fork confluence** is one of the most photographed spots around, and it's easy to reach: take Hwy 199 to South Fork Rd and turn right. Several hundred feet ahead, turn right again; pull off at the next right, just ahead. Bring a picnic.

---

stocks maps and books. Families can borrow free activity backpacks with projects for kids. When the visitors centers are closed, go to Redwood National and State Parks Headquarters in Crescent City (p150).

A mile east of the park in **Hiouchi**, look for **Lunker Fish Trips** (see boxed text, above), one of the North Coast's finest steelhead-fishing guides (fishing is best September to April).

At **Hiouchi Hamlet RV Resort** (☎ 707-458-3321, 800-722-9468; tent sites $19-25, RV sites $33-36; ☎) there is also a small market for supplies and fishing licenses, plus a full-service restaurant. Across the street, the **Hiouchi Motel** (☎ 707-458-3041, 866-446-8244; www.hiouchimotel.com; 2097 Hwy 199; s $50, d $65-70; 🖳) has clean, straightforward rooms. The more expensive option, **Patrick Creek Lodge** (☎ 707-457-3323; www.patrickcreeklodge.net; r $100-130; 🖳) is a 1926 log cabin–style roadhouse that has simple accommodations and serves three surprisingly good meals a day (lunch $6 to $11, dinner $15 to $22).

PELICAN STATE BEACH

Smack dab on the Oregon border, five-acre **Pelican State Beach** (☎ 707-464-6101, ext 5151) is easy to miss. From the south, pull off Hwy 101 just before the state agricultural inspection station. There are no facilities. It's a great beach for kite-flying; pick one up just over the border.

Clifford Kamph Memorial Park (☎ 707-464-7230; 15100 Hwy 101; tent sites $10; 🐾) Though it's within earshot of the road, you can pitch a tent by the ocean here. Pets on-leash welcome, but no RVs.

Sea Escape (☎ 707-487-7333; www.seaescape.us; 15370 Hwy 101 N; r $95-135; ☎) has clean, if a bit frumpy, motel-style suites. Some have ocean views and kitchens.

Casa Rubio (☎ 707-487-4313; 17285 Crissey Rd, www.casarubio.com; r $98-158) Like a distant relative's lovely little summer cottage, this quiet spot rents four ocean-view rooms and offers strolls to the shore or through the garden.

Central Coast

Yes, San Francisco and LA are givens, but no trip to California is worth its salt without a jaunt down the Central Coast. In fact, this stretch has almost everything you've come to California for, at least when it comes to natural beauty: wild Pacific beaches, towering sand dunes, mossy redwood forests where hot springs beckon, and rolling golden hills with ripening vineyards.

In the north, flower-power Santa Cruz stands as the ideological and physical counterpoint to treacly Carmel-by-the-Sea, the gateway to Big Sur country, where Hwy 1 pulls out all the stops scenery-wise. It's an epic journey, past historic lighthouses, California condor habitat and beaches where northern elephant seals sprawl, to can't-miss-it Hearst Castle, a historical monument to personal empire.

The warmth of Southern California begins kissing your skin in the historic college town of San Luis Obispo, aka SLO. It's embraced by the characterful beach towns of Estero and San Luis Bays, stretching from Cayucos Pier past the authentic working fishing harbors of Morro Bay and Avila Beach, down to retro-20th-century Pismo Beach, a pretty idyllic place to lay your head.

SoCal's distinctive Mission-style architecture is laid on extra thick in gracious, moneyed Santa Barbara. North of the city is the cultivated perfection of the wine country that starred in the indie film *Sideways*. To the south waits the primordial rawness of Channel Islands National Park.

Although it's possible to drive through in one ridiculously long day, to do the Central Coast any justice at all, plan on spending at least a week to take advantage of fresh-air opportunities for kayaking, swimming, surfing, snorkeling, diving, hiking, cycling and more.

HIGHLIGHTS

- Cruising the famous ribbon of Hwy 1 where sea meets sky in **Big Sur** (p176)
- Being mesmerized by sea otters and psychedelic jellies inside the **Monterey Bay Aquarium** (p166)
- Screaming your face off aboard a 1924 wooden roller coaster on the **Santa Cruz Beach Boardwalk** (p155)
- Marveling at gorgeously grandiose **Hearst Castle** (p181), overflowing with artistic booty from around the world
- Soaking up the chic culture and endless beaches of posh **Santa Barbara** (p195), aka the American Riviera
- Kayaking around Morro Rock and hiking ocean bluffs in the beach towns of **Estero Bay** (p184)

★ Santa Cruz Beach Boardwalk

★ Monterey Bay Aquarium

★ Big Sur

★ Hearst Castle

★ Estero Bay

Santa Barbara ★

MONTEREY BAY

Monterey Bay is the constant backdrop to life around the peninsula. Along its half-moon coastline, you'll find miles of often-deserted beaches and small towns bubbling over with idiosyncratic character. Even more diverse is the bay itself, protected as the Monterey Bay National Marine Sanctuary, one of the richest and most varied marine environments anywhere on the planet.

SANTA CRUZ

pop 56,925

Anchoring the north end of Monterey Bay, Santa Cruz is counterculture central, a touchy-feely place famous for its leftie-liberal-socialist politics and live-and-let-live ideology – except when it comes to dogs (not allowed off-leash or downtown), parking (meters run seven days a week) and Republicans (allegedly shot on sight). The City Council spends more of its time debating whether medical marijuana dispensaries should be allowed than figuring out ways to help downtown's homeless population.

Local politics aside, Santa Cruz is a crazy-fun city with a carnival-esque downtown. On the waterfront is the famous beach boardwalk and, in the hills, the University of California, Santa Cruz (UCSC). Plan to hang out for a half day, but to truly appreciate the aesthetic of jangly skirts, crystal pendants and waist-length Rastafarian dreadlocks, you'll need to stay longer.

Orientation

Santa Cruz stretches along the coast, blending into Capitola, a low-key beach town, and Aptos beyond. The meandering San Lorenzo River divides the town into a sort of yin and yang. Pacific Ave is downtown's main street. Hwy 1 from the north leads onto Mission St; Hwy 17, the main route from the San Francisco Bay Area, turns into Ocean St. The UCSC campus is uphill, about 2.5 miles northwest of downtown.

Information

Bookshop Santa Cruz (☎ 831-423-0900; www.bookshopsantacruz.com; 1520 Pacific Ave; 🕑 9am-10pm Sun-Thu, 9am-11pm Fri & Sat) Vast selection of new and used books, eclectic magazines and a café; also the city's unofficial cultural center.

FAST FACTS

- **Average temperature low/high in Santa Barbara** January 41/65°F, July 57/77°F
- **San Francisco to Monterey** 120 miles, two to 2½ hours
- **Santa Cruz to Big Sur** 65 miles, 1½ to two hours
- **Big Sur to San Luis Obispo** 115 miles, 2½ to three hours
- **Santa Barbara to Santa Monica** 95 miles, 1½ to 2½ hours

FedEx Office (☎ 831-425-1177; 105 Laurel St; per min 20-30¢; 🕑 7am-11pm Mon-Fri, 9am-9pm Sat & Sun; 💻 📶) High-speed internet workstations.

KPIG 107.5 FM Plays the classic Santa Cruz soundtrack (think Bob Marley, Janis Joplin, the Grateful Dead).

Post Office (☎ 831-426-0144; 850 Front St; 🕑 9am-5pm Mon-Fri)

Visitor Center (☎ 831-425-1234, 800-833-3494; www.santacruz.org; 1211 Ocean St; 🕑 9am-5pm Mon-Fri, 10am-4pm Sat, 11am-3pm Sun; 💻 📶) Free courtesy phones for checking lodgings availability.

Sights

Go strolling, shopping and freak-watching along downtown's Pacific Ave, a 10-minute walk from the beach.

SANTA CRUZ BEACH BOARDWALK

The 1907 **boardwalk** (☎ 831-423-5590; www.beachboardwalk.com; admission free, per ride $2.25-4.50, all-day pass $30; 🕑 seasonal hr vary; 👶) is the West Coast's oldest beachfront amusement park. It has a glorious old-school Americana vibe, with the smell of cotton candy mixing with the salt air, punctuated by the squeals of kiddos hanging upside down on carnival rides. The half-mile-long Giant Dipper, a vintage 1924 wooden roller coaster, and the 1911 Looff carousel are National Historic Landmarks. When you're feeling dizzy, don your flip-flops and plop down your towel on the beach outside. On summer Friday nights, tune in to free concerts by rock veterans you may have thought were already dead.

MUNICIPAL WHARF

You can drive the length of the wharf, where restaurants, gift shops and barking sea lions compete for attention. Some shops

CENTRAL COAST

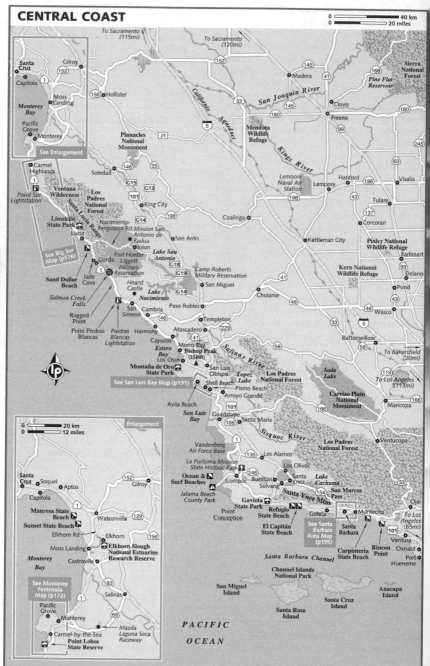

CENTRAL COAST

rent poles and fishing tackle if you're keen to join those patiently waiting patiently for a bite. The views here are first-rate.

WEST CLIFF DRIVE
Bordered by a paved recreation path, this scenic road follows the cliffs southwest of the wharf. Lighthouse Point overlooks **Steamers Lane**, one of the top – and most accessible – surfing spots in California. The lighthouse is home to a tiny **surfing museum** (☎ 831-420-6289; www.santacruzsurfingmuseum.org; 701 W Cliff Dr; donation requested; ☺ noon-4pm Thu-Mon early Sep-early Jul, 10am-5pm Wed-Mon early Jul-early Sep).

Just west of the lighthouse, **Its Beach** is the city's official off-leash beach for dogs (before 10am and after 4pm only). Tops for sunsets, **Natural Bridges State Beach** (☎ 831-423-4609; per car $10; ☺ 8am-sunset; ☂) is at the end of W Cliff Dr, 3 miles from the wharf. There are tidepools for exploring and eucalyptus trees where migratory monarch butterflies roost in big bunches from mid-October through late February.

UNIVERSITY OF CALIFORNIA, SANTA CRUZ
Check it out: a banana slug is the school mascot! Established in the countercultural 1960s, youthful **University of California, Santa Cruz** (UCSC; ☎ 831-459-0111; www.ucsc.edu) is known for its creative and liberal bent. Its rural campus encompasses coast redwoods and architecturally interesting buildings – many made of recycled materials – designed to blend in with the rolling pasture lands. There are two contemporary art galleries, a tranquil **arboretum** (☎ 831-427-2998; 1156 High St; adult/child 6-17 $5/2, free 1st Tue of the month; ☺ 9am-5pm) and several prettily decaying 19th-century structures from the Cowell Ranch, on whichthe campus was built. Agriculture is big here: look for a seasonal **farm cart** (cnr High & Bay Sts; ☺ noon-6pm Tue & Fri mid-Jun–Sep) selling fruit, veggies and flowers grown on campus.

MISSION SANTA CRUZ
Founded in 1791, Mission of the Holy Cross gave the town its name; today it's one of California's most unremarkable missions. The mission fell apart after secularization under Mexican rule and an 1857 earthquake destroyed it completely. Today, Holy Cross Catholic Church stands on the original site. Nearby, the 1931 **mission church** (☎ 831-426-5686; www.holycrosssantacruz.com; 130 Emmet St;

donation requested; ☺ 10am-4pm Tue-Sat, 10am-2pm Sun) is a half-size replica. Around the corner, **Santa Cruz Mission State Historic Park** (☎ 831-425-5849; 144 School St; admission free; ☺ 10am-4pm Thu-Sat, noon-4pm Sun) includes one original structure, the 1791 Neary-Rodriguez Adobe.

MUSEUM OF ART & HISTORY
This smart little downtown **museum** (☎ 831-429-1964; www.santacruzmah.org; McPherson Center, 705 Front St; adult/child 2-17 $5/2, free on 1st Fri of the month; ☺ 11am-5pm Tue-Sun, to 9pm on 1st Fri of the month) is worth a quick look for its rotating displays by contemporary California artists and offbeat local history exhibits.

Activities
SWIMMING & SURFING
Although the northern side of Monterey Bay is warmer than the south, the water here averages a shivery 57°F. Without a wetsuit, various body parts will quickly turn blue.

Surfing is huge in Santa Cruz, especially at **Steamers Lane** (see left). Other fave surf spots are **Pleasure Point Beach** (E Cliff Dr), east of the river, and **Manresa State Beach** (p163). Just west of the municipal wharf, **Cowell Beach** is a popular spot for novice waveriders.

To rent surfboards ($20) and wetsuits ($10), check out women-owned **Paradise Surf Shop** (☎ 831-462-3880; www.paradisesurf.com; 3961 Portola Dr, Capitola; ☺ 10am-6pm Mon-Fri, 9am-6pm Sat & Sun) and internationally renowned **O'Neill Surf Shop** (☎ 831-475-4151; 1115 41st Ave, Capitola; ☺ 9am-8pm Mon-Fri, 8am-8pm Sat & Sun),

---

WHAT THE...?

A kitschy old-fashioned tourist trap, the **Mystery Spot** (☎ 831-423-8897; www.mystery spot.com; 465 Mystery Spot Rd; admission $5; ☺ 10am-6pm Mon-Fri, 9am-7pm Sat & Sun Jun-Aug, 10am-5pm daily Sep-May; ☂) has scarcely changed since the day it opened in 1940. On this steeply sloping hillside, compasses point crazily, mysterious forces push you around and buildings lean at weird angles. Yes, it's silly, but it's also classic Santa Cruz. Make reservations or risk being stuck waiting for a tour. It's 3 miles north of downtown: take Water St east to Market St, turn left and continue on Branciforte Dr into the hills. Parking costs $5. Don't forget your souvenir bumper sticker!

CENTRAL COAST

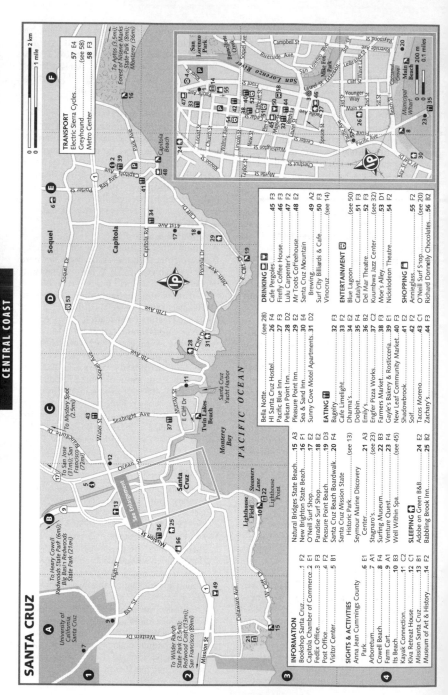

SANTA CRUZ

CENTRAL COAST

INFORMATION
Bookshop Santa Cruz...1 F2
Capitola Chamber of Commerce...2 E1
FedEx Office...3 F3
Post Office...4 F2
Visitor Center...5 B1

SIGHTS & ACTIVITIES
Anna Jean Cummings County Park...6 E1
Arboretum...7 A1
Cowell Beach...8 F4
Farm Cart...9 A1
Its Beach...10 B3
Kayak Connection...11 C2
Kiva Retreat House...12 C1
Mission Santa Cruz...13 B1
Museum of Art & History...14 F2
Natural Bridges State Beach...15 A3
New Brighton State Beach...16 F1
O'Neill Surf Shop...17 E2
Paradise Surf Shop...18 E2
Pleasure Point Beach...19 D3
Santa Cruz Beach Boardwalk...20 F4
Santa Cruz Mission State Historic Park...(see 13)
Seymour Marine Discovery Center...21 A3
Stagnaro's...22 B3
Surfing Museum...23 F4
Venture Quest...(see 45)
Well Within Spa...(see 45)

SLEEPING
Adobe on Green B&B...24 E2
Babbling Brook Inn...25 B2
Bella Notte...(see 28)
HI Santa Cruz Hostel...26 F4
Pacific Blue Inn...27 D2
Pelican Point Inn...28 E2
Pleasure Point Inn...29 E2
Sea & Sand Inn...30 E4
Sunny Cove Motel Apartments...31 D2

EATING
Bagelry...32 F3
Cafe Limelight...33 F2
Dharma's...34 F4
Dolphin...35 B2
Emily's...36 B2
Engfer Pizza Works...37 C2
Farmers Market...38 F3
Gayle's Bakery & Rosticceria...39 E1
New Leaf Community Market...40 F3
Shadowbrook...41 F2
Soif...42 F2
Tacos Moreno...43 C1
Zachary's...44 F3

DRINKING
Cafe Pergoles...45 F3
Firefly Coffee House...46 F3
Lulu Carpenter's...47 F2
Mr Toots Coffeehouse...48 E2
Santa Cruz Mountain Brewing...49 A2
Surf City Billiards & Cafe...50 F3
Vinocruz...(see 14)

ENTERTAINMENT
Blue Lagoon...(see 50)
Catalyst...51 F3
Del Mar Theatre...52 F3
Kuumbwa Jazz Center...(see 32)
Moe's Alley...53 D1
Nickelodeon Theatre...54 F2

SHOPPING
Annieglass...55 F2
O'Neill Surf S-op...(see 20)
Richard Donnelly Chocolates...56 B2

TRANSPORT
Electric Sierra Cycles...57 E4
Greyhound...(see 58)
Metro Center...58 F3

SANTA CRUZ FOR KIDS

Near Natural Bridges State Beach (p157), the **Seymour Marine Discovery Center** (☎ 831-459-3800; www2.ucsc.edu/seymourcenter; off Delaware Ave; adult/child 4-16 $6/4; ☺ 10am-5pm Jun-Aug, 10am-5pm Tue-Sat & noon-5pm Sun Sep-May, tours 1pm, 2pm & 3pm daily; ♿) is part of UCSC's Long Marine Laboratory. Kid-friendly interactive exhibits include touchable tidepools, aquarium tanks and a ginormous blue-whale skeleton outside.

If it's too cold for the beach or your kids aren't up for riding a roller coaster, ride the **Roaring Camp Railroad** (☎ 831-335-4484; www.roaringcamp.com; round-trip fares adult/child 3-12 from $20/14; ☺ seasonal hr vary; ♿), which operates standard-gauge trains from the beach boardwalk up to Felton, 6 miles north of Santa Cruz, where narrow-gauge trains continue up into the redwood forests.

Local moms and dads call the area's best playground, **Anna Jean Cummings County Park** (☎ 831-454-7956; 461 Old San Jose Rd, north of Soquel Dr, Soquel; admission free; ☺ 8am-dusk; ♿), 'Blue Balls Park' after several giant blue balls that appear to be rolling uphill. It's a 10-minute drive east of Santa Cruz, off the Bay/Porter exit from Hwy 1.

where the expert staff have heaps of local knowledge.

Wanna learn to surf? Paradise Surf Shop and **Richard Schmidt Surf School** (☎ 831-423-0928; www.richardschmidt.com) will have you standing and surfing the first day out. Two-hour group lessons average $80 to $100, including equipment rental.

KAYAKING

Kayaking lets you discover the craggy coastline and its kelp beds where sea otters float up close. **Venture Quest** (☎ 831-427-2267; www.kayaksantacruz.com; Municipal Wharf) rents kayaks, provides instruction and leads whale-watching and nature tours as far south as Point Lobos (p174). **Kayak Connection** (☎ 831-479-1121; www.kayakconnection.com; Santa Cruz Harbor, 413 Lake Ave) also offers rentals and tours, including at Elkhorn Slough (p164). Four-hour single/double kayak rentals start at $30/45; lessons and guided tours range from $25 to $95.

WHALE-WATCHING & FISHING

Whale-watching trips and fishing expeditions depart from the municipal wharf. The most popular months for whale-watching trips are December through April, though there's plenty of marine life to see on a summer bay cruise. **Stagnaro's** (☎ tickets 800-979-3370; www.stagnaros.com; Municipal Wharf; scenic cruise adult/child 4-13 from $15/10, whale-watching trip from $41/30, fishing trips $50-75) is a longstanding operator.

CYCLING & HIKING

An easy walk or beach-cruiser ride with million-dollar ocean views – especially at sunset – follows West Cliff Drive (p157). From the boardwalk it's 1 mile to Lighthouse Point and 3 miles to Natural Bridges State Beach. Alternatively, follow E Cliff Dr, stopping at locals' favorite beaches along the way. Nearby state parks offer better hikes, including at **Henry Cowell Redwoods State Park** (☎ 831-335-7077; off Hwy 9; per car $10; ☺ 8am-sunset), near Felton in the Santa Cruz Mountains, where you'll also find **Big Basin Redwoods State Park** (see boxed text, p86); at oceanfront **Wilder Ranch State Park** (☎ 831-423-9703; off Hwy 1; per car $10; ☺ 8am-sunset), also strewn with mountain-biking trails, just north of Santa Cruz; and **Forest of Nisene Marks State Park** (☎ 831-763-7062; Aptos Creek Rd, off Hwy 1; per car $8; ☺ sunrise-sunset), 4 miles north of Aptos (p163).

SPAS

Santa Cruz has a surprising number of spas with private soaking tubs. Locals call them 'soak-and-pokes' (wink, nudge). Sociable **Kiva Retreat House** (☎ 831-429-1142; www.kivaretreat.com; 702 Water St; ☺ noon-11pm Mon-Thu, noon-midnight Fri & Sat, 1:30-11pm Sun, women-only 10:30am-2pm Wed & 9am-1:30pm Sun) offers community (per adult/child eight to 14 $20/5) and private (hourly rental per single/couple from $18/28) hot tubs. **Well Within Spa** (☎ 831-458-9355; www.wellwithinspa.com; 417 Cedar St; ☺ 11am-midnight) rents indoor and outdoor hot tubs and saunas at slightly lower rates. Both spas offer massage appointments. Make reservations.

Festivals & Events

See p163 for events in nearby Capitola and Aptos.

Shakespeare Santa Cruz (☎ 831-459-2159; www.shakespearesantacruz.org) Damn good productions of the Bard in a redwood grove during July and August.

CENTRAL COAST

WOODIES ON THE WHARF Heather Dickson

No need to cover your eyes: it's all about cars here in Santa Cruz. 'Woodies' are those hulking, practical, wooden-bodied beasts developed as commercial station wagons in the 1920s. They became popular with the West Coast surf community in the 1950s and '60s. As Jim Ferdinand, former President of Santa Cruz Woodies, said, 'They were popular with surfers because of their price and the amount of room they had in them – you could fit your board and your buddies.'

On the third Saturday in June, Santa Cruz's **Woodies on the Wharf** (www.santacruzwoodies.com) is the West Coast's premier show for these classic cars. This free, one-day, annual event showcases over 200 vehicles and brings the Beach Boys image back to town. Jim says, 'Lots of the California owners are surfers or past surfers who've tried to recapture their youth, the car they had when they were in high school, or it's just something they've always loved.' As for the cars, many of them are in pristine condition and look like works of art.

Open Studios Art Tour (☎ 831-475-9600; www.ccscc .org) Local artists open their studios for tours over three weekends in October.

Sleeping

Santa Cruz does not have enough beds to satisfy demand: expect outrageous prices for ordinary rooms. Places near the boardwalk run the gamut from friendly to frightening. For straightforward chain and independent motels, check Ocean St downtown and Mission St (Hwy 1) below the UCSC campus.

BUDGET

Book ahead for **state park campgrounds** (☎ reservations 800-444-7275; www.reserveamerica.com; walk-in tent sites $7-35, campsites $35-65) at beaches along Hwy 1 (see p101) and in the redwood forests of the Santa Cruz Mountains off Hwy 9.

HI Santa Cruz Hostel (☎ 831-423-8304, 888-464-4872; www.hi-santacruz.org; 321 Main St; dm $25-28, r $60-100; 🕐 reception 8-11am & 5-10pm; 🖳) This lovely hostel occupies several century-old cottages surrounded by flowering gardens. It's just two blocks from the beach, a 10-minute walk from downtown. Most rooms have shared bath. One bummer: the 11pm curfew. Limited parking costs $1.

Sunny Cove Motel Apartments (☎ 831-475-1741; 21610 E Cliff Dr; r $70-100; 🖳 🐾) It's absolutely nothing fancy, but this tidy hideaway east of downtown is a staunch wallet-saving fave. Long-time Santa Cruzian owners rent retro beach-house units with kitchenettes. Outside is a small pool and barbecue area.

MIDRANGE & TOP END

You'll often find better-value motel and hotel accommodations in Monterey (p169), a 45-minute drive south.

Redwood Croft (☎ 831-458-1939; www.redwood croft.com; 275 Northwest Dr, Bonny Doon; r incl breakfast $145-230; 🐾 🐾) Hidden in redwood groves, about a 25-minute drive north of Santa Cruz, this welcoming B&B with old-fashioned charm has country-kitsch rooms with fireplaces, outdoor hammocks and hot tubs, and a bouncy trampoline for kids.

ourpick Adobe on Green B&B (☎ 831-469-9866; www.adobeongreen.com; 103 Green St; r incl breakfast $149-199; 🛜) Peace and quiet are the mantras here, just a three-block walk from Pacific Ave. Your hosts are practically invisible but their thoughtful touches are everywhere: stylish amenities inside spacious, solar-powered rooms, and breakfast spreads featuring fresh, organic fare.

Pacific Blue Inn (☎ 831-600-8880; http://pacific blueinn.com; 636 Pacific Ave; r incl breakfast $175-225; 🛜) This laidback courtyard B&B near downtown keeps an eco-conscious focus, from energy-efficient lighting and water-saving fixtures to renewable and recycled building materials. Clean-lined rooms have pillow-top beds, fireplaces and flat-screen TVs with DVD players. Free loaner bikes.

Sea & Sand Inn (☎ 831-427-3400; www.santa cruzmotels.com; 201 W Cliff Dr; r $199-359; 🖳 🛜) Perhaps the spiffiest motel in town. Sea & Sand overlooks Main Beach and the wharf and has a grassy lawn at the cliff's edge. Fall asleep to braying sea lions! Rooms are smallish but have solid pine, not veneer, furniture. The pricey views are stellar.

Babbling Brook Inn (☎ 831-427-2437, 800-866-1131; www.innbythesea.com; 1025 Laurel St; r incl breakfast $209-289; 🖳 🛜) With meandering gardens and towering trees, this streamside inn gathers together private rooms in small satellite buildings, decorated with a nod to French-provincial style. Most have gas fireplaces, some have Jacuzzis, and all have feather beds.

Pleasure Point Inn (☎ 831-475-4657; www .pleasurepointinn.com; 23665 E Cliff Dr; r incl breakfast $250-295; ☞) Live out your fantasy of California beachfront living at this luxury inn east of the river. Four contemporary rooms all have hardwood floors, Jacuzzis, kitchenettes and private patios. Climb to the rooftop deck for drop-dead ocean views.

Also recommended:

Pelican Point Inn (☎ 831-475-3381; www.pelican pointinn-santacruz.com; 21345 E Cliff Dr; r $129-199; ☞ ✦) Modest low-lying kitchenette studios and suites near the yacht harbor.

Bella Notte (☎ 831-600-0001, 877-342-3552; http://bellanotteinn.com; 21305 E Cliff Dr; r $159-209; ✦ ☞ ♿) Spacious, if somewhat noisy, hotel rooms near a family-friendly beach.

Eating

Alas, Santa Cruz' food scene lacks luster. If you're grazing, Pacific Ave is lined with restaurants. For cheaper eats, try Mission St (Hwy 1) near UCSC.

ourpick Tacos Moreno (☎ 831-429-6095; 1053 Water St; dishes $2-6; ☷ 11am-8pm) Who cares how long the line is, even at lunchtime when you and every other surfer is starving? You're guaranteed to find *taqueria* heaven here, from marinated pork, chicken and carne asada soft tacos to supremely stuffed burritos.

Emily's (☎ 831-429-9866; 1129 Mission St; items $2-7; ☷ 5:30am-6pm Mon-Fri, 6:30am-6pm Sat & Sun) You'd better believe its motto, which is simply 'good things to eat.' Stop by for hot cheddar-cheese scones, fruity muffins or the day's soup-and-salad combo to nosh with your buddies on the shady creekside porch.

Bagelry (☎ 831-429-8049; 320a Cedar St; bagels $3-6; ☷ 6:30am-5:30pm Mon-Fri, 7:30am-5:30pm Sat, 7:30am-4pm Sun; ☞) The bagels here are real (boiled, then baked) and come with fantastic and quixotic spreads, like hummus with sprouts or Tofutti. Check out the bulletin board for community goings-on.

Zachary's (☎ 831-427-0646; 819 Pacific Ave; mains $3-10; ☷ 7am-2:30pm Tue-Sun) This is the breakfast spot that covetous locals don't want you to know about. Brave the line for huge greasy-spoon portions of sourdough pancakes and artichoke frittatas that'll keep you going all day. 'Mike's Mess' is the kitchen-sink standout.

Soif (☎ 831-423-2020; 105 Walnut Ave; small plates $4-15, mains $20-23; ☷ 5-10pm Mon-Thu, 5-11pm Fri & Sat, 4-10pm Sun) Part wine shop, part wine bar and restaurant, Soif is where *bon vivants* flock for a heady selection of 50 international wines by the glass paired with a sophisticated, seasonally driven, often organic Euro-Cal menu. Expect gastronomic creativity like squid salad with cucumber gazpacho or crispy duck breast with redcurrant gastrique.

Cafe Limelight (☎ 831-425-7873; 1016 Cedar St; dishes $5-10; ☷ lunch Tue-Sun, dinner Tue-Sat; ✦) Simple salads, panini sandwiches, earthy soups, gumbos and stews all done just right, served among tropical foliage inside a cozy brick building. It's even got bottled microbrews and a doggie menu of tasty treats.

Engfer Pizza Works (☎ 831-429-1856; 537 Seabright Ave; pizzas $8-23; ☷ 4-9:30pm Tue-Sun; ♿) Inside an old factory, Engfer crafts addictive wood-oven–fired pizzas using housemade dough and sauces. The specialty 'no-name' pizza is like a giant salad on roasted bread. There's even a vegan pie. Play ping-pong and sip draft microbrews while you wait.

Dolphin (☎ 831-426-5830; Municipal Wharf; mains $10-16; ☷ 8am-9pm; ♿) For seafood on the wharf, this family-owned diner way out at the end of the pier gets mixed reviews. Play it safe and stick with fish and chips or clam chowder in a bread bowl. There's a takeout window and outdoor picnic tables, great for fidgety kids.

For groceries and quick bites:

Farmers market (☎ 831-454-0566; cnr Lincoln & Cedar Sts; ☷ 2:30-6:30pm Wed) For a true taste of the crunchy Santa Cruz vibe.

New Leaf Community Market (☎ 831-425-1793; 1134 Pacific Ave; ☷ 9am-9pm) Downtown's natural-foods store, with a takeout deli and salad bar.

Drinking

Pacific Ave overflows with grungy, hole-in-the-wall bars and eclectic cafés.

ourpick Cafe Pergolesi (☎ 831-426-1775; 418 Cedar St; ☷ 7am-11pm; ☞) Discuss conspiracy theories over stalwart coffee, tea or beer at this way-popular landmark café in a Victorian house with a big ol' tree-shaded veranda overlooking the street. Local art and live music some evenings.

Lulu Carpenter's (☎ 831-429-9804; 1545 Pacific Ave; ☷ 6am-midnight; ☞) If you like to sip

CENTRAL COAST

freshly roasted espresso and spread out with the Sunday papers, try this brick-walled café with casement windows. There's outdoor sidewalk seating on Pacific Ave and a garden patio.

Firefly Coffee House (☎ 831-713-5070; 131 Front St; 🕓 5:30am-4pm; 🛜) Hanging on the southern edge of downtown, not too far from the beach, this indoor/outdoor people's coffee shop brews organic, fair-trade java and delish chai flavored with orange zest and an Indian bazaar's worth of spices.

Surf City Billiards & Cafe (☎ 831-423-7665; 931 Pacific Ave; 🕓 4-11pm Mon-Thu, 4pm-1am Fri & Sat, 1-10pm Sun) Not another funky downtown dive bar (whew!), this shiny-new place has Brunswick Gold Crown tables for shooting stick, pro-level dartboards, big-screen TVs and pretty darn good pub grub.

Vinocruz (☎ 831-426-8466; 725 Front St; 🕓 11am-7pm Mon-Thu, 11am-8pm Fri & Sat, noon-6pm Sun) Airy, welcoming wine shop on Abbott Sq with a sleek stainless-steel tasting bar and an ever-changing line-up of standout vintages from the Santa Cruz Mountains. Hit the outdoor deck in summer.

Santa Cruz Mountain Brewing (☎ 831-425-4900; Swift St Courtyard, 402 Ingalls St; 🕓 noon-10pm; 🐾) Bold, organic brews are proudly poured at this tiny brewpub west of downtown off Mission St (Hwy 1), squeezed between local winery tasting rooms. Oddest flavor on tap? Olallieberry cream ale.

Entertainment

For comprehensive entertainment listings, pick up the free newspapers *Santa Cruz Weekly* (www.metrosantacruz.com) and *Good Times* (www.gtweekly.com).

Kuumbwa Jazz Center (☎ 831-427-2227; www.kuumbwajazz.org; 320 Cedar St) Putting jazz luminaries on stage since 1975, this nonprofit live-music venue pulls in serious jazz cats who come to see big-name performers in an electrically intimate room.

Catalyst (☎ 831-423-1338; www.catalystclub.com; 1011 Pacific Ave) With an 800-seat capacity, Catalyst is a major live-music venue; over the years it's hosted national acts from the Red Hot Chili Peppers and No Doubt to Emmylou Harris. When there's no music, the upstairs bar and pool room remain open.

Moe's Alley (☎ 831-479-1854; www.moesalley.com; 1535 Commercial Way; 🕓 4pm-2am Tue-Sun) A smaller, more casual gathering place,

Moe's will tickle your ears with live bands almost every night of the week. Expect anything from jazz, blues, reggae and salsa to acoustic world-music jams or electronica.

Blue Lagoon (🕓 831-423-7117; 923 Pacific Ave) It used to be a gay dance club till chicks started coming to escape the straight dudes, but the dudes soon followed and now there's hardly a gay boy in sight. The crowd varies with the night's theme, from hip hop to goth industrial. The verdict: it's divey but danceable.

Downtown's **Nickelodeon Theatre** (☎ 831-426-7500; 210 Lincoln St) screens indie and foreign films, while the landmark **Del Mar Theatre** (☎ 831-469-3220; 1124 Pacific Ave) shows midnight and first-run art-house movies.

Shopping

Downtown abounds with locally owned stores – never mind the Gap.

O'Neill Surf Shop (☎ 831-459-9230; 400 Beach St; 🕓 10am-5pm Mon-Fri, 10am-6pm Sat & Sun) If you can't make it to the Capitola mothership, check out the boardwalk branch of this homegrown, internationally renowned brand of surf wear and gear. Graffiti-art fleece hoodie, anyone?

Annieglass (☎ 831-427-4620; 110 Cooper St; 🕓 10am-6pm Mon-Sat, 11am-5pm Sun) Handcrafted sculptural dinnerware and home accents sold in ultrachic New York department stores are made right here in wackadoodle Santa Cruz. Go figure.

Richard Donnelly Chocolates (☎ 831-458-4214; 1509 Mission St; 🕓 10:30am-6pm Tue-Fri, noon-6pm Sat & Sun) The Willy Wonka of Santa Cruz makes chocolates on a par with those in the big city. This guy is an alchemist! Try the cardamom truffles.

Getting There & Around

Santa Cruz is 75 miles south of San Francisco via I-280 to Hwy 85 to Hwy 17, a fast-moving and sometimes perilous route. Monterey is 43 miles south via coastal Hwy 1.

Santa Cruz Experience (☎ 831-426-4514) runs private van shuttles to/from the airports at San Jose (from $60) and San Francisco Oakland (from $110) for up to three passengers.

Greyhound (☎ 831-423-1800; www.greyhound.com; 425 Front St), near downtown's Metro

CENTRAL COAST

Center, has several daily buses to Salinas ($17, 65 minutes), San Francisco ($21, three hours) and Los Angeles ($55, nine hours). To reach Monterey (see p164), change buses in Salinas.

Santa Cruz Metro (☎ 831-425-8600; www.scmtd .com) operates frequent Hwy 17 Express buses between Santa Cruz and San Jose's CalTrain/ Amtrak station ($4, 1¼ hours), connecting with trains to San Francisco. Metro also operates local bus services (single-ride tickets $1.50, day pass $4.50) throughout the county. Many routes converge on downtown's Metro Center between Pacific Ave and Front St, including:

Bus No	Destination
3	Mission St (Hwy 1), Natural Bridges State Beach
7	Beach Boardwalk, Municipal Wharf, Lighthouse
10, 16, 19	UCSC Campus
35	Felton
40	Wilder Ranch State Park

If you're driving, bring quarters for parking meters (per hour 25¢), which operate seven days a week until 8pm. Watch out: meter readers are merciless! Free municipal parking garages downtown usually enforce three-hour limits, except on Sundays.

For renting your own wheels, try **Zipcar** (p290). Between the beach and downtown, **Electric Sierra Cycles** (☎ 831-425-1593; 302 Pacific Ave; bike rental per hr/day from $8/25; ☽ 10am-6pm) rents cruiser bikes in an electrifying rainbow of colors.

SANTA CRUZ TO MONTEREY

Capitola

pop 10,500

Just east of Santa Cruz, the cutesy seaside town of Capitola sees moneyed crowds less inclined to hold drum circles on the beach. Downtown is blissful for strolling, with arty shops inside pretty houses. Sidewalks can get extremely crowded and parking is a nightmare, especially on weekends – try the lot behind City Hall, off Capitola Ave at Riverview Dr.

The **Capitola Chamber of Commerce** (☎ 831-475-6522; www.capitolachamber.com; 716g Capitola Ave) has local tips and information about mid-September's **Capitola Art & Wine Festival** and the **Begonia Festival** held over the Labor Day weekend, with a flotilla of flowered floats on Soquel Creek.

Not far outside town, **New Brighton State Beach** (☎ 831-464-6330; off Hwy 1 exit Park Ave; per car $10; ☽ 8am-sunset) has a fetching blufftop setting backed by pine trees overlooking Monterey Bay. It's incredibly popular for swimming, fishing and **camping** (☎ reservations 800-444-7275; www.reserveamerica.com; campsites $35-50).

For putting together the best beach picnics, head inland to **Gayle's Bakery & Rosticceria** (☎ 831-462-1200; 504 Bay Ave; mains $5-7; ☽ 6:30am-8:30pm; 🚻), with a big deli for scooping up salads and sandwiches. **Dharma's** (☎ 831-462-1717; 4250 Capitola Rd; mains $5-11; ☽ 8am-9pm; Ⓥ 🚻) is a global fusion, 95% vegan fast-food restaurant stuffed full of natural, organic and even gluten-free foods. Back in the 1980s it was called McDharma's – that is, until McDonald's sued 'em and won.

If someone else is picking up the tab, ride the cable car down to **Shadowbrook** (☎ 831-475-1511, 800-975-1511; 1750 Wharf Rd; mains $19-32; ☽ 5-8:45pm Mon-Thu, 5-9:15pm Fri, 4-9:45pm Sat, 4-8:45pm Sun), a huge, old wooden house-turned-restaurant. Open since 1947, it's embraced by vast gardens overlooking Soquel Creek. Alas, the old-school surf-and-turf menu lacks cachet, but the atmosphere is headily romantic.

Catch an organic, shade-grown and fairly traded caffeine buzz while overlooking the creek at **Mr Toots Coffeehouse** (☎ 831-475-3679; 2nd fl, 231 Esplanade; ☽ 7am-10pm; 🛜), which has a local artists' gallery and often live music in the evenings.

South Santa Cruz County

A charming little beach town, **Aptos** boasts a very fun Fourth of July parade (America's shortest!). It's reached from the Aptos/ Seacliff exit off Hwy 1. Nearby is **Seacliff State Beach** (☎ 831-685-6442; off Hwy 1 exit State Park Dr; per car $10; ☽ 8am-sunset). The beach is fetching but the real attraction is the 'cement boat,' a quixotic WWI-era freighter built from concrete, which surprisingly floated just fine, but had a star-crossed life that ended here on the coast as a fishing pier. About 13 miles south of Santa Cruz near Watsonville, the La Selva Beach exit off Hwy 1 leads to **Manresa State Beach** (☎ 831-429-2850; off San Andreas Rd; per car $10) and **Sunset State Beach** (☎ 831-763-7062; off San Andreas Rd; per car $10), where you might have miles of sand and surf all to yourself. All of these state beaches have popular **campgrounds** (☎ reservations 800-444-7275; www.reserveamerica.com; campsites $35-65). For sophisticated French country fare, detour inland to cozy **Cafe Sparrow** (☎ 831-688-6238; 8042 Soquel Dr, off Hwy 1 exit State Park Dr, Aptos; dinner mains $20-30; 11:30am-2pm Mon-Sat, 9am-2pm Sun, dinner from 5pm daily).

Moss Landing & Elkhorn Slough

About 25 miles south of Santa Cruz, Hwy 1 swings back toward the coast at Moss Landing, just south of the Monterey County line. You can poke around several antiques shops, satisfy your hunger at various small cafés and amble around a working fishing harbor – all (unfortunately) in the shadow of a giant power plant.

Perhaps the best reason to visit, **Sanctuary Cruises** (☎ 530-778-3344; www.sanctuarycruises.com; adult/child under 3/child 3-12 $45/10/35) operates whale-watching and dolphin-spotting cruises led by marine biologists. Biodiesel boat tours last four to five hours, which is longer than average, so you've got a better chance of spotting whales. Tours currently depart at 10am on Friday, Saturday and Sunday year-round, but this is highly subject to change and you'll need reservations besides.

Northeast of Moss Landing, nature lovers can hike 5 miles of trails, spot snowy plovers and brown pelicans, and see how Monterey Bay naturally meets the land at **Elkhorn Slough National Estuarine Research Reserve** (☎ 831-728-2822; www.elkhornslough.org; 1700 Elkhorn Rd, off Hwy 1, Watsonville; 9am-5pm Wed-Sun). It's free to enter the visitors center; adults pay $2.50 to hike. Fret not if you forgot your binoculars; borrow a pair, along with a bird book from the visitors center. Call ahead for guided walking-tour schedules. Photographers and wildlife watchers can book seats on a pontoon boat with **Elkhorn Slough Safari** (☎ 831-633-5555; www.elkhornslough.com; adult/child 3-12 $32/24), offering naturalist-guided tours (no children under three allowed).

Kayaking is by far the best way to see the slough, though not on a windy day. Be sure to time your paddling trip to take advantage of the tides. **Kayak Connection** (☎ 831-724-5692; www.kayakconnection.com; 2370 Hwy 1; 4hr s/d kayak rental $35/50, tours $30-65; 9am-5pm Mon, Wed & Fri, 10am-5pm Tue & Thu, 9am-6pm Sat & Sun) and **Monterey Bay Kayaks** (☎ 831-373-5357, 800-649-5357; 2390 Hwy 1; kayak rental per day from $30, tours adult/child 3-12 from $50/30; 9am-7pm Sun-Thu, to 8pm Fri & Sat) can get you out on the water. They're both open shorter hours in winter, so call ahead.

If you're looking for a peaceful place to lay your head, the seaside **Captain's Inn** (☎ 831-633-5550; www.captainsinn.com; 8122 Moss Landing Rd, Moss Landing; r incl breakfast $145-265) is a nautical-themed B&B where living in harmony with nature is key. The tidy rooms aren't as luxurious as the price tag suggests, but some have gas fireplaces, clawfoot tubs and panoramic views of the dunes.

A GRAND CANYON UNDER THE SEA

Starting only a few hundred yards offshore from Moss Landing, the Monterey Canyon plummets to a depth of almost 10,000ft. A mile deep, this submarine canyon is about the same size as the Grand Canyon. Some scientists believe it may also have been carved by the Colorado River during ancient times. Summer's upwelling currents carry cold water from this deep submarine canyon, sending up a rich supply of nutrients toward the surface to feed Monterey Bay's diverse marine life. These frigid currents also account for the bay's lower water temperatures and gloomy fog that often blankets the peninsula during summer.

MONTEREY

pop 28,800

Working-class Monterey is all about the sea. What draws many tourists is the world-class aquarium, overlooking Monterey Bay National Marine Sanctuary, which extends from north of San Francisco's Golden Gate Bridge all the way south beyond Hearst Castle. Once the USA's largest marine sanctuary, it protects dense kelp forests and a stunning variety of marine life, including seals and sea lions, dolphins and whales. Meanwhile, the city itself possesses the best preserved historical evidence of California's Spanish and Mexican periods, with many restored adobe buildings. An afternoon's wander through the town's historic quarter promises to be more edifying than time spent in the tourist ghettos of Fisherman's Wharf and Cannery Row. A snorkeling excursion on the bay? Even better.

CENTRAL COAST

History

The Ohlone people, who had been living on the peninsula since around 500 BC, may have spotted Spanish explorer Juan Rodríguez Cabrillo, the first European explorer to sail by in 1542. He was followed in 1602 by Sebastián Vizcaíno, who landed near the site of today's city and named it after his patron, the Count of Monte Rey.

A long hiatus followed before the Spanish – led by conquistador Gaspar de Portolá and accompanied by Franciscan priest Junípero Serra – returned in 1770 to establish Monterey as their first presidio in Alta (Upper) California. A year later, Serra

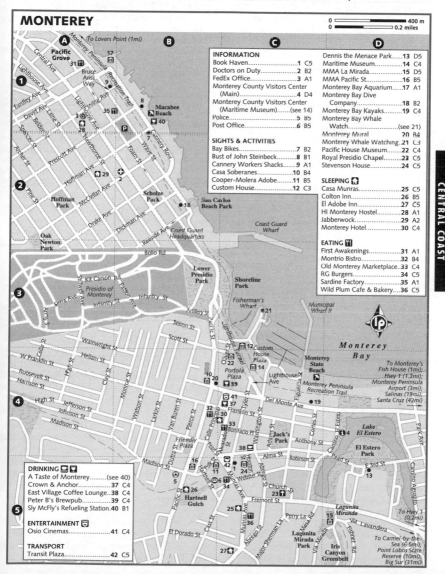

MONTEREY

0 ————— 400 m
0 ————— 0.2 miles

INFORMATION
Book Haven..........................1 C5
Doctors on Duty.................2 B2
FedEx Office.......................3 A1
Monterey County Visitors Center (Main)...............................4 D4
Monterey County Visitors Center (Maritime Museum)......(see 14)
Police..................................5 B5
Post Office..........................6 B5

SIGHTS & ACTIVITIES
Bay Bikes............................7 B2
Bust of John Steinbeck.........8 B1
Cannery Workers Shacks.......9 A1
Casa Soberanes.................10 B4
Cooper-Molera Adobe........11 B5
Custom House.....................12 C3

Dennis the Menace Park......13 D5
Maritime Museum..............14 C4
MMA La Mirada.................15 D5
MMA Pacific St..................16 B5
Monterey Bay Aquarium......17 A1
Monterey Bay Dive Company......................18 B2
Monterey Bay Kayaks.........19 C4
Monterey Bay Whale Watch......................(see 21)
Monterey Mural.................20 B4
Monterey Whale Watching..21 C3
Pacific House Museum........22 C4
Royal Presidio Chapel.........23 C5
Stevenson House................24 C5

SLEEPING
Casa Munras......................25 C5
Colton Inn.........................26 B5
El Adobe Inn......................27 C5
HI Monterey Hostel............28 A1
Jabberwock.......................29 A2
Monterey Hotel..................30 C4

EATING
First Awakenings................31 A1
Montrio Bistro....................32 B4
Old Monterey Marketplace..33 C4
RG Burgers........................34 B5
Sardine Factory.................35 A1
Wild Plum Cafe & Bakery....36 C5

DRINKING
A Taste of Monterey.........(see 40)
Crown & Anchor................37 C4
East Village Coffee Lounge..38 C4
Peter B's Brewpub..............39 C4
Sly McFly's Refueling Station.40 B1

ENTERTAINMENT
Osio Cinemas.....................41 C4

TRANSPORT
Transit Plaza......................42 C5

CENTRAL COAST

decided to separate church and state by shifting the mission to Carmel, a safer distance from the allegedly corrupt military presence.

For a brief spell, Monterey became the capital of Alta California after Mexico declared independence from Spain in 1821. In this newly bustling international port, Yankees from the East Coast mixed with Russian fur traders and merchant seafarers carrying exotic goods from China. In a preamble to war with Mexico, the USA took control of Monterey in 1846. The town spent the next three decades as a backwater, especially after the Gold Rush made everyone run for the Sierra Nevada foothills.

When a luxurious hotel was built by late-19th-century railway entrepreneurs, San Franciscans discovered Monterey as a convenient vacation getaway. Around the same time, fishermen began capitalizing on the teeming marine life in Monterey Bay. By the 1930s, Cannery Row had made the port the 'Sardine Capital of the World,' but overfishing and climatic changes caused the industry's sudden collapse in the 1950s. More recently, the city has been successful in netting enormous schools of tourists.

Orientation & Information

Monterey's historic quarter of downtown is a compact area surrounding Alvarado St, which ends at Portola and Custom House Plazas, near Fisherman's Wharf. This area is known as Old Monterey, as distinguished from Cannery Row, a mile northwest. From Cannery Row, Lighthouse Ave leads west into Pacific Grove (p171), a quiet beach town. Further south on the peninsula lies posh Carmel (p173).

Book Haven (☎ 831-333-0383; 559 Tyler St; ☺ 10am-6pm Mon-Sat) New and used books, including John Steinbeck titles.

Doctors on Duty (☎ 831-649-0770; 501 Lighthouse Ave; ☺ 8am-8pm Mon-Sat, 8am-6pm Sun) Walk-in non-emergency medical clinic.

FedEx Office (☎ 831-373-2298; 799 Lighthouse Ave; per min 20-30¢; ☺ 7am-11pm Mon-Fri, 9am-9pm Sat & Sun; 🖳 🛜) High-speed internet workstations.

Monterey County Visitors Center (☎ 831-657-6400, 877-668-3739; www.montereyinfo.org) Main (401 Camino El Estero; ☺ 9am-6pm Mon-Fri, 9am-5pm Sat & Sun Apr-Oct, closes 1hr earlier Nov-Mar); Maritime Museum (5 Custom House Plaza; ☺ 9am-5pm) The main branch has free courtesy phones for checking accommodations

availability. Ask for the free *Monterey County Film & Literary Map* for self-guided tours.

Police (☎ 831-646-3914; 351 Madison St; ☺ 24hr) For non-emergencies.

Post Office (☎ 831-372-4063; 565 Hartnell St; ☺ 8:30am-5pm Mon-Fri, 10am-2pm Sat)

Sights
MONTEREY BAY AQUARIUM

Monterey's most mesmerizing experience is a visit to the ginormous **aquarium** (☎ 831-648-4888, tickets 866-963-9645; www.montereybayaquarium.org; 886 Cannery Row; adult/child 3-12 $30/18; ☺ 9:30am-6pm Mon-Fri, 9:30am-8pm Sat & Sun May-Sep, 10am-6pm daily Oct-Apr; 🛜 ♿), built on the site of what was once the city's largest sardine cannery. All forms of aquatic creatures are on display, from kid-tolerant sea stars and slimy sea slugs to animated sea otters and surprisingly nimble 800lb tuna. But the aquarium is more than an impressive collection of glass tanks – thoughtful placards underscore the bay's ecological, cultural and historical contexts.

Every minute, upward of 2000 gallons of seawater is pumped into the three-story **kelp forest**, re-creating as closely as possible the natural conditions you see out the windows to the east. The large fish of prey are at their charismatic best during mealtimes; divers hand-feed at 11:30am and 4pm. More giggle-inducing are sea-otter feeding and training sessions at 10:30am, 1:30pm and 3:30pm. Otherwise, the otters can often be seen basking in the **Great Tidepool** outside the aquarium, where they are readied for reintroduction to the wild.

Even new-agey music and the occasional infinity-mirror illusion don't detract from the appeal of the **Jellies Gallery**, where jellyfish show off their mysterious, diaphanous beauty. To see hammerhead sharks, fish and other sea creatures that outweigh you many times over, ponder the awesome **Outer Bay** tank. Nearby you can explore the **Secret Lives of Seahorses**. Throughout the aquarium there are **touch pools**, where you can get close to sea cucumbers, bat rays and various tide-pool creatures. Tots will go nuts in the interactive, bilingual **Splash Zone**, where blackfooted penguin colony feedings happen at 10:30am and 3pm.

A visit can easily become a full-day affair. Get your hand stamped so that you can break up the visit with lunch. (Anyone feel like seafood?) To avoid long lines in summer and on weekends and holidays, buy tickets in advance. Before you leave, make sure you pick up the wallet-sized *Seafood Watch*, an essential seafood-dining guide to keeping the West Coast's fish and shellfish populations sustainable.

CANNERY ROW

Back in John Steinbeck's day, Cannery Row was the epicenter of the sardine-canning industry that was Monterey's lifeblood in the first half of the 20th century. A stinky, hardscrabble melting pot, the area's grit and energy were immortalized in Steinbeck's novel *Cannery Row*. Sadly, there's precious little evidence of that time now, except for the **Cannery Workers Shacks** at the base of flowery Bruce Ariss Way. This small row of even-smaller houses depicts the stark and strenuous lives led by Filipino, Japanese and Spanish laborers during the cannery's heyday. A bronze **bust** of the Pulitzer prize–winning writer sits at the bottom of Prescott Ave, just steps from the unabashedly commercial experience that his row has devolved into. It's chocka-block with touristy restaurants and souvenir shops hawking T-shirts and saltwater taffy.

THE WHARVES

Like its larger namesake in San Francisco, **Fisherman's Wharf** is a tacky tourist trap at heart. It's the jumping-off point for whale-watching expeditions (see p169) and deep-sea fishing trips. The refreshingly authentic **Municipal Wharf II** is a short walk east. There fishing boats bob and sway, painters work on their watercolor canvases and seafood purveyors hawk fresh catches.

MONTEREY STATE HISTORIC PARK

Old Monterey is a collection of lovingly restored 19th-century brick and adobe buildings, all covered by a 2-mile self-guided walking tour called the **Path of History**. All of the historic buildings that make up the park were temporarily closed at press time, following Governor Schwarzenegger's drastic reduction of funding for state parks in 2009, although admission to the gardens was still free. If and when the historic buildings re-open, you can pick up a self-guided touring map at the **Pacific House Museum** (☎ 831-649-7118; 20 Custom House Plaza), which has excellently curated period exhibits on California's colorful multinational history. Following are just a few of the park's many highlights.

Custom House

In 1822, newly independent Mexico ended the Spanish trade monopoly but stipulated that any traders bringing goods to Alta California must first unload their cargoes at the **custom house** (Custom House Plaza) for duty assessment. Restored to the 1940s, the building displays an exotic selection of the goods traders brought in to exchange for California cowhides.

Casa Soberanes

A beautiful garden with meandering walkways paved with abalone shells, bottle-glass fragments and crushed whalebones fronts

CENTRAL COAST

WORTH A TRIP: STEINBECK COUNTRY

The birthplace of John Steinbeck and known as the 'The World's Salad Bowl,' Salinas makes a vivid contrast with the conspicuous affluence of the Monterey Peninsula. A Stanford University dropout who later won a Nobel Prize for Literature, John Steinbeck (1902–68) sensitively portrayed the troubled spirit of poor, rural Americans in novels such as *The Grapes of Wrath* and *East of Eden*. In August, the **Steinbeck Festival** (www.steinbeck.org/festival) pulls together four days of films, lectures, live music, tours and storytelling.

The town's historic center stretches along Main St. At its northern end, the **National Steinbeck Center** (☎ 831-775-4721; www.steinbeck.org; 1 Main St; adult/child 6-12/youth 13-17 $11/6/8; ⏰ 10am-5pm; ♿) will enthrall even those who don't know a lick about Salinas' native son. Interactive, kid-accessible exhibits engagingly chronicle the writer's life and literary works. The on-site agricultural museum takes you on a journey through the modern-day farm industry, from water to pesticides to transportation (trust us, it's more interesting than it sounds).

Steinbeck is buried in the Hamilton family plot at **Garden of Memories Cemetery** (768 Abbott St, off Hwy 101 exit S Sanborn Rd), about 2 miles south of downtown.

For buses to Salinas from Monterey, see p171; from Santa Cruz, see p162.

Casa Soberanes (336 Pacific St), built during the late Mexican period. The interior is adorned with an eclectic mix of New England antiques, 19th-century goods imported on Chinese trading ships and modern Mexican folk art. Across Pacific St, the large and colorful **Monterey Mural** mosaic, adorning the exterior of the Monterey Conference Center, tells the city's history.

Stevenson House

Scottish writer Robert Louis Stevenson came to Monterey in 1879 to court his wife-to-be, Fanny Osbourne, then a married woman (oh, the scandal!). This building, called the French Hotel, was reputedly where he stayed while writing *Treasure Island*. The rooms look primitive, but remember that Stevenson was still a penniless unknown at that time. The **building** (530 Houston St) houses a superb collection of Stevenson memorabilia, including artifacts from Polynesia, where the writer spent his last years.

Cooper-Molera Adobe

This stately 1820s **complex** (☎ 831-649-7111; 525 Polk St; ☺ gift shop 10am-4pm Mon-Sat & 1-4pm Sun) was built by John Rogers Cooper, a New England sea captain, and three generations of his family resided here until 1968. It has been willed to the National Trust, which ensures that its bookshop remains open, selling nostalgic period toys, yesteryear household goods and old-fashioned and contemporary crafts.

MARITIME MUSEUM

Dive right into Monterey's naval history, from the days of early European explorers through the 20th century at this nifty **museum** (☎ 831-372-2608; www.montereyhistory .org; 5 Custom House Plaza; admission free; ☺ 10am-5pm Tue-Sun). Highlights of the seafaring collection include the Fresnel lens from Point Sur Lightstation (p177), a ship-in-a-bottle collection and displays on Monterey's salty past, particularly the rise and rapid fall of the sardine biz.

ROYAL PRESIDIO CHAPEL

Called San Carlos Cathedral nowadays, this graceful sandstone **chapel** (☎ 831-373-2628; www .sancarloscathedral.net; 500 Church St; donation requested; ☺ 10am-noon Wed, 10am-3pm Fri, noon-2pm Sat & 1-3pm Sun, also 10am-noon & 1:15-3:15pm on 2nd & 4th

Mon of the month & 1:15-3:15pm on 2nd & 4th Tue of the month) is California's oldest continuously functioning church. Surrounded by the presidio's fortified walls, the original 1770 mission church stood here before the mission was moved to Carmel (p174). As Monterey expanded under Mexican rule, older buildings were gradually destroyed, eventually leaving this National Historic Landmark as the strongest reminder of the former Spanish colonial presence.

MONTEREY MUSEUM OF ART

With all of its art galleries, it's not surprising that Monterey has a respectable **art museum** (MMA; www.montereyart.org; adult/child under 13 $5/free; ☺ 11am-5pm Wed-Sat, 1-4pm Sun; MMA Pacific Street ☎ 831-372-5477; 559 Pacific St; MMA La Mirada ☎ 831-372-3689; 720 Via Mirada). You can visit both locations on the same day with the same ticket. **MMA Pacific Street** is particularly strong in California contemporary art and modern landscape painters, and photographers like Ansel Adams and Edward Weston. **MMA La Mirada** inhabits a silent film star's villa whose humble adobe origins are exquisitely concealed. Surrounded by lovely rose and rhododendron gardens, it primarily puts on special exhibitions and displays Asian art from MMA's permanent collections. Call ahead to check guided tour schedules and exhibition dates, as the villa is sometimes closed.

Activities

A must for fans of kick-ass playgrounds, **Dennis the Menace Park** (☎ 831-646-3860; 777 Pearl St; ☺ 10am-dusk, closed Tue Sep-May; ⛳) was the brainchild of Hank Ketcham, the classic comic-strip creator. This ain't your standard dumbed-down playground, suffocated by Big Brother's safety regulations. With lightning-fast roller slides, towering climbing walls and hedge mazes, even adults can't resist playing.

CYCLING

With epic scenery and paved bike paths, cycling is quite a popular activity. The **Monterey Peninsula Recreation Trail**, a former railway line, travels for 18 car-free miles along the waterfront from Lovers Point in Pacific Grove, passing Cannery Row and downtown Monterey, en route north to Castroville. Road-cycling enthusiasts with nerves of steel can make the round-trip down to Carmel on the ballyhooed **17-Mile Drive** (p175). For bike rentals and cycling maps, visit **Bay Bikes** (☎ 831-655-2453; www.bay bikes.com; 585 Cannery Row; rentals per hr/day/2 days from $8/32/40; ☾ from 9am daily, closing hr vary seasonally).

WHALE-WATCHING
You can spot whales off the coast of Monterey year-round. Gray whales pass by from mid-December to April, while the season for blue and humpback whales runs from late April through November. Book ahead for basic, three-hour boat tours with **Monterey Bay Whale Watch** (☎ 831-375-4658; http://gowhales.com; 84 Fisherman's Wharf; adult/child 4-12 from $36/25) and **Monterey Whale Watching** (☎ 831-372-2203, tickets 800-979-3370; www.monterey whalewatching.com; 96 Fisherman's Wharf; adult/ child 3-12 $40/30). At Moss Landing, Sanctuary Cruises (p164) runs highly regarded whale-watching tours of Monterey Bay.

DIVING & SNORKELING
Monterey Bay sports world-renowned diving and snorkeling, though the water is pretty chilly. Excellent spots include off Lovers Point in Pacific Grove and at Point Lobos State Reserve (p174), the latter reserved for divers only. Organize a dive or snorkel trip with **Monterey Bay Dive Company** (☎ 831-656-0454; www.montereyscubadiving.com; 225 Cannery Row; 1-person boat dive from $59; ☾ 9am-5pm Mon & Wed-Fri, 6am-5pm Sat, 6am-4pm Sun), which offers instruction and equipment rental. Full standard dive outfits rent for $80 per day, snorkeling kits go for $39. Staff can advise about snorkeling in the inlets of the bay.

KAYAKING
For kayak rentals and weekend instruction courses, **Monterey Bay Kayaks** (☎ 831-373-5357, 800-649-5357; www.montereybaykayaks.com; 693 Del Monte Ave; kayak rentals per day from $30, tours adult/ child 3-12 from $50/30; ☾ 9am-7pm) also leads family-oriented and natural-history tours, including sunset paddles around the bay and full-moon trips to Elkhorn Slough (p164). They're open shorter hours in winter.

Festivals & Events
Marina International Festival of the Winds (www.marinafestival.com; ⊛) Kite-flying, hang-gliding and family fun over Mother's Day weekend in early May.

Castroville Artichoke Festival (www.artichoke festival.org) Cooking demos, 3D 'agro-art' sculptures, and field tours in mid-May.

Red Bull US Grand Prix (www.redbullusgrandprix.com) The largest motorcycle race on the continent is held at the Mazda Laguna Seca Raceway in late July.

Concours d'Elegance (www.pebblebeachconcours.net) Rare and exquisite classic cars on parade at Pebble Beach in mid-August.

Monterey County Fair (www.montereycountyfair.com; ⊛) Old-fashioned carnival rides, wine-tasting competitions and live music at the fairgrounds in mid-August.

Monterey Jazz Festival (www.montereyjazzfestival.org) One of the USA's longest-running jazz festivals (since 1958) happens in mid-September.

Monterey Bay Birding Festival (www.montereybay birding.com) Field trips, workshops and California condor releases in late September.

Monterey Wine Festival (www.montereywine.com) Nonprofit wine-tasting shindig with events held around town in October.

Sleeping
Book ahead for summer visits – the festivals and events listed above can sell out the town remarkably early. Inexpensive chain motels cluster along Munras Ave, just south of downtown, and on N Fremont St, a couple miles east of downtown off Hwy 1. To avoid the tourist circus of Cannery Row, consider staying in Pacific Grove (p171).

Veterans Memorial Park Campground (Map p172; ☎ 831-646-3865; off Skyline Dr; walk-in tent sites per person $5, campsites $25; ⊛) Tucked into thick forest high above downtown, this first-come, first-served municipal campground has 40 well-kept, grassy, if rather open and exposed, sites with coin-op showers, fire pits, BBQ picnic areas and potable water.

HI Monterey Hostel (☎ 831-649-0375, 888-464-4872; www.montereyhostel.org; 778 Hawthorne St; dm $25-28, r with shared bath $59-91; ☾ reception 8am-10pm; 🖳) This well-run, if somewhat basic, hostel with a BBQ patio is just blocks from the aquarium and Cannery Row. Reservations are advised. Take Monterey-Salinas Transit (MST) bus 1 from downtown's transit plaza.

El Adobe Inn (☎ 831-372-5409; http://el-adobe-inn .com; 936 Munras Ave; r incl breakfast $70-155; 🛜 ⊛) This unprepossessing roadside motel offers airy accommodations with just a bit of charm. Rates include use of an outdoor hot tub. Neighboring chain motels may or may not offer cheaper rates.

Colton Inn (☎ 831-649-6500, 800-848-7007; www .coltoninn.com; 707 Pacific St; r incl breakfast $100-325; ☜) Downtown, this champ of a motel prides itself on cleanliness and friendliness, and has earned a solid base of repeat guests. There's no pool and zero view, but staff loan out DVDs and there's even a sauna.

Monterey Hotel (☎ 831-375-3184, 800-966-6490; www.montereyhotel.com; 406 Alvarado St; r incl breakfast $159-319; ☜) Freshly renovated, this 1904 hotel in the heart of downtown is grand in the traditional Victorian manner. As it's a historic building, the drawback is it has no elevator, and thin-walled rooms can be noisy. Booking online can mean huge savings. Valet parking costs $17.

Jabberwock (☎ 831-372-4777, 888-428-7253; www .jabberwockinn.com; 598 Laine St; r incl breakfast $169-299; ▣ ☜) High atop a hill and barely visible through a shroud of foliage, this 1911 Craftsman house hums a playful *Alice in Wonderland* tune through its seven immaculate rooms with names like the Brillig, which flaunts gorgeous hand-painted wallpaper and bay views. All in all, a sublime place to celebrate your un-birthday.

Casa Munras (☎ 831-375-2411, 800-222-2446; www .hotelcasamunras.com; 700 Munras Ave; d $169-319; ▣ ☜ ▨ ❀) Built around an adobe hacienda owned by a 19th-century Spanish colonial don, this historic boutique hotel downtown has chic modern rooms with lofty beds and some fireplaces. Splash in the heated outdoor pool then unwind with a sea-salt scrub in the spa.

our pick **Sanctuary Beach Resort** (off Map p172; ☎ 831-883-9478, 877-944-3863; www.thesanctuary beachresort.com; 3295 Dunes Dr, off Hwy 1 exit Reservation Rd, Marina; r $189-369; ☜ ▨ ♿ ❀) Be lulled to sleep by the surf at this low-lying retreat hidden in the sand dunes north of Monterey. Timeshare townhouses hold petite rooms with gas fireplaces and kitchenettes, plus binoculars to borrow for whale-watching. The beach is an off-limits nature preserve, but there are other beaches and hiking trails nearby.

Eating

Escape Cannery Row for Lighthouse Ave, lined with budget-friendly ethnic eateries serving everything from Hawaiian barbecue to Middle Eastern kebabs, or head over to Pacific Grove (see opposite). The weekly **Old Monterey Marketplace** (☎ 831-655-8070; www.old monterey.org; ☒ 4-8pm Thu) farmers market takes over downtown's Alvarado St.

RG Burgers (☎ 831-372-4930; 570 Munras Ave; items $3-12; ☒ 11am-8:30pm) Next to Trader Joe's grocery store, where you can stock up on trail mix and takeout salads, this locally owned burger shop serves up classic beef, bison, turkey, chicken and veggie falafel patties, sweet tater fries and thick milkshakes.

our pick **First Awakenings** (☎ 831-372-1125; 1st fl, American Tin Cannery, 125 Ocean View Blvd; mains $5-11; ☒ 7am-2pm Mon-Fri, 7am-2:30pm Sat & Sun; ♿) Sweet or savory, but always from scratch, breakfasts and lunches merrily weigh down sunny tables at this hideaway café inside an outlet mall near the aquarium. Try the gigantic blueberry wheat-germ pancake – you'll need only one!

Wild Plum Cafe & Bakery (☎ 831-646-3109; 731b Munras Ave; mains $6-11; ☒ 7am-5pm Mon & Sat, 7am-6:30pm Tue-Fri) Locals crowd into this slender nook for organic-egg breakfasts, seasonal soups, gourmet sandwiches on homemade bread and Mediterranean veggie tacos. Takeout box lunches available for picnickers.

Montrio Bistro (☎ 831-648-8880; 414 Calle Principal; mains $14-38; ☒ 4:30-10pm Sun-Thu, to 11pm Fri & Sat; ♿) It's fitting that Montrio occupies the old firehouse, because this place is hot. Euro-Cal dishes are concocted from mostly organic, market-driven and sustainable local ingredients. Despite its hip interior – think leather walls and iron trellises – the tables still have butcher paper and fat crayons for kids.

Monterey's Fish House (Map p172; ☎ 831-373-4647; 2114 Del Monte Ave, mains $14-40; ☒ lunch 11:30am-2pm, dinner 5-9pm) Ten bucks says you're the only nonlocal in the joint. Dig into spanking-fresh seafood with the occasional Asian twist while being watched over by photos of Sicilian fishermen. Even though it's a casual joint – Hawaiian shirts seem to be *de rigueur* for gentlemen – reservations are essential.

Sardine Factory (☎ 831-373-3775; 701 Wave St; mains $22-47; ☒ dinner) This decades-old institution still prepares passable steaks and seafood, but its real strength lies in its atmosphere and wine list. Each of the dining rooms is ornately and uniquely decorated, with the glass conservatory a crowd-pleasing favorite. Save money with four-course prix fixe dinners (under $20) available in the lounge.

Drinking & Entertainment

Prowl downtown's Alvarado St to find more bars and nightclubs. For encyclopedic entertainment listings, pick up the free tabloid *Monterey County Weekly* (www .montereycountyweekly.com).

East Village Coffee Lounge (☎ 831-373-5601; 498 Washington St; ☼ 6am-late Mon-Fri, 7am-late Sat & Sun) Slick downtown coffeehouse serving fair-trade, organic brews pulls off a big-city lounge vibe with film, live music and DJ nights and, of course, that all-important booze license.

Crown & Anchor (☎ 831-649-6496; 150 W Franklin St; ☼ 11am-2am) Descend into the basement of this British pub and the first thing you'll notice is the red plaid carpeting. At least these blokes do know their way around a bar, though, with dozens of draft beers and single malts, not to mention damn fine fish and chips.

Sly McFly's Refueling Station (☎ 831-649-8050; 700a Cannery Row; ☼ 11:30am-2am) Rubbing against the billiards halls, comedy shops and touristy restaurants of Cannery Row, this waterfront dive has live blues, jazz and rock bands nightly. Skip the food, though.

Osio Cinemas (☎ 831-644-8171; 350 Alvarado St) Downtown's art-house cinema screens indie dramas, cutting-edge documentaries and offbeat Hollywood films. Drop by Cafe Lumiere for decadent cheesecakes, loose-leaf teas and espresso.

More watering holes:

A Taste of Monterey (☎ 831-646-5446; 700 Cannery Row; tasting fee $10-15; ☼ 11am-6pm) Sample medal-winning locally grown wines accompanied by impressive sea views.

Peter B's Brewpub (☎ 831-649-4511; Portola Hotel, 2 Portola Plaza; ☼ 11am-11pm Sun-Thu, to 1am Fri & Sat) Hidden backstreet microbrewery with sports TVs, billiards and outdoor tables.

Getting There & Around

Monterey is 120 miles south of San Francisco via inland Hwys 101 and 156. From Santa Cruz, it's less than an hour's drive south along coastal Hwy 1.

Four miles southeast of downtown off Hwy 68, **Monterey Peninsula Airport** (MRY; ☎ 831-648-7000; www.montereyairport.com; Olmsted Rd) has flights operated by Allegiant Air (San Diego), American Eagle (Los Angeles) and United Express (LA and San Francisco). Major car-rental firms are at the airport.

Monterey/Salinas Airbus (☎ 831-373-7777; www .montereyairbus.com) offers frequent van shuttles to San Jose and San Francisco airports (per person $35 to $45).

If you aren't flying or don't have wheels, getting to the Monterey Peninsula can be tricky. First, take Greyhound or Amtrak to Salinas (p167), then catch MST bus 20 ($2.50, 55 minutes, every 30 to 60 minutes).

Monterey-Salinas Transit (MST; ☎ 831-899-2555, 888-678-2871; www.mst.org; single-ride ticket/day pass from $2.50/6) operates local and regional buses. Many routes converge at downtown's **Transit Plaza** (cnr Pearl & Alvarado Sts), including:

Bus No	Destination
1	Aquarium, Lighthouse Ave, Pacific Grove
4 & 5	Carmel
20 & 21	Salinas
22	Carmel, Point Lobos, Big Sur (summer only)

Between late May and early September, the free Wave trolley bus loops around downtown, Fisherman's Wharf and Cannery Row from 10am to 7pm daily.

You'll find on-street metered parking (up to $1.50 per hour; bring quarters) and parking garages (per day from $7) downtown, around Cannery Row and along Lighthouse Ave.

PACIFIC GROVE
pop 14,700

Founded as a Methodist summer retreat in 1875, Pacific Grove (aka PG) is a tranquil community that maintained a quaint, holier-than-thou attitude well into the 20th century – the selling of liquor was illegal up until 1969, making it California's last 'dry' town. Today, leafy streets are lined by stately Victorian homes, making PG a welcome respite from the touristy Monterey–Carmel hubbub. Its charmingly compact downtown lies along Lighthouse Ave. The **chamber of commerce** (☎ 831-373-3304, 800-656-6650; www.pacificgrove.org; cnr Central & Forest Aves; ☼ 9:30am-5pm Mon-Fri, 10am-3pm Sat) dispenses information.

Sights & Activities

Aptly named **Ocean View Boulevard** affords fine views from Lovers Point west to Point Pinos. There the road becomes the again appropriately monikered **Sunset Drive**, with numerous turn-outs where you can enjoy the

MONTEREY PENINSULA

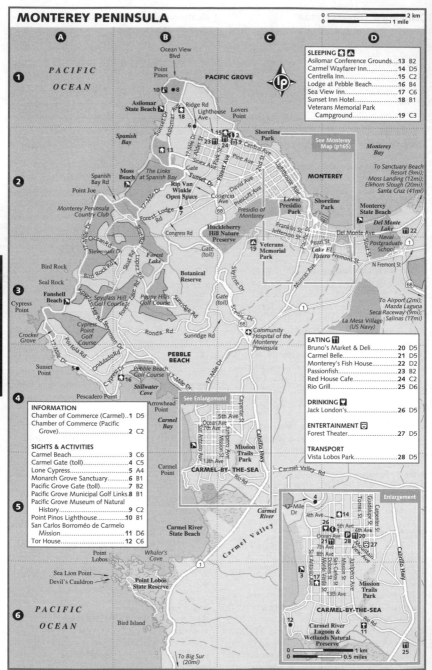

SLEEPING
Asilomar Conference Grounds....**13** B2
Carmel Wayfarer Inn.................**14** D5
Centrella Inn.............................**15** C2
Lodge at Pebble Beach.............**16** B4
Sea View Inn............................**17** C6
Sunset Inn Hotel.......................**18** B1
Veterans Memorial Park
Campground........................**19** C3

EATING
Bruno's Market & Deli...............**20** D5
Carmel Belle.............................**21** D5
Monterey's Fish House..............**22** D2
Passionfish...............................**23** B2
Red House Cafe........................**24** C2
Rio Grill...................................**25** D6

DRINKING
Jack London's...........................**26** D5

ENTERTAINMENT
Forest Theater..........................**27** D5

TRANSPORT
Vista Lobos Park.......................**28** D5

INFORMATION
Chamber of Commerce (Carmel)..**1** D5
Chamber of Commerce (Pacific
Grove)...................................**2** C2

SIGHTS & ACTIVITIES
Carmel Beach...........................**3** C6
Carmel Gate (toll).....................**4** C5
Lone Cypress............................**5** A4
Monarch Grove Sanctuary.........**6** B1
Pacific Grove Gate (toll).............**7** B2
Pacific Grove Municipal Golf Links.**8** B1
Pacific Grove Museum of Natural
History..................................**9** C2
Point Pinos Lighthouse..............**10** B1
San Carlos Borroméo de Carmelo
Mission.................................**11** D6
Tor House................................**12** C6

pounding surf, rocky outcrops and teaming tidepools. The entire route is ideal for walking or cycling (see p169 for bicycle rentals) – we think it surpasses the 17-Mile Drive (p175) for beauty, and it's free.

At the northwestern end of Lighthouse Ave, on the tip of the peninsula, historic **Point Pinos Lighthouse** (831-648-5716; www.pgmuseum.org; donation requested; 1-4pm Thu-Mon) is the oldest continuously operating lighthouse on the West Coast. It has been warning ships off this hazardous point since 1855. Inside are exhibits on its history and its failures: local shipwrecks. The lighthouse grounds provide excellent whale-watching between December and April. They overlook the ocean-view **Pacific Grove Municipal Golf Links** (831-648-5775; 777 Asilomar Ave; green fees $25-48, club rental $40; call for hr), where black-tailed deer freely range.

If you're in town during monarch butterfly season (roughly October through February), the best place to see them cluster is at the **Monarch Grove Sanctuary** (831-648-5716; off Ridge Rd; admission free; dawn-dusk), a thicket of eucalyptus trees off Lighthouse Ave. Kids can learn more about the fluttering creatures' amazing migratory journey then get acquainted with local marine life and Native American cultures at the modest **Pacific Grove Museum of Natural History** (831-648-5716; www.pgmuseum.org; 165 Forest Ave; admission free; 10am-5pm Tue-Sat;).

Sleeping & Eating

PG has no shortage of froufrou B&Bs in gingerbread Victorian houses. Midrange motels shelter off Lighthouse and Asilomar Aves, near the peninsula's western edge.

Asilomar Conference Grounds (831-372-8016, 866-654-2878; www.visitasilomar.com; 800 Asilomar Ave; r incl breakfast $115-185;) This thickly forested state-park lodge boasts buildings designed by architect Julia Morgan, of Hearst Castle (see p181) fame. The historic rooms are tiny and thin-walled but charming nonetheless. The lodge's rec room offers free wi-fi, fireside reading nooks, ping-pong and pool tables, and bicycle rentals.

Centrella Inn (831-372-3372, 800-233-3372; www.centrellainn.com; 612 Central Ave; r incl breakfast $129-229;) For a romantic night inside a Victorian seaside mansion, this turreted National Historic Landmark is dreamy, with enchanting gardens and a player piano. Some of the stately rooms have fireplaces, clawfoot tubs and kitchenettes. Rates include afternoon refreshments and around-the-clock cookies.

Sunset Inn Hotel (831-375-3529; www.gosunsetinn.com; 133 Asilomar Blvd; d $139-219;) At this small motor lodge not far from the beach and golf course, attentive staff will check you into luxuriously redesigned rooms featuring king-sized beds, flat-screen TVs and either a whirlpool tub or rain shower. Some also have romantic gas fireplaces.

Red House Cafe (831-643-1060; 662 Lighthouse Ave; breakfast & lunch $5-12, dinner $13-16; 8:30-11am Sat & Sun, 11am-2pm & dinner from 5pm Tue-Sun;) Always crowded with locals, this 1895 shingled house dishes up comfort food with delightful haute touches, from cinnamon-raisin brioche French toast for breakfast to blue-cheese soufflés and grilled lamb at dinner. Exceptional French tea list.

our pick Passionfish (831-655-3311; www.passionfish.net; 701 Lighthouse Ave; mains $17-24; dinner) Fresh, sustainable seafood is artfully presented in any number of inventive ways, though the seasonally inspired menu also carries slow-cooked meats and vegetarian dishes. The earth-tone decor is spare, with tables squeezed close together. A stellar wine list is temptingly priced at retail, and there are dozens of Chinese teas to pick from. Reservations recommended.

CARMEL-BY-THE-SEA

pop 3928

With impressive coastal frontage, upper-crust boutique shopping and borderline fanatical devotion to its canine residents, Carmel simply glows with smugness. Springing to life as a seaside resort in the 1880s – surprisingly, given that the beach is nearly always clouded over with fog – Carmel attracted famous artists and writers such as Sinclair Lewis and Jack London. Although artistic indulgence survives in the town's 100-plus galleries, sky-high property values have long since obliterated its salt-of-the-earth bohemia.

Today fairytale Comstock cottages, with their characteristic stone chimneys and pitched gable roofs, dot the town. Local bylaws forbid neon signs and billboards; even payphones, garbage cans and newspaper vending boxes are picturesquely shingled. Buildings have no street numbers, so addresses always specify the block and the street, and/or the nearest intersection. All of this quaint charm can wear thin awfully fast so, after seeing the sights, don't blame yourself for not wanting to linger.

Orientation & Information

Ocean Ave is the widest east–west road, with tree-and-flower-filled medians. It's the town's main strip, and the busiest intersection is with San Carlos St. The **chamber of commerce** (☎ 831-624-2522, 800-550-4333; www .carmelcalifornia.com; San Carlos St, btwn 5th & 6th Aves; ☽ 10am-5pm Mon-Sat) hands out maps and art-gallery guides. The free weekly newspaper *Carmel Pine Cone* is packed with local personality and color – the police log is a comedy of manners.

Sights & Activities

Escape the shopping blitzkrieg to amble through tree-lined streets on the lookout for domiciles charming and peculiar. The Hansel-and-Gretel houses at Torres St and Ocean Ave are just how you'd imagine them, while a home at 13th Ave and Monte Verde St is covered in bark. A wicked, cool house in the shape of a ship, made from stone and salvaged ship parts, is near 6th Ave and Guadalupe St. There's more – go find 'em.

Though not always sunny, **Carmel Beach** is still a gorgeous white-sand crescent, where pampered puppies excitedly run off-leash.

SAN CARLOS DE BORROMÉO DE CARMELO MISSION

About a mile south of downtown, this gorgeous Spanish colonial **mission** (☎ 831-624-1271; www.carmelmission.org; 3080 Rio Rd; adult/child 7-17 $6.50/2; ☽ 9:30am-5pm Mon-Sat, 10:30am-5pm Sun) is an oasis of calm and solemnity, ensconced by flowering gardens. Its stone basilica is filled with original art, while a separate chapel protects the tomb of California mission founder Junípero Serra. The original Monterey mission was established by Serra in 1769, but poor soil and the corrupting influence of military troops quickly motivated the move to Carmel.

Museum exhibits are scattered throughout the complex. The bare-bones room, attributed to Serra, looks like something out of *The Good, The Bad and The Ugly*. Don't overlook the gravestone of 'Old

Gabriel,' a Native American convert whom Father Serra baptized personally and whose dates put him at 151 years old when he died. People say he smoked like a chimney and outlived seven wives. There's a lesson in there somewhere.

TOR HOUSE

Even if you've never heard of the 20th-century poet Robinson Jeffers, a pilgrimage to the structures he built with his own hands – **Tor House** (☎ 831-624-1813; www.torhouse .org; 26304 Ocean View Ave; adult/child 12-17 $7/2; ☽ tours 10am-3pm Fri & Sat) and the Celtic-inspired Hawk Tower – offers fascinating insight into both the man and the ethos of the Carmel he embodied, not to mention a host of intriguing architectural aspects. A porthole in the Celtic-inspired Hawk Tower, which is visible from the street, came from the wrecked ship that carried Napoleon from Elba. The only way to see inside is on a tour (advance reservations required).

POINT LOBOS STATE RESERVE

About 4 miles south of town, **Point Lobos** (☎ 831-624-4909; http://pt-lobos.parks.state.ca.us; off Hwy 1; per car $10; ☽ 8am-30min after sunset) has a dramatically rocky coastline. It takes its name from the Punta de los Lobos Marinos, or the 'Point of the Sea Wolves,' named by the Spanish for the howls of the resident sea lions. The full perimeter hike is 6 miles, but several short walks take in the wild scenery. Favorite destinations include **Bird Island**, **Sea Lion Point** and **Devil's Cauldron**, a whirlpool that gets splashy at high tide. **Whaler's Cove** is popular with divers (no snorkeling allowed); diving reservations and **permits** (☎ 831-624-8413; per 2-person team $10, motorized-boat launch fee $5) are required.

Sleeping

You're more likely to see a gray whale breaching in summertime than find cheap rooms in Carmel – ask the chamber of commerce about last-minute deals. A slew of too-quaint B&Bs and small hotels fill up quickly, especially during summer.

Carmel Wayfarer Inn (☎ 831-624-2711, 800-533-2711; www.carmelwayfarerinn.com; cnr 4th Ave & Mission St; r incl breakfast $110-210; ☎ 🐾) None of the charming courtyard rooms or suites in this 1920s apartment complex are quite the same. Some have delightfully retro kitchens

DRIVING TOUR: 17-MILE DRIVE

What to See

Pacific Grove and Carmel are linked by the spectacularly scenic 17-Mile Drive, which meanders through Pebble Beach, a private resort and residential area that epitomizes the peninsula's jaw-dropping wealth. It's no chore staying within the 25mph limit – every curve in the road reveals another postcard-worthy vista, especially when wildflowers bloom. If you're driving, expect to share the road with cyclists, some quite wobbly on their wheels.

Using the free map provided at toll booths, you can easily pick out landmarks such as **Spanish Bay**, where explorer Gaspar de Portolá dropped anchor in 1769; treacherously rocky **Point Joe**, which in the past was often mistaken for the entrance to Monterey Bay and thus became the site of several shipwrecks; and **Bird Rock**, a haven for seals, too. The ostensible pièce de résistance of the drive is the **Lone Cypress**, the trademarked symbol of the Pebble Beach Company, that perches on a seaward rock. Over 250 years old, the tree is now reinforced with wire supports, which fortunately aren't that visible in photographs.

Besides the coast, the real attractions here are the world-famous **golf courses**, including at Pebble Beach, which hosts February's **AT&T Pebble Beach National Pro-Am** (www.attpbgolf.com), a famous golf tournament mixing pros and celebrities. It's easy to picture Don Cheadle driving down the spectacular 18th hole for a victory. The **Lodge at Pebble Beach** (☎ 831-647-7500, 800-654-9300; www.pebblebeach.com; r from $695; ✖ 💻 🛜 🐾) brags about its world-class spa, restaurants and extravagant shops. Even if you're not a trust-fund baby, you can still soak up the rich atmosphere in the resort's art-filled public spaces.

The Route

Open sunrise to sunset, entry to the 17-Mile Drive is controlled by the **Pebble Beach Company** (☎ 831-647-7500; www.pebblebeach.com; per vehicle $9.25, bicycles free). There are five gates; for the most scenic stretch, enter the Pacific Grove Gate off Sunset Dr and exit at the Carmel Gate.

Cycling the drive is enormously popular, but try to do so during the week when traffic isn't as heavy. There's no shoulder on the road, so keep your wits about you. On weekends the flow of bikes goes primarily north to south. For bicycle rentals in Monterey, see p169.

Time & Mileage

This route, which actually measures slightly less than 17 miles these days, could take anywhere from an hour up to a half day, if you stop to mosey around.

and sunset views. Rates include afternoon wine and cheese tastings.

Sea View Inn (☎ 831-624-8778; www.seaviewinncarmel.com; Camino Real btwn 11th & 12th Aves; r incl breakfast $120-195; 🛜) An intimate retreat away from downtown; here cozy fireside nooks are tailor-made for reading or taking afternoon tea. The cheapest country-style rooms are short on cat-swinging space, but it's a short walk over to the beach.

Eating

Not exactly a gourmet ghetto, Carmel has few restaurants worth the price.

Bruno's Market & Deli (☎ 831-624-3821; cnr 6th & Junípero Aves; mains $5-8; ⏰ 7am-8pm) The town's best grocery store, Bruno's has a superb deli for creating picnics. It also stocks kettle-brewed Sparky's root beer from Pacific Grove.

Carmel Belle (☎ 831-624-1600; Doud Craft Studios, cnr Ocean Ave & San Carlos St; mains $5-11; ⏰ 8am-5pm) At this charcuterie, cheese and wine shop hidden in a mini-mall, you'll thank heaven for fresh, often organic, ingredients flowing from local farms onto the tables here. The slow-cooked pork sandwich is a winner.

Rio Grill (☎ 831-625-5436; 101 Crossroads Blvd, off Hwy 1 exit Rio Rd; dinner mains $10-37; ⏰ 11:30am-9pm Mon-Thu, 11:30am-10pm Fri & Sat, 10:30am-9pm Sun; 🚸) At this jazzy bistro, local ingredients find their destiny in flavorful Southwestern, Southern and Cal-Italian dishes. The fire-roasted artichoke and oakwood-smoked baby back ribs will have you licking your fingers.

Drinking & Entertainment

Jack London's (☎ 831-624-2336; Dolores St, btwn 5th & 6th Aves; ⏰ 11:30am-11pm Mon-Fri, 11:30am-midnight Sat & Sun; 🍴) A Carmel mainstay since 1973, Jack's pairs overpriced pub grub with decent microbrews and potent mixed drinks. Service can be snarling but at least there's a crackling fireplace and it's open late.

Forest Theater (☎ 831-626-1681; www.forest theaterguild.org; cnr Mountain View Ave & Santa Rita St; tickets $7-25; ⏰ Apr-Jul) Musicals, drama, comedies and film screenings take place at this enchanting outdoor performance venue, dating from 1910 and anchored by enormous fire pits.

Getting There & Around

Carmel is 5 miles south of Monterey by Hwy 1. There's free unlimited parking beside **Vista Lobos Park** (3rd Ave btwn Torres St & Junípero Ave). MST (see p171) bus 5 runs north to Monterey and south to the mission. Bus 22 passes through four times daily during summer only en route to Big Sur.

BIG SUR TO SAN LUIS OBISPO

On this 125-mile stretch of Hwy 1, you'll snake along the unbelievably picturesque coast southward until it joins with Hwy 101 at San Luis Obispo. Driving along this narrow, two-lane highway is extremely slow going. Even if your driving skills are up for the myriad of hills and switchbacks, others aren't: expect to average under 40mph. Traveling after dark can be perilous, and also futile because you'll miss out on all the grand views. Parts of the road are battle-scarred, evidence of the eternal struggle to keep it open after landslides (for advice about road hazards and conditions, see p291). Watch out for cyclists and always use signposted roadside pull-outs to let faster-moving traffic pass.

BIG SUR

pop 1000

Much ink has been spilled extolling the raw beauty and energy of this stretch of land shoehorned between the Santa Lucia Range and the Pacific Ocean, but nothing quite prepares you for your first glimpse

---

BIG SUR

0 ————— 6 km
0 ————— 4 miles

INFORMATION
Big Sur Ranger Station...1 B3

SIGHTS & ACTIVITIES
Big Sur Discovery
  Center......................2 A3
Bird-Banding Lab........(see 2)
Esalen Institute.............3 B4
Henry Miller Library......4 B3
Molera Horseback
  Tours.....................(see 2)

SLEEPING 🛏 🏠
Andrew Molera State Park
  Campground.............5 A3
Big Sur Campground &
  Cabins....................6 A3
Big Sur Lodge...............7 B3
Deetjen's Big Sur Inn....8 B3
Glen Oaks Motel...........9 B3
Julia Pfeiffer Burns State Park
  Campground..........10 B4
Pfeiffer Big Sur State Park
  Campground.........(see 7)
Post Ranch Inn............11 D3
Ripplewood Resort......(see 9)
Ventana Inn & Spa......12 B3

EATING 🍴
Big Sur Bakery &
  Restaurant.............13 B3
Big Sur River Inn.........14 A3
Café Kevah...............(see 15)
Deetjen's Big Sur Inn...(see 8)
Habanero Burrito Bar..(see 14)
Nepenthe..................15 B3
Sierra Mar...............(see 11)

DRINKING 🍷
Maiden Publick
  House...................(see 14)
Rocky Point...............16 A1

of the craggy, unspoiled coastline. Big Sur is more a state of mind than a place you can pinpoint on a map. It has no traffic lights, banks or strip malls, and when the sun goes down, the moon and stars are the only streetlights – that is, if summer's dense fog hasn't extinguished 'em already.

In the 1950s and '60s, Big Sur – so named by Spanish settlers living in Carmel who referred to the wilderness as *el pais grande del sur* (the big country to the south) – became a favorite retreat for writers and artists, including Henry Miller and the Beat generation. Today it still attracts mystics, artists, hippies and eccentrics looking to contemplate their navels, along with city slickers eager to unplug from their iPhones and reflect deeply on this emerald edge of continent. As you travel through, you'll notice that Big Sur's incomparable redwood forests and backcountry wilderness are still recovering from massive wildfires caused by a lightning storm in 2008.

Orientation & Information
Visitors often wander into businesses along Hwy 1 and ask, 'How much further to Big Sur?' In fact, there is no town of Big Sur as such, though you may see the name on maps. The little commercial activity is concentrated between Andrew Molera State Park to the north and Pfeiffer Big Sur State Park to the south. Sometimes called 'The Village,' this stretch has the post office and the most shops, restaurants and lodgings.

Pick up the comprehensive free *Big Sur Guide*, published by the **Big Sur Chamber of Commerce** (☎ 831-667-2100; www.bigsurcalifornia.org; ❧ 9am-1pm), at local businesses and tourist

---

DON'T MISS: BIG SUR

- **Point Sur Lightstation** (right) Be entranced by moonlight tours.
- **Pfeiffer Beach** (p178) Dramatic surf and purple sand!
- **Nepenthe** (p181) Linger over the sea views.
- **McWay Falls** (p178) Be hypnotized by an oceanside waterfall.
- **Esalen Institute** (p178) Clifftop hot-tub soaks after midnight.

---

spots. Just south of Pfeiffer Big Sur State Park, the **Big Sur Ranger Station** (☎ 831-667-2315; Hwy 1; ❧ 8am-4:30pm) has information and maps for all state parks, the Los Padres National Forest and Ventana Wilderness. South of the Nacimiento-Fergusson Rd turn-off, the US Forest Service (USFS) **Pacific Valley Ranger Station** (☎ 805-927-4211; Hwy 1; ❧ 8:30am-4:30pm) has limited recreational information.

Road and emergency services here are distant – in Monterey to the north or Cambria to the south. Fill up the tank beforehand, and be careful.

Sights & Activities
All of the following are along Hwy 1, listed north to south. Unless otherwise noted, all of Big Sur's state parks are open from 30 minutes before sunrise until 30 minutes after sunset, with 24-hour access for campers. If you pay the entrance fee for one park, you get in free to any others that day – just hang on to your receipt or self-registration payment stub.

BIXBY BRIDGE
Around 13 miles south of Carmel, the landmark Bixby Bridge, spanning Rainbow Canyon, is one of the world's highest single-span bridges; it's over 260ft high. Completed in 1932, it was built by prisoners eager to lop time off their sentences. There's a perfect photo-op pull-off on the bridge's north side. Don't be tricked into thinking that the similar-looking Rocky Creek Bridge further north is the real deal.

POINT SUR STATE HISTORIC PARK
Six miles south of Bixby Bridge, Point Sur looks like a velvet green fortress rising out of the plain. Almost resembling an island, it's actually an imposing volcanic rock connected to the land by a sandbar. Atop the rock sits the 1889 **Point Sur Lightstation** (☎ 831-625-4419; www.pointsur.org; tour adult/child 6-17 from $10/5), which remained in operation until 1974. Ocean views and details of the lighthouse-keepers' lives are engrossing. To join a three-hour guided tour (no reservations accepted) meet at the locked gate on Hwy 1, a quarter-mile north of Point Sur Naval Facility, at 10am or 2pm Saturday or 10am Sunday. Tours also depart some weekdays between April and October, when full-moon

weekend tours are also given. Always call ahead or check the website to confirm current schedules.

ANDREW MOLERA STATE PARK
Named for the farmer who first planted artichokes in California, this oft-overlooked **park** (☎ 831-667-2315; per car $10), 3 miles further south, enjoys a remote and wild setting, with lots of wildlife and great beachcombing. A quarter-mile trail leads from the campground to a beautiful beach where the Big Sur River meets the ocean. **Molera Horseback Tours** (☎ 831-625-5486, 800-942-5486; http://molerahorsebacktours.com; ☼ Mar-Nov) offers guided trail rides to the beach (from $40). Learn more about endangered California condors (see boxed text, p37) at the park's barn-sized **Big Sur Discovery Center** (☎ 831-620-0702; www.ventanaws.org; admission free; ☼ 9am-4pm Fri-Sun; ♿), which leads guided condor-watching tours (per person from $50). You can watch wildlife techs at work in the **bird-banding lab** (☼ sunrise-noon Fri-Sun Apr-May & Sep-Oct, sunrise-noon Thu & Sat Jun-Aug) next door.

PFEIFFER BIG SUR STATE PARK
Four miles further south past the village, **Pfeiffer Big Sur State Park** (☎ 831-667-2315; per car $10; ♿) is Big Sur's largest state park, named after the first European settlers who arrived in 1869. There are miles of pristine hiking trails winding through the redwood groves. The most popular walk – to 60ft-high **Pfeiffer Falls**, a delicate cascade that usually runs from December to May – is an easy, kid-friendly 1.4-mile round-trip.

PFEIFFER BEACH
Just west of Pfeiffer Big Sur State Park, this phenomenal, crescent-shaped **beach** (☎ 831-667-2315; per car $5; ☼ 6am-sunset; ♿) is notable for its huge double rock formation through which waves crash with life-affirming power. It's often windy, and the surf is too dangerous for swimming. Dig down into the wet sand – it's purple! To get there from Hwy 1 south, drive 0.5 miles past Big Sur Ranger Station, then make a sharp right onto Sycamore Canyon Rd, marked by a yellow sign that says 'narrow road.' Follow it for over 2 miles down to the parking lot.

HENRY MILLER LIBRARY
A denizen for 17 years, Henry Miller wrote, 'It was here in Big Sur I first learned to say Amen!' A living memorial, alt-cultural center and bookshop, the nonprofit **Henry Miller Library** (☎ 831-667-2574; www.henrymiller .org; Hwy 1; donation requested; ☼ 11am-6pm Wed-Mon; 💻 📶) is the art and soul of Big Sur bohemia, but was never Miller's home. Inside you'll find all of Miller's written works, many of his paintings and an eye-popping collection of Big Sur and Beat generation material, including copies of the top 100 books Miller claimed most influenced him. Stop by for a browse, some coffee and good conversation. Check the website for upcoming community events including live-music concerts, open-mic nights and outdoor film series. The library is just south of Nepenthe restaurant (p181), over 3 miles south of Pfeiffer Big Sur State Park.

PARTINGTON COVE
From the western side of Hwy 1, a poorly marked steep dirt trail descends a half-mile along Partington Creek to this **cove** (admission free), a little-visited but very beautiful section of Big Sur. During Prohibition it was a landing spot for rum-runners. On the 1-mile round-trip trail you cross a cool bridge and walk through an even cooler tunnel. The cove's water is unbelievably aqua and the kelp forests are incredible. There's no real beach access but you can scamper on the rocks and look for tidepools as waves crash ominously. Look for the trailhead turn-off inside a large hairpin turn, about 6 miles south of Nepenthe restaurant and 2 miles north of Julia Pfeiffer Burns State Park.

JULIA PFEIFFER BURNS STATE PARK
Named for another Big Sur pioneer, this **park** (☎ 831-667-2315; per car $10; ☼ 8am-7pm) hugs both sides of Hwy 1. At the entrance, you'll find picnic grounds along McWay Creek. The highlight is California's only coastal waterfall, **McWay Falls**, which drops 80ft straight into the sea – or onto the beach, depending on the tide. We dare you to take fewer than a dozen photos. To reach the waterfall viewpoint, take the short Over-look Trail west of the parking lot and cross beneath Hwy 1.

ESALEN INSTITUTE
Eleven miles south of Nepenthe, marked only by a small lighted sign, the **Esalen Institute** (☎ 831-667-3000; www.esalen.org; 55000 Hwy 1) is like

a new-age hippie camp for adults. Workshops run the gamut from your standard 'Introduction to Mindfulness Meditation' to the ominous-sounding 'brainwave training.' Fun fact: Gonzo hack Hunter S Thompson was the gun-toting caretaker here in the 1960s.

Esalen's famous hot-springs baths are fed by a natural hot spring and sit on a ledge high above the ocean. Dollars to doughnuts you'll never take another dip that compares view-wise with the one here. Only two small open-air pools perch directly over the waves, so once you've stripped down and taken a lightning-fast shower, zip outside immediately – otherwise, you'll be stuck with a tepid, no-view pool or a rickety bathtub. Clothing-optional 'nightly bathing' is open to the public from 1am to 3am by **reservation** (☎ 831-667-3047; admission $20) only; fees must be paid by credit card.

SOUTHERN BIG SUR
South of Nacimiento-Fergusson Rd, look for the turn-off to **Sand Dollar Beach Picnic Area** (☎ 805-927-4211; per car $5; ☽ 9am-8pm; ☻), almost 10 miles south of Lucia. From the parking lot, it's a five-minute walk down to southern Big Sur's longest sandy beach; leashed dogs are allowed.

Less than a half-mile south of Plaskett Creek Campground, Hwy 1 passes by **Jade Cove** (admission free; ☽ sunrise-sunset), where in 1971 three divers recovered a 9000lb jade boulder that measured 8ft long and was valued at $180,000. The best time to try your luck beachcombing for jade, which is black or blue-green and looks dull until you dip it in water, is during low tide or after a big storm.

If you've got any daylight left, keep trucking past Gorda to **Salmon Creek Falls** (admission free; ☽ sunrise-sunset; ☻), which usually runs from December to May. Tucked up a forested canyon, the double-drop waterfall can be glimpsed from the hairpin turn on Hwy 1, where roadside parking gets crowded. Take the 10-minute walk uphill to splash around in the pools, where kids shriek and dogs happily yip.

Your last taste of Big Sur rocky grandeur comes at **Ragged Point**, a craggy cliff outcropping with fabulous sea views, 15 miles north of Hearst Castle (p181).

Sleeping
Big Sur's lodging ranges from basic four walls and a mattress to glossy mag–worthy resorts. Reservations are essential (even just for camping), especially in summer and on weekends year-round. If everything is booked, the next-closest accommodations are found on the Monterey Peninsula (p169) heading north or San Simeon (p182), just south of Hearst Castle.

BUDGET
Camping is currently available in three of Big Sur's **state parks** (☎ reservations 800-444-7275; www.reserveamerica.com) and at two **USFS campgrounds** (☎ reservations 877-444-6777; www .recreation.gov) further south:

USFS Kirk Creek Campground (www.campone.com; campsites $22) Beautiful, if exposed, ocean-view blufftop campsites with potable water, 2 miles south of Limekiln State Park.

USFS Plaskett Creek Campground (www.campone .com; campsites $22) Forty-four spacious, shaded campsites with potable water in a forested meadow near Sand Dollar Beach.

our pick **Andrew Molera State Park** (tent sites $25) Two dozen first-come, first-served primitive walk-in sites with fire pits and drinking water; no ocean views.

Julia Pfeiffer Burns State Park (tent sites $30) Two small walk-in campsites on a semi-shaded ocean bluff; you must register first at Pfeiffer Big Sur State Park campground, 12 miles north.

Pfeiffer Big Sur State Park (campsites $35-50) Humongous 204-site campground nestled in a redwood-shaded river valley; facilities include drinking water, coin-op showers and laundry, but no RV hookups.

There are a few private campgrounds in Big Sur, most with campsites and cabins crowded uncomfortably close together.

Big Sur Campground & Cabins (☎ 831-667-2322; www.bigsurcamp.com; 47000 Hwy 1; campsites $35-60, cabins $88-360; ☻) Popular with RVers, this well-run private campground has dozens of tent and RV sites with hookups, and also some small tent and A-frame cabins shaded by redwoods, right on the river. It's also got coin-op laundry and hot-shower facilities, a playground and general store.

MIDRANGE
Even if you pay a pretty penny for accommodations, don't expect too many amenities in Big Sur. Most rooms don't have TVs or phones.

CENTRAL COAST

Deetjen's Big Sur Inn (☎ 831-667-2377; www
.deetjens.com; 48865 Hwy 1; r $80-200) Nestled
among redwoods and wisteria along Castro
Creek, this enchanting conglomeration of
rustic, thin-walled rooms and cottages was
constructed by Norwegian immigrant Hel-
muth Deetjen in the 1930s. Some rooms
are warmed by wood-burning fireplaces.
Cheaper ones share bathrooms, but all book
up far in advance.

Ripplewood Resort (☎ 831-667-2242; www
.ripplewoodresort.com; 47047 Hwy 1; d $95-185) Rip-
plewood has struck a blow for fiscal equality
by having the same rates year-round. Rustic
retro-Americana cabins vary in details: all
have private baths; some have kitchens
and fireplaces. The riverside cabins – like
Nos 1 and 2 – are quiet and surrounded by
redwoods; roadside ones can get noisy.

Treebones Resort (☎ 877-424-4787; www.tree
bonesresort.com; 71895 Hwy 1, off Willow Creek Rd; d incl
breakfast $155-245; ⊠ ⛊) Don't let the word
'resort' throw you. Yes, it's got an ocean-
view hot tub and heated pool, but when
was the last time you slept in a yurt? Expect
sumptuous quilt-covered beds, sink vanities
and redwood decks, but little privacy.
Common bathrooms with showers are a
quick stroll away near the main lodge. It's
just north of Gorda, in southern Big Sur.

Glen Oaks Motel (☎ 831-667-2105; www.glen
oaksbigsur.com; Hwy 1; d $195-300; 🛜) At this re-
imagined 1950s redwood-and-adobe motor
lodge, rustic rooms and cabins seem effort-
lessly chic. All of the snug romantic hideaways are equipped with gas fireplaces and
have been dramatically transformed by ecoconscious design elements. The studio
cottage has a kitchenette and delightful
walk-in shower built for two.

Big Sur Lodge (☎ 831-667-3100, 800-424-4787;
www.bigsurlodge.com; 47225 Hwy 1; d $209-369; ⊠)
What you're paying for here is the supre-
mely peaceful location, tucked away inside
the redwood forest of Pfeiffer Big Sur State
Park. Throwback duplex bungalows each
have a deck or balcony; pricier ones may
have kitchenettes and/or wood-burning
fireplaces. Guests enjoy free admission to
all of Big Sur's state parks.

Worth a try if you're stuck:

Ragged Point Inn (☎ 805-927-4502; www.ragged
pointinn.com; 19019 Hwy 1, Ragged Point; r $129-279)
Split-level motel rooms are nothing special, except for
ocean views.

Lucia Lodge (☎ 831-667-2391, 866-424-4787; www
.lucialodge.com; 62400 Hwy 1, Lucia; d incl breakfast
$195-275) Spectacular clifftop views, but only ho-hum
cabin rooms.

TOP END
You can forget all about hippies and
bohemians at these full-service resorts.

Ventana Inn & Spa (☎ 831-667-2331, 800-628-
6500; www.ventanainn.com; 48123 Hwy 1; d incl breakfast
$500-1375; ⊠ 🖥 🛜 ⛊) Romantic Ventana
may wear posh Post Ranch clothes but it
has an Esalen soul, and caters to honey-
mooning couples and paparazzi-fleeing
celebs. Pad from a yoga class to the Japanese
baths and clothing-optional pool, or hole up
all day next to your private wood-burning
fireplace.

Post Ranch Inn (☎ 831-667-2200, 800-527-2200;
www.postranchinn.com; Hwy 1; d incl breakfast $550-2185;
⊠ 🖥 🛜 ⛊) The last word in luxurious
coastal getaways, the legendary Post Ranch
pampers guests with elite lodgings with
features such as slate spa tubs, private
decks, fireplaces and even walking sticks
for those coastal hikes. The mountain-view
tree houses built on stilts do have a bit of
sway. One sour note: the staff can be stiff
and standoffish.

Eating
Like Big Sur lodgings, restaurants are pretty
pricey for what you actually get.

Habanero Burrito Bar (☎ 831-667-2700; Hwy
1; mains $5-7; ☯ 11am-7pm) Beside the Big Sur
River Inn, this made-to-order burrito and
wrap sandwich deli counter also whips
up real fresh-fruit smoothies at the back
of a general store stocked with snacks and
camping supplies.

Big Sur Bakery & Restaurant (☎ 831-667-0520;
Hwy 1; items from $5, mains $14-36; ☯ bakery from 8am
daily, restaurant 11am-2:30pm Tue-Fri, 10:30am-2:30pm
Sat & Sun, dinner from 5:30pm Tue-Sat) This funkily
decorated, warmly lit house behind the
Shell station has expensive menu offerings
that change through the day and season.
Wood-fired pizzas and burgers share the
lineup with refined dishes such as wild
salmon with succotash. Service can be
lackadaisical.

Deetjen's Big Sur Inn (☎ 831-667-2377; 48865
Hwy 1; breakfast $8-12, dinner $12-32; ☯ 8-11:30am,
dinner from 6pm daily) This quaint yesteryear
lodge has a cozy, candle-lit dining room

serving up steaks, cassoulets and other hearty country fare from a daily-changing menu, primarily sourced from organic local produce, hormone-free meats and sustainable seafood.

Big Sur River Inn (☎ 831-667-2700; Hwy 1; breakfast & lunch $8-19, dinner $17-37; ☯ breakfast, lunch & dinner) This roadside inn has a woodsy old supper-club feel with a deck overlooking a creek teeming with throaty frogs. The wedding reception–quality food is classic American, with breakfast the most reliable bet.

our pick **Nepenthe** (☎ 831-667-2345; 48510 Hwy 1; mains $14-37; ☯ 11:30am-4:30pm & 5-10pm, to 10:30pm Jul 4-Labor Day) Nepenthe comes from a Greek word meaning 'isle of no sorrow.' Indeed, it'd be hard to feel blue while sitting on the clifftop ocean-view terrace. The food, while sometimes tasty (try the renowned Ambrosia burger), is secondary to the view and Nepenthe's place in history – Orson Welles and Rita Hayworth bought the place in 1944.

Also recommended:

Café Kevah (☎ 831-667-2345; 48510 Hwy 1; mains $6-15; ☯ 9am-4pm Mar-early Jan) Cheaper eats and much shorter waits, downstairs from Nepenthe.

Sierra Mar (☎ 831-667-2800; Post Ranch Inn, Hwy 1; lunch $19-26, 4-course prix fixe dinner menu $105; ☯ noon-9pm) Modern California cuisine with spirit-lifting romantic ocean views.

Drinking

Maiden Publick House (☎ 831-667-2355; Hwy 1) Close to Big Sur River Inn, the Maiden has a respectable beer bible and motley local musicians jamming their hearts out.

Rocky Point (☎ 831-624-2933; 36700 Hwy 1; ☯ 8:30am-9pm) Detour to the dizzying ocean-view deck for sunset drinks – just ignore the stuffy country-club atmosphere and 1970s-retro menu of appetizers and surf-and-turf.

Getting There & Away

Big Sur is best explored by car because you'll be itching to stop frequently and take in the rugged beauty and stunning vistas that reveal themselves at every turn. MST bus 22 ($2.50, 1¼ hours) travels from Monterey (p171) via Carmel only as far south as Nepenthe restaurant, running thrice daily between late May and early September. Each bus is equipped with a two-bicycle carrying rack.

POINT PIEDRAS BLANCAS

Although many lighthouses still freckle the California coast, few offer such a historically evocative seascape as **Piedras Blancas Lightstation** (☎ 805-927-7361; www.piedrasblancas.org; adult/child 6-17 $10/5; ☯ tours 10am Tue, Thu & Sat). Picturesquely, everything looks much the way it did when the first lighthouse keepers helped ships find safe harbor around the whaling station at San Simeon Bay. Federally designated an outstanding natural area, the grounds of this 1875 lighthouse – incidentally, one of the tallest on the West Coast – have been painstakingly replanted with native vegetation. Knowledgeable volunteers lead walking tours of the property as they chat about marine wildlife, Native American culture and the maritime history of this lonely, windswept coastal spot. Tours currently meet at 9:45am at the old Piedras Blancas Motel, 1.5 miles north of the lightstation. Call ahead to confirm current schedules.

HEARST CASTLE

The most important thing to know is that William Randolph Hearst (1863–1951) did not live like *Citizen Kane*. Not that Hearst wasn't bombastic, conniving and larger than life, but the moody recluse of Orson Welles' movie he was not. Hearst never called his 165-room monstrosity a castle, preferring its official name La Cuesta Encantada (The Enchanted Hill) or more often simply calling it 'the ranch.' From the 1920s to the '40s, Hearst and his long-time mistress Marion Davies (Hearst's wife refused to grant him a divorce) entertained here, seeing a steady stream of the era's biggest movers and shakers. Invitations were highly coveted, but Hearst had his quirks – he despised drunkenness, and guests were forbidden to speak of death.

It's a wondrous, historic (Winston Churchill penned anti-Nazi essays here in the 1930s), over-the-top homage to material excess perched high on a hill, and a visit is a must. Architect Julia Morgan based the main building, or Casa Grande, on the design of a Spanish cathedral, and over decades catered to Hearst's every design whim, deftly integrating the spoils of his fabled European shopping sprees (ancient artifacts, entire monasteries etc) into the whole. The estate sprawls out over acres of bountiful, land-scaped gardens (and, at the time, the world's

CENTRAL COAST

ENORMOUS E-SEALS

Nearly extinct by the late 19th century, northern elephant seals have made a remarkable comeback along California's coast, most famously at **Año Nuevo State Reserve** (p86) north of Santa Cruz. These days a larger, more easily accessible colony of 'e-seals' hangs around Piedras Blancas, including at a well-signposted boardwalk viewpoint 4.8 miles northwest of Hearst Castle, where you'll find interpretive panels and blue-jacketed volunteers from the **Friends of the Elephant Seal** (☎ 805-924-1628; www.elephantseal.org).

During peak winter season, upward of 15,000 elephant seals seek shelter in the coves and beaches along this stretch of coast. On sunny days the seals pretty much 'lie around like banana slugs,' in the words of one volunteer. The behemoth bulls engage in mock – and sometimes real – combat, all while making odd guttural grunts, as their harems of females and young pups look on. You wouldn't think it from just watching them snooze on the sand, but elephant seals can dive deeper (nearly a mile) and for longer (over an hour) than any other mammal.

Always observe elephant seals from a safe distance and do not approach or otherwise harass these unpredictable wild animals. Some of the mature bulls weigh over 2 tons – about the same as those SUVs whizzing by on Hwy 1 – and despite their enormous size, they can move faster on the sand than any human can.

Here's a quick seasonal viewing guide:

- **November and December** Bull seals arrive at the beach, followed by juveniles and mature females already pregnant from last winter's breeding season.

- **January to March** Pregnant seals give birth, peaking in February; after delivering, females mate with the waiting and rather anxious males, who then depart for feeding migrations.

- **April to May** Females wean pups and leave to feed themselves; pups teach themselves how to swim and eventually leave as well.

- **June to October** Seals of all ages return to molt, with females arriving in early summer and males in late summer and early fall.

largest private zoo), accentuated by shimmering pools and fountains, and statues from ancient Greece and Moorish Spain.

Much like Hearst's construction budget, the castle will devour as much of your time as you let it. To see anything of this **state historical monument** (☎ information 805-927-2020, reservations 800-444-4445; www.hearstcastle.com; adult/child from $24/12), you have to take a tour. For most of the year, you'll need tour reservations. In peak summer months and for magical sunset living-history and winter holiday tours, you'll need reservations at least a week or two in advance. Before you leave, or if someone fell down on reservation duty, visit the museum in the back of the visitors center and watch the 40-minute documentary film about the castle and Hearst's life inside the five-story-high National Geographic Theater. The visitors center also has fast-food snacks and gift shop.

Tours start daily at 8:20am, with the last leaving at 3:20pm (later in summer). There are four main tours; for each you depart from the visitors center and make the 10-minute bus ride up the hill. No matter how many tours you go on, you have to make the journey up and down each time. Each of the tours lasts about 1¾ hours, and every tour includes the highlight Neptune and Roman pools. It's best to start with Tour 1, aka the Experience Tour, as you get an overview of the estate. The docents are almost preternaturally knowledgeable – just try and stump 'em. Dress in layers because gloomy fog at sea level can turn into sunny skies on the hilltop, or vice-versa.

Getting to Hearst Castle without your own wheels can be a challenge. San Luis Obispo's RTA (p190) bus 12 makes a couple of daily round-trips north to Hearst Castle ($2.75, two hours) via Morro Bay, Cayucos and Cambria.

AROUND SAN SIMEON

Across Hwy 1 from the entrance road to Hearst Castle, **William Randolph Hearst Memorial State Beach** (☎ 805-927-2035; Hwy 1;

admission free; dawn-dusk;) has a pleasant sandy stretch with rock outcroppings, kelp forests, a wooden fishing pier and picnic areas with BBQ grills. Leashed dogs are OK. On the beach, **See for Yourself Kayak Tours** (805-927-1787, 800-717-5225; www.kayakcambria .com) rents kayaks (per hour from $20), wetsuits ($5), bodyboards ($5) and surfboards ($15), weather permitting. Reserve guided kayaking tours ($45 to $90) in advance. Nearby, Sebastian's historic **general store** (805-927-3307; 442 San Simeon Rd; dishes $6-10; 11am-5pm Tue-Sun) sells beach gear, drinks and giant sandwiches and salads.

Beside the beach parking lot, the **Coastal Discovery Center** (805-927-6575; donation requested; 11am-5pm Fri-Sun mid-Mar–Oct, 10am-4pm Fri-Sun Nov–mid-Mar;), cooperatively run with the Monterey Bay National Marine Sanctuary, has educational displays about this unique meeting point of land and sea, including a talking artificial tidepool, videos of deep-sea divers and a WWII-era shipwreck just offshore, and the lowdown on the Piedras Blancas elephant seal colony (see opposite).

Three miles south of the castle, San Simeon is just a strip of unexciting motels and lackluster restaurants. There are better places to stay and eat in Cambria (see below) and the beach towns of Estero Bay (p184). Two miles south of San Simeon, **Hearst San Simeon State Park** (reservations 800-444-7275; www.reserveamerica.com; San Simeon Creek Rd; off Hwy 1; walk-in tent sites $5, campsites $20-35) has two popular campgrounds with drinking water: developed San Simeon Creek, offering coin-op showers; and primitive Washburn, along a bumpy dirt road.

CAMBRIA
pop 6500

With a whopping dose of natural beauty, the coastal idyll of Cambria is like a lone pearl cast along the coast. Built on lands that once belonged to Mission San Miguel, one of its historical nicknames was Slabtown, after the rough pieces of wood its pioneer buildings were constructed from. Today, just like at Hearst Castle, money is no object in this wealthy retirement community, whose motto 'Pines by the Sea' is affixed to the back of BMWs that tootle around 'the village.'

Cambria has three distinct parts: the tourist-choked East Village, a half-mile off

Hwy 1, with art galleries, antique shops and cafés bordering Main St; the newer West Village, also along Main St off Hwy 1, where you'll find the **chamber of commerce** (805-927-3624; www.cambriachamber.org; 767 Main St; 9am-5pm Mon-Fri, noon-4pm Sat & Sun); and **Moonstone Beach**, along coastal Moonstone Beach Dr, west of Hwy 1. Although its eponymous milky-white moonstones are long gone, the beach still tempts romantic meanderers to stroll along its boardwalk and the scenically rocky shoreline. For more solitude, take the Windsor Rd exit off Hwy 1 and drive down to where the road dead-ends. There you'll find a 2-mile blufftop hiking trail leading across serene **East–West Ranch**.

Sleeping

Most accommodations are expensive motels and hotels fronting Moonstone Beach.

HI Cambria Bridge Street Inn (805-927-7653; www.bridgestreetinncambria.com; 4314 Bridge St; dm $22-25, r with shared bath $40-84; check-in 5-9pm;) Inside an 1895 parsonage, this hostel has grandmotherly character and European-style B&B charm, though shabby-chic rooms are thin-walled and beds could be comfier. There's a communal kitchen – and let's not forget lawn croquet. It's small, so reserve ahead.

Bluebird Inn (805-927-4634, 800-552-5434; http://bluebirdmotel.com; 1880 Main St; d $70-220;) With peaceful gardens, this friendly East Village motel has only basic rooms, but some have fireplaces and private balconies overlooking a bubbling creek. It's a reliable budget-conscious choice. Free wi-fi in lobby.

McCall Farm Bed & Breakfast (805-927-3140; http://mccallfarm.com; 6250 Santa Rosa Creek Rd; r incl breakfast $125-155) Along a rural road lined by citrus orchards, olallieberry fields and fresh-produce stands, this 1895 farmhouse has just two cheery, antique-decorated rooms. Laze on the front porch and watch hummingbirds flutter among the flowers.

Blue Dolphin Inn (805-927-3300, 800-222-9157; www.cambriainns.com; 6470 Moonstone Beach Dr; d incl breakfast $199-329;) Upscale motels along Moonstone Beach Dr are nearly identical, but this one is a stand-out. Beautifully renovated, cozy rooms all have gas fireplaces, pillowtop mattresses and rich-feeling linens. Rates include a breakfast picnic basket and afternoon tea and cookies.

Eating & Drinking

Main St, through the East and West Villages, is stuffed with restaurants.

Lily's Coffeehouse (☎ 805-927-7259; 2028 Main St; items $1-8; ⏰ 8:30am-5pm Wed-Mon; ☏) A community gathering spot, Francophilic Lily's has a peaceful front garden patio and brews robust coffees and teas. Drop by on Saturday between 11am and 4pm for made-to-order crepes.

Linn's Easy as Pie Cafe (☎ 805-924-3050; 4251 Bridge St; dishes $4-10; ⏰ 10am-6pm; ♿ 🚼) If you don't have time to visit Linn's Fruit Bin, the original farm store out on Santa Rosa Creek Rd, you can still fork into famous olallieberry pies and preserves at this takeout counter with a sunny patio in the East Village.

Indigo Moon (☎ 805-927-2911; 1980 Main St; lunch $5-10, dinner $17-23; ⏰ 10am-4pm daily, 5-9pm Wed-Sun) Inside this artisan cheese and wine shop, breezy bistro tables complement market-fresh salads, toasty sandwiches and crunchy sweet-potato fries. Gossip over exquisite local wines by the glass on the back patio.

Wild Ginger (☎ 805-927-1001; 2380 Main St; mains $12-17; ⏰ lunch & dinner Fri-Wed) Owned by a standoffish chef, this cramped café serves up vegetarian-friendly pan-Asian fare, pricey but perfectly seasoned and presented, plus housemade sorbets in exotic flavors like pomegranate and pineapple-coconut. Expect a wait.

ESTERO BAY

This long, shallow bay has the surf town of Cayucos at its northern end and Montaña de Oro State Park to the south. Morro Bay, a deep inlet guarded by gargantuan Morro Rock and separated from the sea by a 12-mile-long sand spit, sits about halfway between the two and has the most of the bay's tourist activity.

San Luis Obispo's RTA (p190) bus 12 travels along Hwy 1 from San Luis Obispo, stopping in Morro Bay ($2.25, 45 minutes). A few daily runs continue up to Cayucos, Cambria and Hearst Castle.

Cayucos

pop 2990

The main drag of amiable, slow-paced Cayucos calls to mind an Old West frontier town, while a block to the west, surf's up.

Ocean Ave, which parallels Hwy 1, maintains historic storefronts and has most of the town's hotels, eateries and antique shops. At the north end of town, fronting a broad beach, is the blissfully uncommercialized, knock-kneed pier, built in 1875 – today, it's favored by fishers and newbie surfers. **Cayucos Surf Company** (☎ 805-995-1000; www.surfcompany.com; 95 Cayucos Dr; ⏰ 9am-6pm) sells and rents surfboards (per half-day $18), wetsuits ($10) and boogie boards ($8); two-hour surfing lessons cost $70, including equipment rental.

SLEEPING

Cayucos doesn't lack for motels or beachfront inns, most of 'em kinda pricey.

Seaside Motel (☎ 805-995-3809, 800-549-0900; www.seasidemotel.com; 42 S Ocean Ave; d $80-155; ☏) You can rest assured of a warm welcome from the hands-on owners of this vintage motel. Country-kitsch rooms are smallish but some have kitchenettes. Keep your fingers crossed for quiet neighbors.

Cayucos Beach Inn (☎ 805-995-2828, 800-482-0555; www.cayucosbeachinn.com; 333 S Ocean Ave; d $145-225; 🐕 ☏ ♿ 🚼) At this remarkably dog-friendly motel, even the doors have special peepholes for your canine. Otherwise, standard rooms are nothing special, but they're airy and well equipped. Look for invitingly grassy picnic areas and BBQ grills out front.

DETOUR: PASO ROBLES WINE COUNTRY

Paso Robles wine country is one of California's fastest-growing, least-pretentious and most under-valued. You could spend days wandering the back roads off Hwy 46, inland from Hwy 1, running both west and east of Hwy 101. Many winemakers have tasting rooms that are open 11am to 4pm daily (some on weekends only); a few offer vineyard tours, and tasting fees are low (usually under $10). Family-owned wineries worth stopping at include Dark Star, Zenaida, Castoro, Eberle and Tobin James, but there are dozens more. Show up for the Zinfandel Festival in March or April, May's Wine Festival and the Harvest Wine Weekend in October. Contact the **Paso Robles Wine Country Alliance** (☎ 800-549-9463; www.pasowine.com) for more details.

Cass House Inn (☎ 805-995-3669; www.casshouseinn
.com; 222 N Ocean Ave; d incl breakfast $165-325; ⌘)
Inside a renovated 1867 Victorian sea
captain's house, five truly luxurious rooms
await, some boasting ocean-view terraces,
soaking tubs and gas fireplaces. All have plush
beds, flat-screen TVs and tasteful accents.

EATING

Ruddell's Smokehouse (☎ 805-995-5028; 101 D St;
dishes $4-10; ⏰ 11am-6pm; ♿) 'Smoker Jim'
transforms fresh-off-the-boat seafood into
succulently smoked slabs. Fish tacos (with
smoked albacore, salmon or ahi) come slath-
ered in a unique relish of mayo, apples and
celery. Scarf it all down at an ocean-view
table outside.

Sea Shanty (☎ 805-995-3277; 296 S Ocean Ave;
mains $6-25; ⏰ 8am-9pm daily, to 10pm Jun-Aug; ♿)
The killer lineup of desserts is what makes
this otherwise ordinary locals' diner awesome – try the strawberry shortcake or
olallieberry cobbler. A bazillion baseball
caps hang from the ceiling; they happily
accept donations in kind.

ourpick **Cass House Restaurant** (☎ 805-
995-3669; 222 N Ocean Ave; 3-/4-course prix fixe dinner
$48/56; ⏰ 5-9pm Thu-Mon) The flawless chef-
driven restaurant at the Cass House Inn
defies expectations. Linger over the locally
sourced, seasonally inspired and eclectic
menu that ambitiously ranges from chile-
spiked watermelon salad to milk-poached
halibut with lemongrass beurre blanc,
all paired with top notch regional wines.
Desserts are artistic.

Morro Bay
pop 10,330
Though home to a commercial fishing
fleet, this beach town's biggest claim to
fame is Morro Rock, a volcanic peak jutting
dramatically from the ocean floor. It's one
of the Nine Sisters, a 21-million-year-old
chain of rocks stretching south to San Luis
Obispo. Morro Bay's less photogenic landmark comes courtesy of the power plant,
which threw up three cigarette-shaped
smokestacks on the north side of town.
In ironic contrast to those artificially ugly
vertical landmarks, Morro Bay harbors
extraordinary natural riches, well worth a
day's exploration, ideally by kayak.

Leading south from Morro Rock is the
Embarcadero, a small waterfront boulevard
packed with souvenir shops and seafood
restaurants. It's also the launchpad for
cruises. The **chamber of commerce** (☎ 805-772-
4467, 800-231-0592; www.morrobay.org; 845 Embarcadero;
⏰ 9am-5pm Mon-Fri, 10am-4pm Sat) is in the thick
of things. Three blocks uphill, Main St is the
less touristy part of downtown.

SIGHTS & ACTIVITIES
Chumash tribespeople are the only people
legally allowed to climb **Morro Rock**, as it's
the protected nesting ground of peregrine
falcons. You can laze at the small beach on
the rock's north side, but you can't drive all
the way around – instead, rent a kayak. Be
aware of the tide schedules: ideally you'll
want to ride the tide out and then back in.
Winds are usually calmest in the morning.

The bay itself is a giant estuary inhabited
by two dozen threatened and endangered
species, including brown pelicans and sea
otters. In winter, over 200 bird species can
be spotted here along the Pacific Flyway.
For views of underwater kelp forests and
schools of fish, take a spin on a semisub-
mersible with **Sub Sea Tours** (☎ 805-772-9463;
www.subseatours.com; 699 Embarcadero; tours adult/child
3-12 $14/7, s/d kayak rental from $9/16; ⏰ 10am-5pm,
departure times vary; ♿). Salty dogs ready for
a little sportfishing should book with **Virg's
Landing** (☎ 805-772-1222; www.morrobaysportfishing
.com; 1215 Embarcadero; trips $49-235).

South of the Embarcadero, **Morro Bay State
Park** (☎ 805-772-2560; www.slostateparks.com; admission
free) encompasses a public **golf course** (☎ 805-
782-8060; 201 State Park Rd; green fees $42-51, ⏰ call for hr)
and a marina with kayak rentals. **Central Coast
Outdoors** (☎ 805-528-1080, 888-873-5610; www.central
coastoutdoors.com; tours from $65) leads kayak tours
(including full-moon paddles) from here, as
well as guided coastal hikes. Over at the
Museum of Natural History (☎ 805-772-2694;
adult/child under 17 $2/free; ⏰ 10am-5pm; ♿), which
has bay-view picture windows, interactive
exhibits geared toward kids demonstrate
how the forces of nature affect us all. Just
north of the museum is a eucalyptus
grove sheltering one of California's last
remaining great blue heron rookeries.

FESTIVALS & EVENTS
Morro Bay Bird Festival (☎ 805-275-4143, 866-
464-5105; www.morrobaybirdfestival.org) Birders flock
together for guided walks, workshops and lectures in
mid-January.

Avocado & Margarita Festival (☎ 800-231-0592; http://morrobay.org) Recipe contests, vats of guacamole and live music in mid-September.

Morro Bay Harbor Festival (☎ 800-366-6043; www .mbhf.com) Maritime-themed family fun, rockin' bands and beer- and wine-tasting in early October.

SLEEPING

Dozens of midrange motels cluster along Main and Harbor Sts, off Hwy 1.

Morro Bay State Park Campground (☎ reservations 800-444-7275; www.reserveamerica.com; campsites $35-50) A short drive south of downtown, 135 woodsy sites are fringed by eucalyptus and cypress trees. There are fire rings, coin-op showers and trails leading to the beach. If it's full, Morro Strand State Beach, north of downtown off Hwy 1, has 76 rather exposed oceanfront sites.

La Serena Inn (☎ 805-772 5633, 800-527-6782; www.laserenainn.com; 990 Morro Ave; r $89-249; 🛜) Large, well-kept rooms at this three-story motel each have a microwave and mini fridge. If you're lucky, you'll get a private balcony with Morro Rock views from where you can hear the gentle clank-clank of boats in the harbor below.

Inn at Morro Bay (☎ 805-772-5651; www.innat morrobay.com; 60 State Park Rd; r $109-279; 🐾) Inside the state park, this two-story waterfront lodge with brick-lined pathways delivers tranquil surroundings. Rooms run the gamut of views and amenities, most furnished with feather beds and fireplaces to ward off chilly fog – avoid the cheapest 'petite queens.' Guests can borrow beach cruisers.

EATING

The downtown **fishermen & farmers market** (☎ 805-772-4467; cnr Main St & Morro Bay Blvd; 🕐 3-6pm Sat) draws a crowd.

Taco Temple (☎ 805-772-4965; 2680 Main St, off Hwy 1 exit San Jacinto St; mains $5-10; 🕐 11am-8:30pm Sun, 11am-9pm Mon & Wed-Sat) Don't be disappointed by the frontage road location, north of downtown. Surfers rave about the gigantic plates of Cal-Mexican grub. Try one of the specials – they deserve the name. Cash only.

Sunshine Health Foods (☎ 805-772-7873; 415 Morro Bay Blvd; mains $5-14; 🕐 11am-5pm Mon-Fri, 9am-5pm Sat; Ⓥ) Stock up on all-natural snacks and groceries here. The mostly organic Shine Café at the back dishes up karma-cleansing grub like tempeh tacos, fresh-squeezed juices and blended smoothies.

Giovanni's Fish Market & Galley (☎ 805-772-2123; 1001 Front St; mains $6-10; 🕐 11am-6pm; 🐾) This family-run place on the Embarcadero is a classic California seafood shack in every good sense of the word. The fish and chips and garlicky fries drive folks mad. Inside there's a market with all the fixin's for a beach barbecue.

Harada (☎ 805-772-1410; 630 Embarcadero; dinner mains $12-36; 🕐 lunch & dinner) Traditional sushi lovers agree: this authentic Japanese restaurant serves up outstanding no-nonsense sashimi, *nigiri* and a tempting array of hot and cold appetizers. It's inside a mini-faux Japanese castle worthy of a Kurosawa movie set.

Montaña de Oro State Park

In spring the coastal hills here are blanketed by bright poppies, mustard and other wild-flowers, giving this **state park** (☎ 805-772-7434; www.slostateparks.com; Pecho Rd, Los Osos; admission free) its Spanish name, meaning 'mountain of gold.' Incredibly windy coastal bluffs are beloved for hiking, mountain-biking and horseback riding. Tucked into a small canyon by the visitor center, a primitive **campground** (☎ reservations 800-444-7275; www.reserveamerica.com; walk-in tent sites $5, campsites $20-25) has pleasantly cool sites with fire rings and potable water.

The northern half of the park features sand dunes and an ancient marine terrace visible due to seismic uplifting. **Spooner's Cove**, once used by smugglers, is now a beautiful sandy beach and picnic area. If you go tide-pooling, only touch the delicate marine creatures such as sea stars, limpets and crabs with the back of one hand to avoid disturbing them. You can hike along the beach and the grassy ocean bluffs, or drive uphill past the visitor center to the start of the hardy 7-mile loop trail tackling **Valencia and Oats Peaks**.

The park boundary is 7 miles southwest of Hwy 1; exit at South Bay Blvd then follow the signs through the town of Los Osos, passing old-world **Carlock's Bakery** (☎ 805-528-1845; 1024 Los Osos Valley Rd; items $1-6; 🕐 6am-6pm Tue-Sat; 🐾). From Hwy 101 south of San Luis Obispo, exit at Los Osos Valley Rd and drive about 12 miles northwest.

SAN LUIS OBISPO
pop 42,960

Almost exactly midway between LA and San Francisco, San Luis Obispo (aka SLO) has long been the classic stopover point for those making the journey along the coast. With no

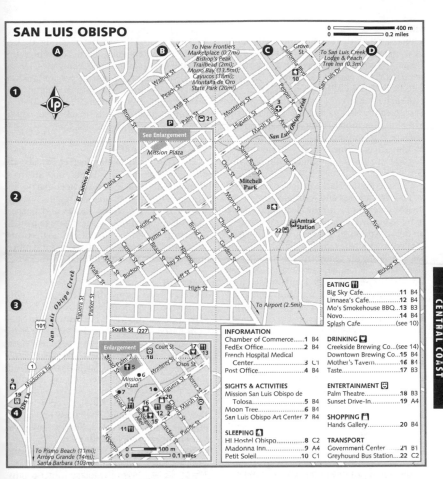

SAN LUIS OBISPO

INFORMATION	
Chamber of Commerce	1 B4
FedEx Office	2 B4
French Hospital Medical Center	3 C1
Post Office	4 B4

SIGHTS & ACTIVITIES	
Mission San Luis Obispo de Tolosa	5 B4
Moon Tree	6 B4
San Luis Obispo Art Center	7 B4

SLEEPING	
HI Hostel Obispo	8 C2
Madonna Inn	9 A4
Petit Soleil	10 C1

EATING	
Big Sky Cafe	11 B4
Linnea's Cafe	12 B4
Mo's Smokehouse BBQ	13 B3
Novo	14 B4
Splash Cafe	(see 10)

DRINKING	
Creekside Brewing Co	(see 14)
Downtown Brewing Co	15 B4
Mother's Tavern	16 B4
Taste	17 B3

ENTERTAINMENT	
Palm Theatre	18 B3
Sunset Drive-In	19 A4

SHOPPING	
Hands Gallery	20 B4

TRANSPORT	
Government Center	21 B1
Greyhound Bus Station	22 C2

must-see attractions, SLO might not seem to warrant much time. But not only does it make an ideal base for coastal explorations, it's one of those small cities that doles out urban pleasures and rural charm in equal measure. Nestled at the base of the Santa Lucia foothills and a grape's throw from a thriving wine industry, SLO gets high marks for livability – to wit: drive-thrus are illegal downtown. California Polytechnic State University (Cal Poly) students keep the streets buzzing during the school year.

Orientation & Information

SLO's downtown is walkable and compact. San Luis Obispo Creek, once used to irrigate mission orchards, flows alongside Higuera St, which runs parallel to Marsh St, but in the opposite one-way direction. Many banks are off Marsh St, near the post office. Most student-friendly cafés have free wi-fi.

Chamber of Commerce (☎ 805-781-2777; http://visitslo.com; 1039 Chorro St; ☽ 10am-5pm Sun-Wed, 10am-7pm Thu-Sat) Free maps and brochures.

FedEx Office (☎ 805-543-3363; 1127 Chorro St; per min 20-30¢; ☽ 7am-11pm Mon-Fri, 9am-9pm Sat & Sun; 🖥 🛜) High-speed internet workstations.

French Hospital Medical Center (☎ 805-543-5353; 1191 Johnson Ave; ☽ 24hr) ER services.

Post Office (☎ 805-541-9138; 893 Marsh St; ☽ 8:30am-5:30pm Mon-Fri, 9am-3pm Sat)

San Luis Obispo Car Free (http://slocarfree.org) Discounts on activities and accommodations for public-transit riders and cyclists.

Sights

Those satisfyingly reverberatory bells you'll hear emanate from **Mission San Luis Obispo de Tolosa** (☎ 805-543-6850; www.missionsanluisobispo.org; 751 Palm St; donation requested; ☷ 9am-4pm). The fifth of the California missions, it was established in 1772 and named for a French saint. Nicknamed the 'Prince of the Missions,' the modest church has an unusual L-shape and whitewashed walls with Stations of the Cross. Tame exhibits depict everyday life during the Chumash and Spanish periods.

Outside, **Mission Plaza** is a shady oasis ringed by restored adobes and fountains overlooking the creek. Look for the **Moon Tree**, a coast redwood grown from a seed that journeyed on board Apollo 14's lunar mission. Nearby the creek, which has shady walking trails, the **San Luis Obispo Art Center** (☎ 805-543-8562; www.sloartcenter.org; 1010 Broad St; admission free; ☷ 11am-5pm Wed-Mon) showcases local artists and traveling exhibits from around California.

SLO's quirkiest attraction is **Bubblegum Alley**, a narrow walkway on the 700 block of Higuera St. Every inch is plastered with ABC gum. Watch your step!

Activities

There are plenty of good hikes around SLO. The most popular trail summits **Bishop's Peak** (1546ft), the tallest of the Nine Sisters, a chain of volcanic peaks stretching up to Morro Bay. The trail (2.2 miles one-way) starts in a grove of live oaks (watch out for poison oak!) and heads along rocky, exposed switchbacks, then scrambles up boulders for panoramic ocean views. Drive northwest from downtown on Santa Rosa St (Hwy 1), turn left onto Highland Dr, take a right onto Patricia Dr and, after a half-mile, look for three black posts and a small trailhead sign on your left.

Festivals & Events

SLO's renowned **farmers market** (☎ 805-541-0286; ☷ 5-9pm Thu; ♿) turns downtown's Higuera St into a giant street party. In the midst of the requisite organic, locally grown fruit and veggie stands and barbecues belching smoke, witness garage bands, salvation peddlers, political signature-collectors, balloon-animal twisters and more free entertainment, intentional or otherwise.

Sleeping

Motels cluster along the northeastern end of Monterey St near Hwy 101 and by the Hwy 101 exit for Hwy 1 at Santa Rosa St.

HI Hostel Obispo (☎ 805-544-4678; www.hostelobispo.com; 1617 Santa Rosa St; dm $24-27, r with shared bath from $45; ☷ reception 8-10am & 4:30-10pm; ▣ ☏) In a converted Victorian house on a tree-lined street by the train station, this solar-powered hostel has a garden patio and indoor games room. Kitchen scraps go to the owner's chickens, linens are line-dried and bikes can be rented. Simply put, you can feel the love. No credit cards.

Peach Tree Inn (☎ 805-543-3170, 800-227-6396; www.peachtreeinn.com; 2001 Monterey St; r incl breakfast $80-200; ▧ ▣ ☏) Friendly, folksy motel rooms (most with air-con) look mighty inviting, especially those right by the creek or with rocking chairs on wooden porches overlooking the grassy lawns, eucalyptus trees and rose gardens. The hearty breakfast comes with homemade breads.

San Luis Creek Lodge (☎ 805-541-1122, 800-593-0333; www.sanluiscreeklodge.com; 1941 Monterey St; r incl breakfast $135-249; ▧ ☏) Squeezed between neighboring motels, this boutique inn has spacious rooms with divine beds (some have gas fireplaces and jetted tubs) in whimsically mismatched buildings evoking Tudor, arts-and-crafts and Southern Plantation styles. Fluffy robes, DVDs, chess sets and board games are free for guests to borrow.

WHAT THE...?

'Oh, my!' is just one of the more printable exclamations overheard at the **Madonna Inn** (☎ 805-543-3000, 800-543-9666; www.madonnainn.com; 100 Madonna Rd; r $179-449; ▧ ▨). You'd expect a place like this in Vegas, not SLO, but here it is, in all its campy, over-the-top extravagance. Japanese tourists, vacationing Mid-Westerners and irony-loving San Francisco hipsters adore the 109 themed rooms – including Yosemite Rock, Caveman and hot-pink Sugar & Spice. Check out photos of the rooms online, or wander the halls and spy into ones being cleaned. The urinal in the men's room is a bizarre waterfall. But the best reason to stop here? Old-fashioned cookies from the fairytale-esque bakery.

Petit Soleil (☎ 805-549-0321, 800-876-1588; www .petitsoleilslo.com; 1473 Monterey St; d incl breakfast $149-289; ☎) This French-themed, gay-friendly 'bed *et* breakfast' charms many travelers, who enjoy the evening wine tastings. Each converted motel room is whimsically decorated according to its name and several – including Chocolat – feature hand-painted murals. Expect some street noise.

Eating

SLO abounds with cheap ethnic eats and student-friendly takeout joints downtown.

Linnaea's Cafe (☎ 805-541-5888; 1110 Garden St; mains $4-8; ☒ 6:30am-10pm; ☎) SLO's first coffeehouse, and the one with the most fervent following, Linnaea's has local art hanging on the walls and live music on weekends. Weeknight menus carry a theme (tamale night, waffle night, etc). Find the petite garden out back.

Mo's Smokehouse BBQ (☎ 805-544-6193; 1005 Monterey St; mains $7-19; ☒ 11am-9pm Mon-Wed, to 10pm Thu-Sun; ☒) Sink your tush into an antique chair before sinking your teeth into some authentic 'cue, hickory-smoked on the premises. You order at the counter, so it's a good option for those short on time. The championship ribs are lip-smacking.

Big Sky Cafe (☎ 805-545-5401; 1121 Broad St; mains $8-20; ☒ 7am-9pm Mon, 7am-10pm Tue-Fri, 8am-10pm Sat, 8am-9pm Sun) Big Sky is a big room, and still the waits can be long – its motto is 'analog food for a digital world.' Fresh, locally sourced breakfasts are delish, but big-plate dinners tend to be bland. Vegetarians will, for once, have more options than meat eaters.

Novo (☎ 805-543-3896; 726 Higuera St; small plates $6-22, dinner mains $16-32; ☒ 11am-10pm Mon-Thu, 11am-midnight Fri & Sat, 10am-10pm Sun) Novo proffers hit-or-miss Mediterranean, Brazilian and Asian-inspired tapas, with an eye toward freshness and artful presentation. Choose from dozens of international beers, wines or sakes as you savor the view from the creekside decks.

For quick eats and takeout:

New Frontiers Marketplace (☎ 805-785-0194; 896 E Foothill Blvd; ☒ 8am-9pm Mon-Fri, 8am-9pm Sat, 9am-8pm Sun) Organic groceries, a takeout deli and a hot-and-cold salad bar.

Splash Cafe (☎ 805-544-7567; 1491 Monterey St; dishes $3-10; ☒ 7am-8:30pm Mon-Thu, 7am-9:30pm Fri-Sun; ☒) Housemade soups, fresh salads, sandwiches and a tempting bakery, too.

Drinking

Higuera St downtown is ground zero for student-centric bars and nightlife.

Downtown Brewing Co (☎ 805-543-1843; 1119 Garden St) More often called just SLO Brew, this study in rafters and exposed brick has plenty of craft beers to go with filling pub grub. Downstairs, you'll find DJs spinning or live bands with names like 'Los Straightjackets' playing most nights.

Mother's Tavern (☎ 805-541-8733; 729 Higuera St; ☎) This cavernous two-story pub draws in the party-hardy Cal Poly masses with its no-cover dance floor and frequent live-music shows. Sunday afternoons are for swingin' big bands.

Creekside Brewing Co (☎ 805-542-9804; 1040 Broad St) Kick back at a sunnyside patio table above the creek near Mission Plaza. It's got its own brews on tap, plus bottled Belgian beers. On Mondays, all pints are just three bucks.

Taste (☎ 805-269-8279; 1003 Osos St) At this high-ceilinged co-op wine-tasting room, take the enomatic wine-dispensing system for a spin with a Riedel glass in hand, then pick up an Edna Valley winery map and go straight to the source.

Entertainment

Palm Theatre (☎ 805-541-5161; www.thepalmtheatre .com; 817 Palm St) The USA's first solar-powered cinema. This old-style movie house showcases foreign and indie films; tickets are a few bucks off on Mondays.

our pick **Sunset Drive-In** (☎ 805-544-4475; 255 Elks Lane, off Hwy 1 exit Madonna Rd; adult/child 5-11 $6/2) Never made out at a drive-in? Here's your chance. The movies are mindless Hollywood blockbusters but the bags of popcorn are bottomless.

Shopping

Downtown has loads of indie boutiques. Brightly lit **Hands Gallery** (☎ 805-543-1921; 777 Higuera St; ☒ 10am-6pm Mon-Wed, 10am-9pm Thu, 10am-8pm Fri & Sat, 11am-5pm Sun) sells fine contemporary craftwork by local artisans, including vibrant jewelry, fiber arts, metal sculptures, ceramics and rainbow-hued blown glass.

Getting There & Around

Three miles southeast of downtown, **SLO County Regional Airport** (SBP; ☎ 805-781-2025; www .sloairport.com; off Broad St; ☎) offers commuter

CENTRAL COAST

flights with United Express (LA and San Francisco).

A half-mile east of downtown, **Amtrak** (1011 Railroad Ave) runs the daily Seattle–LA *Coast Starlight* and twice-daily *Pacific Surfliner*, heading south to Santa Barbara ($30, 2¾ hours), LA ($37, 5¾ hours) and San Diego ($55, 8½ hours). Several daily Thruway buses link to more-frequent regional trains.

From SLO's train station, **Greyhound** (1023 Railroad Ave) has a few daily buses to LA ($38, 5½ hours) via Santa Barbara ($27, 2¼ hours), and to San Francisco ($48, seven hours).

SLO's **Regional Transit Authority** (RTA; ☎ 805-541-2228; www.slorta.org; single-ride fares $1.25-2.75, day pass $4.50) operates several daily bus routes (with limited weekend services) along the coast, including to Pismo Beach, Morro Bay, Cayucos, Cambria and Hearst Castle. Many bus lines converge on downtown's **Government Center** (cnr Palm & Osos Sts).

SLO Transit (☎ 805-541-2877; www.slocity.org) operates city buses ($1.25) and the downtown trolley (25¢) that loops around every 20 minutes from 3:30pm to 9pm Thursday, noon to 9pm Friday and Saturday, and noon to 5:30pm Sunday.

SAN LUIS BAY

This broad bay is home to a string of laid-back little beach towns. If you're looking for a sandy respite from your trip, this is a good spot to break the journey. San Luis Obispo's RTA (see above) operates buses to the bay's Five Cities.

Avila Beach

pop 835

This quaint, sunny town has had a rough shake. In the late 1980s it was discovered that for decades pipes from the nearby Unocal refinery and port had been leaking into the soil, contaminating it with a toxic soup of petroleum products. In 1992 a massive oil spill that occurred while loading a tanker by the beach only added to the misery – not to mention decimated sea-otter populations. In 1999 Unocal began a legal settlement that involved tearing down the town and carting off the beach. Crowds have been lured back by a freshly built seafront commercial district and new sand.

Just west of Hwy 101, **Avila Valley Barn** (☎ 805-595-2810; www.avilavalleybarn.com; 560 Avila Beach Dr; ☷ 9am-6pm daily Jun-Oct, 9am-5pm Thu-Mon Nov-May; ☷) is a good ol' farm stand. Park alongside the sheep and goat pens, lick an ice-cream cone, then grab a basket and walk out into the fields to pick jammy berries, stone fruit and apples in season. Afterward, soak in the lukewarm swimming pool with a seasonal water slide at **Avila Hot Springs** (☎ 805-595-2359; www.avilahotsprings.com; 250 Avila Beach Dr; adult/child under 16 $10/8; ☷ hr vary; ☷) or reserve ahead for a private hillside redwood hot tub at **Sycamore Mineral Springs** (☎ 805-595-7302 ext 375; www.sycamoresprings.com; 1215 Avila Beach Dr; per person per hr $12.50-17.50; ☷ 8am-midnight, last reservation 10:45pm).

Two miles west of downtown, **Port San Luis** (RV sites $25-40) is a hard-working fishing harbor. The barking of sea lions will serenade you on **Harford Pier**, one of the coast's most authentic fishing piers. **Patriot Sportfishing** (☎ 805-595-7200, 800-714-3474; www.patriotsport fishing.com; adult/child 4-12 $45/25) organizes 2½-hour whale-watching cruises from December to April. If you want to paddle out among the sea otters, book ahead with **Central Coast Kayaks** (☎ 805-773-3500; www.centralcoastkayaks .com; 1879 Shell Beach Rd, Shell Beach; s/d kayak rental per 3hr $19/24, tours $60-120).

At the tip of Harford Pier is the **Olde Port Inn** (☎ 805-595-2515; mains $15-35; ☷ 11:30am-9pm Sun-Thu, to 9:30pm Fri & Sat), a seriously old-school seafood restaurant (try the cioppino) with glass-top tables so diners can peer down

---

DETOUR: PORT SAN LUIS LIGHTHOUSE

Ready for an adventure? Visiting this Victorian-era **lighthouse** (☎ 805-546-4904; www.sanluislighthouse.org; hike-in admission adult/child under 12 $5/free), now surrounded by a nuclear power plant, can be a challenge. At press time, the only ways to reach this extremely windy point were by joining a van tour ($20 per person, reservations required – call ☎ 805-540-5771) or hiking a rocky, strenuous 3.5-mile round-trip trail. Guided hikes led by Pacific Gas & Electric docents depart at 9am most Saturday mornings (children must be at least nine years old). Make reservations online at least two weeks in advance, bring plenty of water and expect to return to the harbor parking lot around noon or 1pm.

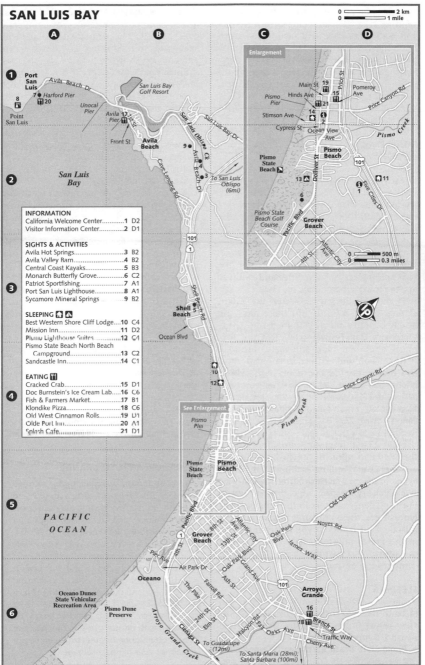

SAN LUIS BAY

0 ▭▭▭ 2 km
0 ▬▬▬ 1 mile

INFORMATION
California Welcome Center............1 D2
Visitor Information Center...........2 D1

SIGHTS & ACTIVITIES
Avila Hot Springs.........................3 B2
Avila Valley Barn.........................4 B2
Central Coast Kayaks.....................5 B3
Monarch Butterfly Grove................6 C2
Patriot Sportfishing......................7 A1
Port San Luis Lighthouse...............8 A1
Sycamore Mineral Springs.............9 B2

SLEEPING
Best Western Shore Cliff Lodge....10 C4
Mission Inn...............................11 D2
Pismo Lighthouse Suites..............12 C4
Pismo State Beach North Beach
   Campground...........................13 C2
Sandcastle Inn..........................14 C1

EATING
Cracked Crab...........................15 D1
Doc Burnstein's Ice Cream Lab....16 C6
Fish & Farmers Market...............17 B1
Klondike Pizza..........................18 C6
Old West Cinnamon Rolls...........19 D1
Olde Port Inn...........................20 A1
Splash Cafe.............................21 D1

into the water. Nearby are scattered shops vending crispy fish and chips, fresh oysters and California-style fish tacos, plus fresh catch right off the boats. Back downtown by the beach, the **Fish & Farmers Market** (4-8pm Fri Apr–mid-Sep) sets up on Avila's oceanfront promenade, lined with boutique shops, cafés and restaurants.

A free trolley loops around town from 9am to 6pm on Saturday and Sunday.

Pismo Beach
pop 8600

Backed by a wooden pier that stretches toward the setting sun, Pismo's beach is wide and sandy. Here James Dean once trysted with Pier Angeli and, in fact, this retro mid-20th-century beach town still feels like somewhere straight out of *Rebel Without a Cause* or *American Graffiti*, especially during mid-June's **Classic at Pismo Beach** (866-450-7469; www.thepismobeachclassic.com), when hot rods and muscle cars line Price and Dolliver Sts, the town's main drags off Hwy 1.

Pismo still likes to call itself the 'Clam Capital of the World,' but these days the beach is pretty much clammed out. Mid-October's **Clam Festival** celebrates the formerly abundant (and still tasty) mollusk with a clam dig, chowder cook-off and live music. For details, contact the **visitor information center** (800-443-7778; www.classiccalifornia.com; 581 Dolliver St; 9am-5pm Mon-Fri, 10am-4pm Sat). There's also a **California Welcome Center** (805-773-7924; 333 Five Cities Dr;) inside Pismo's outlet mall, off Hwy 101.

Over 25,000 migrating monarch butterflies descend upon the town between late October and February, making their winter home in Pismo's **monarch butterfly grove** (www.monarchbutterfly.org; admission free; sunrise-sunset). Forming dense clusters in the tops of eucalyptus trees, these creatures might be easily mistaken for leaves. If you're driving, park in the gravel pull-out off Hwy 1 south of downtown, just past the Pismo State Beach campground entrance.

SLEEPING
Pismo has dozens of motels, but rooms fill fast and rates skyrocket in summer. Ocean-view resort hotels line Price St and Shell Beach Rd north of downtown.

Pismo State Beach North Beach Campground (reservations 800-444-7275; www.reserveamerica.com;

off Hwy 1; campsites $35) A mile south of the pier near the monarch butterfly grove, this state park has 100-plus grassy sites shaded by eucalyptus trees. It offers easy beach access and coin-op showers.

Pismo Lighthouse Suites (805-773-2411, 800-245-2411; www.pismolighthousesuites.com; 2411 Price St; ste incl breakfast $139-229;) It can be hard to tear yourself away from this contemporary all-suites oceanfront hotel with everything a vacationing family needs: in-room Nintendo, a life-sized outdoor chessboard, putting green, ping-pong tables, badminton courts and a heated pool.

Sandcastle Inn (805-773-2422, 800-822-6606; www.sandcastleinn.com; 100 Stimson Ave; r incl breakfast $150-435;) Many of the attractively trim Eastern Seaboard–styled rooms are mere steps away from the sand. The top corner suite is perfect for cracking open a bottle of wine at sunset on the ocean-view patio. Free wi-fi in lobby.

Also recommended:

Best Western Shore Cliff Lodge (805-773-4671, 800-441-8885; www.shorecliff.com; 2555 Price St; r incl breakfast $109-259;) Basic motel rooms with entrancing ocean views from the cliffs.

Mission Inn (805-773-6020, 866-773-6020; www.missioninnpismobeach.com; 601 James Way, off Hwy 101 exit Five Cities Dr; r incl breakfast $119-179;) Oversized hotel-quality rooms, but it's a long way from the beach.

EATING
Start your morning off right with a sugar rush from a pastry at **Old West Cinnamon Rolls**

DETOUR: ARROYO GRANDE

Famous for its swinging bridge, Arroyo Grande is off Hwy 101, just south of Pismo Beach. It's relaxing to stroll the main street past antiques and knick-knack shops, and **Doc Burnstein's Ice Cream Lab** (805-474-4068; 114 W Branch St; items $3-8; noon-9pm;), which scoops up fantastical flavors like petite-syrah sorbet and the peanut butter-banana 'Elvis Special.' Overlooking the creek, Alaskan-run **Klondike Pizza** (805-481-5288; 104 Bridge St; pizzas $12-28; 11am-9pm Sun-Thu, to 10pm Fri & Sat;) is littered with peanut shells on the floor and has nostalgic board games to play while you wait for your reindeer-sausage pie.

(☎ 805-773-1428; 861 Dolliver St; items $3-5; ⏲ 6:30am-5:30pm) bakery.

Splash Cafe (☎ 805-773-4653; 197 Pomeroy Ave; mains $3-10; ⏲ 8am-9pm; ♿) Lines go out and wrap around this boisterous veteran hole-in-the-wall, which makes award-winning clam chowder – in a sourdough bread bowl, naturally – and a long lineup of grilled and fried briny delights. It's open shorter hours in winter.

Cracked Crab (☎ 805-773-2722; 751 Price St; mains $9-48; ⏲ 11am-9pm Sun-Thu, to 10pm Fri & Sat; ♿) Fresh seafood is the staple at this family-owned grill. Watch out: when the famous bucket o' seafood full of flying bits of fish, Cajun sausage, red potatoes and cob corn gets dumped on your butcher paper-covered table, you'd best be wearing one of those silly-looking plastic bibs.

SANTA BARBARA AREA

Frankly put, this area is damn pleasant to putter around. Chic, Mediterranean-style Santa Barbara anchors the region, with a superbly photogenic wine country to the north, Channel Islands National Park to the south and quirky enclaves like new-agey Ojai to the east and Danish-esque Solvang to the west. Or, don't ever leave the beaches – plenty of people don't.

LOS OLIVOS
pop 1100

The bucolic, if somewhat snooty ranch town of Los Olivos is your first stop for exploring Santa Barbara's wine country. The streets are lined with winery tasting rooms, art galleries and cafés. Inside a rickety 19th-century general store, the independent-minded **Los Olivos Tasting Room** (☎ 805-668-7406; 2905 Grand Ave; tasting fee $10; ⏲ 11am-5pm) stocks rare vintages you won't find anywhere else. Servers are by turns loquacious and gruff, but refreshingly blunt in their opinions about local wines. Nibble on Cal-Mediterranean bistro fare at picturesque **Los Olivos Café** (☎ 805-688-7265; 2879 Grand Ave; mains $13-29; ⏲ 11:30am-10pm), which conveniently stays open mid-afternoon for antipasto platters, hearty salads and crispy pizzas. For dinner, giddyup to **Brothers Restaurant at Mattei's Tavern** (☎ 805-688-4820; 2350 Railway Ave; mains $18-44; ⏲ 5-9pm), a late-19th-century stagecoach stop, for boldly flavored nouveau country cooking, anything from spicy dry-rubbed steaks to brandy-glazed pork chops. Reservations are advised.

Los Olivos is 4 miles east of Hwy 101 via Hwy 154.

SOLVANG
pop 5150

Oh, kitschy Solvang. In 1911 bona-fide Danes did indeed found the town – and start a folk school for the preservation of Danish heritage – but the intervening decades have seen Solvang (loosely translated 'Sunny Field') cash in hard on its Euro-charm. Grumpy families and charmed blue-hairs plod down the main drag of Copenhagen Dr, where overpriced trinket shops lurk behind faux-Scandinavian facades and the windmills are, alas, purely decorative. For winery maps, stop by Solvang's **visitor center** (☎ 805-688-6144, 800-468-6765; http://solvangusa.com; 1639 Copenhagen Dr; ⏲ 9am-5pm).

DETOUR: FOXEN CANYON WINE TRAIL

Santa Barbara's wine country, made up of the Santa Maria and Santa Ynez Valleys, unfurls along winding country lanes amid oak-dotted rolling hills that stretch for miles. The 2004 indie hit movie *Sideways* was both a blessing and a curse: local winemakers have found international acclaim, but also huge crowds and tour buses. Free self-guided touring maps from the **Santa Barbara County Vintners' Association** (www.sbcountywines.com) are available at every winery, most found inside the triangle of Hwys 101, 246 and 154. The beautiful **Foxen Canyon Wine Trail** (www.foxencanyonwinetrail.com; Foxen Canyon Rd) curves north of Los Olivos for nearly 30 miles. Seek out big-shouldered giants such as Firestone and Fess Parker or hidden gems like Zaca Mesa, producing Rhône varietals; Foxen, with its corrugated metal-roofed tasting barn; Rancho Sisqouc, where grapevines sprawl across an early-20th-century ranch; or cult winemaker Kenneth Volk. Most tasting rooms are open at least 10am to 4pm daily, keeping shorter hours in winter; tasting fees average $10 to $20, maybe including a souvenir glass.

DRIVING TOUR: HWY 1 IN SANTA BARBARA COUNTY

What to See

You almost expect to have to dodge tumbleweeds as you drive south of Pismo Beach along winding country roads into the agricultural town of Guadalupe, the gateway to North America's largest coastal dunes. The **Dunes Center** (☎ 805-343-2455; www.dunescenter.org; 1055 Guadalupe St, Guadalupe; 🕙 10am-4pm Wed-Sun) has elementary displays on the mystical Dunites who lived here in the 1930s and the so-called **Lost City of DeMille** (www.lostcitydemille.com), the movie set of *The Ten Commandments* (1923) that still lies buried beneath the sands. More recently, scenes from *Pirates of the Caribbean: At World's End* (2007) were shot here. The best dunes access is 3 miles west of town via Hwy 166. Back downtown, dig into juicy steaks and oak-pit barbecue at genuine Old West-flavored **Far Western Tavern** (☎ 805-343-2211; 899 Guadalupe St, Guadalupe; mains $20-32; 🕙 11am-9pm Tue-Thu, to 10pm Fri & Sat, 9am-9pm Sun), which pairs a jukebox and sports TVs with velvet wallpaper, cowhide booths and candlelit tables. Keep motoring south past Vandenberg Air Force Base.

Three miles northeast of Lompoc, beautifully restored **La Purísima Mission State Historic Park** (☎ 805-733-3713; www.lapurisimamission.org; 2295 Purísima Rd, Lompoc; per car $6; 🕙 9am-5pm) is one of California's most evocative Spanish colonial missions, dating from 1787. Guided tours of the flowering gardens, livestock pens and adobe buildings depart at 1pm daily.

Around Lompoc are some truly wild Pacific beaches worth detouring for. **Ocean Beach County Park** (☎ 805-934-6123; www.sbparks.org; admission free; 🕙 8am-sunset) and **Surf Beach** (admission free), with its remote Amtrak train stop, border Vandenberg Air Force Base. On the 10-mile drive west of Lompoc via Ocean Ave (Hwy 246) you'll pass mysterious-looking structures supporting spy and commercial satellite launches. The beaches' dunes are untrammeled and interpretive signs explain the estuary's ecology. Because endangered snowy plovers nest here, vast areas of the beaches may be closed from March to September.

Less than 5 miles south of Lompoc via Hwy 1, Jalama Rd presents 14 miles of twisting tarmac traversing ranch and farmlands before reaching utterly isolated **Jalama Beach County Park** (☎ 805-736-6316; www.jalamabeach.com; 9999 Jalama Beach Rd; per car $8; 🎿). Its **campground** (☎ 805-736-3504; campsites $20-30) is so insanely popular that it doesn't take reservations – look for the 'campground full' sign back near Hwy 1 to save yourself the drive. Otherwise, arrive early in the morning to get your name on the waiting list.

The Route

At Pismo Beach, Hwy 1 ends its brief fling with Hwy 101 that began in SLO as it veers off south to hug the coast. Hwy 1 rejoins Hwy 101 just north of Gaviota State Park.

Time & Mileage

With no detours, it's a 65-mile, two-hour drive, but you should allow at least a half day for sightseeing stops along the way.

The backstreet **Elverhøj Museum** (☎ 805-686-1211; 1624 Elverhoy Way; suggested donation adult/child under 13 $3/free; 🕙 1-4pm Wed-Thu, noon-4pm Fri-Sun) is just about the only spot in town where you can learn about what real Danish life in the area was once like. Along Hwy 246 east of Alisal Rd, **Old Mission Santa Inés** (☎ 805-688-4815; www.missionsantaines.org; 1760 Mission Dr; adult/child under 12 $5/free; 🕙 9am-4:30pm) is a pretty little church that was the stage for a Chumash revolt against Spanish colonial cruelty in 1824.

Solvang's bakeries and pancake houses are almost irresistible, though most aren't that good. Busy **Solvang Bakery** (☎ 805-688-4939; 460 Alisal Rd, Solvang; most items $2-5; 🕙 7am-6pm) is a fortunate exception, selling iced almond butter rings and fresh-baked strudels. Fill your picnic basket at **El Rancho Marketplace** (☎ 805-688-4300; 2886 Mission Dr, Hwy 246; 🕙 6am-10pm), a gourmet supermarket with a fantastic deli case, smokin' barbecue take out, a bargain wine room and an espresso bar.

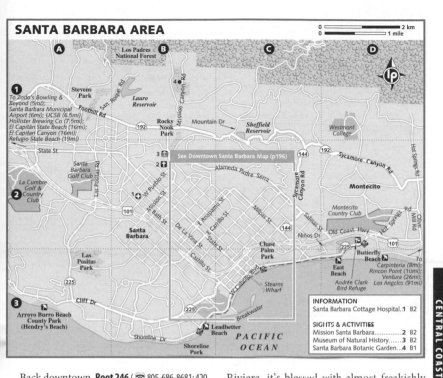

SANTA BARBARA AREA

See Downtown Santa Barbara Map (p196)

INFORMATION	
Santa Barbara Cottage Hospital..1	B2

SIGHTS & ACTIVITIES	
Mission Santa Barbara...............2	B2
Museum of Natural History........3	B2
Santa Barbara Botanic Garden...4	B1

CENTRAL COAST

Back downtown, **Root 246** (☎ 805-686-8681; 420 Alisal Rd; mains $12-35; ☺ lunch Sat & Sun, dinner daily), created by star chef Bradley Ogden and owned by the local Chumash tribespeople, celebrates creative farm-to-table New American cuisine, all with an artful, whimsical touch.

You'll be hard-pressed to find better steaks and chops anywhere than at Buellton's **Hitching Post II** (☎ 805-688-0676; 406 E Hwy 246; mains $20-48; ☺ dinner). This legendary, old-guard country steakhouse serves locally raised meats and makes its own pinot noir (which is damn good, by the way); book ahead or get in line at 4pm.

From Hwy 101, Solvang is 3 miles east of Buellton via Hwy 146. Dozens of merely average motels and hotels charge exorbitant rates, especially on weekends, when you'll need reservations. Try to make this a day trip from Santa Barbara.

SANTA BARBARA

pop 85,680

A 90-minute drive north of LA, Santa Barbara basks smugly in its near-perfection. Nicknamed the American Riviera, it's blessed with almost freakishly good weather and a backdrop of mountains to complement its oceanic foreground. What's apparent as soon as you arrive is the city's iconic architecture. After a 1925 earthquake leveled downtown, planners chose to go with a Mediterranean-style rebuild, thus the city's trademark red-tile roofs, whitewashed adobe walls and waving palm trees. And no one can deny the appeal of the beaches that line the city tip to toe either. Just ignore those pesky oil derricks out to sea.

Orientation

Santa Barbara's coast faces south, not west – that's an important fact to remember when navigating. Downtown is laid out on a grid, with its main artery, State St, running roughly north–south, dividing street addresses between east and west. Lower State St has plenty of student-thronged bars and cheap eats, while upper State St has most of the boutiques, cafés and theaters. Traffic crawls along State St so, if you're driving, pick parallel Chapala St

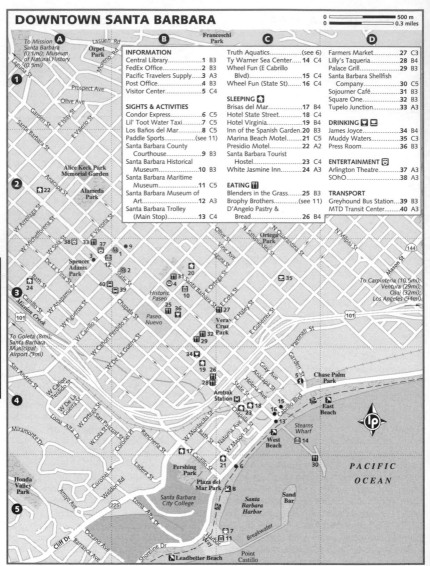

DOWNTOWN SANTA BARBARA

0 ──────── 500 m
0 ──────── 0.3 miles

INFORMATION
Central Library..................1 B3
FedEx Office.....................2 B3
Pacific Travelers Supply....3 A3
Post Office........................4 B3
Visitor Center..................5 C4

SIGHTS & ACTIVITIES
Condor Express..................6 C5
Lil' Toot Water Taxi.............7 C5
Los Baños del Mar............8 C5
Paddle Sports..............(see 11)
Santa Barbara County
   Courthouse...................9 B3
Santa Barbara Historical
   Museum.......................10 B3
Santa Barbara Maritime
   Museum.......................11 C5
Santa Barbara Museum of
   Art...............................12 A3
Santa Barbara Trolley
   (Main Stop)..................13 C4

Truth Aquatics................(see 6)
Ty Warner Sea Center.... 14 C4
Wheel Fun (E Cabrillo
   Blvd)............................15 C4
Wheel Fun (State St)....... 16 C4

SLEEPING
Brisas del Mar................17 B4
Hotel State Street...........18 C4
Hotel Virginia.................19 B4
Inn of the Spanish Garden.20 B3
Marina Beach Motel........21 C5
Presidio Motel................22 A2
Santa Barbara Tourist
   Hostel..........................23 C4
White Jasmine Inn..........24 A3

EATING
Blenders in the Grass.......25 B3
Brophy Brothers............(see 11)
D'Angelo Pastry &
   Bread...........................26 B4

Farmers Market.................27 C3
Lilly's Taqueria................28 B4
Palace Grill.....................29 B3
Santa Barbara Shellfish
   Company......................30 C5
Sojourner Café................31 B3
Square One....................32 B3
Tupelo Junction.............33 A3

DRINKING
James Joyce....................34 B4
Muddy Waters................35 C3
Press Room.....................36 B3

ENTERTAINMENT
Arlington Theatre............37 A3
SOhO.............................38 A3

TRANSPORT
Greyhound Bus Station...39 B3
MTD Transit Center........40 A3

CENTRAL COAST

PACIFIC OCEAN

(one-way northbound) or Anacapa St (one-way southbound). Cabrillo Blvd hugs the coastline and turns into Coast Village Rd in the eastern suburb of Montecito. The University of California, Santa Barbara (UCSB) campus lies west in Isla Vista, near the airport. Many students live in neighboring Goleta.

Information

The helpful websites http://greensanta barbara.com and www.santabarbaracarfree .org offer eco-travel tips and valuable discounts for cyclists and public transit riders.

Central Library (Map p196; ☎ 805-962-7653; www .sbplibrary.org; 40 E Anapamu St; ☽ 10am-8pm

Mon-Thu, 10am-5:30pm Fri & Sat, 1-5pm Sun; 🖳 📶)
Free walk-in internet terminals.

FedEx Office (Map p196; ☎ 805-966-1114; 1030 State
St; per min 20-30¢; 🕓 7am-11pm Mon-Fri, 9am-9pm Sat
& Sun; 🖳 📶) High-speed internet workstations.

Pacific Travelers Supply (Map p196; ☎ 805-963-
4438; 12 W Anapamu St; 🕓 10am-7pm) Guidebooks,
maps and travel accessories.

Post Office (Map p196; ☎ 805-564-2226; 836 Anacapa
St; 🕓 8:30am-6pm Mon-Fri, 9am-2pm Sat)

Santa Barbara Cottage Hospital (Map p195; ☎ 805-
682-7111; cnr Pueblo & Bath Sts; 🕓 24hr) Emergency
room services.

Visitor Center (Map p196; ☎ 805-965-3021; www
.santabarbaraca.com; 1 Garden St; 🕓 9am-5pm Mon-Sat,
10am-5pm Sun; 🖳 📶) Offers maps and themed
self-guided touring brochures.

Sights

THE WATERFRONT
At its southern end, State St runs into
Stearns Wharf. Built in 1872 and once partly
owned by tough-guy actor Jimmy Cagney,
it's the West Coast's oldest continuously
operating wooden pier. There's 90 minutes
of free parking right on the wharf with
validation from any shop or restaurant.

West by the yacht harbor, the interesting
Santa Barbara Maritime Museum (Map p196; ☎ 805-
962-8404; www.sbmm.org; 113 Harbor Way; adult/child
1-5/child 6-17 $7/2/4, free 3rd Thu of the month; 🕓 10am-
5pm Thu-Tue, to 6pm Jun-Aug; 👤) examines
the city's briny history with memorabilia,
hands-on and virtual-reality exhibits, and
a movie theater.

The biodiesel, bright yellow-painted **Lil'
Toot water taxi** (one-way fare adult/child under 13 $4/1)
shuttles between Stearns Wharf and the har-
bor every half hour from noon to 6pm daily.

SANTA BARBARA COUNTY COURTHOUSE
Built in Spanish-Moorish revival style, the
magnificent 1929 **courthouse** (Map p196 ☎ 805-
962-6464; www.santabarbaracourthouse.org; 1100
Anacapa St; admission free; 🕓 8am-5pm Mon-Fri, 10am-
4:30pm Sat & Sun, tours 2pm Mon-Sat & 10:30am Mon,
Tue & Fri) is an absurdly beautiful place to
be on trial (or get married). Marvel at the
hand-painted ceilings, tiles from Tunisia
and Spain, gorgeously kept grounds and the
best view of the city from El Mirador, the
Vertigo-esque clock tower. Peek into the
second-floor mural room depicting California's colonial history and also glimpse
the law library, with its vaulted blue ceiling

---

covered in golden stars. You're free to
explore on your own but the best way to see
the courthouse is on a free guided tour.

MISSION SANTA BARBARA
Nicknamed the 'Queen of the Missions,'
Mission Santa Barbara (Map p195; ☎ 805-682-4713;
www.sbmission.org; 2201 Laguna St; adult/child 6-15 $5/1;
🕓 9am-4:30pm) sits on a hilltop perch northwest of downtown. It's the only California
mission to have twin bell towers, as well as
the sole one to have escaped secularization
under Mexican rule. It has been occupied
without interruption by Franciscans since
its founding in 1786, although the pink
sandstone church dates only from 1820.
Outside is a moody cemetery where an
estimated 4000 Chumash tribespeople lie
buried in unmarked graves.

SANTA BARBARA HISTORICAL MUSEUM
Embracing a romantic cloistered adobe
courtyard, this off-the-beaten-path **museum**
(Map p196; ☎ 805-966-1601; www.santabarbaramuseum
.com; 136 E De La Guerra St; donation requested; 🕓 10am-
5pm Tue-Sat, noon-5pm Sun) has an endlessly
fascinating collection of local memorabilia, ranging from the simply beautiful,
such as Chumash woven baskets and co-

CENTRAL COAST

lonial-era textiles, to the intriguing, such as an intricately carved coffer that once belonged to Junípero Serra. Learn about the city's involvement in toppling the last Chinese monarchy, among other interesting footnotes in local history.

SANTA BARBARA MUSEUM OF ART

Culture vultures will delightedly land at this little **museum** (Map p196; ☎ 805-963-4364; www .sbma.net; 1130 State St; adult/child 6-17 $9/6, Sun free; ☽ 11am-5pm Tue-Sun; ⓖ) specializing in contemporary California artists and big-name modern masters (think Dalí and Picasso), along with a tasteful collection of Asian art, 20th-century photography and classical sculpture. There's an interactive children's gallery, museum store and café.

SANTA BARBARA BOTANIC GARDEN

This stunner of a **garden** (Map p195; ☎ 805-682-4726; www.sbbg.org; 1212 Mission Canyon Rd; adult/child 2-12 $8/4; ☽ 9am-6pm Mar-Oct, to 5pm Nov-Feb, tours 11am Sat & Sun & 2pm daily; ⓖ ⓦ) is devoted to the native plants of California. Rolling miles of trails meander through cacti, redwoods and wildflowers and past the old mission dam and aqueduct, built by Chumash tribespeople to irrigate the mission's fields. Leashed, well-behaved dogs welcome.

Activities

For soaring ocean views, join **Eagle Paragliding** (☎ 805-968-0980; www.eagleparagliding.com) or **Fly Above All** (☎ 805-965-3733; www.flyaboveall.com), which both offer paragliding instruction (introductory lesson $200) and tandem flights (from $100).

BEACHES

Equipped with a playground, **East Beach** (Map p195) is a long, sandy stretch between Stearns Wharf and Montecito. It's Santa Barbara's most popular beach. Chic, but narrow **Butterfly Beach** (Map p195), at its eastern end, is near the Biltmore hotel.

Between Stearns Wharf and the harbor, **West Beach** (Map p196) has calm water and is popular with tourists. **Los Baños del Mar** (Map p196; ☎ 805-966-6110; 401 Shoreline Dr; admission $6; ☽ call for hr; ⓖ) is a municipal outdoor heated-pool complex for recreational and lap swimming. On the other side of the harbor, **Leadbetter Beach** (Map p195) is a good spot for beginner surfers and windsurfers.

WHAT THE...?

The eccentric Madame Ganna Walska bought the 37 acres that make up **Lotusland** (☎ 805-969-9990; www.lotusland.org; adult/child 5-18 $35/10; ☽ tours 10am & 1:30pm Wed-Sat mid-Feb–mid-Nov) in 1941 with money from the fortunes she inherited after marrying – and then divorcing – a string of wealthy men. She spent the next four decades tending and expanding her incredible collection of rare and exotic plants from around the world – there are over 120 varieties of aloe alone. Come when the lotuses bloom, between late June and late August. Reservations are required for the intimate tours; the phone is only attended from 9am to 5pm weekdays, 9am to 1pm Saturday. Directions are provided when you book.

Climbing the stairs on the west end takes you to **Shoreline Park** (Map p195), with picnic tables and awesome kite-flying conditions. Further west near the junction of Cliff Dr and Las Positas Rd, **Arroyo Burro Beach County Park** (Map p195), aka Hendry's, offers romps for kids and dogs and has free parking, a restaurant and a bar.

Twelve miles southeast of Santa Barbara, **Carpinteria State Beach** (per car $10; ☽ 7am-sunset; ⓖ) has calm waters for swimming, wading and tide-pooling. About 25 miles northwest of the city, **Refugio State Beach** (per vehicle $10; ☽ 8am-sunset) is a popular surf spot. It's connected by a recreational cycling path to **El Capitán State Beach** (per car $10; ☽ 8am-sunset; ⓖ), perched on low bluffs 3 miles east. All state beaches are signposted off Hwy 101; call ☎ 805-968-1033 for closure updates.

WHALE-WATCHING & KAYAKING

From the harbor, **Condor Express** (Map p196; ☎ 805-882-0088, 888-779-4253; http://condorcruises .com; 301 W Cabrillo Blvd; adult/child in summer $48/28, in winter $94/50) runs narrated whale-watching catamaran tours year-round.

Kayakers can test the calm waters of the harbor, paddle more secluded coastline, go whale-watching or hitch a ride out to the Channel Islands (p202) for more solitude and sea caves. **Paddle Sports** (☎ 805-899-4925; www.kayaksb.com; 117b Harbor Way; 2hr s/d kayak rental $20/30; ☽ 10am-4pm Thu-Tue, extended daily hr in summer) rents kayaks at the harbor and West

Beach. **Santa Barbara Adventure Co** (☎ 888-773-3239; www.sbadventureco.com; day tours $35-120) also leads guided kayak tours – ask about stargazing floats.

SURFING
Santa Barbara's proximity to the wind-breaking Channel Islands make it a good spot to learn how to ride waves. Unless you're a novice, conditions are too mellow in summer; swells kick back up in winter. **Rincon Point**, 10 miles east of Santa Barbara, has long, glassy, point-break waves for experts, while **Leadbetter Beach** and **Goleta Beach** are best for beginners. Learn to surf with **Santa Barbara Adventure Co** (☎ 888-773-3239; www.sbadventureco.com; 4hr lesson incl equipment rental & lunch $110).

CYCLING
The Cabrillo Blvd **beachfront bike path** runs for 3 miles along the water, between Andrée Clark Bird Refuge and Leadbetter Beach. **Wheel Fun** (Map p196; ☎ 805-966-2282; www.wheel funrentals.com; 23 E Cabrillo Blvd & 22 State St, bike rental per hr from $8; ☼ 8am-8pm) rents bikes and silly-looking surreys (quadracycles). The **Santa Barbara Bicycle Coalition** (www.sbbike.org) offers free printable self-guided road-cycling tours online.

Festivals & Events
Madonnari Italian Street Painting Festival (www .imadonnarifestival.com) Chalk drawings adorn the mission's sidewalks over Memorial Day weekend.
Summer Solstice Celebration (www.solsticeparade .com) Wacky, wildly popular – and just plain wild – performance-art parade in mid-June.
Old Spanish Fiesta Days (www.oldspanishdays-fiesta .org) It's packed in early August for this long-running cultural heritage festival with rodeos, music and dancing.

Tours
Architectural Foundation of Santa Barbara (☎ 805-965-6307; www.afsb.org; adult/child under 12 $10/free) Offers 90-minute docent-guided walking tours of downtown's art, history and architecture, usually on Saturday and Sunday mornings.
Red Tile Walking Tour (www.santabarbaracarfree.org) This self-guided stroll takes in downtown's major sights and historic landmarks, including the courthouse, museums and El Presidio. Pick up a map at the visitors center, or download it online.
Santa Barbara Trolley (Map p196; ☎ 805-965-0353; www.sbtrolley.com; adult/child 3-12 $19/8;

☼ 10am-4pm) A narrated 90-minute one-way loop past Stearns Wharf, Butterfly Beach, the maritime museum, State St and the mission. Hop-on, hop-off tickets are valid all day and entitle you to small discounts at select attractions.

Sleeping
Prepare for sticker shock: basic rooms command over $200 in summer. Don't just show up and expect to find cheap accommodations at the last minute, especially not on weekends. For decent midrange motels and hotels, follow Hwy 101 south to Carpinteria (12 miles) or Ventura (30 miles).

BUDGET
Make **reservations** (☎ 800-444-7275; www.reserve america.com; campsites $35-65) for the developed campgrounds at state beaches off Hwy 101 (see p198).
    Santa Barbara Tourist Hostel (Map p196; ☎ 805-963-0154; www.sbhostel.com; 134 Chapala St; dm $28-35, r $79-95; ☐ ☎) Traveling strangers, roaring trains and a rowdy bar just steps from your door – it's either the perfect country-and-western song or this low-slung bungalow, which feels like a grungy college dorm, next to the Amtrak station.
    Hotel State Street (Map p196; ☎ 805-966-6586; www.hotelstatestreet.net; 121 State St; r with shared bath $69-99; ☐ ☎) Despite the beachy color scheme in the lobby, this hotel-esque hostel has an institutional feel. Many rooms have a sink and TV, but no phone. Only two blocks to the ocean, and even closer to the railroad tracks (bring earplugs).

MIDRANGE
'Motel row' sprawls along upper State St, a couple of miles north of downtown. There is a host of more expensive motels and hotels in the blocks behind West Beach.
    Presidio Motel (Map p196; ☎ 805-963-1355; www .thepresidiomotel.com; 1620 State St; r $100-180; ☒ ☎) What H&M is to shopping, the Presidio is to lodging. Here crisp, modern rooms break the Super 8 mold with funky artwork and interior design. It's north of downtown along noisy State St, but bikes are free to borrow. Its sister motel, the Agave Inn, is cheaper.
    Marina Beach Motel (Map p196; ☎ 805-963-9311, 877-627-4621; www.marinabeachmotel.com; 21 Bath St; r incl breakfast $120-285; ☒ ☐ ☎ ☼) This old-fashioned one-story motor lodge near the ocean has been done up inside and made

CENTRAL COAST

bright. A few of the nothing-special, yet still comfy, rooms come with kitchenettes. Free loaner bikes.

Hotel Virginia (Map p196; ☎ 805-963-9757, 800-549-1700; www.hotelvirginia.com; 17 W Haley St; r incl breakfast $150-200; 🕹 🖵 🛜) Right downtown, this early-20th-century hotel downplays its Holiday Inn Express affiliation. It has heaps of character, starting with the tiled lobby fountain. Tidy rooms have upgrades like flat-screen TVs and CD players.

White Jasmine Inn (Map p196; ☎ 805-966-0589; www.whitejasmineinnsantabarbara.com; 1327 Bath St; r $154-309; 🛜) Whether you bed down in the arts-and-crafts bungalow or Victorian cottage, all of the cozy B&B rooms have romantic gas fireplaces. It's a 10-minute walk west of State St.

Brisas del Mar (Map p196; ☎ 805-966-2219, 800-468 1988; www.sbhotels.com; 223 Castillo St; r incl breakfast $170-265; 🖵 🛜 🐾) Big kudos for all the freebies (DVDs, afternoon wine and cheese, evening milk and cookies) and the new Mediterranean-style front section, although the motel wing is unlovely. The hotel's respectable sister properties, some also near the beach, are lower-priced.

TOP END

our pick **El Capitan Canyon** (off Map p195; ☎ 805-685-3887, 866-352-2729; 11560 Calle Real, Goleta; tents with shared bath $155, cabins from $225; 🛜 🐾 👶) A 20-minute drive northbound up Hwy 101, El Capitan is for those who love to camp but hate to wake up with dirt under their nails. Safari tents are rustic. Creekside cabin amenities vary – some come with fireplaces, kitchenettes, soaking tubs and sleeping lofts – but all have divine beds. You can borrow bikes to pedal over to the beach.

Inn of the Spanish Garden (Map p196; ☎ 805-564-4700, 866-564-4700; http://spanishgardeninn.com; 915 Garden St; d incl breakfast $259-519; 🕹 🖵 🛜 🐾) At this small Spanish revival–style hotel, two dozen romantic rooms and suites have balconies or patios overlooking a gracious fountain courtyard, while palm trees surround an outdoor lap pool. Beds have luxurious linens, bathrooms feature decadent whirlpool tubs, and concierge service is top-notch.

Eating

So-so restaurants abound along State St downtown and by the waterfront. Santa Barbara's **farmers market** (Map p196; ☎ 805-962-

5354; cnr Cota & Santa Barbara Sts; ⌚ 8:30am-12:30pm Sat) also stages a Tuesday afternoon version along the 500 and 600 blocks of State St.

Lilly's Taqueria (Map p196; ☎ 805-966-9180; 310 Chapala St; items from $1.35; ⌚ 11am-9pm Mon, Wed & Thu, 11am-10pm Fri & Sat, 11am-9:30pm Sun) There's almost always a line roping around this taco shack. But the line goes fast, so you'd better be snappy with your order – locals rave about the *adobada* (marinated pork).

D'Angelo Pastry & Bread (Map p196; ☎ 805-962-5466; 25 W Gutierrez St; dishes $2-8; ⌚ 7am-2pm) A retro bakery with shiny-silver sidewalk bistro tables, it's a perfect quick-breakfast spot, whether for a frothy cappuccino and buttery croissant with housemade marmalade or sweet bananas foster French toast.

Blenders in the Grass (Map p196; ☎ 805-962-5715; 720 State St; items $3-6; ⌚ 7am-9pm Mon-Thu, 7am-10pm Fri, 8am-10pm Sat, 8am-9pm Sun) For a quick, healthy burst of energy, pop by this locally owned juice bar and down a wheatgrass shot, blueberry-licious 'Purple Banana' smoothie or date milkshake.

Santa Barbara Shellfish Company (Map p196; ☎ 805-966-6676; 230 Stearns Wharf; dishes $5-15; ⌚ 11am-9pm) 'From sea to skillet to plate' best describes this end-of-the-wharf crab shack that's more of a counter joint. Great lobster bisque, ocean views and the same location for 25 years.

Sojourner Cafe (Map p196; ☎ 805-965-7922; 134 E Cañon Perdido; mains $7-14; ⌚ 11am-11pm Mon-Sat, to 10pm Sun) Hippie Soj has been doing its all-natural, mostly meatless magic since 1978. Globally flavored vegetarian-friendly comfort food sometimes borders on bland, though the gingered tofu wonton pillows are tasty. The dessert list is mostly vegan (though you'd never guess it).

Brophy Brothers (Map p196; ☎ 805-966-4418; 119 Harbor Way; mains $8-20; ⌚ 11am-10pm Sun-Thu, to 11pm Fri & Sat) The seafood at this always-bustling harbor hangout is so fresh that you half expect it to leap straight out of the ocean. Show up at sunset, grab an ocean-view table on the outdoor deck or sit inside at the boisterous bar to knock back Bloody Marys.

Tupelo Junction (Map p196; ☎ 805-899-3100; 1218 State St; mains $12-18; ⌚ 8am-2pm) Busiest at brunch, this sunny café offers Southern-style takes on good ol' comfort-food standards like cinnamon-apple beignets, cheddar hush puppies served with spicy pepper jam or fried-chicken salad topped with herb-buttermilk dressing.

our pick Square One (Map p196; ☎ 805-965-4565; 14 E Cota St; mains $14-25; 5:30-9pm Tue-Sun) A postmodern Californian menu reaches stratospheric heights of inventiveness, piquing even jaded palates with the likes of seafood ceviche with grapefruit gelée or squid-ink ravioli in a delicate sea-urchin broth. Sculpted desserts are sweetly challenging. Svelte wine bar.

Palace Grill (Map p196; ☎ 805-963-5000; 8 E Cota St; dinner mains $16-30; 11:30am-3pm daily, 5:30-10pm Sun-Thu, 5:30-11pm Fri & Sat;) With all the exuberance of Mardi Gras, this N'awlins grill dishes up stiff cocktails, delectable baskets of housemade biscuits and breads, and ginormous plates of jambalaya, blackened catfish and pecan chicken.

Drinking

Santa Barbara's after-dark bar scene revolves around lower State St, where UCSB students run amok. Touristy waterfront bars have ace sunset views.

James Joyce (Map p196; ☎ 805-962-2688; 513 State St) In the thick of the State St drag, this institution's most endearing quality is the inch-thick carpet of peanut shells. Live bands play almost every night.

Press Room (Map p196; ☎ 805-936-8121; 15 E Ortega St) An unpretentious pub attracts local students and a slew of European travelers. There's no better place to catch the game, stuff the jukebox with quarters and be jovially abused by the British bartender.

Muddy Waters (Map p196; ☎ 831-966-9328; 58 E Haley St; 6am-6pm Mon-Sat;) A funkadelic coffeehouse with tattooed baristas, microbrews on tap and anticorporate mottos galore; it's a good place to find out what the young artsy crowd is up to. Live bands some nights after 6pm. Cash only.

Hollister Brewing Co (off Map p195; ☎ 805-968-2810; Camino Real Marketplace, 6980 Marketplace Dr, off Storke Rd, Hwy 101 exit Glen Annie Rd, Goleta; 11am-late) OK, so it's in a shopping plaza, a 15-minute drive west of downtown near the UCSB campus. But beer geeks won't regret making the trip to sample the handcrafted White Star XPA (extra-pale ale), Hip Hop imperial-style ale or 'Barleywhine.' Skip the food, though.

Entertainment

The free weekly *Santa Barbara Independent* (www.independent.com) has complete listings and reviews. The *Santa Barbara News-Press* (www.newspress.com/scene) publishes a daily calendar and Friday's arts-and-entertainment magazine *Scene*.

SOhO (Map p196; ☎ 805-962-7776; www.sohosb .com; 1221 State St; cover $10-20) One unpretentious brick room plus live-music performances almost nightly equals SOhO, hidden behind a McDonald's. Lineups range from indie rock, folk and funk to weekend DJs and jazz every Monday.

Arlington Theatre (Map p196; ☎ 805-963-4408; www.thearlingtontheatre.com; 1317 State St) Harking back to 1931, this mission-style movie palace has a Spanish courtyard, and the gorgeous ceiling is spangled with stars. It's a splendid place to see a concert by anyone from Wynton Marsalis to Pink Martini to Sonic Youth.

Zodo's Bowling & Beyond (off Map p195; ☎ 805-967-0128; 5925 Calle Real, off Hwy 101 exit Fairview Ave, Goleta; 8:30am-2am;) With over 40 beers on tap, pool tables and a video arcade with Skee-Ball, this bowling alley near UCSB is hilarious fun. Call for schedules of open-play lanes, blacklight 'glow bowl' and retro DJ nights.

Getting There & Around

Santa Barbara is bisected by Hwy 101; to reach downtown, take the Garden St or Cabrillo Blvd exits. Municipal parking lots off State St are free for the first 75 minutes; each additional hour costs $1.50. To rent your own wheels, try Zipcar (p290).

Ten miles west of downtown off Hwy 101, **Santa Barbara Municipal Airport** (SBA; ☎ 805-967-7111; www.flysba.com; 500 Fowler Rd, Goleta) has major car-rental firms and is served by American Eagle (LA) and United Express (San Francisco and LA). **Santa Barbara Airbus** (☎ 805-964-7759, 800-423-1618; www.santabarbaraairbus.com) shuttles between Los Angeles International Airport (LAX) and Santa Barbara (one-way/round-trip $48/90, 2½ hours).

Greyhound (Map p196; ☎ 805-965-7551; 34 W Carrillo St) has daily buses to LA ($18, three hours) and San Francisco ($60, nine hours), the latter via San Luis Obispo ($27, 2¼ hours).

Santa Barbara is a stop on the daily Seattle–LA *Coast Starlight*, run by **Amtrak** (Map p196; 209 State St). *Pacific Surfliner* regional

CENTRAL COAST

WORTH A TRIP: OJAI

Ojai (pronounced *oh*-hi, meaning 'moon' to the Chumash) is a town that has long drawn artists and new agers. It's famous for the 'Pink Moment,' a rosy glow that emanates from its mountains at sunset. Hollywood director Frank Capra chose the Ojai Valley to represent the mythical Shangri-La in his 1937 movie *Lost Horizon*. For information and maps, visit the **Ojai Valley Chamber of Commerce** (☎ 805-646-8126; www.ojaichamber.org; 201 S Signal St; ☺ 9am-noon & 1-4pm Mon-Fri).

Arcade Plaza, a maze of Mission-revival–style buildings downtown along Ojai Ave, contains diverting shops, cafés and art galleries. Used-book-lovers will not want to miss rambling **Bart's Books** (☎ 805-646-3755; 302 W Matilija St; ☺ 9:30am-sunset), a few blocks northwest. The ideal vantage point for catching a Pink Moment is the peaceful lookout atop **Meditation Mount**, which closes after sunset. To get there, head east of downtown on Ojai Ave (Hwy 150) for 2 miles, take a left at Boccali's and drive 3 miles up Reeves Rd.

Boccali's (☎ 805-646-6116; 3277 Ojai Ave; mains $7-15; ☺ 4-9pm Mon & Tue, 11:45am-9pm Wed-Sun) farm stand, replete with red-and-white-checkered plastic tablecloths, does simple Italian and does it well. Much of the produce is grown right behind the restaurant, and the fresh-tomato salad is often still warm from the garden. No credit cards.

Ojai is 35 miles east of Santa Barbara via Hwys 101 and 150, or 18 miles north of Ventura via Hwy 33.

trains frequently head south to LA ($25, three hours) and San Diego ($47, six hours), and twice daily north to San Luis Obispo ($30, 2¾ hours). Additional Thruway bus services link Santa Barbara with SLO.

Metropolitan Transit District (MTD; ☎ 805-963-3366; www.sbmtd.gov; 1020 Chapala St; single-ride fares from $1.75) buses travel around the city and surrounding suburbs. MTD's Downtown-Waterfront Shuttle (25¢) hums along State St to Stearns Wharf and by the waterfront between the zoo and Harbor Way.

CHANNEL ISLANDS NATIONAL PARK

Lying off the Southern California coast, these islands are named for the troughs that separate them from the mainland. Rich in unique flora and fauna species, tidepools and kelp forests, they've earned the nickname 'California's Galapagos.' They offer opportunities for hiking, camping, kayaking and scuba diving. Winter is best for wildlife watching, while wildflowers bloom in spring. Though summer is bone-dry, fall sees balmier temperatures and calmer seas.

The National Park Service (NPS) **visitor center** (☎ 805-658-5730; www.nps.gov/chis; 1901 Spinnaker Dr, Ventura; ☺ 8:30am-5pm) is your one-stop shop for books, maps, trip-planning information, natural-history exhibits, a free film and a lookout from where you can see the islands on a clear day. It's at the far end of Ventura Harbor, off Harbor Blvd southwest of Hwy 101.

Sight & Activities

Closest to the mainland, **Anacapa**, which is actually three separate islets, offers a nice, easy introduction to the islands' ecology. Hiking, kayaking, snorkeling and scuba diving are all possible in the rich kelp beds surrounding the island, and boats make the trip year-round.

Santa Cruz, the largest island, is laced with hiking trails. Keep your eyes peeled for archaeological sites from the Chumash tribal and European ranching periods. Popular activities include swimming, snorkeling, scuba diving and kayaking. The island's Painted Cave is one of the planet's largest and deepest sea caves.

Other islands require overnight camping trips and longer channel crossings. Beautiful sandy beaches and nearly 200 bird species are highlights on **Santa Rosa**, a windy place known for its wealth of paleontological and archaeological sites. Come for the rugged hiking, not water sports.

Remote **San Miguel** offers solitude and a wilderness experience, but it's often shrouded in fog and is very windy. There's an interesting caliche forest (made of calcium-carbonate castings of trees) and seasonal colonies of seals and sea lions haul out on shore.

Only 1 square mile in size, isolated **Santa Barbara** is home to a northern elephant seal colony. It's a thriving playground for other marine wildlife and birds, too, satisfying hikers, birders, divers and snorkelers.

CENTRAL COAST

Sleeping

All five islands have primitive **campgrounds** (☎ reservations 877-444-6677; www.recreation.gov; tent sites $15) open year-round (reservations required). Each campground has pit toilets and picnic tables, but you must pack everything in (and out). Water is only available on Santa Rosa and Santa Cruz Islands. Due to fire danger, campfires are not allowed, but campstoves are OK. Be prepared to carry your stuff up to 1.5 miles, possibly uphill, from the boat landing areas.

Getting There & Away

You can only reach the islands by boat or plane. Landings are never guaranteed, again because of changeable weather and surf conditions. Reservations are essential for weekend, holiday and summer trips.

Near the NPS visitor center at Ventura Harbor, **Island Packers** (☎ 805-642-1393; www .islandpackers.com; 1691 Spinnaker Dr, Ventura) offers ferry services (adult/child round-trip from $45/28), day trips including whale-watching cruises year-round, and multiday packages to all the islands. Campers pay extra for their gear. Some boats depart from nearby Oxnard.

Truth Aquatics (Map p196; ☎ 805-962-1127; www .truthaquatics.com; 301 W Cabrillo Blvd, Santa Barbara) offers similar guided tour and activity excursions, but caters mostly to divers and kayakers. Most trips require a minimum number of participants.

Channel Islands Aviation (☎ 805-987-1301; www .flycia.com; half-day tours adult/child 2-12 $160/135) offers island beach excursions, surf-fishing and overnight camping trips to Santa Rosa Island, departing from Camarillo, about 16 miles east of Ventura Harbor via Hwy 101, or Santa Barbara.

VENTURA

pop 106,745

A pushing-off point for Channel Island excursions, San Buenaventura has its own scruffy, ungentrified charms, especially in the historic downtown corridor along Main St, north of Hwy 101 via Seaward Ave. There you'll find a terrific assortment of antique, vintage and secondhand thrift shops. The **Ventura Visitors & Convention Bureau** (☎ 805-648-2075, 800-483-6214; www.ventura-usa.com; 101 S California St; ☀ 8:30am-5pm Mon-Fri, 9am-5pm Sat, 10am-4pm Sun) has free maps and info.

The town's Spanish colonial roots are evidenced by 1782 **Mission San Buenaventura** (☎ 805-643-4318; www.sanbuenaventuramission.org; 211 E Main St; adult/child under 17 $2/50¢; ☀ 10am-5pm Mon-Fri, 9am-5pm Sat, 10am-4pm Sun), the last California mission founded by Junípero Serra. A stroll around this parish church is a mellow experience, leading through a small museum, past statues of saints, centuries-old religious paintings and unusual wooden mission bells, and around a garden courtyard.

Along the waterfront, **San Buenaventura State Beach** (☎ 805-968-1033; Harbor Blvd, off Hwy 101; per car $10; ☀ dawn-dusk; ⛹) is perfect for swimming, surfing or just lazing on the sand. Recreational cycling paths connect to more beaches. Budget motels and high-rise chain hotels cluster off Hwy 101 nearby.

Main St downtown is chockablock with cafés, taco shops and Euro-Cal restaurants. **Mary's Secret Garden** (☎ 805-641-3663; 100 S Fir St; mains $5-12; ☀ 11am-4pm Tue & Wed, to 9:30pm Thu-Sat; Ⓥ) is an internationally spiced vegan haven that also makes fresh juices, smoothies and out-of-this-world cakes. Chef-owned **Brooks** (☎ 805-652-7070; 545 E Thompson Blvd; mains $14-34; ☀ dinner Tue-Sun) restaurant designs top-notch creative New American cuisine like cornmeal-fried oysters, Maryland blue crab ravioli and cinnamon-roll bread pudding.

Laidback **Anacapa Brewing Co** (☎ 805-643-2337; 472 E Main St; mains $9-20; ☀ 11:30am-midnight Tue-Sun) crafts its own microbrews and makes impressive salads and a fine pulled-pork sandwich with crispy sweet-potato fries. Hidden inside a shady brick courtyard, **Zoey's Café** (☎ 805-652-1137, entertainment info 805-652-0091; www.zoeyscafe.com; 451 E Main St; mains $9-12; ☀ 11:30am-3:30pm Mon & Wed-Thu, 11:30am-midnight Fri & Sat) showcases live acts weekly – mostly bluegrass, acoustic folk and comedy – inside a cozy coffeehouse serving hot panini sandwiches, farm-fresh salads and ooey-gooey thick-crust pizzas.

Ventura is 30 miles southeast of Santa Barbara via Hwy 101. It's at least another hour's drive south to Malibu (p214) via Hwys 101 and 1. Daily trains to Santa Barbara ($16, 40 minutes) and LA ($26, 2¼ hours) stop at Ventura's unstaffed **Amtrak station** (cnr Harbor Blvd & Figueroa St). Several daily Coastal Express buses between Ventura and Santa Barbara ($2, one hour) are operated by **Vista** (☎ 800-438-1112; www.goventura.org).

Los Angeles & Orange County

Ah, Los Angeles: land of starstruck dreams and Tinseltown magic, and perhaps the most resented place in California. You may think you know what to expect from LA: earthquakes, floods, fires, traffic, Paris (and Perez) Hilton. Done? Good.

Now here are some other things you should know: LA is America's largest county in terms of population (it would be the eighth-largest state on its own), an economic powerhouse, the hemisphere's largest port and, oh yes, the world's entertainment capital. So, Angelenos philosophize, you take the challenges along with the good.

And there *is* a lot of good: the beaches, the mountains and weeks' worth of culture, food and sheer style. Though you may well find surgically enhanced blondes and Hollywood honchos weaving lanes at 80mph, LA is intensely diverse and brimming with fascinating neighborhoods and characters that have nothing to do with the 'biz.' You owe it to yourself to see LA with your own eyes. You won't need much to act out your own LA story. Credit card, wheels, beach towel, and you're golden. But please leave your preconceptions at home.

There's a sibling-like relationship between LA and its southern neighbor, Orange County. If LA likes to think that it's tortillas, dim sum and margaritas, Orange County is an all-American filet mignon and martini. Both are part arrogance and part truth. Though the OC is, at first glance, a hodgepodge of suburbs, its towns maintain unique personalities, like surf-serious Huntington Beach and gracious Laguna Beach. And let's not forget that high temple of Americana…Disneyland.

HIGHLIGHTS

- Cruising the beachside bike path or riding the ecofriendly Ferris wheel on the pier at **Santa Monica** (p214)
- Joining the human freak parade just south of Santa Monica at the **Venice Boardwalk** (p215)
- Seeing the inner workings of the world's dream factory on a studio tour at **Universal Studios** (p220)
- Browsing the junk, treasure and everything in between on display on Long Beach's **Retro Row** (p216)
- Spending the day gazing at priceless works of art high above LA at the **Getty Center** (p215), in itself a spectacular piece of work
- Screaming through the galaxy on Space Mountain at **Disneyland** (p231), then sticking around for the fireworks display
- Watching the sun dip below the horizon at artsy **Laguna Beach** (p237)

FAST FACTS

- **Average temperature low/high in Los Angeles** January 47/66°F, July 62/82°F
- **LA to Santa Barbara** 95 miles, 1½ to 2½ hours
- **Hollywood to Disneyland** 34 miles, 45 minutes to one hour
- **LA to San Diego** 120 miles, two to three hours
- **Disneyland to Huntington Beach** 16 miles, 20 to 30 minutes

LOS ANGELES

pop city 4,065,000, county 10,393,000

With some 75 miles of coastline, this diverse county offers experiences to match.

From the north, roll into LA on the Pacific Coast Hwy in Malibu, whose very name conjures up both surfers and movie stars. Of the beach towns, Santa Monica is the most tourist friendly and accessible from elsewhere, and, just to its south, everything about Venice is colorful – hippies, murals and boardwalk – making it an especially appealing stop. The South Bay's Manhattan, Hermosa and Redondo Beaches give way to hilltop mansions on the Palos Verdes Peninsula, while San Pedro and Long Beach collectively form LA's southern flank, both port cities with top-rated attractions from military history to a fabulous aquarium and the stately ocean liner *Queen Mary*, plus burgeoning arts districts.

HISTORY

The hunter-gatherer existence of the Gabrieleño and Chumash peoples ended with the arrival of Spanish missionaries and pioneers in the late 18th century. Known as El Pueblo de la Reina de Los Angeles, Spain's first civilian settlement here (1781) remained an isolated farming outpost for decades. LA was incorporated as a California city in 1850, and a series of events caused LA's population to swell by 1930: the collapse of the Northern California Gold Rush, the arrival of the transcontinental railroad, the birth of the citrus industry, the discovery of oil, the launch of the port of LA, the birth of the movie industry and the opening of the California Aqueduct. The city's population has boomed from some 1.5 million in 1950 to over 4 million today.

LA's growth has caused its share of problems, including suburban sprawl and air pollution – though thanks to aggressive enforcement, smog levels have fallen annually since records have been kept – and the occasional earthquake or forest fire. Traffic, a struggling public-education system and a fluctuating real-estate market remain nagging concerns, but with a strong and diverse economy and a decreasing crime rate, all things considered, LA's a survivor.

ORIENTATION

LA County is vast (88 cities on over 4000 sq miles), but the places of visitor interest are fairly well defined in an area shaped roughly like the Big Dipper. Malibu takes up most of the handle, curving round Santa Monica Bay to Santa Monica, Venice, LAX airport and the South Bay. The Palos Verdes Peninsula, San Pedro and Long Beach form the base of the cup. Downtown LA is due north of San Pedro, Hollywood is northwest of Downtown, with West Hollywood and Beverly Hills spreading back toward the coast.

If you're driving, you'll almost certainly be spending some time on LA's freeways. The I-10 (Santa Monica Fwy) heads eastwest, connecting the Pacific Coast Hwy and Santa Monica with Downtown LA. It intersects with I-405 (San Diego Fwy) southbound to Long Beach and Orange County. US-101 (Hollywood Fwy) cuts diagonally through Downtown, merging with I-5 (Golden State or Santa Ana Fwy) to Orange County and San Diego.

INFORMATION

Bookstores

National chains abound, but here are some favorite local bookstores.

Book Soup (Map p212; ☎ 310-659-3110; www.book soup.com; 8818 W Sunset Blvd, West Hollywood; ◷ 9am-10pm) Frequent celeb sightings.

Equator Books (Map pp208-9; ☎ 310-399-5544; www .equatorbooks.com; 1103 Abbot Kinney Blvd; ◷ 9am-10pm Sun-Thu, 9am-11pm Fri & Sat) First editions, out-of-print and rare books on bullfighting, circus freaks, surfing and art, plus an eclectic vinyl selection.

(continued on page 213)

GREATER LOS ANGELES

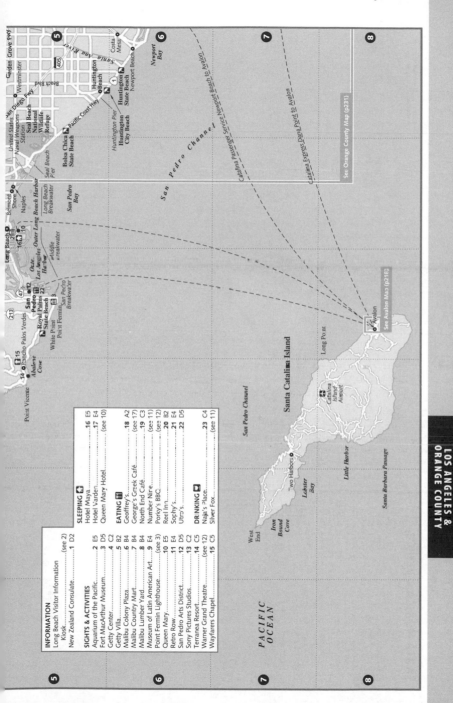

See Orange County Map (p231)

See Avalon Map (p216)

LOS ANGELES &
ORANGE COUNTY

SANTA MONICA & VENICE

LOS ANGELES & ORANGE COUNTY

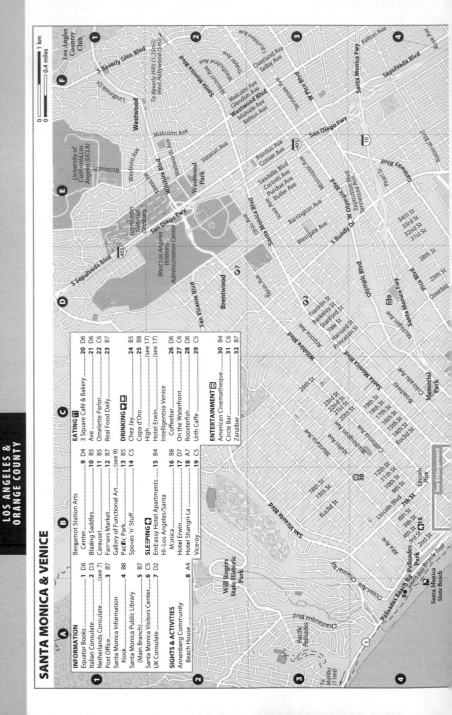

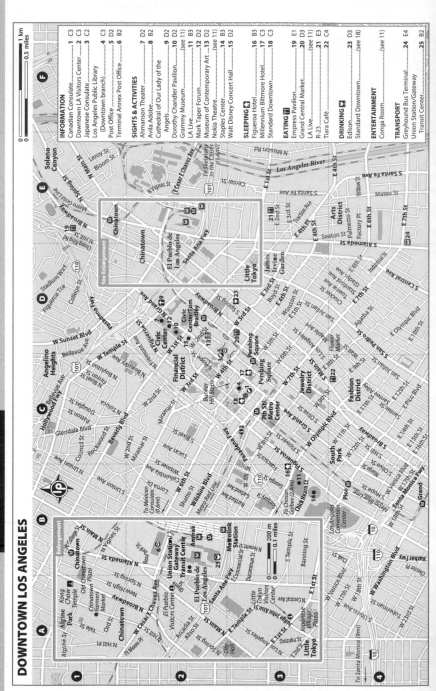

DOWNTOWN LOS ANGELES

See Enlargement

Enlargement

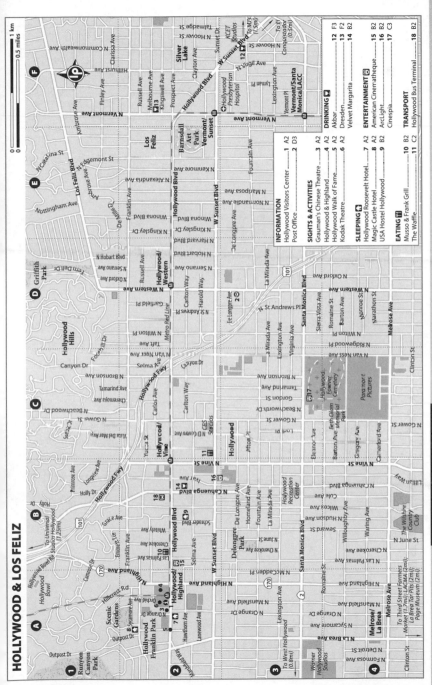

HOLLYWOOD & LOS FELIZ

LOS ANGELES & ORANGE COUNTY

BEVERLY HILLS, WEST HOLLYWOOD & MID-CITY

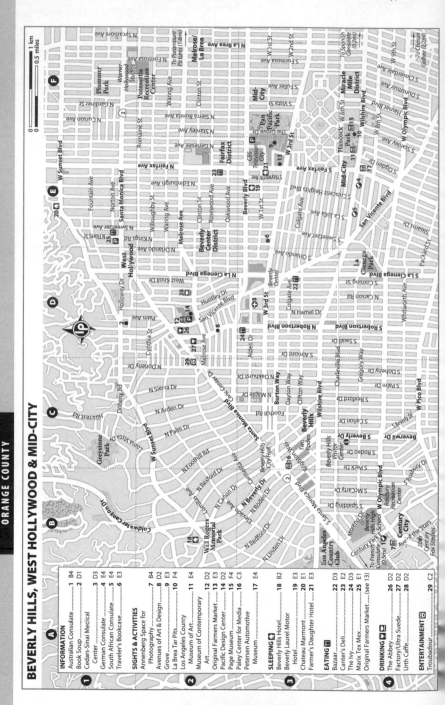

(continued from page 205)

Traveler's Bookcase (Map p212; ☎ 323-655-0575; www.travelbooks.com; 8375 W 3rd St, Mid-City; ☼ 10am-7pm Mon-Sat, 11am-7pm Sun) Just what it says.

Internet Access
For free wi-fi hot-spot locations check www.jiwire.com. Cafes are a good bet, including Coffee Bean & Tea Leaf (www.coffeebean.com), as are libraries (main branches are listed):
Los Angeles Public Library (Map p210; ☎ 213-228-7000; www.lapl.org; 630 W 5th St, Downtown)
Santa Monica Public Library (Map pp208-9; ☎ 310-458-8600; www.smpl.org; 601 Santa Monica Blvd)

Media
KCRW 89.9 FM (www.kcrw.com) Santa Monica-based National Public Radio (NPR) station with cutting-edge music and well-chosen public-affairs programming.
KNX 1070 AM (www.knx1070.com) LA's CBS News affiliate has all-important traffic reports every five minutes.
KPCC 89.3 FM (www.kpcc.org) Pasadena-based NPR station with NPR and BBC programming and intelligent local talk shows.
LA Weekly (www.laweekly.com) Free alternative news and listings magazine.
Los Angeles Magazine (www.losangelesmagazine.com) Glossy lifestyle monthly with useful restaurant guide.
Los Angeles Times (www.latimes.com) The West's leading daily and winner of dozens of Pulitzer prizes.

Medical Services
Cedars-Sinai Medical Center (Map p212; ☎ 310-423-3277; 8700 Beverly Blvd, West Hollywood; ☼ 24hr emergency)

Rite-Aid pharmacies (☎ 800-748-3243; www.riteaid.com; ☼ some 24hr) Call for the nearest branch.

Post
Call ☎ 800-275-8777 for the nearest branch, or see the maps to Downtown LA (Map p210), Hollywood & Los Feliz (Map p211) or Santa Monica & Venice (Map pp208–9) for locations.

Tourist Information
Catalina Visitors Bureau (Map p218; ☎ 310-510-1520; www.catalina.com; Green Pier, Avalon; ☼ hours vary)
Downtown LA Visitors Center (Map p210; ☎ 213-689-8822; http://discoverlosangeles.com; 685 S Figueroa St; ☼ 8:30am-5pm Mon-Fri)
Hollywood Visitors Center (Map p211; ☎ 323-467-6412; Hollywood & Highland complex, 6801 Hollywood Blvd; ☼ 10am-10pm Mon-Sat, 10am-7pm Sun)
Long Beach Visitor Information Kiosk (Map pp206-7; ☎ 562-436-3645, 800-452-7829; ☼ 10am-5pm Jun-Sep, 10am-4pm Fri-Sun Oct-May) Outside the Aquarium of the Pacific.
Santa Monica (☎ 310-393-7593, 800-544-5319; www.santamonica.com) Visitors Center (Map pp208-9; 1920 Main St; ☼ 9am-6pm); Information Kiosk (Map pp208-9; 1400 Ocean Ave; ☼ 9am-5pm Jun-Aug, 10am-4pm Sep-May)

DANGERS & ANNOYANCES
Despite what you may see in the movies, LA is generally safe, especially in the areas covered in this book. Downtown LA, Santa Monica and Venice are home to numerous homeless folks, who generally leave you alone if you do the same.

ACTUALLY, SOME PEOPLE DO WALK IN LA
'No one walks in LA,' the '80s band Missing Persons famously sang. That was then. Fed up with traffic, smog and high gas prices, the city that defined car culture is developing a foot culture. Angelenos are moving into more densely populated neighborhoods and walking, cycling and taking public transit.

The turning point was the extension of the Metro Red Line subway in 2003, connecting Union Station in Downtown LA to the San Fernando Valley via Koreatown, Hollywood and Universal Studios. Stay near one of the arty stations and you may not need a car at all. Particularly convenient stations include Pershing Sq and 7th St/Metro Center in Downtown, and Hollywood/Highland in Hollywood. Unlimited-ride tickets ($5 per day) are a downright bargain, and given LA's legendary traffic it's often faster to travel below ground than above. Light-rail lines connect Downtown with Long Beach and a Culver City branch was due to open as we went to press.

The catch: going further afield. While eventual plans call for a 'Subway to the Sea,' for now you'll be busing it or driving yourself to Mid-City, Beverly Hills and Santa Monica. The easiest transfer is to the Rapid 720 bus (at Wilshire/Vermont station on the Red Line or Wilshire/Western on the Purple Line), which makes limited stops along Wilshire Blvd.

See Getting Around (p230) and visit www.metro.net.

LOS ANGELES IN...

One Day
Fuel up at the **Omelette Parlor** (p225), then go rent bikes at Santa Monica Beach to ride the 22-mile **South Bay Bicycle Trail** (p222) along the oceanfront before the weekend hordes get there (it's least crowded Monday to Friday). Now that you've reached your fitness quota for the day, indulge at one of the fabulous beaches of **Malibu** (see below) or the amusement park of the century-old **Santa Monica Pier** (see below) and lunch at the **Reel Inn** (p225). Midafternoon, head south to the **Venice Boardwalk** (opposite) to see the seaside sideshow, then walk inland to **Abbot Kinney Blvd** (p216) where the fascinating shops compete with tantalizing restaurants, or take a relaxing stroll around the **Venice Canals** (opposite). Watch the sunset or the stars over the ocean at High, the rooftop bar at **Hotel Erwin** (p223).

Two Days
Venture inland to explore what makes LA a world city. Dim sum breakfast at **Empress Pavilion** (p226) is a trip to Hong Kong sans passport. The 'overseas' trek continues at **El Pueblo de Los Angeles** (p219). Then catapult to the future at the dramatic **Walt Disney Concert Hall** (p219) and **Cathedral of Our Lady of the Angels** (p219). Stop for lunch at the new entertainment center **LA Live** (p219), and take in the new **Grammy Museum** (p219). From here, it's a short drive on the Hollywood Fwy to the **Hollywood Walk of Fame** (p220) and **Grauman's Chinese Theatre** (p219) along revitalized Hollywood Blvd. Up your chances of spotting actual celebs by hitting the fashion-forward boutiques on paparazzi-infested **Robertson Blvd** (p229) and having dinner at the **Ivy** (p227).

**LOS ANGELES &
ORANGE COUNTY**

SIGHTS

We've organized LA County's neighborhoods and towns in geographical order, beginning along Santa Monica Bay. Ritzy Malibu kicks things off to the north, followed by Santa Monica and Venice, and around the Palos Verdes Peninsula to San Pedro and Long Beach. Then we head inland to the transit and culture hub of Downtown LA and Hollywood, and curve west again toward the coast, via Mid-City, West Hollywood and Beverly Hills.

Malibu

Malibu, which hugs 27 spectacular miles of Pacific Coast Hwy, has long been synonymous with surfing, stars and a hedonistic lifestyle, but actually looks far less posh than the glossy mags make it sound. Still, it's been celebrity central since the 1930s when money troubles forced landowner May Rindge to lease out property to her Hollywood friends. Leo, Brangelina, Streisand, Cher and other A-listers have homes here and can often be spotted shopping at the village-like **Malibu Country Mart** (Map pp206-7; 3835 Cross Creek Rd; [P]), the new and superchichi **Malibu Lumber Yard** (Map pp206-7; 3939 Cross Creek Rd; [P]) and the more utilitarian

Malibu Colony Plaza (Map pp206-7; 23841 W Malibu Rd; [P]).

Despite its wealth and star quotient, Malibu is best appreciated through its twin natural treasures: the **Santa Monica Mountains National Recreation Area** (Map pp206–7) and the beaches, including **Point Dume**, **Zuma** (this one especially is packed on weekends) and **Surfrider**, a world-famous surf spot. Parking fees vary but average around $8, if you don't strike gold and find a spot on the highway.

Santa Monica

The quintessential LA beach town, Santa Monica melds big-city sophistication with a laid-back, politically progressive, environmentally aware ethos. Bronzed women toting yoga mats share the sidewalk with skateboarding scruffians. It boasts a pleasure pier, pedestrian-friendly Downtown and miles of sandy beaches.

The most recognizable landmark is the **Santa Monica Pier** (Map pp208-09; ☎ 310-458-8900; www.santamonicapier.org; admission free; [♿]), the oldest amusement pier in California (1909), with a vintage **carousel** and small amusement park **Pacific Park** (Map pp208-9; unlimited ride pass adult/child under 7 $20.95/12.95; ⏲ daily in summer, Fri-Sun rest of yr), complete with solar-powered Ferris wheel, a roller coaster and other rides. The city's main **farmers market** (Map pp208-9; Arizona Ave at 3rd St; 8:30am-1:30pm Wed & Sat) is hugely popular and widely considered one of the best in the country.

Meandering under the pier is the 22-mile paved **South Bay Bicycle Trail**. Bike or in-line skate rentals are available on the pier and at beachside kiosks (see p222).

Santa Monica's newest attraction is the seasonally operated **Annenberg Community Beach House** (Map pp208-9; 310-458-4904; www.annenbergbeachhouse.com; 415 Pacific Coast Hwy; admission free, pool adult/child 1-7 $10/4; Jun-early Sep, check website for further details;) on the one-time estate of starlet Marion Davies. Entry is free to the historic mansion, playground and beach, but the lovely pool is open only to holders of a limited number of daily tickets.

The car-free **Third St Promenade** – between Wilshire Blvd and Broadway – is a great place for a stroll and a spot of people-watching. Jugglers, street musicians and Bible-thumpers share space with dinosaur topiaries and (mostly) high-end chain-stores like Anthropologie and Abercrombie & Fitch. For more local flavor, head to celeb-frequented **Montana Av** (Map pp208-9), or down-home **Main St** (Map pp208-9), the neighborhood once nicknamed Dogtown and birthplace of skateboard culture.

Art-lovers should head inland about 2 miles to the **Bergamot Station Arts Center** (Map pp208-9; 2525 Michigan Ave; 10am-6pm Tue-Sat; P), a former rail yard now home to more than 30 avant-garde galleries, including the **Gallery of Functional Art** where clever gifts can be had. To get there, go northeast on Olympic Blvd, turn right on Cloverfield Blvd, and then left on Michigan Ave.

Venice

Venice began as the dream of eccentric tobacco heir Abbot Kinney (1850–1920). Where others saw swampland, he envisioned an amusement park and seaside resort called 'Venice of America' and in the early 1900s carved out canals for Italian *gondolieri* to pole tourists about. Venice faded from the radar until the 1950s and '60s, when its funky vibe drew beatniks and hippies like Jim Morrison. Venice is still a cauldron of creativity, peopled by karmically correct New Agers and a few celebs, including Dennis Hopper and Julia Roberts.

The seaside **Venice Boardwalk** (actually an asphalt beachside strip; Map pp208–9) is a freak show, a human zoo, a wacky carnival and an essential LA experience. Get your hair braided, your karma corrected or a *qi gong* back massage. Encounters with wannabe Schwarzeneggers, hoop dreamers, a Speedo-clad snake charmer or a roller-skating Sikh minstrel are pretty much guaranteed, especially on hot summer afternoons. Alas, the vibe gets a bit creepy after dark.

To escape the hubbub, meander inland to the **Venice Canals** (Map pp208–9), a vestige of Abbot Kinney's dream. Today, ducks preen and locals lollygag in row boats along the serene, flower-festooned waterways.

GET THEE TO THE GETTY

Against its firmament of Hollywood stars, Malibu's cultural star is the **Getty Villa** (Map pp206-7; 310-440-7300; www.getty.edu; 17985 Pacific Coast Hwy; admission free; 10am-5pm Thu-Mon), a hillside replica of a Roman villa that's a fantastic showcase of Greek, Roman and Etruscan antiquities, with stunning sightlines to the shimmering Pacific. Admission is by timed ticket (no walk-ins). MTA bus 534 goes to the villa; be sure to get your ticket punched by the bus driver for admission to the museum.

Further east, the hilltop **Getty Center** (Map pp206-7; 310-440-7300; www.getty.edu; 1200 Getty Center Dr; admission free; 10am-6pm Sun & Tue-Thu, 10am-9pm Fri & Sat) presents triple delights from its perch above the 405 Fwy: a stellar art collection from the Renaissance to David Hockney; Richard Meier's fabulous architecture; and Robert Irwin's seasonally changing gardens. On clear days, add breathtaking views of the city and ocean. Even getting to the 110-acre 'campus' aboard a driverless tram is fun, though you can walk it in 20 minutes. Reach the Getty Center via MTA bus 761.

Parking is $15 at each facility. Parking at the Getty Villa is by reservation only; no reservation is required for the Getty Center.

The hippest shopping strip on LA's west side is funky-sophisticated **Abbot Kinney Blvd** (Map pp208–9), a palm-lined mile of restaurants, yoga studios, art galleries and eclectic shops selling midcentury furniture and handmade perfumes.

There's street parking around Abbot Kinney Blvd and parking lots ($6 to $15) on the beach.

San Pedro

While other LA beachside communities primp, tempt and put on airs, San Pedro (*pee*-droh) feels like what it is: a working port, albeit in the shadow of the ritzy Palos Verdes Peninsula. It began as a lumber port and grew on an influx of Croatian, Italian, Greek, Japanese and Scandinavian fishermen. Today their descendants populate this 90,000-strong enclave, half of the world's third-busiest container port, after Singapore and Hong Kong (the other half is Long Beach). See Tours (p222) for information about cruising the harbor.

San Pedro's symbol is the 1874 **Point Fermin Lighthouse** (Map pp206-7; ☎ 310-241-0684; www.pointferminlighthouse.org; 807 W Paseo del Mar; admission free, donations welcome; ☺ tours 1pm, 2pm, 3pm Tue-Sun), unusually built of wood like a Victorian home. The impressive WWII-era **Fort MacArthur** (Map pp206-7; ☎ 310-548-2631; www.ftmac.org; 3601 S Gaffey St; suggested donation adult/child $3/1; ☺ noon-5pm Tue, Thu, Sat & Sun) displays military history through artifacts and weaponry inside a maze-like battery built into the cliffs.

'Pedro's surfer-meets-sophisticate **Arts District** (Map pp206-7; 6th St btwn Pacific Ave & Palos Verdes St) perks with coffee shops, art galleries, army-surplus stores and restaurants, many in art-deco buildings, including the fabulous 1931 **Warner Grand Theatre** (Map pp206-7; ☎ 310-548-7672, 310-833-8333; www.warnergrand.org; 478 W 6th St).

San Pedro is easiest reached by car. Take the 110 Fwy from either Downtown LA or the 405 Fwy.

Long Beach

LA County's southernmost seaside town hosts the other half of the Port of Los Angeles, but Long Beach's industrial edge has worn smooth in its humming downtown and along the restyled waterfront. Pine Ave is chockablock with restaurants and clubs popular with everyone from coiffed conventioneers to the testosterone-fuelled frat pack.

Long Beach's 'flagship' is the grand (and supposedly haunted!) British ocean liner **Queen Mary** (Map pp206-7; ☎ 562-435-3511; www.queenmary.com; 1126 Queens Hwy; adult/child/senior from $25/13/22; ☺ 10am-6pm), permanently moored here. Larger and fancier than the *Titanic*, it transported royals, dignitaries, immigrants and troops during its 1001 Atlantic crossings between 1936 and 1964. Now visitors can tour its decks, state rooms and dining rooms, and enjoy a meal on board at one of its numerous restaurants. Parking is $12.

Kids will probably have a better time at the **Aquarium of the Pacific** (Map pp206-7; ☎ 562-590-3100; www.aquariumofpacific.org; 100 Aquarium Way; adult/child 3-11/senior over 62 $24/12/21; ☺ 9am-6pm; ♿), a high-tech romp through an underwater world where sharks dart, jellyfish dance and sea lions frolic. Its 12,500 creatures hail from tepid Baja California, the frigid northern Pacific, coral reefs of the tropics and local kelp forests. It's also the only facility in the world that has successfully bred the Seussian-looking weedy sea dragon. Parking is $7. *Queen Mary*/Aquarium combination tickets cost $35 per adult and $19 per child aged three to 11.

A short ride away, the **Museum of Latin American Art** (Map pp206-7; ☎ 562-437-1689; www.molaa.org; 628 Alamitos Ave; adult/child under 12/student/senior $9/free/6/6, Sun free; ☺ 11am-5pm Wed-Sun; Ⓟ) is the only museum in the western USA specializing in contemporary art from south of the border. The permanent collection highlights spirituality and landscapes, and special exhibits are first rate.

Heading east on 4th St brings you to **Retro Row** (Map pp206-7; E 4th St btwn Junipero & Cherry Aves), a hip several blocks of coffee-houses and shops selling vintage clothing and midcentury furniture at prices from 'how much?' to '*how* much?'

I-710, off I-405, reaches Downtown Long Beach as does the MTA Blue Line (p230; 55 minutes from Downtown LA). Once there, Long Beach is easily walkable. Passport mini-buses (www.lbtransit.org) reach all these sights for free except for Retro Row ($1.25).

Santa Catalina Island

Mediterranean-flavored Catalina (population 4000) is just '26 miles across the sea,' as the old song by The Four Preps goes, but it feels an ocean away from LA. Even if it sinks under the weight of day-trippers in summer, stay overnight and you'll feel the ambience go from frantic to romantic.

Part of the Channel Islands (for the national park, see p202), Catalina has a unique ecosystem and history. Until the late 19th century, it was alternately a hangout for sea-otter poachers, smugglers and Union soldiers. Chewing-gum magnate William Wrigley Jr (1861–1932) purchased it in 1919 and brought his baseball team, the Chicago Cubs, here for spring training. In 1924, bison were imported for the shooting of a western (*The Vanishing American*); today their descendants form a managed herd of about 250. Of the island's sun-baked hillsides, valleys and canyons, 88% is owned by the Santa Catalina Island Conservancy, ensuring that most of it remains free of development, though open for visitors.

Tourist activity concentrates in the pint-sized port of Avalon, where a yacht harbor hems in a tiny downtown. Central Avalon is easily traversed on foot in under 10 minutes from the central Green Pier. Avalon's main modes of transportation are golf cart – rent one for about $50 per hour – and the Avalon Trolley (single ride/day pass $2/6).

Avalon's most recognizable landmark is the 1929 art-deco **Casino** (Map p220; ☎ 310-510-0179; 1 Casino Way), not a gambling casino but a cinema and ballroom still in use. Its fabulous murals, twinkling domed ceiling and history can be seen via an amusing one-hour tour (adult/child two to 12 $17.50/14.25). Tour tickets include admission to the **Catalina Island Museum** (Map p218; ☎ 310-510-2414; www.catalinamuseum.org; 1 Casino Way; adult/child 6-15/senior over 60 $5/2/4; ☒ 10am-4pm Apr-Dec, 10am-4pm Fri-Wed Jan-Mar), with modest exhibits about the island's history.

About 1.5 miles inland is the 37-acre **Wrigley Memorial & Botanical Garden** (Map p218; ☎ 310-510-2897; 1400 Avalon Canyon Rd; adult/child $5/free; ☒ 8am-5pm), which has sweeping views,

---

DRIVING TOUR: PALOS VERDES PENINSULA & SOUTH BAY

What to See

Ascending west from San Pedro, the houses thin out and the ocean and sky open up. You'll notice the road rippling and tilting around Portuguese Bend from the earthquake faults below. The **Wayfarers Chapel** (Map pp206-7; ☎ 310-377-7919; www.wayfarerschapel.org; 5755 Palos Verdes Dr S; admission free; ☒ 8am-5pm) is the work of Lloyd Wright (Frank's son), built almost entirely of glass and ensconced in redwoods. Further on, the new **Terranea Resort** (Map pp206-7; ☎ 310-265-2800; www.terranea.com; 6610 Palos Verdes Dr S) perches above the cliffs – stop for lunch at a variety of price points (poolside cafes to pricey fine dining), a walk along its trails or a spa treatment (from $165). As the road swoops north, speed the mansions into the cities of **Redondo Beach, Hermosa Beach** and **Manhattan Beach**, collectively called the South Bay. Manhattan Beach in particular is famous for beach volleyball. At the Redondo Beach Pier, **Naja's Place** (Map pp206-7; ☎ 310-376-9951; 154 International Boardwalk, Redondo Beach; ☒ hours vary) is a beer drinker's nirvana: 77 brews on tap and hundreds more in bottles. Locals flock to **North End Café** (Map pp206-7; ☎ 310-546-4782; 3421 N Highland Ave, Manhattan Beach; mains $6-14; ☒ 8:30am-8pm) for sandwiches, salads and coffees.

The Route

From San Pedro, take Gaffey St south to 25th St and turn right; 25th St becomes Palos Verdes Dr S, heading westward. Past Terranea Resort, the road swings northward and connects with Hwy 1 (Pacific Coast Hwy) south of Redondo Beach. Turn left onto Herondo Ave and right on Hermosa Ave, which parallels the coastline. Veer right onto 27th St, left onto the park-lined Ardmore Ave, left again to Manhattan Beach Blvd, and right onto Highland Ave, the spine of Manhattan Beach.

Time & Mileage

It's around 22 miles from San Pedro to Manhattan Beach on this route, about 50 minutes (outside of rush hour) with no stops. But by all means stop for a beach hike or a bite to eat. You can ride back to San Pedro (via Manhattan Beach Blvd and the 405 Fwy) in about 30 minutes, or continue northward on Hwy 1 (here called Sepulveda Blvd) toward Venice and Santa Monica.

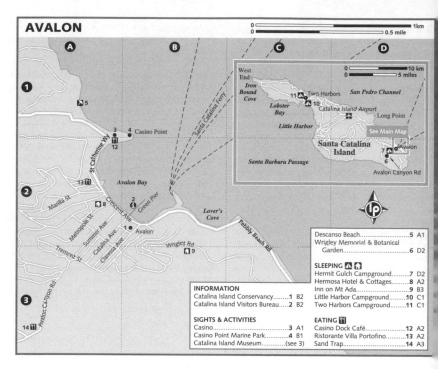

AVALON

INFORMATION
Catalina Island Conservancy........1 B2
Catalina Island Visitors Bureau.....2 B2

SIGHTS & ACTIVITIES
Casino...3 A1
Casino Point Marine Park............4 B1
Catalina Island Museum............(see 3)

Descanso Beach..........................5 A1
Wrigley Memorial & Botanical
Garden.................................6 D2

SLEEPING
Hermit Gulch Campground..........7 D2
Hermosa Hotel & Cottages.........8 A2
Inn on Mt Ada...........................9 B3
Little Harbor Campground.........10 C1
Two Harbors Campground......11 C1

EATING
Casino Dock Café.....................12 A2
Ristorante Villa Portofino.........13 A2
Sand Trap................................14 A3

lots of trails for roaming, handmade local tiles and impressive gardens of cacti and succulents unique to the island.

Avalon's sliver of a beach along Crescent Ave gets packed, and only slightly less so at palm tree–lined **Descanso Beach** (admission $2), a beach club with a bar and restaurant, around the bend from the casino. Better, Avalon has some of Southern California's finest kayaking, and there's snorkeling and scuba diving at Lover's Cove and at Casino Point Marine Park marine reserve. Rent gear at any of these locations or on Green Pier.

Catalina's protected, hilly interior, filled with flora, fauna and memorable vistas of the rugged coast, sandy coves and LA coastline, may only be explored on foot, mountain bike or organized tour. Hikers and cyclists can pick up maps and compulsory permits at the **Catalina Island Conservancy** (Map p218; ☎ 310-510-2595; www.catalinaconservancy. org; 125 Clarissa Ave; biking permit adult/student $35/25, hiking permit free; ☼ 8:30am-4:30pm, closed for lunch). The website has trail details and other locations for permits. Hikers might hop on

the **Airport Shuttle** (☎ 310-510-0143; adult/child round-trip $25/20, reservations required; ☼ from 5 times daily) to the hilltop airport, a popular starting point as you're hiking downhill virtually the whole 10 miles back to Avalon. There's very little shade so bring a hat, sunscreen and plenty of water.

Discovery Tours (☎ 310-510-2500; www.visit catalinaisland.com) and **Catalina Adventure Tours** (☎ 310-510-2888; www.catalinaadventuretours.com) both offer scenic tours ($16 to $70) of Avalon, the canyons, coastline, interior countryside and the fish-rich underwater gardens from a glass-bottom boat.

The following companies operate ferries to Avalon and Two Harbors. Reservations are recommended in summer.
Catalina Express (☎ 310-519-1212, 800-481-3470; www.catalinaexpress.com; adult/child round-trip from $66.50/51) Ferries to Avalon from San Pedro, Long Beach and Dana Point (Orange County) and to Two Harbors from San Pedro (one to 1½ hours, up to 30 daily).
Catalina Marina del Rey Flyer (☎ 310-305-7250; www.catalinaferries.com; adult/child round-trip $83/64) Catamarans to Avalon and Two Harbors from Marina del Rey in LA (one to 1½ hours).

Catalina Passenger Service (☎ 949-673-5245; www.catalinainfo.com; adult/child round-trip $68/51) Catamaran to Avalon from Newport Beach in Orange County (1¼ hours, once daily).

Downtown LA
Downtown is LA's historic core and main business and government district, though for decades it sat empty nights and weekends. A bevy of new cultural, transit and housing options is changing that.

Start by immersing yourself in LA's Spanish Mexican roots, where the city began, at **El Pueblo de Los Angeles**. The 1818 **Avila Adobe** (Map p210; ☎ 213-628-1274; Olvera St; admission free; 🕙 9am-4pm) sits on **Olvera St**, a festive tack-o-rama where you can chomp on tacos and stock up on handmade candy and folkloric trinkets. Nearby the 1939 **Union Station** (Map p210; 800 N Alameda St) is a glamorous edifice of Spanish mission and art-deco design.

The centerpiece of the **Grand Avenue Cultural Corridor** is Frank Gehry's 2003 **Walt Disney Concert Hall** (Map p210; ☎ 323-850-2000; www.laphil.com; 111 S Grand Ave), a gravity-defying sculpture of curving and billowing stainless steel and home of the Los Angeles Philharmonic, now under the baton of Venezuelan phenom Gustavo Dudamel. Tours are available subject to concert schedules.

Rounding out the cultural corridor are the **Museum of Contemporary Art** (MOCA; Map p210; ☎ 213-626-6222; www.moca.org; 250 S Grand Ave; adult/child under 12/student/senior $10/free/5/5, 5-8pm Thu free; 🕙 11am-5pm Mon & Fri, 11am-8pm Thu, 11am-6pm Sat & Sun) and the world-famous stages of the **Dorothy Chandler Pavilion**, **Mark Taper Forum** and **Ahmanson Theater**. Diagonally across from the Ahmanson, architect José Rafael Moneo mixed Gothic proportions with bold contemporary design for his 2002 **Cathedral of Our Lady of the Angels** (Map p210; ☎ 213-680-5200; www.olacathedral.org; 555 W Temple St; admission free; 🕙 6:30am-6pm Mon-Fri, 9am-6pm Sat, 7am-6pm Sun).

Other ethnic enclaves Downtown include **Little Tokyo**, with a contemporary mix of traditional shops, Buddhist temples and restaurants. An increasingly lively **Arts District** (www.ladad.org) is emerging just southeast of Little Tokyo, with some 1200 artists living and working in studios above abandoned warehouses and small factories. **Chinatown** is a few blocks north along Broadway and Hill St, crammed with dim sum parlors,

herbal apothecaries and curio shops. On **Chung King Rd**, an edgy contemporary art gallery scene lures hipsters from around town.

Downtown's newest draw is the $1.7 billion dining and nightlife complex **LA Live** (Map p210), which opened in 2008 at Downtown's southern end, near the convention center. The **Grammy Museum** (Map p210; ☎ 213-765-6800; www.grammymuseum.org; 800 W Olympic Blvd; adult/child 6-17/child under 6/senior over 65/student $14.95/10.95/free/11.95/11.95; 🕙 11:30am-7:30pm Sun-Fri, 10am-7:30pm Sat) offers mind-expanding interative displays of the history of American music and plenty of listening opportunities. Discounted tickets are available through the museum's website. The 7100-seat **Nokia Theatre** (Map p210) hosts the MTV Music Awards and *American Idol* finals. LA Live also includes live-music clubs, a movie megaplex and a dozen restaurants. Across the street, the flying saucer–shaped **Staples Center** (Map p210; ☎ 213-742-7340; www.staplescenter.com; 1111 S Figueroa St) is a sports and entertainment arena with all the high-tech trappings and headliners including the Lakers basketball team and major concert events.

Hollywood, Los Feliz & Silver Lake
First things first: Hollywood the neighborhood is not where one generally goes these days to see stars in the flesh. But even the most jaded visitor may thrill in the famous forecourt of the 1927 **Grauman's Chinese Theatre** (Map p211; ☎ 323-464-6266; 6925 Hollywood Blvd), where generations of screen legends have left their imprints in cement: feet, hands, dreadlocks (Whoopi Goldberg) and even magic wands (the young *Harry Potter* stars). Actors dressed as Superman, Marilyn Monroe and the like pose for photos (for tips).

HOLLYWOOD SIGN FUN FACTS

LA's most recognizable landmark first appeared in 1923 as an advertising gimmick for a real-estate development called Hollywoodland. Over the years the 'land' was dropped, and pranksters have altered the 50ft-tall letters to read 'Hollyweed' and 'Holywood,' among others. A letter mailed to Peg Entwistle (the 24-year-old starlet who jumped from the 'H' in 1932), the day before she killed herself, was an offer to star in a play...about a woman driven to suicide.

Grauman's is on the **Hollywood Walk of Fame** (Map p211), which honors more than 2000 celebrities with stars embedded in the sidewalk between La Brea Ave and Vine St. Real-life celebs sashay along the red carpet for the Academy Awards at the **Kodak Theatre** (Map p211; ☎ 323-308-6363; www.kodaktheatre.com; tours adult/child 3-17/child under 3/senior over 65 $15/10/free/10; ☼ 10:30am-4pm Jun-Aug, 10:30am-2:30pm Sep-May, closed irregularly), open via pricey tours.

The spark plug for the neighborhood's rebirth was **Hollywood & Highland** (Map p211; ☎ 323-467-6412; www.hollywoodandhighland.com; 6801 Hollywood Blvd; admission free; ☼ 24hr), a multistory mall marrying kitsch and commerce. Its plaza is designed to frame views of the **Hollywood Sign** (Map pp206–7).

Following Hollywood Blvd east beyond Hwy 101 (Hollywood Fwy) takes you to the neighborhoods of Los Feliz (lohs *fee*-liss) and Silver Lake, both boho-chic enclaves with offbeat shopping, funky bars and a hopping restaurant scene, as well as resident cool kids like Beck and Flea.

The Metro Red Line (p230) serves Hollywood (Hollywood/Highland station) and Los Feliz (Vermont/Sunset station) from Downtown LA.

Griffith Park

America's largest urban park, **Griffith Park** (Map p211; ☎ 323-644-6661; admission free; ☼ 6am-10pm, trails close at dusk; Ⓟ ♿) is a playground for all age levels and interests. Five times the size of New York's Central Park, it embraces an outdoor theater, zoo, observatory, museum, antique trains, golf, tennis, playgrounds, bridle paths, 53 miles of hiking trails, Batman's caves and even the Hollywood Sign. The **Ranger Station** (4730 Crystal Springs Dr) has maps. Trails include the 3-mile **Mt Hollywood Hiking Trail**, with a spectacular view of the sign.

The **Museum of the American West** (☎ 323-667-2000; www.autrynationalcenter.org; 4700 Western Heritage Way; adult/child 3-12/student/senior over 60 $9/3/5/5, free 2nd Tue each month; ☼ 10am-5pm Tue-Sun, to 8pm Thu Jun-Aug; Ⓟ ♿) exhibits the good, the bad and the ugly of America's westward expansion. Star exhibits include an original stagecoach, a large Colt firearms collection and a nymph-festooned saloon.

On the southern slopes of Mt Hollywood, the 1935 art-deco **Griffith Observatory** (☎ 213-473-0800; www.griffithobservatory.org; 2800 Observatory Rd; admission free, planetarium shows adult/child 5-12/senior over 60 $7/3/5; ☼ noon-10pm Tue-Fri, 10am-10pm Sat & Sun; Ⓟ ♿) has renovated exhibition halls, cutting-edge planetarium technology, shows in the Leonard Nimoy Event Horizon Theater, and opportunities for you to play junior astronomer in its high-power telescopes.

Access to the park is easiest via the Griffith Park Dr or Zoo Dr exits off I-5.

West Hollywood

Rainbow flags fly proudly over Santa Monica Blvd. Celebs keep the gossip rags happy by misbehaving at the clubs on fabled

---

DETOUR: UNIVERSAL STUDIOS HOLLYWOOD

Universal Studios (off Map p211; ☎ 818-622-3801; www.universalstudioshollywood.com; 100 Universal City Plaza; admission over/under 48in $67/57; ☼ hours vary; ♿) first opened to the public in 1915 when studio head Carl Laemmle invited visitors at a quaint 25¢ each (including a boxed lunch) to watch silent films being made. Nearly a century later, Universal remains one of the world's largest movie studios, even if today's visitors are directed to a movie-based theme park where your chances of seeing an actual movie shoot are approximately nil.

Nonetheless, generations of visitors have had a ball here. Start with the 45-minute narrated **Studio Tour** aboard a giant, multicar tram that takes you past working soundstages and outdoor sets like *Desperate Housewives* (when there's no filming). Also prepare to survive a shark attack à la *Jaws* and an 8.3-magnitude earthquake. It's hokey but fun.

Of Universal's thrill rides, top billing goes to the **Simpsons Ride**, a motion-simulated romp 'designed' by Krusty the Clown. **Special Effects Stages** give a glimpse into the craft of moviemaking. **Water World** may have bombed as a movie, but the live action show based on it is a runaway hit, with stunts including giant fireballs and a crash-landing seaplane.

While Universal is generally kid-friendly, Disneyland (p231), Knott's Berry Farm (p234), Legoland (p270) and SeaWorld (p254) are more targeted to the single-digit set.

Parking is $12, or arrive via Metro Red Line.

TOURING THE STUDIOS

Half the fun of visiting LA is hoping you'll see stars. Up the odds by being part of the studio audience of a sitcom or game show, which usually tape between August and March. For free tickets contact **Audiences Unlimited** (☎ 818-260-0041; www.tvtickets.com) or stop by its booth inside Universal Studios Hollywood (p222).

For an authentic behind-the-scenes look, take a small-group tour by open-sided shuttle at **Paramount Pictures** (Map p211; ☎ 323-956-1777; 5555 Melrose Ave, Hollywood; tours $35, minimum age 12; ☒ Mon-Fri) or **Warner Bros Studios** (Map p211; ☎ 818-972-8687; www2.warnerbros.com/vipstudiotour; 3400 Riverside Dr, Burbank, San Fernando Valley; tours $45, minimum age 8; ☒ 8:30am-4pm Mon-Fri, longer in spring & summer) or walking tours of **Sony Pictures Studios** (Map pp206-7; ☎ 323-520-8687; 10202 W Washington Blvd, Culver City; tours $25; ☒ tours at 9:30am, 10:30am, 12:30pm, 1:30pm & 2:30pm Mon-Fri; P). All show you around sound stages and backlots (outdoor sets) and into such departments as wardrobe and make-up. Reservations are required; bring photo ID.

Sunset Strip and browsing sassy and chic boutiques on Robertson Blvd. Welcome to the city of West Hollywood (WeHo), 1.9 sq miles of pure personality.

WeHo's also a hotbed of cutting-edge design for furniture and furnishings, particularly along the **Avenues of Art and Design** (Map p212) around Beverly Blvd and Melrose Ave. Some 130 showrooms fill the monolithic 'blue whale' and 'green whale' of the **Pacific Design Center** (PDC; Map p212; ☎ 310-657-0800; www.pacificdesigncenter.com; 8687 Melrose Ave; ☒ 9am-5pm Mon-Fri), though most sales are to the trade only. A 'red whale' was under construction as we went to press, and there's a small offshoot of the **Museum of Contemporary Art** (MOCA; Map p212; admission free; ☒ 11am-5pm Tue-Fri, 11am-6pm Sat & Sun) behind PDC's main buildings. Parking is $4.50 per hour.

Mid-City

Among LA's dozens of great museums, some of the best line Museum Row, a short stretch of Wilshire Blvd just east of Fairfax Ave.

Los Angeles County Museum of Art (LACMA; Map p212; ☎ 323-857-6000; www.lacma.org; 5905 Wilshire Blvd; adult/child under 17/student/senior $12/free/8/8, 'pay what you wish' after 5pm, 2nd Tue of each month free; ☒ noon-8pm Mon, Tue & Thu, noon-9pm Fri, 11am-8pm Sat & Sun) is one of the country's top art museums and the largest in the western USA. A major 2008 revamp masterminded by Renzo Piano brought the three-story **Broad Contemporary Art Museum** (B-CAM), whose collection includes seminal pieces by Jeff Koons, Roy Lichtenstein, Andy Warhol and Richard Serra.

Elsewhere on LACMA's campus are millennia of paintings, sculpture and decorative arts: Rembrandt, Cézanne and Magritte; ancient pottery from China, Turkey and Iran; photographs by Ansel Adams or Henri Cartier-Bresson; and a jewel box of a Japanese pavilion. There are often headline-grabbing touring exhibits. Parking is $7.

A four-story ode to the auto, the **Petersen Automotive Museum** (Map p212; ☎ 323-930-2277; www.petersen.org; 6060 Wilshire Blvd; adult/child 5-12/senior over 62/student $10/3/5/5; ☒ 10am-6pm Tue-Sun; ☒) exhibits shiny vintage cars galore, plus a fun LA streetscape showing how the city's growth has been shaped by the automobile. Parking is $8.

Between 10,000 and 40,000 years ago, tar-like bubbling crude oil trapped sabertoothed cats, mammoths, dire wolves and other Ice Age critters, still being excavated at **La Brea Tar Pits** (off Map p212). Check out their fossilized remains at the **Page Museum** (Map p212; ☎ 323-934-7243; www.tarpits.org; 5801 Wilshire Blvd; adult/child 5-12/student $7/2/4.50/4.50; ☒ 9:30am-5pm; ☒). An active staff of archaeologists works behind glass. Parking is $6.

Nearby, the **Original Farmers Market** (Map p212; 6333 W 3rd St; P ☒) has plenty of food stalls for a fill-up before hitting the adjacent **Grove** (Map p212), an open-air shopping mall with a musical fountain.

Beverly Hills & Brentwood

The mere words 'Beverly Hills' conjure images of Maseratis, manicured mansions and megarich moguls. Stylish and sophisticated, this is indeed a haven for the well-heeled and famous. See Tours (p222) for guided peeks at stars' homes.

It's pricey and pretentious, but no trip to LA would be complete without a saunter along **Rodeo Drive** (Map p212), the famous three-block ribbon of international style from Armani to Zegna, in killer-design stores.

TV and radio addicts can indulge their passion at the **Paley Center for Media** (Map p212; ☎ 310-786-1000; www.paleycenter.org; 465 N Beverly Dr; suggested donation adult/child under 14/senior/student $10/5/8/8; ⌚ noon-5pm Wed-Sun), a mind-boggling archive of TV and radio broadcasts going back to 1918. Pick your faves, grab a seat at a private console and enjoy.

Several city-owned garages offer two hours of free parking in central Beverly Hills.

Just west of Beverly Hills, in the skyscraper village known as Century City, the **Annenberg Space for Photography** (Map p212; ☎ 213-403 3000; www.annenbergspaceforphotography .org; 2000 Ave of the Stars, No 10; admission free; ⌚ 11am-6pm Wed-Sun) opened in 2009 as the region's first museum of photography, presenting changing shows including the Pictures of the Year exhibit. Parking is $3.50, or $1 on weekends or after 4:30pm daily.

ACTIVITIES
Cycling & In-Line Skating

Skate or ride the paved **South Bay Bicycle Trail** that parallels the beach for 22 miles, from Pacific Palisades (north of Santa Monica) to Torrance in the South Bay. Rentals cost around $7.50 per hour and $18 or $22 per day for in-line skates or bicycles. There are numerous rental shops along the beaches, including the following:

Blazing Saddles (Map pp208-9; ☎ 310-393-9778; Santa Monica Pier, Santa Monica)

Spokes 'n' Stuff (Map pp208-9; ☎ 310-395-4748; 1750 Ocean Front Walk, Santa Monica) On the paved boardwalk behind Loews Hotel.

Hiking

For a quick ramble, head to **Griffith Park** or **Runyon Canyon** (trailhead Fuller St at Franklin Ave). You'll have fine views of the Hollywood Sign, the city and, particularly at Runyon Canyon, eye candy of fitness-obsessed locals and their dogs.

Malibu Creek State Park (Map pp206-7) has a great trail leading to the set of the TV series M*A*S*H, where an old jeep and other relics rust in the sunshine. The trailhead is in the park's main parking lot on Malibu Canyon Rd, which is called

Las Virgenes Rd if coming from Hwy 101 (Ventura Fwy). Parking is $12.

Swimming & Surfing

Top beaches for swimming are Malibu's **Zuma** (Map pp206-7), **Santa Monica State Beach** (Map pp208-9) and **Hermosa Beach** (Map pp206-7).

'Endless summer' is, sorry to report, a myth, so much of the year you'll want to wear a wet suit in the Pacific. Water temperatures become tolerable by June and peak at about 70°F (21°C) in August and September. Water quality varies; for updated conditions check the Beach Report Card at www.healthebay.org.

Good surfing spots for nonbeginners include **Malibu Lagoon State Beach** (Map pp206-7), aka Surfrider Beach, and the **Manhattan Beach** (Map pp206-7) **pier**. Surfing novices can expect to pay about $125 for a two-hour private lesson or $75 for a group lesson, including board and wet suit. The following schools have several beachside locations:

Learn to Surf LA (☎ 310-920-1265; www.learntosurfla .com)

Surf Academy (☎ 877-599-7873; www.surfacademy.org)

TOURS

Esotouric (☎ 323-223-2767; www.esotouric.com; bus tours $58) Hip, offbeat, insightful and entertaining tours themed around famous crime sites (Black Dahlia), literary lions (Chandler to Bukowski) and historical neighborhoods.

Los Angeles Conservancy (☎ 213-623-2489; www .laconservancy.org; tours $10) Thematic walking tours, mostly of Downtown LA, with an architectural focus.

Red Line Tours (☎ 323-402-1074; www.redlinetours .com; tours $25) 'Edutaining' walking tours of Hollywood and Downtown using headsets that cut out traffic noise.

Spirit Cruises (☎ 310-548-8080; www.spiritmarine .com; adult/child $12/6) One-hour boat tours of LA harbor from Long Beach and San Pedro, including shipping terminals and Terminal Island Federal Prison, whose A-list inmates included Al Capone and Timothy Leary.

Starline Tours (☎ 323-463-333, 800-959-3131; www .starlinetours.com; tours from $39) Narrated bus tours of the city, stars' homes and theme parks.

FESTIVALS & EVENTS

LA County has a packed calendar of annual festivals and special events. We've only got space for the blockbusters. For more ideas visit www.culturela.org.

Rose Parade (☎ 626-449-4100; www.tournamentofroses .com) New Year's Day cavalcade of flower-festooned floats along Pasadena's Colorado Blvd, followed by the Rose Bowl football game.

Toyota Grand Prix of Long Beach (☎ 888-827-7333; www.longbeachgp.com) Week-long auto-racing spectacle in mid-April drawing world-class drivers.

Fiesta Broadway (☎ 310-914-0015; www.fiesta broadway.la) Huge street fair along historic Broadway in Downtown, on the last Sunday in April, with performances by Latino stars.

Twilight Dance Series (☎ 310-458-8900; www .santamonicapier.org) Musicians from world beat to world famous perform on the Santa Monica Pier on Thursday evenings from July to early September.

Sunset Junction Street Fair (☎ 323-661-7771; www .sunsetjunction.org) Silver Lake weekend street party in late August, with grub, libations and edgy bands.

West Hollywood Halloween Carnival (☎ 323-848-6400; www.visitwesthollywood.com) Free, rambunctious street fair with eccentric, and often NC-17 rated, costumes on Santa Monica Blvd in WeHo on October 31.

SLEEPING

Your choice of lodging location can be a big part of the LA you experience. For coastal life, base yourself in Santa Monica, Venice or Long Beach. Cool-hunters and party people will be happiest in Hollywood or WeHo, and city-slicker culture-vultures in Downtown. Rates are pretty steep (highest in summer) and further swelled by a lodging tax of 12% to 14%; always ask about discounts.

Santa Monica & Venice

HI-Los Angeles/Santa Monica (Map pp208-9; ☎ 310-393-9913; www.lahostels.org; 1436 2nd St, Santa Monica; dm members/nonmembers $28/31, r with shared bathroom from $104; ☒ ☐ ☎) This 260-bed hostel is in an architecturally interesting building, but it's the killer location – between the beach and Third St Promenade – that really makes it. Rates include linens and continental breakfast.

Hotel Erwin (Map pp208-9; ☎ 310-452-1111; www.jdvhotels.com; 1679 Pacific Ave, Venice; r from $169; ☒ ☐ ☎) Finally, a Venice hotel worthy of the neighborhood. Rooms aren't the biggest and in most there's a low traffic hum, but it's hard to complain when you're steps from the beach and your room features graffiti- or anime-inspired art and honor bar containing sunglasses and '70s-era soft drinks. Its lobby restaurant and rooftop bar are respectively called Hash and High (*nudge, nudge*); the latter boasts spellbinding coastal vistas. Parking is $25.

Embassy Hotel Apartments (Map pp208-9; ☎ 310-394-1279; www.embassyhotelapts.com; 1001 3rd St, Santa Monica; r $175-390; ☒ ☐) This hushed 1927 Spanish colonial hideaway delivers charm by the bucket. A rickety elevator takes you to units oozing old-world flair but equipped with internet. Many rooms have kitchens.

Shangri-La Hotel (Map pp208-9; ☎ 310-394-2791, 877-999-1301; www.shangrila-hotel.com; 1301 Ocean Ave, Santa Monica; r from $305; ☒ ☐ ☎ ☒) This Streamline Moderne building has held court over Ocean Ave since 1929, and finally it is as chic inside as it is outside, thanks to a flashy 2009 redo by the mind behind Downtown's Edison (see p227). Rooms are small, but have a slick design, and some have full kitchens. The party-ready pool deck and rooftop bar host fashion shoots. Parking is $33.

Viceroy (Map pp208-9; ☎ 310-260-7500, 800-622-8711; www.viceroysantamonica.com; 1819 Ocean Ave, Santa Monica; r from $390; ☒ ☐ ☎ ☒) Ignore the high-rise eyesore exterior and plunge into *Top Design*'s Kelly Wearstler's campy 'Hollywood Regency' decor and color palette from dolphin-gray to mamba-green. Look for poolside cabanas, Italian designer linens, and chic bar and restaurant. Parking is $28.

Long Beach

Hotel Varden (Map pp206-7; ☎ 562-432-8950, 877-382-7336; www.thevardenhotel.com; 335 Pacific Ave; r from $109; ☒ ☐ ☎) The designers clearly had a field day performing a modernist renovation in these diminutive rooms in this 1929 hotel near Pine Ave: tiny desks, tiny sinks, lots of right angles, cushy beds, white, white and more white. Rates include simple continental breakfast and wine hour. Parking is $10.

Queen Mary Hotel (Map pp206-7; ☎ 562-435-3511; www.queenmary.com; 1126 Queens Hwy, Long Beach; r $159-259; ☒ ☐ ☎) Take a trip without leaving the dock aboard this grand ocean liner (p216). Staterooms brim with original art-deco details (avoid the cheapest ones, which are on the inside). Rates include admission to guided tours. Parking is $15.

Hotel Maya (Map pp206-7; ☎ 562-435-7676; www.jdvhotels.com; 700 Queensway Dr; r from $189; ☒ ☐ ☎ ☒) Near the *Queen Mary*, the harborside Maya went from noplace to showplace thanks to a recent renovation using natural stone, Mexican tiles and sunny bright colors in the spacious, water-view rooms. Fuego restaurant has bang-on views of Long Beach's downtown. Parking is $10.

Catalina Island

Camping (Map p218; ☎ 310-510-8368; www.visit catalinaisland.com/camping; tent sites per adult/child from $12/6, tent/sleeping bag rentals $16/12) The best way to get up close and personal with the island's natural beauty and possibly bison. There are several campgrounds, including one about 1.5 miles from central Avalon (Hermit Gulch); Little Harbor is especially scenic. Reservations required.

Hermosa Hotel & Cottages (Map p218; ☎ 310-510-1010, 877-453-1313; www.hermosahotel.com; 131 Metropole St; r without bathroom $45-75, cottage with bathroom $65-170) This diver-friendly collection of compact wooden rooms and cottages (some dating back to 1896) is central, tidy and home-style. Rates vary by facilities, including kitchenettes and air-con.

Inn on Mt Ada (Map p218; ☎ 310-510-2030; www.inn onmtada.com; 398 Wrigley Rd; r from $415) This romantic hilltop B&B in the former Wrigley mansion is a worthy splurge for history and unsurpassed views over Avalon. Rates include lots of freebies: golf cart rental, gourmet breakfast, lunch and snacks, and libations all day.

Downtown LA

Millennium Biltmore Hotel (Map p210; ☎ 213-624-1011, 800-245-8673; www.thebiltmore.com; 506 S Grand Ave; r $119-399, ste $460-3000; ✖ 🖥 🛜 🏊) Drenched in tradition and gold leaf, this palatial hotel has bedded stars, presidents and royalty since 1923, although some rooms lack elbow space. The gorgeous art-deco health club takes the work out of workout. Parking is $40.

Figueroa Hotel (Map p210; ☎ 213-627-8971, 800-421-9092; www.figueroahotel.com; 939 S Figueroa St; r $134-164, ste $225-265; ✖ 🖥 🛜 🏊) A rambling 1920s oasis across from LA Live, the Fig welcomes guests with a richly tiled Spanish-style lobby segueing to a sparkling pool and buzzy outdoor bar. Rooms are furnished in a world-beat mash-up of styles (Morocco, Mexico, Japan…) and are comfy but varying in size and configuration. Parking is $12.

Standard Downtown (Map p210; ☎ 213-892-8080; www.standardhotel.com; 550 S Flower St; r from $165; ✖ 🖥 🛜 🏊) This 207-room design-savvy hotel in a former office building goes for a young, hip and party-happy crowd – the rooftop bar fairly pulses – so don't come here with kids or to get a solid night's sleep. Mod, minimalist rooms have platform beds and peek-through showers. Parking is $31.

Hollywood

USA Hostel Hollywood (Map p211; ☎ 323-462-3777, 800-524-6783; www.usahostels.com; 1624 Schrader Blvd; dm incl breakfast & tax from $30-37, r from $70-85; 🖥 🛜) Not for introverts, this energetic hostel puts you within steps of Hollywood's party circuit. Make new friends during staff-organized BBQs, comedy nights and tours, or during free pancake breakfasts in the guest kitchen.

Magic Castle Hotel (Map p211; ☎ 323-851-0800, 800-741-4915; www.magiccastlehotel.com; 7025 Franklin Ave; r from $164; ✖ 🖥 🛜 🏊) Walls are thin, but this renovated former apartment building around a courtyard boasts contemporary furniture, attractive art, comfy bathrobes and fancy bath amenities. Most rooms have separate living room. For breakfast: fresh-baked goods and gourmet coffee on your balcony or poolside. Ask about access to the namesake private club for magicians. Parking is $10.

Hollywood Roosevelt Hotel (Map p211; ☎ 323-466-7000, 800-950-7667; www.hollywoodroosevelt.com; 7000 Hollywood Blvd; r from $399; ✖ 🖥 🛜 🏊) This venerable hotel has hosted elite players since the first Academy Awards were held here in 1929. It pairs a palatial Spanish lobby with sleek Asian contemporary rooms, a busy pool scene and rockin' restaurants. Marilyn Monroe shot her first commercial by the pool. Parking is $30.

West Hollywood, Mid-City & Beverly Hills

Beverly Laurel Motor Hotel (Map p212; ☎ 323-651-2441, 800-962-3824; 8018 W Beverly Blvd; r $109-155; 🅿 ✖ 🛜 🏊) Ride the retro wave on the cheap at this slicked-up 52-room 1950s motel near the Original Farmers Market and Grove. Rooms are just above basic and the pool tiny, but the attached Swingers diner (mains $5 to $11) makes colossal burgers and wicked Bloody Marys.

our pick Farmer's Daughter Hotel (Map p212; ☎ 323-937-3930, 800-334-1658; www.farmersdaughter hotel.com; 115 S Fairfax Ave; r $179-209; ✖ 🖥 🛜 🏊) Opposite the Original Farmers Market, Grove and CBS Studios, this perennial pleaser gets high marks for its sleek 'urban cowboy' look. Adventurous love birds should ask about the No Tell Room. Parking is $17.

Chateau Marmont (Map p212; ☎ 323-656-1010, 800-242-8328; www.chateaumarmont.com; 8221 W Sunset

Blvd; r $345-785;) Its French-flavored indulgence may look dated, but this faux-chateau has long attracted A-listers – Greta Garbo to Bono – with its legendary discretion. The garden cottages are the most romantic, but not everyone is treated like a star. Parking is $28.

Beverly Hills Hotel (Map p212; ☎ 310-276-2251, 800-283-8885; www.beverlyhillshotel.com; 9641 Sunset Blvd; r from $450;) The legendary Pink Palace from 1912 oozes opulence. The pool deck is classic, the grounds lush and the Polo Lounge remains a clubby lunch spot for the well-heeled and well-dressed. Rooms glitter with gold accents and marble tiles. Parking is $33.

EATING
Malibu
Reel Inn (Map pp206-7; ☎ 310-456-8221; 18661 Pacific Coast Hwy; meals $10-32; lunch & dinner;) Across Pacific Coast Hwy from the ocean, this shambling shack with counter service and patio serves up fish and seafood for any budget and in many styles, including grilled, fried or Cajun. The coleslaw, potatoes and Cajun rice (included in most meals) have fans from Harley riders to beach bums and families.

Geoffrey's (Map pp206-7; ☎ 310-457-1519; 27400 Pacific Coast Hwy; mains lunch $14-24, dinner $18-36; 11:30am-10pm Mon-Thu, 11:30am-11pm Fri, 10am-11pm Sat, 10am-10pm Sun) This posh classic has just the right mix of assets for the quintessential Malibu experience: the Pacific Ocean as a back yard, smartly executed Cal-Asian cuisine and a regular clutch of celebrity patrons. In short, it's the perfect date spot, especially at night when romance rules.

Santa Monica & Venice
Omelette Parlor (Map pp208-9; ☎ 310-399-7892; 2732 Main St, Santa Monica; mains $6-12; 6am-2:30pm Mon-Fri, 6am-4pm Sat & Sun;) An institution since when Main St was known as Dogtown, festooned with black-and-whites of old Santa Monica, a soundtrack of oldies and a leafy courtyard out back. Big-as-your-head omelettes and famous waffles for breakfast may last you to dinner.

Axe (Map pp208-9; ☎ 310-664-9787; 1009 Abbot Kinney Blvd, Venice; mains lunch $6-12, dinner $18-26; lunch Wed-Fri, dinner Wed-Sun, brunch 9am-3pm Sat & Sun) An exercise in minimalist refinement, Axe (ah-*shay*) derives from a Yoruba word

meaning 'go with the power of the deities,' presumably derived from the all-organic, farm-fresh ingredients in inventive salads, fab 'flatbread and spreads' plate, or flat iron steak with chimichurri.

Real Food Daily (Map pp208-9; ☎ 310-451-7544; 514 Santa Monica Blvd, Santa Monica; mains $8-17; 11:30am-10pm;) If you're tempted by *tempeh* (soybean cake) or seduced by *seitan* (wheat gluten), or even if you're not, RFD is worth checking out. A vegan place minus the hippie-commune trappings, plus food courtesy of celeb chef Ann Gentry.

3 Square Café & Bakery (Map pp208-9; ☎ 310-399-6504; 1121 Abbot Kinney Blvd, Venice; mains $8-20; breakfast, lunch & dinner) Tiny café and adjacent bakery for devouring Hans Röckenwagner's German-inspired pretzel burgers, gourmet sandwiches and apple pancakes. Bakery shelves are piled high with rustic breads and fluffy croissants.

San Pedro & Long Beach
Utro's (Map pp206-7; ☎ 310-547-5022; Berth 72, San Pedro; dishes $4-12; 11am-4pm Mon-Thu, 11am-7pm Fri-Sun) It doesn't get any more 'Pedro than this longshoremen's hangout, crammed with salty seafarin' types and every inch of wall space covered with memorabilia. It's known for 1/3lb burgers and cold beer; most dishes are under $8.

Sophy's (Map pp206-7; ☎ 562-494-1763; 3240 E Pacific Coast Hwy, Long Beach; mains $6-14; 9am-10pm) North Long Beach is America's largest Cambodian community, with cuisine like a cross between Thai and Vietnamese. Standouts include *such koh ngeat* (beef jerky), beef *lok lak* (in lime and black pepper sauce) and *chanpu* (stir-fried noodles with crabmeat).

Number Nine (Map pp206-7; ☎ 562-434-2009; 2118 E 4th St, Long Beach; mains $7-9; noon-midnight) An enthusiastic, artsy couple of owners serves maximalist portions of Vietnamese noodles in minimalist surrounds on Retro Row. Try the five-spice chicken with egg roll.

George's Greek Café (Map pp206-7; ☎ 562-437-1184; 135 Pine Ave, Long Beach; mains $7-19; 11am-10:30pm Sun-Thu, 11am-11:30pm Fri & Sat) George's is the heart of the Pine Ave restaurant row, both geographically and spiritually. George himself may greet you at the entrance on the generous patio, and locals cry 'opa!' for the *saganaki* (flaming cheese) and lamb chops.

Porky's BBQ (Map pp206-7; ☎ 310-521-9911; www.ribs123.com; 362 W 6th St, San Pedro; mains $7-23; ☽ 11am-9pm Sun-Thu, 11am-10pm Fri & Sat) Between corrugated tin walls or on the teeny tiny terrace in San Pedro's Arts District, enjoy Flintstone-sized sandwiches of brisket or pulled pork, sourdough-style 'Texas toast' and about a dozen slow-cooked, hickory-smoked meats.

Santa Catalina Island

Sand Trap (Map p218; ☎ 310-510-2505; 501 Avalon Canyon Rd; dishes $3-11; ☽ 8am-7pm Wed-Sun) In the shadow of Catalina's golf course, this indoor-outdoor eatery serves burgers and sandwiches, but everyone goes for the award-winning Mexican dishes: tacos, burritos and *huevos rancheros* (ranch-style eggs). The $1 taco happy hour is from 2pm to 7pm.

Casino Dock Café (Map p218; ☎ 310-510-2755; 1 Casino Way; dishes $6-11; ☽ 8am-6pm Apr-Oct) Hoist a beer or indulge in fried seafood at this casual waterside hangout. Live music plays on summer afternoons.

Ristorante Villa Portofino (Map p218; ☎ 310-510-2009; 101 Crescent Ave; mains $15-35; ☽ dinner) The restaurant at the hotel Villa Portofino serves Italian specialties that would be at home at top LA restaurants, such as *mezzeluna di pollo* (chicken-filled pasta) and *vitello al marsala* (veal in mushroom and marsala wine sauce). All served with a view of the harbor.

Downtown LA

Empress Pavilion (Map p210; ☎ 213-617-9898; 3rd fl, Bamboo Plaza, 988 N Hill St; dim sum per plate $2-5, dinner $20-25; ☽ 9am-10pm; **P**) This Hong Kong-style dim sum palace has seating for a small village. Dumplings, wontons, pot stickers, spring rolls, barbecued pork and other delicacies fly off the carts wheeled right to your table by a small army of servers.

Tiara Café (Map p210; ☎ 213-623-3663; 127 E 9th St; sandwiches $8-11, mains $14-16; ☽ 9am-3pm; **V**) Pretty in pink beneath a high ceiling, celeb chef Fred Eric's Fashion District spot feeds designers, sales clerks and bargain hunters with healthy, organic fare: fresh, abundant salads, custom-made sandwiches and lovely, imaginative pizzettes. Check out the amazing collection of anime trinkets.

R-23 (Map p210; ☎ 213-687-7178; 923 E 2nd St; mains lunch $10-15, dinner $40-60; ☽ lunch Mon-Fri, dinner daily) Hidden in the gritty Arts District east of Little Tokyo, R-23 is a fantasy come true for serious sushi aficionados. Not even the bold art and bizarre Frank Gehry–designed corrugated cardboard chairs can distract from the exquisite, ultrafresh treats prepared by a team of sushi masters.

Chosun Galbee (off Map p210; ☎ 323-734-3330 3300 Olympic Blvd, Koreatown; mains $12-24; ☽ 11am-11pm) Great for Korean barbecue virgins as well as serious fanatics. Cook meat on a grill set into your table, preferably on the trendy bamboo-accented terrace. *Galbee* (short rib cubes), *bulgogi* (beef slices) and *dak bukgogi* (chicken) are marinated in tangy soy-sesame sauce. *Panchan* (side dishes included in the price) are varied and excellent: marinated veggies, salads and *kimchi*, Korea's national dish of spicy pickled cabbage.

The stalls of the 1930s **Grand Central Market** (Map p210; ☎ 213-624-2378; 317 S Broadway, Downtown; ☽ 9am-6pm) are atmospheric, historic and tasty. We love Maria's for Ensenada-style fish tacos. Also, browse **LA Live** (Map p210) for about a dozen restaurants from chichi Japanese (Katsuya by Starck) to rockin' fish (Rock'n Fish), Tiki tributes (Trader Vic's) and an all-American beer hall (Yard House).

Hollywood & Los Feliz

The Waffle (Map p211; ☎ 323-465-6901; 6255 Sunset Blvd, Hollywood; most mains $9-12; ☽ 6:30am-2:30am Sun-Thu, 6:30am-4:30am Fri & Sat) After a night out clubbing, do you really feel like filling yourself with garbage? Us too. But the Waffle's 21st-century diner food – cornmeal jalapeño waffles with grilled chicken, carrot cake waffles, mac 'n' cheese, heaping salads – is organic and locally sourced so it's (almost) good for you. Bonus: short but well-chosen wine list.

El Conquistador (off Map p211; ☎ 323-666-5136 3701 W Sunset Blvd, Silver Lake; mains $10-17; ☽ 11am-10pm Sun-Thu, 11am-11pm Fri & Sat) Halloween meets Margaritaville at this campy cantina that's a perfect launchpad for a night on the razzle. Cocktails are ginormous, so be sure to fill up on yummy nachos, quesadillas, enchiladas and other above-average classics.

Musso & Frank Grill (Map p211; ☎ 323-467-7788 6667 Hollywood Blvd, Hollywood; mains $12-35; ☽ 11am-11pm Tue-Sat) Hollywood history hangs thickly in the air at the boulevard's oldest eatery. Waiters balance platters of steaks, chops grilled liver and other dishes harking back to the days when cholesterol wasn't part of our vocabulary. Service is smooth; so are the martinis.

Mid-City & West Hollywood

Canter's Deli (Map p212; ☎ 323-651-2030; 419 N Fairfax Ave, Mid-City; dishes $7-16; 24hr) This institution, open since 1931, is the glue of this Jewish-meets-hipster neighborhood. Intimidated by the phone book–sized menu? Stick to the basics – matzo ball soup, pastrami or corned beef – and you'll be just fine. Service is as sassy as the pickles. The tiny Kibitz Room bar might be showing the game on TV or a rock band.

ourpick Bazaar (Map p212; ☎ 310-246-5555; 465 S a Cienega Blvd, Mid-City; dishes $8-18; dinner nightly, brunch 11am-3pm Sat & Sun) In the SLS Hotel, be dazzled by over-the-top design by Philippe Starck and futuristic tapas by José Andrés: cotton candy foie gras, caprese salad with mozzarella balls that explode in your mouth, and mini-Philly cheesesteaks on 'air bread.' Cocktails and patisserie are similarly *outré*. Caution: those small plates add up.

Marix Tex Mex (Map p212; ☎ 323-656-8800; 1108 N Flores St, West Hollywood; mains $9-19; 11.30am-11pm) Many an evening in Boystown has begun lifting on Marix' patios over kick-ass margaritas, followed by fish tacos, fajitas, chipotle chicken sandwiches, and all-you-can-eat on Taco Tuesdays.

The Ivy (Map p212; ☎ 310-274-8303; 113 N Rob rtson Blvd, West Hollywood; mains $20 29; 11.30am-1pm Mon-Fri, 11am-11pm Sat, 10am-11pm Sun) There always seems to be a paparazzi encampment in the heart of Robertson's fashion frenzy, where the Ivy's picket-fenced porch and rustic cottage are *the* power lunch spot. Chances of catching A-lister babes choke on a carrot stick or studio execs discussing sequels over the lobster omelette are excellent – if you're willing to put up with self-conscious servers and steep prices.

The Original Farmers Market (Map p212; 6333 W rd St; 9am-9pm Mon-Fri, 9am-8pm Sat, 10am-7pm un; P) is a great spot for a casual meal any ime of day.

DRINKING

Cafes

Urth Caffe Santa Monica (Map pp208-9; ☎ 310-314-040; 2327 Main St); West Hollywood (Map p212; ☎ 310-59-0628; 8565 Melrose Ave) Everything costs $1

to $2 more than it should, but consider it the cost of seeing and being seen among hotties, producers and gawkers, over organic libations at these always busy indoor-outdoor cafes. Pastries, salads and panini provide sustenance, and desserts can easily feed two normal people (or nine aspiring actresses).

Intelligentsia Venice Coffeebar (Map pp208-9; ☎ 310-399-1233; 1331 Abbot Kinney Blvd, Venice) Twenty minutes to prepare a cup of joe? In this super-minimalist space, perfectionista barristas ensure that the water temperature is just right before hitting the coffee, and the wait just so before it meets your lips. Less time-intensive beverages are also available.

Bars
SANTA MONICA & VENICE

Chez Jay (Map pp208-9; ☎ 310-395-1741; 1657 Ocean Ave, Santa Monica) Throw your peanut shells on the floor as the managers fill you in on some 50 years of intrigue at this bar-restaurant steps from the Santa Monica Pier. Tales cover Hollywood romance, political machinations and general misbehavior.

Copa d'Oro (Map pp208-9; ☎ 310-576-3030; 217 Broadway, Santa Monica) Chic, small and filled with flattering candlelight, all the better to sip depression-era cocktails mixed by perfectionist yet unpretentious barkeeps. Snack on pressed sandwiches.

On the Waterfront (Map pp208-9; ☎ 310-392-0322; 205 Ocean Front Walk, Venice) Tall glasses of German beer and huge plates of Swiss snackables make for many a memorable afternoon watching the 'bladers, bikers and bohos on the Venice Boardwalk from this indoor-outdoor bar.

See also High, the rooftop bar at Hotel Erwin (p223). Make it part of a pub crawl.

DOWNTOWN LA, HOLLYWOOD & LOS FELIZ
Edison (Map p210; ☎ 213-613-0000; 108 W 2nd St, off Harlem Alley, Downtown; Wed-Sat) *Metropolis* meets *Blade Runner* at this industrial-chic basement boîte where you'll be sipping mojitos surrounded by turbines and other machinery back from its days as a boiler room. Don't worry, it's all tarted up nicely with cocoa leather couches, three cavernous bars and a dress code.

Dresden (Map p211; ☎ 323-665-4294; 1760 N Vermont Ave, Los Feliz) You saw them crooning 'Stayin'

Alive' in *Swingers*; the campy songster duo Marty & Elayne entertains most nights at this retro cool anchor of Los Feliz' coolest strip.

Velvet Margarita (Map p211; ☎ 323-469-2000; 1612 N Cahuenga Blvd, Hollywood) Sombreros, velvet Elvises, cheesy Mexican cult movie projections and margarita-swilling scenesters – it's Cabo San Lucas meets Graceland at this dark palace of kitsch on the Cahuenga Corridor party drag.

See also the rooftop bar at the Standard Downtown (p224).

ENTERTAINMENT

LA Weekly (www.laweekly.com) and the *LA Times* (theguide.latimes.com) have extensive entertainment listings. Snag tickets online, at the box office or through **Ticketmaster** (☎ 213-480-3232; www.ticketmaster.com). Half-price tickets to selected stage shows are available online through **Goldstar** (www.goldstar.com) and, for theater, **LAStageTIX** (www.theatrela.org) and **Plays 411** (www.plays411.com), and in person at the visitors centers in Hollywood and Downtown LA (p213).

LA: SO GAY

Simply put, LA is one of America's gayest cities. The *Advocate* magazine, PFLAG (Parents and Friends of Lesbians and Gays) and America's first gay church and synagogue all started here. Gays and lesbians are woven into every segment of society: entertainment, politics, business and actors/waiters/models.

'Boystown,' Santa Monica Blvd In West Hollywood (WeHo), is gay ground zero. Dozens of high-energy bars, cafés, restaurants, gyms and clubs here are especially busy Thursday through Sunday. Most cater to gay men. Elsewhere, the gay scenes are more laid-back. Silver Lake, LA's original gay enclave, has evolved from largely leather and Levi's to encompass cute multi-ethnic hipsters. Long Beach also has a significant gay community.

LA's Gay Pride celebration (mid-June; www.lapride.org) attracts hundreds of thousands for nonstop partying and a parade down Santa Monica Blvd. Here are some party places to get you started the rest of the year. Freebie listings magazines and the websites www.westhollywood .com and www.gaycities.com have comprehensive listings.

WeHo

The Abbey (Map p212; ☎ 310-289-8410; www.abbeyfoodandbar.com; 692 N Robertson Blvd; mains $9-13; ☽ 8am-2am) From its beginnings as a humble coffeehouse, the Abbey has grown into WeHo's funnest, coolest and most varied bar and restaurant, with dozens of flavored martinis and upscale pub grub. Take your pick of spaces from leafy patio to Goth-mod lounge.

Factory/Ultra Suede (Map p212; ☎ 310-659-4551; www.factorynightclub.com; 652 La Peer Dr) This giant double dance club has an edgy New York feel and sports different stripes nightly, from fashion-forward femmes to male hot bods.

Silver Lake

Akbar (Map p211; ☎ 323-665-6810; www.akbarsilverlake.com; 4356 W Sunset Blvd) Best jukebox in town, casbah atmosphere and a crowd that's been known to change from hour to hour – gay, straight or just hip, but not too-hip-for-you. Some nights the back room's a dance floor; other nights might feature comedy or crafts.

MJ's (off Map p211; ☎ 323-660-1503; www.mjsbar.com; 2810 Hyperion Ave) Popular contempo hangout for dance nights, 'porn star of the week' and cruising. Attracts a younger but diverse crowd.

Beach Cities

Roosterfish (Map pp208-9; ☎ 310-392-2123; www.roosterfishbar.com; 1302 Abbot Kinney Blvd, Venice) The 'Fish has been serving the men of Venice for over three decades, but still feels current and chilled, with a pool table and back patio. Friday nights are busiest.

Silver Fox (Map pp206-7; ☎ 562-439-6343; www.silverfoxlongbeach.com; 411 Redondo Ave, Long Beach) Despite its name, all ages frequent this mainstay of gay Long Beach, especially on karaoke nights. A short drive from shopping on Retro Row.

Cinemas

Angelenos are serious cinephiles, often remaining seated through the end credits. Seeing a flick at **Grauman's Chinese Theatre** (Map p211; ☎ 323-464-6266; 6925 Hollywood Blvd) is a thrill, and any gathering place worth visiting will also have a movie theater; there are 19 screens around Santa Monica's Third St Promenade alone. Here are some other unique venues. Book tickets through **Moviefone** (☎ from any LA area code 777-3456; www.moviefone.com).

American Cinematheque (☎ 323-466-3456; www .americancinematheque.com) Hollywood (Map p211; 6712 Hollywood Blvd); Santa Monica (Map pp208-9; 1328 Montana Ave) Eclectic film fare from around the world.

ArcLight (Map p211; ☎ 323-464-4226; www.arclight cinemas.com; 6360 W Sunset Blvd, Hollywood) A cineaste's favorite, this ultramodern multiplex features assigned seats, the latest technology and no commercials before films (only trailers).

Live Music & Dance Clubs

If you're determined to do the nightclub thing, come armed with a hot bod or a fat wallet to impress the goons presiding over the velvet rope. Covers range from $5 to $20.

Circle Bar (Map pp208-9; ☎ 310-450-0508; 2926 Main St, Santa Monica) This former dive bar has been reincarnated as a sizzling 'meet' market packed with hormone-happy hotties mingling over strong drinks, loud music and a seductive red-on-black decor, but waiting in line to get past the bouncers can be a turn-off.

Conga Room (Map p210; www.congaroom.com; LA Live, Downtown) LA's premier venue for Latin music – partly owned by J-Lo – is right across from the Nokia Theater. Look for sizzling nights courtesy of groups like Ozomatli and Aterciopelados.

Troubadour (Map p212; ☎ 310-276-6168; www troubadour.com; 9081 Santa Monica Blvd, West Hollywood) This legendary rock hall helped catapult the Eagles and Tom Waits to stardom and is still great for catching tomorrow's headliners. A beer-drinking crowd serious about its music keeps attitude to a minimum.

Zanzibar (Map pp208-9; ☎ 310-451-2221; 1301 5th St, Santa Monica; ☟ Wed-Sun) Electronica, Afrobeat and Latin spinmeisters work their turntable magic on throngs of hipsters at this boîte with sensuous African-themed decor. The wraparound bar is great for socializing, while comfy couches invite canoodling.

SHOPPING

Penny-pincher or power shopper, LA bursts with opportunities to drop some cash.

Santa Monica has good boutique shopping on Montana Ave and Main St, while Venice's Abbot Kinney Blvd offers a spirited mix of art, fashion and New Age. If money is no object, Beverly Hills beckons with international couture along Rodeo Dr. Fashionistas (and paparazzi) flock to **Robertson Blvd** (btwn N Beverly & W 3rd St) and **Melrose Ave** (btwn San Vicente & La Brea) in West Hollywood. Silver Lake has cool kitsch and collectibles, especially around **Sunset Junction** (Hollywood & Sunset Blvds), while bargain hunters haunt Downtown's Fashion District.

GETTING THERE & AWAY
Air

LA's main gateway is **Los Angeles International Airport** (LAX; Map pp206-7; ☎ 310-646-5252; www.lawa.org/lax), one of the world's five busiest. All major US carriers and dozens of international airlines fly here. About 22 miles southeast, **Long Beach Airport** (LGB; Map pp206-7; ☎ 562-570-2600; www.longbeach.gov/ airport) is much smaller and easier managed, served by Alaska, Delta, Jet Blue and US Airways. There are occasional fare wars to one airport or the other, though ground transit costs may cancel out any airfare savings.

Bus

The **main Greyhound bus terminal** (Map p210; ☎ 213-629-8401, 800-231-2222; 1716 E 7th St) is in an unsavory part of Downtown, so avoid arriving after dark. Some buses go directly to the **Hollywood bus terminal** (Map p211; ☎ 323-466-6381; 1715 N Cahuenga Blvd). Greyhound buses serve Santa Barbara ($18, three hours), San Francisco ($48, from 7½ hours), San Diego ($18, from two hours) and Anaheim for Disneyland ($10, 40 minutes).

Car

The usual international car-rental agencies have branches throughout LA (see p290 for central reservation numbers). At LAX, if you don't have a prebooking, use courtesy phones in the arrival areas and catch free shuttles to the agencies' off-airport locations. Ecoconscious travelers can try Simply Hybrid (p290) or Zipcar (p290).

Train

Amtrak trains roll into Downtown's historic **Union Station** (Map p210; ☎ 800-872-7245; 800 N Alameda St). The *Pacific Surfliner* travels daily to San Diego ($34, three hours), Santa Barbara ($18, three hours) and San Luis Obispo ($38, 5½ hours).

GETTING AROUND
To/From the Airport

At LAX, door-to-door shuttles operated by **Prime Time** (☎ 800-473-3743; www.primetimeshuttle.com) and **Super Shuttle** (☎ 310-782-6600; www.supershuttle.com) leave from the lower level of all terminals. Typical fares to Santa Monica, Hollywood or Downtown are $21, $26 and $16 respectively. **Disneyland Express** (☎ 714-978-8855; www.grayline.com) travels at least hourly between LAX and Disneyland-area hotels (one way/round trip $22/32).

Curbside dispatchers will summon a taxi for you. There's a flat fare of $46.50 to Downtown LA, and metered fares average $30 to Santa Monica, $42 to Hollywood, and up to $90 to Disneyland. There is a $2.50 surcharge for taxis departing LAX. See below for further information.

LAX Flyaway Buses (☎ 866-435-9529; www.lawa.org/flyaway) depart LAX terminals every 30 minutes from about 5am to midnight, nonstop to Westwood ($5, 30 minutes) and Union Station ($7, 45 minutes) in Downtown LA.

Other public transportation is cheaper but more bother. From the lower level outside terminals, catch a free shuttle bus to parking lot C, from where it is a walk of under a minute to the LAX Transit Center and buses serving all of LA. You can also take shuttle bus G to Aviation Station and the Metro Green Line light rail, from where you can connect to the Blue Line and Downtown LA or Long Beach (40 minutes).

Bicycle

Most buses are equipped with bike racks. Bikes are also allowed on Metro rail trains except during rush hours. For rental places, see p222.

Car & Motorcycle

Parking at motels and cheaper hotels is usually free, while fancier ones charge anywhere from $8 to $30. Valet parking at restaurants, hotels and nightclubs is commonplace, with fees up to about $10, plus a small tip. Keep *plenty* of change in your car for meters. It goes without saying that you should try to avoid driving during rush hours.

Public Transportation

LA's **Metro** (☎ 800-266-6883; www.metro.net) operates about 200 bus lines and six subway and light rail lines including:

Blue Line Downtown (7th St/Metro Center) to Long Beach.
Expo Line Downtown (7th St/Metro Center) to Culver City.
Green Line Norwalk to Redondo Beach.
Purple Line Downtown to Koreatown.
Red Line Union Station to North Hollywood, via Downtown, Hollywood and Universal Studios.

Tickets cost $1.25 per boarding (get a transfer when boarding if needed). There are no free transfers between trains and buses, but 'TAP card' unlimited ride passes cost $5/17 per day/week. Bus drivers sell regular fares and same-day passes (exact fare required). Purchase train tickets at vending machines in stations. Trip planning help is available at ☎ 800-266-6883 or online at www.metro.net.

Local **DASH minibuses** (☎ your area code + 808-2273; www.ladottransit.com; 25¢) serve Downtown and Hollywood. Santa Monica-based **Big Blue Bus** (☎ 310-451-5444; www.bigbluebus.com; 75¢) serves much of western LA and LAX. Its Line 10 Freeway Express connects Santa Monica with Downtown LA ($1.75, one hour).

Taxi

Except for taxis lined up outside airports, train stations, bus stations and major hotels, it's best to phone for a cab. Fares are metered, $2.85 at flag fall plus $2.70 per mile. Taxis serving the airport accept credit cards, though sometimes grudgingly. Some recommended companies:

Checker (☎ 800-300-5007)
Independent (☎ 800-521-8294)
Yellow Cab (☎ 800-200-1085)

ORANGE COUNTY

Although it's 34 independent cities, Orange County (OC) identifies itself as a county more than any other in Southern California

Indulgent TV shows from *The OC* to *Real Housewives* have cemented the county's reputation as a place seething with the spoiled and the rich, and Angelenos poke

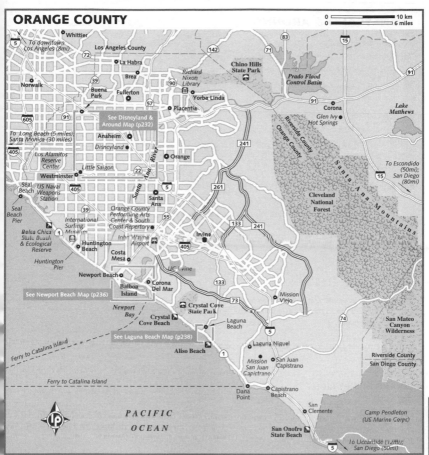

ORANGE COUNTY

fun at their neighbors to the south. 'Behind the Orange Curtain' is a vague reference to the county's brand of conservatism, an amalgam of Christian fundamentalism, materialism, libertarianism and anti-immigrantism. Orange County hurls it right back, with some justification. Laguna Beach supports a flourishing arts community, and the OC's cultural institutions – and beaches – are some of America's best.

Information

The knowledgeable folks at the **Anaheim/Orange County Visitor & Convention Bureau** (Map p232; ☎ 714-765-8888; www.anaheimoc.org; 800 W Katella Ave, Anaheim; ☺ 8am-5pm Mon-Fri) can help plan your OC visit.

DISNEYLAND RESORT

Whether you're as rigid with excitement as the kids or considering repairing to the car to read for 12 hours, there's no denying the saccharine, singsong pull of Disneyland. One simply can't help but be amazed by this alternate universe, where each detail has been carefully 'imagineered,' from the pastel sidewalks to the personal hygiene of the park's 21,000 cast members (read: employees). Disney's California Adventure (DCA) next door pays tribute to the state's history and natural wonders.

Tickets & Opening Hours

Both parks are open 365 days a year, but hours can vary. During peak season (mid-

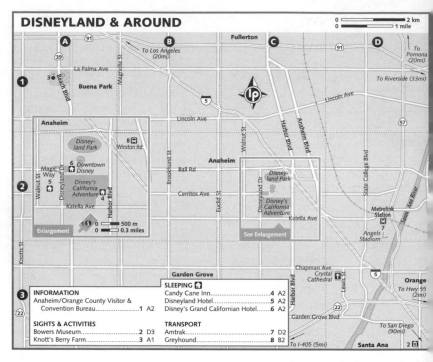

DISNEYLAND & AROUND

INFORMATION
Anaheim/Orange County Visitor &
Convention Bureau........................1 A2

SIGHTS & ACTIVITIES
Bowers Museum................................2 D3
Knott's Berry Farm............................3 A1

SLEEPING 🏠
Candy Cane Inn...............................4 A2
Disneyland Hotel.............................5 A2
Disney's Grand Californian Hotel.......6 A2

TRANSPORT
Amtrak..7 D2
Greyhound.......................................8 B2

DOING DISNEY RIGHT

Here are some tips to help you make the most of your visit:

- Plan on at least one day for each park, more if you want to go on all the rides. Lines are longest during summer and around major holidays. In December and the first week of January crowds pack the resort to see the holiday decorations. In general, visiting midweek is better than Friday, Saturday or Sunday, and arriving early in the day is best.

- Bring a hat, sun block and bottled water.

- If you're not going back to your hotel to eat, make lunch reservations as soon as you arrive.

- Consider returning to your hotel in the heat of the day. The kids can frolic in the pool while you doze with a book on your face. Come 9pm, while you're standing around waiting for the fireworks display, you'll be really glad you did.

June to early September) Disneyland's hours are usually 8am to midnight. The rest of the year it's open from 10am to 8pm or until 10pm. DCA closes at 10pm in summer, earlier in the off-season. Check the current schedule at ☎ 714-781-4565 or www.disneyland.com.

One-day admission to either Disneyland or DCA costs $69 for adults, $59 for children aged three to nine. A Parkhopper ticket (for both parks in one day) costs $94/84 per adult/child. Two- to six-day passes range from $143/123 to $249/219, valid for up to a 13-day period.

The free Fastpass system pre-assigns boarding times for about a dozen attractions. Get tickets from Fastpass machines near the ride entrances, show up at the time printed on the ticket, and go to the Fastpass line. There's still a wait, but it'll be much shorter. Note that you can get only one Fastpass at a time.

Disneyland

Upon entering **Disneyland** (☎ recorded info 714-781-4565, live assistance 714-781-7290; www.disneyland .com; ♿) you're funneled onto Main S

USA, fashioned after Walt's hometown of Marceline, Missouri. Main St ends in the Central Plaza, from which all the 'lands' extend (Frontierland, Tomorrowland etc). Lording over the plaza is one of Disneylands most famous icons, **Sleeping Beauty Castle**, above which nightly fireworks displays take place.

Disney's California Adventure
DCA covers more acres than Disneyland, feels less crowded, and has a mix of attractions and straightforward amusement park–style rides.

The **Hollywood Pictures Backlot** includes a mishmash of building styles. You'll do a serious double-take where a forced-perspective sky-and-land mural makes it look like the street keeps going. The 183ft-tall **Twilight Zone Tower of Terror** is essentially a drop down an elevator chute in a haunted hotel. **California Screamin'** roller coaster covers 10 acres. The **Toy Story Mania** ride feels as if you're in a video game; 3-D glasses give you the illusion of throwing pies and breaking plates to score points.

Sleeping & Eating
Candy Cane Inn (714-774-5284, 800-345-7057; www.candycaneinn.net; 1747 S Harbor Blvd; r $99-189; P X B R) Adjacent to Disneyland's main gate, this might actually be the happiest place around. Guests rave about its sparkling pool and spotless (if a bit cramped) rooms, complimentary continental breakfast and gorgeous gardens.

Disneyland Hotel (714-778-6600; 1150 Magic Way; r $255-345; P X B R) The park's original hotel, with a whopping 969 rooms, hasn't lost its appeal, though its three towers feel a bit retro-mod these days. Turn off the lights in your room and Tinker Bell's pixie dust glows in the dark on the walls. The Neverland-themed pool has a 110ft waterslide, and kids can play aboard Captain Hook's Pirate Ship. Sweet.

our pick **Disney's Grand Californian Hotel** (714-635-2300; 1600 S Disneyland Dr; r from $550; P X B R) Timber beams rise majestically above the cathedral-like lobby of this six-story monument to the American arts-and-crafts movement. Cushy amenities include triple-sheeted beds, custom bedspreads and bathrobes, and a spa. At night kids wind down with bedtime stories by the

lobby's giant stone hearth. Worth visiting even if you don't stay here.

Each of Disney's 'lands' has cafeteria-style eating options, and all Disney restaurants have kids' menus. Call **Disney Dining** (714-781-3463) to make reservations and inquire about character dining – Disney characters work the dining room and greet kids during meals. **Downtown Disney** (www.disneyland.com) shopping district has dozens of choices from fast food to fine dining.

Getting There & Away
The Anaheim Resort is off I-5, about 30 miles south of Downtown LA; exit Disneyland Dr. Enter the 'Mickey & Friends' parking structure from southbound Disneyland Dr at Ball Rd (the largest parking structure in the world, with room for 10,300 vehicles). Parking costs $12.

See p230 for bus services from Los Angeles International Airport.

Two blocks from Disneyland, **Greyhound** (714-999-1256; 100 W Winston Rd) runs frequent departures to/from Downtown LA ($10, 40 minutes).

Amtrak (714-385-1448; www.amtrak.com; 2150 E Katella Ave) trains stop next to Angels Stadium.

Tickets to/from LA's Union Station are $12 (40 minutes).

Getting Around

Many hotels and motels have free shuttles to Disneyland and other area attractions.

Anaheim Resort Transit (ART; ☎ 714-563-5287; www.rideart.org) provides a frequent bus service between Disneyland and nearby hotels. Before boarding pick up an all-day pass ($4) at kiosks or online. Otherwise it's $3 per one-way trip.

HUNTINGTON BEACH

pop 194,000

Welcome to 'Surf City, USA,' officially. In 2006, Huntington Beach (HB) won a drawn-out legal battle with Santa Cruz for that title, a story that neatly symbolizes the distinctly Californian balance between beach-bum blasé and cutthroat competitiveness.

In 1907, to attract home buyers, megadeveloper Henry Huntington brought over Hawaiian-Irish surfing star George Freeth to give demonstrations, an event considered the birth of mainland surfing. Over a century later, HB's 8.5 miles of wide sandy beaches continue to attract both sun-worshippers and surf-worshippers, unperturbed by helicopters roaring overhead or the view of oil pumps. Chances are

you'll understand it too, once you snag a beachside fire pit, watch the sunset and eat s'mores until 10pm.

Huntington Beach Marketing & Visitors Bureau (☎ 714-969-3492; www.surfcityusa.com; Suite 208, 301 Main St; ☼ 9am-5pm Mon-Fri) provides information. An **information kiosk** (1 Main St; ☼ 11am-7pm) at the entrance to the pier is probably more useful, providing maps and info, and able to make hotel and restaurant reservations.

Sights & Activities

Surfing in HB is competitive. Control your longboard or draw ire from locals. **Zack's Pier Plaza** (☎ 714-536-0215; www.beachfoodfun.com; 405 Pacific Coast Hwy; lessons from $75) is a family-owned surf school and bike and boogie board rental shop that can also provide supplies for your beach barbecue. Lessons are also available from **M&M Surfing School** (☎ 714-846-7873; www.mmsurfingschool.com; lessons from $65) in neighboring Seal Beach.

The **International Surfing Museum** (☎ 714-960-3483; www.surfingmuseum.org; 411 Olive Ave; suggested donation $2; ☼ noon-5pm Mon-Fri, 11am-6pm Sat & Sun), off Main St, has exhibits chronicling the sport's history through rotating exhibits of photos, film, music and memorabilia.

Car buffs should get up early for a meander through the **Donut Derelicts Car Show** (www.donutderelicts.com; cnr Magnolia St & Adams Ave; ☼ 6-8:30am Sat), a weekly gathering of

---

DETOUR: KNOTT'S BERRY FARM

If financial, moral or agoraphobic reasons are putting you off a visit to that other theme park, consider smaller, quainter, less commercially frenzied **Knott's Berry Farm** (Map p232; ☎ 714-220-5200; www.knotts.com; 8039 Beach Blvd, Buena Park; adult/child $53/24; ☼ from 10am; ☝). Just 4 miles northwest of Anaheim off I-5, Knott's claims to be America's first theme park, dating from 1934 when Walter Knott's boysenberries (a loganberry-blackberry-raspberry hybrid) and his wife Cordelia's fried-chicken dinners attracted crowds of local farmhands. By 1940 Mr Knott had built an imitation ghost town to keep their guests entertained, which gave way to carnival rides.

The Old West motif is still here, but nowadays thrill rides are the draw, like the **Xcelerator**, a '50s-themed roller coaster that blasts you from 0mph to 82mph in 2.3 seconds. The teeth-chattering **GhostRider** is one of the best wooden roller coasters in California, hurtling along a neck-breaking 4530ft track, at one point plunging 108ft with a G-force of 3.14. For pre- and elementary schoolers, Camp Snoopy has old-fashioned carnival rides themed around the Peanuts gang.

If, after all that, your stomach's up for it, you can still enjoy Mrs Knott's classic fried-chicken dinners (mains $10 to $16, slice of pie $3.75) in a restaurant seating 900.

Halloween is serious business here. In October the park morphs into 'Knott's Scary Farm,' devoted to scaring the bejesus out of visitors, with walk-through mazes, 'scare zones' and countless varieties of the undead on the prowl for fresh blood.

Save time and money by printing tickets online. Parking is $10 (free for restaurant patrons for up to two hours). Closing times vary from 6pm to 1am; check the website.

woodies, beach cruisers and pimped-out street rods.

There are over 50 surfing competitions each year, but the biggest is the **US Open of Surfing** (www.usopenofsurfing.com; ☺ mid-late Jul), which also includes extreme sports like BMX biking in a bowl and even a snowboarding competition on imported snow.

Sleeping & Eating

Shorebreak Hotel (☎ 714-861-4470, 877-744-1117; www.shorebreakhotel.com; 500 Pacific Coast Hwy; r $239-439; 🛄 🖳 🛜) Stow your surfboard (lockers provided) and head inside HB's newest and hippest hotel (opened 2009), a stone's throw from the pier. The Shorebreak spruces things up with an indoor-outdoor fitness center, beach yoga, and bean bag chairs and rattan and hardwood furniture in geometric patterned rooms.

Sugar Shack (☎ 714-536-0355; 213 Main St; dishes $5-8; ☺ from 6am, closing times vary) Arrive at this local icon (since 1967) at 6am to watch surfer dudes don their wet suits, before your huge-portion breakfast. Expect a wait, especially if you want to sit outside. Photos of surf legends (and a bit o' religion) plastering the walls raise it almost to museum status.

Bodhi Tree (☎ 714-969-9500; 501 Main St; dishes $6-14; ☺ 11am-10pm; Ⓥ) Just outside the town center, this 100% vegan Thai-Vietnamese joint carries a huge and varied menu. The orange 'chicken' is delish, as is the Vietnamese sandwich.

Getting There & Away

OCTA (☎ 714-560-6282; www.octa.net) bus 1 connects HB with the rest of OC's beach towns. Maximum parking in municipal lots is $12 per day.

NEWPORT BEACH

pop 86,500

A long peninsula and maze of man-made islands and inlets make Newport Beach one of the largest pleasure harbors on the globe – for the miniscule percentage of humans who can afford to drop anchor here. Indeed, Newport Beach oozes wealth. For the rest of us, the town beckons with family-friendly beaches and several stroll-worthy historical areas.

Newport Beach Conference & Visitors Bureau ☎ 800-942-6278; www.visitnewportbeach.com; 1200 Newport Center Dr, Suite 120; ☺ 8am-5pm Mon-Fri)

> ### CULTURE WITH A BIG C IN THE OC
>
> Orange County may have a reputation for beaches, beemers and mouse-ears, but there's also some surprisingly highbrow culture. In the city of Costa Mesa, next to Newport Beach, **Orange County Performing Arts Center** (☎ 714-556-2777; www.ocpac .org; 600 Town Center Dr, Costa Mesa) hosts the Pacific Symphony and Philharmonic Society of Orange County, and **South Coast Repertory** (☎ 714-708-5555; www.scr.org; 655 Town Center Dr, Costa Mesa) has developed many Pulitzer Prize–winning or –nominated works. In Santa Ana, the county seat, the **Bowers Museum** (Map p232; ☎ 714-567-3600; www .bowers.org; 2002 N Main St; adult/child $12/9; ☺ 11am-4pm Tue-Sun) mounts high-profile exhibits of Californian, Native American and Latin American art that LA museums envy.

---

provides maps, brochures and other tourist information at its main office near Fashion Island shopping center.

Sights

Six miles long, **Balboa Peninsula** has a white-sand beach on its ocean side and a great many stylish homes. Hotels, restaurants and bars cluster around the peninsula's two piers: **Newport Pier**, near its western end, and **Balboa Pier** at the eastern end.

The **Newport Harbor Nautical Museum** (☎ 949-675-8915; www.nhnm.org; 600 E Bay Ave; adult/child/student $5/free/3 ☺ 11am-7pm late Jun-early Sep, 11am-5pm Sun, Wed & Thu, 11am-6pm Sat & Sun early Sep-late Jun) has recently opened in an expanded facility, with a large collection of model ships and a touch tank filled with the prickly, the bumpy, the slick and the slimy. The landmark 1905 **Balboa Pavilion** is illuminated at night, with a historic Ferris wheel nearby.

At the very tip of the peninsula adjacent to West Jetty View Park, the **Wedge** is a famous bodysurfing spot. When the timing's right – in summer – waves bouncing off the jetty meet others barreling in from the sea, and the resulting hollow tunnel can reach 30 bone-crushing feet tall. Watching people get 'thumped' is a popular spectator sport.

In the middle of the harbor sits **Balboa Island**, the little island that time forgot, its streets still largely lined with tightly clustered cottages built in the 1920s and '30s.

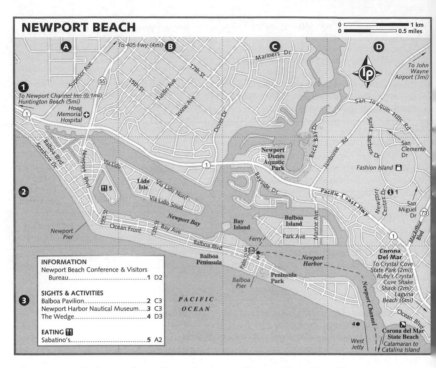

NEWPORT BEACH

| 0 | 1 km |
| 0 | 0.5 miles |

The promenade that circles Balboa Island makes a terrific walk. The island is connected to the mainland by a bridge from Jamboree Rd, or to the peninsula via a tiny car and passenger **ferry** (☎ 949-673-1070; www .balboaislandferry.com; adult/child $1/0.50, car & driver $2; ☼ 6am-2am).

Heading south on Pacific Coast Hwy takes you to Newport Coast, in whose rolling hills nestle pricey condo complexes, which slope down to the intimate Crystal Cove State Park.

Sleeping & Eating
Crystal Cove Beach Cottages (☎ 800-444-7275; www .reserveamerica.com; Crystal Cove State Park; r $33-191; P) These 20 or so shambling beachfront shacks – some little more than dorms with shared facilities – look much as they might have in the 1930s to '50s. Some sleep up to nine people. You'll need to plan carefully in order to snag one though; reservations become available six months ahead of time (on the first day of the month) and are usually gone within hours. Cancellations are sometimes available.

Newport Channel Inn (☎ 949-642-3030, 800-255-8614; www.newportchannelinn.com; 6030 W Coast Hwy; r $119-149; P ⊠) Just across Pacific Coast Hwy from the beach and bike path, this spotless two-story motel offers large rooms with refrigerator and microwave, a big common sundeck and friendly owners. A great deal in this pricey hotel town.

ourpick Resort at Pelican Hill (☎ 949-467-6800, 800-820-6800; www.pelicanhill.com; 22701 Pelican Hill Rd S; r from $695; P ⊠ ▢ ⊜ ▣) At this new Tuscan-themed resort secluded in the hills of Newport Coast, mature trees and Palladian columns line the way to its 204 bungalows and cottages. Pleasures include the world's largest round swimming pool (136ft in diameter), a 36-hole golf course, soothing spa, top-notch Italian fare at Andrea restaurant and staff who define solicitous. Rates are sky high, but the pampering is priceless.

Ruby's Crystal Cove Shake Shack (7703 E Coast Hwy; shakes $5, sandwiches $6-9) This historic spot recently received a face-lift, new first name and menu expansion, and lost some character lines in the process. But the (in)famous – and enormous – date shake is still delicious.

Sabatino's (☎ 949-723-0621; Suite D, 251 Shipyard Way; lunch $10-17, dinner $12-25; ☺ lunch & dinner daily, breakfast Sat & Sun) The claim to fame of this authentic Italian place is its handmade sausage, blended with goat cheese for that cholesterol double-whammy. Family-sized deli sandwiches, spanking-fresh seafood and Sicilian-style pastas keep the locals coming back. It's hard to find; when you get lost, just call.

Getting There & Around
OCTA (☎ 714-560-6282; www.octa.net) bus 1 connects Newport Beach with the rest of OC's beach towns. Bus 71 goes to the end of the Balboa Peninsula.

LAGUNA BEACH
pop 23,700

Secluded down a long canyon and ensconced in wooded hillsides, seaside cliffs, pristine beaches and azure waves, Laguna Beach boasts one of OC's prettiest stretches of coast.

Artist Norman St Clair 'discovered' Laguna around 1910, and soon other artists influenced by French impressionism, who came to be known as the *plein air* school, were setting up camp. By the late '20s, more than half of the town's 300 residents were artists. Real-estate prices make such ratios impossible these days, but the town's artistic heart still beats vigorously. Public sculpture graces the streets and parks, dozens of galleries feature local artists and the city hosts several renowned festivals.

Laguna is also the center of the OC's gay scene. Although the legendary Boom Boom Room club has closed, West St Beach remains a popular summer meeting place.

Orientation & Information
Laguna's beach stretches for 7 miles, but the downtown 'Village' – beguiling shops, restaurants and bars, many hidden in courtyards and funky shacks – occupies about a quarter-mile stretch along three parallel streets: Broadway, Ocean Ave and Forest Ave. S Coast Hwy runs south from the Village, parallel to the water, and N Coast Hwy runs north of the Village.

Pick up info, maps and guides at **Laguna Beach Visitors Bureau** (☎ 949-497-9229, 800-877-1115; www.lagunabeachinfo.com) 252 Broadway (☺ 10am-4pm Mon-Fri); 381 Forest Ave (☺ 10am-5pm Mon-Sat, noon-4pm Sun).

Sights & Activities
Laguna has 30 public beaches and coves. Though many are hidden from view by multimillion-dollar homes, most are accessible by stairs off S Coast Hwy; just look for 'beach access' signs.

Main Beach has volleyball and basketball courts and a playground, and is the best beach for swimming. Northwest of Main Beach, the area is too rocky to surf; tide pooling is best. Tiny **Brown's Park** (551 S Coast Hwy), more of a sculpture-lined garden alley, dead-ends in a deck overlooking Main Beach.

Just northwest of Main Beach, the grassy, bluff-top **Heisler Park** has sweeping views of the craggy coves and deep blue sea. Drop down below the park to **Diver's Cove**, a deep, protected inlet popular with snorkelers and, of course, divers.

Gallery hoppers: on S Coast Hwy, there's a gallery at least every couple of blocks. Of

---

PAGEANT OF THE MASTERS

Laguna Beach's trademark, the **Festival of Arts** (☎ 800-487-3378; www.foapom.com; 650 Laguna Canyon Rd; adult/student $7/4; ☺ from 10am Jul & Aug) is a seven-week juried exhibit of over 140 artists whose work varies from paintings to handcrafted furniture to scrimshaw. Begun in 1932, the festival now attracts patrons and tourists from around the world.

The highlight of the fair is the **Pageant of the Masters** (☎ 949-497-6582, 800-487-3378; www .pageanttickets.com; admission $20-100; ☺ 8:30pm Jul & Aug), in which human models (resident Lagunans) blend seamlessly into re-creations of famous works of art – mostly paintings, but sometimes sculptures, coins, even hood ornaments. The lineup of works changes every year, but The Last Supper is always included. The viewings are accompanied by live orchestral music and engaging narration. Binoculars will enhance the experience, no matter where you're sitting. Bring a jacket; the venue is an outdoor amphitheater.

It's wise to buy Pageant tickets as early as possible; hard-core Pageantistas purchase them when they go on sale each December.

special note is the site of the first 'Whaling Wall,' now a gallery of the marine artist **Wyland** (☎ 949-376-8000; www.wyland.com; 509 S Coast Hwy), whose 100 (and counting) murals of whales adorn buildings worldwide.

The **Laguna Art Museum** (☎ 949-494-8971; www .lagunaartmuseum.org; 307 Cliff Dr; adult/child under 12/ student $15/free/12; ⏰ 11am-5pm, occasional extended hours) has changing exhibits usually featuring California artists, plus a permanent collection heavy on California landscapes and vintage photographs.

Sleeping & Eating

Rates here are for high season (late May to early September) and can fall steeply at other times.

Pacific Edge Hotel (☎ 949-494-8566, 866-932-2896; www.pacificedgehotel.com; 647 S Coast Hwy; r from $149; ⓟ 🖥 🛜 🐾) This cluster of beachside buildings boasts a combined 130 rooms renovated with mid-century furniture and candy colors. About half have ocean views, and many are suites with kitchenettes. Kick back on your deck with brewskis and watch the sun set, or borrow lounge chairs and umbrellas for the hotel's stretch of private beach.

Tides Inn (☎ 949-494-2494, 888-777-2107; www.tides laguna.com; 460 N Coast Hwy; r $175-285; 🖥 🐾) For Laguna this 21-room place is a bargain, especially considering its location three blocks north of the town center, bend-over-backwards service and comfortable rooms – though

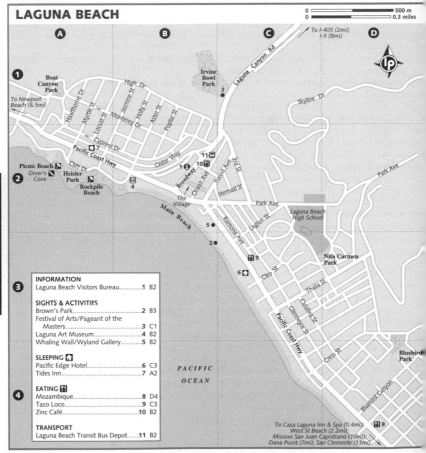

LAGUNA BEACH

INFORMATION	
Laguna Beach Visitors Bureau............1	B2

SIGHTS & ACTIVITIES	
Brown's Park.......................................2	B3
Festival of Arts/Pageant of the	
Masters...3	C1
Laguna Art Museum...........................4	B2
Whaling Wall/Wyland Gallery...........5	B2

SLEEPING 🏠	
Pacific Edge Hotel..............................6	C3
Tides Inn...7	A2

EATING 🍽	
Mozambique......................................8	D4
Taco Loco..9	C3
Zinc Café...10	B2

TRANSPORT	
Laguna Beach Transit Bus Depot......11	B2

DETOUR: SAN JUAN CAPISTRANO

Famous the world over for the swallows that return from their winter migration on the same day every year, the town of San Juan Capistrano is also home to the 'jewel of the California missions.'

Located about 10 miles southeast and inland of Laguna Beach, the **Mission San Juan Capistrano** (off Map p238; ☎ 949-234-1300; www.missionsjc.com; 31882 Camino Capistrano; adult/child/senior $9/5/8; ◷ 8:30am-5pm) was built around a series of 18th-century arcades, each of which enclose charming fountains and lush gardens that range from rose to cactus to water lilies, and are often awash in monarch butterflies. The whitewashed Serra Chapel is considered the oldest building in California and is the only chapel still standing in which Father Junípero Serra (the founder) gave Mass.

To celebrate the swallows' return from their Argentine sojourn, the city puts on the **Festival of the Swallows** every year on March 19. Calling the ceilingless Great Stone Church 'the American Acropolis' is a bit of a stretch, but in its walls is where the beloved swallows make their summer home until around October 23.

From Laguna Beach, take OCTA bus 1 south to K-Mart Plaza, then connect to bus 191/A in the direction of Mission Viejo, which drops you near the mission ($2, about one hour). Drivers should exit I-5 at Ortega Hwy and head west for about a quarter of a mile.

---

some bathrooms are miniscule. Certain rooms have kitchenettes and ocean views. The three rooms on the road can be noisy.

Casa Laguna Inn & Spa (☎ 949-494-2996, 800-233-0449; www.casalaguna.com; 2510 S Coast Hwy; r from $280; P ⊠ ⬚ ☞ ⬚) On a terraced acre of gardens on the south side of town sits this gorgeous 1920s mission-style B&B. Each of the 22 compact rooms is uniquely furnished, but all feature seven layers of bedding; the fastidious attention to detail continues from the gourmet breakfast to the evening cordial. Watch the sun set from the ocean-view tub. A great couple's getaway.

Taco Loco (☎ 949-497-1635; 640 S Coast Hwy; dishes $2.00-12.23; ◷ 11am-midnight Sun-Thu, 11am-2am Fri & Sat; Ⓥ) This taco stand accomplishes the near impossible: good-for-you Mexican food that doesn't suck. A hippie vibe pervades the plastic garden chairs and simple ceramic tables for munching tacos, burritos and quesadillas with fillings from mushroom and tofu to blackened swordfish.

Zinc Café (☎ 949-494-6302; 350 Ocean Ave; dishes $5-10.25; ◷ 7am-4pm Mon & Tue, 7am-9pm Wed-Sun; Ⓥ) On weekends in particular you'll be waiting a while, but in the meantime there will be dogs to pet, bulletin boards to peruse and conversations to eavesdrop on. Once

you're seated on the shady patio, you're ready to order from the relatively limited, all-vegetarian menu. It also has prepared sandwiches for takeout.

Mozambique (☎ 949-715-7777; 1740 S Coast Hwy; dinner mains $18-39; ◷ 4-10pm Mon-Thu, 4pm-midnight Fri & Sat, 11am-10:30pm Sun) African-inspired cuisine as exotic as its name: Durban lamb curry, chicken or shrimp in piquant *peri-peri* sauce and steaks rubbed in special house spices. Most mains are under $30 and are also served upstairs under the chic black-and-white striped canopy of the Shebeen bar.

Getting There & Around

To reach Laguna Beach from I-105, take Hwy 133 (Laguna Canyon Rd) southwest. Laguna is served by OCTA bus 1, which runs along the coast from Long Beach to San Clemente.

Parking is a perpetual problem. Hoard your quarters. Traffic is slow in town in summer, especially on weekend afternoons.

Laguna Beach Transit (☎ 949-497-0746; Broadway & Beach Sts) has its bus center just north of the visitors bureau in the Village. It operates three routes at hourly intervals (approximately 7am to 6pm Monday to Friday, 9am to 6pm Saturday). Rides cost $0.75.

LOS ANGELES & ORANGE COUNTY

San Diego Area

San Francisco has its bohos, Los Angeles its wannabes and Orange County its soccer moms. San Diego, meanwhile, has the valet guy in a polo shirt, khaki shorts and crisp new sneakers. With his perfectly tousled hair, great tan (of course) and puppy-dog enthusiasm, he looks like he's on perennial break from college, and when he wishes you welcome, he really means it.

This may sound pejorative, but our intention is quite the opposite. California's second-largest city and America's eighth largest, San Diego doesn't seduce like San Francisco or thrill like LA, but life here is so persistently pleasant, what with 70 miles of coastline and the nation's most enviable climate, that you won't care much. Small wonder that San Diegans shamelessly yet endearingly promote their hometown as 'America's Finest City.'

For visitors, San Diego bursts with world-famous attractions: the zoo, SeaWorld, Legoland and the museums of Balboa Park (one of the nation's largest urban parks) just for starters. In the heart of downtown is the always-buzzing Gaslamp Quarter, ideal for listening to a live band or dancing 'til the wee hours. Miles of urban beaches reach their apex in the ritzy, picturesque enclave of La Jolla, which boasts pride of place on San Diego's coast. Plus, there's a burgeoning culinary scene.

Spreading north from the city, a necklace of beach communities, collectively called North County, runs up the coast to the Orange County line, with opportunities from bohemian to bourgeois: hiking and snorkeling, power-shopping, excellent dining and, for adrenaline junkies, paragliding and hang gliding.

HIGHLIGHTS

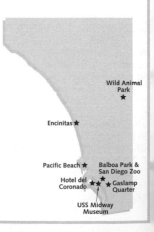

- Checking out the lions, tigers and bears at the world-renowned **San Diego Zoo** (p251) and at **Wild Animal Park** (p270)
- Gorging on knowledge and art at the museums in **Balboa Park** (p249)
- Gaining an appreciation for the defenders of our country at the **USS Midway Museum** (p249)
- Sipping a cocktail at the **Hotel del Coronado** (p261) overlooking the blinding-white beach
- Beach-hopping along the string of easygoing coast towns in North County, such as hippie-dippy **Encinitas** (p269)
- Watching the sunset over the ocean from **Pacific Beach** (p255)
- Enjoying a big – or small – night out in the **Gaslamp Quarter** (p248)

Wild Animal Park ★

Encinitas ★

Pacific Beach ★   Balboa Park & San Diego Zoo
Hotel del ★★ ★ Gaslamp
Coronado   Quarter

USS Midway Museum

FAST FACTS

- **Average temperature low/high in San Diego** January 45/65°F, July 63/75°F

- **San Diego to Los Angeles** 120 miles, two to three hours

- **San Diego International Airport to downtown San Diego** 3 miles, five to 10 minutes

- **Downtown San Diego to La Jolla** 13 miles, 15 to 20 minutes

- **Downtown San Diego to Legoland** 33 miles, 35 to 40 minutes

SAN DIEGO

pop 1.26 million

Its large population and downtown skyscrapers notwithstanding, San Diego retains a laid-back feel. Old Town and the Gaslamp Quarter pull their historical weight. Neighborhoods like Hillcrest, North Park and East Village are luring the young and the hip to a city long mired in a military and blue-hair image. And few cities can compare on the kid-friendly meter, what with a world-famous zoo, an alluring children's museum, naval vessels to explore and SeaWorld. You're never far from water, whether you're whale-spotting on Point Loma, frolicking on Ocean Beach, building a championship-worthy sandcastle on the beach or getting snorkel-happy in La Jolla Cove.

HISTORY

By the time Spanish explorer Juan Rodríguez Cabrillo became the first European to sail into San Diego Bay in 1542, the region was divided peaceably between the native Kumeyaay and Luiseño/Juaneño peoples. Their way of life continued undisturbed until Padre Junípero Serra and Gaspar de Portolá arrived in 1769, founding a mission and a military fort on the hill now known as the Presidio, the first permanent European settlement in California.

The discovery of gold in the hills east of San Diego in 1869 soon brought the railroad, but when the gold played out, the economy took a nosedive and the population plummeted. So when San

Francisco hosted the Panama-Pacific International Exposition in 1914, the next year San Diego responded with its own Panama-California Exposition, hoping to attract investment. Boosters built exhibition halls in the Spanish colonial style that still defines much of the city today.

However, it was the bombing of Pearl Harbor in 1941 that became the catalyst for modern San Diego. The US Pacific Fleet chose the city as its mainland headquarters; the deepwater port affords protection in almost all weather. The military literally reshaped the city, dredging the harbor and building landfill islands.

The opening of the University of California campus in the 1960s heralded a new era as students slowly drove a liberal wedge into the city's homogenous, flag-and-family culture.

ORIENTATION

San Diego is user-friendly, geographically speaking. The airport, train station and bus terminal are within, or very close to, the

(continued on page 247)

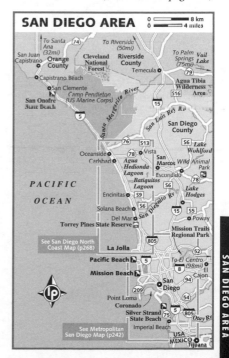

SAN DIEGO AREA

METROPOLITAN SAN DIEGO

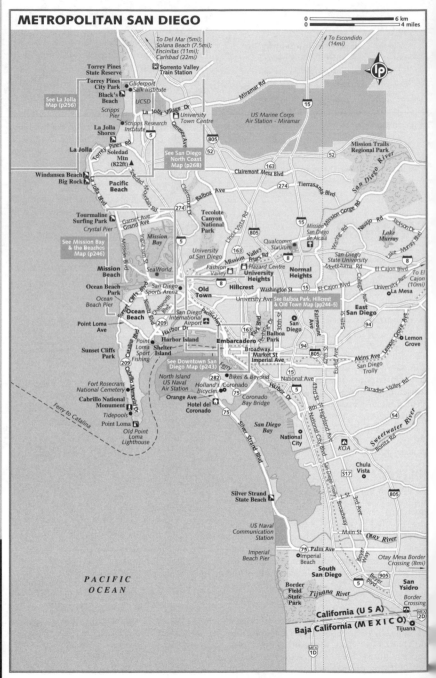

0 _____ 6 km
0 _____ 4 miles

To Del Mar (5mi);
Solana Beach (7.5mi);
Encinitas (11mi);
Carlsbad (22mi)

To Escondido
(14mi)

Torrey Pines
State Reserve

Sorrento Valley
Train Station

Torrey Pines
City Park

Gliderport
Salk Institute

Black's
Beach

Scripps
Pier

UCSD

See La Jolla
Map (p256)

La Jolla Village Dr

University
Town Centre

Miramar Rd

US Marine Corps
Air Station - Miramar

La Jolla Shores

Scripps Research
Institute

La Jolla

Soledad
Mtn
(822ft)

See San Diego
North Coast
Map (p268)

Mission Trails
Regional Park

Windansea Beach
Big Rock

Pacific
Beach

Clairemont Mesa Blvd

Balboa   Ave

Tierrasanta Blvd

Tecolote
Canyon
National
Park

Tourmaline
Surfing Park

Crystal Pier

Garnet Ave
Grand Ave

Mission
Bay

University
of San Diego

Mission San Diego
de Alcalá

San Diego
State University

El Cajon Blvd

Lake
Murray

To El
Cajon
(10mi)

La Mesa

See Mission Bay
& the Beaches
Map (p246)

Mission
Beach

SeaWorld

Fashion
Valley

Hazard Centre

University
Heights

Normal
Heights

Qualcomm
Stadium

Ocean Beach
Park

Ocean
Beach Pier

San Diego
Sports Arena

Old
Town

Hillcrest

Washington St

University Ave

See Balboa Park, Hillcrest
& Old Town Map (pp244–5)

East
San Diego

Point Loma
Ave

San Diego
International
Airport

Harbor Dr

Harbor Island

Embarcadero

San
Diego

Balboa
Park

Lemon
Grove

Sunset Cliffs
Park

Point
Loma
Sport
Fishing

Shelter
Island

See Downtown San
Diego Map (p243)

Broadway

Market St

Imperial Ave

San Diego
Trolly

Akins Ave

Paradise Valley Rd

Fort Rosecrans
National Cemetery

Bikes & Beyond

National Ave

Cabrillo National
Monument

Tidepools

Point Loma

North Island
US Naval
Air Station

Holland's
Bicycles

Coronado

Orange Ave

Hotel del
Coronado

Coronado
Bay Bridge

KOA

Chula
Vista

Old Point
Loma
Lighthouse

Ferry to Catalina

San Diego
Bay

National
City

National City Blvd

San Diego Trolly

Silver Strand Blvd

Silver Strand
State Beach

US Naval
Communication
Station

L St.

Main St

Otay River

Imperial
Beach Pier

Imperial
Beach

Palm Ave

South
San Diego

Otay Mesa Border
Crossing (8mi)

Boyer Way

PACIFIC
OCEAN

Border
Field
State
Park

Tijuana River

California (U S A)

Baja California (M E X I C O)

San
Ysidro

Border
Crossing

Tijuana

SAN DIEGO AREA

DOWNTOWN SAN DIEGO

INFORMATION
Downtown Post Office.....................1 D4
International Visitor Information
  Center...2 A3
Le Travel Store...............................3 C4
San Diego Public Library...............4 D3

SIGHTS & ACTIVITIES
Hornblower Cruises.........................5 A3
Maritime Museum............................6 A3
Museum of Contemporary Art
  San Diego-Downtown.................7 B3
New Children's Museum..................8 B4
Petco Park......................................9 D5
San Diego Harbor Excursion........10 A3
USS Midway Museum....................11 A4

SLEEPING
500 West Hotel.............................12 B3
HI San Diego Downtown Hostel...13 C4
Hotel Indigo.................................14 D4

La Pensione Hotel........................15 B2
Little Italy Inn..............................16 B2
Se San Diego................................17 C3

EATING
Café 222......................................18 C4
Croce's Restaurant & Jazz Bar....19 C4
Filippi's Pizza Grotto...................20 B2
Gaslamp Strip Club......................21 C4

DRINKING
Airport Lounge.............................22 A1
Altitude (inside Marriott Hotel)...23 C5
East Village Tavern & Bowl..........24 D4
Karl Strauss Brewery & Grill........25 B3

ENTERTAINMENT
Anthology....................................26 B3
Arts Tix.......................................27 C3
Casbah..28 A1
Shout House................................29 C4

TRANSPORT
Ferry Landing..............................30 A3
Greyhound Station.......................31 C3
Santa Fe Train Depot (Amtrak)....32 B3
Transit Store................................33 C3
West Coast Rent a Car................34 B2

BALBOA PARK, HILLCREST & OLD TOWN

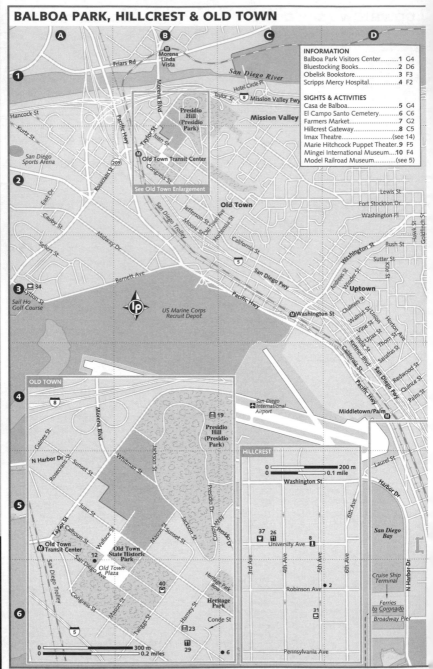

INFORMATION
Balboa Park Visitors Center...........1 G4
Bluestocking Books........................2 D6
Obelisk Bookstore.........................3 F3
Scripps Mercy Hospital..................4 F2

SIGHTS & ACTIVITIES
Casa de Balboa.............................5 G4
El Campo Santo Cemetery.............6 C6
Farmers Market............................7 G2
Hillcrest Gateway.........................8 C5
Imax Theatre..........................(see 14)
Marie Hitchcock Puppet Theater.9 F5
Mingei International Museum...10 F4
Model Railroad Museum...........(see 5)

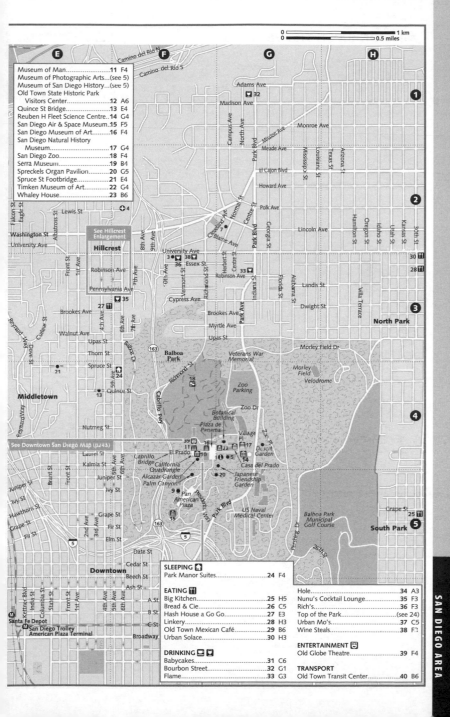

Museum of Man..........................**11** F4
Museum of Photographic Arts...(see 5)
Museum of San Diego History...(see 5)
Old Town State Historic Park
   Visitors Center......................**12** A6
Quince St Bridge.....................**13** E4
Reuben H Fleet Science Centre..**14** G4
San Diego Air & Space Museum.**15** F5
San Diego Museum of Art.........**16** F4
San Diego Natural History
   Museum...............................**17** G4
San Diego Zoo.........................**18** F4
Serra Museum..........................**19** B4
Spreckels Organ Pavilion..........**20** G5
Spruce St Footbridge...............**21** E4
Timken Museum of Art.............**22** G4
Whaley House..........................**23** B6

SLEEPING 🛏
Park Manor Suites.............................**24** F4

EATING 🍴
Big Kitchen.......................................**25** H5
Bread & Cie.......................................**26** C5
Hash House a Go Go..........................**27** E3
Linkery..**28** H3
Old Town Mexican Café......................**29** B6
Urban Solace.....................................**30** H3

DRINKING 🍸 🍷
Babycakes...**31** C6
Bourbon Street..................................**32** G1
Flame..**33** G3

Hole..**34** A3
Nunu's Cocktail Lounge.....................**35** F3
Rich's...**36** F3
Top of the Park.............................(see 24)
Urban Mo's.......................................**37** C5
Wine Steals.......................................**38** F3

ENTERTAINMENT 🎭
Old Globe Theatre.............................**39** F4

TRANSPORT
Old Town Transit Center.....................**40** B6

MISSION BAY & THE BEACHES

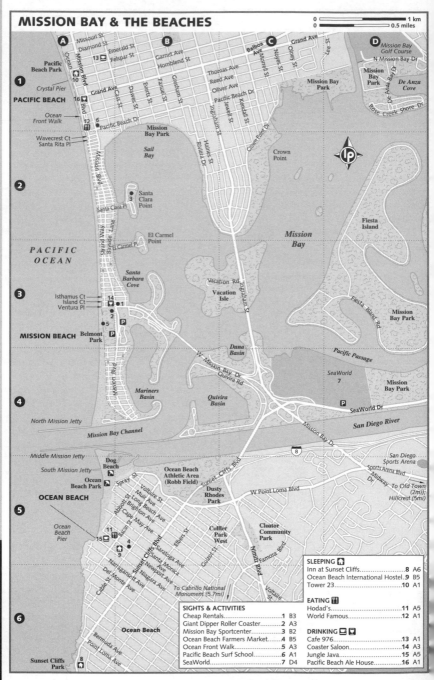

SAN DIEGO AREA

SIGHTS & ACTIVITIES
Cheap Rentals..........................1 B3
Giant Dipper Roller Coaster..........2 A3
Mission Bay Sportcenter..............3 B2
Ocean Beach Farmers Market..........4 B5
Ocean Front Walk.....................5 A3
Pacific Beach Surf School.............6 A1
SeaWorld...............................7 D4

SLEEPING 🏠
Inn at Sunset Cliffs...................8 A6
Ocean Beach International Hostel..9 B5
Tower 23..............................10 A1

EATING 🍴
Hodad's...............................11 A5
World Famous.........................12 A1

DRINKING 🍷
Cafe 976.............................13 A1
Coaster Saloon.......................14 A3
Jungle Java...........................15 A5
Pacific Beach Ale House..............16 A1

(continued from page 241)

city center. (You'll get used to the planes' alarmingly low landing patterns.) San Diego's downtown, a compact grid north-east of San Diego Bay, revolves around the historic Gaslamp Quarter, a beehive of restaurants, bars and boutiques; the convention center sits to its southwest along the water, and office towers rise to the north. Within the city center, north–south 'avenues' are numbered (1st, 2nd etc), while east–west 'streets' are lettered (A, B, C etc) heading south and named for trees in alphabetical order (Ash, Beech etc) heading north.

I-5 is the main north–south freeway, connecting San Diego County with Orange and Los Angeles Counties; I-8 runs east from Ocean Beach, up Mission Valley. The Cabrillo Fwy (CA 163) heads north from downtown through Balboa Park.

Waterfront attractions along the Embarcadero lie just west of the downtown grid, and upscale Coronado is reached via a bridge south of downtown or a short ferry ride. North of downtown are San Diego's Little Italy and museum-rich Balboa Park, home of the San Diego Zoo. The historic park at Old Town is northwest of downtown, and lesbi-gay Hillcrest and boho North Park form the park's northern flank. East of downtown is the up-and-coming East Village neighborhood.

INFORMATION
Bookstores
Book hounds should peruse the old, new and rare offerings of bookstores on 5th Ave between University and Robinson Aves in Hillcrest.

Bluestocking Books (Map pp244-5; ☎ 619-296-1424; 3817 5th Ave, Hillcrest; ⊙ 11am-7pm Tue-Thu, 9am-9:30pm Fri-Mon) Despite the name, this isn't a 'women-only' bookstore, but a funky, all-encompassing spot with new and used tomes.

DG Wills Books (Map p256; ☎ 858-456-1800; 7461 Girard Ave, La Jolla; ⊙ 10am 7pm Mon-Sat, 11am-6pm Sun) A fixture in the area, and a must for those of bookish bent.

Le Travel Store (Map p243; ☎ 619-544-0005; 745 4th Ave; ⊙ 10am-6pm Mon-Sat, noon-6pm Sun) Excellent source for maps, travel guides and accessories.

UCSD Bookstore (Map p256; ☎ 858 534-7323; 9500 Gilman Dr; ⊙ 8am-6pm Mon-Fri, noon-5pm Sat & Sun) Excellent stock and helpful staff, also sells clothing and computers.

Internet Access
For wi-fi hot-spot locations, check www .jiwire.com and see cafes (p265).

San Diego Public Library (Map p243; ☎ 619-236-5800; www.sandiego.gov/public-library; 820 E St,

---

SAN DIEGO IN...

One Day
Start with breakfast and espresso at an outdoor cafe on Little Italy's **India St** (p249) Then make your way to **Balboa Park** (p249). Pick a museum or two that interests you and have lunch at one of the cafés or restaurants, detouring to the gardens along the way. Devote the afternoon to the **San Diego Zoo** (p251), among the world's best. For dinner and a night out on the town, head to the **Gaslamp Quarter** (p248); many restaurants have terrace seating for people-watching, and the partying ranges from posh to raucous.

Two Days
Take the ferry to Coronado for a sea-view breakfast at the **Hotel del Coronado** (p261), before a drive up to **La Jolla** (p255). Explore **Torrey Pines State Reserve** (p257), the **Birch Aquarium** (p257) or edgy **Black's Beach** (p257); explore the **underwater coast** (p258) with a snorkel or dive or try a **glider ride** (p259). Head to **La Jolla Village** (p255) to browse the 1920s Spanish revival landmarks, the **Museum of Contemporary Art** (p256) or the boutiques along Girard Ave – you'll have plenty of choice for a lunch or snack. As the sun begins its descent over the ocean, continue to Del Mar, where you can cheer or snuggle from one of the cafés on the roof of **Del Mar Plaza** (p268) as the sky turns brilliant orange and fades to deepest blue.

To add a third and fourth day, include **SeaWorld** (p254) and the **San Diego Wild Animal Park** (p270).

SAN DIEGO AREA

Downtown; ⊗ noon-8pm Mon & Wed, 9:30am-5:30pm Tue & Thu-Sat, 1-5pm Sun; ▢ ⊚) Free wi-fi access. Call or check the website for branch locations.

Internet Resources

Accessible San Diego (www.asd.travel) Excellent resource for barrier-free travel around San Diego.
Gaslamp.org (www.gaslamp.org) Everything you need to know about the bustling Gaslamp Quarter.
San Diego Convention & Visitors Bureau (www .sandiego.org) Search for hotels, sights, restaurants, rental cars and more, and make reservations.
SanDiego.com (www.sandiego.com) Comprehensive ad-based portal to all things San Diegan, from fun stuff to serious business.

Media

Gay & Lesbian Times (www.gaylesbiantimes.com) Free weekly.
KPBS 89.5 FM (www.kpbs.org) National Public Radio (NPR) affiliate.
San Diego Magazine (www.sandiegomagazine.com) Glossy monthly.
San Diego Reader (www.sdreader.com) Free tabloid-sized listings magazine.
San Diego Union-Tribune (www.signonsandiego.com) The city's major daily.

Medical Services

Rite-Aid Pharmacy (☎ 800-748-3243; www.riteaid .com; ⊗ some 24hr) Call for the nearest branch.
Scripps Mercy Hospital (Map pp244-5; ☎ 619-294-8111; 4077 5th Ave, Hillcrest; ⊗ 24hr emergency room)

Post

For local post office locations, call ☎ 800-275-8777 or log on to www.usps.com.
Downtown post office (Map p243; ☎ 619-232-8612; 815 E St; ⊗ 9am-5pm Mon-Fri)

Tourist Information

Balboa Park Visitors Center (Map pp244-5; ☎ 619-239-0512; www.balboapark.org; 1549 El Prado; ⊗ 9:30am-4:30pm) In the House of Hospitality. Sells park maps and the Passport to Balboa Park (adult/child three to 12 $39/21, with zoo admission $65/36), which allows one-time entry to 13 of the park's museums within seven days.
San Diego Convention & Visitors Bureau (☎ 619-236-1212, 800-350-6205; www.sandiego.org); Downtown (Map p243; cnr W Broadway & Harbor Dr; ⊗ 9am-5pm Jun-Sep, 9am-4pm Oct-May); La Jolla (Map p256; 7966 Herschel Ave; ⊗ 11am-4pm, possibly longer Jun-Sep & Sat & Sun) Handles inquiries for the entire county. The downtown location is also known as the International Visitors Information Center.

DANGERS & ANNOYANCES

Serious crime is relatively rare, even in downtown San Diego. Aggressive panhandling is the most common problem, and there are a fair number of vagrants in and around the Gaslamp Quarter.

SIGHTS
Downtown

Just south of the city's stretch of skyscrapers lies the historic Gaslamp Quarter. Closer to the bay and near the city's mammoth convention center looms Petco Park, San Diego's baseball stadium, which has helped seal downtown's renewal. To the west lies the Embarcadero district, a fine place for a bayfront jog by historic battleships. A short walk north lands you in Little Italy, where mom-and-pop eateries alternate with high-end design stores.

GASLAMP QUARTER

Founded in 1867, the Gaslamp Quarter has, almost since its inception, catered to the vices of travelers. During San Diego's Gold Rush of the 1870s, the neighborhood quickly degenerated into a string of saloons, bordellos, gambling halls and opium dens. In San Diego's postwar boom, the Victorian and beaux-arts buildings were left to molder while the rest of downtown was razed and rebuilt. When developers started to eye the area in the early 1980s, preservationists organized to save the old brick and stone facades from the wrecking ball.

These days, the Gaslamp Quarter is again the focus of the city's nightlife, though of a significantly tamer variety; much of the business comes from conventioneers at the nearby convention center and, especially on weekend nights, hordes of visitors flash their plastic money (and plastic cleavages).

PETCO PARK

Just a quick stroll southeast of the Gaslamp is downtown's newest landmark, the San Diego Padres' **baseball stadium** (Map p243; ☎ 619-795-5011; www.padres.com; 100 Park Blvd; adult/child under 12/senior over 60 $9/5/6; ⊗ tours 10:30am, 12:30pm & 2:30pm Tue-Sun May-Aug, 10:30am & 12:30pm Tue-Sun Apr & Sep, subject to game schedule; ⛶). Even if the Padres are perennial basement-dwellers in the standings, their stadium rocks, incorporating some architecturally significant structures. Take an 80-minute behind-the-scenes tour.

MUSEUM OF CONTEMPORARY ART SAN DIEGO – DOWNTOWN

This **museum** (MCASD; Map p243; ☎ 858-454-3541; www.mcasd.org; 1001 & 1100 Kettner Blvd; adult/25 & under/senior $10/free/5; ☺ 11am-5pm Thu-Tue, to 7pm 3rd Thu each month, with free admission 5pm-7pm) completed work on an ambitious expansion in 2007 and now comprises two buildings, a section of the former Santa Fe Rail Depot (with permanent works by Jenny Holzer and Richard Serra) and a three-story contemporary art space, which adds a modern counterpoint to the station's mission-style architecture. MCASD is the downtown branch of the La Jolla-based institution (p256) that has brought groundbreaking art to San Diegans since the 1960s. Tickets are valid for seven days in all locations.

While here, peek in at the depot itself (aka Union Station), which looks a lot like a piece from a model railway, with Spanish-style tilework and an historic Santa Fe Railway sign on top. It was built in conjunction with the 1915 exposition in the hope that the Santa Fe Railway would make San Diego its terminus, although that designation eventually went to LA.

NEW CHILDREN'S MUSEUM

San Diego's **New Children's Museum** (Map p243; ☎ 619-233-8792; www.thinkplaycreate.org; 200 W Island Ave; adult/senior over 65/child over 1 $10/5/10; ☺ 10am-4pm Mon, Tue, Fri & Sat, 10am-6pm Thu, noon-4pm Sun; ☺) is new both chronologically (opened 2008) and conceptually. Installations are designed by artists, so tykes can learn principles of movement and physics while simultaneously being exposed to art and working out the ants in their pants. Exhibits change every 18 months or so, but if we mention a climbing wall covered with graffiti art, a pillowfight in a room with mattress-like walls and human-powered 'legway' scooters, do you get the idea?

LITTLE ITALY

Italian immigrants, mostly fishermen, began settling this rise of land just up from San Diego Bay in the 19th century. The community had its heyday in the 1920s, when Prohibition opened up new 'business opportunities' (read 'bootlegging'). Although construction of I-5 tore apart Little Italy's cultural fabric, the hardiest of the old family businesses have survived and, thanks

to the city's recent urban renaissance, gained new clientele. Now old-world grocery stores alternate with slick cafes and high-end boutiques.

Embarcadero

The 100ft masts of the square-rigger *Star of India* will help you spot the **Maritime Museum** (Map p243; ☎ 619-234-9153; www.sdmaritime .com; 1492 N Harbor Dr; adult/child 6-17/senior over 62 $14/8/11; ☺ 9am-8pm, to 9pm late May-early Sep; ☺). Launched in 1863, the tall ship plied the England–India trade route and carried immigrants to New Zealand. The museum takes you on a journey through the history of water voyage, plus a fair amount of navy stuff.

The main attraction, though, is the **USS Midway Museum** (Map p243; ☎ 619-544-9600; www .midway.org; Navy Pier; adult/child 6-17/senior over 62/ student $17/9/13/13; ☺ 10am-5pm; ☺) aboard the Navy's longest-serving aircraft carrier (1945–91). A self-guided audiotour takes in berthing spaces, galley, sick bay and, of course, the flight deck with its restored aircraft, including an F-14 Tomcat. Allow at least two hours. Parking costs from $5.

Balboa Park

After receiving her botany degree in 1881, Kate O Sessions came to San Diego as a teacher but soon began working as a horticulturist, establishing gardens for the fashionable homes of the city's emerging elite. In 1892, in need of space for a nursery, she suggested to city officials that they allow her the use of 30 acres of city-owned Balboa Park in return for planting 100 trees a year and donating 300 others for placement throughout San Diego. The city agreed, and within a decade Balboa Park had shade trees, lawns, paths and flowerbeds. Today it's one of the country's finest urban parks, with flower gardens and shaded walks, tennis courts and swimming pools, museums and theaters, a velodrome, golf courses, an outdoor organ and one of the world's great zoos. The park is also the city's premier cultural center, with a cluster of theaters and museums along the El Prado promenade.

To visit everything would take a full two days, but most visitors pick and choose. Get information and discount passes to the park and zoo at the **Balboa Park Visitors Center** (p248) in the House of Hospitality. Some museums occasionally have free admission on Tuesday – find out which ones from the visitors center.

Balboa Park is easily reached from downtown on bus 7, 7A or 7B along Park Blvd. By car, Park Blvd provides easy access to free parking areas. From the west, El Prado is an extension of Laurel St, which crosses Cabrillo Bridge.

The free minibus called the Balboa Park Tram makes a continuous loop through the main areas of the park.

EL PRADO

Originally built for the 1915–16 Panama-California Exposition (see p241), these Spanish colonial buildings are particularly beautiful in the morning and evening. The original exposition halls, which were mostly constructed out of stucco, chicken wire, plaster, hemp and horsehair, were only meant to be temporary. However, they proved so popular that, over the years, they have been gradually replaced with durable concrete replicas. The complex houses a number of museums.

California Building & Museum of Man

As you enter Balboa Park via Laurel St, you cross the picturesque Cabrillo Bridge and then pass under an archway and into an area called the California Quadrangle, home to the **Museum of Man** (Map pp244-5; ☎ 619-239-2001; www.museumofman.org; Plaza de California; adult/child 6-12/child 13-17 & senior $10/5/7.50; ☼ 10am-4:30pm), which specializes in Native American artifacts from the American Southwest. The California Building's richly decorated **Tower of California** has become a symbol of San Diego itself. The museum exhibits world-class pottery, jewelry, baskets and other artifacts of cultures as diverse as the Mayans, ancient Egyptians and Native Americans of the Southwest.

Old Globe Theatre

Built in the style of Shakespeare's Globe in London, this **theater** (Map pp244-5; ☎ 619-234-5623; www.oldglobe.org; 1363 Old Globe Way) won a Tony award in 1984 for its ongoing contribution to theater arts. You can catch performances year round of plays by Shakespeare and others, on three stages.

San Diego Museum of Art

The city's largest **museum** (Map pp244-5; ☎ 619-232-7931; www.sdmart.org; Plaza de Panama; adult/child 6-17/student/senior over 65 $10/4/7/8; ☼ 10am-5pm Tue-Sat, noon-5pm Sun, to 9pm Thu) has no truly famous works in its permanent collection, but includes a decent survey of European masters from the Renaissance to modernism, as well as some noteworthy American landscape paintings and Asian art. It was designed by San Diego architect William Templeton Johnson in the 16th-century Spanish style. The facade is particularly ornate, with sculptures depicting Spanish artists. The **Sculpture Garden** has pieces by Alexander Calder and Henry Moore.

Mingei International Museum

The **museum** (Map pp244-5; ☎ 619-239-0003; www.mingei.org; 1439 El Prado, Plaza de Panama; adult/child 6-17/senior $7/4/5; ☼ 10am-4pm Tue-Sun) exhibits folk art, costumes, toys, jewelry, utensils and other handmade objects from traditional cultures around the globe.

Timken Museum of Art

Distinctive for *not* being in imitation Spanish style, the **Timken** (Map pp244-5; ☎ 619-239-5548; www.timkenmuseum.org; 1500 El Prado; admission free; ☼ 10am-4:30pm Tue-Sat, 1:30-4:30pm Sun) houses a significant collection of works by Rembrandt, Rubens and El Greco. There's also a remarkable selection of Russian icons. The museum is named after the Timken family, who rode to fame and fortune on the invention of the roller bearer used in horse-drawn carriages.

Casa de Balboa

There are three museums in the Casa de Balboa, located at 1649 El Prado.

The permanent collection at the stellar **Museum of Photographic Arts** (Map pp244-5; ☎ 619-238-7559; www.mopa.org; adult/child under 12/student/senior $6/free/4/4; ☼ 10am-5pm) traces the history of photography in terms of both technology and aesthetics, with particular strengths in social documentary and photojournalism.

The **Museum of San Diego History** (Map pp244-5; ☎ 619-232-6203; www.sandiegohistory.org; adult/child 6-17/student/senior $5/2/4/4; ☼ 10am-5pm Tue-Sun) features changing exhibits, including historical costumes and a cool interactive walk-on map of San Diego.

Downstairs, the **Model Railroad Museum** (Map pp244-5; ☎ 619-696-0199; www.sdmrm.org; adult/senior/student $6/3/5; ⏰ 11am-4pm Tue-Fri, 11am-5pm Sat&Sun; ♿), is reputedly the largest indoor model-railroad display in the world, with working models of real railroads in Southern California, past and present. Awesome.

San Diego Natural History Museum

Kids dig this temple to the natural world, which has a particular focus on the ecosystems of Southern California and the Baja California peninsula, as well as the requisite dinos. Giant-screen films are included in the admission to the **museum** (Map pp244-5; ☎ 619-232-3821; www.sdnhm.org; 1788 El Prado; adult/child 3-12/youth 13-17/senior over 62 $16/10/11/14; ⏰ 10am-5pm; ♿). Opposite is the **Reuben H Fleet Science Center** (Map pp244-5; ☎ 619-238-1233; www.rhfleet.org; 1875 El Prado; adult/child 3-12 & senior over 65 $10/8.75; ⏰ 9:30am, closing times vary; ♿), a family-oriented, hands-on museum-cum-**Imax theater** (Map pp244-5; adult/child 3-12 incl Science Center $14.50/11.75, additional films $5; ♿).

SPRECKELS ORGAN PAVILION

Heading south from Plaza de Panama, you can't miss the extravagantly curved colonnade that provides shelter for one of the world's largest **outdoor organs** (Map pp244-5). Donated by the Spreckels family of sugar fame, the organ has some 4400 pipes, the smallest the size of a pencil and the largest nearly 32ft long. Free concerts are held at 2pm on Sunday and 7:30pm on Monday from mid-June to August.

SAN DIEGO AIR & SPACE MUSEUM

This **museum** (Map pp244-5; ☎ 619-234-8291; www.aerospacemuseum.org; 2001 Pan American Plaza; adult/child 3-11/student/senior $15/6/12/12; ⏰ 10am-5:30pm Jun-Aug, to 4:30pm Sep-May; ♿) offers a fun-filled look at the history and mystique of flight. Highlights include an original Blackbird SR-71 spy plane and a replica of Charles Lindbergh's *Spirit of St Louis*, and simulators that require an extra charge.

MARIE HITCHCOCK PUPPET THEATER

This **theater** (Map pp244-5; ☎ 619-685-5990; www.balboaparkpuppets.com; 2130 Pan American Place; adult/child $5/3; ♿) puts on shows at 11am, 1pm and 2:30pm Wednesday to Sunday (reduced show times in winter).

SAN DIEGO ZOO

If it slithers, crawls, stomps, swims, leaps or flies, chances are you'll find it in this justifiably world-famous **zoo** (Map pp244-5; ☎ 619-231-1515; www.sandiegozoo.org; 2920 Zoo DR; adult/child 3-11 $28.50/18.50, with guided bus tour & aerial tram ride $35/26; ⏰ from 9am, closing times vary; Ⓟ ♿) on some 100 acres in northern Balboa Park. It's home to more than 3000 animals – representing more than 800 species – in a beautifully landscaped setting, including the new 7.5 acre Elephant Odyssey.

The zoo shines for its pioneering methods of housing and displaying animals to mimic their natural habitats, leading to a revolution in zoo design and, so the argument goes, to happier animals. The zoo also plays a major role in the protection of endangered species.

In its efforts to re-create those habitats, the zoo has also become one of the country's great botanical gardens, tricking San Diego's near-desert climate into yielding everything from bamboo and eucalyptus to mini African rainforests.

It's wise to arrive early, as many of the animals are most active in the morning, and many are fed between 9am and 11am. Animal shows are held in the two amphitheaters (no extra charge). A big, free parking lot is off Park Blvd. Bus 7 will get you there from downtown.

The 'deluxe admission package' includes a 40-minute guided bus tour and a round-trip on the Skyfari aerial tram. The extras probably aren't worth it, unless you have sore feet or are in a hurry. A combined ticket to visit both the San Diego Zoo and the Wild Animal Park (p270) within a five-day period costs $54.50/33.50 for an adult/child.

Old Town

In 1769 Junípero Serra and Gaspar de Portolá established the first Spanish settlement in California on **Presidio Hill**, overlooking the valley of the San Diego River, though it was later moved to a more ready source of water (see p254). Until the 1860s, the cluster of wood and adobe buildings here, just below Presidio Hill, pretty much was San Diego. Today this area is called Old Town, and it's good for those who need to quell their beach-guilt with a spot of history.

Old Town State Historic Park Visitors Center (Map pp244-5; ☎ 619-220-5422; Wallace St; ⏰ 10am-5pm) houses a California history slide show and a neat model of Old Town. Several guided tours of Old Town leave daily in summer. Other buildings around Old Town Plaza are a mix of historic and commercial: old dentist's office, tinsmith, shops selling candles and moccasins, early courthouse and Wells Fargo Bank, and the Casa de Estudillo, the adobe home of an early commandant.

Two blocks from the Old Town perimeter sits **Whaley House** (Map pp244-5; ☎ 619-297-7511; 2482 San Diego Ave; admission $5; ⏰ 10am-10pm in summer, to 4:30pm rest of year), the city's oldest brick building, having served as courthouse, theater and private residence. In the '60s it was officially certified as haunted by the US Department of Commerce. Inside, the period furniture is watched over by knowledgeable costumed docents. Ask one of them about the theater's slanted stage.

El Campo Santo Cemetery (Map pp244-5), between Arista and Conde Sts on San Diego Ave, is a tiny, touching cemetery dating back to the earliest Spanish settlers. One grave near the gate was so placed because the man, 'Jesus the Indian,' died while 'completely drunk.' The construction of San Diego Ave accidentally covered many resting spots, so you may notice some medallions marking grave sites embedded in the street.

The walk from Old Town along Mason St to Presidio Hill (now Presidio Park) rewards you with views of the bay. On the site of the original mission stands the handsome **Serra Museum** (Map pp244-5; ☎ 619-297-3258; 2727 Presidio Dr; adult/child 6-17/student/senior $5/2/4/4; ⏰ irregular hr), which highlights life during the city's rough-and-tumble early period.

The Old Town Transit Center, on the trolley line at Taylor St, is a stop for the Coaster commuter train, the San Diego Trolley (orange and blue lines) and buses 4 and 5 from downtown. Free parking lots surround the park.

Uptown, Hillcrest & North Park

Uptown consists roughly of the triangle north of downtown, east of Old Town and south of Mission Valley. As you head north from downtown along the western side of Balboa Park, you arrive at a series of bluffs that, in the late 19th century, became San Diego's most fashionable neighborhood –

only those who owned a horse-drawn carriage could afford to live here. Known as Bankers Hill after some of the wealthy residents, these upscale heights had unobstructed views of the bay and Point Loma before I-5 went up.

As you head northward toward Hillcrest, detour across the 375ft **Spruce St Footbridge** (Map pp244–5), a 1912 suspension bridge built over a deep canyon between Front and Brant Sts. The nearby **Quince St Bridge** (Map pp244–5), between 3rd and 4th Aves, is a wood-trestle structure built in 1905 and refurbished in 1988.

Just up from the northwestern corner of Balboa Park, you hit **Hillcrest**, the heart of Uptown. The neighborhood began its life in the early 20th century as a modest middle-class suburb, and it has evolved into a well-tended bohemian neighborhood with a large gay population. The **Hillcrest Gateway** (Map pp244–5), a neon sign that arches over University Ave at 5th Ave, marks the center of the action: coffeehouses, thrift shops and excellent restaurants in all price ranges. Hillcrest's **farmers market** (Map pp244-5; 5th Ave, cnr Normal & Lincoln Sts; ⏰ 9am-1pm Sun) is tops for people-watching.

The bohemian vibe continues as you head east on University Ave to 30th St, where the North Park neighborhood is to San Diego what Brooklyn has become to New York City: an enclave of young bohemians making the world a better place through food, art and music. There are no sights per se here, but it's worth a stroll or a night out.

Coronado

Directly across the bay from downtown San Diego, protecting the harbor from the ocean, Coronado is a civilized escape from the jumble of the city or the humble of the beaches. Follow the tree-lined, manicured median strip of Orange Ave toward the commercial center, Coronado Village, around the Hotel del Coronado. Then park your car; you won't need it again until you leave.

The story of Coronado is in many ways the story of that hotel. When the 'Hotel Del' was built in 1888, it was designed to 'be the talk of the western world.' While that's surely an exaggeration these days, the Del has plenty of lore to go along with its 26 acres of grounds overlooking an impossibly white beach. Its main building is a sprawling timber palace with billowing turrets, dramatic ballrooms and nearly 700 rooms, all connected by a maze of dark corridors, bright courtyards, and elegantly carved stairways. Though it has hosted presidents, celebrities and royalty, the Del achieved its widest exposure in the 1959 movie *Some Like It Hot*, which earned it a lasting association with Marilyn Monroe. For details on the hotel, see p261.

The soaring 2.12-mile-long Coronado Bay Bridge opened in 1969 and joins Coronado to San Diego; Silver Strand, a long, narrow sand spit, runs south to Imperial Beach and connects Coronado to the mainland (though people still call it 'Coronado Island' in honor of its original status). Bus 901 from downtown San Diego runs the length of Orange Ave to the Hotel del Coronado.

Alternatively, the hourly **Coronado Ferry** (☎ 619-234-4111; www.sdhe.com; adult/child under 4 $3.25/free; ☽ 9am-10pm) shuttles between the Broadway Pier on San Diego's Embarcadero (Map p243) to the ferry landing at the foot of Orange Ave in Coronado (Map p242), from where it's about 1.5 miles to the Village. At the ferry landing, **Bikes & Beyond** (Map p242; ☎ 619-435-7180; rental per hr/day from $7/30; ☽ 9am-8pm, call for seasonal hr) is the most convenient place that rents out bicycles, or you can catch the hourly bus 904 to the rest of the island.

Point Loma

On the southern tip of Point Loma, west of Old Town and north of the airport, you'll find **Cabrillo National Monument** (Map p242; ☎ 619-557-5450; admission per car $5, on foot or bicycle $3; ☽ 9am-5pm), offering fine views across the bay to San Diego's downtown; you can also see sailboats and battleships coming in and out of the harbor. It's also the best place in San Diego to see the gray-whale migration (January to March) from land. The 1854 **Old Point Loma Lighthouse** (now a museum), dramatically situated at the top of the hill, was so prone to fog that a new, lower lighthouse took over duty 36 years later. On the ocean side of the point, you can drive to the **tidepools** (☽ 9am-4:30pm) to look for anemones, starfish, crabs, limpets and 'dead man's fingers,' best seen in low tide in winter; you could walk it, but it's a steep mile down and you have to get back up.

See the driving tour (p254) for further details about Cabrillo.

If you're not driving, the monument can be reached by bus 84 from Old Town Transit Center.

Ocean Beach

Ocean Beach, San Diego's most bohemian seaside community, is the Santa Cruz of the south, with OBecians proudly flouting the conservatism of inland San Diego – when they can find the time between waves, that is. Newport Ave, which runs perpendicular from the beach, is a jumble of tattoo parlors, surf shops, coffee shops and no-shirt-no-shoes-no-problem bars sprinkled amid the 'Newport Ave Antique Mall' (not a mall but a collection of shops). The street ends a block from the half-mile-long **Ocean Beach Pier**.

The other action lies on the sands, of course. Just north of the pier is the headquarters for the beach scene, with volleyball courts and sunset BBQ. Further up you'll reach **Dog Beach** (Map p246), where pooches can run unleashed around the marshy area. A few blocks south of the pier, you'll find **Sunset Cliffs Park**, a great spot to watch the sun dipping below the horizon.

If you're here on a Wednesday afternoon, stop by the **Ocean Beach farmers market** (Map p246; ☽ 4-7pm, to 8pm Jun-Sep) to see street performers and sample fresh food.

Mission Bay & the Beaches

In the 18th century, the mouth of the San Diego River formed a shallow bay when the river flowed and a marshy swamp when it didn't – the Spanish called it False Bay. After WWII, a rare combination of civic vision and coastal engineering turned the swamp into a 7-sq-mile playground, with 27 miles of shoreline and 90 acres of public parks. The river was channeled to the sea, the bay was dredged and millions of tons of sludge were used to build islands, coves and peninsulas.

The attractions of Mission Bay run the gamut from luxurious resort hotels to free outdoor activities. Kite flying is popular in Mission Bay Park, beach volleyball is big on Fiesta Island, and there's delightful cycling and in-line skating on the miles of smooth bike paths. Sailing, windsurfing and kayaking dominate the waters in northwest Mission Bay. For equipment-rental information, see p258.

SAN DIEGO AREA

DRIVING TOUR: SAN DIEGO HISTORY

What to See

This route traces San Diego's evolution from its European 'discovery' to the mission era. Start at the **Cabrillo National Monument** (see p253), where Portuguese explorer Juan Rodríguez Cabrillo first laid eyes on San Diego. Its **visitors center** (☎ 619-557-5450; ✆ 9am-5pm) has an excellent, old-school presentation on Cabrillo's 1542 voyage up the California coast, plus good exhibits on the native inhabitants and the area's natural history.

After leaving the national monument, stop at **Fort Rosecrans National Cemetery** (Map p242), just under a mile from the gate, which although not connected to the city's earliest history is significant nonetheless. Some 99,000 war dead are memorialized here, including military members whose remains have not been recovered. The views alone are quite a tribute, with the ocean on one side and the harbor on the other.

In 1769, a band of missionaries led by the Franciscan friar Junípero Serra founded the first of the 21 California missions, on San Diego's Presidio Hill, and a small *pueblo* (village) grew around it. Now that village is known as Old Town, and the **Old Town State Historic Park** (p252) is an excellent place to browse for an hour or two. Walk or drive up Mason St to **Presidio Hill** to get the views the old padres had. San Diego Ave, east of the historic park, is packed with restaurants for a snack, meal or margarita.

The original mission site turned out to be less than ideal, and in 1774 the mission was moved about 7 miles upriver, closer to a steady water supply and fertile land in what's now called Mission Valley. Here the **Mission Basilica San Diego de Alcalá** (Map p242; ☎ 619-281-8449; www .missionsandiego.com; 10818 San Diego Mission Rd at Friars Rd; adult/child/student/senior $3/1/2/2; ✆ 9am-4:45pm) is a modest rectangle embracing a tranquil garden, far from the city's bustle. Unfortunately, reaching it requires passing through the valley itself, via the unlovely I-8 freeway, flanked by massive shopping malls and hotels.

The Route

From the gate of the Cabrillo National Monument, the Fort Rosecrans National Cemetery is about 0.8 miles along Cabrillo Monument Dr; the main entrance will be on your left. Continuing on, Cabrillo Monument Dr becomes Catalina Blvd. Bear right when you reach Chatsworth Blvd, follow it 2.2 miles through this mostly residential neighborhood, and turn left on Rosecrans St. Bear right on Rosecrans St where the road forks and, after the freeway overpass and Old Town Transit Center, turn right onto Congress Ave, where there are several free parking lots for Old Town. From Old Town, return to the Transit Center and turn right on Taylor St, which merges onto I-8 East in less than a mile. After 4.5 miles, exit Fairmount Ave, turn left and it changes names to Mission Gorge Rd; at the car dealerships, turn left onto San Diego Mission Rd, and the mission is about 0.4 miles ahead on your right.

Time & Mileage

It's about 16 miles one way. With no traffic, the drive takes about 30 minutes, but you'll want to allow at least half a day for stops at these worthy locales.

SEAWORLD

Along with the zoo, **SeaWorld** (Map p246; ☎ 619-226-3901, 800-257-4268; www.seaworld.com/seaworld/ca; 500 SeaWorld Dr; adult/child 3-9 $65/55; ✆ 9am-11pm Jul–mid-Aug, shorter hr rest of year; ⏲) is one of San Diego's most popular attractions. There's no denying that SeaWorld has an overtly commercial feel, with corporate logos slapped on every available surface, but it's entertaining and it can even be educational.

The biggest draws are live-animal shows, particularly Believe, featuring Shamu, the world's most famous killer whale, and his killer whale amigos leaping, diving and gliding. Some may find the presentation a little, well, awww, but the animals induce awe. Dolphin shows are also popular. Avoid marked 'soak zones' near the tanks or you will get wet. There are also zoo-like animal exhibits, such as petting pools where you can touch the slippery surface of a dolphin or manta ray, along with a few amusement park–style rides, such as the Journey to Atlantis flume. Lines can be long in summer and around holidays.

By car, take Sea World Dr off the I-5 less than a mile north of where it intersects with I-8. Parking is $12. Take bus 9 from Old Town.

MISSION BEACH & PACIFIC BEACH
Between the South Mission Jetty and Pacific Beach Point stretch 3 miles of pure, unadulterated SoCal beach scene. **Ocean Front Walk** (Map p246) bristles with joggers, in-line skaters and cyclists – the perfect place for scantily clad, pretty people-watching. Back from the beach, Mission Blvd consists of block after block of surf shops, burger joints and beer busts. Down at the Mission Beach end, beach bums pool their resources to rent small houses and apartments for the summer season.

The surf is good for beginners, bodyboarders and bodysurfers.

The family-style amusement park **Belmont Park** (Map p246; ☎ 858-488-0668; www.belmontpark .com; admission free; ☑ check website) has been at the southern end of Mission Beach since 1925. One of the highlights is the classic wooden **Giant Dipper roller coaster** (Map p246; admission $6; ☑ from 11am).

Up in Pacific Beach (PB) the activity spreads further inland, especially along

Garnet Ave (Map p246), with bars, restaurants and vintage-clothing stores. At the ocean end of Garnet Ave, **Crystal Pier** (Map p250) is worth a gander. Built in the 1920s, it's still home to a cluster of rustic cabins built out over the waves.

Tourmaline Surfing Park (Map p242), at the far northern end of the beach, is particularly popular with longboarders. For information on equipment rentals, see p258.

To get around, consider renting a bike or in-line skates. **Cheap Rentals** (Map p246; ☎ 800-941-7761, 858-488-2453; www.cheap-rentals.com; 3689 Mission Blvd; ☑ 9am-7pm daily Mar-Aug, to 5pm Mon-Fri Sep-Feb) has low prices and rents out everything from bikes and skates (per hour/day $5/15) to surf equipment and baby joggers; it also accepts advance reservations.

La Jolla
Though technically part of San Diego, La Jolla feels a world apart because of both its conspicuous wealth and its location above San Diego's most photogenic stretch of coast. With upscale boutiques, immaculate parks, sandy coves and turquoise waters, you can understand why locals say La Jolla is Spanish for 'the jewel.' But some challenge this claim, saying that the indigenous peoples who inhabited the area until the mid-19th century called it Mut la Hoya (Place of Many Caves). Either way, it's pronounced 'la hoy-ya.'

Bus 30 connects La Jolla to downtown via the Old Town Transit Center. **La Jolla Visitors Center** (Map p256; ☎ 619-236-1212; Suite A, 7966 Herschel Ave; ☑ 11am-4pm, extended summer hr) is in the center of town.

DOWNTOWN LA JOLLA
The compact downtown sits atop a bluff lapped by ocean waves. Regrettably, there's little interaction between downtown and the sea, though you can catch lovely glimpses of the Pacific between buildings. The main thoroughfares, Prospect St and Girard Ave, are San Diego's favorite places for high-end shopping.

The **Athenaeum Music & Arts Library** (Map p256; ☎ 858-454-5872; www.ljathenaeum.org; 1008 Wall St; admission free; ☑ 10am-5:30pm Tue-Sat, to 8:30pm Wed), housed in a graceful Spanish Renaissance structure, is devoted exclusively to art and music. Its reading room is a lovely place to relax and read.

SEALS vs SWIMMERS

La Jolla's **Children's Pool** was created in the early 1930s when the state deeded the area to the city as a public park and children's pool. Then came the seals, drawing tourists but gradually nudging out swimmers completely by 1997. Opposing parties duked it out in court: animal-rights groups fought to protect the cove as a rookery, while swimmers and divers wanted the seals removed (their presence raises bacteria in the waters to unsafe levels). State and federal courts have consistently ruled the seals must go, but enforcement by means of a consistent police presence and piped-in sounds of barking dogs may prove difficult, and Mother Nature may yet have the last word.

The small but excellent **Museum of Contemporary Art San Diego – La Jolla** (MCASD: Map p256; ☎ 858-454-3541; www.mcasd.org; 700 Prospect St; adult/student/senior $10/free/5, free 5-7pm on 3rd Thu of each month; ☺ 11am-5pm Thu-Tue, to 7pm 3rd Thu of each month) supports a permanent post-1950s collection especially strong in minimalist, pop and California art. The same ticket is

good for both here and the downtown San Diego branches of the museum (p249).

LA JOLLA COASTLINE
A wonderful walking path skirts the La Jolla shoreline for half a mile. Its western end is at the **Children's Pool** (Map p256), where a jetty protects the beach from big waves.

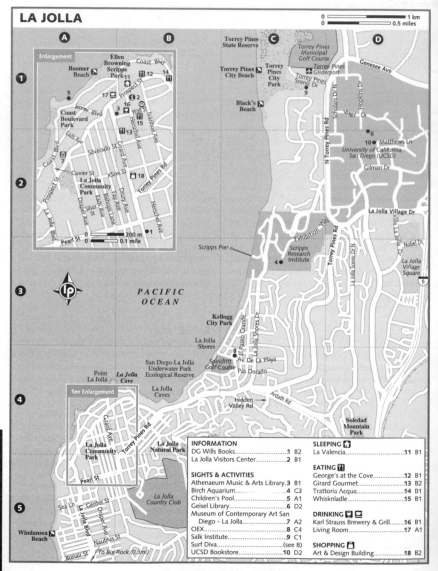

LA JOLLA

0 ———————— 1 km
0 ———————— 0.5 miles

PACIFIC OCEAN

INFORMATION		
DG Wills Books	1	B2
La Jolla Visitors Center	2	B1

SIGHTS & ACTIVITIES		
Athenaeum Music & Arts Library	3	B1
Birch Aquarium	4	C3
Children's Pool	5	A1
Geisel Library	6	D2
Museum of Contemporary Art San Diego - La Jolla	7	A2
OEX	8	C4
Salk Institute	9	C1
Surf Diva	(see 8)	
UCSD Bookstore	10	D2

SLEEPING		
La Valencia	11	B1

EATING		
George's at the Cove	12	B1
Girard Gourmet	13	B2
Trattoria Acqua	14	B1
Whisknladle	15	B1

DRINKING		
Karl Strauss Brewery & Grill	16	B1
Living Room	17	A1

SHOPPING		
Art & Design Building	18	B2

Atop Point La Jolla, at the path's eastern end, **Ellen Browning Scripps Park** (Map p256) is a tidy expanse of green lawns and palm trees, with views of **La Jolla Cove** to the north. The cove's gem of a beach provides access to some of the best snorkeling around.

Experienced surfers can head to **Windansea Beach** (Map p256), 2 miles south of downtown (take La Jolla Blvd south and turn west on Nautilus St). If you can brave the ire of the locals, you'll find that the surf's consistent peak works best at medium to low tide. You'll find a more civilized welcome immediately south at **Big Rock**, California's version of Hawaii's Pipeline.

LA JOLLA SHORES
Called 'the Shores,' this area northeast of La Jolla Cove is where La Jolla's cliffs meet the wide, sandy beaches that stretch north to Del Mar. To reach the **beach** (Map p256), take La Jolla Shores Dr north from Torrey Pines Rd and turn west onto Av de la Playa. The waves here are gentle enough for beginner surfers, and kayakers can launch from the shore without much problem.

Some of the best beaches in the county are north of the Shores in **Torrey Pines City Park** (Map p256), which covers the coastline from the Salk Institute up to the Torrey Pines State Reserve. **Torrey Pines Gliderport** (Map p256), at the end of Torrey Pines Scenic Dr, is the place for hang gliders and paragliders to launch themselves into the sea breezes that rise over the high cliffs. Tandem flights are available if you can't resist trying it. Down below – there's a path to the south from the parking lot – is **Black's Beach** (Map p256), one of America's most renowned clothing-optional beaches.

BIRCH AQUARIUM
Off N Torrey Pines Rd, **Birch Aquarium** (Map p256; ☎ 858-534-3474; www.aquarium.ucsd.edu; 2300 Exhibition Way; adult/child 3-17/student/senior $12/ 8.50/9/10; ☺ 9am-5pm; ℗ ♿) isn't as blatantly razzle-dazzle – or immense – as those other aquariums you'll find in Monterey or Long Beach, but this top-notch educational and research institution has brilliant displays on marine life. Marine scientists were working here as early as 1910 and it has grown to be one of the world's largest marine-research institutions. It is now part of the University of California, San Diego

(see below), and its pier is a landmark on La Jolla's coast.

The staff have the time and the inclination to answer any underwatery question you can throw at them. Check out the tidepool overlooking the ocean where visitors can touch animals, and don't leave without glimpsing the diminutive weedy sea dragons in the Art of Deception hall.

SALK INSTITUTE
In 1960 Jonas Salk, the pioneer of polio prevention, founded the **Salk Institute** (Map p256; ☎ 858-453-4100; www.salk.edu; 10010 N Torrey Pines Rd; free tours at noon Mon-Fri) for biological and biomedical research. Louis Kahn designed the building, completed in 1965, as a masterpiece of modern architecture. It features a classically proportioned plaza made of travertine marble and cubist, mirror-glass laboratory blocks framing a perfect view of the Pacific. Stand on the plaza's eastern end and let your eye follow the 'river of life,' representing knowledge, as it 'connects' with the ocean. There are three floors of laboratories, and above each of them is an entire floor used to house the necessary utilities. You can tour the Salk Institute for free with a guide; call (ext 1287) or go online for reservations.

TORREY PINES STATE RESERVE
Encompassing the land between N Torrey Pines Rd and the ocean from the Torrey Pines Gliderport to Del Mar, this **reserve** (Map p256; ☎ 858 755-2063; www.torreypine.org; ☺ 9am-sunset) preserves the last mainland stands of the Torrey pine (*Pinus torreyana*), a species adapted to sparse rainfall and sandy, stony soils. The views over the ocean and north to Oceanside are superb.

Parking costs $10 per car, but admission is free if you enter on foot. Several walking trails wind through the reserve and down to the beach. If you want to hike, park near the driving range on N Torrey Pines Rd and take the paved path northwest until you reach a box of trail maps at the beginning of the Broken Arrow Trail.

UNIVERSITY OF CALIFORNIA, SAN DIEGO (UCSD)
The 26,000 lucky students of University of California, San Diego live and study among the campus' rolling coastal hills, which are

SAN DIEGO AREA

covered in fragrant eucalyptus trees. By far its most distinctive structure is the **Geisel Library** (Map p256), an upside-down multi-leveled pyramid of glass and concrete whose namesake, Theodor Geisel, is better known as Dr Seuss, creator of the *Cat in the Hat*. He and his wife contributed substantially to the library, and there is a collection of his drawings and books on the ground level.

From the eastern side of the library's 2nd level, an allegorical snake created by artist Alexis Smith winds around a native California plant garden, past an enormous marble copy of John Milton's *Paradise Lost*. The piece is part of the Stuart Collection of outdoor sculptures spread around campus. The **UCSD bookstore** (Map p256; ☎ 858-534-7323; 9500 Gilman Dr; ⊙ 8am-6pm Mon-Fri, noon-5pm Sat & Sun) has excellent stock and helpful staff.

The best access to campus is off La Jolla Village Dr or N Torrey Pines Rd (bus 30 from the Old Town Transit Center); parking costs $1/6 per hour/day, free on weekends.

ACTIVITIES

If you love surf and sky, you'll go nuts in coastal San Diego. For information on biking, see p288. For the latest beach, weather and surf reports, call the **City Lifeguard** (☎ 619-221-8824).

Surfing

In general, San Diego is a great place for surfers of any skill level, though the water can get crowded and several spots, particularly Sunset Cliffs and Windansea, are somewhat 'owned' by locals, which means they'll heckle you unless you're an awesome surfer.

Fall brings strong swells and the off-shore Santa Ana winds. In summer swells come from the south and southwest, and in winter from the west and northwest. Spring brings more frequent onshore winds, but the surfing can still be good.

Beginners looking to rent equipment should head to Mission or Pacific Beaches, where the waves are gentle. North of Crystal Pier, Tourmaline Surfing Park is an especially good place to take your first strokes. **Pacific Beach Surf School** (Map p246; ☎ 858-373-1138; www.pacificbeachsurfschool.com; 4150 Mission Blvd, Pacific Beach; private lessons per person $75-85; ⊙ call for details) provides instruction and

---

> **BEST SURF BREAKS**
>
> The best San Diego County (Map p244) surf breaks, from south to north, are at Imperial Beach (especially in winter); Point Loma (reef breaks, which are less accessible but less crowded, best during winter); Sunset Cliffs in Ocean Beach; Pacific Beach; Big Rock (California's Pipeline); Windansea (hot reef break, best at medium to low tide); La Jolla Shores (beach break, best in winter); and Black's Beach (a fast, powerful wave). In North County (Map p271), there are breaks at Cardiff State Beach, San Elijo State Beach, Swami's, Carlsbad State Beach and Oceanside.
>
> The bodysurfing is good at Coronado, Pacific Beach, Boomer Beach near La Jolla Cove (for the experienced only, best with a big swell) and La Jolla Shores. To get into the whomp (the forceful tubes that break directly onshore), know what you're doing and head to Windansea or the beach at the end of Sea Lane (both in La Jolla).

---

wetsuits for rent and both soft (foam) and hard (fiberglass) boards. See also Cheap Rentals (p255) in Mission Beach. Rental rates vary depending on the quality of the equipment, but generally soft boards cost about $10 to $16 per half-day and $15 to $25 per full day; wetsuits cost $5 per hour, $10 per half-day.

In La Jolla, the women at **Surf Diva** (Map p256; ☎ 858-454-8273; www.surfdiva.com; 2160 Av de la Playa, La Jolla; classes from $60, workshops around $165; ⊙ call for details) offer basic classes for guys and gals, or two-day weekend workshops for women. Also check out Aloha Surfer Girls (p41).

Diving & Snorkeling

San Diego County divers will find kelp beds, shipwrecks and canyons deep enough to host bat rays, octopus and squid. You'll find some of California's best and most accessible diving (no boat needed) in the **San Diego-La Jolla Underwater Park Ecological Reserve** (Map p256), accessible from La Jolla Cove. With an average depth of 20ft, the 6000 acres of look-but-don't-touch underwater real estate are great for snorkeling, too. Ever-present are the spectacular, bright orange garibaldi fish, a protected species.

Further out, you'll see forests of giant California kelp (which can increase in length by up to 3ft per day) and the 100ft-deep La Jolla Canyon.

A number of commercial outfits conduct scuba courses, sell or rent equipment, fill tanks and run boat trips to nearby wrecks and islands. A snorkel and fins cost around $20; scuba-gear rental packages cost about $60; and guided dives run at about $120. Try **OEX** (Map p256; ☎ 858-454-6195; www.oeexpress .com; 2158 Av de la Playa, La Jolla).

Kayaking

You can rent kayaks and canoes on Mission Bay. Try **Mission Bay Sportcenter** (Map p246; ☎ 858-488-1004; www.missionbaysportcenter.com; 1010 Santa Clara Pl; single/tandem kayaks per hr $13/18).

Ocean kayaking is a great way to see marine life and explore cliffs and caves inaccessible from land. **Family Kayak** (☎ 619-282-3520; www.familykayak.com; 3 hrs from $55) has guided single- and multi-day trips and classes. See also OEX (above) in La Jolla.

Whale-Watching

Gray whales pass San Diego between mid-December and late February on their way south to Baja California, and again in mid-March on their way back to Alaskan waters. Their 12,000-mile round-trip journey is the longest migration of any mammal on earth.

Cabrillo National Monument (p253) is the best place to see the whales from land, where you'll also find exhibits, whale-related ranger programs and a shelter from which to watch the whales breach (bring binoculars).

Half-day whale-watching boat trips generally cost $20 to $30 for adults and $15 for children for a three-hour excursion, and most companies give you a free pass to return again if you don't spot any whales. From late December through late March **San Diego Harbor Excursion** (Map p243; ☎ 619-234-4111; www.sdhe.com; 1050 N Harbor Dr; ☻ vary by tour and season) offers 3½-hour trips guided by Birch Aquarium (p257) naturalists.

Hang Gliding & Paragliding

For a memorable fly-like-a-bird experience – and perhaps the most expensive 20 minutes of your life – head to **Torrey Pines Gliderport** (Map p256; ☎ 858-452-9858; www.flytorrey.com; 2800 Torrey Pines Scenic Dr; tandem hang-gliding flights per person per 20 min $175, paragliding tandem $150) in La Jolla, a world-famous gliding location and one of the best gliding schools in the country. Even if you have no intention of going up, swing by and watch the fun.

TOURS

Hike, Bike, Kayak San Diego (☎ 858-551-9510, 866-425-2925; www.hikebikekayak.com; 2246 Av de la Playa, La Jolla) Just what it says. Kayak tours from £35 per person.

Hornblower Cruises (Map p243; ☎ 888-467-6256; www.hornblower.com; 1066 N Harbor Dr; adult $20-$25, child 4-12 $10-$12.50) Operates boat tours of San Diego Harbor. One- and two-hour sightseeing tours leave from the Embarcadero (near the *Star of India*).

Old Town Trolley Tours (☎ 619-298-8687; www .trolleytours.com; adult/child 4-12 $32/16) Makes a hop-on-hop-off loop around the main attractions near downtown and in Coronado, via open-air trolley buses.

FESTIVALS & EVENTS

San Diego County Fair (☎ 858-755-1161; www .sdfair.com) Huge county fair held from mid-June to July 4; features headline acts and hundreds of carnival rides and shows at the Del Mar Fairgrounds.

US Open Sandcastle Competition (☎ 619-424-6663; www.usopensandcastle.com) You won't believe what can be made out of sand at the amazing sandcastle-building competition held mid-July at Imperial Beach, south of Coronado.

Comic-Con International (☎ 619-491-2475; www .comic-con.org) America's largest event for collectors of comic, pop culture and movie memorabilia, at the San Diego Convention Center in late July.

Del Mar Horse Racing (☎ 858-755-1141; www.dmtc .com) The well-heeled bet on the horses at the gorgeous Del Mar Racetrack. Mid-July to mid-September.

Old Globe Festival (☎ 619-239-2255; www.oldglobe .org) Renowned Shakespeare festival at the Old Globe Theatre in Balboa Park during August.

Fleet Week (☎ 800-353-3793; www.fleetweeksandiego .org) From September into November, the US military shows its might in a parade of ships and the signature Blue Angels air show.

SLEEPING

Wherever you're looking to stay, San Diego has a variety of lodgings across all budget categories. If you're staying in Ocean Beach, near the flight path of San Diego International Airport, you might wish to bring earplugs. Always ask about discounts; some are available only online.

SAN DIEGO AREA

Budget

Ocean Beach International Hostel (Map p246; ☎ 619-223-7873, 800-339-7263; www.californiahostels .com; 4961 Newport Ave, Ocean Beach; dm $17-24; 🖵 🛜) OBI Hostel is a friendly, laid-back place popular with Europeans, and only a couple of blocks from the water. Perks include complimentary transport from the airport or bus and train stations, and free breakfast and wi-fi. Private rooms are first-come, first-served.

HI San Diego Downtown Hostel (Map p243; ☎ 619-525-1531, 888-464-4872, ext 156; www.sandiego hostels.org; 521 Market St, Gaslamp Quarter; dm/d/tr members $25/55/78, nonmembers $28/58/81; 🖵 🛜) Centrally located in the Gaslamp Quarter, this HI facility is conveniently near to public transportation and nightlife, and has a wide range of rooms. It provides a make-your-own pancake breakfast and has 24-hour access.

ourpick 500 West Hotel (Map p243; ☎ 619-234-5252, 866-315-4251; www.500westhotel.com; 500 W Broadway, Downtown; s/d/tw with shared bath $59/69/79; 🖵 🛜) Inside the elegant beaux-arts former YMCA (the Y gym is still in the building; guests pay $5 per day for access), this place is almost too good to be true – tiny rooms are decked out with playful modern furniture, flat-screen TVs and platform beds. The catch: bathrooms are shared, though they're private once you get inside and they are cleaned fastidiously round the clock.

La Pensione Hotel (Map p243; ☎ 619-236-8000, 800-232-4683; www.lapensionehotel.com; 606 W Date St, Little Italy; r from $95; 🅿 🖵) All 75 rooms at this four-story, dramatically lit hotel in the heart of Little Italy have a queen-size bed, a fridge and charming black-and-white photos of the neighborhood. You'll feel like you're in the Old Country as you take your morning coffee in the courtyard. Parking is free, but there are only 24 spaces.

Midrange

Little Italy Inn (Map p243; ☎ 619-230-1600, 800-518-9930; www.littleitalyinn.com; 505 E Grape St, Little Italy; r $89-199; 🛜 🛜) It may lie in the shadow of the I-5, but this utterly charming boutique hotel manages to pull off 'urban getaway,' regardless. Staff go out of their way to make you feel at home, and the 23 uniquely decorated rooms are all tastefully appointed, with luxuries like plush bathrobes. Most rooms have private bathrooms, and others

boast indulgent in-room spa bathrooms. Stylish continental breakfast included. Note: rooms facing Grape St are subject to traffic noise.

Park Manor Suites (Map pp244-5; ☎ 619-291-0999, 800-874-2649; www.parkmanorsuites.com; 525 Spruce St, Hillcrest; r from $139; 🅿 🖵 🛜) This gay-friendly place, facing Balboa Park and a reasonable walk to central Hillcrest, used to be an apartment building, meaning mostly large rooms with kitchens and vast closets. Staff call the room decor 'old world,' though we'd say 'old' – take your pick. Breakfast is served on the top floor, with sweeping downtown-to-ocean views.

Inn at Sunset Cliffs (Map p246; ☎ 619-222-7901, 866-786-2543; www.innatsunsetcliffs.com; 1370 Sunset Cliffs Blvd, Ocean Beach; r from $175; 🅿 🖵 🛜 🛜 🛜) Hidden away from the hustle and bustle and right on the ocean (though with no beach access), this child-friendly motel has a courtyard terrace with great ocean views. Some rooms are small and look tired, but are clean. Ask about rooms with full kitchens. The free computer in the lobby is a welcome perk.

Top End

Tower 23 (Map p246; ☎ 866-869-3723; www.t23hotel .com; 723 Felspar St, Pacific Beach; r from $199; 🖵 🛜) Mod and modernist showplace for a contempo-cool beach stay, with lots of teals and mint blues, fabbo bar and restaurant, and a sense of humor. There's no pool, but dude, you're right on the beach. Parking is $20.

Hotel Indigo (Map p243; ☎ 619-727-4000, 877-846-3446; www.hotelindigo.com/sandiego; 509 9th Ave, Downtown; r from $200; 🛜 🖵 🛜 🛜) San Diego's first hotel to be Leadership in Energy and Environmental Design–certified green, the Indigo (opened 2009) proves that environmentally friendly can still be comfy. This pet-friendly property has green roofs, sustainable materials in its construction, windows that open (there's a concept!) and cheery design motifs inspired by local waters and California poppies. Bonus: when the Padres are playing (p248), you get to watch the game from your room or the roof deck.

Se San Diego (Map p243; ☎ 619-515-3000; www.se sandiego.com; 1047 5th Ave, Downtown; r from $249; 🖵 🛜 🛜) This new hotel brings Hollywood glam to San Diego. The 9000lb bronze front door pivots to reveal Nepalese carpets and walls covered in silver leaf, and the texture fest continues with crystal beads, stingray skin and woven leather. There's doting service, a chic restaurant, a lovely spa and, should you need it, a music studio. Parking is $36.

La Valencia (Map p256; ☎ 858-454-0771, 800-451-0772; www.lavalencia.com; 1132 Prospect St, La Jolla; r from $295; 💻 🎧 🏊) Publicity stills of Lon Chaney, Lillian Gish and Greta Garbo line the hallways of this 1926 landmark: pink-walled, Mediterranean-style, and designed by William Templeton Johnson. Among its 116 rooms, the ones in the main building are rather compact (befitting the era), but villas are spacious and, in any case, the property wins for Old Hollywood romance. If you don't stay, consider lifting a toast – and a pinkie – to the sunset from its Spanish-revival lounge, La Sala. Parking is $25.

Hotel del Coronado (Map pp244-5; ☎ 619-435-6611, 800-468-3533; www.hoteldel.com; 1500 Orange Ave, Coronado; r from $380; 💻 🎧 🏊) San Diego's iconic hotel, the Del provides more than a century of history, tennis courts, spa, shops, splashy restaurants, manicured grounds and a white-sand beach. Some rooms are in a 1970s seven-story building; book the original building. Parking is $25. For more on the Del's history, see p252.

EATING

Downtown restaurants tend to cater to conventioneers and businessfolk, but that doesn't mean you have to sacrifice in quality or atmosphere. You'd expect – and you'll find – Italian cuisine in Little Italy, hoppy, happy places in Hillcrest and high-toned dining in La Jolla. But don't overlook Old Town, touristy though it may be, for Mexican fare, and North Park is an up-and-coming neighborhood bubbling with eager gourmets.

Budget
Bread & Cie (Map pp244-5; ☎ 619-683-9322; 350 University Ave, Hillcrest; pastries $2.50-5, sandwiches $7-8; 🕐 7am-7pm Mon-Fri, to 6pm Sat, 8am-6pm Sun; 🅿) This clattery, chattery cafeteria-size bakery-deli makes the best bread around (with flavors like lemon sage, anise and fig, and caramelized onion), and carries a limited assortment of gourmet sandwiches. It's an

excellent spot to eavesdrop on locals, especially in the mornings. The name 'Cie' is pronounced 'sea.'

Girard Gourmet (Map p256; ☎ 858-454-3321; 7837 Girard Ave, La Jolla; mains $4-8; 🕐 7am-8pm Mon-Sat, to 7pm Sun) Fresh, affordable no-nonsense quiches, soups and sandwiches, plus daily hot-plate specials like salmon penne pasta. If you bring the kids, don't expect to escape without buying one of the huge clownfish cookies.

Hodad's (Map p246; ☎ 619-224-4623; 5010 Newport Ave, Ocean Beach; burgers $4-9; 🕐 11am-9pm Sun-Thu, 11am-10pm Fri & Sat) Ocean Beach's legendary burger joint serves great shakes, massive baskets of onion rings and succulent hamburgers wrapped in paper. The walls are covered in license plates, grunge/surf-rock plays (loud!) and your bearded, tattooed server might sidle into your booth to take your order.

Big Kitchen (Map pp244-5; ☎ 619-234-5789; 3003 Grape St, South Park; mains $4-9.50; 🕐 7am-2pm Mon-Fri, 7:30am-3pm Sat & Sun; ♿) The heart and soul of funky South Park, just to the east of Balboa Park at 30th Ave, Big Kitchen welcomes all to its enclave of food, art, music and civic bonhomie. The omelets are stupendous, as is the challah French toast, and there's a whole page of breakfast combos named after regulars including Whoopi Goldberg, who used to wait tables here.

Café 222 (Map p243; ☎ 619-236-9902; 222 Island Ave, Downtown; mains $6-11; 🕐 7am-1:45pm) Downtown's favorite breakfast place for pumpkin waffles, buttermilk orange-pecan or granola pancakes, and scrambled eggs or eggs Benedict. There are lunchtime sandwiches and salads, but we can't get enough of the breakfast (available until closing).

Midrange
Old Town Mexican Cafe (Map pp244-5; ☎ 619-297-4330; 2489 San Diego Ave, Old Town; dishes $3-14; 🕐 7am-midnight) Watch the staff turn out fresh tortillas in the window while waiting for a table. Besides breakfast (great *chilaquiles* – soft tortilla chips in mole), there's a big bar (try the Old Town ultimate margarita) and rambling dining room serving famous *machacas* (shredded pork with onions and peppers).

Filippi's Pizza Grotto (Map p243; ☎ 619-232-5095; 1747 India St, Little Italy; dishes $5-17; 🕐 9am-10pm Sun & Mon, 9am-10:30pm Tue-Thu, 9am-11:30pm Fri & Sat; ♿)

SAN DIEGO AREA

There are often lines out the door for Filippi's old-school Italian cooking (pizza, spaghetti and ravioli) served on red and white–checked tablecloths in the dining room. The front of the shop is an excellent Italian deli.

Hash House a Go Go (Map pp244-5; ☎ 619-298-4646; 3628 5th Ave, Hillcrest; breakfast $8-16; ☺ 7.30am-2pm Tue-Fri, 7.30am-2.30pm Sat-Mon, dinner Tue-Sun) This buzzing bungalow makes biscuits and gravy straight outta Carolina: towering eggs Benedict, large-as-your-head pancakes and – wait for it – hash seven different ways. Come hungry. Eat your whole breakfast and you may not need dinner.

our pick Urban Solace (Map pp244-5; ☎ 619-295-6464; 3823 30th St, North Park; lunch $8-16, dinner $9-18; ☺ 11:30am-10pm Mon-Thu, 11:30am-11pm Fri, 5-11pm Sat, 5-9pm Sun) You know those hip young gourmets in North Park? Here's where you'll find them, reveling in creative comfort food: meat loaf of ground lamb, fig, pine nuts and feta; mac 'n' cheese with duck confit; chicken and dumplings. The setting's surprisingly chill for such great eats; maybe it's the cocktails, like a mojito made with bourbon.

Linkery (Map pp244-5; ☎ 619-255-8778; 3794 30th St, North Park; mains $9-20; ☺ 5.30-11:30pm daily, lunch Fri-Sun) A daily changing menu of house-made sausages and hand-cured meats from sustainably raised animals is the thing here – on a roll, in tacos, on a board with cheese or in *choucroute* (French stew). Vegetarians: don't worry; you're covered too.

World Famous (Map p246; ☎ 858-272-3100; 711 Pacific Beach Dr, Pacific Beach; breakfast & lunch $8-15, dinner $10-24; ☺ 7am-11pm) Watch the surf while enjoying 'California coastal cuisine,' an ever-changing menu of inventive dishes from the sea (think banana rum mahi, bacon and spinach–wrapped scallops), plus steaks, salads, lunchtime sandwiches and burgers, and breakfasts like the Newport omelet, with crab, shrimp and spicy sauce.

Gaslamp Strip Club (Map p243; ☎ 619-231-3140; 340 5th Ave, Gaslamp Quarter; mains $14-24; ☺ kitchen 5-10pm Sun-Thu, 5pm-midnight Fri & Sat, bar open later) No, not that kind of strip...the New York steak kind. Pull a bottle from the wine vault then char your own favorite cut of steak, chicken or fish on the open grills in this retro Vegas dining room. Fab, creative martinis, 'pin-up' art by Alberto Vargas and reasonable prices. No one under 21 allowed.

Top End

Croce's Restaurant & Jazz Bar (Map p243; ☎ 619-233-4355; 802 5th Ave, Downtown; breakfast & lunch $7-19, dinner $23-35; ☺ 5:30pm-midnight Mon-Fri, 10am-midnight Sat & Sun) This sizzling restaurant is a pioneer of the Gaslamp. It's also Ingrid Croce's tribute to her late husband, singer Jim Croce. The contemporary American menu hits few false notes, nor do the musicians who perform nightly at the jazz bar.

our pick Whisknladle (Map p256; ☎ 858-551-7575; 1044 Wall St, La Jolla; dishes $9-30; ☺ lunch & dinner) This newcomer has earned plenty of kudos for its 'Slow Food' preparations of local, farm-fresh ingredients, served on a breezy covered patio. The menu changes daily, but it's always clever. So are the cocktails (the London's Burning mixes gin and jalapeño water).

Trattoria Acqua (Map p256; ☎ 858-454-0709; 1298 Prospect St, La Jolla; lunch $10-18, dinner $17-35; ☺ lunch & dinner; **P**) Lovely by day, dreamy by night, Trattoria Acqua is set into the hillside like an ocean-view treehouse. There's scrumptious northern Italian cuisine with coastal Cali touches: salad of crab, avocado, tomato and mango; ravioli filled with butternut squash and crushed Amaretto cookies; lobster pot pie.

George's at the Cove (Map p256; ☎ 858-454-4244; www.georgesatthecove.com; 1250 Prospect St, La Jolla; mains $11-48; ☺ 11am-11pm) If you've got the urge to splurge, the Euro-Cal cooking here is as dramatic as the oceanfront location thanks to the bottomless imagination of chef Trey Foshee. George's has graced just about every list of top restaurants in California, and indeed the USA. Three venues allow you to enjoy it at different price points: Ocean Terrace, George's Bar and George's California Modern.

DRINKING

In the Gaslamp Quarter of downtown, the center of the city's (straight) nightlife, the line between restaurant, bar and club often gets blurry after 10pm.

Cafes

Jungle Java (Map p246; ☎ 619-224-0249; 5047 Newport Ave, Ocean Beach; ☺ 7am-9pm Sun-Thu, to 10pm summer, winter varies; ☎) Funky-dunky, canopy-covered cafe and plant shop, crammed with crafts and art treasures. A perfect microcosm of Ocean Beach.

Café 976 (Map p246; ☎ 858-272-0976; 976 Felspar St, Pacific Beach; ☯ 7am-11pm; ☞) Not everyone in Pacific Beach spends the days surfing; some drink coffee and read books at this side-street cafe in a converted old house with green plants.

Living Room (Map p256; ☎ 858-459-1187; 1010 Prospect St, La Jolla; ☯ 6am-1am; ☞) This popular cafe serves sandwiches and has a great, central position in the heart of La Jolla Village.

Bars

Altitude (Map p243; ☎ 619-696-0234; 660 K St, Downtown) The Marriott's rooftop bar is the best of the lot. It may have the de rigueur firepits and sleek decor but, unlike other open-air lounges, the vibe is friendly. Sightlines to Petco Park are superb.

East Village Tavern & Bowl (Map p243; ☎ 619-677-2695; 930 Market St, East Village; ☯ 11:30am-1am, from 10am Sat & Sun) This large sports bar a few blocks from Petco Park has six bowling lanes (thankfully, behind a wall for effective soundproofing). A pub menu (dishes $6 to $11; pulled pork sliders, applewood BLT etc) is served all day.

Wine Steals (Map pp244-5; ☎ 619-295-1188; 1243 University Ave, Hillcrest; cheese & charcuterie boards $10-13; ☯ 11am-11pm Sun, 4-11pm Mon, 11am-midnight Fri & Sat; ℗) Gay, straight, not sure, who cares… This place gets elbow to-elbow with a stylish but laid back crew for affordable wine tastings which you can pair with cheese-charcuterie boards.

Nunu's Cocktail Lounge (Map pp244-5; ☎ 619-295-2878; 3537 5th Ave, Hillcrest) Dark and divey, this hipster haven started pouring when JFK was president and still looks the part with its curvy booths, big bar and lovably kitsch decor. Smoking patio.

Airport Lounge (Map p256; ☎ 619-685-3881; 2400 India St, Little Italy) The clientele is Euro-cool, the DJs hot, the design mod, the drinks strong and the servers dressed like flight attendants at this buzzy watering hole in the flight path of San Diego Airport.

Coaster Saloon (Map p246; ☎ 858-488-4438; 744 Ventura Pl, Mission Beach) This old-fashioned neighborhood dive bar has front-row views of the Belmont Park roller coaster and draws an unpretentious crowd. Good margaritas.

ENTERTAINMENT

Check the San Diego *Reader* or the Thursday edition of the San Diego *Union-Tribune* for the latest happenings around town. **Arts Tix** (Map p243; sdartstix.com; 3rd Ave & Broadway, Downtown; ☯ 11am-6pm Tue-Thu, 10am-6pm Fri & Sat, 10am-5pm Sun), in a kiosk on Broadway outside Horton Plaza, has half-price tickets for same-day evening or next-day matinee performances and discounted tickets to all types of other events. **Ticketmaster** (☎ 619-220-8497; www.ticketmaster.com) and **House of Blues** (www.hob.com) sell other tickets.

Anthology (Map p243; ☎ 619-595-0300; www.anthologysd.com; 1337 India St, Downtown; cover free-$60) Near Little Italy, Anthology presents live

---

SURF & SUDS

'The beer that made San Diego famous' may not quite roll off the tongue, but never mind: America's Finest City is home to some of America's finest brewpubs. The San Diego Brewers Guild (www.sandiegobrewersguild.org) counts some 40 member establishments, serving a variety of grub to accompany handcrafted brews. Hop over to the guild's website (get it?) or pick up one of its pamphlets around town. Here are some pubs to get you started:

- **Karl Strauss Brewery & Grill** (www.karlstrauss.com) Downtown (Map p243; ☎ 619-234-2739; 1157 Columbia St; mains $9-29; ☯ hrs vary) La Jolla (Map p256; ☎ 858-551-2739; cnr Wall St & Herschel Ave; mains $9-29; ☯ hrs vary) San Diego meets Bavaria at this longtime favorite, where wait staff will instruct you which beers pair with your food choices. Go on Thursday 'cask nights.'

- **Pacific Beach Ale House** (Map p246; ☎ 858-581-2337; www.pbalehouse.com; 721 Grand Ave, Pacific Beach; mains $9-25; ☯ 11am-2am) Contempo-cool setting and a huge menu including lobster mac 'n' cheese, steamed clams and bistro meat loaf.

- **Pizza Port** (Map p268; ☎ 760-720-7007; www.pizzaport.com; 571 Carlsbad Village Dr, Carlsbad; pizzas $8-23; ☯ 11am-11pm; Ⓥ) Rockin' and raucous barn of a space with surf art and 'anti-wimpy' pizzas to go with the signature 'Sharkbite Red' brew.

GAY & LESBIAN SAN DIEGO

Ironically, given the gay community's recent uneasy relationship with America's armed forces, historians trace the roots of San Diego's thriving gay community to the military. During WWII, amid the enforced intimacy of military life, gay men from around the country were suddenly able to create strong if clandestine social networks. After the war, many of these new friends stayed.

In the late 1960s, a newly politicized gay community began to make the Hillcrest neighborhood its unofficial headquarters, and it still has the highest concentration of bars, restaurants, cafés and bookstores catering to lesbians and gays. The scene is generally more casual and friendly than in San Francisco or LA.

San Diego's **Gay Pride festival** (www.sdpride.org) takes over Hillcrest and Balboa Park in late July.

Pick up the free, widely available, *Gay and Lesbian Times*.

Bookstore

- **Obelisk Bookstore** (Map pp244-5; ☎ 619-297-4171; 1029 University Ave, Hillcrest) Large gay, lesbian, bisexual and transgender selection.

Cafe

- **Babycakes** (Map pp244-5; ☎ 619-296-4173; www.babycakessandiego.com; 3766 5th Ave, Hillcrest; 🕙 9am-11pm Sun-Thu, 9am-midnight Fri & Sat; 📶) Hillcrest location, palmy, tropical garden, exotic cupcakes and wi-fi. Truly, darling, what more could you ask?

Bars & Clubs

- **Bourbon Street** (Map pp244-5; ☎ 619-291-4043; www.bourbonstreetsd.com; 4612 Park Blvd, University Park) Away from Hillcrest's central strip, this gay bar's layout of rooms and courtyards, bar and dance floor, makes for easy mingling during bingo and guest DJ nights and wicked-cheap martini happy hours.

- **Hole** (Map pp244-5; ☎ 619-225-9019; 2820 Lytton St, Point Loma) This gay dive near Point Loma is surrounded by auto repair shops, all the better for camo. Head down to the patio to find manly men enjoying Sunday beer bust, wet underwear contests and more.

- **Rich's** (Map pp244-5; ☎ 619-295-2195; 1051 University Ave, Hillcrest; 🕙 Tue-Sun) DJs shower the crowd with Latin, techno, pop and house at this gay dance institution.

- **Top of the Park** (Map pp244-5; ☎ 619-291-0999, 525 Spruce St, Hillcrest; 🕙 Fri evening) Start your weekend off big with after-work cocktails surrounded by a veritable gaggle of gays in the penthouse restaurant of the Park Manor Suites hotel (p263).

- **Urban Mo's** (Map pp244-5; ☎ 619-491-0400; 308 University Ave, Hillcrest) Equal parts bar and restaurant, Mo's isn't particularly known for great food, service or prices, but it's popular nonetheless for its thumping club beats, casual vibe, dance floor and happy hours.

jazz in a swank supper-club setting, both up-and-comers and big-namers.

Casbah (Map p243; ☎ 619-232-4355; 2501 Kettner Blvd, Little Italy; cover free-$15) Liz Phair, Alanis Morissette and the Smashing Pumpkins all rocked this funky Casbah on their way up the charts, and it's still a good place to catch local acts and tomorrow's headliners.

Shout House (Map p243; ☎ 619-231-6700; 655 4th Ave, Downtown; cover free-$10) Dueling pianos entertain at this rowdy but basically innocent Gaslamp bar. Pianists have an amazing repertoire: standards, rock and more; we once heard the cult comedy number 'D*ck in a Box.'

SHOPPING

Little Italy (www.littleitalysd.com) is the de facto design district, heaped high with browse-worthy home-furnishings shops, from antiques and architectural salvage to cutting-edge modern ware. For bikinis and surfboards, head to Garnet Ave in Pacific Beach or Newport Ave in Ocean Beach.

They also have good thrift and vintage shops, but the best are along Hillcrest's 5th Ave. Given that adventure sports gods Tony Hawk and Shawn White are San Diegans, surf and skate clothing are natural purchases. Gaslamp City Sq (cnr 5th Ave and J St) is de facto HQ for extreme-sports wear.

At the other end of the scale, La Jolla's skirt-and-sweater crowd pays retail for cashmere sweaters and expensive tchotchkes, particularly along Girard Ave and Prospect St. Paintings, sculpture and decorative items, and small boutiques fill the gaps between hoity-toity national chains like Talbot's, Ralph Lauren and Armani Exchange. The **Art & Design Building** (Map p256; 7661 Girard Ave, La Jolla) is one-stop shopping for art, furniture and adventurous textiles from a half-dozen galleries and studios.

Mall shoppers can choose from **Westfield Horton Plaza** (Map p243; ☎ 619-239-8180; www .westfield.com/hortonplaza; 324 Horton Plaza) and three large malls in Mission Valley: **Fashion Valley** (Map p242; ☎ 619-688-9113; www.simon.com; 7007 Friars Rd); **Westfield Mission Valley** (☎ 619-296-6375; www.westfield.com/missionvalley; 1640 Camino del Rio N) and **Hazard Center** (Map p242; ☎ 619-543-8111; www.hazardcenter.com; 7676 Hazard Center Dr). **Westfield University Towne Center** (Map p242; ☎ 858-546-8858; www.westfield.com/utc; 4545 La Jolla Village Dr, La Jolla) sits outside of central La Jolla.

GETTING THERE & AWAY
Air
All major US carriers (see p285) serve **San Diego International Airport** (SAN; Lindbergh Field; Map p242; ☎ 619-400-2400; www.san.org; 3665 N Harbor Dr), about 3 miles west of downtown; planespotters can experience the thrill of watching jets come in for a landing over Balboa Park. If coming from LA, air fares fluctuate and it may be less expensive to travel by bus or train. Ground transportation may also makes more sense after allowing for check-in times for the 30-minute flight.

Bus
Greyhound (Map p243; ☎ 800-231-2222, 619-239-3266; 120 W Broadway) serves San Diego from cities all over North America (see p287).

To and from LA (one way and round trip fares are $16.50 and $28; the journey takes 2¼ to four hours and buses leave almost every half hour), trip times vary depending on the number of stops enroute. Buses to Anaheim, home of Disneyland, run nine times per day for the same price.

Services between San Francisco and San Diego (one way and round trip are $63 and $124; it takes 11 hours and there are nine daily) usually require a transfer in LA.

Greyhound also has direct services from San Diego to Tijuana, across the border in Mexico (one way and round-trip are $12 and $24; it takes one hour and buses leave hourly on the half hour).

Train
Amtrak (p292) trains arrive at and depart from the lovely **Santa Fe Train Depot** (Map p243; 1050 Kettner Blvd) at the western end of C St. Amtrak's *Pacific Surfliner* runs several times daily to LA ($34, three hours) and Santa Barbara ($47, six hours).

GETTING AROUND
Car is the main mode of transport, but you can reach most places on public transportation. Local buses and trolley lines are run by the **Metropolitan Transit System** (MTS; ☎ 619-233-3004; 24hr recorded info 619-685-4900; www .sdmts.com), and several other bus companies serve surrounding areas. All sorts of local public-transportation tickets, maps and information are available from the **Transit Store** (Map p243; ☎ 619-234-1060; 102 Broadway; ⏰ 9am-5pm Mon-Fri).

To/from the Airport
Bus 992 ('the Flyer,' $2.25) operates at 10- to 15-minute intervals between the airport and downtown, with stops along Broadway. Buses leave between 5am and 1am and make several stops before heading north on Harbor Dr to the airport.

Airport shuttles such as **Super Shuttle** (☎ 800-974-8885; www.supershuttle.com) charge about $13 to downtown, but these tend to travel at their own pace, often making stops en route. If you're going to the airport, call the shuttle a day ahead. The taxi fare to downtown from the airport is $10 to $15.

Bicycle
Coastal San Diego has wonderful areas for biking. All public buses are equipped with bike racks and will transport two-wheelers for free. Inform the driver before boarding, then stow your bike on the rack on the back

of the bus. For more information phone ☎ 619-685-4900.

The following are just two companies that rent out various types of bicycles, from mountain and road bikes to kids' bikes and cruisers. In general, expect to pay about $7 per hour, $10 to $14 per half-day (four hours) and up to $30 per day.

Cheap Rentals (Map p246; ☎ 800-941-7761, 858-488-2453; www.cheap-rentals.com; 3689 Mission Blvd; ◷ 9am-7pm daily Mar-Aug, to 5pm Mon-Fri Sep-Feb)

Holland's Bicycles (Map p242; ☎ 619-435-3153; 977 Orange Ave, Coronado; ◷ 10am-6pm Mon-Sat, 10am-5pm Sun)

Boat

San Diego Harbor Excursion (☎ 619-234-4111; www .sdhe.com; one way $3.25; ◷ vary) runs hourly ferries between Broadway Pier in San Diego's Embarcadero and the San Diego Convention Center and Coronado. It also operates a **water taxi** (☎ 619-235-8294; per person $7; ◷ 9:30am-8pm Mon-Fri, 9:30am-10pm Sat & Sun) connecting San Diego, Coronado and other shore points, by reservation.

Bus

The Metropolitan Transit System (p265) operates local buses. The system is most convenient if you're going to/from downtown and not staying out late. Most bus tickets cost $2.25. The Old Town Transit Center (Map pp244–5) is an important hub.

The Transit Store (p265) has route maps, tickets and day passes for $5/9/12/15 for one/two/three/four days. Single-day passes are available for purchase on board buses.

Useful routes to/from downtown include the following:

No 2 South Park, North Park
No 3 Balboa Park, Hillcrest, UCSD Medical Center
No 7, 7A, 7B Balboa Park, Zoo, Hillcrest
No 9 Old Town to Pacific Beach, SeaWorld

No 11 Hillcrest, Adams Ave Antique Row
No 30 Old Town, Pacific Beach, La Jolla, University Towne Centre
No 35 Old Town to Ocean Beach
No 901 Coronado

Car

All the big-name rental companies have convenient desks at the airport. The western terminal at the airport has free direct phones to a number of car-rental companies – you can call several and then get a courtesy bus to the company of your choice.

For contact details of the big-name rental companies, including Avis, Budget and Hertz, see p290. Some of the smaller, independent companies – such as **West Coast Rent a Car** (Map p243; ☎ 619-544-0606; 834 W Grape St) in Little Italy – may have lower rates and offer more relaxed conditions. Ecoconscious travelers can try Zipcar (p290).

Taxi

Taxi flag fall is $2.40, plus $2.60 for each additional mile. Some established companies:

San Diego Cab (☎ 619-226-8294)
Yellow Cab (☎ 619-234-6161)

Train

A commuter train service, the Coaster, leaves Santa Fe Train Depot (Map p243) and runs up the coast to North County, with stops including Solana Beach, Encinitas, Carlsbad and Oceanside. In the city of San Diego, it stops at the Sorrento Valley station (where there's a connecting shuttle to UCSD) and Old Town. Tickets are available from vending machines at stations, payable with cash, Visa, MasterCard and most debit cards. Fares range from $5 to $6.50 depending on distance. There are about 20 trains daily in each direction Monday to Friday, 10 on Saturday and none on Sunday.

Bicycles are permitted on board Coaster trains.

For information, contact **Regional Transit** (☎ 619-233-3004, from North County 511; http:// transit.511sd.com).

Trolley

Municipal trolleys (not to be confused with Old Town Trolley tourist buses) operate on three main lines. From the transit center across from the Santa Fe Train Depot, Blue

Line trolleys go south to San Ysidro (Mexico border) and north to the Old Town Transit Center. The Green Line runs from Old Town east through Mission Valley including to Mission San Diego de Alcalá (p254). The Orange Line connects the Convention Center with the rest of downtown, but otherwise it's less useful for visitors. Trolleys run between about 4:15am and 1am daily at 15-minute intervals during the day, and every 30 minutes in the evening. The Blue Line continues limited all-night service on Saturday. Fares are $2.50 per ride, valid for two hours from the time of purchase at vending machines on the station platforms.

For information, contact **MTS** (☎ 619-233-3004, 24hr recorded info 619-685-4900; www.sdmts.com).

NORTH SAN DIEGO COUNTY COAST

North of La Jolla, the coastal cliffs shrink quickly, making way for a series of wide, inviting beaches that stretch nearly unbroken all the way to Camp Pendleton, the marine corps base that takes up the northwestern corner of the county.

Known locally as 'North County,' this region resembles the San Diego of 40 years ago, though more and more development, especially east of I-5, has turned much of it into a giant bedroom community. Stick close to the water for the best ambience.

Getting There & Around

From the south, take N Torrey Pines Rd to Del Mar for the most scenic approach to North County. Continue along the coast on S21 (which changes its name from Camino del Mar to Pacific Coast Hwy to Coast Hwy 101, going north). The I-5 is quicker and continues to LA. Rush hour is 7am to 10am and 3pm to 7pm Monday to Friday.

Bus 101 departs from University Towne Centre near La Jolla and follows the coastal road to Oceanside; for information call the **North County Transit District** (NCTD; ☎ 760-966-6500; www.gonctd.com; single ride/day pass $2/5). NCTD also operates the Coaster commuter train, which originates in San Diego and makes stops in Solana Beach, Encinitas, Carlsbad and Oceanside. All NCTD buses and trains have bike racks. Greyhound buses stop at Oceanside and San Diego but not in between.

TIJUANA, MEXICO

Times are tough in Tijuana. For years, 'TJ' was a cheap, convivial borderland escape for hard-partying San Diegans, Angelenos, sailors and college kids. But a triple-whammy of drug-related violence (see also p287), global economic downturn and the 2009 H1N1 swine-flu virus has turned once-bustling tourist areas into ghost towns. Local authorities have taken steps to turn things around, but heavily armed soldiers in bulletproof vests tend not to inspire confidence.

If you go, the San Diego Trolley runs from downtown to San Ysidro ($3, 30 minutes). Cross the border on foot, and pick up a map at the border station for the approximately one-mile walk; follow signs reading 'Centro Downtown.' If traveling by taxi, take a white-and-green one (these have meters). If you're planning on driving across the border, see p286.

Avenida Revolución ('La Revo') is the main tourist drag. Other sightseeing highlights include **Museo de las Californias** (inside Centro Cultural Tijuana; ☎ 011-52-664-687-9695; cnr Paseo de los Heroes & Av Independencia; adult/child $2/1.50, free Sun; ☺ 10am-7pm Tue-Sun), for an excellent history of Baja California from prehistory to the present; there's signage in English. **Catedral de Nuestra Señora de Guadalupe** (Cathedral of our Lady of Guadalupe; Av Niños Héroes & Calle 2a) is Tijuana's oldest church. **Mercado El Popo** (Calle 2a & Av Constitución) is a colorful market selling needs from tamarind pods to religious iconography.

For a meal, try **La Especial** (☎ 011-52-664-685-6654; Av Revolución 718; breakfast $5-12, mains $6-17; ☺ 9am-10pm Sun-Thu, 9am-11:30pm Fri & Sat), a woodsy dining room in a shopping arcade below Hotel Lafayette, serving classics like *carne asada* (thinly sliced beef served with tortillas and sides). The venerable though shopworn **Hotel Caesar** (☎ 011-52-664-685-1606; Av Revolución 827; Caesar salad $6; ☺ 9am-midnight) is the 1920s birthplace of the Caesar salad.

See p286 for passport and customs information.

DEL MAR

pop 4400

The rich and famous – and those who aspire to be – have been flocking to Del Mar since at least 1937, when a prestigious group including Bing Crosby and Jimmy Durante founded a racetrack 'where the turf meets the surf.' Del Mar's been the ritziest of North County's seaside suburbs ever since. There's a Tudor aesthetic that should feel out of place but somehow doesn't, good (if pricey) restaurants and high-end boutiques. Downtown Del Mar (sometimes called 'the village') extends for about a mile along Camino del Mar. North of the town center, the racetrack is also the site of the annual **county fair** (p259).

The **Del Mar Racetrack & Fairgrounds** (☎ 858-755-1141; www.delmarracing.com; races from $5; ☺ mid-Jul–early Sep) is one of the most beautiful structures on the coast, with Spanish-style architecture and lush gardens. Opening day is the highlight of the social calendar, the equine pageantry enhanced by a spectacle of hats and the hoi-polloi. Driving here on opening day…just don't.

At the end of 15th St, **Seagrove Park** abuts the beach and overlooks the ocean. This little stretch of well-groomed beachfront lawn is a community hub and perfect for a picnic.

Best Western Stratford Inn (☎ 858-755-1501, 800-446-7229; www.pacificahost.com; 710 Camino Del Mar; r $165-250; P ⏸ 🛜 🐾 ♿) The sprawling Stratford has large, handsome rooms (many with new carpeting and bathroom fixtures), lots of wood in its construction, a spa for foot and body treatments, laundry facilities and two pools. A few have kitchenettes and distant ocean views.

L'Auberge Del Mar Resort & Spa (☎ 858-259-1515, 866-835-8145; www.laubergedelmar.com; 1540 Camino Del Mar; r $350-540; ⏸ 🛜 🐾) On the grounds of the historic Hotel del Mar, where 1920s Hollywood celebrities once frolicked, L'Auberge continues a tradition of European-style elegance, with luxurious linens, creamy-dreamy colors, generous deck space, a spa and lovely grounds. It feels so intimate and the service is so individual, you'd never know there are 120 rooms.

Across the street is the shopping center **Del Mar Plaza** (1555 Camino Del Mar) where you can pick up groceries and sandwiches (about $6) for the beach at **Harvest Ranch**

Market (☎ 858-847-0555; ☺ 8am-9pm). Or check out the rooftop patio and its swank restaurants for North County's best vantage points, especially at sunset:

Il Fornaio (☎ 858-755-8876; lunch $11-23, dinner $12-34; ☺ 11:30am-10pm Mon-Fri, 10am-10pm Sat & Sun) Classic trattoria-style pizzas, pastas and salads.

Pacifica Del Mar (☎ 858-792-0476; lunch $10-25, dinner $18-35; ☺ 11:30am-10pm Mon-Fri) Fresh seafood and inventive preparations. Arrive by 6pm for the two-course prix fixe menu for $21.75.

SOLANA BEACH

pop 13,500

Solana Beach has a more homey, walkabout feel than Del Mar, with good beaches as well as the **Cedros Design District** (Cedros Ave),

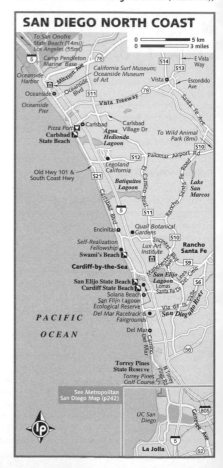

SAN DIEGO NORTH COAST

SAN ELIJO LAGOON ECOLOGICAL RESERVE

Between Solana Beach and Encinitas, in the town of Cardiff-by-the-Sea, community outcry in the 1960s saved this wetlands from the sort of development that's occurred on the rest of North County's coast. Although it's bisected by the I-5, US Hwy 101 and railroad tracks, the 1000-plus-acre reserve performs vital environmental functions for shore life. Learn about it at the new **nature center** (☎ 760-634-3026; www.sanelijo.org; 2710 Manchester Ave, Cardiff-by-the-Sea; admission free; ◷ 9am-5pm; **P**) and then go exploring along its 7 miles of footpaths.

which has a glut of home-furnishing stores, architecture studios, antiques shops and clothing boutiques.

Vegetarians visit **Zinc Café** (☎ 858-793-5436; 132 S Cedros Ave; mains $6-9; ◷ 7am-4pm Mon-Thu, to 5pm Fri & Sat; **V**) and either order at the counter or sit outside. It serves a gourmet, Cal-Ital menu with precious dishes like the potato and arugula pizzette. Join yoga-holics, crunchy surf dudes and moms and babies on the shaded, sidewalk-adjacent patio.

The crowd at the converted warehouse and bar **Belly Up Tavern** (☎ 858-481-9022, 858-481-8140; 143 S Cedros Ave) gets down to folks like Neko Case, Blackalicious and Calexico.

ENCINITAS

pop 59,300

Since Paramahansa Yoganada founded his **Self-Realization Fellowship Retreat & Hermitage** here in 1937, the town has been a magnet for healers and seekers. The gold lotus domes of the hermitage – conspicuous on Coast Hwy 101 – mark the southern end of Encinitas. Somehow it's fitting that the nearby **Swami's Beach** is a powerful reef break favored by territorial locals. Parking is free.

Sights

A highlight is the hermitage's intimate **Meditation Garden** (☎ 760-753-2888; 215 K St; ◷ 9am-5pm Tue-Sat, 11am-5pm Sun), with magical ocean vistas, multitiered koi ponds and a palpable tranquility. The entrance is west of Coast Hwy 101. In keeping with the swami-surf theme, nearby **Hansen Surfboards** (☎ 760-

753-6595; 1105 S Coast Hwy 101) is the county's largest surf shop, renting boards for $20 per day.

The heart of Encinitas lies north of the hermitage on Coast Hwy 101 between E and D Sts. Apart from the outdoor cafes, bars, restaurants and surf shops, the town's main attraction is **La Paloma Theater** (☎ 760-436-7469; 471 S Coast Hwy 101), built in 1928.

The 35-acre **Quail Botanical Gardens** (☎ 760-436-3036; www.qbgardens.org; 230 Quail Gardens Dr; adult/child 3-12/student $12/6/8, free 1st Tue each month; ◷ 9am-5pm; **⅋**) nurtures the largest variety of bamboo plants in North America. Its interactive garden for kids, Seeds of Wonder, is an award-winning romp. To get there, take the Leucadia Blvd exit from I-5 and head east for 0.5 miles. Parking is $2.

A few miles east of central Encinitas, the new **Lux Art Institute** (☎ 760 436-6611; www.luxart institute.org; 1550 S El Camino Real; admission $10 for up to 2 visits per person; ◷ 1-5pm Thu & Fri, 11am-5pm Sat; **P**) offers a unique perspective on the creative process. An artist in residence crafts major pieces, from concept to construction, while spectators watch in the 'green' studio building. Creative types will want to make a bee-line for it. From Encinitas, take Encinitas Blvd east and turn right onto S El Camino Real, for about 1.3 miles.

Sleeping & Eating

Leucadia Beach Inn (☎ 760-943-7461; www.leucadia beachinn.org; 1322 N Coast Hwy; r $85-145; **P** **⊠** **⊚** **⅋**) All 21 sparkling-clean rooms in this charming 1920s hostelry have Spanish tile floors, and many have full kitchenettes. The beach is a few blocks' walk. Book early for a summer visit.

Swami's Café (☎ 760-944-0612; 1163 S Coast Hwy 101; mains $5-9; ◷ 7am-sunset; **P** **V** **⅋**) For pancakes and waffles, burritos (for breakfast or lunch), salads, three-egg omm-lets (sorry, we couldn't resist) and an entire menu of smoothies, you can't beat this indoor-outdoor roadside shack. There's a laid-back, good-for-you vibe and lots of options for vegetarians.

El Callejon (☎ 760-634-2793; 345 S Coast Hwy 101; mains $5-23; ◷ 11am-10pm; **P**) Local favorite El Callejon is a raucous, fun Mexican joint at the northern end of the town center. The menu is as long as the phone book of a small village in Jalisco, and it would take you over two years of a different variety every day to go through their tequila list.

CARLSBAD
pop 92,900

Besides fine beaches, Carlsbad is home to the kitschy but fun Legoland. The town got its start when the train service arrived in the 1880s. As a result, it has a solid downtown of four square blocks rather than stretching along the highway like most North County towns. Homesteader John Frazier claimed his well water had identical mineral content to the spa water of Karlsbad (now in the Czech Republic), hence the name.

Legoland California (☎ 760-918-5346; www .legoland.com/california; 1 Legoland Dr, Carlsbad; adult/ child 3-12 $65/55; ☽ opens 10am, closing hours vary, closed most Tue & Wed Sep-May; ⓖ) is a fantasy environment built largely of those little colored plastic blocks. Many rides and attractions are targeted to elementary schoolers: a junior 'driving school,' a jungle cruise lined with Lego animals, pedaling wacky 'sky cruiser' cars on a track, and fairytale, princess, pirate, adventurer and dino-themed escapades. Sign up budding scientists (age 10 and over) on arrival at the park for an appointment for Mindstorms, where they can make computerized Lego robots. There are also lots of low-thrill activities like face painting.

Happy kids generally mean happy grown-ups, and the whole family will probably get a kick out of Miniland, re-creating the skylines of New York, Washington, San Francisco and Las Vegas entirely out of Lego blocks. New York's 25ft Freedom Tower was built according to the real Freedom Tower's winning design, years before the actual building will be complete. Check the website for information on two-day and combination tickets with the adjacent, low-key Sea Life Aquarium (adult/ child $18.95/11.95).

Driving from downtown San Diego (about 32 miles), take the I-5 Fwy north to the Cannon Rd E exit. Parking is $12. Alternatively, take the Coaster commuter train (p266) to Carlsbad Village Station; from here bus 321 operated by **North County Transit District** (☎ 619-233-3004; from North County 800-266-6883; www.gonctd.com) goes to the park ($2, 20 minutes, hourly at 55 minutes past the hour Monday to Friday).

Approximately 80 percent of all poinsettias sold worldwide originate in commercial flower farms in San Diego's inland hills, notably from Encinitas-based **Paul Ecke Poinsettia Ranch** (☎ 760-753-1134; www.ecke.com), established in 1923. In spring, ranunculus on its 50-acre **Flower Fields** (adult/child 3-10 $10/5; ☽ 9am-6pm Mar-early May, weather permitting; ⓖ) in Carlsbad burst into rainbows of color. It's a great place to photograph your kids. Call for directions.

About halfway between Legoland and Carlsbad Village, the independently run, 86-room **West Inn & Suites** (☎ 866-375-4705, 760-208-4929; 4970 Av Encinas; r incl breakfast from $169; Ⓟ ⊠ ▣ ▣ ⓖ) caters in equal parts to

---

DETOUR: SAN DIEGO WILD ANIMAL PARK

Since the early 1960s, the San Diego Zoological Society has been developing the **Wild Animal Park** (off Map p268; ☎ 760-747-8702; www.sandiegozoo.org; 15500 San Pasqual Valley Rd, Escondido; adult/ child 3-11 $28.50/18.50, incl tram $35/26; ☽ from 9am, closing times vary; ⓖ), an 1800-acre, open-range zoo where herds of giraffes, zebras, rhinos and other animals roam the open valley floor. For an instant safari feel, board the Journey to Africa tram ride, which tours you around the second-largest continent in under half an hour.

Elsewhere, animals are in enclosures so naturalistic it's as if the humans are guests, and there's a petting enclosure and animal shows; pick up a map and schedule. Special programs, like a 'photo caravan,' zip-lining and even sleepovers (yowza!) are available for an additional fee. A combined ticket for unlimited visits to both San Diego Zoo and the Wild Animal Park within a five-day period costs $60/43 per adult/child.

The park's just north of Hwy 78, 5 miles east of I-15 from the Via Rancho Pkwy exit. Plan a 45-minute transit by car from San Diego, except in rush hour when that figure can double. Parking is $9. For transit information contact **North San Diego County Transit District** (☎ 619-233-3004; from North County 800-266-6883; www.gonctd.com).

business folk (note the computer and fitness centers) and vacationing families (note the sparkling pool and shuttle service to the beach and Legoland). It's not dirt cheap, but as you enjoy your king-size bed, fresh orchids, Aveda bath products and 30in flat-screen TV, you'd think you'd be paying a lot more.

Carlsbad Inn Beach Resort (☎ 760-434-7020, 800-235-3939; www.carlsbadinn.com; 3075 Carlsbad Blvd; r from $240; P ✕ 🖥 ⚓ 👶) A faux-Tudor upper-end-tourist-class hotel cum time-share property on the beachfront, in the center of Carlsbad Village, this inn has oodles of activities for kids from ceramics to Ping Pong tourneys. The location makes up for the whiff of indifference from some staff.

French Pastry Cafe (☎ 760-729-2241; 1005 Carlsbad Village Dr; mains $6; 🕑 7am-6pm) In a drab-looking shopping center just off I-5, this is the real deal for croissants and brioches baked daily and kick-start espresso, plus omelets, salads and sandwiches until 2:30pm.

Fidel's Norte (☎ 760-729-0903; 3003 Carlsbad Blvd; mains $9-15; 🕑 lunch & dinner; 👶) Heavy wood booths inside and classic cantina wrought-iron patio furniture are the backdrop for Carlsbad's Mexican restaurant of record. The La Pachanga plate lets you sample Cal-Mex classic appetizers, or create your own combination. Sure, it's touristy, but locals like it too.

Le Passage (☎ 760-729-7097; 2961 State St; lunch $8-16, dinner $16-20; 🕑 lunch Tue-Fri, dinner Tue-Sun) Escape the fray on the intimate back patio of this country French bistro. All the better to enjoy baked brie or lavender-roasted chicken.

OCEANSIDE
pop 165,800

Oceanside lies just outside the Camp Pendleton Marine Base, with all that entails. While it lacks the effervescence of its coastal neighbors, the surf is great and the streets sure are safe. The **California Welcome Center** (☎ 760-721-1101, 800-350-7873; www.visitoceanside .org; 928 N Coast Hwy; 🕑 9am-5pm) has helpful staff, coupons for local attractions, maps and information.

The wooden **Oceanside Pier**, which extends more than 1900ft out to sea, is so long that an electric shuttle transports people to the end ($0.50).

The **California Surf Museum** (☎ 760-721-6876; www.surfmuseum.org; 312 Pier View Way; adult/child under 12/student $3/free/1, free on Thu; 🕑 10am-4pm daily, to 8pm Thu) relocated into tubular new digs in 2009. Exhibits change annually along different themes (eg women of surfing) and include a timeline of surfing history, surf-themed art, and a radical collection of boards.

The **Museum of Art** (☎ 760-435-3720; www.oma -online.org; 312 Pier View Way; adult/student/senior $8/3/5; 🕑 10am-4pm Tue-Sat, 1-4pm Sun) also underwent a recent revamp and it now stands at an impressive 16,000 sq ft. There are about 10 rotating exhibits a year, with an emphasis on SoCal artists (especially from the San Diego region) and local cultures.

At the northern end of the waterfront, the extensive Oceanside Harbor provides slips for hundreds of boats. **Helgren's** (☎ 760-722-2133; www.helgrensportfishing.com; 315 Harbor Dr S) leads a variety of charter trips including whale-watching (adult/child $30/20).

101 Café (☎ 760-722-5220; 631 S Coast Hwy; most mains $4-10; 🕑 breakfast, lunch & dinner; P 👶), a tiny 1928 Streamline Moderne diner, serves the classics: omelets, burgers etc. If you're lucky, you'll catch the owner and can quiz him about local history.

Stare right at the pier from **333 Pacific** (☎ 760-433-3333; 333 N Pacific St; lunch $13-20, dinner $21-43; 🕑 lunch Tue-Sun, dinner nightly; P) in the Wyndham Hotel, but also take time to look at the slick decor around you…and on your plate. Lunch is a better deal (with arguably more interesting fare – kobe or ahi sliders, chimichurri fish tacos, crab-shrimp cheddar melt) than the undoubtedly fine steaks and seafood for dinner.

Directory

CONTENTS

ACCOMMODATIONS

Lodging in Coastal California is expensive and reservations are recommended year-round. Accommodations in this book fall into one of three categories: budget (double-occupancy rooms less than $100); midrange ($100 to $185); and top end (over $185). Rates are generally highest in summer. They spike even higher around major holidays such as Memorial Day, Independence Day and Labor Day, when minimum-night stays often apply. Prices listed in this guide reflect peak-season rates but don't include accommodation taxes of 10% to 16%, unless otherwise stated.

You can almost always do better than the published rates, particularly midweek or during the off-season (ie winter). Always ask about discounts, packages and promotional rates. Also check the web: some lodgings give better rates if you book

online. Auto-club members (p289) get discounts at many motels and some hotels, which may also publish discount coupons in flyers available at highway rest areas, gas stations and tourist information offices (or online at www.roomsaver.com).

More and more properties are providing wireless-internet access (🛜), handy if you travel with a laptop. Accommodations that provide internet access for travelers without their own computers are indicated in this guide with an internet (🖳) icon. Lodgings that cater to families are marked with the child-friendly (🐾) icon. For eco-friendly accommodations, turn to the GreenDex (p302).

If you smoke, ask about the availability of smoking rooms. Many lodgings in California are exclusively nonsmoking. In Southern California, nearly all lodgings have air-conditioning but in Northern California, where it rarely gets hot, the opposite is true. If it matters, inquire when making reservations.

If you book a room over the phone, get a confirmation number, and always ask about the cancellation policy before you give your credit-card number. If you plan to arrive late in the evening, call to reconfirm on the day of arrival. Hotels may overbook but if you've guaranteed the reservation with a credit card, they should accommodate you somewhere else. If they don't, squawk.

Where available, we have listed a property's toll-free reservation number. If you're having trouble finding accommodations, consider booking online with travel agencies like **Orbitz** (www.orbitz.com), **Travelocity** (www.travelocity.com) and **Expedia** (www.expedia.com), or travel discounters **Hotels.com** (www.hotels.com), **Hotwire** (www.hotwire.com) and **Priceline** (www.priceline.com).

BOOK ACCOMMODATIONS ONLINE

For more accommodations reviews and recommendations by Lonely Planet authors, check out www.lonelyplanet.com/hotels. You'll find the true, insider lowdown on the best places to stay. Reviews are thorough and independent. Best of all, you can book online.

PRACTICALITIES

- AC 110V is standard; you'll need adapters to run most non-US electronics.

- Major daily newspapers include the *Los Angeles Times, San Francisco Chronicle* and *San Jose Mercury News.*

- For news, National Public Radio (NPR; www.npr.org) and Public Radio International (PRI; www.pri.org) are at the lower end of the FM dial.

- Major broadcast TV channels include: ABC, CBS, NBC, FOX and PBS (public broadcasting). Major cable channels include: CNN (news), ESPN (sports), HBO (movies) and the Weather Channel.

- NTSC standard is incompatible with PAL or SECAM. DVDs are coded Region 1 (US and Canada only).

- The imperial system is used for weights and measures; see the inside front cover for conversions.

B&Bs

If you want an atmospheric, often romantic, alternative to impersonal motel or hotel rooms, stay at a B&B. They're typically in restored old houses with floral wallpaper and antique furnishings, and charge well over $100 per couple. Rates normally include breakfast, but rooms with TV and telephone are the exception, not the rule; some may share bathrooms. Most B&Bs require advance reservations, though some will accommodate the occasional drop-in guest. Smoking is prohibited. A two- or three-night minimum stay usually applies. Many belong to the **California Association of Bed & Breakfast Inns** (☎ 800-373-9251, www.cabbi.com).

Camping

Campgrounds abound in Coastal California, with most open year-round. Facilities vary widely. Primitive campgrounds usually have toilets, fire pits, picnic benches and sometimes drinking water; they're most common in national forests and on Bureau of Land Management (BLM) land. State and national park campgrounds are usually better equipped, featuring flush toilets and sometimes hot showers and RV hookups. Overnight fees range from under $5 for walk-in, tent-only 'envirosites' up to $65 for developed beachfront campsites with hookups. For a complete list of state-park campgrounds and overnight fees, browse www.parks.ca.gov.

You can usually camp in national forests and on BLM land in any area where you can safely park your vehicle next to a road

without blocking traffic. You are not allowed to park off undesignated roads (ie roads not shown on maps that do not have signs identifying a road number). Campfires may require a permit, usually available for free from any ranger station. Dispersed camping is not permitted in state or national parks, except for backpackers holding the appropriate permits. Check with a ranger station or visitor center if you're unsure about where to camp.

For camping reservations, which are strongly recommended in summer, try:
Kampgrounds of America (KOA; ☎ 888-562-0000; http://koa.com) National network of full-service private campgrounds.

Recreation.gov (☎ 518-885-3639, 877-444-6777; www.recreation.gov) Camping reservations for national parks, national forests and BLM land.

ReserveAmerica (☎ 800-444-7275; www.reserve america.com) For state-park campgrounds that accept reservations.

Hostels

At the time of writing, Coastal California has 20 hostels affiliated with **Hostelling International USA** (HI-USA; ☎ 301-495-1240, reservations 800-909-4776; www.hiusa.org; annual membership adult/child/senior $28/free/18). You don't need a membership card in order to stay at an HI hostel but having one saves you $3 per night. You can buy one at the hostel when checking in.

There are a growing number of independent hostels, particularly in cities, which have more relaxed rules and typically no curfew. Most independent hostels are convivial places, often with organized events and activities. Some include a light

DIRECTORY

breakfast or other meals in their rates, arrange local tours and may pick up guests at transportation hubs.

Some hostels say they accept only international travelers, basically to keep out destitute locals – American travelers who look like they'll fit in with other guests may be admitted. A passport, HI-USA card or international plane ticket should help establish your credentials.

Reservations are always recommended, especially in peak summer season.

Motels & Hotels

Motels surround a parking lot and usually have some sort of a lobby. Hotels provide extra services and amenities, but these can be expensive. If you walk in without reservations, always ask to see a room before paying for it, especially at motels.

Rooms are often priced by the size and number of beds in a room, rather than the number of occupants. A room with one double or queen-size bed usually costs the same for one or two people, while a room with a king-size bed or two beds costs more. There is often a surcharge for a third or fourth person. 'Suites' may simply mean oversized rooms, not necessarily two separate rooms, so ask.

Room location may affect price. Renovated or larger rooms, or those with a view, are likely to cost more. Beware that 'oceanview,' 'oceanfront' and 'partial oceanview' labels are liberally used and may require a periscope to spot the waves.

As a rule, motels offer the best lodging value for the money. Rooms won't often win design awards, but they're usually comfortably furnished and cleanish. Amenities vary, but expect a telephone, TV, alarm clock and private bathroom. Some provide an in-room mini-fridge, coffeemaker and microwave.

Better motels and many hotels offer swimming pools with hot tubs, self-service laundry, internet access and a complimentary continental breakfast that varies from stale donuts and coffee to full-on buffets. Upscale hotels add concierge services, fitness and business centers, spas, restaurants and bars.

Make reservations at chain motels and hotels online or by calling their central reservation lines, but to learn about specific amenities and additional discount promotions, call the property directly. Every listing in this book includes local direct numbers.

ACTIVITIES

Coastal California offers all kinds of activities for outdoor enthusiasts, from surfing and kayaking to whale-watching and hiking. Turn to the Coastal California Outdoors chapter (p39) for ideas and inspiration; for specific outfitters, see the destination chapters. Most outdoor outfitters provide instruction and hand-holding for newbies, or they'll simply rent equipment for do-it-yourself types. Co-op retailer **REI** (☎ 253-891-2500, 800-426-4840; www.rei.com) sells and rents outdoor-activity equipment and offers lessons, workshops and adventure tours. In Southern California, also try **Adventure 16** (☎ 619-283-2362; www.adventure16.com).

BUSINESS HOURS

Unless otherwise noted, standard business hours in this guide are as follows.

Shops are open from 10am to 5pm or 6pm (often until 9pm at malls), except Sunday when hours are noon to 5pm (malls to 6pm). Businesses are open 9am to 5pm Monday to Friday. Post offices are open 8am to 4:30pm or 5:30pm Monday to Friday. Banks are open 8:30am to 4:30pm Monday to Thursday, until 5:30pm Friday. Some post offices and banks are also open until noon, 1pm or 2pm Saturday. In cities, some supermarkets and restaurants stay open 24 hours.

At restaurants, breakfast is served 7am to 10:30am Monday to Friday, with weekend brunch from 9am to 2pm Saturday and Sunday; lunch runs 11:30am to 2:30pm Monday to Friday; and dinner is served 5pm to 10pm daily, sometimes later on Friday and Saturday. Bars and pubs typically open 5pm to midnight, extended to 2am on Friday and Saturday. In cities, nightclubs and dance clubs open by 10pm and close around 2am, sometimes later on weekends.

CHILDREN

Coastal California is a tailor-made destination for traveling with kids. For general information, advice and anecdotes, read Lonely Planet's *Travel with Children* by Cathy Lanigan. Helpful online resources include www.visitcalifornia.com, www.travel withyourkids.com, www.parentsconnect.com

and www.thefamilytravelfiles.com. To find child-friendly sights, activities, hotels, restaurants and entertainment, look for the 👶 icon throughout the destination chapters.

Practicalities

Children's discounts are widely available for everything from museum admissions and movie tickets to bus and train fares and motel stays. The definition of a child varies – in some places anyone under 18 is eligible, while in others it's only toddlers or infants.

Most hotels and motels allow children to share a room with their parents for free or for a modest surcharge, although a roll-away bed or cot may cost extra. This practice is rare in B&Bs, many of which don't allow children. Larger hotels often have an on-call babysitting service. Otherwise, hotel staff may be able to help you make arrangements. Be sure to ask whether sitters are licensed and bonded, what they charge per hour, whether there's a minimum fee and if they charge extra for meals and transportation. Remember to tip.

Most car-rental agencies (p290) have children's safety seats, but be sure to book them in advance. The same goes for high-chairs and cribs; they're common in many restaurants and hotels but numbers are limited. It's perfectly fine to bring kids, even toddlers, along to casual restaurants, but not to upscale places at dinner. Many family-style restaurants and diners break out paper placemats and crayons for drawing. Ask about cheaper children's menus.

Most women are discreet about breast-feeding in public. You'll find baby food, infant formulas, soy and cow's milk, disposable diapers (nappies) and other necessities in supermarkets and drugstore chains. Diaper-changing stations exist in many public toilets in malls, department stores, airports and even some restaurants and gas stations.

Sights & Activities

Coastal California offers lots for kids to do. Families flock to Anaheim's **Disneyland** (p231), **Universal Studios Hollywood** (p220) in LA, **Legoland** (p270) near San Diego and **Fisherman's Wharf** (p63) and the **Exploratorium** (p64) in San Francisco, just to name a few. At national and state parks, ask at visitors centers about 'Junior Ranger' programs, in which kids earn themselves a badge and

certificate to take home after completing an activity booklet that's fun for all ages. Many outdoor outfitters and tour operators have specially tailored gear and activities for kids, depending on how little they are – see the destination chapters for more details.

CLIMATE CHARTS

For advice about seasonal travel in Coastal California, see p14.

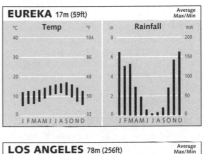

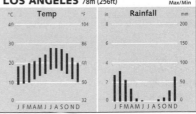

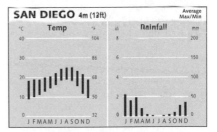

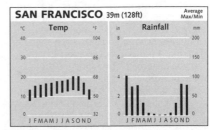

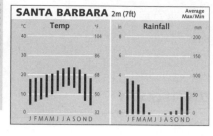

SANTA BARBARA 2m (7ft)

COURSES

The big three coastal cities – San Francisco, LA and San Diego – are the best places to take a class. Pick up the local alternative weekly newspapers for current listings of drop-in classes. For cooking courses, see p46. For outdoor outfitters that also offer lessons (eg surfing), see p39.

DANGERS & ANNOYANCES

By and large, California is not a dangerous place. The most publicized problem is violent crime, but this is pretty much confined to areas not on the itinerary of most visitors. Traffic accidents pose a potential danger and, of course, there is always the dramatic, albeit unlikely, possibility of a natural disaster, such as an earthquake. Prepare for the worst, but expect the best.

Crime

Most cities have 'bad' neighborhoods to avoid, particularly after dark. In the destination chapters, the Dangers & Annoyances sections provide some details. If you're worried, quiz hostel and hotel staff, locals and police about the latest no-go zones.

If you find yourself in a neighborhood where you'd rather not be, look confident. Don't keep stopping to look at your map, and hail a taxi if you can. Use ATMs during daylight hours in well-trafficked areas. Exercise caution in parking lots and garages, especially at night. If your car is bumped from behind by another vehicle in a remote area, keep going to a well-lit public place like a police or gas station.

If you're accosted by a mugger, there's no 100% recommended plan of action. Don't carry valuables or an excess of cash, and don't put it all in the same pocket, wallet or bag. Keep some money separate, and hand it over fast – it's better than getting attacked. Muggers are not too happy to find their victims penniless.

That said, don't obsess about crime. Just protect yourself as best you can.

Earthquakes

Earthquakes (p35) happen frequently in Coastal California, but most are so tiny they can only be detected by sensitive seismological instruments. If you're caught in a serious earthquake, stand inside a doorway or get under a desk or table. Protect your head and stay clear of windows, mirrors or anything that might fall. Don't head for elevators or go running into the street. If you're in a shopping mall or large public building, expect the alarm and/or sprinkler systems to come on.

If outdoors, get away from buildings, trees and power lines. If you're driving, pull over to the side of the road away from bridges, overpasses and power lines; stay inside the car until the shaking stops. If you're on a sidewalk near buildings, duck into a doorway to protect yourself from falling bricks, glass and debris. Prepare for aftershocks. Use the telephone only if absolutely necessary. Turn on the radio and listen for news bulletins.

Wildlife

For safety advice for drivers, see p291.

Never feed or approach wild animals, because it causes them to lose their innate fear of humans, which in turn makes them more aggressive, and eventually they may have to be killed. Feeding or otherwise harassing specially protected wildlife is a crime, subject to huge fines. Black bears are often attracted to campgrounds where they may find food, trash and any other scented items left out on picnic tables or stashed in tents and cars. Always use bear-proof boxes where they're provided.

Attacks on humans by mountain lions – also called cougars or pumas – are rare. Stay calm if you encounter a mountain lion, pick up small children, stand your ground – unless you've cornered the animal, in which case give it an escape route – and appear as large (and confident) as possible by raising your arms or grabbing a stick. If the lion gets aggressive or attacks, fight back, shout and throw objects at it.

Snakes and spiders are found throughout California, not just in wilderness areas, but they prefer warmer inland areas.

Attacks or fatalities are exceedingly rare; the following descriptions are necessarily general. If you get bitten, seek medical attention immediately.

Watch your step when hiking as rattlesnakes may bask in the middle of the trail. Most rattlesnakes have roughly diamond-shaped patterns along their backs. Bites are rarely fatal; antivenin is available in most hospitals. Always wear hiking boots and, if you're worried, stomp your feet and stay out of thick underbrush and tall grass.

Scorpions spend their days under rocks or woodpiles. The long stinger curving up and around the back is characteristic of these animals. Stings can be very painful but almost never fatal; however, bear in mind that small children are at highest risk.

The most dangerous spider is the black widow. The female has a small, round body marked with a red hourglass shape under its abdomen. She makes very messy webs, so avoid these, as the normally shy spider will bite only if harassed. The bite emits neurotoxins; they're painful but rarely fatal.

The large (up to 4in long) and hairy tarantula looks much worse than it is – it very rarely bites, and then usually only when it is roughly handled. The bite is not fatal, although it is quite painful and can cause infections.

DISCOUNT CARDS

For automobile association member discounts, see p289.

Available at universities and student-oriented travel agencies, an **International Student Identity Card** (ISIC; www.isic.org) entitles you to some discounts on transportation and admission to sights and attractions. For nonstudents under 26, the International Youth Travel Card (IYTC) offers some of the same savings. If you're a US student, always carry your school or university ID card. Registered students can also buy the **Student Advantage Card** (☎ 877-256-4672; www.studentadvantage.com; 1-year card $20) for worthwhile discounts on trains, buses, airfares and shopping.

People over the age of 62 (sometimes 55 or 60) often qualify for the same discounts as students; any ID showing your birth date should suffice as proof of age. Members of the **American Association of Retired Persons** (AARP; ☎ 888-687-2277; www.aarp.org; 1-year membership $12.50), an advocacy group for those aged 50 years and older, qualify for small discounts on hotels, car rentals, attractions and entertainment venues.

For tourists, local discount cards include the **Go San Diego Card** (www.gosandiegocard.com adult/child from $65/50), the **Go Los Angeles Card** (www.golosangelescard.com; adult/child from $60/50) and **CityPass** (www.citypass.com; adult/child from $59/39) valid for San Francisco, Hollywood or Southern California. These discount passes will save you money only if you're doing lots of sightseeing in a short time, however.

FESTIVALS & EVENTS

Check with local visitor information centers or chambers of commerce, or contact the California Travel & Tourism Commission (p283) for even more current events. See also Holidays (below).

January & February
Tournament of Roses (☎ 877-793-9911; www.tournamentofroses.com) Famous New Year's Day parade of flower-coated floats, marching bands and equestrians, held in the LA suburb of Pasadena.
Chinese New Year Held in late January/early February with firecrackers, parades, lion dances and lots of food; the biggest celebrations are in San Francisco and LA.

March & April
San Diego Latino Film Festival (☎ 619-230-1938; www.sdlatinofilm.com) Screens films from throughout Latin America and the US in mid-March.
Toyota Grand Prix of Long Beach (☎ 888-827-7333; www.gplb.com) Week-long auto-racing spectacle through city streets draws world-class drivers to LA in mid-April.
San Francisco International Film Festival (☎ 415-561-5000; www.sffs.org) California's longest-running film festival, held from late April to early May.

May & June
Kinetic Grand Championship (☎ 707-822-3619; http://kineticgrandchampionship.com) Over Memorial Day weekend, quirky human-powered contraptions of all sorts ride from Arcata to Ferndale in the North Coast's wackiest event.
San Francisco Pride (☎ 415-864-0831; www.sfpride.org) USA's biggest lesbian, gay, bisexual and transgender pride parade attracts over a million participants in late June.

July
Festival of Arts & Pageant of the Masters (☎ 800-487-3378; www.foapom.com) Exhibits by hundreds of artists and a pageant of art masterpieces 're-created'

DIRECTORY

using real people during July and August in Laguna Beach, Orange County.

US Open Sandcastle Competition (☎ 619-424-6663; www.usopensandcastle.com) Amazing sandcastle competition held in mid-July at Imperial Beach, south of San Diego.

Carmel Bach Festival (☎ 831-624-1521; www.bach festival.com) If you love baroque music, come to Carmel for recitals, films and behind-the-scenes peeks in mid-July and early August.

Mendocino Music Festival (☎ 619-937-4041; www.mendocinomusic.com) Orchestral, chamber, opera, jazz and world music concerts on the North Coast headlands, with children's matinees and open rehearsals, in mid-July.

August

Reggae on the River (☎ 707-923-3368; www.reggae ontheriver.com) Draws huge crowds for reggae and world music shows, arts-and-craft fairs, camping and swimming outside Garberville in NorCal in early August.

Old Spanish Days Fiesta (☎ 805-962-8101; www .oldspanishdays-fiesta.org) A celebration of early rancho culture with parades, rodeo, crafts exhibits and shows in Santa Barbara in early August.

Steinbeck Festival (☎ 831-775-4721; www.steinbeck .org) Celebrates California's literary Nobel laureate with films, theater, storytelling and tours in Salinas in early August.

Concours d'Elegance (☎ 831-622-1700; www.pebble beachconcours.net) Showcases vintage vehicles to modern concept cars in Pebble Beach in mid-August.

September

San Francisco Fringe Festival (☎ 415-673-3847; www.sffringe.org) This theater marathon in mid-September attracts a variety of performers from around the world.

Monterey Jazz Festival (☎ 831-373-3366; www .montereyjazzfestival.org) This big-name festival in mid-September celebrates both traditional and modern styles of jazz.

Fleet Week (☎ 619-232-3101; www.fleetweeksandiego .org) US military shows off its might with a parade of ships, air shows and concerts in San Diego from mid-September to early October.

Simon Rodia Watts Towers Jazz Festival (☎ 213-847-4646; www.parks.ca.gov) Features jazz, gospel, R&B and other sounds in the shadow of LA's Watts Towers, usually on the last weekend of September.

October

San Francisco Jazz Festival (☎ 415-788-7353, 866-920-5299; www.sfjazz.com) Features live performances by top and new artists throughout the Bay Area from early October to early November.

World Championship Pumpkin Weigh-Off (☎ 650-726-9652; www.miramarevents.com) In Half Moon Bay, south of San Francisco, this competition among West Coast pumpkin growers happens in mid-October.

LitQuake (☎ 415-750-1497; www.litquake.org) Author readings, discussions and literary events like the legendary pub crawl; held in San Francisco in mid-October.

November

Diá de los Muertos (☎ 415-391-2000; www.dayof thedeadsf.org) Party to wake the dead on November 2, with costume parades, sugar skulls and fabulous altars, including in San Francisco's Mission district and across SoCal.

Hollywood Christmas Parade (☎ 323-469-8311; www.hollywoodchristmasparade.org) Features celebrities waving at fans lining LA's Hollywood Blvd, plus classic cars, floats and marching bands, on the first Sunday after Thanksgiving.

December

Christmas Boat Parade (☎ 949-729-4400; www .christmasboatparade.com) A parade of 150 or so brightly illuminated boats, including multimillion-dollar yachts, floating at Orange County's Newport Beach.

First Night Alcohol-free New Year's Eve street festivals, featuring dance, theater and live music suitable for families, take place in many coastal cities.

FOOD

Restaurant reviews in this guide are ordered by price: budget (mains under $10), midrange (mains $10 to $20) and top end (mains over $20). Prices do not include drinks, appetizers, desserts, taxes or tip, unless otherwise stated. For more on Coastal California's food culture, see p46.

GAY & LESBIAN TRAVELERS

The mayor of San Francisco declared same-sex marriage legal in 2004, but statewide voters overturned it in 2008 (court challenges are still pending, see p13). So make no mistake, bigotry persists. Californians tend to be tolerant, although there have been cases of bashings even in metropolitan areas. In small towns, 'tolerance' may come down to a don't-ask-don't-tell policy. The age of sexual consent, regardless of gender or sexual orientation, is 18.

San Francisco has its famed Castro district (p80); San Diego's hottest gay neighborhood is Hillcrest (p264); and in LA it's West Hollywood and Silver Lake (p228). All three cities have gay and alternative newspapers that cover what's going on and provide contact information for local GLBT organizations.

Damron (www.damron.com) publishes the classic gay travel guides, but they're advertiser-driven and sometimes outdated. Check out **OutTraveler** (www.outtraveler.com), **Gay. com** (www.gay.com/travel) and **PlanetOut** (www .planetout.com/travel) for loads of online travel information. **Purple Roofs** (www.purpleroofs.com) lists gay-owned and gay-friendly hotels, B&Bs and inns statewide.

If you're looking for a gay mechanic or florist, consult the **Gay & Lesbian Yellow Pages** (www.qayyellow.com). For counseling or referrals, call the **GLBT National Hotline** (☎ 888-843-4564; www.glnh.org; ☯ 1-9pm Mon-Fri, 9am-2pm Sat).

HOLIDAYS

Thanksgiving and Christmas are the biggest holiday travel times, when you'll overpay for airfare and still be squeezed onto an overbooked flight. On the upside, people usually spend these holidays with family, so city hotels stand nearly empty and may offer fantastic room rates. On summer holiday weekends (ie Memorial Day, Fourth of July, Labor Day), everywhere is crowded and overpriced.

On the following national holidays, banks, schools and government offices (including post offices) close, and transportation, museums and other services operate on a Sunday schedule. Holidays falling on a weekend are usually observed the following Monday.

New Year's Day January 1
Martin Luther King Jr Day 3rd Monday in January
Presidents' Day 3rd Monday in February
Memorial Day last Monday in May
Independence Day July 4 (aka Fourth of July)
Labor Day 1st Monday in September
Columbus Day 2nd Monday in October
Veterans' Day November 11
Thanksgiving Day 4th Thursday in November
Christmas Day December 25

Colleges usually take a one- or two-week 'spring break' in March or April, when many beach hotels and resorts, especially in SoCal, raise their rates. For students of all ages, summer vacation runs from June to August, making these the busiest travel months in Coastal California.

INSURANCE

No matter how long you're traveling for, it's smart to buy travel insurance. Worldwide travel insurance is available at www.lonely planet.com/travel_services. You can buy, extend and claim online anytime – even if you're already on the road.

At minimum you'll need coverage that includes treatment for medical emergencies. The best policies also extend to the worst possible scenario, such as an accident that requires hospitalization and a return flight home. Medical care in California is prohibitively expensive and some providers demand payment up-front. Be sure to keep all receipts and documentation so you can make a claim later. Some policies ask you to phone a call center for an immediate assessment of your problem before seeking medical care. Some also specifically exclude 'dangerous activities' such as scuba diving and motorcycling. US citizens should check with their medical insurer at home to see if they already have coverage in California.

Also consider coverage for luggage theft or loss and trip cancellation. If you already have a home-owner's or renter's policy, see what it will cover and consider getting supplemental insurance to cover the rest. If you have prepaid a large portion of your trip, cancellation insurance may be a worthwhile expense. If you're driving, you must carry liability insurance, offered by car-rental agencies and some credit cards (see p290).

INTERNATIONAL VISITORS
Entering the Country

Getting into the USA can be a bureaucratic nightmare, depending on your country of origin, as the rules keep changing. All travelers should double-check current visa and passport regulations *before* coming to the USA. For updated information, check the website of the **US Department of State** (http://travel.state.gov/visa) and the travel section of the **US Customs & Border Protection** (www.cbp .gov) website.

The Department of Homeland Security (DHS) registration program, **US-VISIT** (www .dhs.gov/us-visit), currently includes 327 ports of air, land and sea entry. For foreign visitors (excluding, for now, most Canadian and some Mexican citizens), registration consists of having a digital photo taken and

DIRECTORY

electronic (inkless) fingerprints made of each index finger; the process takes less than a minute.

PASSPORTS & VISAS

Currently, most Canadian citizens arriving from anywhere in the Western hemisphere are exempt from visa requirements. However, a Canadian passport, cross-border Trusted Traveler Program card or an enhanced driver's license or photo ID that complies with the USA's Western Hemisphere Travel Initiative (WHTI) is now required. For details, consult www.cbp.gov.

All visitors to the USA from other countries must have a machine-readable passport that is valid for six months longer than their intended stay and meets current US standards. If your passport was issued after October 26, 2006, it must be an e-Passport with a digital photo and an integrated RFID chip containing biometric data. For more information, consult www.cbp.gov.

Currently under the Visa Waiver Program (VWP), citizens of the following countries may enter the USA without a visa for stays of 90 days or fewer (no extensions allowed): Andorra, Australia, Austria, Belgium, Brunei, Czech Republic, Denmark, Estonia, Finland, France, Germany, Hungary, Iceland, Ireland, Italy, Japan, Latvia, Liechtenstein, Lithuania, Luxembourg, Malta, Monaco, the Netherlands, New Zealand, Norway, Portugal, San Marino, Singapore, Slovakia, Slovenia, South Korea, Spain, Sweden, Switzerland and the UK.

Under the VWP program, you must have a passport that meets current US standards and either a round-trip or onward ticket to any foreign destination, other than a territory bordering the US (ie Mexico and Canada). This ticket must be nonrefundable in the USA. You must also get approval from the Electronic System for Travel Authorization (ESTA) in advance. Register online with DHS at https://esta.cbp.dhs.gov at least 72 hours before arrival. Once travel authorization is approved, your registration is valid for two years.

All other foreign visitors must obtain a visa from a US consulate or embassy in their own country, a process that costs at minimum a nonrefundable $131, involves a personal interview and can take several weeks; apply at home as early as possible.

CUSTOMS REGULATIONS

You may import duty free 1L of alcohol, if you're over 21; 200 cigarettes (one carton) or 50 cigars (not Cubans), if you're over 18; and $100 worth of gifts ($800 for US citizens). Amounts in excess of $10,000 in cash, traveler's checks, money orders and other cash equivalents must be declared. Unless you're curious about US jails, don't even think about bringing in illegal drugs, drug paraphernalia, firearms or other weapons. For full details and the latest regulations, contact **US Customs & Border Protection** (☎ 703-526-4200, 877-227-5511; www.cbp.gov).

California is an important agricultural state. To prevent the spread of pests and diseases, certain food items (including meats, fresh fruit and vegetables) may not be brought into the state. If you drive into California across the border from Mexico or the adjacent states of Oregon, Nevada and Arizona, you may have to stop for a quick vehicle inspection by California Department of Food and Agriculture officials.

Embassies & Consulates

Most foreign embassies are in Washington, DC, but many countries have consular offices in LA and San Francisco. To get in touch with an embassy in Washington, DC, call that city's **directory assistance** (☎ 202-555-1212). For more foreign consulates

---

TIPPING

Gratuities are not optional in the US; service-industry workers rely on tips as their primary source of income. Only withhold tips in cases of outrageously bad service, which rarely happens.

Airport & hotel porters $2 per bag, minimum per cart $5

Bartenders 10–15% per round, minimum per drink $1

Concierges Nothing for simple information like directions, up to $20 for securing restaurant reservations or sold-out show tickets

Hotel maids $2-4 per night, left under the card provided

Parking valets At least $2 when handed back the keys

Restaurant servers 15-20%, unless a gratuity is already charged on the bill

Taxi drivers 10-15%, rounded up to the next dollar

in California, click to www.sos.ca.gov/business/ibrp/consulates.htm.

Australia Los Angeles (Map p212; ☎ 310-229-2300; Century Plaza Towers, 31st fl, 2029 Century Park E); San Francisco (Map pp58-9; ☎ 415-536-1970; 575 Market St, Suite 1800)

Canada Los Angeles (Map p210; ☎ 213-346-2700; 550 S Hope St, 9th fl); San Francisco (Map pp58-9; ☎ 415-834-3180; 580 California St, 14th fl)

France Los Angeles (☎ 310-235-3200; 10390 Santa Monica Blvd, Suites 115 & 410); San Francisco (Map pp58-9; ☎ 415-397-4330; 540 Bush St)

Germany Los Angeles (Map p212; ☎ 323-930-2703; 6222 Wilshire Blvd, Suite 500); San Francisco (☎ 415-775-1061; 1960 Jackson St)

Ireland San Francisco (☎ 415-392-4214; 100 Pine St, Suite 3350)

Italy Los Angeles (Map p208; ☎ 310-820-0622; 12400 Wilshire Blvd, Suite 300); San Francisco (☎ 415-931-4924; 2590 Webster St)

Japan Los Angeles (Map p210; ☎ 213-617-6700; 350 S Grand Ave, Suite 1700); San Francisco (☎ 415-777-3533; 50 Fremont St, Suite 2300)

Mexico Los Angeles (☎ 213-351-6800; 2401 W 6th St); San Francisco (☎ 415-354-1700; 532 Folsom St)

Netherlands Los Angeles (Map p208; ☎ 877-388-2443; 11766 Wilshire Blvd, Suite 1150)

New Zealand Los Angeles (Map pp206-7; ☎ 310-566-6555; 2425 Olympic Blvd, Suite 600e)

South Africa Los Angeles (Map p212; ☎ 310-651-0902; 6300 Wilshire Blvd, Suite 600)

Spain Los Angeles (☎ 323-938-0158; 5055 Wilshire Blvd, Suite 860); San Francisco (Map pp58-9; ☎ 415-922-2995; 1405 Sutter St)

UK Los Angeles (Map p208; ☎ 310-481-0031; 11766 Wilshire Blvd, Suite 1200); San Francisco (Map pp58-9; ☎ 415-617-1300; 1 Sansome St, Suite 850)

It's important to realize what the embassy of the country of which you are a citizen can and can't do. Generally speaking, it won't be much help in emergencies if the trouble you're in is remotely your own fault. Remember, you're bound by local laws and embassy officials won't be sympathetic if you've committed a crime in California, even if such actions are legal in your own country. If you have all your money and documents stolen, they will assist you in getting a new passport, but forget about a loan for onward travel.

INTERNET ACCESS
California leads the world in internet technology, so it's pretty easy to stay connected. This guide uses the internet icon (🖳) wherever public internet terminals are available and the wi-fi icon (📶) to denote wireless internet access, whether free or fee-based.

There are internet cafes in cities and towns, charging $3 to $12 per hour for on-line access. Better cybercafes and full-service copy shops like **FedEx Office** (☎ 800-463-3339; www.fedex.com) also provide stations for printing digital-camera photos and/or burning photo CDs. At public libraries, internet terminals and wi-fi access are typically free but may be subject to registration requirements, time limits, queues and slow connections, with access to some websites blocked; out-of-state visitors must sometimes pay a nominal fee. Most coffee shops, including Starbucks, and some airports, bars and even museums have wi-fi hot spots, either free or for an hourly/daily access fee.

Many motels and most hotels provide guests with high-speed internet connections (sometimes wired, but increasingly wireless) and/or a place to log on to the internet, such as a self-serve lobby terminal or full-fledged business center. Fees range from nothing to more than $10 per day. These days, you can even connect in the woods: private campgrounds and RV parks increasingly offer wi-fi, as do dozens of state parks (www.parks.ca.gov), usually near to the ranger station or in campgrounds and picnic areas.

If you're visiting from abroad, remember that you will need an AC adapter and a plug adapter for US sockets. Both are sold in larger electronics stores such as **Best Buy** (☎ 888-237-8289; www.bestbuy.com).

See p17 for useful California travel websites.

LEGAL MATTERS
If you are stopped by the police for any reason, there is no system of paying fines on the spot. Attempting to pay the fine to the officer may lead to a charge of attempted bribery. There is usually a 30-day period to pay a fine. For traffic offenses, the police officer will explain the options to you. Most matters can be handled by mail.

If you are arrested for more serious offenses, you have the right to remain silent and are presumed innocent until proven guilty. There is no legal reason to speak to a police officer if you don't wish. All persons who are arrested are legally allowed the

THE LEGAL AGE FOR...

■ Drinking alcohol: 21

■ Driving a car: 16

■ Smoking tobacco: 18

■ Consensual sex (heterosexual or homosexual): 18

Travelers should note that they can be prosecuted under the laws of their home country regarding age of consent, even while traveling abroad.

right to make one phone call. If you don't have a lawyer, friend or family member to help you, call your embassy. The police will give you the number upon request. If you can't afford a lawyer, a public defender will be appointed to you free of charge.

At bars, restaurants, nightclubs and liquor stores, you may be asked for photo ID to prove you are of legal age to buy and consume alcohol. Stiff fines, jail time and other penalties can be incurred for driving under the influence (DUI) of alcohol or drugs. A blood-alcohol content of 0.08% or higher is illegal. Penalties for DUI range from license suspension and fines to jail time. It is also illegal to carry open containers of alcohol inside a vehicle, even if they are empty. Containers that are full and sealed may be carried, but if they have ever been opened, they must be stored in the trunk.

During holidays and festive events, police roadblocks are sometimes set up to deter DUI. Officers can give roadside sobriety checks to assess if you've been drinking or using drugs. If you fail, they'll require you to take a breath, urine or blood test to determine the level of alcohol in your body. Refusing to be tested is treated the same as taking and failing the test. If you're in a group, choose a 'designated driver' who agrees not to consume alcohol or drugs.

In California, possession of less than 1oz of marijuana is a misdemeanor, punishable by up to one year in jail, though first-time offenders may be eligible for community service and counseling. Possession of any other illegal drug, including cocaine, heroin, ecstasy, hashish or more than an ounce of weed, is a felony, punishable by lengthy jail sentences. For foreign visitors, it's grounds for deportation.

MAPS

Visitors centers and chambers of commerce stock basic local and regional maps, often free. Gas stations, convenience shops and bookstores sell low-cost folding maps of local areas that include street-name indexes. Members of automobile associations (p289) can obtain free maps from local offices. For a map atlas, the gold standard is Benchmark Press' *California Road & Recreation Atlas* (www.benchmarkmaps.com; $24.95), which shows *every* road in the state, as well as campgrounds, trailheads, ski areas and hundreds of other points of interest. For detailed trail and topographical maps, stop by state and national park visitors centers, USFS ranger stations or outdoor retailers like **REI** (☎ 800-426-4840; www.rei.com). The best topo maps are published by the **US Geological Survey** (USGS; ☎ 877-275-8747; www.usgs.gov), available online. For GPS and laptop users, National Geographic (☎ 800-962-1643; www.natgeomaps.com) publishes the Topo! series of outdoor recreation mapping software, with a complete CD-ROM set available for California ($100).

PETS

Traveling with your canine companion is no more difficult in Coastal California than in the rest of the USA. Look for the 🐾 icon, highlighting pet-friendly businesses in the destination chapters. For general travel tips and even more dog-friendly accommodations, restaurants, beaches and off-leash parks, browse www.dogfriendly.com.

Many motels and hotels have pet-friendly accommodations, although these are often smoking rooms and pets may never be left unattended; a nightly surcharge (ranging from nominal to outrageously expensive) and maximum weight restrictions may apply. Dogs are sometimes welcome on outdoor patios or at sidewalk tables at restaurants and cafes, but ask first. Dogs are not usually allowed on public transportation or inside shops, though exceptions may be made for 'pocket pooches' being toted around in designer handbags, especially in chi-chi neighborhoods.

Few beaches allow dogs, and then usually only if they're leashed; check posted signs carefully. If you're planning to visit state or national parks, consider leaving Fido at home – dogs are rarely, if ever, allowed on hiking trails, and may not be left alone tied up at public campgrounds. Never leave your pet unattended inside a locked vehicle with the windows rolled up – temperatures inside can quickly become lethal.

SOLO TRAVELERS

Coastal California can be a meditative journey for solo travelers. In general, don't advertise where you are staying or that you are traveling alone. If someone invites you to his or her home, let someone (eg hostel staff) know where you're going. This advice also applies if you go for a long hike by yourself. If something happens and you don't return as expected, you want someone to notice and begin looking for you. For more advice for women travelers, see p284.

TIME

California is in the Pacific time zone, eight hours behind GMT/UTC. Daylight Saving Time (DST), when clocks move ahead one hour, runs from the second Sunday in March to the first Sunday in November.

TOURIST INFORMATION

The **California Travel & Tourism Commission** (☎ 916-444-4429, 877-225-4367; www.visitcalifornia .com) has an excellent website packed with useful pretrip planning information, plus a free downloadable annual visitors' guide. It also maintains 12 regional **California Welcome Centers** (www.visitcwc. com). Staff dispense maps and brochures and can help with accommodations. Look for CWCs in San Francisco (p54); Oceanside (p271), north of San Diego; Pismo Beach (p192) on the Central Coast; and Arcata (p138) on the North Coast. Local tourist information offices are listed throughout the destination chapters.

TOURS

For city tours and guided outdoor activities that you can sign up for after arrival in Coastal California, see the destination chapters.

Backroads (☎ 510-527-1555, 800-462-2848; www .backroads.com) Bicycling, hiking, kayaking and multisport tours of the California coast, with deluxe camping and inn stays.

Elderhostel (☎ 978-323-4141, 800-454-5768; www .elderhostel.org) Nonprofit organization offers 'learning adventures' throughout California for active travelers aged 55 and up.

Green Tortoise (☎ 415-956-7500, 800-867-8647; www .greentortoise.com) Budget-minded trips for independent travelers utilizing converted sleeping-bunk buses; the 'Coastal Crawler' route connects San Francisco and LA.

Trek America (☎ 800-873-5872; www.trekamerica .com) Offering outdoors-focused trips for small groups along the coast, including camping and national parks.

TRAVELERS WITH DISABILITIES

If you have a physical disability, California can be an accommodating place. The Americans with Disabilities Act (ADA) requires that all public buildings (including hotels, restaurants, theaters and museums) be wheelchair-accessible, and buses and trains must have wheelchair lifts. Telephone companies are required to provide relay operators (available via TTY numbers) for the hearing impaired. Many banks now provide ATM instructions in Braille or via earphone jacks for hearing-impaired customers, and you'll find audible crossing signals at many intersections.

Larger chain motels and hotels often have specially equipped rooms and suites for guests with disabilities. If you're worried about stairs, ask about the availability of an elevator, especially at independent lodgings. Major car-rental agencies offer hand-controlled vehicles and vans with wheelchair lifts at no extra charge, but you must reserve them well in advance.

Wheelchair Getaways (☎ 800-642-2042; www .wheelchairgetaways.com) rents out wheelchair-accessible vans in San Francisco, LA and San Diego.

All major airlines, Greyhound buses and Amtrak trains will assist travelers with disabilities, as long as you notify them 48 hours in advance. Service animals (such as guide dogs) are allowed to accompany passengers, but you must have documentation. Airlines and Greyhound buses accept wheelchairs as checked baggage, while Amtrak allows standard wheelchairs on trains. On Amtrak, travelers with documented disabilities receive discounts off regular fares when booking in person or by phone.

Most national and some state parks and recreation areas have paved, graded-dirt or boardwalk nature trails. For free admission to national parks, US citizens and permanent residents with permanent disabilities can get a free 'America the Beautiful' Access Pass. **California State Parks** (☎ 916-445-8949; http://access.parks.ca.gov/) has a detailed online accessibility guide with a searchable regional directory. The **California State Coastal Conservancy** (☎ 510-286-1015; www .scc.ca.gov) offers free downloadable wheelchair riders' guides to the San Francisco Bay Area and the LA and Orange County coasts.

For local access guides, contact visitor information centers listed throughout the destination chapters. Other helpful resources for travelers with disabilities:

Access-Able Travel Source (☎ 303-232-2979; www .access-able.com) General travel website with useful tips and links, including the Travelin' Talk Network.

Disabled Sports USA Far West (☎ 530-581-4161; www.dsusafw.org; annual membership $25) Organizes adaptive sports and outdoor recreation programs.

Mobility International USA (☎ 541-343-1284; www .miusa.org) Advises disabled travelers on mobility issues and runs educational international-exchange programs.

Moss Rehabilitation Hospital (☎ 800-225-5667; www.mossresourcenet.org/travel.htm) Extensive links and tips for accessible travel.

VOLUNTEERING

Volunteering might provide some of your most memorable experiences – you'll get to interact with Californians and the land and sea in ways you never would just passing through. Casual, drop-in volunteer opportunities are most common in cities.

Register online with organizations like **One Brick** (www.onebrick.org), **HandsOn Bay Area** (www .handsonbayarea.org), **LA Works** (www.laworks.com) or **Volunteer San Diego** (www.volunteersandiego.org). These nonprofit groups are also a great way to meet locals and socialize. For more opportunities, browse local alternative weekly newspapers and **Craigslist** (www.craiglist.org).

WOMEN TRAVELERS

California is a reasonably safe place to travel, even if you're flying solo (see p283). Just use the same common sense as you would anywhere. The website www.journeywoman .com facilitates women exchanging travel tips and links to helpful resources. The booklet 'Her Own Way,' published by the Canadian government, is filled with general travel tips, useful for any woman; click to www.voyage.gc.ca, then under Resources select Publications and download the PDF.

Planned Parenthood (☎ 800-230-7526; www .plannedparenthood.org) offers referrals to low-cost women's health clinics throughout California. If you are sexually assaulted, consider contacting a rape-crisis center before calling the police, unless you are in immediate danger, in which case call ☎ 911. Not all police have as much sensitivity training and/or experience in assisting sexual assault survivors, whereas rape crisis–center staff will actively advocate on your behalf and act as a link to other community services, including hospitals and the police. Telephone books have listings of local rape-crisis centers, or contact the 24-hour **National Sexual Assault Hotline** (☎ 800-656-4673; www.rainn.org). Alternatively, go straight to a hospital emergency room.

Transportation

GETTING THERE & AWAY

Flights and tours can be booked online at www.lonelyplanet.com/travel_services.

AIR

Domestic airfares vary hugely depending on the season, day of the week, length of stay and flexibility of the ticket for changes and refunds. Still, nothing determines fares more than demand, and when business is slow, airlines lower fares to fill seats. Airlines are competitive and at any given time any one of them could have the cheapest fare. Expect less fluctuation with international fares.

International passengers arriving in Los Angeles disembark at the Tom Bradley International Terminal of **Los Angeles International Airport** (LAX; ☎ 310-646-5252; www.lawa.org/lax), 19 miles southwest of Downtown. Most international flights to the San Francisco Bay Area land at **San Francisco International Airport** (SFO; ☎ 650-821-8211, 800-435-9736; www.flysfo.com), 15 miles south of downtown. Bay Area airports in **Oakland** (OAK; ☎ 510-563-3300; www.flyoakland.com) and **San Jose** (SJC; ☎ 408-277-4759; www.sjc.org) are important domestic gateways with limited international services. **San Diego International Airport** (SAN; ☎ 619-400-2400; www.san.org), aka Lindbergh Field, has flights to Canada and Mexico.

Smaller regional airports mainly for domestic travel:

Arcata/Eureka Airport (ACV; ☎ 707-839-5401; http://co.humboldt.ca.us/aviation) On the North Coast.
Bob Hope Airport (BUR; ☎ 818-840-8840; www.burbankairport.com) In Burbank.
Jack McNamara Field Airport (CEC; ☎ 707-464-7229; www.co.del-norte.ca.us) In Crescent City.
John Wayne Airport (SNA; ☎ 949-252-5200; www.ocair.com) In Orange County.
Long Beach Airport (LGB; ☎ 562-570-2600; www.longbeach.gov/airport) In LA County.
Monterey Peninsula Airport (MRY; ☎ 831-648-7000; www.montereyairport.com) On the Central Coast.
San Luis Obispo County Regional Airport (SBP, ☎ 805-781-5205; www.sloairport.com) On the Central Coast.
Santa Barbara Municipal Airport (SBA; ☎ 805-967-7111; www.flysba.com) On the Central Coast.

Major domestic airlines serving California:

Alaska Airlines/Horizon Air (☎ 800-252-7522, 800-547-9308; www.alaskaair.com)
American Airlines (☎ 800-433-7300; www.aa.com)
Continental Airlines (☎ 800-523-3273; www.continental.com)
Delta Air Lines (☎ 800-221-1212; www.delta.com)
Frontier Airlines (☎ 800-432-1359; www.frontierairlines.com)
Hawaiian Airlines (☎ 800-367-5320; www.hawaiianair.com)
JetBlue Airways (☎ 800-538-2583; www.jetblue.com)
Northwest Airlines (☎ 800-225-2525; www.nwa.com)
Southwest Airlines (☎ 800-435-9792; www.southwest.com)
Spirit Airlines (☎ 800-772-7117; www.spiritair.com)
United Airlines (☎ 800-864-8331; www.united.com)

THINGS CHANGE...

The information in this chapter is particularly vulnerable to change. Check directly with the airline or a travel agent to make sure you understand how a fare (and ticket you may buy) works and be aware of the security requirements for international travel. Shop carefully. The details given in this chapter should be regarded as pointers and are not a substitute for your own careful, up-to-date research.

TRANSPORTATION

US Airways (☎ 800-428-4322; www.usairways.com)
Virgin America (☎ 877-359-8474; www.virginamerica
.com)

Major international airlines serving California:
Aeroméxico (☎ 800-237-6639; www.aeromexico.com)
Air Canada (☎ 888-247-2262; www.aircanada.com)
Air France (☎ 800-237-2747; www.airfrance.com)
Air New Zealand (☎ 800-262-1234; www.airnew zealand.com)
Alitalia (☎ 800-223-5730; www.alitaliausa.com)
British Airways (☎ 800-247-9297; www.britishairways .com)
Cathay Pacific Airways (☎ 800-233-2742; www .cathaypacific.com)
Iberia Airlines (☎ 800-772-4642; www.iberia.com)
Japan Airlines (☎ 800-525-3663; www.japanair.com)
KLM (☎ 800-225-2525; www.klm.com)
Lufthansa (☎ 800-399-5838; www.lufthansa.com)
Mexicana Airlines (☎ 877-801-2010; www.mexicana .com)
Qantas Airways (☎ 800-227-4500; www.qantas.com)
Singapore Airlines (☎ 800-742-3333; www.singapore air.com)
V Australia (☎ 800-444-0260; www.vaustralia.com)
Virgin Atlantic (☎ 800-821-5438; www.virgin-atlantic .com)
WestJet Airlines (☎ 888-937-8538; www.westjet.com)

LAND
Border Crossings

Mexico and California share a border. Tijuana is the closest Mexican city, accessible via San Ysidro, the world's busiest border crossing. Open 24 hours a day, the border is 17 miles south of downtown San Diego. For more info about day-tripping to Tijuana, see p267.

US citizens or permanent residents not intending to go past the border zone (ie beyond Ensenada), or stay in the border zone for more than 72 hours, don't need a visa to enter Tijuana. To re-enter the USA, US citizens are required to carry a passport or US federal government-certified equivalent (for a list, see http://travel.state.gov). A driver's license is no longer proof enough. Children under 16 need only to show a US birth certificate. Non-US citizens may be subject to a full immigration inspection upon returning to the US, so bring your passport and US visa (if required).

Unless you're planning an extended stay in Tijuana, taking a car across the border is probably more hassle than it's worth. Instead, take the trolley or a taxi from downtown San Diego or leave your car on the US side of the border, then walk or take a shuttle across. Several parking lots

---

CLIMATE CHANGE & TRAVEL

Climate change is a serious threat to the ecosystems that humans rely upon, and air travel is the fastest-growing contributor to the problem. Lonely Planet regards travel, overall, as a global benefit, but believes we all have a responsibility to limit our personal impact on global warming.

Flying & Climate Change

Pretty much every form of motor travel generates CO_2 (the main cause of human-induced climate change) but planes are far and away the worst offenders, not just because of the sheer distances they allow us to travel, but because they release greenhouse gases high into the atmosphere. The statistics are frightening: two people taking a return flight between Europe and the US will contribute as much to climate change as an average household's gas and electricity consumption over a whole year.

Carbon Offset Schemes

Climatecare.org and other websites use 'carbon calculators' that allow jetsetters to offset the greenhouse gases they are responsible for with contributions to energy-saving projects and other climate-friendly initiatives in the developing world – including projects in India, Honduras, Kazakhstan and Uganda.

Lonely Planet, together with Rough Guides and other concerned partners in the travel industry, supports the carbon offset scheme run by climatecare.org. Lonely Planet offsets all of its staff and author travel.

For more information check out our website: lonelyplanet.com.

WARNING

In 2009 the **US State Department** (http://travel.state.gov) issued a travel alert about increasing Mexican drug cartel violence and crime along the US–Mexico border. Travelers should exercise extreme caution in Tijuana (see p267), avoid large-scale gatherings and demonstrations, and not drive after dark, especially in cars with US license plates.

(charging around $10 or less per day) are located off the Camino de la Plaza exit off I-5, south of San Diego.

If you decide to drive across, you must get Mexican car insurance (available from around $15 per day) either beforehand or at offices off I-5 exits near the border. Expect long waits at the border, as US security has tightened in recent years. Traffic in Tijuana is frenetic, parking is competitive, and there will likely be an even longer wait to cross back into the US.

If you're renting a car or motorcycle, find out if the agency's insurance policy covers driving to Mexico. Chances are it doesn't. If that's the case, don't risk it: if anything happens to the car, you'll be responsible for all damages or loss.

Bus

The main national bus carrier, **Greyhound** (☎ 800-231-2222; www.greyhound.com), operates to cities and towns in Coastal California from

around the US. See p289 for information about domestic fares, seating and reservations. Buses also connect with **Greyhound Canada** (☎ 800-661-8747; www.greyhound.ca) and **Greyhound México** (☎ 800-710-8819; www.greyhound.com.mx) routes.

If California is part of a wider North American itinerary, you might save money with a Greyhound **Discovery Pass** (www.discoverypass.com), valid for unlimited travel in the US and Canada for seven ($199), 15 ($299), 30 ($399) or 60 ($499) consecutive days. Purchase passes online in advance or, for travel starting in the US, at any Greyhound bus terminal.

Car & Motorcycle

Though each US state legislates its own rules of the road, there's little variation. For advice about driving in California, see p289.

If you're interested in driving someone else's car to California to save money, **Auto Driveaway** (☎ 800-346-2277; www.autodriveaway.com) has dozens of offices nationwide, or browse www.movecars.com.

Train

Amtrak (☎ 800-872-7245; www.amtrak.com) operates a fairly extensive rail system throughout the US. Trains are comfortable, if slow, and equipped with dining and lounge cars on long-distance routes. Fares vary according to the type of train and seating. You can travel in reserved or unreserved coach seats,

ROAD DISTANCE CHART (MILES)

	Crescent City	Eureka	Los Angeles	Mendocino	Monterey	San Diego	San Francisco	San Luis Obispo	Santa Barbara
Crescent City	---								
Eureka	85	---							
Los Angeles	727	644	---						
Mendocino	227	143	526	---					
Monterey	468	387	321	266	---				
San Diego	848	765	121	647	442	---			
San Francisco	356	275	380	154	112	505	---		
San Luis Obispo	585	500	201	383	145	322	230	---	
Santa Barbara	688	604	97	487	248	218	337	104	---

Distances (miles) are approximated values, due to variations in route direction and selection.

business class or first class, which includes sleeping compartments.

Long-distance trains to/from California:

California Zephyr Daily service between Chicago and Emeryville (from $145, 53 hours) near San Francisco, via Denver and Salt Lake City.

Coast Starlight Travels the West Coast daily between LA and Seattle (from $98, 35 hours), via Oakland, Sacramento and Portland.

Southwest Chief Daily departures between Chicago and LA (from $143, 43 hours), via Kansas City, Albuquerque and Flagstaff.

Sunset Limited Thrice-weekly service between New Orleans and LA (from $133, 48 hours), via Tucson and El Paso.

See p292 for more intra-California routes.

Amtrak's USA Rail Pass is valid for coach-class travel for 15 (per adult/child $389/195), 30 ($579/290) or 45 ($749/375) days, limited to eight, 12 or 18 one-way 'segments,' respectively. A segment is *not* the same as a one-way trip. If reaching your destination requires riding more than one train, you'll have to use multiple pass segments. Purchase passes either online or through international travel-agency representatives. For Amtrak's California Rail Pass, see p292.

GETTING AROUND

AIR

If you have limited time and want to cover great distances quickly, fly. Depending on the departure airport, destination, time of year and booking date, air travel can be less expensive than bus, train or rental car. California airports are listed on p285.

Flights between the Bay Area and Southern California take off every hour from 6am to 10pm from SFO and OAK. It's possible to show up at the airport, buy your ticket and hop on, though competitive fares require advance purchase, and you'll have to set aside time to contend with security lines. Flights to smaller airports can be fairly pricey, because fewer airlines compete on these routes.

Several major US carriers (see p285) fly within California, though flights are often operated by their regional subsidiaries, such as American Eagle, Delta Connection and United Express. Southwest is the most popular low-cost airline. Alaska Airlines and Horizon Air also have a substantial intra-California network.

BICYCLE

Bicycling Coastal California requires a high level of fitness and focused awareness. Coastal highways climb up and down wind-blown bluffs above the ocean and along narrow stretches of winding road with fast-moving traffic. Nonetheless, bicyclists are fairly common, and the ride is incredibly rewarding. Cars pose the greatest hazard.

You can rent bikes by the hour, day, week or month. Buy them new at specialty bicycle shops, sporting-goods stores or outdoor outfitters like co-op **REI** (☎ 800-426-4840; www.rei.com), or used at flea markets and from notice boards at hostels and universities. Also check online bulletin boards like **Craigslist** (www.craigslist.org).

Cyclists must follow the same rules of the road as vehicles, but don't expect drivers to always respect your right of way. Bicycling is permitted on all roads and highways – even along freeways if there's no designated alternative, such as a smaller parallel route (all mandatory exits are marked). The **Adventure Cycling Association** (☎ 406-721-1776, 800-775-2453; www.adv-cycling.org) is an excellent source for bicycle touring maps covering the entire Pacific Coast.

If you tire of pedaling, some local buses are equipped with bike racks; call the transportation company to check. To transport bikes on airplanes, Greyhound buses and Amtrak trains, contact the respective company to ask about reservations, excess-baggage surcharges and whether you'll need to disassemble the bike and box it.

For coastal cycling enthusiasts, perhaps the best-kept secret is those specially designated 'hike & bike' campsites available at some California State Parks (see p273). There you can roll (or walk) right into your campsite and set up a tent for just $5 to $10 per night.

San Francisco, Arcata, Santa Cruz, San Luis Obispo and Santa Barbara rank among Coastal California's most bike-friendly communities. The **California Department of Transportation website** (www.dot.ca.gov/roadsand traffic.html) has links to cycling advocacy groups statewide. For more inspiration and practical information for recreational cycling and mountain biking, see p43.

TRANSPORTATION

To avoid all-too-common bicycle theft, use a good, heavy-duty lock. Always wear a helmet – they're mandatory for anyone under 18. Ensure you have proper lights and reflective clothing at night. Carry water and a repair kit for flats. Emergency roadside assistance is available from **Better World Club** (see right).

BOAT

You can't travel around Coastal California by boat, although there are a few public ferry services, including to Santa Catalina Island (p216), off the Los Angeles and Orange County coasts, and Channel Islands National Park (p202), offshore from Ventura County. Also, commuter ferries operate throughout the San Francisco Bay Area.

BUS

Often the cheapest way to get around California, **Greyhound** (☎ 800-231-2222; www .greyhound.com) runs several daily buses along highways between coastal cities, stopping at some smaller towns along the way. Frequency of service varies, but the most popular routes operate every hour or so, sometimes around the clock.

As a rule, Greyhound buses are reliable, cleanish and comfortable, with air-con, barely reclining seats, onboard lavatories and no smoking on board. Sit toward the front, away from the bathroom. Long-distance buses stop for meal breaks and driver changes every few hours, usually at fast-food restaurants or truck stops.

Bus stations are dreary places, often in sketchy urban areas. In small towns, where there is no station, buses stop in front of a specific business – know exactly where and when the bus arrives, be obvious as you flag it down, and be prepared to pay with exact change.

It's easiest to buy tickets online with a major credit card, and then pick them up by showing photo ID at the bus terminal's ticket counter. You can also buy tickets over the phone or through an agent. For tickets by mail, order at least 10 business days in advance.

For the lowest fares, buy tickets online at least seven days in advance. Also check the Greyhound website for special promotional deals. Children aged two to 11 get 40% off;

seniors over 62 qualify for 5% discounts. Students who have a Student Advantage Discount Card (see p277) receive 15% off regular fares, or 10% with any valid student ID. If you're traveling with friends or family, Greyhound's companion fares allow up to three additional travelers to get 50% off with a minimum three-day advance purchase.

Note your ticket does not reserve or guarantee a seat on a bus. Seating is normally first-come, first-served. Arrive at least an hour before departure to get a seat; allow more time on weekends and holidays. Now available in Sacramento, San Diego, San Francisco and LA, priority seating (surcharge $5) guarantees you a seat and lets you board ahead of other passengers.

For details about Greyhound's multiday Discovery Pass, see p287.

CAR & MOTORCYCLE

Neither buses nor trains access large swaths of California's coast, so plan on driving if you want to visit small towns, isolated beaches or far-flung forests. Independence costs you, since rental rates and gas prices will eat a good chunk of a travel budget. For recommended maps, see p282.

Automobile Associations

For 24-hour roadside assistance, free maps and trip-planning services, and travel discounts on accommodations, attractions, car rentals and more, try:

American Automobile Association (AAA; ☎ 800-874-7532; www.aaa.com) Has reciprocal agreements with some international auto clubs (bring your membership card from home).

Better World Club (☎ 866-238-1137; www.betterworld club.com) This ecofriendly alternative supports environmental causes and offers cyclists roadside assistance (see left).

Driver's License

Foreign visitors may legally drive a car in the USA for up to 12 months using their home driver's license. However, an International Driving Permit (IDP) will simplify the car-rental process, especially if your license doesn't have a photo or isn't written in English. To drive a motorcycle, you will need either a valid US state motorcycle license or a specially endorsed IDP.

TRANSPORTATION

CALIFORNIA DRIVIN'

Three major north–south routes run the length of California. CA Hwy 1 is the most scenic, but the slowest. From LA to San Francisco, the trip takes seven hours via US Hwy 101, a mostly four-lane highway, but 10 hours via Hwy 1, which runs along high bluffs for much of its serpentine course. If winding roads make you carsick, take Hwy 101. The fastest route, inland I-5 (which is boring), takes six hours.

In Southern California, Hwy 101 ends in Los Angeles; Hwy 1 merges with I-5, which hugs the coastline to San Diego. North of LA around Ventura, Santa Barbara and San Luis Obispo, Hwys 1 and 101 merge. On the far north coast, Hwy 1 merges with Hwy 101 at Leggett, where Hwy 101 continues north to Oregon. For all about the Pacific Coast Highway, see p65.

LA's tangled freeways can be confusing. The most important thing to know is that they go by names *and* numbers. Hwy 101, for example, is called the Ventura Freeway heading north, but the Hollywood Freeway heading south.

Insurance

Liability insurance is required by law, but is not automatically included in California rental contracts because some Americans are covered for rental cars under their personal car-insurance policies. If you're not already covered, expect to pay about $15 per day. Insurance against damage to the car itself, called Collision Damage Waiver (CDW) or Loss Damage Waiver (LDW), costs an additional $15 or so per day, usually with an initial deductible of $100 to $500 for any repairs.

Some credit cards cover CDW for rentals of up to 15 days, provided you charge the entire cost of the rental to the card. But if there's an accident, you may have to pay the car-rental agency first, and then seek reimbursement from the credit-card company. There may also be exceptions that are not covered, such as 'exotic' rentals (eg 4WDs, convertibles). Check with your credit-card company in advance.

Rental

Most international car-rental agencies have desks at major airports, in all coastal cities and some smaller towns. For rates and reservations, go online or call toll-free:

Alamo (☎ 877-222-9075; www.alamo.com)
Avis (☎ 800-331-1212; www.avis.com)
Budget (☎ 800-527-0700; www.budget.com)
Dollar (☎ 800-800 3665; www.dollar.com)
Enterprise (☎ 800-261-7331; www.enterprise.com)
Fox (☎ 800-225-4369; www.foxrentacar.com)
Hertz (☎ 800-654-3131; www.hertz.com)
National (☎ 877-222-9058; www.nationalcar.com)
Rent-A-Wreck (☎ 877-877-0700; www.rent-a-wreck.com)
Thrifty (☎ 800-847-4389; www.thrifty.com)

Car Rental Express (www.carrentalexpress.com) rates and compares independent agencies, and is especially useful for searching out cheaper long-term rentals.

Rental rates vary wildly, depending on the car type, rental location, drop-off location, number of drivers etc. Rates peak during summer and around holidays, when demand skyrockets. For a midsize car expect to pay $30 to $75 per day or $200 to $500 per week. Rates usually include unlimited mileage, but not taxes, fees or insurance (see left). You must have a driver's license to rent a car; most agencies also require a major credit card, *not* a debit or check card. Typically drivers must be at least 21 years old; those under 25 may incur a daily surcharge of around $25.

Some major car-rental agencies, including Avis, Budget and Hertz, now offer 'green' fleets of hybrid rental cars, as does LA-based **Simply Hybrid** (☎ 323-653-0011, 888-359-0055; www.simplyhybrid.com). Expect to pay significantly more for hybrid models. In San Francisco, LA, San Diego, Santa Barbara and Santa Cruz, **Zipcar** (☎ 866-494-7227; www.zipcar.com) charges hourly/daily car-sharing fees, which includes free gas, insurance and limited mileage; apply online (foreign drivers OK).

MOTORCYCLES

Motorcycle rentals and insurance are not cheap, especially if you've got your eye on a Harley-Davidson. Expect to pay from $100 to $175 per day (excluding taxes and fees), depending on the rental location, size of the bike and length of the rental. Rates sometimes include helmets, unlimited miles and liability insurance; collision insurance (CDW) costs extra.

Motorcycle rental agencies in Coastal California:

Dubbelju Motorcycle Rentals (Map pp58-9; ☎ 415-495-2774, 866-495-2774; www.dubbelju.com; 698a Bryant St, San Francisco) Rents BMWs, Triumphs and Harley-Davidson motorcycles and Yamaha scooters.

Eagle Rider (☎ 310-536-6777, 888-900-9901; www.eaglerider.com) Has 12 outlets in California, including in LA, San Diego and San Francisco; one-way rental surcharge from $150 to $300.

RECREATIONAL VEHICLES

Gas-guzzling RVs remain popular with Coastal California travelers despite high fuel prices. It's easy to find campgrounds with electricity and water hookups, but in big cities, RVs are nothing but a nuisance, because there are few places to park or plug them in. Although cumbersome to navigate, they do solve transportation, accommodation and cooking needs in one fell swoop.

RV rental agencies with branches in Coastal California:

Cruise America (☎ 480-464-7300, 800-671-8042; www.cruiseamerica.com)

El Monte RV (☎ 562-483-4956, 888-337-2214; www.elmonterv.com)

Happy Travel Campers (☎ 310-675-1335, 800-370-1262; www.camperusa.com) Based in LA.

Road Conditions & Hazards

Drivers should watch for stock and deer on coastal highways. Hitting a large animal at 55mph will total your car, kill the animal and perhaps seriously injure you as well. Thick fog may also impede driving – slow down, and if it's too soupy, pull off the road. Watch out for fallen rocks, which can damage or even disable your car if struck. For statewide road conditions contact **Caltrans** (☎ 800-427-7623; www.dot.ca.gov).

Hwy 1 hugs the coastal bluffs along dramatic stretches of coastline, particularly between San Luis Obispo and Big Sur, and north of San Francisco. Not for the faint of heart, these precarious cliffsides often wash out in winter. Caltrans always seems to be repairing Hwy 1, and every couple of years, stretches close for months at a time. Hwy 101 north of Leggett (where Hwy 1 ends) is particularly prone to slides where it runs between the Eel River Gorge and unstable slopes.

When you see signs that read, 'Expect long delays 40 miles ahead,' or 'Hwy 1 closed north of Hearst Castle,' heed their warnings but don't panic. They sometimes overstate the situation to deter unnecessary travel. If you have hotel reservations, call the innkeeper. Local folk *always* know precisely what's happening with Hwys 1 and 101, which may be their only connections to the outside world.

Road Rules

The *California Driver Handbook* and *California Motorcycle Handbook* explain everything you need to know about driving here. They're available free from any Department of Motor Vehicles (DMV) office or download the PDFs from www.dmv.ca.gov.

Talking on a handheld cell (mobile) phone while driving is illegal in California; use a handsfree device (ie Bluetooth headset) instead. Drivers, front-seat passengers and children under 16 must wear a seatbelt at all times. Children under six years old, or those weighing less than 60lb, must ride in approved child-safety seats; most car-rental agencies rent these for around $10/50 per day/week, though you must reserve them when booking. All motorcyclists must wear helmets.

In winter months along the coast, avoid high-mountain inland routes unless you have a 4WD vehicle. If it's raining on the coast in January, chances are it's snowing in the mountains. Chains may be required at any time. Take note of weather forecasts.

Californians drive on the right-hand side of the road. On interstate highways, the speed limit is sometimes raised to 70mph. Unless otherwise posted, the speed limit is 65mph on freeways, 55mph on two-lane undivided highways, 35mph on major city streets and 25mph in business and residential districts and near schools. It's forbidden to pass a school bus when its lights are flashing.

Unless otherwise posted, you may turn right on red after stopping, so long as you don't impede intersecting traffic, which has the right of way. You may also make a left on red at two intersecting one-way streets. At four-way stop signs, cars proceed in the order in which they arrived. If two cars arrive simultaneously, the one on the right

TRANSPORTATION

has the right of way. When in doubt, just politely wave the other person ahead.

When emergency vehicles (ie police, fire or ambulance) approach, pull over and get out of their way. On freeways you may pass slower cars on either the left or the right lane, but try to pass on the left. If two cars are trying to get into the same central lane, the one on the right has priority. Carpool lanes marked with a diamond symbol are reserved for cars with multiple passengers. Fines for driving in these lanes without the minimum number of passengers are prohibitively stiff.

California has strict anti-littering laws. If you are seen throwing anything from a vehicle onto the roadway, you may be fined up to $1000. Littering convictions are shown on your driving record the same as other driving violations. When parking read all posted regulations and pay attention to colored curbs, or you may be towed. For laws regarding transporting alcohol and driving while under the influence of alcohol or drugs, see p281.

LOCAL TRANSPORTATION

California's major cities all have local bus, cable-car, trolley, train, light-rail and/or subway systems. Larger coastal towns and counties operate commuter-bus systems, usually with limited evening and weekend services. Inexpensive water taxis ply San Diego, Long Beach and Santa Barbara harbors. For local transportation details, see the destination chapters.

TRAIN

Amtrak (☎ 800-872-7245; www.amtrak.com) operates intra-California routes, with Thruway buses providing connections to smaller towns.

Sometimes you'll only spend an hour on the train, then four hours on a bus, but it's more civilized than Greyhound.

The sleek, double-decker *Pacific Surfliner* operates a two-class train service between San Luis Obispo (SLO) and San Diego. A dozen daily trains ply the San Diego-LA route ($34, three hours) via Anaheim, with five trains continuing north to Santa Barbara ($38, 5½ hours) and two to SLO ($55, 8½ hours). Tracks hug the coastline for beautiful vistas.

The long-distance *Coast Starlight* travels daily between LA and Seattle, stopping along the coast at Santa Barbara (from LA $20, 2½ hours), SLO ($38, 5¼ hours) and Oakland ($52, 11¼ hours). Despite its romantic name, it travels on not-so-scenic inland rails north of SLO, but it's a comfortable alternative to taking the bus between the San Francisco Bay Area and LA. For other long-distance train routes, see p287.

Reserve as far in advance as possible to ensure a seat and a good fare. Fares are usually higher in summer, from late May to early September. Year-round, seniors receive a 15% discount, AAA members (see p289) save 10%, children aged 2 to 15 get 50% off and students with a Student Advantage Card (see p277) get a 15% discount. Check the Amtrak website for more promotional deals.

Valid for seven days of travel within a 21-day period, Amtrak's California Rail Pass (per adult/child $159/80) can be used on *Pacific Surfliner* trains, the *Coast Starlight* within California, and most connecting Thruway bus services. Buy passes online, by phone or in person. You must make separate seat reservations for each leg of travel. For Amtrak's USA Rail Pass, see p288.

The Authors

SARA BENSON
Coordinating author, Central Coast

Sara jumped on a plane to California after college with just one suitcase and $100 in her pocket. She landed in San Francisco, and has bounced around the Golden State ever since, including stints in LA and SLO County. Sara is an avid outdoor enthusiast and has worked as a national park ranger in the Sierra Nevada. Her travel writing features on popular websites and in magazines and newspapers from coast to coast, including the *Los Angeles Times* and *San Francisco Chronicle*. Already the author of dozens of travel and nonfiction books, Sara has also written for Lonely Planet's *California, California Trips* and *USA* guides. Follow her adventures online at www.indietraveler.blogspot.com and @indie_traveler on Twitter.

ANDREW BENDER
Los Angeles & Orange County, San Diego

Yet another LP author with an MBA, this native New Englander first came to Los Angeles after B-school to work in film production, but he ended up leaving the industry to do what every MBA (and production dude) secretly dreams of: travel and write about it. Since then, his writing and photography have appeared in the *Los Angeles Times, Forbes, Hemispheres* (United Airlines in-flight magazine), *SilverKris* (Singapore Airlines in-flight magazine), some two dozen LP titles including *Los Angeles and Southern California,* and his blog, www.wheres-andy-now.com. When not on the road, he can be seen biking the beach in Santa Monica and discovering LA's next greatest ethnic joint.

ALISON BING
San Francisco & the Bay Area

Over 15 years in San Francisco, Alison has done everything you're supposed to do here and many things you're not, including falling in love on the 7 Haight bus and gorging on Mission burritos before Berlioz symphonies. Alison holds degrees in art history and international diplomacy – respectable diplomatic credentials she regularly undermines with outspoken culture commentary for foodie magazines, radio, TV and books, including Lonely Planet's San Francisco Encounter and City guides.

THE AUTHORS

NATE CAVALIERI
North Coast

Nate Cavalieri has lived in, camped on and biked through Coastal California for the past five years. For this project, he packed his tent and researched the North Coast chapter by bicycle and public transportation. His other titles for Lonely Planet include guides to Chicago, Puerto Rico, California and *Volunteer: A Traveler's Guide to Making a Difference Around the World*. Determined to practice what he preaches, he's currently traveling and volunteering on an open-ended trip around the world.

JOHN A VLAHIDES
San Francisco & the Bay Area

John A Vlahides lives in San Francisco. He co-hosts the TV series *Lonely Planet: Roads Less Traveled* on National Geographic Adventure. He is also co-founder of the California travel site 71miles.com. John studied cooking in Paris with the same chefs who trained Julia Child, and is a former luxury-hotel concierge and member of the prestigious Les Clefs d'Or, the international union of the world's elite concierges. He spends free time singing with the San Francisco Symphony, sunning on the nude beach beneath the Golden Gate Bridge, skiing the Sierra Nevada, and touring California on his motorcycle.

THE AUTHORS

Behind the Scenes

THIS BOOK

This 3rd edition of *Coastal California* was written by Sara Benson (also the coordinating author), Andrew Bender, Alison Bing, Nate Cavalieri and John A Vlahides. John A Vlahides and Alex Hershey wrote the previous edition. This guidebook was commissioned in Lonely Planet's Oakland, California, office and produced by the following:

Commissioning Editors Suki Gear, Kathleen Munnelly
Coordinating Editor Karen Beaulah
Coordinating Cartographer Damien Demaj
Coordinating Layout Designer Paul Queripel
Managing Editor Melanie Dankel
Managing Cartographer Shahara Ahmed
Managing Layout Designer Tim Newton
Assisting Editors Michala Green, Emma Sangster, Ceinwen Sinclair, Kelly Walker
Assisting Cartographers Ildiko Bogdanovits
Assisting Layout Designers Trevor Double
Cover Naomi Parker, lonelyplanetimages.com
Internal image research Jane Hart, lonelyplanetimages.com
Indexer Marie Lorimer
Project Manager Anna Metcalfe

Thanks to Lucy Birchley, Ross Butler, Helen Christinis, Michelle Glynn, Sally Darmody, Annelies Mertens

THANKS
SARA BENSON

Thanks to Suki Gear, Kathleen Munnelly and everyone at Lonely Planet for making this book happen. Without such talented California co-authors, I could never have coordinated this guide – thank you, Andy, John, Nate and Alison. I'm grateful to everyone out on the road who shared their local expertise and tips, from park rangers and long-distance cycling fiends to my rabble-rousing, peripatetic friends and family scattered from San Diego up into the Humboldt Nation, especially those who opened their homes: the Picketts, Connollys Sr, Boyles, Starbins, Blues and Dan Mulholland. PS to Mike Connolly Jr: next time, no wildfires!

ANDREW BENDER

Carol Martinez, Robin McClain, Megan Rodriguez, Madison Fisher, Joe Timko, Kate Buska, Erik Dahlerbruch and Jared Ruplinger, and, in house, Suki Gear, Kathleen Munnelly and Sara Benson for the opportunity and their good cheer and advice.

ALISON BING

Many thanks and California bear hugs to: editorial superhero Suki Gear; SF co-conspirator John A Vlahides and coordinating author Sara

THE LONELY PLANET STORY

Fresh from an epic journey across Europe, Asia and Australia in 1972, Tony and Maureen Wheeler sat at their kitchen table stapling together notes. The first Lonely Planet guidebook, *Across Asia on the Cheap*, was born.

Travelers snapped up the guides. Inspired by their success, the Wheelers began publishing books to Southeast Asia, India and beyond. Demand was prodigious, and the Wheelers expanded the business rapidly to keep up. Over the years, Lonely Planet extended its coverage to every country and into the virtual world via lonelyplanet.com and the Thorn Tree message board.

As Lonely Planet became a globally loved brand, Tony and Maureen received several offers for the company. But it wasn't until 2007 that they found a partner whom they trusted to remain true to the company's principles of traveling widely, treading lightly and giving sustainably. In October of that year, BBC Worldwide acquired a 75% share in the company, pledging to uphold Lonely Planet's commitment to independent travel, trustworthy advice and editorial independence.

Today, Lonely Planet has offices in Melbourne, London and Oakland, with over 500 staff members and 300 authors. Tony and Maureen are still actively involved with Lonely Planet. They're traveling more often than ever, and they're devoting their spare time to charitable projects. And the company is still driven by the philosophy of *Across Asia on the Cheap*: 'All you've got to do is decide to go and the hardest part is over. So go!'

Benson; fearless leaders Brice Gosnell and Heather Dickson; the Sanchez Writers' Grotto for steady inspiration; and Marco Flavio Marinucci, for the best-ever bus ride.

NATE CAVALIERI
Warm thanks to Sara Benson, Suki Gear and my other inspiring colleagues at Lonely Planet. Thanks also to Florence for the watchful proofreading and support, and to the many great folks who offered rides, campsites, directions and friendly conversation during research.

JOHN A VLAHIDES
John A Vlahides is grateful to his co-author Sara Benson, commissioning-editor Suki Gear, cartographer Alison Lyall, and regional-publisher Brice Gosnell for being so damn wonderful to work with. And thanks to Jim Aloise for encouraging me to get out of my mind. But I'm most grateful to you, dear reader. Enjoy this book and have a blast in California.

OUR READERS
Many thanks to the travelers who used the last edition and wrote to us with helpful hints, useful advice and interesting anecdotes:
Marco Bianchi, Steve Blood, Del Draper, Laura English-Rose, Rod Marett, Al Mercado, Jan Moyle, Ruth Wood

ACKNOWLEDGMENTS
Many thanks to the following for the use of their content:

Globe on title page ©Mountain High Maps 1993 Digital Wisdom, Inc.

SEND US YOUR FEEDBACK

We love to hear from travelers – your comments keep us on our toes and help make our books better. Our well-traveled team reads every word on what you loved or loathed about this book. Although we cannot reply individually to postal submissions, we always guarantee that your feedback goes straight to the appropriate authors, in time for the next edition. Each person who sends us information is thanked in the next edition – and the most useful submissions are rewarded with a free book.

To send us your updates – and find out about Lonely Planet events, newsletters and travel news – visit our award-winning website: **lonelyplanet.com/contact**.

Note: we may edit, reproduce and incorporate your comments in Lonely Planet products such as guidebooks, websites and digital products, so let us know if you don't want your comments reproduced or your name acknowledged. For a copy of our privacy policy visit lonelyplanet.com/privacy.

Index

GREENDEX

GreenDex

It seems like almost everyone in California is going 'green' these days. But how can you know which businesses really are ecofriendly, and which are simply jumping on the 'greenwashing' bandwagon?

We've done our homework. All of these sights, attractions, activities, tour operators, outdoor outfitters, nonprofit organizations, festivals, restaurants, coffeehouses, shops, lodgings and transportation providers have been hand-picked by our authors for acting in harmony with sustainable tourism goals. Some top picks are involved in environmental education, conservation and cleanup. Others are locally owned and operated, helping to preserve California's homegrown arts and cultural identities, especially that of Native Americans.

We want to keep developing our sustainable tourism content. If you think we've omitted some where that should be listed here, or if you disagree with our choices, email us at www.lonelyplanet .com/contact and set us straight for next time. For more information about sustainable tourism and Lonely Planet, see www.lonelyplanet.com/about/responsible-travel.

MAP LEGEND

ROUTES

.... Freeway
.... Primary
.... Secondary
.... Tertiary
.... Lane
.... Under Construction
.... Unsealed Road

.... One-Way Street
.... Mall/Steps
.... Pedestrian Overpass
.... Walking Trail
.... Walking Path
.... Track

TRANSPORT

.... Ferry
.... Bus Route

.... Rail

HYDROGRAPHY

.... River, Creek
.... Swamp
.... Reef

.... Water
.... Lake (Dry)
.... Lake (Salt)

BOUNDARIES

.... International
.... State, Provincial

.... Regional, Suburb
.... Cliff

AREA FEATURES

.... Airport
.... Area of Interest
.... Beach, Desert
.... Building
.... Campus
.... Cemetery, Christian

.... Forest
.... Land
.... Market
.... Park
.... Sports
.... Urban

POPULATION

◎ CAPITAL (NATIONAL)
● Medium City
○ Town, Village

● Large City
○ Small City

SYMBOLS

Sights/Activities
.... Beach
.... Christian
.... Golf
.... Hindu
.... Islamic
.... Monument
.... Museum, Gallery
● Point of Interest
.... Ruin
.... Winery, Vineyard
.... Wildlife/
Game Reserve

Eating
.... Eating

Drinking
.... Drinking

.... Café

Entertainment
.... Entertainment

Shopping
.... Shopping

Sleeping
.... Sleeping
.... Camping

Transport
.... Airport, Airfield
.... Border Crossing
.... Bus Station
.... Parking Area
.... Petrol Station
.... Taxi Rank

Information
$ .... Bank, ATM

.... Embassy/Consulate
.... Hospital, Medical
.... Information
.... Internet Facilities
.... Police Station
.... Post Office, GPO
.... Telephone

Geographic
.... Lighthouse
.... Lookout
▲ .... Mountain, Volcano
.... National Park
.... Pass, Canyon
.... River Flow
.... Shelter, Hut
+ .... Spot Height
.... Waterfall

LONELY PLANET OFFICES

Australia
Head Office
Locked Bag 1, Footscray, Victoria 3011
☎ 03 8379 8000, fax 03 8379 8111
talk2us@lonelyplanet.com.au

USA
150 Linden St, Oakland, CA 94607
☎ 510 250 6400, toll free 800 275 8555
fax 510 893 8572
info@lonelyplanet.com

UK
2nd fl, 186 City Rd,
London EC1V 2NT
☎ 020 7106 2100, fax 020 7106 2101
go@lonelyplanet.co.uk

Published by Lonely Planet Publications Pty Ltd
ABN 36 005 607 983

Although the authors and Lonely Planet have taken all reasonable care in preparing this book, we make no warranty about the accuracy or completeness of its content and, to the maximum extent permitted, disclaim all liability arising from its use.